W9-ALN-488

Issues for Debate in American Public Policy

SIXTH EDITION

CQ PRESS

A Division of Congressional Quarterly Inc. Washington, D.C.

SELECTIONS FROM THE **CQ RESEARCHER**

CQ Press
1255 22nd Street, NW, Suite 400
Washington, DC 20037

Phone: (202) 729-1900; toll-free, 1-866-427-7737 (1-866-4CQ-PRESS)

Web: www.cqpress.com

Title page photo: Scott Ferrell, Congressional Quarterly Inc.
Cover photo: Photodisc Green/Getty Images

♾ The paper used in this publication exceeds the requirements of the American National Standard for Information Sciences—Permanence of Paper for Printed Library Materials, ANSI Z39.48-1992.

Printed and bound in the United States of America

09 08 07 06 05   2 3 4 5

A CQ Press College Division Publication

Director	Brenda Carter
Acquisitions editor	Charisse Kiino
Marketing analyst	Bonnie Erickson
Production editor	Belinda Josey
Cover designer	Kimberly Glyder
Composition	Olu Davis
Print and design manager	Margot Ziperman
Sales manager	James Headley

ISSN: 1543-3889
ISBN: 1-933116-03-X

Contents

ANNOTATED CONTENTS   vii

PREFACE   xiii

CONTRIBUTORS   xv

EDUCATION

1   No Child Left Behind   **1**

    Has No Child Left Behind raised
student achievement?   4

    Are too many schools being labeled
"in need of improvement?"   7

    Is No Child Left Behind improving the
quality of teaching?   8

    Is No Child Left Behind adequately funded?   12

    Background   13

      Federal Reforms   13

      Achievement Gaps   16

    Current Situation   16

      States Push Back   16

      Teachers' Union Sues   18

      War of Words   18

    Outlook: Reform Unlikely?   19

    Notes   19

    Bibliography   21

2   Rising College Costs   **23**

    Are tuitions rising because colleges waste
money?   26

    Should government increase funding for
higher education?   29

    Should colleges be penalized for
raising prices?   32

    Background   33

      Exclusive Clubs   33

      Need-Blind Aid   33

    Current Situation   38

      Colleges Cut Costs   38

    Outlook: Tight Budgets   42

    Notes   43

    Bibliography   45

HEALTH CARE

3   Marijuana Laws   **47**

    Should marijuana be legally available by
prescription for medical purposes?   51

    Should marijuana be legal for adults and
regulated like alcohol and tobacco?   54

    Background   58

      Ancient Remedy   58

      DEA Debate   59

    Current Situation   60

      Research Efforts   60

      States' Rights   62

    Outlook: Supreme Court Ruling   64

    Notes   65

    Bibliography   66

4 Sexually Transmitted Diseases 69

Should abstinence be the sole focus of
sex education? 72

Is the United States doing enough to
prevent STDs? 76

Will President Bush's abstinence-only
policy hurt the global effort to
prevent AIDS? 82

Background 85

Early Anti-STD Efforts 85

AIDS Leads to Restraint 86

Young People at Risk 88

Current Situation 88

Focus on Vaccines 88

Research Funding 89

Teachers' Reaction 89

Abstinence Funding 89

Outlook: New Focus on Women 90

Notes 91

Bibliography 93

SOCIAL POLICY

5 Child Welfare Reform 97

Do state and local governments do
enough to keep families together? 101

Does the federal government give state and
local child welfare agencies enough
financial support and flexibility? 103

Does the child welfare system prepare
foster adolescents for adulthood? 105

Background 107

Orphan Trains 107

Child Abuse and Crack 110

Current Situation 111

Rigid Rules and Budgets 111

Whole Child Approach 112

Outlook: Hope and Fear 115

Notes 116

Bibliography 117

6 Social Security Reform 121

Does Social Security face an immediate
funding crisis? 124

Would privatization be good for
future retirees? 127

Are benefit cuts or payroll-tax increases
better alternatives to privatization? 128

Background 131

Roots in Industrialization 131

Social Security Act 133

Later Amendments 134

Current Situation 135

Privatization 135

Eroding Pensions 136

Budget Concerns 138

Outlook: Campaign Debate 139

Notes 139

Bibliography 140

CIVIL LIBERTIES, CIVIL RIGHTS AND JUSTICE

7 Right to Die 143

Are "living wills" effective? 147

Should Congress regulate end-of-life
decisions? 148

Should states permit physician-assisted
suicide for terminally ill patients? 150

Background 151

Processes of Dying 151

Politics of Dying 153

"Culture of Death"? 156

Current Situation 157

Federal Standards Eyed 157

Assisted Suicide Argued 160

Outlook: Understanding Death? 161

Notes 162

Bibliography 163

8 Supreme Court's Future 165

Has William Rehnquist been a
successful chief justice? 168

Will President Bush change the balance of
power on the Supreme Court? 171

Should the Senate limit filibusters
against judicial nominees? 172

Background 175

"Storm Centre" 175

Rehnquist's Court? 177

Bush's Judges 179

Current Situation 180

Rampant Speculation 180

Business as Usual? 182

Outlook: Waiting and Watching   183
Notes   184
Bibliography   185

9 Gang Crisis   **187**
Is government doing enough to
  combat the problem?   189
Should gun laws be tightened to
  combat gang violence?   192
Should more minors be tried as adults
  for gang crimes?   194
Background   197
  Early Gangs   197
  Seeking Respectability   199
  War Refugees   201
Current Situation   202
  Invisible Crisis   202
  National Gang Policy?   202
Outlook: More Violence?   204
Notes   205
Bibliography   207

ENVIRONMENT

10 Alternative Energy   **209**
Will hydrogen replace fossil fuels as
  America's predominant energy source? 212
Are efforts to develop hydrogen technology
  diverting funds from more promising
  energy sources?   214
Is the United States losing its competitive
  edge in developing alternative-energy
  sources?   215
Background   217
  Mixed Messages   217
  Bush's Energy Policy   219
  Hydrogen Initiative   220
Current Situation   222
  Ambivalent Consumers   222
  State Alternatives   224
Outlook: Energy Bill   226
Notes   227
Bibliography   228

11 Smart Growth   **231**
Do smart-growth policies contain sprawl? 236

Does managed growth reduce the
  supply of affordable housing?   238
Are Americans wedded to suburban life? 239
Background   241
  Early American Cities   241
  Cars Drive Development   241
  Anti-Sprawl Measures   244
  New Urbanism   245
Current Situation   246
  Policy Challenges   246
  Federal Impact   248
  Anti-Sprawl Movement   248
Outlook   249
  More Roads?   249
  Aging Baby Boomers   249
Notes   250
Bibliography   251

BUSINESS AND THE ECONOMY

12 Big-Box Stores   **253**
Do big-box retailers hurt locally
  owned businesses?   256
Do big-box retailers make communities
  less livable?   258
Do big-box retailers benefit
  local economies?   261
Background   263
  Early Retailers   263
  Backlash   263
  Rise of the Discounters   265
  Wal-Mart Emerges   266
Current Situation   268
  Union Busting?   268
  Strike in California   268
  Zoning Lawsuits   270
  Ballot Battles   271
Outlook: More Expansion   271
Notes   272
Bibliography   273

13 Privatizing the Military   **277**
Can the military do its job without
  military contractors?   279
Does privatization save taxpayers money? 282
Should there be more oversight of
  private military contractors?   284

Background   285
   Mercenary Armies   285
   Citizen Armies   287
   Downsizing the Military   289
Current Situation   291
   Modern Mercenaries   291
   Cheney and Halliburton   292
   Tightening Oversight   294
Outlook: After the Handover   295
Notes   295
Bibliography   297

FOREIGN POLICY

14 International Law   **299**
   Should the United States give more
     weight to international law in
     foreign policy?   302
   Should the Supreme Court consider
     international and foreign law in
     making decisions?   303
   Should U.S. courts hear suits for
     human rights violations abroad?   306
Background   307
   "The Law of Nations"   307
   The Rule of Law   309
   The Post-9/11 World   311
Current Situation   312
   Policies Challenged   312
   Death Case Reviewed   314
Outlook: Preventive Action   316
Notes   317
Bibliography   319

15 Middle East Peace   **321**
   Does Arafat's death make Palestinian
     statehood more likely?   324

Has the U.S. allied itself too closely
   with Israel?   325
Should Israel pull its settlers out of
   the Gaza Strip?   327
Background   328
   Old Conflict   328
   David vs. Goliath?   329
   Peace Efforts   331
   The "Roadmap"   333
Current Situation   336
   U.S. Policy   336
   Abbas and Hamas   336
   The Occupied Territories   338
Outlook: Many Uncertainties   339
Notes   340
Bibliography   342

16 Exporting Democracy   **345**
   Should the United States be
     trying to export democracy?   348
   Is democracy taking root in Iraq and
     Afghanistan?   351
   Is the Bush administration making America
     safer by exporting democracy? 353
Background   355
   Wilsonian Idealism   355
   Idealists vs. Realists   355
   Republican Transition   356
Current Situation   358
   Politics Amid War   358
   People Power   359
   Tough Realities   360
   Paying the Bills   362
Outlook: If at First. . .   363
Notes   364
Bibliography   366

Annotated Contents

The 16 *CQ Researcher* reports reprinted in this book have been reproduced essentially as they appeared when first published. In the few cases in which important new developments have since occurred, updates are provided in the overviews highlighting the principal issues examined.

EDUCATION

No Child Left Behind

More than three years have passed since President George W. Bush signed the No Child Left Behind Act, the most recent reauthorization of the Elementary and Secondary Education Act. The nearly 1,000-page bill increases funding for schools that serve poor students, mandates highly qualified teachers in every classroom and holds schools that take federal funds accountable for raising student achievement across income brackets and racial groups. As schools and districts try to meet the demands of the law, the debate about its fairness and merit is intensifying. States and school districts want more flexibility and more funding, and some are going to court to challenge the law, while supporters worry that it is in danger of being significantly diluted.

Rising College Costs

Tuition and fees at public colleges and universities soared by 10.5 percent from the last academic year to this year, continuing a quarter-century trend of higher-education costs rising faster than inflation. The average total cost of attending a private school jumped to $27,516 annually—far beyond the means of most American families. However, the size of federal grants to students has not kept pace with rising prices, and state appropriations to colleges have not adjusted to burgeoning enrollments. Colleges have asked for increased government spending on higher education, but Republican congressional leaders are skeptical about the need for more federal aid and whether such aid would solve the problem. To cope with the financial crunch, more and more colleges are turning to innovative uses of technology to reduce their costs.

HEALTH CARE

Marijuana Laws

A dozen states have adopted legislation in recent years allowing patients with certain illnesses to use marijuana as a medicine, even though these measures clearly conflict with federal anti-marijuana laws. In California, federal drug agents have raided the homes of patients using medical marijuana, claiming federal law superceded California's law permitting compassionate use of marijuana. Recently, two medical marijuana users challenged Washington's authority to overrule a state's law, but the U.S. Supreme Court ruled in favor of the federal government in June 2005. Meanwhile, some studies show that marijuana is less addictive than caffeine, and legalization proponents argue that it should therefore be available to adults for personal use. The U.S. government and other critics continue to insist that marijuana should remain illegal because it is not an effective medicine, and it is dangerous both in its own right and as a "gateway" drug to cocaine and other more addictive and harmful drugs.

Sexually Transmitted Diseases

The United States has the highest rate of sexually transmitted diseases (STDs) of any industrialized nation. Yet some experts contend the United States has no concerted, national campaign to prevent and cure infection. Although the number of new AIDS cases has fallen dramatically in the United States, adolescents, minorities and women suffer disproportionately high rates of all sexual infections. The Bush administration argues that abstinence is the only completely effective approach to avoiding STDs and bars any organization receiving federal funding for abstinence-only education from discussing contraceptives, except to point out their failure rates. But public health officials see condoms as an essential protective measure against STDs. They say the abstinence-only message deprives teenagers of crucial, potentially life-saving information and makes little sense in developing countries, where married women are the fastest-growing group infected with AIDS.

SOCIAL POLICY

Child Welfare Reform

The U.S. child welfare system is designed to protect the nation's children, but in recent years it has been rocked by horror stories of children who were physically and sexually abused and even murdered. However, a nationwide reform movement offers hope for the future. Welfare agencies across the country are focusing more on keeping families together and quickly moving the nation's 500,000 foster children into permanent homes. Although the foster care rolls are dropping, unadopted foster teens still must struggle with a lonely transition to adulthood after leaving the system. State programs still fall short; not one has passed a federal review, but states are hitting improvement targets in follow-up checks. Social workers continue to complain that they are underpaid and overworked. Meanwhile, Congress is divided over a Bush administration plan that would give states more flexibility in using federal funds but end the guarantee of federal support for every foster child.

Social Security Reform

Social Security has provided a guaranteed income for retirees, widows and disabled individuals for almost 70 years. But unless changes are made to the taxpayer-funded system, Social Security will begin paying more in benefits than it collects in payroll taxes in about 15 years. That's when the retirement of millions of baby boomers will overwhelm the system's pay-as-you-go funding mechanism. Moreover, by 2052, the program's trillion-dollar trust fund is expected to run dry. Experts continue to debate the seriousness of the program's problems and the best way to strengthen it. Three years ago, President George W. Bush called for bolstering Social Security funding by allowing workers to invest part of their payroll contributions in personal investment accounts. Since his reelection, Bush has put Social Security reform at the top of his legislative agenda.

CIVIL LIBERTIES, CIVIL RIGHTS AND JUSTICE

Right to Die

Terri Schiavo lay in a "persistent vegetative state" for 15 years until she died on March 31, 2005, after hospice staff removed her life-sustaining feeding tube. Schiavo's case touched off a wrenching nationwide debate that continues in political, legal and medical circles over when, if ever, to withdraw life support from incapacitated patients unable to express their own wishes. Many advocates and experts used the case to emphasize the need to write a "living will" and designate a "health-care proxy" to help make such decisions, but only a small minority of Americans have taken either step. Some members of Congress want to make it harder to remove life support, but others say that no legal changes are needed and the issue is for the states to decide, not the federal government. Meanwhile, the U.S. Supreme Court is preparing to hear the Bush administration's attempt to thwart the Oregon law legalizing physician-assisted suicide—a law twice approved by the state's voters but strongly opposed by right-to-life and disability-rights groups.

Supreme Court's Future

For the past 18 years, Chief Justice William H. Rehnquist has led a Supreme Court with a tenuous conservative majority and a cohesive liberal bloc. Now battling cancer, Rehnquist is widely expected to retire soon, perhaps before the end of the court's current term this summer. That would allow President George W. Bush to put his stamp on the court, which has had no vacancies for more than 10 years. Other justices are also nearing the end of their tenure, including the court's most liberal member, John Paul Stevens. Bush has promised to nominate conservative jurists to the court, which could start fierce confirmation fights in the closely divided Senate. Republicans are already angry with Democrats' tactics in blocking votes on Bush's nominees for lower courts. Meanwhile, the court's calendar includes controversial cases on the death penalty, church-state relations and property rights.

Gang Crisis

Once an urban problem, street gangs have now infiltrated U.S. communities large and small. Gang experts say at least 21,500 gangs—with more than 731,000 members—are active nationwide. Long-established domestic gangs like the Bloods and the Crips remain powerful, but the problem has worsened dramatically in recent years. Heavy immigration, particularly from Latin America and Asia, has introduced highly violent gangs like Mara Salvatrucha and the Almighty Latin Kings Nation. Bound by tight ethnic and racial ties, they often stymie police investigations by assaulting or killing potential witnesses. Having already diversified from illegal drugs into auto theft, extortion, property crimes and home invasion, some East Coast gangs have started trafficking in fraudulent identification papers that could be used by terrorists. While experts agree that gangs are more pervasive than ever, few agree on a remedy. Proposed legislation would increase penalties for gang membership and gang crimes, but critics say it won't solve the problem.

ENVIRONMENT

Alternative Energy

Recent breakthroughs in hydrogen fuel-cell technology offer new hope that the United States could one day end its dependence on fossil fuels. Proponents of renewable fuels say non-polluting hydrogen could both help end U.S. reliance on Middle Eastern oil and dramatically reduce air pollution and emissions of carbon dioxide, the main greenhouse gas linked to global warming. The Bush administration is intensifying its support for fuel cells, including a proposal to spend $1.2 billion on hydrogen research over the next five years. But critics, even those who foresee a major role for hydrogen fuel cells, note the administration is also proposing increases in domestic production of highly polluting fossil fuels to generate electricity and power cars as well as to produce the hydrogen itself. Critics also say the administration is continuing to reject caps on carbon emissions and underfund subsidies for wind power and other renewable-energy technologies.

Smart Growth

Sprawling suburbs, increasing traffic congestion, strip malls surrounded by acres of parking lots: Are these long-standing features of the modern American landscape only going to get worse? Without a shift in priorities, projected population increases over the next few decades are expected to accelerate the spread of development away from city and town centers. Critics contend that sprawl eats up valuable open space, worsens air and water pollution and destroys Americans' sense of community. They champion policies that encourage "smart growth"—compact neighborhoods that combine housing, offices, schools and other amenities linked by public transportation and sidewalks. Developers and land-rights advocates call such policies intrusive social engineering and say sprawl is unstoppable—a sign of American prosperity and an efficient market responding to the growing demand for a piece of the American dream.

BUSINESS AND THE ECONOMY

Big-Box Stores

America is teeming with Wal-Marts, Home Depots and other "big-box" chain stores—some larger than five football fields. Millions of consumers like the low prices, free parking and one-stop shopping convenience offered by the megastores, while policymakers say the stores create jobs, enable customers to save money for other expenditures and pump much-needed tax dollars into community coffers. Critics say big-box stores actually harm local economies and flourish only because they receive public subsidies, pay low salaries and benefits and utilize unethical and possibly illegal practices to drive smaller, locally owned competitors out of business. Critics also say the stores cause added traffic congestion and suburban sprawl, force U.S. companies to ship high-paying manufacturing jobs overseas and cost more in local services than the taxes they generate. Communities increasingly are passing special ordinances to keep the big retailers out, but the chains are fighting back, saying they are simply giving consumers what they want.

Privatizing the Military

Since the Cold War ended, a downsized U.S. military has increasingly turned to private contractors to fill positions once held by military personnel. In U.S.-occupied Iraq, most of the jobs involve logistical support, but several thousand contractors also work as armed security guards or help interrogate Iraqi prisoners. The privatiza-tion trend went largely unnoticed until April 2004, when insurgents in Fallujah murdered four civilian security guards and burned and mutilated their bodies. Soon afterward, at least two contract interrogators were implicated in prisoner abuses at Baghdad's Abu Ghraib prison. The incidents have renewed questions about the effectiveness and legal status of private contractors operating in war zones and the wisdom of the Pentagon's increasing reliance on private contractors. Supporters of privatization say the military's use of contractors saves taxpayers money and improves efficiency by freeing up soldiers for strictly combat operations.

FOREIGN POLICY

International Law

The Bush administration has been widely condemned for skirting international law in its harsh handling of enemy combatants after the war in Afghanistan and bypassing the United Nations in the invasion of Iraq. Critics at home and abroad say the policies weakened international support for U.S. actions and could endanger any U.S. service members captured in future conflicts. Liberal advocacy groups are urging the U.S. Supreme Court to consider foreign and international law in making decisions and the lower courts to be open to suits against foreign officials or multinational corporations for human rights violations abroad. Conservatives counter that foreign law has no role in U.S. constitutional issues and are joining with business groups to urge U.S. courts to restrict litigation for overseas offenses. Meanwhile, there is growing concern that international trade laws grant dispute-settlement tribunals powers so broad they can challenge U.S. court decisions and domestic laws that protect health, safety, the environment and workers' rights.

Middle East Peace

After more than four years of violence and little negotiation, the Middle East is abuzz with new hopes for peace. In the first leadership change in decades, moderate politician Mahmoud Abbas has been chosen as Palestinian president following the death of Yasser Arafat, who was long considered the primary obstacle to peace by Israel and the United States. Prime Minister Ariel Sharon is planning to unilaterally withdraw Israeli settlements from the Gaza Strip, and President George W. Bush has committed the United States to helping resolve the conflict. These developments may revive peace talks focusing on the eventual creation of an independent Palestinian state. However, skeptics argue the physical and psychological foundations needed for peace are being eroded by Palestinian suicide bombings and harsh Israeli reprisals, confiscations of Palestinian farmland, expansion of Israeli settlements and the erection of an immense barrier between Palestinian and Israeli lands.

Exporting Democracy

At his second inauguration in January 2005, President George W. Bush vowed "to seek and support the growth of democratic movements and institutions in every nation." Although critics from Russian President Vladimir Putin to political scientist Francis Fukuyama said the president was taking on too great a challenge and that similar efforts in the past have failed, the president's backers urged him to stay the course. Successful elections in Iraq and Afghanistan and promising pro-democracy activities in Lebanon, Egypt, Ukraine, Kyrgyzstan and other nations seemed to prove Bush correct. Still, Bush's campaign to promote global democracy faces challenges, including forming an interim government in violence-torn Iraq. Moreover, skeptics say, establishing a true government of the people requires civil liberties for women as well as men, a free press, an independent judiciary and the other institutions that make up a democracy.

Preface

D oes Social Security face an immediate funding crisis? Should the Senate limit filibusters against judicial nominees? Is democracy taking root in Iraq and Afghanistan? These questions—and many more—are at the heart of American public policy. How can instructors best engage students with these crucial issues? We feel that students need objective, yet provocative, examinations of these issues in order to understand how they affect citizens today and will for years to come. This annual collection aims to promote in-depth discussion, facilitate further research, and help readers formulate their own positions on important subjects. Get your students talking both inside and outside the classroom about *Issues for Debate in American Public Policy.*

This sixth edition includes 16 up-to-date reports by *CQ Researcher,* an award-winning weekly policy backgrounder that brings complicated issues down to earth. Each report chronicles and analyzes executive, legislative and judicial activities at all levels of government. This collection is divided into seven diverse policy areas to cover a range of issues studied in most American government and public policy courses: education, health care, social policy, civil liberties, civil rights and justice, the environment, business and the economy, and foreign policy.

CQ RESEARCHER

CQ Researcher was founded in 1923 as *Editorial Research Reports* and was sold primarily to newspapers as a research tool. The publication was renamed and redesigned in 1991 as *The CQ Researcher.* Although the *Researcher* is still used by hundreds of journalists and newspapers, many of which reprint portions of the reports, its main subscribers are now high school, college and public libraries, and its primary audience is students. In 2002, the *Researcher* won the American Bar Association's coveted Silver Gavel award for magazine excellence for a series of nine reports on civil liberties and other legal issues.

Researcher staff writers—all highly experienced journalists—sometimes compare the experience of writing a *Researcher* report to drafting a college term paper. Indeed, there are many similarities. Each report is as long as many term papers—about 11,000 words—and is written by one person without any significant outside help. One of the key differences is that the writers interview leading experts, scholars and government officials for each issue.

Like students, staff writers begin the creative process by choosing a topic. Working with the *Researcher*'s editors, the writer identifies a controversial subject that has important public policy implications. After a topic is selected, the writer embarks on one or two weeks of intense research. Articles are clipped, books are ordered and information is gathered from a wide variety of sources, including interest groups, universities and the government. Once the writer feels well informed, he or she begins the interview process. Each report requires a minimum of 10 to 15 interviews with academics, officials, lobbyists and people working in the field. After all interviews are completed, the writer develops a detailed outline. Only then does the writing begin.

CHAPTER FORMAT

Each issue of *CQ Researcher*, and therefore each selection in this book, is structured in the same way. Each begins with an overview, which briefly summarizes the areas that will be explored in greater detail in the rest of the chapter. The next section, "Issues," is the core of each chapter. It chronicles important and current debates on the topic under discussion and is structured around a number of key issue questions, such as "Has the U.S. allied itself too closely with Israel?" and "Does the child welfare system prepare foster adolescents for adulthood?" These questions are usually the subject of much debate among practitioners and scholars in the field. Hence, the answers presented are never conclusive but detail the range of opinion on the topic.

Next, the "Background" section provides a history of the issue being examined. This retrospective covers important legislative measures, executive actions and court decisions that illustrate how current policy has evolved. Then, the "Current Situation" section examines contemporary policy issues, legislation under consideration and legal action being taken. Each selection concludes with an "Outlook" section, which addresses possible regulation, court rulings and initiatives from Capitol Hill and the White House over the next five to 10 years.

Each report contains features that augment the main text: two or three sidebars that examine issues related to the topic at hand, a debate between two experts with opposing views on the topic, a chronology of key dates and events and an annotated bibliography that details the major sources used in writing the article.

ACKNOWLEDGMENTS

We wish to thank many people for helping to make this collection a reality. Tom Colin, managing editor of *CQ Researcher*, gave us his enthusiastic support and cooperation as we developed this sixth edition. He and his talented staff of editors and writers have amassed a first-class library of *Researcher* reports, and we are fortunate to have access to that rich cache. We also thankfully acknowledge the advice and feedback from current readers and are gratified by their satisfaction with the book.

Some readers may be learning about *CQ Researcher* for the first time. We expect that many readers will want regular access to this excellent weekly research tool. For subscription information or a no-obligation free trial of the *Researcher*, please contact CQ Press at www.cqpress.com or toll-free at 1-866-4CQ-PRESS (1-866-427-7737).

We hope that you will be pleased by the sixth edition of *Issues for Debate in American Public Policy*. We welcome your feedback and suggestions for future editions. Please direct comments to Charisse Kiino, CQ Press, 1255 22nd Street, NW, Suite 400, Washington, DC 20037, or *ckiino@cqpress.com*.

—The Editors of CQ Press

Contributors

Thomas J. Colin, managing editor of *CQ Researcher*, has been a magazine and newspaper journalist for more than 25 years. Before joining Congressional Quarterly in 1991, he was a reporter and editor at the *Miami Herald* and *National Geographic* and editor in chief of *Historic Preservation*. He holds a bachelor's degree in English from the College of William & Mary and a bachelor's degree in journalism from the University of Missouri.

Mary H. Cooper recently retired after 22 years as a *CQ Researcher* staff writer specializing in environmental, energy and defense issues. She formerly was a reporter and Washington correspondent for the Rome daily newspaper *l'Unità* and is the author of *The Business of Drugs* (CQ Press, 1990). Cooper graduated from Hollins College with a bachelor's degree in English.

Nicole Gaouette is a Washington writer who has served as a correspondent for the *Christian Science Monitor* in the Middle East, Tokyo and Boston. She has also been a Tokyo-based editor for Knight Ridder Financial News. She received a bachelor of arts degree in East Asian studies from McGill University and a master of science degree in journalism from Columbia University.

Sarah Glazer specializes in health, education and social policy issues. Her articles have appeared in the *Washington Post*, *Glamour* and *The Public Interest*, as well as in *Gender and Work*, a book of essays. Glazer covered energy legislation for the Environmental and Energy Study Conference and reported for United Press International. She holds a bachelor of arts degree in American history from the University of Chicago.

Brian Hansen is a former *CQ Researcher* staff writer who now is a Washington reporter for McGraw-Hill. He previously reported for the *Colorado Daily* in Boulder and the *Environment News Service*. He has received the Scripps Howard Foundation award for public service reporting and the Education Writers Association award for investigative reporting. He holds a bachelor of arts degree in political science and a master of arts degree in education from the University of Colorado

Kenneth Jost, associate editor of *CQ Researcher*, graduated from Harvard College and Georgetown University Law Center, where he is an adjunct professor. He is the author of *The Supreme Court Yearbook* and editor of *The Supreme Court A to Z* (both published by CQ Press). He was a member of the *CQ Researcher* team that won the 2002 American Bar Association Silver Gavel Award.

Peter Katel is a veteran journalist who previously served as the Latin America bureau chief for *Time* in Mexico City and as a Miami-based correspondent for *Newsweek* and the *Miami Herald*'s *El Nuevo Herald*. He also worked as a reporter in New Mexico for 11 years and wrote for several nongovernmental organizations, including International Social Service and the World Bank. He has won several awards, including the Interamerican Press Association's Bartolome Mitre Award. Katel is a graduate of the University of New Mexico with a degree in university studies.

Barbara Mantel is a freelance writer in New York City whose work has appeared in the *New York Times, Journal of Child and Adolescent Psychopharmacology* and *Mamm Magazine*. She is a former correspondent and senior producer for National Public Radio and has won several journalism awards, including the National Press Club's Best Consumer Journalism Award and Lincoln University's Unity Award. She holds a bachelor of arts degree in history and economics from the University of Virginia and a master of arts degree in economics from Northwestern University.

Patrick Marshall is a freelance writer based in Bainbridge Island, Wash., who writes about public policy and technology issues. His recent *CQ Researcher* reports include "Policing the Borders" and "Civil Liberties in Wartime."

Tom Price is a Washington-based freelance journalist who writes regularly for *CQ Researcher*. Previously he was a correspondent in the Cox Newspapers Washington Bureau and chief politics writer for the *Dayton Daily News* and the *Journal Herald*. He is the author of two Washington guidebooks: *Washington, D.C., for Dummies* and the *Irreverent Guide to Washington, D.C.* His work has appeared in *The New York Times, Time, Rolling Stone* and other periodicals. He earned a bachelor of science degree in journalism at Ohio University.

Amy Standen is a writer, editor and public radio producer in San Francisco. She is also the author of *Maggie Taylor's Landscape of Dreams* (2005).

William Triplett is a veteran writer and former *CQ Researcher* staff writer who is now the Washington correspondent for *Variety*. He previously covered science and the arts for such publications as *Smithsonian, Air & Space, Washingtonian, Nature* and the *Washington Post*. He holds a bachelor of arts degree in journalism from Ohio University and a master of arts degree in English literature from Georgetown University.

1

No Child Left Behind

Barbara Mantel

President Bush visits with students in St. Louis, Mo., on Jan. 5, 2004, the second anniversary of the No Child Left Behind Act. Bush has called the sweeping overhaul of federal education policy the start of "a new era, a new time in public education." But today the bipartisan legislation is under heavy criticism from Republicans and Democrats alike. Besides seeking exemptions from parts of the law, legislators are pressing Congress for more money to implement the act.

From *CQ Researcher*, May 27, 2005.

Politics indeed makes for strange bedfellows: There was President Bush standing on a Boston stage flanked by four jubilant legislators, two Republicans and two Democrats, including liberal lion Sen. Edward M. Kennedy of Massachusetts. The occasion was the signing on Jan. 8, 2002, of the No Child Left Behind Act — a sweeping, bipartisan overhaul of federal education policy.

Cheering crowds greeted Bush and the four lawmakers that day as they touted the new law on a whirlwind, 12-hour tour of three states, with the president calling the legislation the start of "a new era, a new time in public education."

Kennedy, who played a key role in negotiating the bill's passage, told Bush: "What a difference it has made this year with your leadership." [1]

The law is actually the most recent reauthorization of the Elementary and Secondary Education Act (ESEA), which since 1965 has tried to raise the academic performance of all students.

"This legislation holds out great promise for education," said education researcher G. Gage Kingsbury, director of research at the Northwest Evaluation Association, in Lake Oswego, Ore. "But it also has strong requirements and includes a host of provisions that have never been tried on this scale before." [2]

No Child Left Behind (NCLB) increases the reach of the federal government into the management of local schools and raises the stakes for schools, districts and states. It increases funding for schools serving poor students, mandates "highly qualified" teachers in every classroom and holds schools that accept federal funds accountable for raising the achievement of all students. Schools that

Few States Make the Grade on Teacher Quality

Only three states — Connecticut, Louisiana and South Carolina — received a grade of A for their efforts to improve teacher quality, according to a 2005 assessment by *Education Week*. In every state except New Mexico, more than 50 percent of secondary teachers majored in the core academic subject they teach. But only eight states had more than 75 percent of secondary school teachers who majored in their core subject.

Rating State Efforts to Improve Teacher Quality

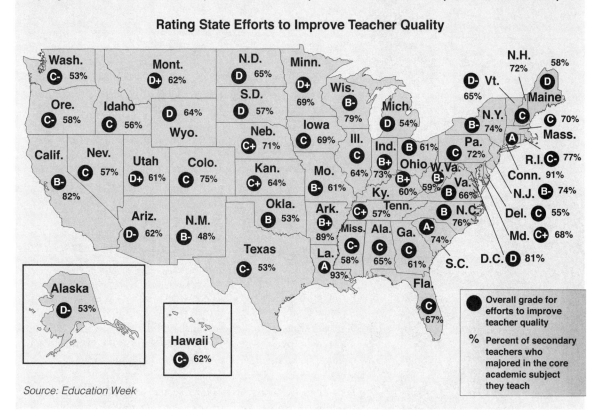

Source: Education Week

don't meet state benchmarks two years in a row are labeled "in need of improvement" and suffer sanctions.

Most significantly, NCLB sets a deadline: By 2014 all students must be grade-level proficient in reading and math — as evidenced by their scores on annual tests in grades 3-8, and once in high school. (*See sidebar, p. 3.*)

But more than three years after its passage, the bipartisan accord that produced the bill appears badly frayed. Kennedy now says No Child Left Behind "has been underfunded, mismanaged and poorly implemented and is becoming the most spectacular broken promise of this Republican administration and Congress. "America's children deserve better." [3]

In the states, politicians from both parties are equally unhappy, including GOP legislators from some "red states" that overwhelmingly supported Bush in last year's presidential election. "I wish they'd take the stinking money and go back to Washington," said state Rep. Steven Mascaro, R-Utah. [4]

"We have to fight back," Gov. John Baldacci, D-Maine, said. "We have to tell them we're not going to take it any more." [5]

It hasn't been just talk. In early May, Utah's Republican governor signed legislation giving precedence to the state's education policies when they conflict with NCLB, and in the past year and a half more than 30 states have introduced bills that would release them from some of the law's requirements.

The ABCs of NCLB

Here are the basic provisions of the No Child Left Behind Act, which spells out its standards and requirements in more than 1,000 pages of regulations:

Standards and Testing — As in the previous version of the law, each state must adopt challenging standards for what its students should know and be able to do. Academic standards must contain coherent and rigorous content and encourage the teaching of advanced skills. States must also develop tests aligned to the standards and establish cutoff scores that classify student achievement as basic, proficient or advanced. What has changed is the amount of testing states must do. Beginning in September 2005, states must test children annually in grades 3-8 and once in high school. Previously, schoolchildren had to be tested only four times in grades K-12.

Public Reporting — For the first time, states must publicly report their test results, with student scores broken down into four subgroups: economically disadvantaged students; major racial and ethnic groups; students with disabilities and students with limited English proficiency. States must report each school's progress in raising student performance and the difference in teacher qualifications in high-poverty versus low-poverty schools.

Accountability — All students must reach proficiency in reading and math by 2014. States must establish annual benchmarks for their schools, with special emphasis on closing achievement gaps between different groups of students. Since 1994 states had been required to make "adequate yearly progress" (AYP) in raising achievement, but there was no firm timetable or deadline for students reaching proficiency. Now if a school does not make AYP, the state and district must develop a two-year plan to help the school improve.

Sanctions — If a school receiving Title I funds — designed to improve the performance of low-income students — does not make AYP in raising student performance for two years in a row, the state must designate it a school "in need of improvement." [1] Most states are applying this rule to all schools in a Title I district, even those that do not take Title I money. Students in these schools must be given the option of transferring out, and if a school fails to achieve its AYP for three consecutive years, it must pay for tutoring, after-school programs and summer school for those low-income students who remain. After four years, the state must restructure the school.

Teachers — For the first time, teachers must be "highly qualified," meaning they have a college degree and are licensed or certified by the state. Newly hired middle-school teachers must have a major or pass a test demonstrating their knowledge in the subjects they teach. Veteran teachers can do the same or demonstrate their competency through an alternative system developed by each state.

---

[1] About 55 percent of the schools in the nation's 100 largest districts were eligible for Title I funds in the 2001/2002 school year; http://nces.ed.gov/pubs2003/100_largest/table_05_1.asp.

Besides seeking exemptions from parts of the law, legislators are pressing Congress for more money to implement the act. Much of the controversy stems from the fact that Congress has appropriated $27 billion less than it authorized for the law's implementation.

But the act's supporters say enough money is being provided, pointing out that federal funding for public education has increased by more than 30 percent since the NCLB was enacted. "The education reforms contained in the No Child Left Behind Act are coupled with historic increases in K-12 funding," according to the Web site of Sen. Judd Gregg, R-N.H., who made the whirlwind trip with Bush and Kennedy three years ago. [6]

Nevertheless, in April the National Education Association, the nation's largest teachers' union, sued the Department of Education on the grounds that the act is not properly funded. In addition, Connecticut also is threatening to sue, estimating that NCLB will cost the state an extra $41.6 million dollars in the next few years. The atmosphere has gotten so disagreeable at times that Secretary of Education Margaret Spellings angrily called Connecticut officials "un-American."

Part of the states' resentment stems from the fact that Congress provides only 8 percent of total funding for public education — $501.3 billion in the last school year — but since the 1960s has passed laws giving the Department of Education increasing powers over the nation's 96,000 schools. [7] The NCLB is the most far reaching yet.

Supporters of the act say it represents an evolutionary change, while critics say it is a revolutionary incursion of the federal government into the historic domain of the states.

"I don't know any educator or parent who doesn't think our schools should be accountable," said state Rep. Margaret Dayton, R-Orem. "The question is: To whom should they be accountable? Under No Child Left Behind our local schools are accountable to Washington, D.C., and here in Utah, we think our schools should be accountable to the parents and the communities where they are." [8]

Even supporters acknowledge that NCLB's provisions have been overwhelming for states without the administrative staff to implement the law.

In 2004, No Child Left Behind became "a significant force affecting the operations and decisions of states, school districts and schools," according to the Center on Education Policy, an independent advocate for public education. [9] For example, the law has compelled states and school districts to step up efforts to test students in more grades and put "highly qualified" teachers in every classroom. In addition, for the first time entire school districts have been labeled "in need of improvement."

However, as the law's requirements take hold, the debate about its fairness and efficacy has been escalating. Besides the debate over funding, critics argue that the law is too rigid and that too many schools — even good schools — are being told they need to improve. This has sparked widespread opposition to President's Bush's proposal to extend the law's annual testing requirements to high school students. (*See "At Issue," p. 17.*)

On the other side of the debate, many of NCLB's staunchest defenders worry that the Department of Education has become too flexible in implementing the law, citing a recent relaxation of requirements for testing disabled students and department approval of what some see as lax state plans to ensure that veteran teachers are "highly qualified."

And voices from all sides call for more guidance and technical support to localities from the Department of Education.

As the public discussion grows louder leading up to the law's reauthorization fight in 2007, coalitions have begun to form. The American Association of School Administrators, the Children's Defense Fund, the Learning Disabilities Association of America, the National Education Association and several other groups joined together last fall to call for significant revisions in the law. Proponents — including the Citizens' Commission on Civil Rights, the National Alliance of Black School Educators, Just for Kids, the Education Trust and the Business Roundtable — formed their own coalition, called the Achievement Alliance, to vigorously defend the law.

Here are some of the questions parents, educators, children's advocates, lawmakers, and researchers are asking:

Has No Child Left Behind raised student achievement?

The goal of the NCLB law is to ensure that by 2014 all children are at grade-level proficiency in reading and math. The law requires states to measure student achievement by testing children in grades 3-8 every year, and once in high school.

But each state determines its own academic standards, the courses taught, the standardized tests used and the cutoff scores that define a student as proficient. Thus, the rigor varies between the states, making it impossible to compare one state to another. Colorado may have reported 87 percent of its fourth-graders proficient in reading in 2003 and Massachusetts 56 percent, but no one knows what that says about the relative achievement of their students. [10]

It is possible, however, to look at student achievement within a state and ask, for example, how this year's fourth-graders compare to last year's.

With a growing number of states administering annual tests, researchers have conducted some preliminary studies. They all show that student achievement, for the most part, is improving.

The Center on Education Policy surveyed states and a sampling of school districts and reported that 73 percent of states and 72 percent of districts said student achievement is improving. In addition, states and districts were more likely to say that achievement gaps between white and black students, white and Hispanic students, and English-language learners and other students were narrowing rather than widening or staying the same. [11]

Similarly, the Council of the Great City Schools, a coalition of 65 of the nation's largest urban school systems, reported that while math and reading scores in

Thousands of Schools Missed Progress Targets

Eleven thousand public schools — or nearly 12 percent of the nation's 96,000 public schools — failed in 2004 for the second year in a row to meet "adequate yearly progress" (AYP) targets set by the No Child Left Behind law. Such schools are labeled "in need of improvement" and must offer all students the right to transfer; after missing AYP for three consecutive years, they must offer low-income students supplemental services, like after-school tutoring. After four years, the state must restructure the school.

Number of Public Schools Needing Improvement
(based on failure to meet "adequate yearly progress" targets)

Wash.	166
Mont.	40
N.D.	21
Minn.	71
N.H.	71
Vt.	28
Maine	50
Ore.	328
Idaho	71
Wyo.	64
S.D.	106
Wis.	51
Mich.	450
N.Y.	713
Mass.	381
Iowa	66
Pa.	333
Calif.	1626
Nev.	122
Utah	16
Colo.	129
Neb.	N/A
Ill.	694
Ind.	77
Ohio	487
W.Va.	37
R.I.	39
Conn.	134
Kan.	21
Mo.	40
Ky.	130
Va.	113
N.J.	520
Ariz.	184
N.M.	124
Okla.	146
Ark.	305
Tenn.	165
N.C.	160
Del.	43
Texas	199
Miss.	132
Ala.	83
Ga.	413
S.C.	208
Md.	256
La.	75
D.C.	79
Fla.	965
Alaska	179
Hawaii	138

Source: Education Week

urban schools remain lower than national averages, they are rising and achievement gaps are narrowing. [12]

The Education Trust, a nonprofit advocate of school reform, also analyzed proficiency rates since No Child Left Behind took effect. It found that in most states it studied, achievement scores of elementary school students had risen, and achievement gaps had narrowed. But when the Trust looked at middle and high schools, the results were more mixed. While the majority of states in the study reported an increase in the percentage of proficient students, there was much less success in narrowing achievement gaps. [13]

Delaware is a case in point. The state has made some of the largest strides in raising achievement and narrowing gaps among elementary students. For instance, the gap in Delaware between the percentage of reading-proficient white and Hispanic fifth-graders narrowed from 31 points in 2001 to less than five points in 2004, and for African-American students, the gap narrowed from 22 points to 16. [14] But in middle schools, achievement gaps have actually widened.

"It is a little harder to get a reform groundswell in middle schools and high schools," says Delaware's Secretary of Education Valerie Woodruff. "In math, for

Is Testing Crowding Out Art and Recess?

Testing required by the No Child Left Behind Act is taking a toll on education, says George Wood, an Ohio high school principal and director of The Forum for Education and Democracy. "School people are no fools," Wood wrote in the 2004 book *Many Children Left Behind.* "Tell them what they will be measured on, and they will try to measure up."

"Test preparation crowds out much else that parents have taken for granted in their schools," Wood said. Recess for elementary school students, nap time for kindergartners and music and art for middle school students are some of the things being eliminated from the school day, he contends, along with reductions in class time for social studies and creative writing.

Diane Rentner, project coordinator at the Center on Education Policy, says the cutbacks haven't been too bad so far. "It's not huge, it's not a revolution yet," she says. In a March 2005 survey of school districts, the center found "a slight movement toward cutting down on other subjects to focus on reading and math," Rentner says.

More than two-thirds of districts reported that instructional time on subjects other than math and reading had been reduced minimally or not at all. However, 27 percent of the districts reported that social studies class time had been reduced somewhat or to a great extent, and close to 25 percent said instruction time in science, art and music had been reduced.

While the center's findings don't support a revolutionary shift in class time, Rentner still calls the trend worrisome and expects that as state proficiency benchmarks rise, there may be additional pressure on schools to focus more time on reading and math. "It would be sad if there were no arts in the schools, and students didn't learn civic education," she says.

Rentner also points out another potentially troubling survey result: The poorer the school district, the more likely it was to require schools to allot a specific amount of time to math and reading. "You could jump to the next conclusion that low-income kids are receiving a less rich curriculum," Rentner says. While that might be necessary in the short term to bring kids closer to proficiency in math and reading, Rentner hopes that it doesn't have to continue.

It is this impact on low-income and minority schools that most concerns Wood. An opponent of NCLB, Wood calls for a moratorium on high-stakes testing until more research shows it to have some link to student success after leaving high school.

But Daria Hall, a policy analyst at the Education Trust, which generally supports the goals and methods of No Child Left Behind while criticizing the government's implementation of the law, says that's the wrong response. "We don't deny that focusing so much on math and reading means that other subjects might not receive the attention they deserve," says Hall. But that doesn't have to happen, she says, citing schools, many in poor districts, that have integrated math and reading instruction into their other subjects.

"So, for example, there is no need to give short shrift to social studies," she claims. "We can teach the content of social studies while at the same time covering state standards on reading." The same can be done, she says, with math and science.

But it's not something that one teacher or even one school can do alone, Hall adds. "There needs to be research from the U.S. Department of Education on how to effectively integrate standards across the curriculum," she says. "It needs to really be a systemic effort."

example, we don't have enough well qualified teachers at the middle school level."

The fundamental question is how much of the documented improvement is a result of No Child Left Behind. Daria Hall, a policy analyst at the Education Trust, says it is a significant amount. Educators "are using the standards to develop a challenging curriculum for all students," she says. "They are using assessment results to inform their instruction in the classroom."

NCLB, Hall says, gives administrators leverage to make needed changes.

Diane Rentner, project coordinator at the Center on Education Policy, is hearing something different. The center did not specifically ask state and district officials if they thought the law was responsible for achievement gains. But Rentner says district officials later said they "were almost offended that No Child Left Behind would be viewed as this great catalyst of change because they felt like they had been working for years to improve student achievement."

"Our math curriculum has been completely reviewed from K-12 and in the majority of cases exceeds state standards," says Margo Sorrick, an assistant superintendent in Wheaton, Ill. For instance, the district now requires three years rather two years of math for high school graduation. "These changes have nothing to do with No Child Left Behind," says Sorrick.

But the law does shine a new light on those reforms. Now that states must report their progress in raising student achievement, the press routinely covers the release of so-called state report cards. Stiffening graduation requirements, revising the curriculum and replacing staff at the worst schools have taken on more urgency, Rentner says. "We jokingly say the news media have become the enforcer of the law," she adds.

But trying to figure out the law's exact impact is still all but impossible. Besides the difficulty of teasing out the roles of pre- and post-NCLB reforms, there are gaps in the data. Most states started testing students only six or seven years ago, and many changed their tests, making before-and-after comparisons unreliable.

Several experts also warn that initial gains in achievement scores may be deceptive. Brian Stecher, a senior social scientist at the Rand Corporation, a nonprofit research organization, says that on new, high-stakes tests teachers often feel pressure to coach students in test-taking skills and to teach the material emphasized on the test. "That can allow you to get initially a relatively big gain in scores," Stecher says, "and then the increase tapers off."

That's of particular concern to states because the pace of recent improvement is not fast enough to ensure 100 percent student proficiency by 2014. "Progress needs to be accelerated," Hall says bluntly.

Are too many schools being labeled "in need of improvement?"

Holding states accountable for student achievement is central to No Child Left Behind. The law gives states a firm goal and a firm deadline, and to reach it each state must come up with annual benchmarks. In Wisconsin, for instance, 67.5 percent of a school's students must be proficient in reading this school year, 87 percent six years later and finally 100 percent in 2014. [15]

But it's not enough for a school to look at its students as a single, undifferentiated block. NCLB requires schools to divide students into subgroups — ethnic, racial, low-income, disabled and English-language learner — and each must meet the proficiency benchmarks as well.

Schools also must test at least 95 percent of students in a subgroup, meet state-determined attendance requirements and improve high school graduation rates.

Schools that meet all of these targets are deemed to have made "adequate yearly progress" (AYP). But if a school misses just one target it doesn't make AYP, and the district and state must create a two-year intervention plan. Options include reducing class size, providing extra help for disadvantaged students and increasing professional development for teachers. Local and state officials decide on the details, and the federal government provides extra funding.

Sanctions prescribed by the law, however, kick in when a school doesn't make AYP for two consecutive years. Such schools, if they take Title I funds, are labeled "in need of improvement" and must offer all students the right to transfer; after missing AYP for three consecutive years, they must offer low-income students supplemental services, like after-school tutoring. After four years, the state must restructure the school.

This system of accountability is among the most contentious elements of NCLB. While praising the overall goals of the law, the National Conference of State Legislatures called the system rigid and overly prescriptive. Too many schools, it said, are being labeled "in need of improvement," and the law, therefore, "spreads resources too thinly, over too many schools, and reduces the chances that schools that truly are in need can be helped." [16]

Last year, 11,008 public schools — nearly 12 percent of the nation's total — were identified as needing improvement. [17] Critics of the law see that number rising dramatically. "Essentially, all schools will fail to meet the unrealistic goal of 100 percent proficient or above," wrote testing expert Robert Linn, "and No Child Left Behind will have turned into No School Succeeding." [18]

But Keri Briggs, senior adviser to Acting Deputy Secretary of Education Raymond Simon, strongly disagrees. "We have identified schools that have beat expectations; there are several in many states," says Briggs. "We know it's possible."

Critics, however, say the accountability system has several flaws, such as not recognizing progress made by schools that start with large numbers of low-performing students. A school that significantly raises the percentage of students reading at proficiency, for example, would still not make AYP if that percentage remains below the state benchmark. Such schools "should be given credit," says Scott Young, a senior policy specialist at the National Conference of State Legislatures.

But the law does provide a so-called safe harbor alternative for these schools: If a subgroup of students falls short of the benchmark, the school can still make AYP if the number below the proficiency level is decreased by 10 percent from the year before. But according to Linn, that's something even the best schools would have difficulty accomplishing. "Only a tiny fraction of schools meet AYP through the safe-harbor provision because it is so extreme," Linn wrote. [19]

After protests from both Republican and Democratic governors, Secretary Spellings announced in April she would appoint a panel to consider allowing states to use a "growth model" to reward schools whose students make significant progress but that still miss AYP. Such a model would follow individual students as they move from grade to grade. By contrast, the current system compares the current fourth-grade class, for example, with last year's fourth-graders.

Kingsbury, at the Northwest Evaluation Association, likes the growth-model idea but says goals and timetables are needed. Otherwise, Kingsbury explains, "there is no guarantee students will end up at a high level of proficiency when they graduate."

Another frequent complaint is that the accountability system is too blunt an instrument. "The problem," says Patricia Sullivan, director of the Center on Education Policy, "is the lack of distinction between the school that misses by a little and the school that misses by a lot." The school that misses the benchmark for one subgroup for two consecutive years is identified as needing improvement just like the school that misses the benchmark for several subgroups. Both face the same sanction: All students would have the option to transfer.

Since urban schools tend to be more diverse and have more subgroups, it is harder for them to make AYP. But the Education Trust's Hall says those who complain care more about the adults working in urban schools than the kids. "Is it fair to expect less of schools that are educating diverse student bodies?" Hall asks. "Is it fair to those students? Absolutely not."

The Department of Education has signaled its willingness to compromise, to a degree. Many districts have complained that requiring all students with disabilities to be grade-level proficient by 2014 is unfair and unrealistic. The law does allow 1 percent of all students — those with significant cognitive disabilities — to take alternative assessments. Secretary Spellings recently declared that another 2 percent — those with persistent academic disabilities — could take alternative tests, geared toward their abilities and not necessarily at grade level. States would have to apply to the Department of Education in order to use this option.

The reaction from educators was muted. Betty J. Sternberg, Connecticut's education commissioner, said, "The percentages are fine. They help us. The problem may be in the details of what they are requiring us to do to have access to the flexibility." [20]

But advocates for disabled students worry that the department is backpedaling. Suzanne Fornaro, board president of the Learning Disability Association of America, is particularly concerned about students with learning disabilities: "If the changes result in lowering expectations, they might result in decreasing a student's access to the general curriculum and high-quality instruction."

Is No Child Left Behind improving the quality of teaching?

Teaching quality may be the single most important in-school factor in how well students learn. While it's difficult to know precisely what makes effective teachers, there are some common yardsticks, including mastery of their subject area. Yet government surveys show that, "One out of four secondary classes (24 percent) in core academic subjects are assigned to a teacher lacking even a college minor in the subject being taught." (*See map, p. 2.*) That figure rises to 29 percent in high-minority schools and 34 percent in high-poverty schools. [21]

No one blames teachers. It's rarely by choice that teachers are assigned to a subject out of their field. But NCLB requires a "highly qualified" teacher in every classroom by the end of the 2005/2006 school year. Highly qualified teachers must have a bachelor's degree, be licensed or certified by the state and demonstrate that they know each subject they teach. New teachers can qualify by either passing a state test or having completed a college major in their subject area. Veteran teachers have a third option: an alternative evaluation created by each state, known by the acronym HOUSSE (high objective uniform state standard of evaluation).

Most states are likely to claim success by the deadline. Many say they are already close. But whether teaching actually will have changed is less certain. In "Quality Counts 2005," a report by *Education Week*, researchers graded states on their efforts to improve teacher quality, looking at the amount of out-of-field teaching allowed, the quality of the state certification process and the amount and quality of professional development. (*See map, p. 2.*) Only three states got As, 14 got Bs and the rest received Cs and Ds. [22]

No Child Left Behind's ability to alter the picture may be limited, critics say. They point to the problems rural and urban schools are having recruiting and retaining skilled teachers and to many states' less-than-rigorous HOUSSE plans.

"I love my job. I know how kids learn," says Jon Runnalls, Montana's "Teacher of the Year" in 2003, "and for someone to come and say that now I'm not highly qualified, that's a slap in the face." Runnalls has taught middle school science for 31 years, but his college degree is in elementary education with an emphasis in science. According to NCLB, he'd have to go back to school, take a state test or pass the state's alternative evaluation. But Montana doesn't have a test, and its HOUSSE plan has not yet been approved by the Department of Education. It's really not a plan at all; it simply says that a veteran certified teacher is, by default, highly qualified.

Not surprisingly, Montana reports 98.8 percent of its classes are taught by highly qualified teachers.

Ten other states, like Montana, don't evaluate veteran teachers, arguing that the state certification process is a rigorous enough hurdle. But even many of the states that do have more elaborate HOUSSE plans have faced criticism.

Most states use a system in which veteran teachers accumulate points until they have enough to be considered highly qualified. "The most prevalent problem is that states offer too many options that veteran teachers can use to prove they are highly qualified — options that often have nothing to do with content knowledge," says Kate Walsh, president of the National Council on Teacher Quality. While states give points for university-level coursework, states also give them for sponsoring a school club, mentoring a new teacher and belonging to a national teacher organization. Teachers also get points for experience.

But according to Walsh, "The purpose of HOUSSE is to ensure that teachers know their content, not to count the number of years in the classroom." [23]

Even with the flexibility offered by the HOUSSE option, some schools in rural and urban areas are struggling to meet the law's requirements, although the Department of Education has given rural districts a three-year extension. After studying a rural district in Alabama that offered a $5,000 signing bonus to new teachers, researchers from the Southeast Center for Teaching Quality noted: "Central office staff told us that to ensure the bonus worked, they could only require recipients work two years. Most teachers take the bonus, serve their two years and leave." Urban districts the researchers studied struggled to find experienced teachers prepared to work with few resources and students with diverse learning and emotional needs. [24]

As a result, rural and urban schools are more likely to assign teachers to instruct in multiple subjects, often outside their field. These schools are also more reliant on teachers who have entered the profession through some alternative route, usually with little or no classroom experience. No Child Left Behind says such teachers are highly qualified if enrolled in an intensive induction and mentoring program and receiving high-quality professional development.

But Tom Blamford, an associate director at the National Education Association, says the quality of these programs is often poor. "We know what it takes to change classroom practice," Blamford says. "It has to do with knowledge, coaching, feedback and more knowledge, and it's a cyclical process. It's very rare that professional development meets those standards." Usually, he says, it's someone standing in front of a group of teachers lecturing them.

What rural and urban schools need to do, according to Scott Emerick, a policy associate at the Southeast Center for Teaching Quality, is use federal funds more effectively to improve working conditions, design better professional-development programs and devise sophisticated financial incentives to attract and retain teachers. But Emerick says they often don't know how, and the federal government is not providing enough guidance.

"These districts need on-the-ground assistance beyond accessing a federal Web site that tells you what other people are doing," he says.

1950s-1960s *A legal challenge and federal legislation initiate an era of education reform.*

1954 In *Brown v. Board of Education*, the Supreme Court decides "separate educational facilities are inherently unequal."

1958 Congress passes National Defense Education Act in response to the Soviet launch of *Sputnik*.

1965 President Lyndon B. Johnson signs Elementary and Secondary Education Act (ESEA) providing funds to school districts to help disadvantaged students.

1966 Congress amends ESEA to add Title VI, establishing grants for the education of handicapped children.

1966 Sociologist James S. Coleman's "Equality of Educational Opportunity" report concludes that disadvantaged black children learn better in well-integrated classrooms, helping to launch an era of busing students to achieve racial balance in public schools.

1968 Congress amends ESEA to add Title VII, called the Bilingual Education Act.

1970s-1980s *Studies criticize student achievement, and the standards movement gains momentum.*

1975 Coleman issues a new report concluding busing had failed, largely because it had prompted "white flight."

1980 U.S. Department of Education is established, ending education role of Department of Health, Education, and Welfare.

1983 National Commission on Excellence's "A Nation at Risk" report warns of a rising tide of mediocrity in education and recommends a common core curriculum nationwide.

1989 President George H.W. Bush convenes nation's governors in Charlottesville, Va., for first National Education Summit, which establishes six broad objectives to be reached by 2000.

1989 National Council of Teachers of Mathematics publishes *Curriculum and Evaluation Standards for School Mathematics*.

1990s-2000s *Congress requires more standards, testing and accountability from the states.*

1994 President Bill Clinton signs the Goals 2000: Educate America Act, which adopts the goals of the first National Education Summit. The act creates the National Education Standards and Improvement Council with the authority to approve or reject states' academic standards. The council, however, becomes ineffective after Republicans take control of Congress during midterm elections and object to the increasing federal role in education. . . . Clinton later signs Improving America's Schools Act of 1994, requiring significantly more testing and accountability than the original ESEA.

Jan. 8, 2002 President George W. Bush signs No Child Left Behind Act, increasing funding to states while also increasing federal mandates and sanctions to an unprecedented degree. States must increase student testing, place "highly qualified" teachers in every classroom and meet state-determined annual targets for student proficiency in reading and math. By 2014, all students must be 100 percent proficient. Title I schools not meeting annual targets must offer transfers to students and provide supplemental services, like tutoring.

April 7, 2005 Secretary of Education Margaret Spellings announces her willingness to provide some flexibility to states in meeting the requirements of No Child Left Behind.

April 19, 2005 Republican-dominated Utah legislature passes a bill giving priority to state educational goals when those conflict with No Child Left Behind and ordering officials to spend as little state money as possible to comply with the federal law.

April 20, 2005 The nation's largest teachers' union and eight school districts in Michigan, Texas and Vermont sue the Department of Education, accusing the government of violating a No Child Left Behind Act provision that states cannot be forced to spend their own money to meet the law's requirements.

Are Schools' Graduation Rates Accurate?

The No Child Left Behind Act holds schools accountable not just for student achievement but also for graduation rates. High schools must raise their graduation rates if they are to make adequate yearly progress. Increasing the percentage of graduates is a worthy goal, but it serves another purpose as well. The requirement is designed to prevent schools from improving achievement scores by encouraging their lowest-performing students to leave.

The system depends, of course, on accurate reporting. But researchers say that high school graduation rates reported by most states are just not believable.

The problem: States don't really know how many kids are dropping out of school.

States "consistently underestimate the number of dropouts, thereby overstating the graduation rates, sometimes by very large amounts," says Jay P. Greene, a senior fellow at the Manhattan Institute for Policy Research. In a recent report, Greene called some states' rates "so improbably high they would be laughable if the issue were not so serious." [1]

Although a few school districts have been accused of falsifying dropout data, researchers don't believe deception is at the root of the problem. Rather, they say the cause is more benign: Most schools don't know what happens to students who leave. Did a student transfer to another school? Move to another state? Or really drop out? Trying to answer those questions may be a secretary or clerk who often has other responsibilities as well.

"You basically have to do detective work," says Christopher Swanson, a senior research associate at The Urban Institute's Education Policy Center. "That takes time, effort and resources that may not be available to the school." Swanson says schools don't have an incentive to distinguish dropouts from transfers if it means that the graduation rates they report will be lower as a result.

Even states with sophisticated systems to track individual students over time — and there are a handful — can still report inflated graduation numbers. Texas, which reported an 84.2 percent graduation rate for its Class of 2003, counts as graduates students who have left school and either received or are working toward a General Educational Development certificate (GED). [2] No Child Left Behind prohibits the practice.

Both Swanson and Greene have developed methods for estimating how many students are actually graduating that do not rely on dropout data. Instead, they use two pieces of basic information they say are less subject to manipulation: the number of students enrolled in high school and the number of graduates. Their formulas differ, but both researchers come up with similar graduation rates that are far lower than those published by the states.

For example, South Carolina reported a high school graduation rate of 77.5 percent for the class of 2002; [3] Greene calculated the rate as 53 percent. [4] California reported a 2002 graduation rate of 87 percent; Greene put it at 67 percent. Indiana reported a graduation rate of 91 percent; Greene says it was 72 percent.

To fix the problem, Greene would like to see all states assign each student a unique identifying number for tracking their school careers, with reasonable definitions of who is a dropout and who is a graduate and an auditing program to ensure the quality of the data.

"Starbucks knows exactly what sells," Greene says. "Wal-Mart knows what inventory it has in every store. Schools have no idea."

Some states are developing such systems, but doing so will be time consuming and costly. In the meantime, some critics of the current reporting methods want the Department of Education to require states to estimate graduation rates using methods similar to Greene's or Swanson's. "The department's role does not end with the collection of data," the Education Trust says. "It must ensure that state calculations are accurate, complete and accessible to the public." [5]

However, federal education officials believe the responsibility lies elsewhere. While the Department of Education will provide technical assistance to states as they create more sophisticated systems for tracking students, it believes that the quality of the data is the states' responsibility. "Anytime there is a problem in the states, parties are always prone to point the finger," says Deputy Assistant Secretary for Policy Darla Marburger. "And folks point the finger at the U.S. Department of Education. But it is not really a problem in our house."

---

[1] Jay P. Greene, "Public High School Graduation and College Readiness Rates: 1991-2002," Education Working Paper No. 8, Manhattan Institute for Policy Research, p. 2, February 2005.

[2] www.tea.state.tx.us/peims/standards/wedspre/index.html?r032.

[3] Education Trust, "Telling the Whole Truth (or Not) About High School Graduation," December 2003, p. 4.

[4] Greene, *op. cit.*, Table 1.

[5] Education Trust, *op. cit.*

AP Photo/Daily Herald/Matt Smith

Gov. Jon Huntsman, R-Utah, prepares to sign a state measure on May 2, 2005, defying the No Child Left Behind Act, aided by a Provo elementary school student. In the past year and a half, more than 30 states have introduced bills that would release them from some of the law's requirements.

Is No Child Left Behind adequately funded?

The funding question is so contentious it has divided former congressional supporters of the law and prompted both Republican and Democratic state lawmakers to introduce bills exempting their states from portions of the law.

The issue also has generated nearly two-dozen studies from think tanks, lobbying groups, school districts and states. Their conclusions about the adequacy of funding range from modest surpluses to shortfalls of millions, and in a few cases, even billions of dollars.

Beneath the competing claims are radically different estimates of the costs of implementing the law. Researchers can't even agree on what costs should be included, let alone their size. Adding to the problem, said a study, "is the evolving nature of the regulations, guidance and other advisories issued by the U.S. Department of Education." [25]

After reviewing the studies, the National Conference of State Legislatures concluded a shortfall is more likely and released a report in February calling for change. "We would ask Congress to do one of two things," says senior policy specialist Young. "Either increase funding to levels that would allow states to meet the goals of the law or

provide states waivers from having to meet requirements where there is insufficient funding."

In response, the Education Department embraced the studies projecting plenty of funds. "The perpetual cry for more money . . . simply does not comport with the facts: Since taking office, President Bush has increased education funding by . . . 33 percent," said a department press release.

To understand the debate, it is helpful to break down the costs of implementing the law into two categories: complying with the letter of the law versus bringing students to grade-level proficiency by 2014, which several states claim may be much more costly.

To comply with the letter of the law, states must establish academic standards, create assessments, monitor schools' progress, help schools needing improvement, pay for students to transfer and receive tutoring and place a highly qualified teacher in every classroom. Connecticut recently called its estimate of these costs "sobering." The state said that through fiscal 2008 it would have to spend $41.6 million of its own money to comply with the law. [26] Minnesota said its cost would be $42 million. [27]

Other states go even further. They say doing what's explicitly called for in the law will not be enough to bring 100 percent of students to proficiency in reading and math by 2014. In order to reach that goal, several states say they'll have to do much more. "It might involve after-school services and making sure children are well nourished," Young says. "Early-childhood education is a big one, essential to preventing the achievement gap from occurring."

Ohio commissioned a study that adopted an expanded notion of costs and included summer school, an extended school day and intensive in-school student intervention. The study calculated the annual cost of fully implementing NCLB at $1.5 billion; the additional federal funding that Ohio receives through the law, however, is only $44 million. [28]

The authors of the Ohio study acknowledged, "the task of assigning costs to the requirements of No Child Left Behind presents a formidable challenge." [29] Their assumptions, and the assumptions of other state studies, have come under attack.

A report in *Education Next*, a journal devoted to education reform, last spring accused the state studies of gross exaggeration. The authors, including the chairman of the Massachusetts Board of Education, contended that while there may be a shortage of money to evaluate schools and help those that need intervention, the gap can be filled by giving states more flexibility to shift existing federal money around. And it concludes, "No one — neither critics nor supporters of NCLB — really has any idea what it would cost to bring all students to proficiency by 2014, or even if it can be done at all." [30]

Accountability Works, a nonprofit research and consulting firm, goes a step further, concluding there is "little solid evidence that NCLB is insufficiently funded." In fact, the firm concluded some states might even have surpluses.

Echoing *Education Next*, Accountability Works said the reports claiming NCLB provides insufficient funding contain significant flaws. "Often, expenditures that are not required by NCLB are included in the calculations," the report said. "In other cases, such studies included expenditures that were required by prior federal law." [31]

Given the huge range of estimates and the fact that some of the repercussions of the law are just beginning to be felt, it may take years for the true costs of implementation to become clear.

But one thing is clear: State education departments are often overwhelmed. Many don't have the staff or the expertise to effectively carry out No Child Left Behind's requirements: creating data systems to monitor each school's adequate yearly progress; putting teams together to help schools in need of improvement and, as more fail, to restructure schools; and evaluating outside suppliers of tutoring services. Many states have never had to do these things, on this scale, before, and the alarm has been sounded not only by the states but also by private researchers and even the Government Accountability Office.

The Department of Education's Briggs says the federal government is helping. "We have held conferences where we have tried to bring states together to learn together."

But many states say the problem is rooted in past state budget cuts and resulting staff reductions. The extra money provided by NCLB is being used to create assessment tests or reduce class size, with little left over to hire administrative staff. That's the case in Idaho, says Allison Westfall, public information officer at the state Department of Education. "We have a very small Title I staff — we're down to five people now — who are often on the road visiting schools," she says. "So we've had to bring in people from other departments, and we're stretched really thin." And there are no plans to hire.

"This lack of capacity — not a lack of will — on the part of most states is the single, most important impediment to achieving the gains of No Child Left Behind," said Marc Tucker, president of the National Center on Education and the Economy, a research group. On average, state education departments have lost 50 percent of their employees in the past 10 years, he says, calling it "the hidden issue." [32]

BACKGROUND

Federal Reforms

On April 11, 1965, President Lyndon B. Johnson returned to the Texas school he had attended as a child to sign the nation's first comprehensive education law, the Elementary and Secondary Education Act. "As president of the United States," he declared, "I believe deeply no law I have signed or will ever sign means more to the future of America." [33]

The primary assumption in ESEA — enacted as part of Johnson's War on Poverty — was that higher-quality education would move poor students out of poverty.

With ESEA, the federal government began to address the causes of the achievement gap. In the process, the federal role in education policy — until then a strictly local affair handled by the nation's 15,000 independent school districts — expanded dramatically. ESEA's signature program, Title I, initially allocated more than $1 billion a year to school districts with high concentrations of low-income students. To administer the program, federal and state education bureaucracies grew, as did the federal and state roles in local school districts.

During the next decade, minority achievement improved marginally, but dissatisfaction with public education grew faster, as did resentment over federal infringement on local education affairs. In 1981, President Ronald Reagan took office vowing to abolish the U.S. Department of Education.

The next year, Reagan and Secretary of Education Terrell Bell appointed the National Commission on Excellence in Education to report on the quality of public education. Eighteen months later, the commission's explosive report, "A Nation at Risk," declared, "the educational foundations of our society are presently being eroded by a rising tide of mediocrity that threatens our very future as a Nation and a people." [34]

'These Are the Very Weakest Programs Offered'

Arthur E. Levine, president of Teachers College, Columbia University, led a four-year assessment of the 1,200 university programs that prepare most of the nation's school principals and administrators. Released in March 2005 by Levine's Education Schools Project, the study, "Educating School Leaders," says most university-based preparation programs for administrators range in quality from "inadequate to appalling." Levine recently discussed the report with writer Barbara Mantel.

CQ: Does No Child Left Behind make the issue of how we train school leaders more urgent?

AL: No Child Left Behind demands assessment; it demands effective curricula that will move students to achievement of standards and requires that all students achieve those standards. Principals and superintendents have to lead that transformation of the schools, which requires a very different set of skills and knowledge from their predecessors.

CQ: What is your overall characterization of university-based programs that train school administrators?

AL: The quality is very weak. These are the very weakest programs offered by America's education schools. While a relatively small proportion could be described as strong, the majority vary in quality from inadequate to appalling.

CQ: Do most principals and superintendents come through these programs?

AL: I can't give you numbers on superintendents. For principals, it is 89 percent.

CQ: In what areas do these programs fall short?

AL: First of all, the curriculum for the master's degree is irrelevant to the job of being a principal, appearing to be a random grab bag of survey courses, like Research Methods, Historical and Philosophical Foundations of Education and Educational Psychology.

CQ: Your report also talks about admission standards.

AL: The standardized test scores for students in leadership programs are among the lowest of all students at graduate schools of education, and they're among the lowest in all academe. But the larger problem is that the overwhelming majority of students in these programs are in them primarily for a bump in salaries. All 50 states give salary increases for educators who take master's degrees or graduate credits. So people want quickie programs and easy degrees. There is a race to the bottom among programs as they compete for students by dumbing down the curriculum, reducing the length of the program, cutting the number of credits required to graduate and lowering expectations of student performance.

CQ: Your report also says the degrees offered don't make sense.

AL: Generally the master's degree is considered prepa-

The report focused on how poorly American students compared with students from other countries; the steady decline in science scores; a drop in SAT scores; the functional illiteracy of too many minority students; and complaints from business and military leaders about the poor quality of U.S. high school graduates.

To overcome the problems, the report called for rigorous and measurable academic standards, establishment of a minimum core curriculum, lengthening of the time spent learning that curriculum and better teacher preparation.

"A Nation at Risk" marked the beginning of a movement for national standards and testing. Over the next decade, seven groups received federal financing to develop standards for what students should know, including the National Council of Teachers of Mathematics, the National History Standards Project and the National Standards in Foreign Language. [35]

In September 1989, President George H.W. Bush — the self-described "education president" — convened an education summit in Charlottesville, Va. Ignoring traditional Republican reluctance to actively involve Washington in education policy, Bush teamed with the president of the National Governors' Association — Democratic Gov. Bill Clinton, who had been active in education reform in his home state of Arkansas.

"The movement gained momentum with the 1989 education summit," wrote Andrew Rudalevige, an associate professor of political science at Dickinson College, in Carlyle, Pa. [36] Bush and the governors set broad performance goals for American schools to reach by the year 2000. It was hoped that all children would attend preschool, that 90 percent of all high school students would graduate, that all students would be proficient in core subjects, that U.S. students would be first in the

ration for principalship and the doctorate for a superintendency. Why does anybody need a doctorate to be a superintendent? A doctorate is a research degree. What does that have to do with running a school system?

CQ: What are some of your key recommendations?

AL: States and school boards should eliminate salary increases based on taking degrees. Or they can give people raises based on master's degrees but require that the field be germane to their work. If you're a math teacher, I can understand giving an increase in salary for taking a degree in mathematics or advanced teaching skills. Number two: close down failing programs. States can clean this up if they want to. They are in charge of the authorization of university programs and the licensure of school administrators. But I would like to see universities try first before the states step in.

CQ: How much time would you give the universities to do this?

Arthur E. Levine, president, Teachers College, Columbia University

Columbia University

AL: I would give universities two years to clean up their house, and then the state has an obligation to step in if they fail to do that.

CQ: What other recommendations do you have for universities?

AL: Eliminate the current master's degree and put in its place something I've been calling a master's of educational administration, which would be a two-year degree combining education and management courses, theory and practical experience. The doctor of education degree (EdD) would be eliminated. It has no integrity and no value. The PhD in education leadership should be reserved for the very tiny group of people who wish to be scholars and researchers in the field.

CQ: And your last recommendation?

AL: There is a tendency of universities to use these programs as cash cows. They encourage these programs to produce as much revenue as possible by reducing admission standards, using adjuncts and lowering academic standards for graduation in order to get enough cash to distribute to other areas. Universities need to stop doing that.

world in science and math, that every adult would be literate and every school free of drugs and violence.

In 1994, President Clinton signed the Goals 2000: Educate America Act, which adopted the summit's ambitious agenda and provided federal funds to help states develop standards. The real sea change came later that year, Rudalevige wrote, when reauthorization of ESEA "signaled a nationwide commitment to standards-based reform." [37] The law required states to develop content and performance standards, tests aligned with those standards and a system to measure a school's "adequate yearly progress" in bringing all students to academic proficiency. But there was no deadline, and it took several years for the Education Department to develop the accompanying regulations and guidelines. By 1997, only 17 states were fully complying with the law, according to Krista Kafer, senior education policy analyst at the Heritage Foundation. [38]

In January 2001 former Texas Gov. George W. Bush became president, having made education a centerpiece of his campaign. Three days after his inauguration, he proposed what became the blueprint for No Child Left Behind. Its standards-and-testing strategy wasn't new, but accountability provisions were. They significantly raised the stakes for states, local districts and schools.

The proposal called for annual testing in grades 3-8, school and state report cards showing student performance by ethnic and economic subgroups, a highly qualified teacher in every classroom and sanctions for schools not showing progress in bringing students to proficiency.

Congress finally passed NCLB after nearly a year of intense debate and political horse-trading, which included the elimination of private school vouchers, increases in funding and addition of a provision requiring that all students reach proficiency in math and reading in 12 years.

"The political compromises written into No Child Left Behind make the regulatory process crucial," said Rudalevige. [39] That's because the law grants the secretary of Education the power to grant waivers and interpret the rules and, until the bill is reauthorized, determine the flexibility states will have to meet their goals.

Achievement Gaps

Most educators say the best thing about No Child Left Behind is its focus on minorities and low-income students.

"When you say to a school that you expect every sub-group of kids to meet standards," says Delaware Education Secretary Woodruff, "that really makes schools pay closer attention to all kids." It is now possible, for instance, to track how minority and low-income students perform on state tests at each school and to calculate the achievement gaps between them and their peers. The fundamental goal of No Child Left Behind is to close these gaps while raising the achievement of all students, which has been the goal of education reforms for decades.

But to get a sense of how students have been performing historically, researchers must look to national data, because state testing is too new.

To get that information, the U.S. Department of Education has been measuring American students' achievement levels since 1969 through its National Assessment of Educational Progress (NAEP). NAEP periodically administers what it calls a "trend assessment" to a nationally representative sample of students at ages 9, 13 and 17 and breaks down the results for white, black and Hispanic students.

The data show that black and Hispanic students have made long-term gains, thus narrowing the achievement gap. From 1971 to 1999 for example, the last year for which data is available, the difference between the average reading scores of 13-year-old white and black students shrank from 39 points to 29 points. In math, the gap plummeted 14 points — from 46 points to 32 points. [40]

However, most of the reductions in the achievement gap occurred during the 1970s and 1980s, as minorities made notable gains while white students' average achievement increased slightly or not at all. Then, in the 1990s, the gap stopped shrinking; in fact, in many cases it grew. Black and Hispanic students continued making modest gains in math and Hispanic students in reading, but those improvements no longer exceeded those of whites. [41]

"When achievement goes up for all groups," the Center on Education Policy noted, "African-American and Hispanic students must improve at a faster rate than others for the gap to close." [42]

While still smaller than decades ago, the achievement gap remains quite large. For instance, the 32-point difference in math scores for black 13-year-olds and their white peers in 1999 is the equivalent of roughly three grade levels. [43]

"What, then, are the most probable explanations for the achievement gap?" asked the Center on Education Policy in a report examining minority achievement. "A complex combination of school, community and home factors appear to underlie or contribute to the gap," it answered. [44]

CURRENT SITUATION

States Push Back

Mounting state resistance to NCLB — including its level of funding and strict achievement timetables — has led to a mini-revolution in the states.

In 2004, legislatures in 31 states introduced bills challenging aspects of the law. [45] This year, so far, 21 states have either introduced or reintroduced legislation, and the numbers are likely to grow if more states decide to test Education Secretary Spellings' promise to take a "common sense" approach to enforcing the law. [46]

In Colorado, Republican state Sen. Mark Hillman proposed allowing school districts to opt out of No Child Left Behind if they forgo Title I funds; he suggested a tax increase to replace the lost federal funds. In Idaho, two Republican state senators introduced legislation demanding that predominantly rural states be exempt from the law. In Maine, Democratic state Sen. Michael Brennan sponsored a bill directing the state's attorney general to sue the federal government if federal funding is insufficient to implement No Child Left Behind.

Despite the blizzard of proposals, only three states actually passed legislation. The Republican-dominated Utah legislature passed a bill on April 19 — and the governor signed it on May 2 — allowing schools to ignore NCLB provisions that conflict with state education laws or require extra state money to implement. Spellings has warned that Utah could lose $76 million of the $107 million it receives in federal education funding.

"I don't like to be threatened," an angry state Rep. Mascaro told *The New York Times*. [47]

AT ISSUE

Should annual testing be extended to high school?

YES   Bob Wise
President, Alliance for Excellent Education

Written for The CQ Researcher, May 5, 2005

Achieving the national goal of building a better educated, more competitive work force for the 21st century requires effective tools. With two-thirds of high school students either dropping out or graduating unprepared for college, the majority of our nation's young people need more support than they are currently getting from their secondary schools and teachers. An increased number of required tests at the high school level could help to leverage the academic assistance many students require, if those tests are designed and implemented appropriately.

Last fall, President Bush set off a major debate when he proposed extending the reading and math tests required by the No Child Left Behind Act for third- through eighth-graders and in one year of high school to students in grades nine, ten and eleven. "We need to be sure that high school students are learning every year," he said.

At the Alliance for Excellent Education, we believe all children deserve an excellent education that prepares them for the economic and social challenges that follow high school. And we agree with the president that our schools must be held accountable for providing that high-quality education. Testing students during their high school years has the potential to provide needed data about their progress — as a whole, and by gender, race and ethnicity — and could allow us to better measure the effectiveness of the schools supposed to be preparing all of our young people to become productive members of American society.

But tests should help schools understand and address the needs of their students. If we are going to hold schools accountable for their students' ability to perform at high academic levels, we must also give them the resources necessary to provide the additional, targeted instruction that many teens need to become proficient in reading, writing, math and other subjects.

To be taken seriously by students, tests need to be relevant. High school tests should be aligned to the expectations of colleges and employers and provide both educators and students with a gauge to measure progress toward a successful transition to postsecondary education, technical training or rewarding jobs.

Finally, the federal government should fully cover the cost of designing and administering the exams, thus ensuring that states can adequately and effectively implement the tests they are required to give.

Tests alone won't make a difference. But as a part of a toolkit designed to improve the nation's graduation and college-readiness rates, they are worthy of our consideration.

NO   Paul Houston
Executive Director, American Association of School Administrators

Written for The CQ Researcher, April 27, 2005

High school reform should not focus on a test but rather on what is being learned. I recently visited the Olathe, Kan., school district to learn more about a series of programs called 21st Century Schools, which have been implemented in all the high schools. These are "vocational" schools. In other words, they are focused on the future work life of students, and the programs are very rigorous and produce great results. But more important, the programs are meaningful, engaging and hands on, using the students' motivation to create a vehicle for excellence.

As I walked through Olathe Northwest High School, I saw students and teachers engaged in hard work. In one classroom, they were constructing a "battlebot," a robot that is used in gaming to battle other robots — with the last one running being the winner. The students were looking forward to taking their creation to a national competition later this year. While this sounds fun (some may say "frivolous"), what is really happening is that students are experiencing deep learning about metallurgy, structures, engines, insulation and a hundred other things I didn't understand. They were excited and knowledgeable about what they were doing — and about how much fun they were having with the learning process.

There were about a dozen students who stayed after the bell to talk with me, and every one of them plans to attend college and study engineering. There is no shortage of engineering candidates in Olathe. I asked them why they liked what they were doing, and the answer was simple. One told me he got to use what he was learning in class. "Telling me that calculus is good for me isn't very meaningful," he said. "Now I see how I can use it."

I would suggest to those who want to reform high schools that the place to start is in places like Olathe, where the school district has figured out that the best way to get students to learn more is to give them engaging, imaginative work that creates meaning for them. And we must give schools adequate resources to provide state-of-the-art opportunities for students to receive hands-on learning.

Those who are interested in reform should focus on getting schools the resources they need to do the job and then challenging them to make schools interesting and engaging places. Reform will not be achieved by mandating more testing. Education has always been about the whole child, and unless we take that into consideration, the current effort to reform high schools will be just as unsuccessful as the others that preceded it.

Raul Gonzales, legislative director at the National Council of La Raza, which advocates for Hispanic-Americans, agrees that money is tight in states still suffering from a four-year-long budget crisis. [48] "States are trying to implement this law on the cheap," Gonzales says, "because there isn't really enough money."

For example, under the law states are allowed to test English-language learners for up to three years in their native language, but most states don't have reading tests in native languages. "We're not accurately measuring what kids can do because we're using the wrong tests," he says.

Perry Zirkel, a professor of education and law at Lehigh University, in Bethlehem, Pa., says the states' resistance to the law is still mostly "sparks, not fire." He points out that New Mexico, Virginia and Utah are the only states to pass legislation.

"Despite all the talk," Zirkel says, "I don't think there has been sufficient momentum to convince the majority of the public that No Child Left Behind is, on a net basis, a bad law."

Moreover, a coalition of Hispanic, African-American and other educators have voiced concerns that the Utah legislature's effort to sidestep provisions of the federal law might allow minority students to fall through the cracks. [49]

Teachers' Union Sues

One day after the Utah legislature made its move, the NEA and eight school districts in Michigan, Texas and Vermont sued the Department of Education, contending it is violating an NCLB provision that says states cannot be forced to use their own money to implement the law:

"Nothing in this Act shall be construed to authorize an officer or employee of the Federal Government to mandate, direct, or control a State, local education agency, or school's curriculum, program of instruction, or allocation of State or local resources, or mandate a State or any subdivision thereof to spend any funds or incur any costs not paid for under this Act."

"We don't disagree when the Department of Education says federal funding has increased," explains NEA spokesman Dan Kaufman. "We just don't believe that the funding has been enough for the types of really strict, comprehensive things that it requires states to do." The teachers' union would like to see Congress appropriate the full amount it authorized when passing the bill. So far, it is $27 billion short.

"We . . . look forward to the day when the NEA will join us in helping children who need our help the most in classrooms, instead of spending its time and members' money in courtrooms," the Department of Education said in response. [50]

The lawsuit was filed in the U.S. District Court for the Eastern District of Michigan, which has jurisdiction over one of the school districts joining the suit. The suit asks the court to declare that states and school districts do not have to spend their own funds to comply with NCLB and that failure to comply for that reason will not result in a cutoff of federal education funds.

Some legal experts say that, regardless of its merits, the lawsuit could be dismissed on procedural grounds. First of all, the teachers' union may not have the legal standing to bring suit because it doesn't have a direct stake in the outcome, even though its members do. The experts also say the court could rule that the lawsuit is premature, and that NCLB does not specify that there is a right to sue.

Moreover, several legal experts said, courts typically don't want to take on messy political debates. Just deciding the facts and determining the costs of No Child Left Behind would be extremely complex.

"The courts' view is that if you have problems with this law, then go lobby Congress to change it," Lehigh's Zirkel says. In fact, the lawsuit may actually be an indirect way to lobby Congress, he adds, and it may be more effective because it's more public.

War of Words

Zirkel says Connecticut's threat to sue may also be an indirect attempt at lobbying Congress. In early April, Connecticut Attorney General Richard Blumenthal announced he would sue the Department of Education on grounds that the federal government's approach to the law is "illegal and unconstitutional." [51] Connecticut's argument is essentially the same as the teachers' union's, but the state — which has a direct stake in the outcome — has better legal standing, Zirkel says. Blumenthal has estimated the annual testing required by the law would create an additional financial burden for the state, which now tests students every other year.

While a few school districts have sued the government over the law, Connecticut would be the first state to do so, but as of May 25, Blumenthal had yet to act.

Meanwhile, the state's dispute with the Education Department has become very public. "We've got better things to spend our money on," Connecticut Education

Commissioner Sternberg said in explaining her opposition to annual testing. "We won't learn anything new about our schools by giving these extra tests." [52]

But Secretary Spellings clearly will not compromise on annual testing, consistently calling it one of the "bright lines" of NCLB. She and Sternberg have been having a war of words, with Spellings calling the law's opponents "un-American" and Sternberg demanding an apology.

Spellings also has accused Connecticut of tolerating one of the nation's largest achievement gaps between white and black students. Sternberg has said the huge gap was due to the extraordinary performance of white students in Connecticut's affluent suburbs.

The two finally met in mid-April, but the meeting was inconclusive.

OUTLOOK

Reform Unlikely?

If the NEA's lawsuit and Connecticut's threat to sue are indirect ways of lobbying Congress, their timing may be off.

Jeffrey Henig, a professor of political science and education at Columbia University's Teachers College, says some constituents in prosperous suburban school districts are beginning to grumble as well-regarded schools fail to make "adequate yearly progress" because one or two subgroups of students miss proficiency targets.

"But I don't think it has really gelled into clear, focused pressure on Congress to reform the law," Henig says, adding that the situation could change if more schools fall into that category.

But lawmakers are extremely reluctant to revisit the law before it comes up for reauthorization in 2007, Henig says. Moderate Democrats are committed to the law's focus on raising achievement levels for minority, low-income and disabled students, he says, and they fear that any reworking could result in easing the pressure on states to shrink the achievement gap. And a core group of Republicans is committed to the law's tough accountability provisions. Both groups, Henig says, would prefer "to hold to the legislation and to placate any dissatisfied groups through the regulatory process."

The Department of Education has already amended the law's regulations, guidelines and enforcement. For instance, in 2003 and 2004 it allowed English-language learners to be tested in native languages for their first

three years, gave rural districts more time to place highly qualified teachers in classrooms and allowed some flexibility on testing participation rates.

In April, Spellings — then in her new job as secretary for just three months — told states they could apply to test a greater portion of disabled students using alternative assessments. In addition, Spellings said she would grant states flexibility in other areas if they could show they were making real progress in closing achievement gaps and meeting proficiency targets.

But Young of the National Conference of State Legislatures says states are trying to decipher what she means. "There is no indication of what that flexibility would include," he says, "and there is no indication of how states would be judged by these indicators."

So far, Spellings is holding firm on annual testing, but she did grant North Dakota a waiver temporarily allowing new elementary school teachers to be rated highly qualified without taking a state test.

"The Department of Education is really feeling the heat and is trying to compromise," says educational consultant Scott Joftus, former policy director at the Alliance for Excellent Education.

The department also has allowed some states to lower the cutoff point for proficiency on their student assessment tests and to use averaging and other statistical methods to make it easier for schools to make adequate yearly progress. Young calls it gaming the system and expects it to continue unless Congress reforms No Child Left Behind.

In 2007, when the law comes up for reauthorization, Congress could negotiate changes, but the process could take years. Last time, it took two-and-a-half extra years.

NOTES

1. Dana Milbank, "With Fanfare, Bush Signs Education Bill," *The Washington Post*, Jan. 9, 2002.

2. Northwest Evaluation Association, "The Impact of the No Child Left Behind Act on Student Achievement and Growth: 2005 Edition," April 2005, p. 2.

3. http://kennedy.senate.gov/index_high.html.

4. Sam Dillon, "Utah Vote Rejects Parts of U.S. Education Law," *The New York Times*, April 20, 2005.

5. "Governor worried about costs of Bush education reform law," The Associated Press State & Local Wire, April 26, 2005.

6. http://gregg.senate.gov/forms/myths.pdf.

7. www.ed.gov/nclb/overview/intro/guide/guide_pg11.html#spending.

8. National Public Radio, "Talk of the Nation," May 3, 2005.

9. Center on Education Policy, "From the Capital to the Classroom: Year 3 of the No Child Left Behind Act," March 2005, p. v.

10. *Ibid.*, p. 4.

11. *Ibid.*, p. 1.

12. Council of the Great City Schools, "Beating the Odds: A City-By-City Analysis of Student Performance and Achievement Gaps on State Assessments," March 2004, pp. iv-vi.

13. The Education Trust, "Stalled in Secondary: A Look at Student Achievement Since the No Child Left Behind Act," January 2005, p. 1.

14. University of Delaware Education Research and Development Center, "Awareness To Action Revisited: Tracking the Achievement Gap in Delaware Schools, State of Delaware Report," March 2005, p. 2.

15. www.dpi.state.wi.us/dpi/esea/pdf/wiaw.pdf.

16. National Conference of State Legislatures, "Task Force on No Child Left Behind: Final Report," February 2005, p. vii.

17. http://edcounts.edweek.org.

18. Center for the Study of Evaluation, "Test-based Educational Accountability in the Era of No Child Left Behind," April 2005, p. 19.

19. *Ibid.*, p. 14.

20. Susan Saulny, "U.S. Provides Rules to States for Testing Special Pupils," *The New York Times*, May 11, 2005, p. A17.

21. The data are from 2000, the most recent available. See The Education Trust, "All Talk, No Action: Putting an End to Out-of-Field Teaching," August 2002, p. 4.

22. Education Week Research Center, "Quality Counts 2005," January 2005, p. 92. www.edweek.org/rc/index.html.

23. National Council on Teacher Quality, "Searching the Attic," December 2004, p. 12.

24. Southeast Center for Teaching Quality, "Unfulfilled Promise: Ensuring High Quality Teachers for Our Nation's Students," August 2004, pp. 8-9.

25. Augenblick, Palaich and Associates, Inc. "Costing Out No Child Left Behind: A Nationwide Survey of Costing Efforts," April 2004, p. 1.

26. Connecticut State Department of Education, "Cost of Implementing the Federal No Child Left Behind Act in Connecticut," March 2, 2005, p. iii.

27. Center on Education Policy, *op. cit.*

28. Ohio Department of Education, "Projected Costs of Implementing The Federal 'No Child Left Behind Act' in Ohio," December 2003, p. vi.

29. *Ibid.*

30. James Peyser and Robert Castrell, "Exploring the Costs of Accountability," *Education Next*, spring 2004, p. 24.

31. Accountability Works, "NCLB Under a Microscope," January 2004, p. 2.

32. Joetta L. Sack, "State Agencies Juggle NCLB Work, Staffing Woes," *Education Week*, May 11, 2005, p. 25.

33. www.lbjlib.utexas.edu/johnson/archives.hom/speeches.hom/650411.asp.

34. www.ed.gov/pubs/NatAtRisk/risk.html.

35. For background, see Kathy Koch, "National Education Standards," *The CQ Researcher*, May 14, 1999, pp. 401-424, and Charles S. Clark, "Education Standards," *The CQ Researcher*, March 11, 1994, pp. 217-240.

36. www.educationnext.org/20034/62.html.

37. *Ibid.*

38. Heritage Foundation, "No Child Left Behind: Where Do We Go From Here?" 2004, p. 2.

39. www.educationnext.org/20034/62.html.

40. National Center for Education Statistics, "Trends in Academic Progress: Three Decades of Student Performance," 2000, p. 39.

41. *Ibid.*, p. 33.

42. Center on Education Policy, "It takes more than testing: Closing the Achievement Gap," 2001, p. 2.

43. *Ibid.*, p. 1.

44. *Ibid.*, p. 3.

45. National Conference of State Legislatures, "No Child Left Behind Quick Facts: 2005," April 2005.

46. www.nea.org/lawsuit/stateres.html.

47. Dillon, *op. cit.*

48. For background, see William Triplett, "State Budget Crisis," *The CQ Researcher*, Oct. 3, 2003, pp. 821-844.

49. Dillon, *op. cit.*

50. U.S. Department of Education, "Statement by Press Secretary on NEA's Action Regarding NCLB," April 20, 2005, p. B1.

51. Sam Dillon, "Connecticut to Sue U.S. Over Cost of School Testing Law, *The New York Times*, April 6, 2005.

52. Michael Dobbs, "Conn. Stands in Defiance on Enforcing 'No Child'," *The Washington Post*, May 8, 2005, p. A10.

BIBLIOGRAPHY

Books

Meier, Deborah, and George Wood, eds., *Many Children Left Behind: How the No Child Left Behind Act Is Damaging Our Children and Our Schools*, Beacon Press, 2004.
Meier, the founder of several New York City public schools, and Wood, a high school principal and the founder of The Forum for Education and Democracy, and other authors argue that the law is harming the ability of schools to serve poor and minority children.

Peterson, Paul E., and Martin R. West, eds., *No Child Left Behind: The Politics and Practice of School Accountability*, Brookings Institution Press, 2003.
Peterson, director of the Program on Education Policy and Governance at Harvard, and West, a research fellow in the program, have collected essays that examine the forces that gave shape to the law and its likely consequences.

Rakoczy, Kenneth Leo, *No Child Left Behind: No Parent Left in the Dark*, Edu-Smart.com Publishing, 2003.
A veteran public school teacher offers this guide to parents for becoming involved in their children's education and making the most out of parent-teacher conferences in light of the new law.

Wright, Peter W. D., Pamela Darr Wright and Suzanne Whitney Heath, *Wrightslaw: No Child Left Behind*, Harbor House Law Press, 2003.
The authors, who run a Web site about educational law

and advocacy, explain the No Child Left Behind Act for parents and teachers.

Articles

Dillon, Sam, "New Secretary Showing Flexibility on 'No Child' Law," *The New York Times*, Feb. 14, 2005, p. A18.
Education Secretary Margaret Spellings has shown a willingness to work with state and local officials on No Child Left Behind, saying school districts need not always allow students in low-performing schools to transfer to better ones if it caused overcrowding.

Friel, Brian, "A Test for Tutoring," *The National Journal*, April 16, 2005.
Friel examines the controversy surrounding some of the outside tutoring firms providing supplemental services to students under provisions of No Child Left Behind.

Hendrie, Caroline, "NCLB Cases Face Hurdles in the Courts," *Education Week*, May 4, 2005.
Hendrie describes the hurdles facing the National Education Association's lawsuit against the Department of Education.

Ripley, Amanda, and Sonja Steptoe, "Inside the Revolt Over Bush's School Rules," *Time*, May 9, 2005.
The authors examine efforts by states to seek release from aspects of No Child Left Behind and the teachers' union's lawsuit against the federal government.

Tucker, Marc S., and Thomas Toch, "Hire Ed: the secret to making Bush's school reform law work? More bureaucrats," *Washington Monthly*, March 1, 2004.
The authors discuss staffing shortages at state departments of education that are slowing implementation of No Child Left Behind.

Reports and Studies

Center on Education Policy, *From the Capital to the Classroom: Year 3 of the No Child Left Behind Act*, March 2005.
The center examines the implementation of No Child Left Behind at the federal, state and local levels and points out positive and negative signs for the future.

Citizens' Commission on Civil Rights, *Choosing Better Schools: A Report on Student Transfers Under the No Child Left Behind Act,* **May 2004.**
The commission describes the early efforts to implement the school-choice provision of No Child Left Behind, calling compliance minimal.

National Conference of State Legislatures, *Task Force on No Child Left Behind: Final Report,* **February 2005.**
The panel questions the constitutionality of No Child Left Behind and calls it rigid, overly prescriptive and in need of serious revision.

Northwest Evaluation Association, *The Impact of No Child Left Behind Act on Student Achievement and Growth: 2005 Edition,* **April 2005.**
The association reports the percentage of proficient students is rising on state tests but also notes the disparity between the achievement growth of white and minority students.

Southeast Center for Teaching Quality, *Unfulfilled Promise: Ensuring High Quality Teachers for Our Nation's Students,* **August 2004.**
The center finds that rural and urban schools don't have the skills and training to recruit and retain highly qualified teachers and offers recommendations for change.

For More Information

Achieve, Inc., 1775 I St., N.W., Suite 410, Washington, DC 20006; (202) 419-1540; www.achieve.org. A bipartisan, nonprofit organization created by the nation's governors and business leaders that helps states improve academic performance.

Alliance for Excellent Education, 1201 Connecticut Ave., N.W., Suite 901, Washington, DC 20036; (202) 828-0828; www.all4ed.org. Works to assure that at-risk middle and high school students graduate prepared for college and success in life.

Center on Education Policy, 1001 Connecticut Ave., N.W., Suite 522, Washington, DC 20036; (202) 822-8065; www.cep-dc.org. Helps Americans understand the role of public education in a democracy and the need to improve academic quality.

Council of the Great City Schools, 1301 Pennsylvania Ave., N.W., Suite 702, Washington, DC 20004; (202) 393-2427; www.cgcs.org. A coalition of 65 of the nation's largest urban public school systems advocating improved K-12 education.

Editorial Projects in Education Inc., 6935 Arlington Rd., Suite 100, Bethesda, MD 20814-5233; (301) 280-3100; www.edweek.org. A nonprofit organization that publishes *Education Week, Teacher Magazine,* edweek.org and *Agent K-12.*

Education Commission of the States, 700 Broadway, Suite 1200, Denver, CO 80203-3460; (303) 299-3600; www.ecs.

org. Studies current and emerging education issues.

The Education Trust, 1250 H St., N.W., Suite 700, Washington, DC 20005; (202) 293-1217; www2.edtrust. org/edtrust. An independent nonprofit organization working to improve the academic achievement of all students.

National Conference of State Legislatures, 7700 East First Pl., Denver, CO 80230; (303) 364-7700; www.ncsl.org. A bipartisan organization serving the states and territories.

Northwest Evaluation Association, 5885 Southwest Meadows Rd., Suite 200, Lake Oswego, OR 97035; (503) 624-1951; www.nwea.org. A national nonprofit organization dedicated to helping all children learn.

Southeast Center for Teaching Quality, 976 Airport Rd., Suite 250, Chapel Hill, NC 27514; (919) 951-0200; www.teachingquality.org. A regional association dedicated to assuring all children have access to high-quality education.

U.S. Department of Education, No Child Left Behind Web site, www.ed.gov/nclb/landing.jhtml?src=pb. Describes the provisions of the No Child Left Behind law.

Wrightslaw, www.wrightslaw.com. Provides information about effective advocacy for children with disabilities, including "Wrightslaw: No Child Left Behind."

2

Rising College Costs

Tom Price and Amy Standen

Incoming freshmen gather for their next orientation event at the University of Illinois Urbana-Champaign campus in June 2003. Democratic Illinois Gov. Rod Blagojevich signed legislation in July 2003 guaranteeing that the tuition for in-state undergraduate students will not be raised at a state institution beginning in 2004. Across the country, tuition and fees at public colleges soared a near-record 10 percent in 2004.

From *CQ Researcher,*
Originally published December 5, 2003.
(Updated May 2005.)

The average undergraduate racks up student debts totaling about $18,900. [1] And then there's Erin Sandonato. In 1997, she launched her college career at Georgia Southern University, in Statesboro, confident she would not be straining her family's pocketbook.

As a Georgia high-school graduate with at least a "B" average, she qualified for the state's HOPE scholarship program, which pays for tuition, fees and books at any public university in Georgia.

But when her parents moved to Florida, Sandonato transferred to the University of Central Florida to be closer to them. Since their income was too high to let her qualify for Florida grants — but not high enough to pay all her bills — she worked full time.

"Physically and financially, I just couldn't work 40 hours a week and take a full class load," she recalls. So after her sophomore year, she dropped out and worked for a year and a half, waiting tables and clerking in a mall.

When Sandonato returned to classes, her energy and bankroll replenished, she picked Broward Community College, in Fort Lauderdale, because "it was a lot less expensive" than a four-year university.

Last spring, she finally finished her bachelor's degree in public relations at the University of West Florida, in Fort Myers. Now she ponders how to pay back the $45,000 in debt she says she acquired during her six undergraduate years.

"I would have been a lot better off financially if I had stayed in Georgia," she says. "I had absolutely no idea the financial obligations that college actually has until I was in the middle of it."

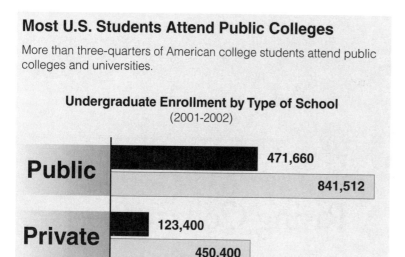

Most U.S. Students Attend Public Colleges

More than three-quarters of American college students attend public colleges and universities.

Undergraduate Enrollment by Type of School
(2001-2002)

Public
471,660
841,512

Private
123,400
450,400

■ 2 years ☐ 4 years

Sources: The College Board; Digest of Education Statistics, 2002

The increases raise the total cost — tuition, fees and room and board — of attending a residential, four-year state school by 7.8 percent and 5.6 percent at private institutions. The cost of attending an elite private university now can approach an eye-popping $40,000 a year, while the average private school costs $27,516 (of which $20,082 is for tuition and fees). In-state students at public four-year institutions pay an average of $11,354 (including $5,132 for tuition and fees).

These increases are just the latest hikes in a quarter-century trend of higher-education prices rocketing far above the inflation rate. Over the last decade, tuition increases at public, private and two-year institutions exceeded inflation by between 22 and 47 percent.

As prices rise, critics charge that colleges are wasting money on extravagant facilities, overpaid administrators and underworked faculty. Some students complain that reductions in course offerings — another troublesome issue, considering that education costs are rising — are preventing them from graduating on time. This, in turn, results in their needing to stay in school longer and the accumulation of more debt. And high-school graduates from lower-income families are finding it harder to get to college at all.

Last year, Congress failed to pass the Higher Education Act — the primary source of federal aid for higher education — after a bitter election-year fight over interest rates on student loans, ever-mounting tuition costs and levels of federal support. After a year of partisan stalling, some are arguing that it is time for legislators to take a step back and build an efficient, effective federal funding program for college education. "They must move beyond polarized debates," said Sandy Baum, senior policy analyst at the College Board, "and consider creative new measures if they are to fulfill the act's fundamental intent: to increase access to college for all students, particularly those who can't afford it."

After several bleak years, the overall fiscal outlook for state schools has improved modestly. But their budget

College prices have been steadily rising, and millions of students like Sandonato are feeling the pinch. Indeed, her story touches on many of the major issues accompanying the soaring price of higher education, including the:

- Plight of middle-income families;
- Trend away from need-based financial aid and toward merit-based aid;
- Strains of combining work with study;
- Burden of debt;
- Difficulty in understanding the complexity of tuition pricing; and the
- Relatively low tuitions at public institutions — especially community colleges.

Tuition and fees at public colleges and universities — which award most U.S. bachelor's degrees — soared by 10.5 percent from the last academic year to this year, according to the College Board's annual report on higher-education prices. Consider, however, that that's a drop of almost 4 percent over the previous year's increase, which was the sharpest in three decades. Community colleges increased tuition and fees by 8.7 percent (the 2003-4 increase was 13.8 percent), while costs at private four-year schools rose 6 percent. [2]

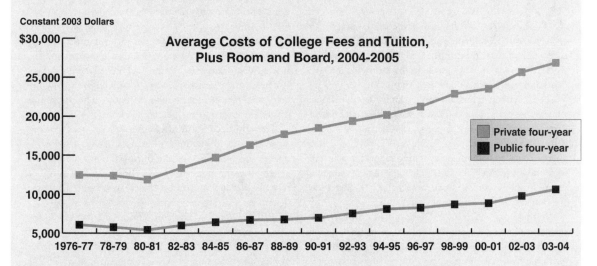

Costs Rose Faster at Private Schools

The inflation-adjusted cost of a four-year education at a private university more than doubled since the mid-1970s and jumped 75 percent at public schools.

Constant 2003 Dollars

Average Costs of College Fees and Tuition, Plus Room and Board, 2004-2005

Legend: Private four-year / Public four-year

* In constant 2004 dollars; over ten year period ending in 2004-2005; average tuition rose 51 percent at public schools, 36 percent at private schools.

Source: College Board report. Trends in college pricing, 2004

woes continue: Educators note that state appropriations to higher-education institutions have not kept up with enrollment increases, especially since the weakening national economy began putting strains on state tax receipts beginning in about 2001. [3]

"The states have been running away from higher education," complains Terry Hartle, senior vice president for government and public affairs at the American Council on Education. "In 1980, about 48 percent of the revenue at public colleges came from state appropriations. In 2000, it was only 35 percent."

College budgets also have been squeezed by the stock market collapse — which crunched endowments — and the sputtering economy, which has taken a toll on fundraising. Donations to colleges declined by 1.2 percent in 2002, the first drop in 14 years. [4] Fortunately, the tide may be changing, albeit slowly: In 2004, donations to colleges increased 3.4 percent, thanks to a spike in contributions by individuals. [5]

As rising college prices have outpaced student aid, the proportion of American high-school graduates enrolling in college also has dropped — to 61.7 percent in 2001 from a peak of 67 percent in 1997. In 2000, the United States fell to 13th place compared with other nations in the percentage of the population studying for a bachelor's degree or higher and seventh place in the proportion pursuing a lesser degree. [6]

Still, more money is available in grants and loans today than at any time in history. Nearly $46 billion in grants was shared by 60 percent of the nation's students in the 2003-4 academic year. [7] But advocates for the poor worry that a trend away from basing aid on need is reducing assistance available to lower-income students.

Because grants and college price tags vary widely, however, the averages paint only a fuzzy picture of how individual students fare, making it difficult for families to make informed financial decisions about college. The confusion can lead lower-income families to give up on higher education, even though grants and loans could make it affordable. At the same time, many middle-income families feel overburdened because they don't qualify for substantial grants.

Loans Provide Most Financial Aid

More financial aid — $122 billion — was available to U.S. college students last year than ever before. More than half of the aid was in the form of loans, and $48 billion came from grants. [1] Students also received and earned more than $1 billion from college work-study jobs. In addition, federal tax breaks saved students and their parents more than $6 billion.

The federal government provides about two-thirds of all student aid, most in the form of loans. Colleges and universities themselves pass out the biggest proportion of scholarships and other grants — about $23 billion. State governments, which provide operating support to state colleges and universities, also distribute more than $6 billion in grants. Private-sector loans total more than $10 billion a year.

Here are the top sources of student aid: [2]

Pell Grants — The federal government's primary contribution of grants to lower-income students totaled more than $12.7 billion last year. Most go to undergraduates, although some are awarded to postgraduates enrolled in teacher-certification programs. Pell Grant recipients often receive other forms of aid as well. The maximum grant this academic year is $4,050, the minimum $400. The average grant last year was $2,466. [3] A grant's size is based on a student's financial circumstances and the cost of attending his school. The program is named for former Sen. Claiborne Pell, D-R.I.

Subsidized Stafford Loans — The largest, single, source of federal education aid totaled more than $25 bil-

lion last year. They are awarded on the basis of student need. The maximum provided in a year ranges from $2,625 for a freshman to $8,500 for a graduate student. The federal government pays the interest until six months after the student stops attending school at least half time, and the student doesn't have to begin repaying the loan until then. Payment can be deferred longer, or even forgiven, for graduates who take certain public-service jobs. The program is named for former Sen. Robert T. Stafford, R-Vt.

Unsubsidized Stafford Loans — These loans are similar to the subsidized Stafford loans, but the government does not pay the interest, and the maximum loan available is $18,500 for a graduate student. Borrowers can postpone repaying the loan until after they leave school. The same deferment and forgiveness provisions apply.

PLUS Loans — These unsubsidized federal loans are made to parents. Repayment begins when the loan is made. The variable interest rate is capped at 9 percent. Deferment or forgiveness for public-service employment is available.

Perkins Loans — The federal government and a higher-education institution jointly finance these loans, which are awarded by the school to needy students. Undergraduates can borrow up to $4,000 annually, graduate students up to $6,000. Repayment begins nine months after the student stops attending school at least half time. Repayment can be deferred or forgiven if the student takes certain public-service employment. The program is named for the late Rep. Carl D. Perkins, D-Ky.

As the size of individual grants lags behind the price increases, students like Sandonato are graduating with ever-higher debt loads, and a sense that working their way through school robbed them of an essential part of college life.

Sandonato talks wistfully of having wanted to "experience college not just in the classroom but in activities outside of the classroom." Instead, she says, she had time only to "work full time, take classes and worry about exams."

As families, university administrators and members of Congress wrestle with the issue of rising college costs, here are some of the questions they are debating:

Are tuitions rising because colleges waste money?

When *The New York Times* reported in 2003 on opulent

new amenities at American colleges, leaders of the House Education Committee quickly sent copies to every representative and to journalists who cover education. In a cover letter, Chairman John A. Boehner, R-Ohio, and Higher Education Subcommittee Chairman Howard "Buck" McKeon, R-Calif., lamented "the increasing availability of lavish facilities on campuses across America and how this trend is driving up the cost of higher education." [8]

Similarly, when the College Board's 2003 report on college prices noted the relationship between declining state appropriations and rising tuition at public schools, Boehner immediately issued a statement decrying higher education's reluctance to admit its own responsibility for the soaring cost of college.

Supplemental Educational Opportunity Grants — Undergraduate students with exceptional financial need are eligible for these grants, which range from $100 to $4,000 a year and are funded by the federal government and awarded by colleges and universities.

Work-Study — Colleges disperse these funds for the federal government to students who work to pay a portion of their college expenses. Students must be paid at least the minimum wage, and schools are encouraged to place students in public-service jobs or jobs related to their course of study, often on campus. The amount a student can earn is based on financial need.

HOPE Scholarship Tax Credits — First- or second-year college students — or their parents — can use these credits to reduce their federal income tax payments by up to $1,500 a year, depending on financial need, college costs and other available financial aid. [4]

Lifetime Learning Credit — Tax credits of up to $2,000 are available to students who are beyond the second year of college or are taking classes parttime to upgrade their job skills. Amounts depend on financial need, college costs and other available financial aid. [5]

Institutional Grants — Colleges offer these scholarships from their own funds. Some are based on financial need. Others, awarded on merit, go to athletes, outstanding scholars and other students who are particularly attractive to college admissions and financial-aid officers. On private campuses, nearly 60 percent of students received institutional grants last year.

State Grants — States are shifting away from awarding grants on the basis of need: 90 percent of all state grants a decade ago were need-based, compared with 75 percent last year. While state grants overall are only one-third the size of the federal grant programs, state grants have grown twice as fast over the last decade. Grants vary from state to state. Georgia's HOPE program, for instance, pays for tuition, fees and books at any public higher-education institution in the state for any graduate of a Georgia high school with at least a "B" average who maintains a "B" average and Georgia residency while in college. [6] New York's Tuition Assistance Program, which awards annual scholarships worth up to $5,000, is based on need. [7]

[1] "Trends in Student Aid, 2004," The College Board. Available online at www.collegeboard.com/prod_downloads/press/cost04/TrendsinStudentAid2004.pdf; "The Student Guide 2004-2005: Federal Student Aid at a Glance." http://studentaid.ed.gov/students/publications/student_guide/2004_2005/english/glance.htm.

[2] Unless otherwise noted, financial aid information is from the U.S. Education Department Web site: http://www.ed.gov/finaid/landing.jhtml?src=rt.

[3] Statistics from "Trends in Student Aid, 2003," and the Education Department Web site, *op. cit.*

[4] Department of Education, "The HOPE Scholarship and Lifetime Learning Credits;" online at http://ed.gov/offices/OPE/PPI/HOPE/index.html; National Association of Student Financial Aid Administrators, Parent and Student Guide to Federal Tax Benefits for Tuition and Fees (for tax year 2004) http://www.nasfaa.org/annualpubs/taxbenefitsguide.html.

[5] Department of Education, "The HOPE Scholarship and Lifetime Learning Credits;" online at http://ed.gov/offices/OPE/PPI/HOPE/index.html; notice 97-60, Lifetime Learning Credit. http://www.irs.gov/individuals/article/0,,id=96273,00.html#QA9.

[6] Georgia Student Finance Commission, "Georgia's Hope Scholarship Program." Available online at http://www.gsfc.org/HOPE/Index.cfm.

[7] New York Higher Education Services Corp., "Tuition Assistance Program: New York's TAP Can Help You Pay for College!" Available online at http://www.hesc.com/bulletin.nsf/0/3CA243796A98D19D85256D88006B4AD3?OpenDocument&a=PF.

"Hyperinflation in college costs has been pummeling parents and students for more than a decade," he said, "and the problem has not been a lack of spending by the states or federal government. Even when states were increasing their investment in higher education in recent years, college tuition was skyrocketing."

Referring to the *Times* report, Boehner charged that "extravagant spending by institutions for everything from super-size Jacuzzis and sunbathing decks to massage facilities and rock-climbing walls is contributing significantly to the soaring cost of college."

Adding to the allegations of extravagance are periodic reports about high-paid athletic coaches and college presidents, along with questions about generous faculty salaries and light workloads.

Salaries for college presidents at both public and private institutions have soared over the last few years. *The Chronicle of Higher Education* has reported that seven private college presidents earned more than $800,000 in 2003 (up from four in 2002), and 42 earned at least $500,000, which is 15 more than just a year earlier. In 2002, two liberal arts college presidents earned more than $400,000. [9] In 2003, at least ten surpassed that amount. [10]

Such reports make college administrators and their supporters cringe. They say, for example, that many students (and parents) want fancy amenities, and that colleges must compete for the best students.

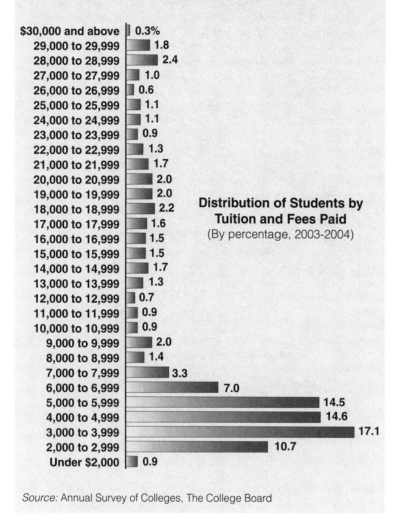

Most Students Pay Less Than $7,000

Two-thirds of the full-time undergraduates at American four-year colleges pay less than $7,000 a year in tuition and fees. About 14 percent spend at least $20,000.

$30,000 and above	0.3%
29,000 to 29,999	1.8
28,000 to 28,999	2.4
27,000 to 27,999	1.0
26,000 to 26,999	0.6
25,000 to 25,999	1.1
24,000 to 24,999	1.1
23,000 to 23,999	0.9
22,000 to 22,999	1.3
21,000 to 21,999	1.7
20,000 to 20,999	2.0
19,000 to 19,999	2.0
18,000 to 18,999	2.2
17,000 to 17,999	1.6
16,000 to 16,999	1.5
15,000 to 15,999	1.5
14,000 to 14,999	1.7
13,000 to 13,999	1.3
12,000 to 12,999	0.7
11,000 to 11,999	0.9
10,000 to 10,999	0.9
9,000 to 9,999	2.0
8,000 to 8,999	1.4
7,000 to 7,999	3.3
6,000 to 6,999	7.0
5,000 to 5,999	14.5
4,000 to 4,999	14.6
3,000 to 3,999	17.1
2,000 to 2,999	10.7
Under $2,000	0.9

Distribution of Students by Tuition and Fees Paid
(By percentage, 2003-2004)

Source: Annual Survey of Colleges, The College Board

institutions are labor intensive with unique expenses.

"Higher education is a people-heavy business," says Travis Reindl, director of state policy analysis at the American Association of State Colleges and Universities. "And it's not just about paying them. It's also about employee benefits. Look at where health-care costs have gone in the last few years. Talk about being above the rate of inflation!"

Colleges also come under fire because of the seemingly light workloads enjoyed by high-priced, tenured faculty. A 1998 survey by the National Center for Education Statistics (NCES) concluded that the average classroom-teaching load was 11 hours a week. [11]

But while professors may spend only 11 hours in the classroom, according to the NCES survey, they work an additional 45.6 hours each week on research, administration, advising students and other duties. [12]

Overall, though, college faculty salaries are a different story altogether: In 2005, college professors received a 2.8 percent raise, trailing inflation for the first time in eight years. The average salary for all professors was $68,505. [13]

Because colleges are so labor intensive, they have trouble increasing productivity, says Naomi Richman, manager of the higher-education rating team at Moody's Investors Service.

At the same time, they insist that institutions have to pay top dollar to get top-quality executives. But, they point out, in the context of total college costs, presidential pay has no real impact on prices. And besides, relatively few institutions acquire lavish recreational facilities or extravagantly paid executives anyway, they say.

It's not fair to compare college prices to the overall inflation rate, college executives add, because educational

"In most areas of the economy, you have productivity gains over time, so a factory can produce the same amount of widgets at lower cost," she says. "If teachers are teaching 20 kids in the classroom, if they [start teaching 30], that's considered watering down the product."

Many college employees also require expensive tools, pointed out Ronald Ehrenberg, director of the Cornell Higher Education Research Institute. "Theoretical scientists, who in a previous generation required only desks and pencils and papers, now often require supercomputers," Ehrenberg noted. "Experimental scientists increasingly rely on sophisticated laboratory facilities that are increasingly expensive to build and operate." [14]

Moreover, college executives tend to be paid less than their counterparts in private industry, according to Sandy Baum, a Skidmore College economics professor who analyzes higher-education finance for the College Board. For most teachers, she adds, "making a decision to be a faculty member is a decision that money is not what your life is about." Teachers "work very hard," she says. "They put a lot of time into their teaching and research — and research is a very important part of what faculty members do."

"I don't think higher education has done a very good job of explaining its efforts to hold down costs," University System of Maryland Chancellor William Kirwan said at a roundtable hosted by McKeon's subcommittee on Sept. 30, 2003. Because of state subsidy cuts, "we eliminated 800 positions — about 4 percent of our staff. We have not had raises for faculty and staff going on three years."

Nevertheless, some education scholars say colleges could still make themselves more efficient. "There's less innovation in higher education" than in other organizations, says Patrick M. Callan, president of the National Center for Public Policy and Higher Education. "Recessions usually force choices on organizations and squeeze out excess. But in higher education, we simply shift the [burden to pay] onto the students."

Carol Twigg, executive director of Rensselaer Polytechnic Institute's Center for Academic Transformation, is demonstrating how innovation with information technology can cut costs and improve teaching effectiveness. The center is helping colleges redesign courses to cut the time teachers spend lecturing, grading tests and carrying out administrative tasks. Retooling the teaching process is enabling teachers to teach more students and in most cases teach them more effectively.

Thirty demonstration projects have cut costs an average of 40 percent, Twigg says. Meanwhile, "significant increases in student learning" were measured in 22 of the projects, and the others matched the effectiveness of traditional teaching methods.

Should government increase funding for higher education?

Nearly $13 billion was appropriated during the 2003-4 academic year for Pell Grants, the primary source of fed-

AP Photo/Gene Boyars

Freshmen Lauren Bassos, left, and Jennifer Buono attend Brookdale Community College, in Lincroft, N.J., instead of a four-year college. Community and online institutions are becoming increasingly popular as costs at four-year public and private schools outpace inflation.

eral grants for low-income students. [15] This is a smaller increase than in recent years, but part of a long-term increase in these federal grants: The amount represents a more than 50 percent inflation-adjusted increase in a decade. [16]

"If anyone told me 15 years ago that we'd have $12 billion in Pell Grants by now," Callan says, "I'd have said we'd probably pretty much have solved the problems of access to education."

But the access is not there, spurring debate about whether state and federal governments are short-changing America's institutions of higher education. Even though federal spending on higher-education grants has increased substantially, it has not kept pace with rapidly rising cost, prices and enrollments.

The inflation-adjusted price of attending college — tuition, fees and room and board — rose between 26 and 51 percent over the last 10 years, with the smallest percentage increase occurring at public two-year institutions and the highest at public four-year schools. And while Pell Grant funds increased 6 percent in the last year, there was a 7 percent increase in the number of Pell recipients, which means that the average grant fell by 1 percent, the first decline in inflation-adjusted value of Pell Grants since 1999-2000. Last year, the average Pell Grant was $2,466, enough to pay about a third of a

Size of Pell Grants Has Dropped

The total amount spent on Pell Grants for low-income students has risen over the last 30 years (top graph), but due to rising enrollments the inflation-adjusted amount of the maximum grant (bottom graph) has declined since peaking in 1975-76.

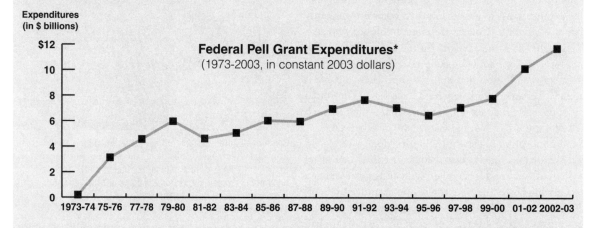

Expenditures (in $ billions)

Federal Pell Grant Expenditures*
(1973-2003, in constant 2003 dollars)

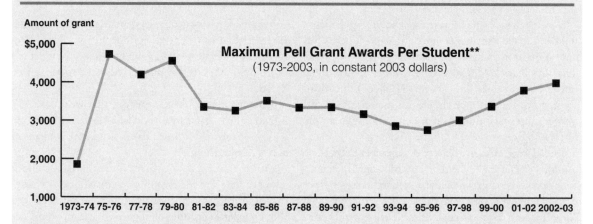

Amount of grant

Maximum Pell Grant Awards Per Student**
(1973-2003, in constant 2003 dollars)

* Federal Pell Grant Expenditures (in constant 2003 dollars): 2003-2004: $12.7 billion spent on Pell Grants.

** Maximum Pell Grant Awards per student (remains $4050, but is less in 2003 dollars): 2003-2004: The '03-'04 inflation-adjusted amount is a 1 percent decline from '02-'03 number.

Source: The College Board

commuter student's tuition and fees at the typical community college. But it paid less than a quarter of the average tuition, fees and room and board at four-year state schools, and covered less than one-tenth of those charges at the average private college. [17] In 1980-81, by contrast, the average Pell Grant covered 35 percent of the cost of a four-year state school.

And the $4,050 maximum available under a Pell Grant — available only to dependent students from families whose income is around $20,000 or less — falls far short of most students' expenses, says Reindl of the American Association of State Colleges and Universities. "The size of available grants declines as family income rises, up to $50,000, at which point, "you're pretty much out of it," Reindl explains. The maximum amount was frozen at $4,050 for the third year in a row in 2004.

As a result, more students are borrowing more money: Loans comprised 56 percent of student aid last year, [18] up from about 45 percent a decade earlier. In the 2003-4 academic year, more than 90,000 students or potential students in the huge California community-college system alone dropped out or failed to enroll because of tuition hikes and course cuts caused by inadequate state support, according to Chancellor Thomas Nussbaum. "The very idea of what public higher education should be is being eroded," he complained. "That's 100,000 people. Gone." [19]

Meanwhile, state appropriations — the largest source of revenue for public colleges — have not kept up with enrollment increases either. In fact, as enrollments have been increasing, the states' share of higher-education budgets has dipped to "a dangerously low point," College Board president and former West Virginia Gov. Gaston Caperton said at an Oct. 21, 2003, press conference.

Over the last several years, states faced a collective $200 billion budget gap, largely due to already enacted tax cuts, the sluggish economy and pressures from a growing anti-tax movement. [20] Schools reliant on state funding had one of their worst years ever in 2003-4: aggregate appropriations for higher education fell 2.1 percent, to $60.3 billion, possibly one of the largest cuts ever. [21] But there has been some recovery: In the 2004-5 fiscal year, state funding increased 3.8 percent.

Higher-education advocates want the state and federal governments to jack up their education spending, particularly for Pell Grants and other aid to lower-income students. The Coalition for Better Student Loans — including financial-aid administrators, parents, lenders and higher-education organizations — wants federal loan programs for other students enhanced as well. The group asked Congress for larger subsidized loans, reduced fees, more flexible repayment options and an additional $1 billion to forgive loans to graduates who take hard-to-fill jobs at modest pay, such as teaching in low-income communities.

Many state officials would increase higher-education spending if their state budgets would allow it, and leading congressional Democrats want to raise federal assistance. But Republican leaders in Congress are skeptical about the need for more U.S. aid for higher education.

> **"Higher education is kind of in the driver's seat right now. Families that have a generation or two of experience with college understand that the worst thing that could happen to your child is not to go to college. We're sort of the cartel that controls access to the middle class, and we're taking the opportunity to leverage up prices, as any private-sector, for-profit enterprise would."**
>
> — **Patrick M. Callan,**
> President, National Center for
> Public Policy and Higher Education

The federal government provided more than 67 percent of all student aid last year: that's $81 billion, 70 percent of which was given in the form of loans. [22] Those amounts represent a substantial increase above inflation in all categories over the decade, the GOP lawmakers note.

"We have been putting more and more money into higher education, and we just can't keep up" with rising college prices, McKeon says. "We fall further and further behind as the schools increase their tuition and fees, and as the states lower their help for schools."

The pattern makes McKeon wonder if raising federal aid to students actually encourages colleges to raise prices so they can gobble up the federal increase. Boehner entertains similar thoughts about state spending decisions. "It does seem pretty clear that the more the federal government was doing, the states looked over and said, 'Maybe we don't have to do as much,' " Boehner says.

some federal funds to institutions that raise tuition and fees substantially above the overall inflation rate. [24]

The measure called for a "College Affordability Index," defined as twice the Consumer Price Index. If a college raised tuition and fees by more than the index over a two-year period — with some exceptions — it would be required to explain to the U.S. Education Department the reasons for the price hike and provide a plan for holding down prices in the future.

If the college continued to exceed the index for three more years, it would lose any federal student aid dispersed on campus, such as work-study funds and Perkins loans. The federal government would continue to offer students direct aid, such as Pell Grants and Stafford loans, although the size of the loans could be restricted.

But the idea was always controversial, and McKeon dropped it in March 2004, saying that it may no longer be necessary to penalize high-tuition schools. "More and more institutions today are announcing voluntary steps to avoid excessive tuition hikes that hurt parents and students." [25]

McKeon and other Republicans, however, would still like to create the watch list of universities that raise tuition by more than twice the rate of inflation for three years in a row. And if the current Higher Education Act is passed, they'll get it.

As Callan points out and as a former clothing store owner like McKeon can appreciate, when demand goes up in a free market, there is no natural incentive to lower prices. "Higher education is kind of in the driver's seat right now," Callan says. "Families that have a generation or two of experience with college understand that the worst thing that could happen to your child is not to go to college. We're sort of the cartel that controls access to the middle class, and we're taking the opportunity to leverage up prices, as any private-sector, for-profit enterprise would.

"Right now, hardly any college that's very attractive feels that it's going to lose enrollment by raising prices."

Despite its demise, the legislation did succeed in sparking a debate over ever-increasing college tuition. "I sympathize," says Peter Magrath, president of the National Association of State Universities and Land Grant Colleges. "I think he is right to raise the issue. He's got our attention, and rightly so."

But some opponents of McKeon's bill argue that the legislation struck at the wrong target. "Increases in

The Ohio State Buckeyes play the Michigan Wolverines in front of 112,118 fans at Michigan Stadium on Nov. 22, 2003. Critics oppose big athletic programs as well as lavish college facilities like Jacuzzis and rock-climbing walls. But educators say sports programs and fancy amenities cost relatively little and are necessary to attract students.

The Bush administration appears to be of a similar mind. "The color of change is not always green," Deputy Assistant Education Secretary Jeffrey Andrade told an independent advisory committee on financial aid in April 2003. "I urge the committee not to take the easy way out and argue that all we need is money." [23]

Should colleges be penalized for raising prices?

For a time, House Republicans considered taking a stick to rising college prices.

The Affordability in Higher Education Act, introduced by McKeon in October 2003, would have denied

tuition in community colleges are the direct result of cutbacks in state appropriations," says George Boggs, president and chief executive officer of the American Association of Community Colleges. "It doesn't make any sense to penalize those colleges or their students — who are among the most needy students in higher education — because of something they can't control."

BACKGROUND

Exclusive Clubs

For 300 years, America's college campuses remained fairly exclusive venues, even though Ann Radcliffe set up a scholarship fund at Harvard College in 1643, the North Carolina General Assembly chartered a state university in 1789 and the Morrill Act supplied federal support for practical education at public universities in 1862. [26]

By 1869, approximately 52,000 students were enrolled at U.S. colleges — about as many as now attend the University of Texas in Austin. About 9,300 of the students were awarded bachelor's degrees the following spring, and one got a Ph.D. [27]

In 1901, access to education broadened with the opening of the first public "junior" college in Joliet, Ill. — a partnership of the University of Chicago and Joliet Township High School. [28] The number of two-year schools grew rapidly, and by 1940 students were studying on 575 two-year campuses across the country. But most were private institutions, and many were highly selective. [29]

Congress' decision after World War II to underwrite college educations for returning veterans established today's widespread belief that every American should be able to attend college and the federal government should help make that possible. The Servicemen's Readjustment Act of 1944 — known as the GI Bill — provided that aid, and vets by the millions grabbed at the opportunity.

By 1947, college attendance had soared to 2.3 million from 1.5 million in 1939. A growing proportion of students became the first from their families to study beyond high school. By 1952, public institutions eclipsed private schools as the primary place to earn a degree as working- and middle-class students took advantage of lower public school tuition. That trend would accelerate in succeeding decades.

The returning soldiers also fathered children in record numbers, setting the stage for another enrollment boom that a generation later would combine with President Lyndon B. Johnson's Great Society programs to make federal funds even more important to higher education.

The Soviet Union's 1957 launch of the first satellite, Sputnik, spurred Congress to pass the National Defense Education Act the next year. The bill created the National Defense Student Loan Program for studying in fields considered critical to the national defense, such as math, science and foreign languages. The loans — the first federal aid to students who were not military veterans — later were renamed National Direct Student Loans.

In 1963, the Higher Education Facilities Act authorized $1.2 billion in federal spending over three years for college and university construction projects, with 40 percent set aside to help states build new community and technical colleges. In 1964, Congress passed the Economic Opportunity Act, which created the college work-study program within its anti-poverty provisions.

In 1965, for the first time, the number of public two-year community colleges exceeded the number of public four-year schools, although — as today — full-time-equivalent enrollment (FTE) remained higher at the four-year institutions. Thanks to their affordability, convenient locations and evening classes, community colleges attracted lower-income, live-at-home students and older working students.

Also that year, Congress passed the Higher Education Act, which today remains the primary source of federal money for colleges, universities and their students. The law authorized Education Opportunity Grants, allocated to colleges for distribution among lower-income students, and created Guaranteed Student Loans, which later were named for Sen. Robert T. Stafford, R-Vt.

In 1972, Congress established direct federal grants to lower-income students, later named for a key supporter, Sen. Claiborne Pell, D-R.I. The federal government also began to provide matching funds for state financial-aid plans and created the Student Loan Marketing Association (now known as SLM Corp., or Sallie Mae) to facilitate the student-borrowing market by buying and selling the debts.

Need-Blind Aid

With middle-class families increasingly complaining about rising college prices, Congress in 1978 passed the

CHRONOLOGY

1800s *Federal government steps into public higher education.*

1862 Congress passes the Morrill Act to help states establish public universities.

1869 About 52,000 students are enrolled in U.S. colleges.

1900-1960 *Higher education begins to become mass education.*

1901 University of Chicago and Joliet Township High School establish first public junior college, in Joliet, Ill.

1939 College enrollment hits 1.5 million.

1940 Students take courses at 575 two-year colleges. Most are private institutions; many are highly selective.

1944 Congress passes "GI Bill," giving returning World War II veterans the wherewithal to attend college.

1947 College enrollment hits 2.3 million.

1950 Students pay less than 9 percent of cost of public College education.

1952 For first time, more students attend public colleges than private ones.

1959 College enrollment hits 3.6 million.

1960-1980 *Federal government becomes a big-time higher-education bankroller.*

1963 Congress authorizes $1.2 billion for three years of college construction projects, 40 percent earmarked for community and technical colleges.

1964 Federal work-study program begins. Four-year public college tuition and fees average less than $300 a year.

1965 Congress passes Higher Education Act, creating Guaranteed Student Loans, later named for Sen. Robert T. Stafford, R-Vt. For the first time, a majority of high school graduates goes on to college.

1969 College enrollment reaches 8 million, an unprecedented and unrepeated 122 percent increase in 10 years.

1972 Congress establishes federal grants for lower-income students, later named for Sen. Claiborne Pell, D-R.I.

1976 Tuition and fees for one year cost about $600 at average public four-year college.

1978 Middle-class students share in federal assistance, as Congress expands eligibility for Pell Grants and makes student loans available for all income levels.

1980-2003 *College prices skyrocket and governments provide more aid to middle and upper classes.*

1980 Parent Loans for Undergraduate Students — PLUS Loans — enable parents to borrow for their children's education, regardless of family income. States appropriate 44 percent of state colleges' spending.

1990 College enrollment hits 13.8 million.

1993 Georgia establishes HOPE Scholarship Program for "B"-or-better students regardless of financial need, establishing model for other states and federal government.

1997 Federal government provides more federal aid for middle class through tax credits, deductions for student loan interest and tax-free college savings accounts. Two-thirds of high school graduates attend college — a historical high.

1999 State appropriations to public colleges drop to 32.3 percent of the schools' budgets. Students' share of public college cost rises to 18.5 percent.

2000 Colleges enroll 15.3 million.

2001 Percentage of high-school grads attending college drops to 61.7.

2002 Need-blind state grants account for 24 percent of all state grants, up from 10 percent 10 years earlier.

2003 Tuition and fees at public four-year colleges average $4,694, more than 15 times higher than in 1964. Private four-year colleges average $19,710, two-year public schools, $1,905.

Middle Income Student Assistance Act, which expanded eligibility for Pell Grants and made federal loans available to students of all income levels. In the late '80s and throughout the '90s, Congress created several tax benefits to mitigate higher-education expenses — measures that benefit the middle and upper classes more than the poor.

To counter a "brain drain" of promising students leaving their home states for college, several states created scholarship programs that weren't based on need. Some were available to any high-school graduate who qualified for college. Others were merit-based.

Some advocates for the poor warned that providing aid for the middle class would divert aid from the poor and make it more difficult for needy students to attend college. But tax breaks and merit scholarships "have become enormously popular with middle-class families who also tend to be voters," notes Sandra Ruppert, a program director with the Education Commission of the States. Need-blind state grants increased from 10 percent of all state grants in 1992 to 24 percent in 2002, the latest year for which records are available. [30]

The combination of new federal-aid provisions, expanded state facilities and the arrival on campus of the Baby Boomers sent enrollments skyrocketing — from 3.6 million in the fall of 1959 to 8 million in 1969, an unprecedented 122 percent jump that would never be surpassed. Over the next 30 years, growing at slower rates, enrollments reached 15.3 million in 2000.

From an enclave for the elite, the college campus evolved into the normal next stop for the typical high-school graduate. In 1965, for the first time, a majority of high-school grads enrolled in college. By 1997, two-thirds were taking that step.

Federal financial aid soared along with enrollments. Spending on Pell Grants, for instance, rose from $48 million in the 1973-74 academic year to the current $12.7 billion. During the 30-year period, the minimum grant increased faster than inflation — from $50 to $400 this year, as did the maximum grant, which went up from $452 to $4,050. But, because of year-to-year fluctuations in funding, inflation-adjusted grants generally had more purchasing power in the '70s than today, and the minimum grants were worth more through most of the '90s than they are now.

State appropriations to public colleges also tended to increase over the years, with variations among the states

President Bush, House Education Committee Chairman John Boehner, R-Ohio, and Sen. Edward M. Kennedy, D-Mass., share a laugh before Bush signed the landmark No Child Left Behind Act in January 2003 at Hamilton High School, in Hamilton, Ohio. Boehner has been critical of colleges and universities for not holding costs down.

according to economic conditions. From 1980-81 to 1999-2000, for instance, state appropriations increased from $19 billion to nearly $51 billion, a pace more than a third faster than inflation.

Yet college spending rose even faster. Four-year state colleges spent $34.7 billion in 1980-81 and nearly $125 billion in 1999-2000, an increase more than 50 percent above the inflation rate. Even accounting for rising enrollments, spending-per-student exceeded inflation by a third on both four-year and two-year campuses.

Thus, even though state appropriations went up, states' share of college budgets declined from 44 percent in 1980-81 to 32.3 percent in 1999-2000. And, in the last few years, declining tax receipts have led many states to reduce appropriations.

So students — or their parents — have had to make up the difference. When the first Baby Boomers hit campus in 1964, average tuition and fees were less than $300 a year at public four-year schools, and the full cost of tuition, fees, room and board was less than $1,000. [31]

Since then, according to a College Board study, the full price for a four-year degree has increased at more than twice the inflation rate on private campuses and at 75 percent above inflation at public schools. [32] Over the last decade, tuition at public four-year schools rose four times faster than the median family income. [33]

Innovation Cuts Costs — and Improves Teaching

The Math Emporium at Virginia Polytechnic Institute and State University in Blacksburg, Va., is open 24 hours a day, nearly 365 days a year. Sprawling over the vast, acre-plus first floor of a remodeled department store, the facility provides math students with 500 desk-top computers. Opened in 1997, the facility enabled Tech to redesign its math courses to cut costs, free teachers from routine work and turn out better-educated, happier students.

Up the East Coast in Connecticut, Fairfield University biology students participate in inter-active computer exercises during lectures and use their laptops — rather than scalpels — to dissect animals during lab sessions. By conveying information more efficiently, computers have cut the time students must spend in introductory courses, thus reducing the Jesuit school's need for adjunct professors.

Down south at Florida Gulf Coast University in Fort Myers — the self-proclaimed "fastest growing public university in the nation" — the introductory Understanding the Visual and Performing Arts class is taught with CD-ROMs, videotapes and Web pages. The electronic tools enable each faculty member to teach more students while giving students a more vivid understanding of the arts. The electronic approach has cut the use of adjunct teachers and boosted average student grades by a full letter. [1]

Across the country, colleges and universities are seeking to innovate their way to lower costs — and many are discovering they can improve educational quality at the same time. The trend has mounted a frontal assault on the traditional notion that colleges can't become more productive because faculty can teach only a certain number of students at a time.

"Higher-education leaders say you can't do anything about costs because they honestly believe it," says Carol Twigg, executive director of the Center for Academic Transformation at Rensselaer Polytechnic Institute in upstate New York. Innovators are "trying to change the nature of the conversation and say 'you can reduce costs, and there are lots of ways you can do it.'"

Wielding grants from the Pew Charitable Trusts, the center is encouraging schools to apply technology to the cause of academic productivity. "Higher education has a flawed production mode," Twigg says. "We teach classes in repetitive little cells. With the typical freshman English course or algebra course in a large institution, you've got 50 classes with 50 faculty members all doing the exact same thing — standing in front of a class of 30 students."

But much content delivery can be shifted from faculty lectures to interactive computer programs, she says. The computers can quiz the students and immediately tell them how well they're grasping the subject matter. The students can work with the computers whenever it's most convenient while interacting with teachers when they need personalized help.

"You utilize technology to take on tasks the technology can take on and free up faculty time and enable them to do other things," Twigg explains.

Courtesy University of Alabama

The Mathematics Technology Learning Center at the University of Alabama offers 240 computers 70 hours a week. The program has boosted passing grades in intermediate algebra by 50 percent.

About half of the class hours in community colleges and a third in four-year institutions are consumed in just 25 core courses, Twigg says. Many are introductory courses with high failure rates — 50 to 60 percent at community colleges and from 15 to 40 percent at four-year schools. Making these courses less labor-intensive and more effective can have a huge impact on college costs, and student success.

Virginia Tech is a leader in course redesign. The Mathematics Department began computer teaching in two freshman calculus courses in 1992. The approach proved so popular and effective that the department began redesigning other courses. Five years later, the Emporium was launched.

Tech math students can use any Internet connection to access self-paced tutorials, teachers' notes and streaming video lectures. In the Emporium, they can get around-the-clock help from faculty members and tutors.

Tech, Fairfield and Florida Gulf Coast are among 30 schools that received $200,000 Pew grants to work with Twigg's program. The redesigned courses have reduced costs an average 40 percent, Twigg says, while doing a better job of teaching than traditional courses.

The 500-computer Math Emporium at Virginia Polytechnic Institute and State University in Blacksburg, Va., helps cut costs, free teachers from routine work and turn out better students.

Courtesy Virginia Polytechnic Institute

On 22 of the campuses, students in redesigned courses tested better than students in traditional courses, she says. At the eight other schools, the students scored about the same.

On benchmark exams at Fairfield, for instance, students in redesigned courses got 88 percent of the questions correct compared with 79 percent in traditional courses. The redesigned courses experienced a 3 percent dropout rate compared with 8 percent in previous years. Eighty-five percent of students enrolled for a second semester of biology after taking the redesigned first-semester course, up from 75 percent.

At Florida Gulf Coast, 54 percent of students in the redesigned course earned "A" or "B" grades, up from 31 percent in the traditional course. "D"s and "F"s dropped to 21 percent from 45 percent.

But course redesign is not the only cost-cutting innovation on campus. Members of the Wisconsin Association of Independent Colleges and Universities, for instance, are collaborating on back-office operations to tap economies of scale they can't produce individually. The schools anticipate savings on such areas as health insurance, information technology, purchasing, travel management, billing, staff training and financial administration. [2]

Other institutions are offering tuition discounts to encourage students to take evening, weekend and summer classes to make better use of facilities.

Meanwhile, the cell phone is playing an increasingly important role on campuses, as it is everywhere else. Long-distance calling from dormitory telephones has faded as a source of college revenue now that most students carry their own cell phones. During the 2001-2 academic year, for instance, Miami University of Ohio's phone income dropped $300,000.

So schools are taking a new tack: This year, in an effort to recoup its losses, Miami joined a growing number of schools that — like the corner grocery store — are selling cell phone plans to their students. [3]

---

[1] Information about these and other innovative uses of information technology can be found on the Web site of the Center for Academic Transformation, Rensselaer Polytechnic Institute: http://center.rpi.edu.

[2] Rolf Wegenke, president, Wisconsin Association of Independent Colleges and Universities, testimony before the House Education and the Workforce Committee, 21st Century Competitiveness Subcommittee, July 10, 2003. Available online at http://edworkforce.house.gov/hearings.

[3] Mary Beth Marklein, "Colleges Catch Cellphone Wave," *USA Today*, Oct. 29, 2003, p. 5D.

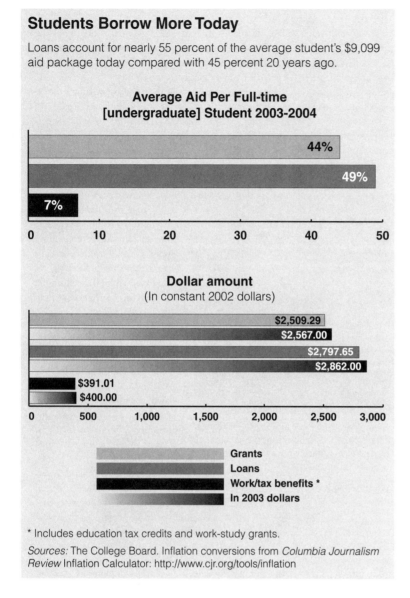

Students Borrow More Today

Loans account for nearly 55 percent of the average student's $9,099 aid package today compared with 45 percent 20 years ago.

Average Aid Per Full-time [undergraduate] Student 2003-2004

44%

49%

7%

0   10   20   30   40   50

Dollar amount
(In constant 2002 dollars)

$2,509.29

$2,567.00

$2,797.65

$2,862.00

$391.01

$400.00

0   500   1,000   1,500   2,000   2,500   3,000

Grants
Loans
Work/tax benefits *
In 2003 dollars

* Includes education tax credits and work-study grants.

Sources: The College Board. Inflation conversions from *Columbia Journalism Review* Inflation Calculator: http://www.cjr.org/tools/inflation

as large a portion of college charges as they did in the program's early years.

CURRENT SITUATION

The 2004 Higher Education Act was shelved in the midst of a heated election year, but Republicans introduced a bill in February that would mirror many of the same provisions outlined in that act. [34] Most controversial is a provision (familiar from 2004 version) that would make it harder for students to lock in their loans at low, fixed interest rates.

Rep. John A. Boehner, the Ohio Republican who introduced the legislation, says that the money the federal government spends subsidizing those low rates is better spent on expanding Pell Grants to more students. Democrats opposing the bill say that it will effectively make college more expensive for students.

The revised act also requires that colleges that continue to hike tuition above a certain formula must provide a detailed accounting of those costs and expenditures. And if the current bill passes, Pell Grants would get something of a makeover, upgrading the maximum grant amount for the first time in years, and expanding the months of a year during which students are eligible for them.

Thus, as states' share of college budgets declined, the proportion covered by students' tuition and fees more than doubled, from less than 9 percent in 1950 to 18.5 percent in 1999. The rest was covered by federal and local governments, private gifts, endowment earnings and charges for products and services, such as room and board.

In the final analysis, public schools no longer offer the same bargain for middle-class students they did when the first boomers plunked down $300 for tuition and fees. And federal grants for lower-income students don't cover

Meanwhile, realizing that they aren't likely to get much from the current administration and Congress, college executives are searching for new ways to cut costs and raise funds. At the same time, schools in several states are fending off lawsuits aimed at undoing recent price hikes.

Colleges Cut Costs

Well aware of the congressional majority's sentiment, college executives have intensified efforts to cut costs, as students recover from the record-setting price hikes of the past couple years. "If American Airlines hired an outside consultant to tell them how to increase profits, and the suggestion was only to raise prices, the consultant probably would be fired," Mark Yudof, chancellor of the Texas University System, said of the need for colleges to do more than hike tuition. [35]

Murray State University President Alexander described cutbacks typical of those implemented by colleges across the country. [36] Over the last few years, he said, his Kentucky school:

- Froze and eliminated faculty positions;
- Eliminated positions for administrators, professionals, support staff and graduate assistants;
- Closed the campus television station;
- Reduced the number of classes;
- Halted heating and cooling system upgrades;
- Reduced travel; and
- Restricted overtime.

Colleges also are exploring innovative ways to reduce expenses and increase revenues. "Colleges need to think about quality in ways that don't start with the assumption that cost-effectiveness and quality are always in direct opposition," says Callan of the National Center for Public Policy and Higher Education.

The American Association of Community Colleges' Boggs sees two-year schools' approaches to the challenge as "very innovative and creative and entrepreneurial." Community colleges are partnering with other institutions, businesses, industries and governments, Boggs explains. "They have offered classes on weekends and evenings for a long time. A growing number are putting courses online — or at least information, study guides and other materials to help the students in the traditional program."

In Charlotte, N.C., for example, Boggs says, Central Piedmont Community College recruited businesses to sponsor courses. And two-year schools are cooperating with high schools on what Callan describes as "increasing student productivity" — encouraging students to take courses for college credit while still in high school.

Gov. Mark Warner, D-Va., wants all of his state's public high schools to take part in what he calls "a dramatic reform" of the senior year.

"For students not going on to higher education, we'll work with them to get an industry-recognized certificate" in a trade, such as auto mechanics, Warner said of his Senior Year Plus proposal. "For the college-bound, we'll

Vanderbilt University Chancellor Gordon Gee earns $852,023. He is one of seven presidents of private universities who were paid more than $800,000, according to *The Chronicle of Higher Education*. Educators say they have to pay top dollar to get top executives and that, in the context of total college costs, presidential pay has little impact on prices.

offer every high-school senior the opportunity to acquire a full semester of college credit" through dual college-high school enrollment and advanced-placement courses. "It will save $5,000 on college costs for the family, $3,000 for the state."

Callan calls it an example of how actions to address the cost problem can also be "educationally compelling" ideas. "We have a huge amount of research that says the senior year in high school is a horrible waste of time," Callan explains. "When kids who are ready to do college work are offered the chance, we find the families and the students jump at it. It cuts costs and it educationally makes sense."

Some institutions are being forced to make their prices more appealing to students and parents. For instance, an Illinois law guarantees that the tuition for in-state undergraduate students will not be raised at a state institution once they enroll. [37] Other state legislatures have imposed — and later lifted — price freezes or caps in the past. Gov. Robert Ehrlich, Jr., R-Md. said he may propose a cap on tuition at state schools, possibly tying it to inflation. State budget cuts in Maryland led public institutions to raise tuition by an average of 19 percent in 2003-4 alone. [38]

Should the federal government penalize colleges and universities for significant tuition increases?

YES
Rep. Howard "Buck" McKeon, R-Calif.
Chairman, House Education Subcommittee on Higher Education

Written for The CQ Researcher, November, 2003

America's higher-education system is in crisis as a result of explosive price increases that are jeopardizing the dream of a college education for millions of students across America. According to the Advisory Committee on Student Financial Assistance, cost factors prevent 48 percent of all qualified, low-income high-school graduates from attending a four-year college and 22 percent from attending any college at all. At this rate, by the end of the decade, over 2 million qualified students will miss out on the opportunity to go to college.

As chairman of the House Subcommittee on 21st Century Competitiveness, I have made college affordability a top priority. In 1997, I created the National Commission on the Cost of Higher Education to study tuition increases and rising administrative costs and to make policy recommendations on how to hold down these increases. Throughout my eight-year chairmanship, I have worked hard to increase the maximum Pell Grant from $2,000 to $4,050 and have fought to drive down interest rates to make student loans more affordable. Nevertheless, tuition has not dropped, but instead has skyrocketed beyond our most liberal projections.

To place higher education back within the reach of our nation's youth, last month I introduced the Affordability in Higher Education Act. The measure, among other things, sanctions colleges and universities that boldly increase tuition and fees at hyper-inflationary rates year after year. My bill states that, beginning in 2008, if an institution increases its tuition and fees more than twice the rate of inflation for an interval of three years, it could be removed from participation in programs within Title IV of the Higher Education Act, which would exclude them from receiving direct aid through their students' Pell Grants and Stafford and Direct Loans.

It is a shame that tuition has spiraled so far out of the reach of America's students that it is necessary to introduce legislation to penalize colleges into compliance. However, drastic times call for drastic measures. My legislation will give colleges plenty of time to react before any sanctions are imposed (in 2011).

I hope that no schools are sanctioned as a result of my bill. However, I refuse to sit idly by and endlessly subsidize colleges without holding them accountable for extraordinary price increases that prevent our nation's brightest from pursuing higher education.

NO
Travis Reindl
Director, State Policy Analysis, American Association of State Colleges and Universities

Written for The CQ Researcher, November, 2003

Sanctioning institutions for tuition increases will not change state or campus behavior. Thirty years ago, federal lawmakers put financial aid in the hands of students rather than institutions. As a result, any significant attempt to use federal student aid as a "carrot" or a "stick" will disproportionately impact students.

Such an approach fails to recognize basic realities: In the public sector, most colleges do not set their own tuition rates. Those rates are largely influenced by state funding (which has fallen more than $3 billion over the past two fiscal years).

Moreover, making the Department of Education responsible for hundreds of institutional-management reviews does not seem to be the most effective use of scarce federal resources, particularly with a Pell Grant shortfall approaching $3 billion.

Washington can, however, help students and their families through improved institutional disclosure and consumer information. By moving beyond "sticker prices" and percentage increases to metrics such as average/median net price and average/median loan debt per graduate, the federal government can equip students and families with data about how institutions are spending their money and about what the average student can expect to pay at a particular campus.

Making such information broadly available will result in better-informed consumers and more accountable institutions — a true "win-win." More important, the Department of Education and other agencies already collect value-added data elements such as those listed above, so there is no good reason why they couldn't — or shouldn't — be disseminated as soon as possible.

By focusing on areas where it does not have effective leverage, Congress also leaves aside the types of fundamental policy questions that Higher Education Act reauthorization is meant to engage. For example, what is Congress' priority in federal student-aid programs — ensuring access or subsidizing choice? At what point does excessive student indebtedness become a drag on the formation of economic and social capital?

These and other questions deserve to be tackled by lawmakers, particularly as the aging of the Baby Boomers threatens an unprecedented strain on the federal budget, and student borrowing/debt reaches record levels.

College affordability is a crucial issue, and members such as Rep. Howard "Buck" McKeon deserve credit for their persistence and candor. Congress, however, should focus its limited time, energy and resources where they will yield the greatest result.

Should governments reduce financial aid for middle-income students in order to provide more college grants to the poor?

YES   Sandy Baum
Economics Professor, Skidmore College; Co-author, "Trends in College Pricing" and "Trends in Student Aid," Published annually by the College Board

Written for The CQ Researcher, November 2003

Providing adequate aid to qualified low-income students should be a high priority for the federal government. The diversion of student subsidies in recent years away from low-income students and toward middle-income students reduces both our economic efficiency and the equity of our society.

To be efficient, public subsidies must alter behavior in socially meaningful ways. While middle-income students face pressures meeting the rapidly rising price of a college education, it is usually their choice of institution — rather than their access to higher education — that is at issue. In contrast, for low-income students the question often is whether or not they will go to college at all and, if they do enroll, whether they will graduate.

College attendance rates disturbingly correlate with family income. While virtually all high-income students with the highest test scores go to college about a quarter of those from low-income families with the same test scores do not. And those low-income students who do go to college disproportionately attend two-year colleges and are much less likely to earn bachelor's degrees.

Denying educational opportunity to qualified students not fortunate enough to be born into comfortable financial circumstances is unfair under almost any reasonable definition of equity, but it also reduces our economy's productive capacity. College graduates earn more than high-school graduates, contribute more to society and receive fewer social services.

In recent years, the federal government has aimed an increasing portion of higher-education subsidies at more affluent families through tax preferences for college savings and other tax-based policies. This shifting focus of federal policy, along with the movement of states away from need-based aid, reduces the effectiveness of student subsidies.

There are many areas of federal expenditures more deserving of cuts than middle-income student assistance — and elimination of recent tax cuts for the most fortunate Americans would certainly be a better trade-off. But grants for low-income students must be at the top of the higher-education policy agenda.

NO   Scott Ross
Executive Director, Florida Student Association

Written for The CQ Researcher, November 2003

The concept of need-based financial aid should not be ignored by either the federal or state governments, but it should not be created at the expense of middle-income students.

Three groups of students attend college in this country. The first is made up of students who generally have the means to attend college at their own or their parents' expense. They generally do not require financial aid. The second group includes those unable to pay for any of their education. Through the Free Application for Federal Student Aid (FAFSA), these students are deemed to have financial need and are usually awarded significant funds to pursue their education.

Middle-income students comprise the third group, which includes the majority of students applying to college. They usually cannot obtain any financial aid because their parents or providers earn just enough to exclude them from receiving any need-based financial aid.

To create more need-based financial aid at the expense of these middle-income students would be devastating to thousands of students who want to pursue their education. When most of these students seek help, the only answer they are given is, "Take out a student loan."

While nobody can argue that student loans have become an almost necessary part of financing a student's education, these middle-income students are being sent into the work force with debt that is almost unmanageable. This tremendous debt load forces students to seek employment entirely based on financial reward and prevents them from accepting jobs in education or other critical jobs.

The cost of education in the United States is rising at an astronomical rate. Each and every day, some of our best and brightest students are being "priced out" of an opportunity to attend college.

If we continue to neglect middle-income students and ask them to take on a financial burden that is beyond their means, we are essentially choosing one student over another, thus contradicting the actual intent of need-based financial aid: to give all students an opportunity to pursue their educational dreams.

Students Share of College Costs Rose

Over the past 20 years, the share of college costs paid by state governments dropped by a fifth while students' share (tuition and fees) jumped by more than 40 percent.

Sources of Public College Revenue
(By percentage of total costs)

1980-1981

- 12.9%
- 45.6%
- 26.2%

1999-2000

- 18.5%
- 35.8%
- 30.1%

■ Tuition and fees　　■ States　　□ Other*

* Includes private gifts, some federal payments to universities and room and board fees.

Source: National Center for Education Statistics

And students in at least four states have asked courts to roll back college-price increases. In September 2003, students in Maryland and California filed a lawsuit alleging that state institutions breached contracts by raising prices after students had enrolled on the basis of lower advertised charges. The California court has not ruled. A judge granted summary judgment for the University of Maryland, and the students have appealed.

Students and alumni won their suit in Missouri, where a 19th-century law required that "all youths resident of the state" be admitted to the University of Missouri "without payment of tuition." The university didn't charge tuition until 1987, and the legislature repealed the law in 2001, after the suit was filed. But the trial court ruled in favor of about 114,000 students who paid tuition in the interim, and the state Supreme Court refused the university's appeal. Robert Herman, the plaintiffs' lawyer in the class-action suit, says the university owes the plaintiffs "well over $1 billion."

The court has not decided on a remedy. Herman suggests paying the plaintiffs with vouchers that they could use to purchase university services over time. Some might donate their awards back to the university, he says. Others might use the vouchers to pay for their children's education, to take classes themselves or to "sell them on eBay."

OUTLOOK

Tight Budgets

College soothsayers don't like what they're reading in their tea leaves. Converging trends dictate that upward pressures on college costs will endure for the foreseeable future. Educators will have to find innovative ways to hold down costs in order to avoid pricing ever-larger numbers of potential students out of the higher-education market.

Republican leaders in Congress oppose any significant increase in federal aid to higher education, and states won't find it easy to significantly raise their appropriations to colleges. While state appropriations have improved modestly, it's far too early to predict the kinds of increases that would take public colleges out of their current financial straits.

"States, and higher education in particular, are likely to face very tight budget conditions for the next decade," said Dennis Jones, president of the National Center for Higher Education Management Systems. "All but a handful of states will find it impossible to maintain current levels of public services within their existing tax structures." [39]

Colleges' declining share of state budgets is widely attributed to increased state spending on K-12 education and increased costs for Medicaid, law enforcement and prisons at a time of strong opposition to tax increases and support for tax cuts. Unlike the federal government, every state but Vermont is constitutionally required to balance its books. [40]

"Higher education is a discretionary part of the budget, and that's not true for Medicaid, corrections, police and that type of stuff," says Magrath, of the National Association of State Universities and Land Grant Colleges.

In addition, says the Education Commission of the States' Ruppert, legislators are "well aware that there are other sources of revenue for colleges in tuition and fees and donations and endowments and grants."

Legislators, therefore, find it easier to balance tight budgets on higher education's back. And "this danger is likely to become even more pronounced in the future because of further projected increases in Medicaid costs and because of demographic shifts over the next decade and beyond," Kane and Orszag wrote.

The Congressional Budget Office estimates that Medicaid will consume 2.8 percent of gross domestic product in 2030 — up from 1.2 percent now — as the Baby Boomers grow old and the cost of health care continues to rise. The states' Medicaid burden will jump substantially as well, they added, and as a result, "state support for higher education is likely to come under increasing pressure, even as state revenues recover."

As this is occurring, notes Callan of the National Center for Public Policy and Higher Education, "In 2009 we're going to have the biggest high-school graduating class in the history of the country." And they will be "the poorest as well as the most ethnically and racially

> ## "Hyperinflation in college costs has been pummeling parents and students for more than a decade . . . Extravagant spending by institutions for everything from super-size Jacuzzis and sunbathing decks to massage facilities and rock-climbing walls is contributing significantly to the soaring cost of college."
>
> **— Rep. John H. Boehner, R-Ohio,**
> Chairman, House Education Committee

heterogeneous generation of students to appear on the doorstep of American higher education." [41]

The increase in enrollments will require more staff and facilities, and the lower-income students will be more likely to need remedial education and, therefore, be more expensive to educate. And they will need financial aid.

Callan worries: "If we continue the trajectory of cost increases and price increases for much longer, there will not be enough financial aid — even in the most generous circumstances — to cover the needs."

NOTES

1. "College on Credit: How Borrowers Perceive Their Education Debt Results of the 2002 National Student Loan Survey," Dr. Sandy Baum and Marie O'Malley, February 2003. http://www.nelliemae.com/library/research_10.html

2. All figures on college prices in this section are from "Trends in College Pricing 2004," College Board; www.collegeboard.com.

3. For background, see William Triplett, "State Budget Crises," *The CQ Researcher*, Oct. 3, 2003, pp. 821-844.

4. Goldie Blymenstyk, "Donations to Colleges Decline for the First Time Since 1988," *The Chronicle of Higher Education*, March 21, 2003, p. 29.

5. News, The Council for Aid to Education, March 2, 2005. http://www.cae.org/content/display_press.asp?id=57&ref=5

6. Sandra S. Ruppert, "Closing the College Participation Gap," Education Commission of the States, October 2003, p. 2. Available online at www.communitycollegepolicy.org.

7. College Board, "Trends in College Pricing, 2004."

8. Greg Winter, "Jacuzzi U? A Battle of Perks to Lure Students," *The New York Times*, Oct. 5, 2003, p. A1.

9. Blymenstyk, *op. cit.*

10. *Chronicle of Higher Education*, November 19, 2004.

11. Linda J. Zimbler, "Background Characteristics, Work Activities, and Compensation of Faculty and Instructional Staff in Postsecondary Institutions: Fall 1998," Department of Education, National Center for Education Statistics; http://nces.ed.gov/pubs2001/2001152.pdf.

12. *Ibid.*

13. "Off the Pace," *Chronicle of Higher Education*, April 22, 2005.

14. Address to 2003 annual meeting of the American Educational Finance Association; www.ilr.cornell.edu/cheri/wp/cheri_wp32.pdf.

15. "Trends in Student Aid, 2004," The College Board; www.collegeboard.com.

16. *Ibid.*

17. *Ibid.*

18. *Ibid.*

19. Scott Jaschik, "Match the Mission To the Tuition," *The Washington Post*, Oct. 26, 2003, p. B1.

20. Triplett, *op. cit.*

21. "State Appropriations: Improving, but Tempered by Rising Costs," *The Chronicle of Higher Education*, January 7, 2005.

22. "Trends in Student Aid, 2004."

23. Stephen Burd, "Bush's Next Target?" *The Chronicle of Higher Education*, July 11, 2003, p. A18.

24. 108th Congress, First Session, H.R. 3311, the Affordability in Education Act of 2003; http://frwebgate.access.gpo.gov.

25. "House G.O.P. to Drop Idea of Penalty for Steep Rises in Tuition," *The New York Times*, March 3, 2004.

26. "Ann Radcliffe Trust," in Handbook for Students 2002-2003, Faculty of Arts and Sciences, Harvard University; www.registrar.fas.harvard.edu/handbooks; William S. Powell, "Carolina — A Brief History," University of North Carolina at Chapel Hill, www.unc.edu/about/history.html; for background, see Scott W. Wright, "Community Colleges," *The CQ Researcher*, April 21, 2000, p. 338.

27. Enrollment figures are from the "Digest of Education Statistics, 2002," U.S. Department of Education, National Center for Education Statistics; http://nces.ed.gov/pubs2003/digest02/index.asp.

28. Wright, *op. cit.*

29. Historical information in this section is derived in part from: Wright, *op. cit.*; Mary H. Cooper, "Paying for College," *The CQ Researcher*, Nov. 20, 1992, pp. 1001-1024; "History of Student Financial Aid," from the Web site FinAid: The Smart Student Guide to Financial Aid, www.finaid.org. "The Higher Education Act: A History," *The Chronicle of Higher Education*, July 11, 2003, p. A8.

30. Financial aid information is from "Trends in Student Aid," *op. cit.*

31. Unless otherwise noted, college finance information comes from "Digest of Education Statistics, 2002," *op. cit.*

32. "Trends in College Pricing," *op. cit.*

33. Ruppert, *op. cit.*, p. 4.

34. "Republican Bill to Renew Higher-Education Act Mirrors Last Year's Legislation," *The Chronicle of Higher Education*, February 11, 2005.

35. Quoted in Sara Hebel, "The Future of Tuition," *The Chronicle of Higher Education*, Sept. 19, 2003, p. A10.

36. Alexander, *op. cit.*

37. Susan C. Thomson, "SIU Plans for Freeze on Tuition Beginning Next Year," *St. Louis Post-Dispatch*, Sept. 12, 2003, p. B1; "States Move to

Limit Increases in Tuition," *The Chronicle of Higher Education*, March 5, 2004.

38. Lori Montgomery and Amy Argetsinger, "Ehrlich Says He May Seek Tuition Cap At Colleges," *The Washington Post*, Oct. 31, 2003, p. B1.

39. Dennis Jones, "State Shortfalls Projected Throughout the Decade," National Center for Public Policy and Higher Education, February 2003; www.highereducation.org/pa_0203/index.html.

40. Ruppert, *op. cit.*, p. 4.

41. Patrick M. Callan, "A Different Kind of Recession," College Affordability In Jeopardy, a supplement of National Crosstalk, National Center for Public Policy and Higher Education, Feb. 11, 2003; www.highereducation.org.

BIBLIOGRAPHY

Books

Cohen, Arthur M., and Florence B. Brawer, *The American Community College*, 4th ed., Jossey-Bass, 2002.
This standard reference by a UCLA higher-education professor (Cohen) and the research director of the Center for the Study of Community Colleges (Brawer) analyzes the history and contributions of community colleges.

Ehrenberg, Ronald G., *Tuition Rising: Why College Costs So Much*, Harvard University Press, 2002.
The director of Cornell's Higher Education Research Institute delineates causes of escalating college price increases, including the costs of buildings, personnel, supplies, technology and the desire to score well in U.S. News & World Report 's annual college review.

McPherson, Michael S., and Morton Owen Schapiro, *The Student Aid Game*, Princeton University Press, 1997.
Current (Schapiro) and former (McPherson) college presidents explore the intricacies of higher-education finance and lay out policy options for governments and institutions.

Pittinsky, Matthew (ed.), *The Wired Tower: Perspectives on the Impact of the Internet on Higher Education*, Financial Times Prentice Hall, 2002.
As chairman and a founder of Blackboard Inc., a major supplier of information technology to education, Pittinsky speaks from experience. Other contributors include college administratiors and financiers.

Articles

"Education Life," *The New York Times*, Nov. 9, 2003. Available, for a fee, at www.nytimes.com/indexes/2003/11/09/edlife/index.html.
This issue of *The Times*' education section contains several timely stories about rapidly rising college prices and the debate about what should be done.

"The Future of Tuition," *The Chronicle of Higher Education*, Sept. 19, 2003.
This special report in the weekly higher-education journal provides both news reports and several commentaries on such topics as the "public-private quality gap," aid for the poor and inadequate planning and budgeting.

"Holding on to HOPE," *The Atlanta Journal and Constitution*, Sept. 9-11, 2003.
This three-day series about Georgia's HOPE scholarship program for "B"-or-better students says it is running out of money. HOPE gives most of its aid to Georgians who would attend college anyway, the report says.

"Learning the Hard Way," *Newsweek*, Sept. 15, 2003, p. 50.
A survey of global education conditions asserts that despite lamentations about problems facing U.S. colleges, it's instructive to observe how they are envied elsewhere.

Reports and Studies

Boehner, John, and Howard McKeon, "The College Cost Crisis," House Committee on Education and the Workforce, Sept. 3, 2003. Available at http://edworkforce.house.gov/issues/108th/education/highereducation/CollegeCostCrisisReport.pdf.
Committee Chairman Boehner and McKeon, who chairs the Higher Education Subcommittee, argue that colleges overcharge.

Jones, Dennis, "State Shortfalls Projected Throughout the Decade," National Center for Public Policy and Higher Education, February 2003. Available at www.highereducation.org/pa_0203/index.html.
The president of the National Center for Higher Education Management Systems warns that public colleges

shouldn't expect significant increases in state support over the next 10 years. Most states will not even be able to maintain current services with existing tax structures, he says.

"Straight Talk About College Costs and Prices: The Final Report and Supplemental Material from the National Commission on the Cost of Higher Education," American Council on Education/Oryx Press, 1998.
A congressionally mandated commission warns: "If colleges and universities do not take steps to reduce their costs, policymakers at the federal and state levels will intervene and take up the task for them."

"Trends in College Pricing 2003", *The College Board.* **Available at www.collegeboard.com/prod_downloads/ press/cost03/cb_trends_pricing_2003.pdf.**
This is the most-quoted annual report on the cost of attending college.

"Trends in Student Aid, 2003," *The College Board.* **Available at www.collegeboard.com/prod_downloads/ press/cost03/cb_trends_aid_2003.pdf.**
A companion to "Trends in College Pricing" summarizes recent and historical information about grants and loans.

For More Information

American Association of Community Colleges, 1 Dupont Circle, N.W., Suite 410, Washington, DC 20036-1193; (202) 728-0200; www.aacc.nche.edu. The primary advocacy organization for the nation's community colleges.

American Association of State Colleges and Universities, 1307 New York Ave., N.W., Washington, DC 20005-4704; (202) 293-7070; www.aascu.org. Represents more than 430 public colleges and universities in the United States and its territories; lobbies for programs that strengthen academic quality, promote access and inclusion and facilitate educational innovation.

American Council on Education, 1 Dupont Circle, N.W., Suite 800, Washington, DC 20036-1193; (202) 939-9300; www.acenet.edu. Conducts and publishes research and lobbies on issues relating to women and minorities in higher education and management of higher-education institutions.

The College Board, 45 Columbus Ave., New York, NY 10023-6992; (212) 713-8000; www.collegeboard.com. Promotes high learning standards, equity of opportunity and financial support for needy college students.

Education Commission of the States, 700 Broadway, Suite 1200, Denver, CO 80203-3460; (303) 299-3600; www.ecs.org. A clearinghouse that provides state policymakers and education leaders with independent research and analysis on issues facing all levels of the education system.

Education and Workforce Committee, U.S. House of Representatives. The GOP-led panel maintains a Web site, "College Cost Central," which it calls "A Resource for Parents, Students, & Taxpayers Fed Up With the High Cost of Higher Education;" available at http://edwork- force.house.gov/issues/108th/education/highereducation/c ollegecostcentral.htm/

Institute for Higher Education Policy, 1320 19th St., N.W., Suite 400, Washington, DC 20036; (202) 861-8223; www.ihep.com. Studies the rising costs of a college education and government regulatory issues facing colleges and universities.

National Association for Equal Opportunity in Higher Education, 8701 Georgia Ave., Suite 200, Silver Spring, MD 20910; (301) 650-2440; www.nafeo.org. Represents public and private historically black colleges and universities.

National Association of Independent Colleges and Universities, 1025 Connecticut Ave., N.W., Suite 700, Washington, DC 20036-5405; (202) 785-8866; www.naicu.edu. Represents private colleges and universities on policy issues such as student aid, taxation and government regulation.

National Association of State Universities and Land-Grant Colleges, 1307 New York Ave., N.W., Suite 400, Washington, DC 20005-4722; (202) 478-6040. Serves as a clearinghouse for issues involving public higher education.

National Center for Public Policy and Higher Education, 152 North Third St., Suite 705, San Jose, CA 95112; (408) 271-2699; www.highereducation.org. An independent, nonpartisan think tank that promotes public policies that enhance students' opportunities to pursue high-quality education and training beyond high school.

United Negro College Fund, 8260 Willow Oaks Corporate Dr., P.O. Box 10444, Fairfax, VA 22031; (800) 331-2244; www.uncf.org. Represents private, historically black colleges and universities.

3

Marijuana Laws

Patrick Marshall

Angel Raich, who has a brain tumor, and Diane Monson, right, who suffers from chronic back pain, sued to prevent the federal government from blocking their use of marijuana, which is permitted by California's medical marijuana law if recommended by a physician. The two women sued after federal drug agents raided Monson's home and took her six plants. The Supreme Court ruled that the federal law against marijuana takes precedence over the state's decision to allow its use for medical purposes.

Getty Images/Mannie Garcia

From *CQ Researcher*,
Originally published February 11, 2005.
(Updated June 2005.)

Diane Monson had been using marijuana since 1999 to treat her chronic back pain and spasms. No other prescription medication worked. But on Aug. 15, 2002, agents from the federal Drug Enforcement Administration (DEA) and Butte County sheriff's deputies raided Monson's home in Oroville, Calif. Although the local district attorney agreed that Monson's six medical cannabis plants were lawful under local guidelines and California's Compassionate Use Act, the DEA agents destroyed Monson's plants; the DEA has yet to file charges against Monson.

Angel Raich suffers from an inoperable brain tumor, chronic pain and a number of other conditions that her doctor says defy conventional treatments. At one point, the Oakland, Calif., mother of two teenagers was so weak she had to use a wheelchair. With no way to relieve her pain — and because California voters had approved the medical use of marijuana in 1996 — she decided, at her doctor's suggestion, to give marijuana a try." [1]

The drug worked wonders, Raich says. Her symptoms eased, and she even retired her wheelchair.

Raich and Monson sued the U.S. government to stop the federal drug raids. In June 2005, however, the U.S. Supreme Court ruled that the federal ban trumps the state's medical marijuana law.

Recent opinion polls indicate strong public support for medicinal marijuana. A November 2003 Gallup Poll found that 75 percent of U.S. adults favor allowing patients with a doctor's prescription to possess and use marijuana. Moreover, at least 10 other states besides California have passed medical marijuana laws since 1996: Alaska, Colorado, Hawaii, Maine, Maryland, Montana, Nevada, Oregon, Vermont and Washington. And last November,

Marijuana Use Continues to Decline

Marijuana use among eighth, 10th and 12th-grader dropped from 2003 to 2004, continuing a decline that began in the mid-1990s. Past-month use of marijuana among eighth-graders declined significantly.

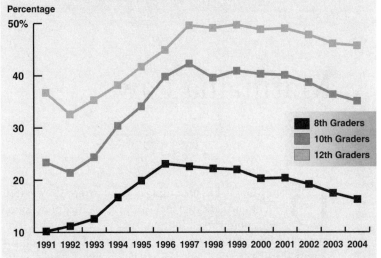

Marijuana Use Among Students, 1991-2004
(by the percentage who used in the past month)

Percentage

- 8th Graders
- 10th Graders
- 12th Graders

Source: Monitoring the Future survey, December 2004; the survey of 50,000 public and private-school students is conducted by the University of Michigan's Institute for Social Research and funded by the National Institute on Drug Abuse.

voters passed 17 initiatives calling for reduced marijuana penalties in Alaska, Montana, Oregon, Ann Arbor, Mich., Columbia, Mo., and several state districts in Massachusetts.

"Every, single ballot initiative on medical marijuana that has been out there has won, often by very substantial margins," says Ethan Nadelmann, director of the Drug Policy Alliance, which supports legalizing marijuana for medical purposes and personal use by adults. "I think it's now safe to say that majorities in every state of the country support making marijuana legal for medical purposes."

But Robert L. DuPont, president of the Institute for Behavior and Health and former director of the National Institute on Drug Abuse (NIDA), disagrees. "Smoked marijuana is the cause of many serious health problems, and it is the solution to none," he told a congressional subcommittee last year. "There are more effective, safer

and better-tolerated medicines now available for all of the illnesses for which the marijuana advocates propose using smoked marijuana." [2]

Meanwhile, Canada recently began allowing patients — with a doctor's recommendation — to legally possess marijuana. (See sidebar, p. 57.) And Israel, which has been in the forefront of research on pharmaceutical uses for marijuana, last August began testing the therapeutic effects of certain ingredients in marijuana on soldiers suffering from acute combat-related stress disorders. [3]

Although the public may support medical use of marijuana, many government officials and some researchers say marijuana is both dangerous and not viable as a medicine. "It is a patent medicine of the 19th century hawked by carnival barkers," says David Murray, special assistant to the director of the Office of National Drug Control Policy (ONDCP), the federal government's lead drug policy group. "People feel good after they take it, but they don't get better."

Not only is smoked marijuana not an effective medicine, say opponents of medical marijuana and NIDA, but it is addictive, carcinogenic, damages the body's respiratory, immune and reproductive systems, affects short-term memory and ability to learn and is a "gateway" to harder narcotics use. [4]

Moreover, Murray and other opponents contend that supporters of medical marijuana have a hidden agenda — legalization of marijuana for recreational purposes. "It is not the medical community that is pushing for this," he says. "Activists, legalizers and other political-pressure groups are using the name of the medical community and/or patients to push for their objectives."

According to the DEA, "The campaign to allow marijuana to be used as medicine is a tactical maneuver in an overall strategy to completely legalize all drugs. Pro-legalization groups have transformed the debate from decriminalizing drug use to one of compassion and care for people with serious diseases." [5]

Indeed, when Nadelmann was asked if legalizing marijuana for medical purposes would help lead to overall legalization, he said, "I hope so." [6]

But Nadelmann notes that billionaire investment fund manager George Soros, a major supporter of the Drug Policy Alliance, among other marijuana reformists, does not support across-the-board legalization efforts.

Indeed, many medical marijuana advocates vehemently deny that their fight has anything to do with legalizing the drug for general use. "We're not fighting for legalization overall," says Hilary McQuie, political director of Americans for Safe Access, a medical marijuana advocacy group in Berkeley, Calif. If a good alternative medication is developed, she adds, "I would be ready to stop the fight for medical marijuana."

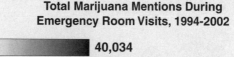

Emergency Room 'Mentions' Rose

The number of emergency room visits in which marijuana use was mentioned rose to nearly 120,000 in 2002, triple the number in 1994. Opponents of legal marijuana use cite "marijuana mentions" as an indication of the drug's harmfulness.

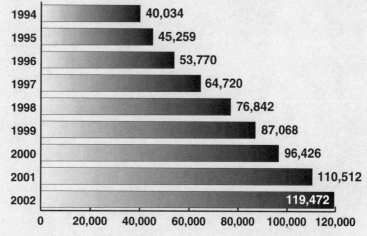

Total Marijuana Mentions During Emergency Room Visits, 1994-2002

Year	Mentions
1994	40,034
1995	45,259
1996	53,770
1997	64,720
1998	76,842
1999	87,068
2000	96,426
2001	110,512
2002	119,472

Source: Substance Abuse and Mental Health Services Administration

Steve Fox, director of government relations at the Washington, D.C.-based Marijuana Policy Project, which advocates general decriminalization of marijuana, calls the DEA's position "nonsensical." He cites a broad array of medical publications and organizations that have endorsed the medical use of marijuana — including the New York State Medical Society, the American Academy of Family Physicians, the American Nurses Association and even the authoritative *New England Journal of Medicine* — none of which advocates full legalization.

"Federal authorities should rescind their prohibition of the medical use of marijuana for seriously ill patients and allow physicians to decide which patients to treat," the journal editorialized. [7]

The California Medical Association and the California Nurses Association echoed those sentiments when they joined an *amicus* brief to the U.S. Supreme Court in support of the Oakland Cannabis Buyers' Cooperative — a group that grew and distributed marijuana for patients with a doctor's recommendation but was shut down by the DEA in 1998. The cooperative then sued the federal government in a case that was appealed to the Supreme Court. The high court ruled that medical necessity was not a defense against federal anti-marijuana laws (*see p. 60*).

"Neither federal prosecutors nor the courts should impede a desperate patient who has tried all conventional treatments without success and, acting with the advice and approval of his or her physician, seeks to alleviate his or her serious suffering by using a non-conventional treatment that has been reasonably shown to be effective in his or her case," the two organizations urged. [8]

Meanwhile, recent studies show that fewer teens are using marijuana and that usage rates among adults have remained steady even though marijuana abuse and dependence have been increasing, particularly among African Americans and Hispanics.

In December 2004, the University of Michigan's annual Monitoring the Future survey of nearly 50,000 secondary-school students showed that marijuana use among eighth, tenth and 12th graders had continued its

At Last, an Honest Politician.

"You bet I did. And I enjoyed it."

It's NORML to Smoke Pot.

www.NORML.org
National Organization for the Reform of Marijuana Laws Foundation

New York City Mayor Michael Bloomberg acknowledged he had smoked pot in a full-page ad in *The New York Times* on April 9, 2002, sponsored by the National Organization for the Reform of Marijuana Laws.

"Quite possibly, the media campaign aimed at marijuana use that has been undertaken by the White House Office of Drug Control Policy, in collaboration with the Partnership for a Drug Free America, has been having its intended effect," said University of Michigan researcher Lloyd Johnston, the study's principal investigator. "I am not aware of any other social influence process that could explain these changes in how young people view marijuana." [10]

In a related study published in the *Journal of the American Medical Association* (*JAMA*) in May 2004, researchers found that adult marijuana abuse and dependence increased during the 1990s. Addiction researchers at the National Institutes of Health found that the number of people reporting that they used marijuana in 1991-1992 and 2001-2002 remained about the same in both time periods. But the study found that marijuana abuse or dependence rose 22 percent during the decade, largely due to a 224 percent increase among African-Americans ages 18 to 29 and a 148 percent jump among young Hispanic men in the same age range. [11]

"Marijuana is the most commonly used illegal substance in the United States, and its use is associated with educational underachievement, reduced workplace productivity, motor vehicle accidents, and increased risk of use of other substances," says NIDA Director Nora D. Volkow. "This study suggests that we need to develop ways to monitor the continued rise in marijuana abuse and dependence and strengthen existing prevention and intervention efforts, particularly developing and implementing new programs that target African-American and Hispanic young adults."

"The increase in potency of marijuana over the last decade may be partly responsible for the drug's increased abuse and dependence, particularly since marijuana-use patterns have not changed over this period," the authors wrote. However, no single factor can account entirely for the increases seen in minority populations, they added, because numerous cultural, psychosocial, economic and lifestyle factors likely play roles.

Aside from medical considerations, some marijuana-law reformers argue that marijuana should be generally available. "Adults should be allowed to possess virtually anything without the government interfering," says David Boaz, executive vice president of the Cato Institute, a libertarian, public policy group. "The federal government has no constitutional authority to deal with possession of marijuana."

slow, steady decline since 1996. [9] In 2003 and 2004, the study found, the proportion of students seeing marijuana use as dangerous has increased, and personal disapproval of marijuana use increased in 2004 — which the authors said could explain some of the decline in use.

But Murray of the Office of National Drug Control Policy says flatly, "Marijuana is illegal because it is harmful." Furthermore, he adds, legalizing and regulating marijuana like alcohol and tobacco would be impossible because marijuana can be easily grown in one's back yard, while alcohol and tobacco require complicated distilling and curing. "You'd get an increase in availability and an increase in accessibility," Murray says.

Critics say that's nonsense, first of all because alcohol, like marijuana, can be created at home. "We saw what happened when there was alcohol prohibition," Fox says. "People were creating bathtub gin that was leading to the death of users. It created enormous organized crime problems, which is what they're doing right now with marijuana. If we take marijuana off the streets and regulate it, we will diminish organized crime problems."

Some critics of the government's opposition to legalization of marijuana speculate that it is grounded more on political and cultural biases than medical or scientific evidence.

"There is an identification of drugs, in particular with marijuana, with the counterculture," says Rep. Barney Frank, D-Mass. "How do you account for the prohibitionist mentality toward marijuana compared to alcohol, which does a great deal more damage? The answer is that middle-aged white guys drink, but they don't smoke marijuana. It's seen as the drug of choice of the counterculture."

Nadelmann agrees, but he also sees a darker motive behind the opposition. "We have private indications that many Republicans [in Congress] are sympathetic to medical marijuana," he says, "but they are feeling pressure from the White House to oppose it so that "the more reactionary side of the conservative movement can use the drug issue to advance its broader political agenda."

As the debate over marijuana policy continues, here are some of the questions being asked:

Should marijuana be legally available by prescription for medical purposes?

The Controlled Substances Act of 1970 categorized drugs into five "schedules" based on their medicinal value, potential danger and potential for abuse or addiction. Marijuana is listed in Schedule 1, which is reserved for drugs that have no recognized medical use and are considered highly dangerous and addictive, including

freevibe.com

Just tell your parents you were stoned. They'll understand.

r·e·s·p·o·n·s·i·b·i·l·i·t·y
YOUR ANTI-DRUG.

Office of National Drug Control Policy/Partnership for a Drug-Free America

Declining marijuana use among secondary-school students may reflect the national media campaign mounted by the White House Office of Drug Control Policy and the Partnership for a Drug-Free America.

heroin. As a Schedule 1 drug, marijuana cannot be legally possessed, prescribed or distributed. [12]

Critics of medical uses for marijuana contend that marijuana has no medicinal value. "We don't have a body of evidence from a scientific perspective that supports that smoked medical marijuana brings any benefits to an individual," says Arthur T. Dean, chairman of the Community Anti-Drug Coalitions of America (CADCA).

The ONDCP's Murray stresses that medicinal marijuana has not been approved by the Food and Drug Administration (FDA) because advocates have thus far failed to convince the FDA of its medical value. "Marijuana is not being treated differently than any other drug that applies to be a medicine through the FDA," Murray says. "It has to go through independent,

Cannabis Among Least Addictive Drugs

LSD, MDMA and cannabis were rated by addiction researchers and clinicians as significantly less addictive than nine other drugs. Crack cocaine, nicotine and heroin were rated the most addictive.

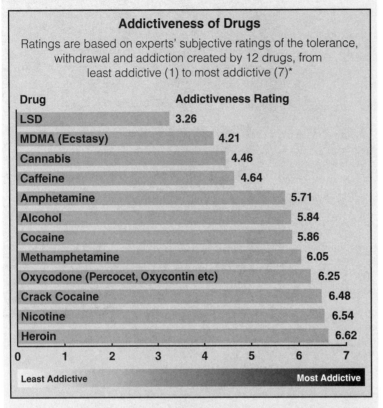

Addictiveness of Drugs

Ratings are based on experts' subjective ratings of the tolerance, withdrawal and addiction created by 12 drugs, from least addictive (1) to most addictive (7)*

Drug	Addictiveness Rating
LSD	3.26
MDMA (Ecstasy)	4.21
Cannabis	4.46
Caffeine	4.64
Amphetamine	5.71
Alcohol	5.84
Cocaine	5.86
Methamphetamine	6.05
Oxycodone (Percocet, Oxycontin etc)	6.25
Crack Cocaine	6.48
Nicotine	6.54
Heroin	6.62

Least Addictive — Most Addictive

Source: Robert Gore and Mitch Earleywine, "Addiction Potential of Drugs of Abuse: A Survey of Clinicians and Researchers," Department of Psychology, University of Southern California, October 2004. The survey included 746 addiction researchers, clinicians specializing in addiction and generalist psychotherapists.

marijuana, says Mitch Earleywine, a noted drug researcher and director of clinical training in psychology at the University of Southern California. A 1999 study by the American Medical Association and the government's own Institute of Medicine (IOM) also supported medicinal marijuana, he adds. [13]

"Limited, controlled evidence supports the view that smoked marijuana and THC [a potent chemical in marijuana] can provide symptomatic relief in patients with MS, spinal cord injury and other causes of spasticity," said a 2001 report by the Council on Scientific Affairs of the American Medical Association (AMA). "Smoked marijuana stimulates appetite and increases caloric intake in normal subjects," which is why patients say it helps relieve their chemotherapy-induced nausea and the wasting effects of AIDS. [14]

The IOM report also found evidence of potential medical benefits from marijuana, especially certain components. "Scientific data indicate the potential therapeutic value of cannabinoid drugs, primarily THC, for pain relief, control of nausea and vomiting, and appetite stimulation," said the report, which surveyed the results of available studies. [15]

Moreover, in their *amicus* brief in the *Raich* case, the California Medical Association and California Nurses

new drug trials. It has to go through clinical trials. It has to have multiple patients and analyses for medical conditions. It has never attained that standing."

But advocates of medical marijuana say the government itself has prevented such trials because it alone controls the legal supplies of research-quality marijuana, and has rejected most applications to study the medicinal qualities of marijuana.

Meanwhile, "thousands of medical users around the country" dispute the idea that there are no medical uses for

Association point out that "the government does not dispute the facts that the plaintiffs here suffer painful, debilitating diseases that have not responded to conventional medicines, and that have responded to medical cannabis. Thus, the factual record is clear that for these patients, the use of medical cannabis ameliorates their suffering and pain, and affirmatively improves their condition."

USC's Earleywine notes that the IOM report was "pretty clear" that certain ingredients of marijuana, particularly THC, "have some medicinal value." But he acknowl-

Penalties for Possession Vary Widely

Possession of marijuana is a crime under federal law. But in several states and local jurisdictions, possessing marijuana can lead to a friendly wave from a police officer or time in jail.

Under federal law, possession of any amount of marijuana can result in up to a year in jail and a $1,000 fine for a first offense. For a second conviction, the penalties increase to a 15-day mandatory minimum sentence and a maximum of two years in prison and a fine of up to $2,500. In California, by contrast, a first offense brings no jail time and up to a $100 fine.

In many cases, a state has declined to prosecute an individual only to have federal authorities step in. Shortly after California's medical marijuana law was passed in 1996, Todd McCormick, a cancer patient who used marijuana to reduce nausea and pain, was growing marijuana at his Bel Air home, and local authorities had taken no action. In July 1997, however, federal agents raided his home. Under a plea agreement, he was sentenced to five years in federal prison. He was released in December 2003.

Moreover, writes author Eric Schlosser, "A person may even be tried twice for the same drug crime: After being found innocent by a state jury, marijuana growers can be — and have been — subsequently convicted in federal court."

Schlosser also notes, "There are no established criteria for when a U.S. attorney will enter a marijuana case. The federal government could prosecute any and every marijuana offender in America if it so desired, but in a typical year it charges less than 2 percent of those arrested. In some districts there is a policy that the U. S. attorney will enter cases involving more than a hundred plants or a hundred pounds. In others, a federal prosecutor may simply take a special interest in a case." [1]

Schlosser cites the case of Edward Czuprynski, a liberal activist in Michigan, who was convicted in federal court of possession of 1.6 grams of marijuana, approximately the amount used in a single marijuana cigarette. "Under Michigan law he most likely would have received a $100 fine," writes Schlosser. "But in federal court, Czuprynski was sentenced to 14 months in prison. His license to practice law was suspended. His successful law firm closed down."

To further complicate matters, marijuana laws vary widely from region to region. While getting caught with an ounce of marijuana in California brings a misdemeanor charge and no jail time, for example, conviction in Alabama brings up to a year in jail and a $2,000 fine. Similarly, cultivating any amount of marijuana in California (except when it is recommended for a patient or caregiver) is a felony that can bring 16 months in prison, while cultivating 2.2 pounds to 100 pounds in Alabama means a mandatory minimum of five years in prison and a $50,000 fine.

In Texas, penalties start out on the tough side and get harsher. Possession of up to two ounces of marijuana is punishable by 180 days in jail and up to a $2,000 fine. For more than two ounces, the penalty rises to a year in jail and a fine of up to $4,000.

In addition to the patchwork of state laws, federal law requires anyone convicted of a drug offense to lose his or her student aid, notes Rep. Barney Frank, D-Mass. "I've been trying to repeal that." Frank points out that convictions for other crimes, such as armed robbery, do not necessarily result in a loss of aid.

And convictions for possession of marijuana can be counted as parole or probation violations, resulting in jail time. "There are no hard numbers on any of that," says Ethan Nadelmann, director of the Drug Policy Alliance, but when you talk to people in probation and parole, they say it is massive. That gives the lie to the argument there aren't a lot of people behind bars for marijuana offenses."

---

[1] Eric Schlosser, "Marijuana and the Law," *The Atlantic Monthly*, September 1994.

---

edges that opponents of medical marijuana interpreted the IOM report differently. "The Institute of Medicine report has turned into kind of a Rorschach test, with people grabbing onto parts that support their argument," he says.

In fact, the IOM report made a sharp distinction between the benefits and safety of smoked marijuana versus the benefits and safety of potential cannabis-type drugs. For patients with AIDS or undergoing chemotherapy, who simultaneously suffer from severe pain, nausea and appetite loss, "cannabinoid drugs might offer broad-spectrum relief not found in any other single medication," the report said.

"But it does not follow from this that smoking marijuana is good medicine." Besides delivering carcinogenic substances to the lungs, marijuana plants vary in potency and cannot provide a precisely defined dosage, it said.

"For those reasons, there is little future in smoked marijuana as a medically approved medication," the report said, recommending instead that research focus on developing a non-smoked, rapid-onset delivery system. [16]

Moreover, the DEA's fact sheet on marijuana states that other studies have shown smoked marijuana can cause "a variety of health problems, including cancer, respiratory problems, loss of motor skills and increased heart rate." It also can impair the ability of the immune system to fight off infections, potentially doing "more harm than good in people with already compromised immune systems." [17]

While neither the IOM nor AMA studies called for a rescheduling of marijuana, both advocated more study and research into the development of drugs derived from marijuana that would presumably not carry the dangers posed by smoked marijuana — which stem mostly from inhaling the smoke and the difficulties of delivering consistent dosages quickly. Until then, the IOM said, some patients have no viable alternatives to smoking marijuana. "Until a non-smoked rapid-onset, cannabinoid drug-delivery system becomes available, we acknowledge that there is no clear alternative for people suffering from chronic conditions that might be relieved by smoking marijuana, such as pain or AIDS wasting," the report notes. [18]

Despite the calls for more study, advocates of medical marijuana say the U.S. government rejects most applications to study the drug's potential medicinal uses.

Opponents of legalizing medical marijuana point out that there is already a medication containing THC — Marinol — that has been approved by the FDA. However, advocates of medical marijuana say that because Marinol is delivered in pill or suppository form, patients cannot get it into their systems quickly or adjust the dose easily. What's more, THC is only one of the potentially therapeutic substances in marijuana, they say.

Meanwhile, Great Britain and Canada are on the verge of developing another marijuana extract — Sativex — that looks more promising. Its developers — GW Pharmaceuticals of Great Britain — say it offers the full spectrum of marijuana's active ingredients, delivered in a spray. Absorbed under the tongue, the medication is easier to take than Marinol and faster acting.

Earleywine, however, is not sure Sativex would be any better than regular marijuana smoked through a vaporizer to remove carcinogens. Both Earleywine and McQuie of Americans for Safe Access are concerned about drawbacks to the "pharmaceuticalization" of marijuana.

"Given its effectiveness and safety, being able to grow your own medicine and not having to pay prescription drug prices is a huge benefit for people," says McQuie, pointing out that Marinol costs about $300 a month, and no one knows how much Sativex will cost. "A lot of people believe they should have the right to use marijuana as a sole remedy."

Some medical marijuana advocates contend the federal government's reluctance to allow patients to use marijuana has more to do with protecting the pharmaceutical industry than with medical concerns.

"The real problem with allowing patients to use cannabis as a medication is economics," Claudia Jensen, a California physician who supports the use of marijuana to treat attention deficit disorder (ADD), told a congressional hearing last April. "If cannabis were approved for use in just the [ADD] market alone, it could significantly impact the $1 billion a year sales for traditional [attention deficit disorder] pharmaceuticals. . . . Multiply those numbers by the tens of medical diagnoses that are effectively treated by cannabis — for example chronic pain, which is a much bigger business than the treatment of ADD; or glaucoma, or multiple sclerosis — and it is easy to see the pharmaceutical industry would suffer beyond calculation." [19]

The ONDCP's Murray says the government has no bias against marijuana. "We have no fear of marijuana," he says, noting that many other dangerous substances with high potential for abuse have been approved once they have gone through clinical trials and demonstrated medicinal utility.

But advocates of medical marijuana say sick patients shouldn't be asked to wait for the "ideal" solution — whether it be a pharmaceutical extract of marijuana or FDA approval of the plant form of the drug. "A federal policy that prohibits physicians from alleviating suffering by prescribing marijuana to seriously ill patients is misguided, heavy-handed, and inhumane," the *New England Journal of Medicine* editorialized. [20]

Should marijuana be legal for adults and regulated like alcohol and tobacco?

Some medical marijuana advocates argue that the recognition of marijuana's medicinal value and low level of addictiveness indicate that it is long overdue for being reclassified — or rescheduled — to a less restrictive category under the Controlled Substances Act and even made available to adults for recreational purposes.

"Clearly, cannabis does not belong on Schedule 1. Its addictive potential is right around caffeine's," Earleywine says.

Neither the AMA nor the Institute of Medicine recommended that marijuana be legalized or rescheduled. However, says McQuie of Americans for Safe Access, "The fact that the IOM stated that marijuana had medical value should take it out of Schedule 1 in and of itself." To be classified as Schedule 1, a drug must have no medicinal value, be highly addictive and dangerous.

The National Organization to Reform Marijuana Laws (NORML) argues that no one has ever died from an overdose of marijuana but that 50,000 Americans die from alcohol poisoning and another 400,000 die from cigarette smoking every year. [21]

"The smoking of cannabis, even long term, is not harmful to health," wrote the editors of the British medical journal *Lancet*, arguing for decriminalization of marijuana. "Leaving politics aside, where is the harm in decriminalising cannabis? There is none to the health of the consumers." [22]

But parents' groups and the U.S. government continue to warn that marijuana is dangerous. "Marijuana is an addictive drug," says Calvina Fay, executive director of the Drug Free America Foundation, in St. Petersburg, Fla. "It's a dangerous drug. It's a harmful drug. It's currently classified as being illegal. We don't see anything good that can come from legalizing it."

Indeed, opponents contend that marijuana is carcinogenic, harms the body's respiratory, immune and reproductive systems, affects short-term memory and ability to learn and is a "gateway" to harder narcotics use. [23]

Proponents of legalization argue, however, that while marijuana smoke does contain concentrations of carcinogens at least as high as tobacco, smokers tend to inhale much less marijuana smoke over their lifetimes than tobacco smokers.

But Fay and other opponents of legalizing marijuana say comparing marijuana to alcohol and tobacco misses the point: Those drugs should be illegal as well, they argue, but given their historical acceptance that is not a practical goal. "If we had known what we know today about the scientific evidence of the harms of alcohol, I don't think we would have ever legalized it," Fay says. "When we ended prohibition, we didn't have the scientific evidence that we have today."

Moreover, "very heavy lobby groups" are working hard to ensure that alcohol and tobacco remain legal, she adds. "That is one of the dangers when you open Pandora's box. It's really hard to put the bugs back in."

The ONDCP's Murray agrees that the legality of alcohol doesn't make a good case for legalizing marijuana. "That is hardly an argument: That because you dropped an anvil on your foot then you should drop a tire iron on your other foot," Murray says.

Critics also argue that marijuana is a gateway to more dangerous drugs. "It's not that every kid who smokes marijuana goes on to use heroin or cocaine," Murray says. "But you hardly find anyone using cocaine and heroin today who did not start with marijuana. The risk of developing a dependency later in life on cocaine is 15 times greater for those who were early, young marijuana smokers than for those who did not smoke marijuana."

But proponents of legalization say that virtually all scientific studies refute or fail to confirm that the use of marijuana leads to harder drugs. "Most users of other illicit drugs have used marijuana first," the IOM report's authors acknowledge. But, "most drug users begin with alcohol and nicotine before marijuana — usually before they are of legal age." Thus, they conclude, "There is no conclusive evidence that the drug effects of marijuana are causally linked to the subsequent abuse of other illicit drugs." [24]

What's more, advocates of legalization argue, marijuana — like alcohol and tobacco — is a historical fact. Its usage is so widespread, they say, that criminalizing it does more harm than good.

The Cato Institute's Boaz agrees, citing the nation's attempt at alcohol prohibition in the 1920s. "We tried that experiment [with alcohol] and it didn't work," he says. "We're having the same thing now with marijuana."

Criminalizing marijuana use only creates crime and an unregulated black market, say legalization advocates, while costing billions of dollars in law enforcement and inconvenienced or ruined lives due to criminal penalties — all while failing to prevent people from using it.

"Prohibition and the resulting black market enriches criminals and terrorists, results in gang warfare, encourages the recruitment of youth to sell drugs, provides youth with easier access to drugs, corrupts government officials, destabilizes governments and undermines the rule of law," Scott Ehlers, a senior policy analyst at the Drug Policy Foundation, told a congressional hearing in 1999." [25]

Criminalization has also kept the government from helping addicts kick the habit, he said. "If drug use and addiction were treated as a health problem," Ehlers said, "you would have health-care workers reaching out to drug users, rather than the police actively seeking out and arresting people for possessing personal quantities of drugs. With the threat of

CHRONOLOGY

1764-1969 *Marijuana use spreads in the United States, prompting government regulation.*

1764 Marijuana appears in *The New England Dispensatory*, a pharmaceutical guide.

1854 Poet John Greenleaf Whittier describes marijuana as an intoxicant.

1860 Ohio State Medical Society holds first clinical marijuana conference.

1932 National Conference of Commissioners on Uniform State Laws drafts a Uniform Narcotic Drug Act that includes marijuana. By 1937, all states prohibit marijuana use.

1937 Federal Marijuana Tax Act requires anyone who cultivates, distributes or uses marijuana to pay a high tax.

1938 Food, Drug and Cosmetic Act (FDCA) creates a drug-testing procedure regulated by the Food and Drug Administration (FDA).

1960s *Marijuana use spreads from minorities, musicians and artists to the middle classes via the military and college students.*

1970-1996 *Federal government crackdown on marijuana use spurs advocates of legalization to seek reforms.*

1970 Federal Controlled Substances Act prohibits marijuana possession.

1972 President Richard M. Nixon's National Commission on Marihuana and Drug Abuse recommends decriminalizing marijuana for personal use. . . . National Organization for the Reform of Marijuana Laws (NORML) petitions Drug Enforcement Administration to reclassify marijuana as a Schedule 2 drug so physicians can prescribe it.

1985 FDA approves dronabinol (Marinol), a synthetic THC, for cancer patients.

1986 DEA holds public hearings on dronabinol, even though it still hasn't held hearings on the 1972 petition for rescheduling marijuana.

1988 Administrative law Judge Francis Young rules the DEA shouldn't "continue to stand between those sufferers and the benefits of this substance in light of the evidence in this record." DEA rejects Young's finding.

1992 First Bush administration cancels a "compassionate use" program that provided government-grown marijuana to a small group of patients.

1996-Present *Medical marijuana becomes a major issue as states pass initiatives, and cases land in the courts.*

1996 Arizona and California pass laws allowing possession of marijuana with a doctor's recommendation. . . . Office of National Drug Control Policy threatens action against physicians who recommend or prescribe marijuana. . . . California doctors and patients sue federal government in 1997.

1998 Federal government shuts down six marijuana cooperatives in California that provide the drug to patients. In 2001, the U.S. Supreme Court holds in *United States v. Oakland Cannabis Buyers' Cooperative* that medical necessity is not sufficient grounds to violate the federal law against marijuana possession.

March 17, 1999 U.S. Institute of Medicine report finds some medical benefits in marijuana but also warns that the smoke can be toxic.

2003 U.S. Supreme Court, by declining to reverse a lower court's decision in *Conant v. McCaffrey*, allows physicians to recommend, but not prescribe, marijuana to patients.

2004 On June 28, the U.S. Supreme Court agrees to hear a federal appeal of a lower-court decision protecting patients from federal laws against possession of marijuana. . . . In November, voters across the country pass 17 initiatives aimed at liberalizing marijuana laws.

June 2005 U.S. Supreme Court rules, 6-3, that federal ban overrides state laws permitting medical use of marijuana (*Gonzales v. Raich*).

Canada and the Netherlands Lighten Up

Marijuana laws in Canada and the Netherlands are among the most liberal in the industrialized world, along with those in Switzerland, Spain and England and other countries in Western Europe.

Although it is still illegal to buy marijuana in the Netherlands, the government in 1976 began permitting possession and sale of small quantities of the drug, and in the next few years it began to be sold in licensed coffee shops and pharmacies. Criminal action is taken only if the quantity purchased is more than five grams per person. And, marijuana cannot be advertised or sold to persons under age 18.

Possession is also still illegal in Canada, but regulations adopted in 2001 allow possession and use of marijuana for medical purposes if a patient has a doctor's recommendation.

But David Murray, special assistant to the director of the U.S. Office of National Drug Control Policy, says the Canadian law has had unexpected repercussions. Canadians "have been stunned" to discover that the new policy has sparked an increase in marijuana usage and in illegal cultivation and distribution, he says.

"They had thought of marijuana as this sort of mom-and-pop thing with no real victims. What they're finding out is that indoor growers have sort of taken over and muscled in. Criminal elements — Mafia, Asian gangs, biker gangs — are using violence to take control of the marijuana situation. You don't eliminate the criminality [with legalization] but you do get an increase in use."

The Canadian Addiction Survey recently found that the number of Canadians using marijuana had doubled over the past 10 years: 14 percent of Canadians said they used the drug in 2004, compared to 7.4 percent in 1994. [1] Opponents of legalization worry that legalizing marijuana for the general population — not just for medical users — would trigger more marijuana use.

Eugene Oscapella — a founder of the Canadian Foundation for Drug Policy, which favors reform of marijuana laws — agrees there have been unforeseen impacts. "Let's not forget the drug-prohibition industry is a big industry," says Oscapella, an attorney. "It's an industry for organized crime. It's an industry for politicians. There also are all these mom-and-pop operations across the country.

They're making $50,000 or $60,000 a year growing something in the back yard. And they're quite happy with the law the way it is."

As for the apparent increase in usage, Oscapella says no one knows how much of the increase is the result of users feeling freer to report their actual usage more honestly under Canada's new, more liberal policies.

Rather than reimposing restrictions on marijuana, legalization advocates like Oscapella say legalizing and licensing marijuana cultivation would "threaten the market" for criminal elements.

But the Canadian Professional Police Association, representing 54,000 members, vigorously opposes decriminalization, saying police should have the discretion to arrest anybody — not just issue tickets.

Legalization proponents concede that marijuana usage has increased in Canada and the Netherlands since liberalization but cite a recent study showing that rates in those countries have not risen higher than U.S. usage levels. Data analyzed by Common Sense for Drug Policy show that 36.9 percent of Americans have used marijuana during their lifetime, compared to 17 percent in the Netherlands. [2]

Neither Canada nor the Netherlands has seen increased calls for tighter regulation of marijuana; instead, there has been pressure for greater liberalization. In 2002, Canada's Senate Special Committee on Illegal Drugs issued a detailed report on marijuana, which recommended legalization of the drug.

"In effect, the main social costs of cannabis are a result of public policy choices, primarily its continued criminalization, while the consequences of its use represent a small fraction of the social costs attributable to the use of illegal drugs," the report said. [3] "The prohibition of cannabis does not bring about the desired reduction in cannabis consumption or problematic use. However, [prohibition] does have a whole series of harmful consequences."

---

[1] CBC News, Nov. 24, 2004, www.cbc.ca/story/canada/national/2004/11/24/ drugstudy041124.html.

[2] www.drugwarfacts.org/thenethe.htm.

[3] "Cannabis: Our Position for a Canadian Public Policy," Senate Special Committee on Illegal Drugs, September 2002, p. 29.

---

criminal sanctions gone, many more people with substance-abuse problems would seek medical assistance rather than hiding out of fear of arrest and imprisonment."

Not everyone agrees. "Because of regulations against

marijuana, we're constraining it to a smaller population," Murray says. "Keeping marijuana illegal strengthens our ability to regulate a dangerous substance that is, in fact, quite problematic for young people."

Oakland medical marijuana advocate Ed Rosenthal celebrates with his wife and daughter after he was sentenced in June 2003 to just one day in jail on federal marijuana charges; prosecutors had sought a five-year sentence. Several jurors later said they would have acquitted him if testimony had been permitted revealing he grew marijuana for medical purposes under California law.

And even if marijuana were appropriate for adults, it might send the wrong message to children if it were legalized, say some opponents of legalization. "All of the adults debating this are not sending the right message to kids," says Sue Thau, a CADCA policy analyst.

But Nadelmann says the message being sent to kids is that adults are hypocritical, because they ban a substance that is less addictive than coffee while allowing alcohol and tobacco to be traded freely.

"Tens of billions of taxpayer dollars [are sent] down the drain each year," writes Nadelmann. "People losing their jobs, their property, and their freedom for nothing more than possessing a joint or growing a few marijuana plants. And all for what? To send a message? To keep pretending that we're protecting our children? Alcohol prohibition made a lot more sense than marijuana prohibition does today — and it, too, was a disaster." [26]

BACKGROUND

Ancient Remedy

The marijuana — or hemp — plant has been used by humans for at least 10,000 years. Archaeologists in Taiwan have found strands of the plant decorating clay pots dating back to 8000 B.C. Over the following centuries, it spread throughout Asia and Europe, thanks primarily to its utility as a fiber for making rope.

The first record of human consumption of marijuana for medicinal or recreational purposes dates back to 2737 B.C., when the Chinese emperor Shen Neng recorded the use of cannabis to treat gout, malaria, beriberi, rheumatism and poor memory.

By 1400 B.C., marijuana was being used as a medicine in India and by 70 A.D. it had been listed in a Greek pharmacopoeia. European doctors began taking note of the plant by the early 1500s.

During the Middle Ages, marijuana and hashish, a concentrated form of the drug made from marijuana resin, was widely used in the Middle East as both a medicine and an intoxicant. But Muslim societies in the Middle East at the time punished recreational smokers with 40 to 80 lashes while exempting from punishment those using the drug for medicinal purposes. [27]

Marijuana first came to the United States in the mid-1800s and was used both as an intoxicant and a medicine. The first mention of marijuana as an intoxicant by an American author appears in a poem by John Greenleaf Whittier in 1854. Soon after, in 1860, the Ohio State Medical Society held the first clinical conference on marijuana.

During the 19th and early 20th centuries, Mexican immigrants brought marijuana into the country and made it popular among immigrants, jazz musicians and African-Americans. Many local governments, particularly in areas with extensive immigration, passed their own anti-marijuana laws.

By the turn of the 20th century, marijuana use in the United States was generally limited to lower socioeconomic groups. "Few people in the United States actually [smoked] marijuana, but those who did were not members of mainstream, Protestant, Caucasian society," writes Earleywine." [28]

The federal government did show more concern with regulating drugs in the early 20th century. An exposé of the patent medicine industry's scams in 1905 helped prompt passage of the Pure Food and Drug Act of 1906, establishing the Bureau of Chemistry — the forerunner of the FDA — and forcing manufacturers to disclose ingredients of their medicines and stop making unsubstantiated claims about their benefits. The law was superseded in 1938 by the Food, Drug and Cosmetic Act (FDCA), which set up the FDA's procedure for testing drugs for safety and efficacy. Many cannabis extracts were being used even as late as the 1930s, produced by such respectable pharmaceutical firms as Eli Lilly and Parke-Davis. [29]

In 1932, the National Conference of Commissioners on Uniform State Laws drafted a proposed Uniform Narcotic Drug Act that called for making marijuana illegal. Public opinion had turned dramatically against smoked marijuana in the '30s following a concerted federal public education — some say a misinformation campaign — calling marijuana a "killer drug in which lurks murder, insanity and death." Lurid newspaper accounts, heavily tinged with racism and anti-immigrant sentiment, blamed the "marijuana menace" for causing users to commit heinous crimes. The controversial 1936 government-commissioned documentary "Reefer Madness" depicted high school students who smoked the "devil weed" going insane and killing their parents. [30]

By 1937, every state had prohibited marijuana use, either by adopting the Uniform Act or by passing separate legislation.

The first federal legislation directly concerned with marijuana was the Marihuana Tax Act (adopting the drug's Spanish spelling) — passed in 1937. It did not prohibit marijuana production or use but required anyone who cultivated, distributed or used it to pay a $1-an-ounce tax for industrial or medicinal uses and $100-an-ounce for recreational use. The tax was high enough that marijuana's popularity as a medicine and a recreational drug waned. By 1942, the drug was rarely prescribed.

However, marijuana was still legal under federal law. It did not gain widespread popularity again until the 1960s, when it became popular with veterans returning from Vietnam — where it had been plentiful — and youths.

Rising public sentiment about the nation's drug problem resulted in passage in 1970 of the Controlled Substances Act, which for the first time prohibited marijuana possession under federal law. Possession for sale or distribution became a felony, while possession for personal use was a misdemeanor punishable by up to one year in jail and a $1,000 fine for a first offense.

The National Commission on Marihuana and Drug Abuse — established by President Richard M. Nixon in 1972 — decided Congress had gone too far. The panel proposed decriminalizing possession of marijuana for personal use and also recommended that "casual distribution of small amounts of marijuana for no remuneration, or for insignificant remuneration not involving profit, would no longer be an offense." [31]

The commission's findings were largely ignored.

DEA Debate

Also in 1972, the National Organization for the Reform of Marijuana Laws (NORML) petitioned the DEA asking that marijuana be reclassified as a Schedule 2 drug so physicians could prescribe it. It took several years and a court order before the government responded to NORML's request.

Meanwhile, a 1982 IOM report on medicinal marijuana, "Marijuana and Health," said cannabis and its derivatives have "shown promise in the treatment of a variety of disorders," including some kinds of glaucoma, severe asthma, chemotherapy-induced nausea, seizures and other nervous-system disorders. [32] As information about marijuana's reputed medicinal benefits spread, sick Americans began being arrested for marijuana possession and public pressure led numerous states, beginning with New Mexico in 1978, to recognize marijuana's medicinal value.

But the laws were largely symbolic because possession of marijuana — still a Schedule I drug — remained a federal crime. In 1986, the DEA finally held public hearings on NORML's rescheduling request, and in 1988 Administrative Law Judge Francis L. Young called marijuana "one of the safest therapeutically active substances known to man." While marijuana can be abused, he wrote, "the same is true of dozens of drugs or substances listed in Schedule 2" that are routinely prescribed by physicians. [33]

"Marijuana has been accepted as capable of relieving distress of great numbers of very ill people, and doing so with safety under medical supervision," Young continued. "It would be unreasonable, arbitrary and capricious for DEA to continue to stand between those sufferers and the benefits of this substance in light of the evidence in this record." [34]

However, in an unusual move, then-DEA Administrator John Lawn overruled Judge Young's ruling, saying, "The evidence presented . . . was limited to testimony of individuals who had used marijuana for those conditions and the testimony of the psychiatrists or general practice physicians. There is not a shred of credible evidence to support any of their claims." An appeals court upheld Lawn's power to overrule an administrative law judge in 1994. [35]

In 1977, President Jimmy Carter called for decriminalization of marijuana possession, but by 1978-79 — as drug use among youths was reaching its peak in America — an anti-drug backlash developed. The backlash was led by a "parents movement," which later morphed into

Opposing sides in the ongoing medical marijuana debate demonstrate outside the U.S. Supreme Court following arguments on Nov. 29, 2004. The government argued that the federal Controlled Substance Act of 1970 can be used to block laws in California and other states that permit physician-prescribed use of marijuana for medical purposes.

the influential Atlanta-based anti-drug lobbying group, National Families in Action.

Frustrated in their efforts at the federal level, advocates of legalizing marijuana turned to the states. Since 1973, 12 states have enacted laws in some way decriminalizing marijuana. All call for no jail time for simple marijuana possession.

In the early 1980s, the state/federal Investigational New Drug program (IND) was launched in which six states began clinical trials on the medicinal use of marijuana — using pot grown by a federal government facility in Mississippi.

In recent years, the federal government has aggressively confronted the challenges from the states. In 1996, just after passage of medical marijuana laws in Arizona and California, the ONDCP threatened to take action against any physician who recommended or prescribed marijuana to patients. A group of doctors and patients in California sued the federal government to block such action. The case, *Conant v. McCaffrey*, was finally concluded in October 2003 when the U.S. Supreme Court let stand a 9th U.S. Circuit Court of Appeals ruling allowing physicians to recommend marijuana to patients.

Thus blocked by the 9th Circuit, federal officials next filed suit in January 1998 to shut down six California marijuana cooperatives that provided the drug to patients. The defendants in the case, *United States v. Oakland Cannabis Buyers' Cooperative*, argued that "medical necessity" exempted them from federal laws against growing marijuana. [36]

The 9th Circuit court agreed. The case, however, was appealed to the U.S. Supreme Court and, in May 2001 the high court ruled medical necessity was not a valid exemption from federal drug laws. [37]

CURRENT SITUATION

Research Efforts

Although some states and cities have loosened restrictions on medical marijuana and possession of small amounts of the drug for recreational use, the only marijuana that is legal under federal law is grown by the University of Mississippi for a handful of patients who still receive a supply under the discontinued IND program and a small number of scientists conducting federally approved research.

And despite some popular notions to the contrary, marijuana laws are being widely enforced in most of the country. More than 755,000 marijuana arrests were made in 2003, according to the Federal Bureau of Investigation — a number that has nearly tripled over the past 15 years. [38]

However, marijuana is still widely available. In 2001, approximately 83 million Americans said they had tried marijuana at least once. [39] Moreover, a Gallup Poll showed that three-quarters of U.S. adults favor legalizing marijuana for medical use, and a recent poll conducted by AARP — a 38-million member organization for people over age 50 — found that 72 percent of Americans over 45 favor allowing marijuana to be used for medical purposes. [40]

That public opinion has not been reflected in Congress, however, which has been particularly inhospitable to proposals to protect medical users of marijuana, according to Allen St. Pierre, executive director of NORML. "The people's house once again blindly did not look at this issue last year," he says, adding that Congress has become more closed to the idea since President Bush was elected.

"Even under [former House Speaker Newt] Gingrich [R-Ga.], there were subcommittee hearings on [marijuana] legislation," St. Pierre says. "Yes, they were 'dog and pony shows' and, yes, we got the crap beat out of us every time. But at least we had hearings."

Rep. Maurice Hinchey, D-N.Y. has routinely introduced — and plans to reintroduce in the current Congress — an amendment to Justice Department appropriations legislation that would prohibit the use of federal funds to interfere with state medical marijuana laws. More than two-thirds of House Democrats have voted in favor of the legislation two years in a row. The so-called Hinchey amendment "is a way to get a vote on it and stop the federal government from preventing states from carrying out their lawful authority under the Constitution," Hinchey says.

He concedes it would be more straightforward to simply pass legislation reclassifying marijuana as a Schedule 2 drug, thus allowing doctors to legally prescribe it, "but the leadership of the House will not allow that particular attempt to come to vote."

Dean, of the Community Anti-Drug Coalitions of America, calls Hinchey's amendment "a propaganda campaign" and says the FDA rather than Congress should determine how best to deal with marijuana.

However, there's a Catch-22 to that argument, according to advocates for legalizing marijuana: They note the FDA won't approve a schedule change for marijuana until studies demonstrate its efficacy and relative safety, but the federal government controls the only legal supplies of marijuana for research, and isn't allowing researchers to obtain the marijuana they need to conduct such studies.

"I understand that the FDA in particular wants to have randomized clinical trials," says Earleywine, of the University of Southern California. "That's fine. Let us do it. But they are not letting us do it."

The federal government did approve one marijuana study in 1997 — a project examining the effects of smoked marijuana, oral THC and a placebo in HIV patients — after delays of more than three years since it was first proposed and its protocol was approved by the FDA. According to the Marijuana Policy Project, which helped fund the two-year study, conducted by Dr. Donald Abrams at the University of California at San Francisco, this was the first clinical trial in 15 years in the United States "that would obtain any data whatsoever on marijuana's medical effectiveness." [41]

In December 2003, most recently, the government rejected a University of Massachusetts request to grow marijuana for FDA-approved research. The university had submitted the proposal nearly four years earlier and only received the DEA's decision after filing suit to demand a response. (The DEA declined requests for comment.)

"By denying the application, the DEA effectively is prohibiting research that might eventually lead to FDA approval of cannabis as a federally authorized prescription drug," editorialized California's *Orange County Register*. "The decision said, in effect, that the feds don't approve of the medicinal use of marijuana and they will block any research that might challenge that predetermined opinion." [42]

"The only producer of marijuana right now is the farm at the University of Mississippi," says Fox of the Marijuana Policy Project. "They are the only ones growing it, and they are not applying for FDA approval. In order to get FDA approval you have to manufacture or produce the drug so that you know the exact makeup of the drug, then you test it, and then you apply for FDA approval. There is no entity right now that can produce marijuana and do their research and apply for approval. It's really impossible."

In fact, as Fox points out, any research with marijuana has to meet standards that are required of no other drug research. "The federal government believes that marijuana is so dangerous that medical marijuana research has to go through a special panel for approval," Fox says. In addition, "You have to show the marijuana would be a more effective treatment for a condition than other drugs out there, which is a standard that is not applied to any other new drug proposal."

The government, says Fox, "is not being honest about what it is doing."

While the DEA and the FDA declined to comment, Murray of the Office of National Drug Control Policy rejects the charges. "There you get into the conspiracy theory," he says. "The argument is made that 'marijuana is highly effective, and we know this, but the government won't let us prove it.' On the other hand, they say, 'We need more research on this, but the government won't let us do it.' On the face of it, that is wrong."

Murray concedes that not many medical marijuana studies have been approved, but he faults the researchers. "There is, in fact, a difficulty for some researchers to get access to the marijuana they would like to use," says Murray. "The primary reason is that they do not submit protocols of research that meet NIDA's standards for any drug application." For example, he says, some research proposals did not provide for control groups and involved people taking multiple drugs simultaneously.

"These are scientific problems," Murray says, "not government suppression problems."

States' Rights

Historically, "states' rights" has been a call to arms for conservatives and libertarians, who think the federal government, for the most part, should not be telling the states what to do. "We have a variety of different [state] systems," the Cato Institute's Boaz says. "Sometimes we decide that we have different cultural views here in Utah than they have in California. So we have different rules."

But when it comes to marijuana laws, those who favor liberalization find themselves on the side of states' rights, while conservatives argue for strong federal drug laws — even if they conflict with state laws. [43]

"Drug laws should be on the national level," says CADCA's Thau. "Otherwise, people cross state lines to do stuff that they wouldn't be allowed to do in their own state."

DuPont, of the Institute for Behavior and Health, agrees, but for slightly different reasons. "It's a scary concept to have states approve medicines," he says. "It's also very scary to have medicines approved on the basis of ballot initiatives. This is not a good way to have public policy. It's a national issue. There's no question about it."

Fox of the Marijuana Policy Project, however, says states should be free to establish their own policies on marijuana, whether that means legalizing it or banning it — although he thinks banning it would be a mistake because it would increase organized crime. "But the states should be allowed to experiment."

The Framers of the Constitution expected the federal government to have very limited powers, but that point has long since passed. In considering the *Raich* case, the Supreme Court was essentially asked to decide whether there were limits to the federal government's power over state drug laws.

In oral arguments before the court last Nov. 29, the federal government said it has the power under the 1970 Controlled Substances Act to prohibit marijuana possession by individuals — even when it is allowed and regulated under a state law and even if that possession occurs without a commercial transaction or interstate commerce having occurred. Congress' authority to pass the act was based upon its constitutional power — under the so-called Commerce Clause — to regulate interstate commerce. (The marijuana used in the case was grown and consumed by individuals locally and without sales.)

Raich's attorney, Randy E. Barnett, a law professor at Boston University, told the justices that if California patients grow modest amounts of marijuana for their own use, it doesn't fall under federal jurisdiction, and any attempt by the government to enforce the Controlled Substances Act against them is unconstitutional. "The class of activities involved in this case are non-economic and wholly intrastate," Barnett told the justices. [44]

The Supreme Court has ruled in the past that non-commercial activities that significantly affect interstate markets can be governed by federal law. And the federal government claims in *Raich* that it must have the power to regulate all use of marijuana if it is to control the interstate market in the drug.

But Barnett argued that allowing patients to smoke homegrown marijuana won't impact federal efforts to control the illegal interstate market in marijuana. "The federal prohibition of this class of activities is not essential — is not an essential part of a larger regulatory scheme that would be undercut unless the intrastate activity were regulated," Barnett said.

Rep. Mark E. Souder, R-Ill., and several of his colleagues disagree. In a brief to the Supreme Court they argued: "Permitting even the limited marijuana cultivation and distribution allegedly at issue in this case would undermine drug regulations by (1) giving drug traffickers a new strategy to evade arrest; (2) creating geographic 'safe havens' for drug dealers to base their operations; (3) increasing the risk of diversion from 'medical' use to purely recreational trafficking; (4) increasing the supply and lowering the price of marijuana; and (5) potentially increasing the demand for the drug through reduced public perception of marijuana's harms."

However, fear that the federal government might, under the authority of the Commerce Clause, regulate even non-economic activities within the states raises concerns even among parties who don't support medical marijuana. The state of Alabama, for example, filed an *amicus* brief in support of Raich, even though Alabama does not have medical marijuana laws.

AT ISSUE

Should marijuana laws be relaxed?

YES   Paul Armentano
Senior policy analyst, The NORML Foundation

Written for The CQ Researcher, February 2005

Scott Bryant had just settled down to watch TV with his 7-year-old son on the night of April 17, 1995, when 13 Wisconsin sheriff's deputies burst through his front door looking for marijuana. Bryant, 29, who was unarmed, was shot and killed as his young son helplessly looked on. Police seized less than three grams of marijuana in the no-knock raid. On review, the county district attorney ruled that the shooting was "not in any way justified."

Scott Bryant was a victim — not of marijuana, but of marijuana prohibition. During the past decade, more than 6.5 million Americans have been arrested on marijuana charges, more than the entire combined populations of Alaska, Delaware, the District of Columbia, Montana, North Dakota, South Dakota, Vermont and Wyoming. As in Bryant's case, nearly 90 percent of these arrests were for the simple possession of marijuana for personal use, not for cultivation or sale.

Annually, state and local justice for marijuana arrests are now estimated to cost $7.6 billion, or approximately $10,400 per arrest. However, despite this massive expenditure and the threat of arrest, approximately 80 million Americans, including former President Bill Clinton and former House Speaker Newt Gingrich, self-identify as having used marijuana at some point in their lives. Nearly 15 million Americans admit to being current users of cannabis. It is time for America's marijuana laws to reflect this reality, not deny it.

Critics of liberalizing America's marijuana laws argue that marijuana isn't a "harmless" substance. They're correct; marijuana isn't harmless. In fact, no substance is, including those that are legal. However, as acknowledged by a study in the current issue of *Current Opinion in Pharmacology*, "Overall, by comparison with other drugs used mainly for 'recreational' purposes, cannabis [is] rated to be a relatively safe drug." Indeed, by far the greatest danger to health posed by the adult use of cannabis stems from a criminal arrest and incarceration.

Speaking before Congress on the 40th anniversary of marijuana prohibition, Aug. 2, 1977, former President Jimmy Carter stated: "Penalties against drug use should not be more damaging to an individual than use of the drug itself. Nowhere is this more clear than in the laws against the possession of marijuana in private for personal use."

More than 25 years later, the time has come to heed his advice and to stop arresting the millions of otherwise law-abiding adults who use marijuana.

NO   Robert L. DuPont, M.D.
President, Institute for Behavior and Health; former director, National Institute on Drug Abuse (NIDA), and White House drug czar for Presidents Nixon and Ford

Written for The CQ Researcher, February 2005

Marijuana is a dangerous drug that is prohibited not only in the United States but throughout almost all of the rest of the world — for sound public health reasons.

First, let's dispense with the myth that many marijuana users end up in prison. Under the Controlled Substances Act of 1970, only possession of marijuana with intent to sell is a felony. Federal prosecution for marijuana possession is limited to major drug traffickers. Thus, in 2001 only 2.3 percent of defendants sentenced in federal court for a marijuana offense were sentenced for simple possession — 186 people. In state prisons in 2002, only 8,400 prisoners (about 0.7 percent of the total prison population of 1.2 million) were serving time for possession marijuana, and only half of those were incarcerated for a first offense. Prison is not a realistic risk for American marijuana users unless they also are drug sellers. Drug trafficking, including the sale of marijuana, is a serious crime deserving of stiff punishments.

The collective national judgment about marijuana is expressed in the nation's democratically enacted laws. Like speeding, drunken driving, smoking cigarettes in elevators and failing to buckle your seat belt in a car, possessing and selling marijuana are prohibited in order to protect the public health.

Moreover, marijuana use is dangerous. MayoClinic.com reported that marijuana use reduces memory, inhibits driving ability, limits attention span, increases the risk of schizophrenia, generates paranoia, anxiety and panic attacks and causes breathing trouble. That same report stated, "Burning marijuana smoke contains higher amounts of some cancer-causing chemical than does tobacco smoke. Smoking marijuana increases your risk of cancer of the mouth, larynx and lungs."

The risk of arrest and a fine — but not prison — for the possession of marijuana is also real but small. The health risk from using marijuana is also real but by no means small. For American youth, marijuana use leads to more drug-abuse treatment than all other drugs and alcohol combined. It also leads to more than 100,000 emergency room episodes per year.

The ongoing debate over marijuana laws is healthy. When all of the facts are carefully considered, I am confident that legislators across the country will see the wisdom of continuing to prohibit the use and sale of marijuana. The goal of this legal prohibition is to reduce the levels of marijuana use and the serious harm caused by that use.

"The question presented here is not whether vigorous enforcement of the nation's drug laws is good criminal policy," Alabama's brief said. "It most assuredly is. The question, rather, is whether the Constitution permits the federal government, under the guise of regulating interstate commerce, to criminalize the purely local possession of marijuana for personal medicinal use. It does not." The brief also noted that California's law would not have a negative impact on Alabama.

"If the court holds that Congress does have the power to reach non-commercial use of medical marijuana, then it is difficult to see how there are any meaningful limits on Congress' commerce power," says Jonathan Adler, associate professor of law and associate director of the Case School of Law in Cleveland.

"The Controlled Substances Act was written when people had forgotten that Congress has limited and enumerated powers. That's part of what creates this problem," Adler explains. "Now the courts have to confront what Congress did." The act also bumped up against what has traditionally been the realm of the states: regulation of medical treatment, he says.

Trevor Morrison, an assistant professor of law at Cornell University, agrees. "In some ways, Raich is kind of a reckoning point for the court since it started to establish the new limits on Congress in the mid-1990s," Morrison says. "I guess a question like this has been inevitable. The question is just how robust to make these new limits. The court has articulated a concern that it needs to impose limits on legislative authority in order to ensure that there continues to be some kind of division between federal power and state power."

The California Medical Association (CMA) is pretty clear about where it believes the line should be drawn with respect to doctor-patient issues.

"Although the federal government has a significant role to play in ensuring that manufacturers who claim that their products will accomplish particular medical results are held to a high level of accountability of efficacy and safety, that consumer-protection role has never justified interfering with a specific doctor's recommendation to a specific patient about how best to treat or help alleviate a particular condition," said the *amicus* brief submitted to the 9th Circuit court by the CMA. [45]

OUTLOOK

Supreme Court Ruling

Convinced that the federal government opposes their efforts, advocates for liberalizing marijuana laws have increasingly turned to the states and the courts.

"The reality is this Congress is not going to pass medical marijuana legislation," says St. Pierre of NORML. "It leaves us the courts. It leaves us [statewide voter] initiatives." That's a shame, he says, since the issue really belongs in the legislature. "Legislators are supposed to do things responsibly. I think that they have so terribly punted this issue."

Rep. Frank agrees that prospects for the near term are dim. "If we had a Democratic House, we might be able to move it," he says, "But not with a Republican House."

In its decision, the Supreme Court said the issue was one for lawmakers, not judges. For the majority, Justice John Paul Stevens said the case was "troubling" because Monson and Raich said nothing but marijuana worked to alleviate their symptoms. But he said Congress could use its power over interstate commerce to ban marijuana even when grown within a state for medicinal, not commercial, purposes. Local cultivation for personal use, he said, "may have a substantial impact on the interstate market for this extraordinarily popular substance."

Still, Stevens closed by noting that the government could reclassify marijuana to allow medical use or that Congress could revisit the issue.

For her part, Justice Sandra Day O'Connor wrote in dissent that the ruling "extinguishes" California's "experiment" on medical marijuana without any proof that the law would affect interstate commerce. While noting that she herself would have voted against the California law, O'Connor said the decision "stifles an express choice by some States, concerned for the lives and liberties of their people, to regulate medical marijuana differently" than the federal government.

Despite the setback, medical marijuana advocates stressed that the state laws remained on the book and the federal government has only limited resources to go after the estimated 100,000 people already issued cards for medicinal use of the substance.

Some experts say that the medical marijuana issue may soon change dramatically in any case, thanks to the impending introduction of cannabis-based drugs such as Sativex.

Medically effective pharmaceutical versions of marijuana could, says Fox of the Marijuana Policy Project, have widespread impact. "On the one hand, it could make it more difficult to pass new state medical marijuana laws," he notes, "because legislators may say you don't need to grow it yourself since you can buy it at the pharmacy."

At the same time, he says, if marijuana is acknowledged as a medicine, the obvious question would be: Does it make sense to arrest people who are using the same thing but growing it themselves? Homegrown marijuana is likely to be much cheaper than pharmaceutical versions, and Fox says that for some people the smoked variety works better.

"I would expect that the pharmaceutical companies would want to be against any law that made marijuana legal to be used if you grow it yourself," Fox adds.

Nadelmann, of the Drug Policy Alliance, is convinced that, despite setbacks in Congress and the courts, marijuana eventually will be available to adult Americans. "The positive part of the story is that the numbers are trending our way," he says. "The generation of Americans who came of age before the '60s is dying out. The generation of Americans who do not know the difference between marijuana and heroin is no longer such a big proportion of the population.

"Meanwhile, roughly 50 percent of all Americans between ages 16 and 50-something have tried marijuana at least once."

NOTES

1. Evelyn Nieves, "'I Really Consider Cannabis My Miracle': Patients Fight to Keep Drug of Last Resort," *The Washington Post*, Jan. 1, 2005, p. A3.

2. Testimony before House Government Reform Subcommittee on Criminal Justice, Drug Policy and Human Resources, April 1, 2004.

3. Barbara Opall-Rome, "Israel tests pot's effect on trauma from war," *Air Force Times*, Sept. 6, 2004, p. 23.

4. See National Institute on Drug Abuse (NIDA) Info Facts, "Marijuana," at www.nida.nih.gov/Infofax/marijuana.html. Also see "Exposing the Myth of Medical Marijuana," U.S. Drug Enforcement Administration (DEA), www.usdoj.gov/dea/ongoing/marijuanap.html.

5. *Ibid*, DEA.

6. Christopher S. Wren, "Small but Forceful Coalition Works to Counter U.S. War on Drugs," *The New York Times*, Jan. 2, 2000, p. A1.

7. *The New England Journal of Medicine*, Jan. 30, 1997, pp. 366-367.

8. *Amicus curiae* brief submitted by the California Medical Association. Appeal from order modifying injunction by the U.S. District Court, Case No. C 98-0088 CRB. Jan. 11, 2000.

9. L.D. Johnston, *et al.*, "Overall teen drug use continues gradual decline; but use of inhalants rises," University of Michigan News and Information Services, Dec. 21, 2004; www.monitoringthefuture.org.

10. *Ibid*.

11. "New Research Study in JAMA Shows Adult Marijuana Abuse and Dependence Increased During 1990s," NIDA press release, May 4, 2004, www.nida.nih.gov/Newsroom/04/nr5-4.html.

12. There are two exceptions. A handful of patients continues to receive federally provided marijuana under a program managed by NIDA that was discontinued in 1992. And a small number of researchers have been able to obtain federally grown marijuana for research studies.

13. John A. Benson Jr., *et al.*, eds., *Marijuana and Medicine: Assessing the Science Base*, Institute of Medicine, 1999.

14. Council on Scientific Affairs, American Medical Association, "Report 6," 2001 AMA annual meeting.

15. Benson, *op. cit.*

16. *Ibid.*, DEA.

17. DEA, *op. cit.*

18. Benson, *op. cit.*

19. Statement of Claudia Jensen before Committee on House Government Reform Subcommittee on Criminal Justice, Drug Policy and Human Resources, April 1, 2003.

20. *The New England Journal of Medicine, op. cit.*

21. www.norml.org/index.cfm?Group_ID=3476.

22. "Deglamorizing cannabis," *The Lancet*, Vol. 346, No. 8985, Nov. 11, 1995, p. 1241.

23. For background, see Kathy Koch, "Medical Marijuana," *The CQ Researcher*, Aug. 20, 1999, pp. 705-728.

24. Benson, *op. cit.*, p. 6.

25. Testimony of Scott Ehlers before Subcommittee on Criminal Justice, Drug Policy, and Human Resources Hearing on "Drug Legalization, Criminalization, and Harm Reduction," June 16, 1999.

26. Ethan Nadelmann, "An End to Marijuana Prohibition: The Drive to Legalize Picks Up," *National Review*, July 12, 2004, p. 4.

27. Mary Lynn Mathre, ed., *Cannabis in Medical Practice* (1997), pp. 35-36.

28. Mitch Earleywine, *Understanding Marijuana: A New Look at the Scientific Evidence* (2002), p. 23.

29. Koch, *op. cit.*

30. *Ibid.*

31. "Marihuana: A Signal of Misunderstanding," National Commission on Marihuana and Drug Abuse, 1972, http://www.druglibrary.org/ schaffer/library/studies/nc/ncmenu.htm.

32. Koch, *op. cit.*

33. Cited in R.C. Randall, ed., *Marijuana, Medicine and the Law*, Vol. II (1989), p. 445.

34. Docket No. 86-22, Opinion and Recommended Ruling, Findings of Fact, Conclusions of Law and Decision of Administrative Law Judge Francis L. Young, Sept. 6, 1988, p. 34.

35. Koch, *op. cit.*

36. The citation is 532 U.S. 483 (2001).

37. The 9th Circuit's decision is *Conant v. McCaffrey*, 309 U.S. F3d 629 (Oct. 29, 2002); the government's petition for *certiorari* was filed under the name *Walter v. Conant*, 03-40; the court denied *certiorari* on Oct. 14, 2003; a transcript of arguments before U.S. Supreme Court, Nov. 29, 2004, is at www.supremecourtus.gov.

38. "Crime in the United States: 2003," Federal Bureau of Investigation.

39. Summary of findings from the 1999 "National Household Survey on Drug Abuse," Department of Health and Human Services, 2000.

40. "AARP Poll Shows Most Support Legalizing Medicinal Marijuana," The Associated Press, Dec. 19, 2004.

41. Available at www.mpp.org/archive/abrams 98.html.

42. *Orange County Register*, Dec. 23, 2004.

43. For background, see Kenneth Jost, "The States and Federalism," *The CQ Researcher*, Sept. 13, 1996, pp. 793-816.

44. Argument before U.S. Supreme Court, Nov. 29, 2004, No. 03-1454.

45. *Amicus* brief of the California Medical Association and the California Nurses Association in Support of Plaintiffs-Appellants Angel McClary Raich and Diane Monson, On Appeal from the United States District Court for the Northern District of California, Case No. C02-4872MJJ, March 5, 2003.

BIBLIOGRAPHY

Books

Benson, John A. Jr., *et al.*, eds., "Marijuana As Medicine: Assessing the Science Base," National Academy Press, March 1999.
Advocates and critics of medical marijuana alike cite this 267-page report as support for their arguments. While Institute of Medicine researchers indicated that the toxicity of marijuana smoke limited its role as a medicine, they said compounds in marijuana apparently offer some medicinal value. The report recommends more research, especially directed toward developing pharmaceuticals derived from marijuana.

Earleywine, Mitch, *Understanding Marijuana: A New Look at the Scientific Evidence*, Oxford University Press, 2002.
An associate professor of clinical science at the University of Southern California provides a balanced, detailed and easy-to-understand look at the medical, legal and political issues surrounding marijuana.

Husak, Douglas, *Legalize This! The Case for Decriminalizing Drugs*, Verso, 2002.
A professor of philosophy and law at Rutgers University argues that criminalizing marijuana and other drugs fosters corruption and organized crime and that public resources would be better directed at education and treatment.

Iversen, Leslie L., *The Science of Marijuana*, Oxford University Press, 2000.
A professor of pharmacology at the University of Oxford examines marijuana's medicinal potential, possible toxic effects and use as a recreational drug.

Zimmer, Lynn, and John P. Morgan, *Marijuana Myths/Marijuana Facts*, The Lindesmith Center, 1997.
Zimmer, an emeritus associate professor of sociology at the City University of New York, and Morgan, emeritus professor of pharmacology at the university's medical school, debunk 20 so-called myths about marijuana and its purported impact on memory, crime and pregnancy. The Lindesmith Center is now part of the Drug Policy Alliance, which advocates reform of marijuana laws.

Articles

Kassirer, Jerome P., "Federal Foolishness and Marijuana," *The New England Journal of Medicine*, Jan. 30, 1997, p. 366.
The prestigious journal comes out strongly in favor of legalizing medical marijuana in a groundbreaking editorial, declaring that "a federal policy that prohibits physicians from alleviating suffering by prescribing marijuana for seriously ill patients is misguided, heavy-handed, and inhumane. Marijuana may have long-term adverse effects and its use may presage serious addictions, but neither long-term side effects nor addiction is a relevant issue in such patients."

Nadelmann, Ethan A., "An End to Marijuana Prohibition: The Drive to Legalize Picks Up," *National Review*, July 12, 2004.
The founder and executive director of the Drug Policy Alliance summarizes recent efforts to legalize marijuana, backing up his argument for legalization with considerable documentation. A follow-up debate between Nadelmann and John Walters, head of the Office of National Drug Control Policy, appeared in the Sept. 27, 2004, issue.

Schlosser, Eric, "Marijuana and the Law," *The Atlantic Monthly*, September 1994.
Journalist Schlosser argues that federal marijuana policies calling for prison time end up ruining lives and are, in many cases, not appropriate to the crime.

Reports and Studies

"2003 National Household Survey," Department of Health and Human Services, Substance Abuse and Mental Health Services Administration, Office of Applied Studies, 2004.
This annual report provides a wealth of survey data on Americans' use of illegal drugs, as well as alcohol and tobacco. The report contains data collected from interviews with 70,000 individuals ages 12 and older. This most recent edition contains data collected in 2001.

Abraham, Manja D., *et al.*, "Licit and Illicit Drug Use in Amsterdam III: Developments in Drug Use 1987-1997," Centre for Drug Research (CEDRO), University of Amsterdam, 2000.
The CEDRO report is the Dutch equivalent of the National Household Survey in the United States and is a must read for any policy makers or analysts considering decriminalizing marijuana.

"Marijuana: Early Experiences with Four States' Laws That Allow Use for Medical Purposes," Report to the Chairman, Subcommittee on Criminal Justice, Drug Policy and Human Resources, Committee on Government Reform, U.S. House of Representatives, November 2002, GAO-03-189.
A congressional subcommittee describes in detail the medical marijuana programs in four states.

For More Information

Americans for Safe Access, 1322 Webster St., Suite 208, Oakland, CA 94612; (888) 929-4367; www.safeaccessnow.org. Advocates "safe, legal access to marijuana for all who are helped by it" and provides legal training for lawyers and patients as well as medical information for doctors and patients.

Canadian Foundation for Drug Policy, 70 MacDonald St., Ottawa, Ontario, Canada K2P 1H6; (613) 236-1027; www.cfdp.ca. Supports reforming drug policies "to make them more effective and humane."

Common Sense for Drug Policy, 3220 N St., N.W., Suite 141, Washington, DC 20007; (202) 299-9780; www.csdp.org. Advocates the "regulation and control of marijuana in a manner similar to alcohol and clear federal guidelines for the practice of pain management."

Community Anti-Drug Coalitions of America, 625 Slaters Lane, Suite 300, Alexandria, VA 22314; (800) 542-2322; http://cadca.org. Seeks "to create safe, healthy and drug-free communities" by eliminating drug use among children.

Drug Enforcement Administration, 2401 Jefferson Davis Highway, Alexandria, VA 22301; (800) 882-9539; www.usdoj.gov/dea/. Enforces the nation's controlled-substances laws.

Drug Free America Foundation, P.O. Box 11298, St. Petersburg, FL 33733-1298; (727) 828-0211; www.dfaf.org. Opposes efforts to legalize or decriminalize illicit drugs.

Drug Policy Alliance, 925 15th St., N.W., 2nd Floor, Washington, DC 20005; (202) 216-0035; www.drugpolicy.org. Created by the merger of the Drug Policy Foundation and Lindesmith Center, works to "promote alternatives to the war on drugs based on science, compassion, health and human rights."

Institute for Behavior and Health, 6191 Executive Blvd., Rockville, MD 20852; (301) 231-9010; www.ibhinc.org. Works to improve drug-abuse treatment programs and encourage student drug testing.

Marijuana Policy Project, P.O. Box 77492, Washington, DC 20013; (202) 462-5747; www.mpp.org. Lobbies for liberalization of marijuana laws.

National Families in Action, 2957 Clairmont Road, N.E., Suite 150, Atlanta, GA 30329; (404) 248-9676; www.nationalfamilies.org/about.html. A nonprofit drug-prevention organization made up of parent volunteers.

National Institute on Drug Abuse, 6001 Executive Blvd., Suite 5213, Bethesda, MD 20892-9561; (301) 443-1124; http://www.nida.nih.gov/. Part of the National Institutes of Health, NIDA seeks "to lead the nation in bringing the power of science to bear on drug abuse and addiction."

National Organization for the Reform of Marijuana Laws, 1600 K St., N.W., Suite 501, Washington DC 20006-2832; (202) 483-5500; www.norml.org. NORML is a leading advocate for legalization of marijuana.

Office of National Drug Control Policy, 750 17th St., N.W., Washington, DC 20503; (202) 395-6700; www.whitehousedrugpolicy.gov/. The ONDCP establishes policies and priorities for federal drug control efforts and seeks to ensure cooperation among federal, state and local entities involved with drug policies.

4

High school students in the Children's Aid Society's sexuality-education program in New York City visit Binghamton University last summer. The "abstinence-plus" program has been called the nation's most successful approach to reducing teen sex and pregnancy. It urges youths to wait until they are older to have sex and then to use contraceptives conscientiously. The Bush administration says abstinence is the only 100 percent effective approach to avoiding STDs and is providing funding to spread the message in U.S. schools and overseas.

From *CQ Researcher,*
December 3, 2004.

Sexually Transmitted Diseases

Sarah Glazer

The United States has the highest rates of sexually transmitted diseases (STDs) of any industrialized nation, and sexually active youth account for about half the new cases of infection occurring annually. Indeed, more than half of all Americans will get an STD at some point in their lifetime. [1] Yet the nation has no concerted, national campaign to prevent, treat and cure these infections, according to the American Social Health Association, a public health advocacy and information group in Research Triangle Park, N.C. [2]

What the public needs is more information — not less, many public health advocates argue. Not much has changed since 1997, when "The Hidden Epidemic," a report by the Institute of Medicine (IOM), singled out secrecy as a major societal obstacle to curbing a problem that costs the United States up to $15.5 billion annually in direct medical expenses." [3] (*See chart, p. 71.*)

The shame Americans feel about sex-related infection continues to inhibit people from talking about it to their sexual partners, a crucial factor in preventing it from spreading. It also prevents doctors from asking their patients about their sexual history and doing the kind of testing that could catch many of these infections in the early stages when they are easily curable, says Edward Hook, a professor of medicine at the University of Alabama, who served on the IOM committee.

"There is this really curious American ambivalence about sex being everywhere — from the sidelines of the football game to merchandising — but we can't advertise doing it safely or the untoward consequences of doing it unsafely," Hook says. "If I had one thing I could change it would be the stigma." In other developed countries, people are more likely to tell their partners if they're infected

STD Rates in U.S. Are Higher

The reported rates of curable STDs in the United States are several times higher than in other developed countries, according to the most recent available data.

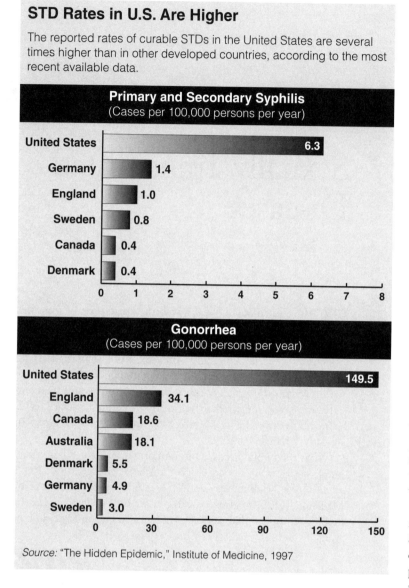

Primary and Secondary Syphilis
(Cases per 100,000 persons per year)

United States	6.3
Germany	1.4
England	1.0
Sweden	0.8
Canada	0.4
Denmark	0.4

Gonorrhea
(Cases per 100,000 persons per year)

United States	149.5
England	34.1
Canada	18.6
Australia	18.1
Denmark	5.5
Germany	4.9
Sweden	3.0

Source: "The Hidden Epidemic," Institute of Medicine, 1997

Similarly, many of the other most common STD infections — including genital herpes and human papillomavirus (HPV) — have few if any recognizable symptoms, another serious obstacle to rousing public awareness. (*See chart, p. 74.*)

STDs have been around for centuries but were once fewer and curable. Syphilis and gonorrhea, two of the oldest, are deadly bacterial diseases that were almost eliminated after the discovery of antibiotics. But both have recently made a comeback, most notably in the gay community. With the rise of drug-resistant strains of gonorrhea, the number of effective antibiotics against that infection is dwindling, posing a potential public health crisis. Moreover, in recent decades, the variety of viral STDs — like herpes and HPV, which are treatable but not curable — has multiplied.

If left untreated, STDs can produce tragic results, especially for women — including infertility, tubal pregnancy and cervical cancer. In some cases, pregnant women can transmit the infection to their babies, which can be life threatening.

And most Americans underestimate their risk of contracting an STD. According to recent survey data, only 14 percent of men and 8 percent of women think they are at risk of being infected. [4]

and talk to their doctors about it, he maintains, because there is less shame.

Most young girls won't even know they have chlamydia, one of the most common and curable STDs, unless their doctor tests them for it. In approximately three-quarters of infected men and women, this bacterial infection has no early symptoms, but it can be easily cured with antibiotics if caught early. If not, in 10 percent of girls it can lead to serious consequences like infertility or a tubal pregnancy years later.

Meanwhile, despite dire predictions in the 1980s of a growing AIDS epidemic, the number of new HIV infections diagnosed in the United States each year appears to have stabilized during the 1990s to about 40,000 new infections. [5] While still unacceptably high, it is a remarkable decrease from more than 150,000 cases a year in the mid-1980s. [6]

That success story has included dramatic decreases in HIV among gay men, injection drug users and newborn infants. Recent reports of rising syphilis and HIV rates in the male, gay community have some experts worried, however, about the possibility of a new resurgence of HIV, which is more easily transmitted among people with STDs.

AIDS also remains among the top three causes of death for African-American women between ages 35 and 44 and African-American men 25 to 54. During the televised vice presidential debate, a question from moderator Gwen Ifill, senior correspondent of PBS' "The NewsHour with Jim Lehrer," drew national attention to the fact that African-American women are diagnosed with AIDS at a rate 23 times higher than white women and die from AIDS at a much higher rate than their white counterparts.

African-Americans also have the poorest survival rate of all racial and ethnic groups, according to the Centers for Disease Control and Prevention (CDC). [7] One possible reason for the lower survival rate: Blacks have a much higher rate than whites of other STDs — 20 times more gonorrhea and five times more syphilis.

Women and adolescents are also disproportionately affected by STDs. Worldwide, approximately half the new HIV infections are occurring among women, and the rate of HIV infection is growing faster in women than in men. [8]

Because of the inconsistent reporting system for STDs in this country, it's unclear whether STD rates are on the rise among young Americans. Some experts worry that rising chlamydia rates among young people indicate a growing number may be turning to hormonal birth control, which doesn't protect against STDs, instead of condoms, which do. But those rates may be merely a result of increased testing, according to government officials.

On the whole, teens are engaging in less risky sexual behavior than in previous years, possibly in response to widespread public education campaigns about HIV. A recent study found that more than half of sexually active teenage girls now use condoms. [9] Indeed, among 15-to-24-year-olds, HIV is far less common than chlamydia, genital herpes, HPV or gonorrhea.

STDs Cost U.S. $15.5 Billion Annually

The direct cost of eight major STDs among Americans ages 15-24 was $6.5 billion in 2000. Overall, STDs cost the U.S. $15.5 billion. The CDC estimates that 19 million STD infections occur annually, almost half among youth ages 15-24.

STD	Total Cost
Sexually transmitted HIV	$3 billion
Human papillomavirus (HPV)	$2.9 billion
Genital Herpes	$292.7 million
Chlamydia	$248.4 million
Gonorrhea	$77 million
Trichomoniasis	$34.2 million
Hepatitis B	$5.8 million
Syphilis	$3.6 million
Total	$6.5 billion*

* Does not add up exactly due to rounding.
Source: The Alan Guttmacher Institute

The stunning 33 percent decline in teen pregnancy rates between 1991 and 2000 appears to have been driven as much by teens' concerns about STDs as their fear of becoming pregnant, a recent CDC study suggests. According to the analysis, delaying the age of first intercourse and improved contraceptive use both contributed equally to the drop in teen pregnancy. The proportion of teenagers who ever had sexual intercourse by the time they finished high school dropped from 51 percent in 1991 to 43 percent in 2001. [10]

Abstinence advocates credit this trend at least in part to "virginity pledges," a church-led movement in which teens pledge publicly to abstain from sex until marriage. But a recent study found that teens who took the pledge had the same rate of STDs and pregnancy as those who didn't, probably because they were less likely to use contraception the first time they had sex and less likely to seek medical treatment. (*See sidebar, p. 84.*) [11]

Sarah Brown, director of the National Campaign to Prevent Teen Pregnancy, suggests that abstinence has become increasingly cool because of the way it's portrayed in the media. On TV, "You see hot characters saying 'No.' So I'm not surprised to see a few more young people delaying sexual activity."

Black Women Have Highest AIDS Rate

Experts are still trying to puzzle out why African-American straight women are contracting AIDS faster than any other demographic group. Black women are 23 times more likely to have AIDS than white women.

The Centers for Disease Control and Prevention (CDC) suggests that the higher rate of poverty among blacks might contribute to the higher infection rates, because poverty limits access to the quality health care that could help prevent progression of the disease.

In addition, black men in heterosexual relationships may be more likely to secretly engage in risky anal sex — known as sex "on the down low" — with other men than white men. A higher percentage of black males have used intravenous drugs and spent time in prison, where they are likely to be exposed to anal sex, increasing their risk of contracting HIV. [1]

Finally, black men and women have the highest sexually transmitted disease (STD) rates of any ethnic group in the nation. Compared to whites, blacks are 20 times more likely to have gonorrhea and five times more likely to have syphilis. [2] Open sores caused by STDs like herpes can serve as an entry point for HIV, and the presence of certain STDs can increase the chances of contracting HIV by three- to fivefold, according to recent studies. Similarly a person infected with both HIV and another STD has a greater chance of spreading HIV to other sexual partners.

---

[1] See, Jon Cohen, "A Silent Epidemic," www.slate.com, Oct. 27, 2004.

[2] CDC, "STD Surveillance 2003," www.cdc.gov.

Sex education advocates forecast doom as programs preaching abstinence-until-marriage proliferate with the prod of greatly expanded federal funding under the Bush administration. Such programs are not permitted to instruct students about condoms or contraception except to discuss their failure rates.

"There's a real danger that many people are not getting the information they need to protect themselves against sexually transmitted diseases," says Cynthia Dailard, senior public policy associate at the Alan Guttmacher Institute, a private research organization in New York, who has surveyed sex education in the schools.

Abstinence advocates argue that condoms are not 100 percent effective against all STDs, as abstinence is, and that teaching kids about the benefits of condoms gives them a mixed moral message about premarital sex.

It's like an anti-drug program that says, "Here are the drugs just in case you decide to do it," argues Leslee Unruh, executive director of the Abstinence Clearinghouse, a private group in Sioux Falls, S.D., that promotes abstinence education. "We've been doing sex education in our schools for almost 30 years, and what's happened?" she asks, noting that the variety of sexually transmitted diseases has proliferated over that period.

The evaluations Brown's organization has sponsored have so far found no abstinence program to be effective in reducing risky behavior. But she is skeptical that teenage ignorance is a real danger in an age when teens spend more time in front of the computer and TV than in school. "A lot of us underestimate the number of sources young people draw on for information," she says.

As President Bush begins his second term with a strengthened mandate, here are some of the issues being debated in Congress, the schools and the media:

Should abstinence be the sole focus of sex education?

There's little dispute that avoiding sex is the only 100 percent certain way to avoid getting a sexually transmitted disease. But the question is whether educational programs designed to convey this message almost exclusively are successful in reducing both intercourse and risky sexual behavior that exposes teens to infection.

The most rigorous evaluations have not found a single abstinence-only program that is effective in reducing the kind of behavior that leads to STDs. In May 2001, a National Campaign to Prevent Teen Pregnancy report concluded that programs that emphasized abstinence as the best and safest approach but that also stressed using protection against pregnancy and STDs were the most effective in reducing teen pregnancy or reducing risky sexual behavior. The widely publicized report was backed up by a research task force that included outspoken advocates of abstinence-only education, such as Texas ob-gyn Joe S. McIlhaney, Jr., president of the Austin-based pro-abstinence Medical Institute for Sexual Health and a member of the Presidential Advisory Council on HIV/AIDS, as well as representatives from groups that favor contraceptive education, such as the Guttmacher Institute — the former research arm of Planned Parenthood. [12]

According to report author Douglas Kirby, senior research scientist at ETR Associates in Scotts Valley, Calif., so-called "abstinence-plus" programs were effective in producing four types of changes in behavior known to lower the risk of STDs:

- delaying first intercourse;
- reducing the number of sex partners;
- reducing the frequency of sex, or
- increasing condom use.

The most impressive results came from an after-school program that provides tutoring, counseling and medical services in addition to sexuality education. The program, run by the Children's Aid Society in New York City, delayed the date of first intercourse and reduced pregnancy rates among girls by 50 percent. Participants in the program were also more likely than a comparison group to be vaccinated for hepatitis B, which can be sexually transmitted. (*See sidebar, p. 80.*)

Blacks Have Highest Gonorrhea Rate

Gonorrhea rates among African-Americans are 20 times higher than rates among whites and 9 times higher than rates for Hispanics. The higher rates are most likely due to differences in access to prevention and treatment services. A bacterial infection curable with antibiotics, gonorrhea most easily infects adolescent girls because of changes in the cervix due to puberty. Public health officials warn of growing problems with drug-resistant gonorrhea.

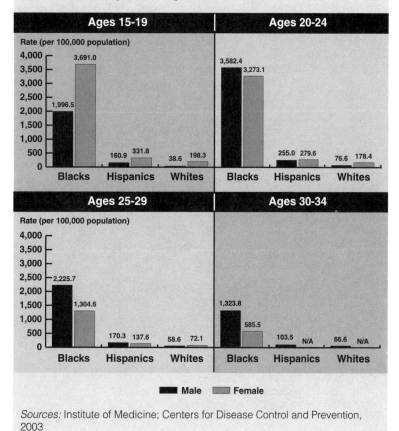

Sources: Institute of Medicine; Centers for Disease Control and Prevention, 2003

But none of the abstinence-only programs Kirby studied produced those kinds of results. "I'm in the process of doing an international search and have not found any abstinence-only programs that delay the initiation of sex," Kirby says of studies of sex-education curricula. "That is not to say they do not work; it's mostly due to the fact that there are very few studies that meet reasonable criteria. So the jury is still out."

Advocates of abstinence education reject the conclusion that abstinence-only programs are ineffective. But they do acknowledge that so far there have been only a

handful of studies that meet the most rigorous research standard: assigning students randomly to a group that receives the program and a control group that does not.

According to Robert Rector, senior research fellow at the conservative Heritage Foundation in Washington, D.C., a number of programs show results that are not statistically significant "but close." Rector, who has conducted his own survey of sex-education studies, says, "Certainly by the time we get as many studies as we have on the other side, abstinence is going to look pretty good."

Common STDs and Their Outcomes

STD	Symptoms	Curable	Long-Term Outcomes
Chlamydia	Women usually have no symptoms; men may have a penile discharge.	Yes.	In women, may cause pelvic inflammatory disease (PID), which can lead to infertility, tubal pregnancy and chronic pain. In men, may cause scrotal infection. In infants, may cause eye and lung infections.
Genital herpes	May cause no symptoms, or itching, irritation or painful blisters. The disease is chronic, so symptoms can recur with subsequent outbreaks.	No. Medicines can help manage outbreaks.	Most cases are mild. If a woman acquires herpes during pregnancy, the virus can be life-threatening for the infant.
Gonorrhea	Women usually have no symptoms; men may have a penile discharge.	Yes. But new strains are becoming antibiotic-resistant	In women, may cause PID, which can lead to infertility, tubal pregnancy and chronic pain. In men, may cause scrotal infection.
Hepatitis B	May cause no symptoms, or "yellow jaundice" or abdominal problems.	No. Can be prevented with a vaccine.	May lead to liver cancer and sometimes death.
HIV/AIDS	HIV may cause no symptoms but may progress to AIDS. In AIDS, the body's immune system is compromised, so it cannot fight off many infections and cancers.	No. Medicines may extend life.	Opportunistic infections and cancers may lead to death. Pregnant women may transmit HIV to the fetus or infant.
Human papillomavirus (HPV)	Untreated, some HPV types may lead to cervical abnormalities or genital warts.	No, but the immune system may suppress or eliminate the virus.	Untreated, some HPV types may lead to cervical cancer or genital warts. Pap testing can usually detect cervical disease in time to prevent cancer. Genital warts can be treated.
Syphilis	Painless sores and rashes that go away without treatment.	Yes.	Untreated, may cause serious neurological, cardiac and other diseases, or death. Increases risk of contracting or transmitting HIV. In pregnancy, can lead to severe abnormalities or death of infant.
Trichomoniasis	In women, may cause heavy discharge and genital irritation. Men may have no symptoms.	Yes.	Could have no long-term consequences; may cause adverse pregnancy outcomes.

Source: J. R. Cates, *et al.*, "Our Voices, Our Lives, Our Futures: Youth and Sexually Transmitted Diseases," School of Journalism and Mass Communication, University of North Carolina at Chapel Hill, 2004

Abstinence advocates also argue that abstinence-plus curricula contain very little emphasis on abstinence, "other than a random sentence or two which says, 'The safest thing you can do is abstain; now let's talk about where to get your condoms,' " according to Rector. A Heritage Foundation analysis of nine programs described by Kirby as abstinence-plus concluded that only 4.7 percent of the curricula's content discusses abstinence compared to 71 percent in an "authentic" abstinence program. [13]

"There's no moral message that says, 'We really want you to abstain' even through high school — or even until marriage," Rector maintains. "They have a lot of content that's nearly pornographic; it's just completely outrageous and unacceptable to most parents."

If traditional sex education is so successful, asks Unruh of the Abstinence Clearinghouse, why is there such a high rate of STDs among teens?

"We continue to promote sex and sex education in the schools and make the kids feel like there's something wrong with them if they're not having sex; that's why," she says, answering her own question.

"There's no such thing as responsible sex outside of marriage," she stresses, echoing the prime warning of abstinence educators. "If you are a person having sex outside marriage, a condom may break or may come off; you may be allergic to latex. HPV [human papillomavirus] is caused by skin-to-skin contact; a condom will not protect against that."

Unruh's statement that condoms won't protect against HPV is only partially correct. According to the American Social Health Association (ASHA), "Using condoms consistently and correctly can reduce the risk of getting HPV-related diseases such as genital warts and cervical cell abnormalities. However condoms do not protect against all genital areas and therefore, cannot completely prevent the spread of HPV." [14]

Statements like Unruh's about HPV are actually dangerous, because they leave out or distort important information teens need to protect themselves, public health experts say. In a recent review of abstinence-until-marriage programs around the country, the Sexual Information and Education Council of the United States (SIECUS), a private group in New York that advocates contraceptive instruction in the schools, charged that the programs are "based on religious beliefs, rely on fear and shame, omit important information, include inaccurate information and present stereotypes and biases as fact." [15]

As an example, SIECUS cites this statement from the abstinence-only FACTS * curricula, which is taught in Arizona, Nebraska, Oregon and Utah: "You know people talk about you behind your back because you have had sex with so many people. . . . Finally you get sick of it and commit suicide." [16]

Concerns have heightened with the expansion of federally funded programs that bar any mention of contraception except to discuss failure rates. "Our tradition of commitment to truth-telling makes those programs immoral," says the Rev. Debra Haffner, a Unitarian-

Universalist minister and director of the Religious Institute, which represents 2,300 religious leaders from more than 40 denominations in the United States that support sexuality education. [17]

Some experts are disturbed by the psychological effects such programs could have on teens. "What does it mean to sit in a classroom and be told to be abstinent after you've already had sex? How does that help you?" asks Deborah L. Tolman, professor of Human Sexuality Studies at San Francisco State University and author of the 2002 book *Dilemmas of Desire: Teenage Girls Talk about Sexuality*.

"I have concerns about a lot of the abstinence programs, because the ultimate result is going to be a generation that's terrified of sexuality, unable to embrace their sexuality. At what point does it become a good thing, and how do you make yourself and your body go from bad to good?" asks Tolman, observing that many people don't get married until their mid- to late-20s, and 90 percent will have had intercourse by age 20.

Abstinence advocates counter that their message does not prevent teenagers from getting information about contraception and protection about STDs in other ways. "Most kids get several hits of sex education" in health and science classes, maintains Rector, including information about contraception. But he says "on the three days that they're taught about abstinence, do you also want them to be taught about contraception? An abstinence provider would say that's the worst thing you could do — to send a very strong mixed message at that point."

Counters Tolman: "If you take abstinence-only money, you can't talk about contraception anywhere in the school." Of Rector's assertion that kids will get sex education in other classes, she says, "It's an acknowledgement of the profound need for the information and the sense of responsibility ultimately for public education to provide the information."

But the Campaign to Prevent Teen Pregnancy's Brown cautions against dismissing abstinence-only sex education. "The Bush administration has tapped into a widely shared value: Most people would prefer teenagers not to have sex in middle school or high school." She adds, "The idea that nobody can get teens to delay first intercourse with a strong abstinence-only program doesn't strike me as reasonable."

An answer should be forthcoming in the next three to four years, after ongoing evaluations of abstinence-only programs funded by the federal government are completed.

---

* Family Accountability Communicating Teen Sexuality.

Syphilis Poses New Threat

A recent rise in syphilis cases among gay men is raising concern that the trend may signal a return to promiscuous, unprotected sex and possibly to a new surge in sexually transmitted diseases (STDs) reaching beyond the gay community.

Although the number of new syphilis cases remains relatively low — about 7,000 new cases a year — recent studies suggest that syphilis is on the rise for the third consecutive year. And more than 60 percent of syphilis cases in 2003 occurred among men who have sex with men, researchers at the Centers for Disease Control and Prevention (CDC) estimate. [1]

"There's a lot of concern this may be a warning signal that risky behavior in subsets of gay men may be increasing, potentially leading to increasing rates of HIV transmission," says John Douglas, director of the CDC's Division of STD Prevention.

Untreated syphilis can cause serious neurological, cardiac and other diseases. It also increases the risk of getting or transmitting HIV. In pregnancy, syphilis can lead to severe infant abnormalities or even death.

Use of the illegal recreational drug crystal methamphetamine and the prescription impotence drug Viagra appears to be fueling increases not only in syphilis but also in HIV and other STDs among gay men, according to CDC

researchers. When crystal meth users get high from the drug, they are twice as likely as non-users to engage in anal intercourse without a condom. Condoms are protective against both HIV and syphilis. [2]

Now that anti-retroviral therapy has made living with HIV possible, some experts speculate that complacency about HIV may be behind the increases in unsafe sex.

"People without HIV are saying, "I see these people [treated with anti-retroviral therapy] walking around, climbing mountains and looking great; maybe I don't need to be so worried anymore," Douglas suggests.

The annual number of new HIV infections in the United States appears to have stabilized during the 1990s to about 40,000 new infections each year, a significant decrease from more than 150,000 cases a year in the mid-1980s. Still, King K. Holmes, director of the Center for AIDS and STD at the University of Washington, Seattle, notes that "40,000 cases a year of a fatal disease is disastrous."

---

[1] CDC press release from 2004 National STD Prevention Conference, "New U.S. Data Show Fewer Americans Have Herpes but Rates of Other Sexually Transmitted Diseases High," March 8, 2004.

[2] "Viagra, Methamphetamine, Internet Use Linked to Increase in Number of Syphilis, HIV Cases Among MSM, Studies Say," *Kaiser Daily HIV/AIDS Report*, March 11, 2004. at www.kff.org.

Is the United States doing enough to prevent STDs?

The values war over abstinence also has invaded the nation's public health campaign to prevent STDs. For years, a central message of government health campaigns has been that condoms are a crucial weapon in the war against HIV and other STDs. But in the last two years, social conservatives have claimed that condoms are not very effective against sexually transmitted diseases and have pressed federal agencies to adopt this viewpoint, sometimes successfully.

For example, until recently a CDC Web page said that education about condom use did not lead young people to earlier or increased sexual activity, a statement that conflicted with the views of abstinence-only advocates. In October 2002, however, the CDC dropped that information, which was based on several studies, from a revised version of its online fact sheet about condoms. It also dropped

instructions on condom use and specific information on the effectiveness of different types of condoms. [18]

The revised fact sheet posted on the Web site emphasizes condom failure rates and the effectiveness of abstinence, beginning in boldface: "The surest way to avoid transmission of sexually transmitted diseases is to abstain from sexual intercourse or to be in a long-term mutually monogamous relationship with a partner who has been tested and you know is uninfected. . . . [C]ondom use cannot guarantee absolute protection against any STD." [19]

The Democratic staff of the House Government Reform Committee has charged these revisions were made under pressure from conservative Republicans. "Under the Bush administration, scientific evidence on the effectiveness of condoms has been suppressed or distorted" in support of the claim that condoms are not very effective in preventing sexually transmitted diseases, charges the staff

Web site sponsored by Rep. Henry A. Waxman, ranking California Democrat on the committee. [20]

Conservatives like Rep. Mark Souder, R-Ind., have focused their criticism on HPV, a common STD that can lead to cervical cancer in a small percentage of women. Because HPV is transmitted by skin-to-skin contact and because condoms do not cover all the areas of skin where HPV manifests itself — in genital warts, for example — they may not provide the same protection as they do against STDs transmitted by bodily fluids, according to the CDC. [21]

A law authored by former Rep. Tom Coburn, R-Okla., and signed by President Bill Clinton days before leaving office in 2001 requires the CDC and the Food and Drug Administration (FDA) to inform the public about the "effectiveness of condoms to protect against HPV" and "to determine if condom labels are medically accurate."

"Nearly 5,000 women die every year in the U.S. as a result of HPV-related cancers, and millions more are treated for other health conditions related to HPV infection," Souder says. "This is a serious health issue, and Congress passed and President Clinton signed the HPV prevention law four years ago specifically because FDA and CDC had failed to properly address it. These agencies continue to thumb their nose at Congress and undermine their own scientific integrity and — most importantly — the health of the public with their continued cover-up of the HPV epidemic."

In March, Souder called hearings to confront the CDC and FDA with his contention that the agencies had not complied with the law. A fact sheet from his office claims that government Web sites "continue to omit" medically accurate information, including "the lack of effectiveness of condoms in preventing infection." He also charges that the FDA has yet to rewrite condom labels to ensure that they "reflect the effectiveness or lack of effectiveness in preventing HPV and other STDs." [22]

But as news reports noted at the time of the hearings, this debate is as much about ideology — premarital abstinence vs. condom use — as it is about preventing disease. [23]

"People like Rep. Souder are taking this small piece of the puzzle and running with it, saying condoms don't work . . . instead of saying condoms are really good at preventing HIV and other diseases," said Julie Davids, executive director of CHAMP, a New York-based HIV/AIDS organization that cosponsored a March rally protesting the Souder hearings. [24]

A member of the U.S. teen-celibacy group Silver Ring Thing waits for customers at its merchandise table at a church in Claygate, England, during the group's tour of the United Kingdom. Abstinence advocates credit stunning declines in teen pregnancy rates in recent years in part to "virginity pledges" until marriage.

As evidence of condoms' alleged ineffectiveness, for example, the Abstinence Clearinghouse in its promotional materials prominently cites a 2001 study by the National Institutes of Health, which concluded, "There is no scientific evidence that condoms prevent the transmission of most sexually transmitted disease, including chlamydia, syphilis, chancroid, trichomoniasis, genital herpes and HPV." [25]

What it doesn't say is that the study found strong evidence for condoms' effectiveness against HIV and gonorrhea. And a January 2004 CDC report notes that there is evidence that condom use may actually reduce the risk of cervical cancer, public health advocates note. [26]

"If we want to beat cervical cancer, we must focus on making sure all women have access to cervical cancer screening and follow-up care instead of turning cervical cancer into an excuse to disparage condoms," said James R. Allen, president and CEO of ASHA.

"Scaring sexually active individuals away from using condoms will not reduce the prevalence of HPV," says Theresa Raphael, executive director of the National Coalition of STD Directors. "Instead, it will put millions of Americans at risk of contracting a range of preventable STDs."

As for the other diseases, the study was inconclusive. "Scientifically, this is an enormously difficult thing to

CHRONOLOGY

1940s-1950s *Penicillin contributes to aggressive public health treatment of venereal disease.*

1941 Penicillin becomes the first modern antibiotic found effective against bacterial infections.

1946 Early-stage syphilis peaks in U.S. at 94,957 cases.

1956 Drop to 6,392 cases of syphilis spurs reduction in funding for public health treatment.

1960s-1970s *Complacency about venereal disease leads to resurgence; birth control pill, sexual revolution and gay liberation movement increase promiscuous sexual behavior.*

1961 Early-stage syphilis cases nearly triple from low point in mid-1950s.

1962 Food and Drug Administration (FDA) approves birth control pill.

1969 Riot at gay Stonewall Bar in New York City's Greenwich Village marks beginning of gay rights movement.

1980s *AIDS (Acquired Immune Deficiency Syndrome) discovered in gay men; spreads to intravenous (IV) drug users; chlamydia rises; gonorrhea rates decline; U.S. government begins campaign against AIDS; syphilis rates climb in minorities, fueled by crack cocaine epidemic.*

1981 Centers for Disease Control (CDC) reports rare form of pneumonia in five gay men, later determined to be AIDS; program to promote teen chastity begun under Adolescent and Family Life Act.

1982 AIDS officially recognized by CDC.

1983 CDC adds female sex partners of men with AIDS as risk group.

1984 HIV (Human Immune Deficiency Virus) isolated as cause of AIDS.

1987 AZT, the first anti-retroviral drug against AIDS, comes on the market.

1990s *AIDS deaths peak, then fall with new therapy; sexual behavior in U.S. becomes less risky following public health campaigns; federal government expands sexual-abstinence programs.*

1992 AIDS becomes No.1 cause of death in U.S. for men ages 25-44.

1995 FDA approves first protease inhibitor, ushering in new era of highly effective anti-retroviral AIDS therapy.

1996 Welfare reform act signed into law, funding states for new abstinence-until-marriage initiative; number of new AIDS cases declines for first time, but AIDS remains leading cause of death for African-Americans ages 25-44.

1997 AIDS deaths decline by more than 40 percent over previous year due to anti-retroviral therapy.

1998 First large-scale human trials for HIV vaccine begin.

2000s *AIDS begins infecting large numbers of women; President Bush expands funding for abstinence, worldwide AIDS program; scientists make breakthroughs in developing HPV (human papillomavirus) vaccine.*

October 2001 Bush administration creates third grant program for abstinence education.

2002 U.N. reports women comprise half of all adults with HIV/AIDS.

Jan. 28, 2003 Bush announces $15 billion plan for AIDS relief overseas during his State of the Union address.

2004 Bush global AIDS program begins first round of funding. . . . In October GlaxoSmithKline announces it will bring HPV vaccine to market in 2006 . . . . On Nov. 20, Congress passes omnibus spending bill increasing abstinence funding for fourth consecutive year. . . . On Nov. 23, U.N. reports a record 39.4 million people are living with AIDS worldwide and that the number of women with HIV/AIDS is increasing throughout world.

study; people aren't guinea pigs; you can't put people in cages and expose them to STDs with and without condom use," explains John Douglas, director of the CDC's Division of STD Prevention. He notes that more recent studies have found condoms reduce the risk of herpes and chlamydia. While "condoms are not perfect, "he says," it's quite clear that the absence of their use is worse than using them imperfectly."

When asked about the CDC's new abstinence emphasis and removal of condom information from in its Web site, Douglas sounds like a government official caught between a rock and a hard place. "I feel the fact sheet we have up there is an accurate fact sheet; it does take more pains to point out the imperfections of condoms than previous fact sheets." As for the impact of the controversy over condoms' effectiveness, he says, "I don't have any data that condom use has diminished because of that, but we have lots of concerns that it could be."

Ideally, the best way to prevent sexually transmitted diseases would be to develop vaccines. The only STD for which a vaccine is currently available is hepatitis B. The recent flu vaccine crisis has demonstrated that the nation can no longer rely on pharmaceutical companies to develop vaccines, some researchers argue, because the profit margins just aren't big enough. Vaccines against HPV and herpes are currently in the final phase of clinical trials.

"Pharmaceutical companies don't want to invest in something that would be high-risk for liability and low-risk for profitability," says Willard "Ward" Cates Jr., president and CEO of the Institute for Family Health, Family Health International in Research Triangle Park, N.C., which has conducted research to bring new contraceptive products to market. He says his organization has not been able to find a pharmaceutical company to underwrite similar research efforts in the area of HIV and genital herpes vaccines.

Given the industry's lack of interest, the federal government should step up to the plate and fund special research institutes around the country to develop vaccines against STDs, argues Lawrence Corey, professor of medicine at the University of Washington in Seattle and principal investigator in HIV vaccine trials funded by the National Institutes of Health (NIH).

"There's no culture that has controlled an STD without a vaccine," contends Corey. In the case of genital herpes, for example, 22 percent of the population has it, according to one recent study Corey cites, but 95 percent of those who

A mobile AIDS testing lab waits for customers on a busy street in Los Angeles last spring. The number of new HIV infections in the United States appears to have stabilized during the 1990s to about 40,000 new infections each year, down from more than 150,000 cases a year in the mid-1980s.

have it don't know it. Consequently, "You can't screen and test everybody," Corey says. But work on developing a herpes vaccine has been extremely slow. The third pharmaceutical company to work with Corey's group on a herpes vaccine recently dropped out, he says, "because the risk is high and the amount of capital they can put into it is low."

The NIH is currently sponsoring a large clinical trial of a herpes vaccine that appears to work in women, but not men. So even if this trial proves successful after three or four years, it's not the ultimate solution, Corey observes.

Of course, the kind of commitment that Corey is talking about would take a lot more federal funding. In the world of medical researchers, "You get a grant for $350,000 it's a big grant; $1 million is a huge grant," says Corey. By contrast, he notes, "If a company is doing vaccine development, it's 5, 8, 10 million dollars a year." Today's limited government funding means that vaccine development will be slower than if the government made a big commitment, he argues. Worldwide, barely 20 researchers are working on a herpes vaccine, Corey estimates. "What kind of a commitment is that?" he asks.

HIV vaccine research has more generous government funding and more interest from pharmaceutical companies than other STDs partly because HIV is fatal, while most other STDs are not. Corey's group is starting a trial this month in cooperation with drug maker Merck, which will be the first to test the efficacy of a vaccine for

This Sex-Education Program Works

Joel, a high school senior with a mop of curly black hair, wears hip-hop-style jeans favored by many teenagers in Washington Heights, a low-income New York City neighborhood heavily populated with Dominican immigrants.

But unlike many of his peers, he plans to apply for college. He also has a different attitude about sex than most of his buddies. "I'd like to try it, but if I get a girl pregnant, I don't know what I would do. I'm putting it on pause," Joel says, adding that he plans to wait to have sex until he is 18 or 19 — "when I'm more mature." (Joel is a pseudonym.)

Since the sixth grade, Joel has participated every day after school in a sexuality-education program run by the Children's Aid Society, a curriculum used at several schools around the country. It is the nation's most successful program for reducing teen sex and pregnancy, according to a three-year study of 600 children — half in the program and half randomly assigned to a control group. Girls in the program had one-third of the pregnancies and half as many births as the comparison group. Teens in the program, who are mainly minority and low-income, also waited until they were older to have sex for the first time and used contraceptives more conscientiously when they did have sex. [1]

"Paradoxically, we are the only proven program that has abstinence-only results but we can get no money from the federal government," observes the program's founder, Michael A. Carrera, director of the National Adolescent Sexuality Training Center at Children's Aid. The program is ineligible for federal funding because it instructs teens in the importance of condoms and birth control and also pro-vides contraceptives as part of its comprehensive package of medical and dental services.

The program has not had a single case of HIV in its 20 years, according to Carrera. The rate of other STDs has not been evaluated, but teens in the program were more likely to have received a hepatitis B vaccine. Boys also were more likely to make regular medical visits and discuss sexual health with a doctor, according to Jackie Williams Kaye, who co-directed the evaluation for Philliber Research Associates in New York.

Carrera said he developed his comprehensive approach because, after decades as a traditional sex-education teacher, he felt that his message wasn't really sticking with kids. "What I learned," Carrera says, "was that I was separating it from all the other things that make a kid whole" — most significantly, their hopes for the future.

Joel, for example, is getting preparation for the future that includes one-on-one tutoring to prepare him for the manda-tory state graduation test; visits to colleges; and meetings with a college adviser — all services supplied by the program.

"When young people feel there's hope in the future and possibilities, then they themselves will take many of the steps to avoid the risks," Carrera maintains. One indication may be that 61 percent of the program's high school grad-uates enrolled in college, compared to 39 percent of their peers from similar backgrounds.

But not everyone is convinced the program is a success. "Carrera believes kids will be sexually active and that it's pointless to spend much effort trying to teach them to delay," says Robert Rector, senior research fellow at the

HIV based on T-cell responses, currently seen as a highly promising approach. But the HIV vaccine search has run into failure before and remains a difficult scientific prob-lem. As a result most medical researchers, who survive by applying for grants based on past successes, are reluctant to devote themselves to it full time, he says.

"If you put people full time in a risky venture, you've got to give them some job security. You can't continue to have negative data; no one will keep on funding you," Corey says. "So you've got to be like a broker; you diver-sify your portfolio so you can have a success. But that's not the best way to make a vaccine. So we have a lot of people spending 25 percent of their time on it; it would move a lot quicker if we had people spending 100 per-cent of their time on it."

Researchers like Cates say STDs have been the poor stepchild of HIV ever since HIV was recognized as the most serious global disease. "You have HIV getting bil-lions of dollars and STDs tens of millions of dollars," he estimates, even though herpes causes premature death in infants, and untreated HPV can lead to cervical cancer in women. Moreover, having an STD can increase the risk of HIV transmission. "Is it fatal? No. Is it serious? Absolutely," he says.

conservative Heritage Foundation, who favors preaching abstinence.

Carrera also prefers that kids delay sex, but adds, "Look, if our own children decided, against whatever we said, that they were going to do something their own way, we would make sure they wouldn't get hurt or hurt somebody else," by providing contraceptives.

However, the dramatic drops in unintended pregnancies were not replicated among the boys, leading Kaye to speculate that perhaps the boys were having sex with girls outside the program who were not getting its message.

Rector suggests the program's success with girls is "because they shoot the girls up with Depo-Provera," a contraceptive hormone. Kaye says fewer than a quarter of the girls in the program use the hormone, a rate that is admittedly higher than the Depo-Provera usage rate among their peers who are not in the program. Eighty-five percent of the teens in both groups used condoms.

Moreover, older teens who already have had sex are harder to engage, and boys who had already had sex were the

The Children's Aid Society's Millennium after-school sexuality program in New York City teaches about postponing sex and also using contraceptives.

least conscientious attendees and showed the least success, according to the evaluation. In response to that finding, the program has shifted its focus to including sixth- and seventh-graders, who are on the verge of puberty.

Can Carrera's success be replicated elsewhere? A similar program in Florida failed to achieve the same success, according to evaluator Douglas Kirby, senior research scientist at ETR Associates in Scotts Valley, Calif. But Carrera did not personally provide the training, Kirby says, adding, "Michael Carrera is very charismatic, and he certainly enters into the equation."

Carrera agrees, to some extent. The Florida program was not an exact replica of his approach, he says. He says that only 21 of the 50 programs in 20 states that claim to use his curriculum are exact replications. The others have not been able to raise enough money — $4,000 per child annually — to include all the services. But at $17 a day, Kaye says, it's a bargain for a program proven to work, compared to other highly regarded after-school programs.

[1] Children's Aid Society, "2001 Data," fact sheet on findings from evaluation by Philliber Research Associates. See Douglas Kirby, "Emerging Answers," May 2001, National Campaign to Prevent Teen Pregnancy, at www.teenpregnancy.org.

When it comes to prevention, years of inadequate flat funding at both federal and state levels (*see p. 89*) have forced numerous cutbacks in the public health system's ability to prevent STDs at clinics throughout the country, says Gail Bolan chair of the national Coalition of STD Directors and chief of the STD Control Branch at the California Department of Health Services.

In California, the number of publicly funded clinics that specialize in STDs has dwindled, and the health department has difficulty getting the word out to doctors about growing problems with drug-resistant gonorrhea, according to Bolan. With bioterrorism at the top of the

agenda, public health staff is increasingly diverted from routine public health problems like STDs, federal and state officials say.

Regarding inadequately funded STD prevention, the CDC's Douglas says, "We have a lot of social and health issues in this country and lots of choices to make, and those choices are getting tougher all the time. It's rare for any program to get to all the funding it needs to address the problem. STDs are not an exception. We're using the resources we have to reach those people at the greatest risk."

But he adds, "In this country we put greater priorities on the things we see than the things we don't see. The

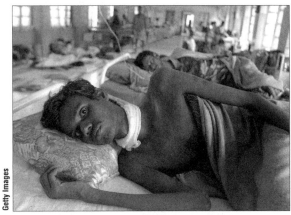

Men and women with HIV or AIDS crowd a hospital ward in India's Tamil Nadu state. President Bush's $15 billion plan to tackle AIDS overseas requires that one-third of the prevention funds be spent on encouraging abstinence. But several groups that battle AIDS overseas say that preaching abstinence to unmarried, sexually active teens in the developing world is pointless since adolescents often marry and have children.

public sees curative medicine in all of its glorious forms in a much clearer light than they do the background work of public health; clean water is not as sexy as organ transplants."

Some experts say the government should urge mass screening for STDs, especially when a patient has no symptoms. In the case of chlamydia, the CDC and other prominent medical organizations are now recommending that sexually active women up to age 25 be screened for chlamydia. But less than half of the nation's medical providers follow those guidelines. Experts say doctors feel uncomfortable suggesting a patient is sexually active or even promiscuous.

"I've had providers say, 'I don't have those kinds of patients in my practice,' " recalls Bolan.

Similarly, controversy continues about whether all adults should be tested routinely for herpes. "People concerned about the spread of herpes have been saying we have to do a better job of identifying people affected," says Charles Ebel, senior director of program development at ASHA.

"We have some blood tests that work well to identify HSV-2 [the most common type of genital herpes] with people who have ambiguous symptoms or are in situations suggestive of being at risk — because they have a past or present partner with herpes — but don't have symptoms," Ebel notes. "But a lot of people in clinical care don't want to have to identify someone and tell them they have an STD when the person ostensibly doesn't have any problem, because there's a social stigma associated with STDs and a certain psychological and social distress burden experienced by those diagnosed."

Proponents of mass screening point out that herpes affects one in five American adults, and open herpes sores can increase the risk of getting HIV. "It's not the most severe disease, but in the long term it could be important in controlling HIV rates and in minimizing neonatal infection because sometimes it is transmitted from mother to baby," Ebel says.

Similar issues have been raised when it comes to routinely running a DNA test that is now available to test for HPV, a mostly benign infection that in a small percentage of women can lead to cervical cancer later on. Running the test requires doctors to explain that HPV is sexually transmitted.

"If they have to go there with patients, they have to get into the whole sexual-history piece, which is complicated, time-consuming, sometimes embarrassing and relates back to the social stigma," Ebel says. "There's controversy about how much these DNA tests should be used and how much clinicians should be expected to bite off counseling about this."

"It's a total waste of money to get tested for strains of HPV," Cates argues, because HPV is so widespread. In the majority of cases, HPV goes away on its own without the patient even being aware she had it. "In this country, using the Pap smear as the main cancer control approach is the most cost-efficient, time-efficient way for clients to proceed."

Will President Bush's abstinence-only policy hurt the global effort to prevent AIDS?

President Bush's five-year, $15 billion plan to tackle AIDS overseas requires that one-third of the prevention funds be spent on encouraging abstinence. The Global AIDS bill, the legal mandate for the strategy, would provide a minimum of $133 million annually to abstinence-until-marriage programs in 15 countries. The administration points to Uganda's stunning success in reducing HIV as the justification, saying it wishes to replicate its approach.

In the most dramatic decline seen in any country, Uganda's HIV prevalence decreased from a peak of 15 percent of the population in 1991 to 5 percent in 2001. Most experts attribute that drop to the high-visibility campaign waged personally by President Yoweri K. Museveni known as ABC — in which A stands for abstinence, B stands for Be faithful and C stands for condoms. [27]

William Shepherd Smith, president of the Institute for Youth Development, a pro-abstinence group in Sterling, Va., says he has traveled to African countries like Mozambique, where HIV rates have been as high as 40 percent among young people. "The message we saw was condoms, condoms and more condoms," an approach he says was failing. By contrast, he says, the answer in Uganda was to get young people to wait till marriage to have sex. "It wasn't ABC take your pick; it was A to young people, B to couples and C 'If you don't have self control, yes use a condom,' " with condoms particularly targeted to promiscuous groups like prostitutes and truck drivers.

Indeed, a video about Uganda made by Sterling's group emphasizes the role of abstinence and plays down the role of condoms, quoting Harvard medical anthropologist Edward Green saying, "Rates were coming down in 1993, and very few people were using condoms." Smith says in the video, "Much of the message to young people is about character development, about making the right choices in life." [28]

The abstinence emphasis of Bush's program, which also plans to rely heavily on faith-based groups, smacks of religion to some critics, who say the administration is neglecting the important role of condoms. Deborah Arrindell, senior director of health policy at ASHA, calls the policy "exporting ideology."

William Smith, director of public policy at SIECUS, charges, "These funds are going to missionary groups that haven't done public health in these countries; so again, the Bush administration is building up an entire new industry to promote an ideology of marriage promotion just like they've done here."

Several groups that work with AIDS in the developing world say the concept of preaching abstinence to unmarried, sexually active teens is a supremely American idea. "It's not valid for millions of adolescents in the developing world, because they're married. In the developing world, teen pregnancy is a concept that occurs within marriage," says Geeta Rao Gupta, president of the International Center for Research on Women (ICRW)

in Washington, D.C., a private research organization. [29] Married women are the fastest-growing group of people being infected with HIV in India, which will soon outpace South Africa as the country with the world's highest infection rate. [30] In fact, marriage does not appear to be a protective factor in these countries as abstinence advocates often assume.

"Young married girls are more likely to be HIV-positive than their unmarried peers because they have sex more often, use condoms less often, are unable to refuse sex and have partners who are more likely to be HIV-positive," according to a report by ICRW citing research in Kenya and Zambia. [31] Young women are expected to prove their fertility quickly once married and rarely have the social status to insist that their husbands abstain or put on a condom, Gupta points out.

Experts at the Alan Guttmacher Institute argue that all three components of ABC were important in reducing Uganda's HIV rates. The abstinence message appears to have had a strong impact on young people. The median age at which young women began having sex rose from 15.9 in 1988 to 16.3 in 1995.

But experts now think a reduction in partners may be the most important behavior change. The "Be Faithful" message produced increasing levels of monogamy among sexually active men and women of all ages; the unmarried particularly were less likely to have more than one sexual partner in 1995 than in 1989. Condom use rose steeply among unmarried sexually active men — from 2 percent in 1989 to 22 percent in 1995. [32]

In Zambia, where HIV rates also appear to be declining among urban youth, The Guttmacher Institute gives much of the credit to a program that promotes both abstinence and condom use, noting that young people exposed to a U.S. Agency for International Development-funded media campaign are 67 percent more likely to have used a condom than those not exposed.

A field study published earlier this year charges that the administration's Global AIDS program puts excessive emphasis on abstinence and discriminates against any group that provides information on safe abortion. The United States "is prohibiting organizations from providing condoms or condom information," said Jodi Jacobson, executive director of the Center for Health and Gender Equity, an international reproductive health and rights organization based in Takoma Park, Md., which authored the study. [33]

Do Virginity Pledges Reduce STD Risks?

Lifeway Christian Resources, the world's largest provider of religious products, initiated a movement in 1993 called "True Love Waits," which encourages adolescents to pledge to abstain from sex until marriage. The goal: follow "God's plan for purity." [1] Within two years, an estimated 2.2 million teens — 12 percent of all American adolescents — had taken the pledge, often in church-sponsored gatherings.

In 2000, the first study of the sexual behavior of virginity pledgers found that they waited 18 months longer than non-pledgers to have their first sexual intercourse, had fewer sexual partners and married earlier. [2] Advocates of the faith-based approach to reducing teen pregnancy seized on the results as proof that the program works to both reduce pregnancy and sexually transmitted diseases (STDs).

But Columbia University sociology Professor Peter Bearman, who conducted the survey, found just the opposite when he did a follow-up study with more than 11,000 pledgers between the ages of 18 and 24. [3]

Urine samples revealed that pledgers were just as likely to have sexually transmitted diseases as non-pledgers. Communities in which at least 20 percent of teens had been pledgers had higher rates of STDs than other communities, according to the study. The study also found that pledgers were less likely to use condoms the first time they had inter-course, and were less likely to have ever been tested for an STD or to have seen a doctor over worry about an STD.

Bearman speculates that if teens are breaking their public virginity pledges, they will hide the fact. In addition, there will probably be less discussion of sex and STDs among pledgers in schools with large numbers of pledgers.

"If they have burning urination, and there's no discussion in the peer community about what it means as an STD symptom, there's generalized ignorance," he suggests. Pledgers who remained virgins were also more likely to have oral and anal sex, which can increase teens' risk of acquiring STDs, the study found.

Public health officials are most concerned about untreated human papillomavirus (HPV), which affects 20-25 percent of girls in the age group studied. Untreated HPV cases can "facilitate cancer in early adulthood," Bearman notes.

Virginity-pledge advocates say Bearman's study doesn't represent their personal experience. "I've met these kids," says Leslee Unruh, director of the Abstinence Clearinghouse in Sioux Falls, S.D. "We had pictures of their weddings; we saw their purity rings."

She cites a study by Robert Rector, a senior research fellow at the conservative Heritage Foundation, which found that virginity pledgers are less likely to engage in unpro-

The organization contends that the Bush strategy limits condom use to narrowly defined "high risk" groups, including prostitutes and substance abusers. By so stigmatizing condoms, the group argues, it contributes to the perception that risk is something that only occurs outside of marriage. For example, in a recent survey of 300 HIV-positive married women in Zimbabwe, the majority of the women knew about HIV but did not insist on condom use with their husbands or partners because they thought that condom use was only for those who visited prostitutes. [34] Faith-based groups that receive U.S. funds may exclude information about contraceptive methods, including condoms, if such information is inconsistent with their religious beliefs, the group said.

Government officials have stated that abstinence will be only one part of a broad-based strategy and have denied the claims that the program is discriminating against groups that provide abortion. Since only 20 percent of the entire program is slated for prevention, the one-third devoted to abstinence represents a very small fraction of the entire effort, they say.

"To say that condoms alone are going to solve this problem is crazy," Mark Dybul, the plan's deputy chief medical officer, said in response to the recent study from the Center for Health and Gender Equity. "You need the full ABC message, which was really initiated by President Museveni of Uganda." [35]

In an interview earlier this year, the Bush administration's point man, Ambassador Randall L. Tobias, U.S. Global AIDS Coordinator, answered criticisms that some groups couldn't get access to funding because they wanted to emphasize condoms as a prevention approach. "The

tected sex or experience teen pregnancy. [4] Bearman calls that study "a nonsense analysis of our data" and says he found no difference in the pregnancy rate.

Rector counters that while it's true that pledgers aren't particularly good about using contraception the first time they have intercourse, over time they use protection at the same rates as non-pledgers. He says he has been unable to replicate Bearman's finding that teens who take the pledge have as high a rate of STDs as teens who don't.

Olympic champion Carl Lewis addresses a True Love Waits rally held during the 2004 summer Olympics in Athens, Greece.

Both sides agree, however, that delaying sex is beneficial from a developmental perspective. One out of five adolescents has sex before age 15, a trend that disturbs experts on both sides of the virginity divide. [5]

"A lot of kids have sex way before they're able to handle relationships and intimacy," Bearman agrees. But he stresses that the two big public health concerns — STDs and teen pregnancy — are not affected by virginity pledges and may even be exacerbated by them. "The pledge doesn't really help kids," he says.

[1] See www.lifeway.com.

[2] Peter S. Bearman and Hannah Bruckner, "Promising the Future: Virginity Pledges as They Affect Transition to First Intercourse," July 15, 2000.

[3] Peter Bearman and Hannah Bruckner, "After the Promise: The STD Consequences of Adolescent Virginity Pledges," Sept. 2, 2004. Forthcoming in the *Journal of Adolescent Health*.

[4] Robert Rector, *et al.*, "Teens Who Make Virginity Pledges Have Substantially Improved Life Outcomes," Heritage Foundation, Sept. 21, 2004.

[5] National Campaign to Prevent Teen Pregnancy, "14 and Younger: The Sexual Behavior of Young Adolescents," 2003, at www.teenpregnancy.org.

U.S. doesn't discourage that; we're buying as many condoms now as has ever been the case," he said. "But . . . the evidence really shows that condoms have never been effective anywhere in the world in curtailing broad-based general epidemics in the broad population." [36]

He added, "Changing behavior is what is really making the difference in Uganda and other places, and that means getting people to do two things: To delay the age at which they become sexually active, and then reducing the number of partners they have when they are sexually active."

Smith, of the Institute for Youth Development, argues that it's highly unlikely that public health officials will be able to persuade a man to wear a condom if he's irresponsible enough to be promiscuous. "Irresponsible men like them less," he says. "The better message to these same men is if you want to live and have a lot of sex, 'Reduce part-

ners.' " He adds that handing out condoms is "an absurd approach but the approach we've bought into because we don't want to give a moralistic message. We should have recognized that it was the right public health message — not a religious message — to reduce partners."

BACKGROUND

Early Anti-STD Efforts

Some sexually transmitted diseases, such as syphilis and gonorrhea, have been known for centuries while others, such as HIV, have only been identified in the past few decades. STDs are caused by more than 25 infectious organisms, and as more organisms are identified, the number of STDs continues to expand.

In the early part of the 20th century, syphilis was responsible for populating the mental hospitals with victims who suffered dementia and for the deaths of adults or babies (who caught it in utero).

The social hygiene movement of the early 1900s, which sought to unite moral cleanliness with health, tried to combat these deadly diseases by arguing that prostitution spread venereal disease, and by preaching the values of sexual abstinence and self-discipline. [37] In the 1930s many hospitals refused to admit patients with venereal disease because they considered the sufferers immoral, a lack of treatment that contributed to a growing epidemic. [38]

With the advent of penicillin in the 1940s, the control of the disease shifted from moralistic preaching to medical treatment. Syphilis can be cured by antibiotics in its early stages. If left untreated, late-stage syphilis can cause paralysis, blindness, dementia and death.

Beginning in the late 1940s and continuing through the early 1950s, aggressive national programs against syphilis succeeded in nearly eliminating early-stage syphilis in the United States. By the mid-1950s, the apparent success of the program led to sharp funding reductions for combating it. But within a few years of the funding reductions, the number of primary and secondary syphilis cases in the United States nearly tripled. [39]

"Historically, anytime we start to pat ourselves on the back and think control efforts have helped, the diseases come back," notes the university of Alabama's Hook. "In the U.S., we thought we eliminated syphilis three times, in 1997 most recently." But recent statistics indicate syphilis is on the rise again.

The sexual revolution that began in the 1960s with the birth control pill, gay liberation and the cocaine epidemic were all factors that contributed to an epidemic of STDs and the spread of HIV during the 1970s and '80s. In the United States and Britain, symptomatic genital herpes and genital warts increased up to 15-fold during the '70s and '80s. During the '70s, chlamydial infections became the most prevalent bacterial STD in the developed world. [40]

AIDS Leads to Restraint

AIDS first came to the attention of the health community in 1981, when CDC scientists reported a strange immune-system disorder in five homosexual men from Los Angeles. The following year, when new cases of the disease appeared in heterosexual women, drug users and Haitian immigrants, the CDC officially recognized it as a new disease and named it Acquired Immune Deficiency Syndrome (AIDS).

From the mid-1980s to the '90s, public health campaigns against HIV urged the use of condoms and the reduction of sexual partners. Sexual behavior over that period, especially among young people, became more moderate, with greater use of condoms and later initiation of sex. [41] The waning of the cocaine epidemic, which many believe helped fuel unprotected sex by loosening inhibitions, and improvements in diagnosing STDs also contributed to the decline of STDS and AIDS through this period.

For example, cases of gonorrhea, a bacterial infection curable with antibiotics, fell 59 percent between 1978 and 1994 through a combination of public health programs, safer sexual practices stemming from concerns about HIV and changes in contraceptive methods, according to the Institute of Medicine. [42] However, gonorrhea remained high among minorities and adolescents. [43]

In 1987, the first anti-AIDS drug, AZT, came on the market. The next big advance in AIDS treatment came in 1995 when drug companies released a new class of medicines known as protease inhibitors, ushering in the new era of highly effective anti-retroviral therapy. Researchers found that protease inhibitors were most effective when patients were given a cocktail of three or four types at a time. Since then, the FDA has approved other drugs to be given in combination. Although not a cure, anti-retroviral therapy has permitted many people with AIDS to live longer, high-quality lives.

In 1997, an expert committee organized by the Institute of Medicine issued a report warning that STDs were "hidden epidemics" that represented "a growing threat to the nation's health." The committee estimated the annual direct and indirect cost of STDs, including HIV, was $17 billion. The committee singled out the social stigma attached to STDs and the resulting secrecy surrounding the subject as one of the primary obstacles to curbing the epidemic — both historically and today. [44] It noted that this view was particularly evident early in the AIDS epidemic, when some considered the disease a symbol of deviant sexual behavior. [45]

King K. Holmes, director of the Center for AIDS and STDs at the University of Washington and a member of the IOM Committee, worries that the abstinence-only movement is a return to the moralistic approach of old. "What we need is less of these simplistic approaches — abstinence only or condom only," he says. "We need

Is "abstinence-only" the best sex-education policy for schools to implement?

YES

Elizabeth Bradley
Math Teacher, Lewiston High School, Lewiston, Maine; 2000 Presidential Award Recipient

From National Education Association Web Site,
www.nea.org/neatoday/0302/debate.html

Consider this: "Good morning, class. Today we're going to talk about how to drive a car safely, even if you've been drinking. Now, it's really better not to drink and drive, because you might end up dead, but there are some ways to do it so that you cut your risk of becoming injured or dying."

The fact is that the true message sent by adults, the media, and the schools is the exact opposite: "Don't drink and drive." And we don't offer training in how to do it safely.

Now, let's change the scene just a little.

"Good morning, class. Today we're going to learn how to have safe sex (now referred to as 'safer sex' because safe sex doesn't really exist).

"We'll show you how to put a condom on a banana, and some other things you can do to minimize your risk of contracting an incurable disease, which may make you sterile (chlamydia), be a precursor to cervical cancer (HPV) or cause death (HIV).

"Oh, and you might end up pregnant. Then your choices are abortion ('one dead, one wounded,' to quote a recent bumper sticker), adoption (a lifelong hole in your heart), or parenthood (a 24/7 commitment that will make school, college, work, independence and emotional stability very difficult)."

Why can't we take the drinking-and-driving approach of "Just don't do it"? Statistics show that kids do care about what the adults in their lives have to say.

To me, teen promiscuity is in the same category as Russian roulette, and promoting safe sex is just handing them the gun.

If you knew that within the next 12 months your child would have a child, an incurable disease or be HIV positive, how far would you be willing to go today to prevent that? [Four] million teens a year [must] deal with these consequences.

Let's raise the standard and tell kids, unequivocally, what is in their best interest.

Why is it that we want so much to protect their sexual activity, but not their very lives?

NO

Eileen Toledo
English Teacher, Pablo Avila Junior High School, Camuy, Puerto Rico; Administers the "Baby, Think It Over" program

From National Education Association Web Site,
www.nea.org/neatoday/0302/debate.html

More students are becoming sexually active at earlier ages. As an educator, I had to get involved. I have been using "Baby, Think It Over" at my junior high school for five years. Pregnancy dropped from 15 the first year, to three last semester, and zero this year!

This program has a "baby" simulator. Students, male and female, are given "baby" to take home for five days. They experience the endless cries, waking at night, feeding, changing diapers.

Meanwhile, at school, we talk about child abuse, how to place babies to sleep correctly, and more. Students budget the weekly costs of caring for a baby. They inquire about jobs available to them at their age (13-16). Students realize how hard raising a baby can be for them.

One girl who loved baby-sitting became so frustrated after two days that "baby" was thrown in a clothes hamper and covered to drown out the cries. Her parents explained the consequences had this been a real baby. The student learned that this is not the time for her to become a parent.

We also discuss STDs, and we talk about how making love is different from sex, which is what teens are having. Making love is a beautiful experience in a true relationship between adults ready and able to take on responsibilities. . . .

We do role-plays: You're with your boyfriend, lose control, go all the way and don't even think about birth control, and a while later the girl is pregnant and all dreams are now put on hold. Or, things get hot but you stop and say, "Wait a second, I'm not ready for this."

Yet, I cannot be so naive [as] not to see that most teens become sexually active at an early age. So I must also talk about birth control. But schools that accept federal "abstinence-only" funds are not allowed to teach any factual information about the effectiveness of any form of birth control.

Students who have complete information about disease transmission and contraceptive use are the most likely to remain abstinent and will protect themselves if they choose to be sexually active.

We have worked with more than 400 students, and only three became pregnant in high school.

multi-component interventions like ABC together with biomedical interventions and services for kids with STDs."

Young People at Risk

The number of people infected with STDs in the United States is difficult to determine, and trends over time are even more difficult to discern. Only some STDS — chlamydia, gonorrhea, HIV and AIDS, hepatitis B and syphilis — are nationally "reportable," which means that state health authorities report the number of cases to the CDC. However, the reports are generally believed to be an undercount of the actual number of cases. [46] As a result of expanded screening programs and improved detection tests, there has been some improvement in tracking these diseases since 1996.

Bacterial STDs such as gonorrhea and chlamydia can be cured. Viral STDs — such as herpes, hepatitis B and HIV — can be effectively treated but at present there is no cure for them.

Sexually active youth have the highest STD rates of any age group in the country. By age 25, at least half of sexually active youth will have acquired an STD. Almost half of the approximately 18.9 million new cases of STDs occurring annually are among 15-to-24-year-olds. Three types of infection (HPV, chlamydia and trichomoniasis) account for 88 percent of all new cases in this age group. [47]

Females are particularly prone to STD infection because of the anatomy of the female reproductive tract. STDs are more easily passed from men to women, which results in higher female rates of infection. Moreover, the consequences of untreated STDS are often more serious for women ranging from infertility, tubal pregnancy and chronic pain to other complications.

Some STDs are especially common among young people for biological reasons. The bacterial infections chlamydia and gonorrhea most easily infect adolescent girls because of changes in the cervix during puberty. Young people are also more likely to be unmarried, to have more than one partner over time or have a partner who has an STD.

CURRENT SITUATION

Focus on Vaccines

The budget for prevention of STDs, directed by the CDC, remained flat over the past two years at $168 million. Congress just passed a $2.4 million dollar increase for FY 2005, but it still falls far short of what is needed to promote awareness and screening, according to public health advocates. [48]

ASHA was pushing for another $115 million, which it says is needed to help prevent STDs in women, adolescents and people of color, groups that are disproportionately impacted by STDs. "If these were common ear infections that could lead to pain and hearing loss, screening would be part of every physical," says the ASHA's Arrindell, who argues that because of squeamishness about sexual matters they're not.

For example, even though the CDC has made a big push to get sexually active young women tested for chlamydia, it is estimated that less than half of them do. Public health experts blame the expense of the tests, lack of awareness among young people and the reluctance of doctors to imply that an unmarried patient is sexually active.

"Every time a teenage girl gets chlamydia, she has a 10 percent chance of being infertile or having an ectopic pregnancy," complications that won't become apparent for years or decades, Hook notes. Yet only about 40 percent of primary-care providers are following the CDC's recommendation to test sexually active young women annually, Hook says, a reluctance he attributes at least partly to embarrassment.

Given how difficult it is to nudge both patients and doctors toward regular testing for these often-silent diseases, many experts agree the ultimate preventive solution is vaccines. Currently the only STD for which a vaccine exists is hepatitis B, a virus that can result in cirrhosis of the liver, liver cancer and even death.

Although the vaccine has been available for years, few adults availed themselves of it when it was advertised as effective against an STD. "Now in the 1990s, when it's been made into a baby shot and people are not told [hepatitis B is] an STD, rates are declining, and we're making a huge difference," Hook says.

Recently, breakthroughs were announced in the development of a vaccine for women against HPV strains linked to cervical cancer. The pharmaceutical company GlaxoSmithKline announced in October that it had moved up its government filing date to 2006, two years ahead of schedule, for a vaccine that could prevent 70 percent of all cervical cancers worldwide. Merck and Co. is developing a similar vaccine that industry analysts expect to be filed late in 2005. [49]

Progress remains frustratingly slow, however, in the search for a vaccine against HIV and herpes.

Research Funding

The federal government is currently spending $18.5 billion on HIV/AIDS, with the largest wedge of the pie going into health care for people living with HIV/AIDS in the United States. About 15 percent of the total, or $3 billion, is allocated to research. President Bush proposed a 7 percent increase for fiscal 2005 for the entire AIDS budget, mostly for mandatory funding for domestic care and for his global AIDS program. [50]

Congress allocated a total of $2.3 billion for the global fight against HIV and AIDS, tuberculosis and malaria in fiscal 2005. This is $99 million more than the president requested and $690 million more than last year. [51]

By contrast, research funding for other STDs at the National Institute of Allergies and Infectious Diseases was $51.5 million in fiscal 2004 with only a $1 million increase requested by the administration for 2005.

The so-called values debate has also threatened research into risky sexual behavior. Last year, the Traditional Values Coalition, an organization of 43,000 churches, publicly objected to some $100 million worth of government-backed research, much of it on sexual behavior. It compiled a "hit list" of 150 researchers who had done sex studies that looked, for example, at behavior that puts people at risk for STDs.

In July 2003, Rep. Patrick J. Toomey, R-Pa., introduced an amendment to withdraw financing from a list of more than 200 studies on the hit list. The proposal fell short on the House floor by two votes. [52]

The University of Washington's Holmes called this the latest example of moralistic blocking of basic scientific research — and "frightening." [53]

Teachers' Reaction

Much of the controversy over the Bush administration's expansion of abstinence programs stems from a definition in the 1996 welfare reform act (Temporary Assistance to Needy Families Act), to which all federally funded abstinence programs must adhere. The definition requires that programs have as their "exclusive purpose" to teach the benefits of abstaining from sexual activity. Among other things, the definition requires programs to teach "sexual activity outside of marriage is likely to have harmful psychological and physical effects."

Teaching about contraceptives is not permitted except in the context of their failure rates, according to federal officials, a guideline that has raised the hackles of some states and educators. California was for many years the only state that did not apply for funds under this act, because state laws authorized comprehensive sexuality-education programs that teach about contraception. California had experimented with its own abstinence-only initiative in the early 1990s. The program was terminated in February 1996, when evaluation results found the program to be ineffective. [54] Governors in Arizona and Pennsylvania also rejected those funds last year.

The restrictions have had a "chilling effect" on teachers of sexuality education, according to David Hoover, a senior project coordinator and clinical social worker with the National Education Association (NEA), which represents teachers. "Teachers are often forbidden to answer questions" from students about condoms and birth control, Hoover says. "It's about the only topic we approach where we say people shouldn't know anything."

Unruh of the Abstinence Clearinghouse claims the chilling effect works in the opposite direction, too. According to Unruh, school administrators in liberal "blue" states like New York are barring abstinence programs from their doors. "We don't want to give out names of teachers that are having us come in [to discuss abstinence] because we know they'll give them a hard time."

Abstinence Funding

Despite the lack of definitive studies showing that they work, President Bush has proposed a major boost for two of the three programs that fund abstinence programs. Although the welfare reform act has expired, Congress has authorized the welfare system and the abstinence funding within it to continue unchanged. The initiative has channeled $50 million per year for five years into the states. States that choose to accept the funds are required to match every four federal dollars with three state-raised dollars and then disperse the funds to schools and community organizations.

Bush proposed doubling funding this year for the largest abstinence program, Special Projects of Regional and National Significance (SPRANS), to $186 million from last year's level of $76 million. The program already has grown exponentially during the Bush's administration from a mere $20 million in 2001, its first year. Congress provided $105 million for the program for fiscal 2005 in an omnibus-spending bill passed last month. [55]

Bush also proposed doubling funding to $26 million for programs under the Adolescent and Family Life Act, the first of the three federal program designed to prevent teen pregnancy by promoting chastity. However, Congress appropriated $13 million, the same as last year.

It is unclear exactly how many schools receive federally funded abstinence-only programs since private groups that are the direct grant recipients often provide instructors and curriculum to the schools. According to Unruh, 700 groups receive funding under welfare reform, 119 under SPRANS and 58 under the Adolescent and Family Life Act.

According to the most recent data, compiled by the Alan Guttmacher Institute in 1999, 35 percent of school districts with a sex-education policy taught an abstinence-only curriculum. According to the CDC, 96 percent of the nation's high schools taught abstinence as the best way to prevent HIV.

Even before the Bush administration expanded funding, schools were already moving toward an abstinence philosophy during the 1990s, according to the Guttmacher Institute. "It was a time when social conservatives were getting organized from the school-board level on up," says study author Dailard. "Schools were reacting to the vocal minority. It's why we see teachers not being able to teach contraception in the classroom — either because of school district policy that prevented them or because they feared possible community reprisal."

According to Dailard, 22 states have a sex-education mandate. But that policy, she cautions, may not tell the whole story about what schools are teaching because the real decision-making occurs at the local level. According to a survey by the institute, four in 10 sex-education teachers either do not teach about contraceptives at all or teach they are ineffective in preventing pregnancy and STDs. [56] That number has risen from one in 50 at the beginning of the decade, according to Dailard.

OUTLOOK

New Focus on Women

Worldwide, the focus is shifting to women as the fastest-growing group contracting HIV. The number of women with HIV has risen in every region in the world, according to a United Nations report released last month; women account for nearly 60 percent of infected people in Africa, the most heavily affected continent. [57]

Microbicides — gels and creams under development that women could use on themselves to prevent STDs instead of depending on men to use condoms — could eliminate the disease in the future, advocates claim.

"When 50 percent of the new infections worldwide are happening among women, and the rate of new infection among women is increasing more rapidly than among men, that tells us there's a big gap in our prevention strategy," says Anna Forbes, a program coordinator for the Global Campaign for Microbicides, headquartered in Washington, D.C. "A condom can only go so far. When the man refuses to wear a condom and it's left in the drawer, it's not protective."

Microbicides could be invaluable for married women in the developing world who want protection against HIV but want to bear more children, Forbes adds.

Although microbicides are being developed primarily to prevent HIV, several under development would also protect against other STDs. Some advocates say a commercial product could be as close as five years away; other experts are more skeptical. Since 1990, five clinical trials have found the now commercially available microbicide Nonoxynol 9 was not effective against HIV and in some cases increased the risk, according to the University of Washington's Holmes, who participated in the first such study. Other microbicides have proven effective against HIV in the laboratory and in animals but have yet to be proven in clinical trials with people.

Other solutions — vaccines — will depend on funding and biological breakthroughs. Most experts think it will be at least a decade before a safe, affordable HIV vaccine can be developed, according to the American Foundation for AIDS Research. [58]

In the meantime, experts are concerned about growing rates of STDs in the gay community and high rates among poor people and minorities. Considering the growing numbers of the medically uninsured, Hook says, there's a question about how they will obtain either preventive care or treatment if they become infected. And the homeless and indigent are likely to have the most trouble sticking to the complex treatment regimen required for treating HIV.

While increases in syphilis and HIV are currently confined to the gay community, some experts worry the trend could spread to the general population.

"We're not yet seeing major increases in adolescents," says Holmes, "but it would not be surprising if we saw this phenomenon become more generalized if we don't strengthen our interventions." Moreover, over the past five years, heterosexuals have accounted for the greatest proportionate increase of reported AIDS cases in the United States. [59]

The increasingly female face of HIV means that more advocates from all sides and international groups like the U.N. are recognizing prevention efforts will have to change to take women's situation into account. Paradoxically, some abstinence advocates are singing the same song as women's advocates about the dangers women face in trying to influence men's sexual behavior, especially in societies where violence against wives is accepted.

"The woman who demands that the partner wear a condom will subject herself to great abuse," says abstinence proponent Smith of the Institute for Youth Development. But Smith vehemently rejects a biomedical breakthrough like microbicides as the solution. In fact, he says, "It worries me. We have to change the fundamental behaviors of men and women to be abstinent until they meet that partner in a faithful, lifetime way. If we don't, and we develop microbicides, another disease will come along that we won't have a microbicide for."

In many ways the same debate is being played out domestically in the debate over whether STDs should be prevented through a moral strategy — abstinent behavior — or modern science — through vaccines.

"We also believe it's important to delay sexual activity," SIECUS' Smith says of high school teens. But he contends the abstinence movement's approach is "to censor; to not give people information. Ours is to respect that young people are sexual beings and need information to protect themselves for lifelong sexual health."

As the recent presidential election showed, the country is deeply divided over moral values. And one might assume that division extends to sex education — except if one looks at the polls. Over 90 percent of adults and teens say it is important for teens to be given a strong message from society that they should not have sex until they are at least out of high school. A hefty majority also wishes that teens were getting more information not just about abstinence but also about contraception and protection against sexually transmitted diseases. And most adults don't think it's a "mixed message" to stress abstinence while also providing information about using birth control and protection against infection. [60]

As a parent, the University of Alabama's Hook sees the importance of both. "I have 12-year-old and 9-year-old girls. I think abstinence is great. I'm all for it; that's what I'm promoting in my kids," he says. "At the same time, if my kids make a wrong decision, I don't want to penalize them and have them not talk to me about it."

Moreover, Hook notes, "We're now seeing the resurgence of diseases like gonorrhea and syphilis in gay men, and that is happening because of the perception that modern treatment has transformed a previously fatal disease to a disease that can be managed as chronic illness."

NOTES

1. American Social Health Association, "Overview Fact Sheet on Sexually Transmitted Diseases," at www.ashastd.org.

2. *Ibid.*

3. Thomas R. Eng and William T. Butler, eds., *The Hidden Epidemic, Institute of Medicine* (1997); See also www.cdc.gov.

4. American Social Health Association, *op. cit.*

5. For background, see Adriel Bettelheim, "AIDS Update," *The CQ Researcher*, Dec. 4, 1998, pp. 1049-1072.

6. Centers for Disease Control and Prevention (CDC), "HIV/AIDS Among African Americans," at www.cdc.gov/hiv/pubs/Facts/afam.htm.

7. *Ibid.*

8. For background, see David Masci, "Global AIDS Crisis," *The CQ Researcher*, Oct. 13, 2000, pp. 809-832.

9. John S. Santelli, *et al.*, "Can Changes in Sexual Behaviors among High School Students Explain the Decline in Teen Pregnancy Rates in the 1990s?" *Journal of Adolescent Health*, August 2004, pp. 80-90, see p. 89.

10. *Ibid.*

11. Peter Bearman, "After the Promise: The STD Consequences of Adolescent Virginity Pledges," *Journal of Adolescent Health*, March 2005, pp. 271-278. For background, see Kathy Koch, "Encouraging Teen Abstinence," *The CQ Researcher*, July 10, 1998, pp. 577-600.

12. Douglas Kirby, "Emerging Answers," May 2001, National Campaign to Prevent Teen Pregnancy, at www.teenpregnancy.org.

13. Shannan Martin, *et al.*, "Comprehensive Sex Education vs. Authentic Abstinence: A Study of Competing Curricula," Heritage Foundation, 2004.

14. ASHA, "Fact Sheet on HPV," www.ashastd.org.

15. SIECUS press release, "SIECUS Releases Review of Fear-Based, Abstinence-Only-Until-Marriage Curricula Used in Federally-Funded Programs," Sept. 29, 2004. Full report at www.siecus.org/reviews.html.

16. *Ibid.*

17. See www.religiousinstitute.org.

18. See "Condom Effectiveness," Politics and Science Web site, and Adam Clymer, "U.S. Revises Sex Information and a Fight Goes on," *The New York Times*, Dec. 27, 2002.

19. CDC, "Male Latex Condoms and Sexually Transmitted Diseases," at www.cdc.gov/nchstp/od/latex.htm.

20. "Condom Effectiveness," at http://democrats.reform.house.gov/features/politics_and_science/example_condoms.htm.

21. Abby Christopher, "Hearing Addresses Condoms for HPV Prevention," *Journal of the National Cancer Institute*, July 7, 2004, p. 985.

22. "Status of HPV-related Provisions of Public Law 106-554," fact sheet from office of Rep. Mark Souder, e-mailed Nov. 2004.

23. Abby Christopher, "Hearing Addresses Condoms for HPV Prevention," *Journal of the National Cancer Institute*, July 7, 2004, p. 985.

24. "200 Public Health Advocates Rally Against Bush's Abstinence-Only Sex Education Policy at Close of STD Conference," March 11, 2004, *Kaiser Daily HIV/AIDS Report* at www.kff.org.

25. National Institutes of Health, "Scientific Evidence on Condom Effectiveness for STD Prevention," 2001.

26. ASHA, "Major Health Organizations Call for Science — Not Politics — to Drive Sexual Health Policy," press release, March 11, 2004.

27. U.S. Agency for International Development, "What Happened in Uganda?" *Project Lessons Learned Case Study*, September 2002.

28. Institute for Youth Development, "What Happened in Uganda?" (Video), March 2004.

29. See www.icrw.org.

30. Dara Mayers, "Our Bodies, Our Lives," *Ford Foundation Report*, summer 2004, pp. 8-13.

31. See Susan A. Cohen, "Delayed Marriage and Abstinence-until-Marriage: On a Collision Course?" June 2004, *The Guttmacher Report on Public Policy*, June 2004.

32. *Ibid.*

33. Robert Walgate, "Bush's AIDS plan criticized for emphasizing abstinence and forbidding Condoms," *British Medical Journal*, July 24, 2004. at www.bmj.com.

34. "Debunking the Myths in the U.S. Global AIDS Strategy: An Evidence Based Analysis," Center for Health and Gender Equity, March 2004.

35. Walgate, *op. cit.*

36. Interview on "The NewsHour with Jim Lehrer," May 18, 2004.

37. Elizabeth Feder, "Social Hygiene," Reader's Companion to U.S. Women's History (on-line).

38. Eng and Butler, *op. cit.*, p. 88.

39. *Ibid*, p. 208.

40. Willard Cates, Jr., "Treating STDs to Help Control HIV Infection," *Contemporary OB/GYN*, Oct. 1, 2001.

41. See Nina Bernstein, "Behind Fall in Pregnancy, a New Teenage Culture of Restraint," *The New York Times*, March 7, 2004.

42. Eng and Butler, *op. cit.*, p. 208.

43. Cates, *op. cit.*

44. Eng and Butler, *op. cit.*, pp. 1, 88.

45. *Ibid.*, pp. 88-89.

46. Cates, J. R. *et al.*, "Our Voices, Our Lives, Our Futures: Youth and Sexually Transmitted Diseases, School of Journalism and Mass Communication, University of North Carolina at Chapel Hill, February 2004.

47. These figures are for 2000. Hillard Weinstock, *et al.*, "Sexually Transmitted Diseases Among American Youth: Incidence and Prevalence Estimates, 2000," *Perspectives on Sexual and Reproductive Health*, January/February 2004, pp. 6-10.

48. Some funding for HIV/AIDS is also included in CDC's HIV/AIDS, STD and TB prevention program, which has also been level-funded at $1.1 billion for the last two years. Congress passed an increase of about 4 percent over last year's budget for CDC overall for FY 2005, more than the president requested.

49. Reuters, "Glaxo Vaccine Stops Virus Linked to Cancer-Study," Nov. 12, 2004.

50. Kaiser Family Foundation, "HIV/AIDS Policy Fact Sheet: Federal Funding for HIV/AIDS: The FY 2005 Budget Request," February 2004 at www.kff.org.

51. Katharine Q. Seelye and David E. Rosenbaum, "Big Spending Bill Makes a Winner of Mars Program but Many Losers Elsewhere," *The New York Times*, Nov. 23, 2004.

52. Benedict Carey, "Long After Kinsey, Only the Brave Study Sex," *The New York Times*, Nov. 9, 2004, p. F1.

53. For background, see William Triplett, "Science and Politics," *The CQ Researcher*, Aug. 20, 2004, pp. 661-684.

54. Debra Hauser, "Five Years of Abstinence-only-Until-Marriage Education: Assessing the Impact," Advocates for Youth, 2004, at www.advocatesforyouth.org.

55. Seelye and Rosenbaum, *op. cit.*

56. Alan Guttmacher Institute, "Sex Education: Needs, Programs and Policies," April 2004, p. 21, at www.agi-usa.org.

57. Lawrence K. Altman, "AIDS Infections Reach Record High, U.N. Says," *The New York Times*, Nov. 23, 2004.

58. www.amfar.org.

59. Willard Cates, *op. cit.*

60. The National Campaign to Prevent Teen Pregnancy, "Teens Continue to Express Cautious Attitudes Toward Sex," press release, Dec. 16, 2003. Available at www.teenpregnancy.org.

BIBLIOGRAPHY

Books

Eng, Thomas R., and William T. Butler, eds., *The Hidden Epidemic: Confronting Sexually Transmitted Diseases*, **National Academy Press, 1997.**
An Institute of Medicine panel called secrecy one of the biggest obstacles to curbing a hidden epidemic of STDs.

Richardson, Justin, and Mark A. Schuster, *Everything You Never Wanted Your Kids to Know About Sex (but Were Afraid They'd Ask): The Secrets to Surviving Your Child's Sexual Development from Birth to the Teens,* **Crown, 2003.**
Two Harvard-trained doctors provide a humorous, compassionate and informative guide for parents.

Articles

Bernstein, Nina, "Behind Fall in Pregnancy, a New Teenage Culture of Restraint," *The New York Times*, **March 7, 2004.**
In tracing the romance of two 16-year-old sweethearts in the Bronx, Bernstein cites a new interest in virginity as one of the reasons teen pregnancy rates are falling.

Cohen, Jon, "A Silent Epidemic," Oct. 27, 2004, www.slate.com.
Cohen reviews possible explanations for the high percentage of HIV and AIDS among black women.

Epstein, Helen, "The Fidelity Fix," *The New York Times Magazine*, **June 13, 2004, p. 54.**
Reducing the number of sexual partners, especially through fidelity in marriage, has helped reduce HIV in Uganda.

Lane, Earl, "White House Policy: Aiding Abstinence," *Newsday*, **Oct. 22, 2004.**
The Bush administration has exhibited an unusual interest in ideological purity for its appointees, critics charge.

Santelli, John, "Can Changes in Sexual Behaviors Among High School Students Explain the Decline in Teen Pregnancy Rates in the 1990s?" *Journal of Adolescent Health*, **May 11, 2004, at www.teenpregnancy.org.**
Santelli concludes that 53 percent of the recent decline in teen pregnancy can be attributed to abstinence and 47 percent to increased contraceptive use.

Weinstock, Hillar, *et. al.*, **"Sexually Transmitted Diseases Among American Youth: Incidence and Prevalence Estimates, 2000,"** *Perspectives on Sexual and Reproductive Health*, **January/February 2004, pp. 6-10. at www.agi-usa.org.**
CDC researchers conclude that Americans between 15 and 24 account for nearly half the new cases of STDs.

Reports and Studies

Alan Guttmacher Institute, "Sex Education: Needs, Programs and Policies," April 2004.
The latest information about sex education as it relates to STDs. At www.agi-usa.org.

Bearman, Peter S., and Hannah Bruckner, "Promising the Future: Virginity Pledges as They Affect Transition to First Intercourse," July 15, 2000, at http://www. sociology.columbia.edu/people/faculty/bearman/papers/ virginity.pdf
Teens who took virginity pledges delayed their first sexual intercourse by many months, a study found.

Cates, J.R., *et al.*, "Our Voices, Our Lives, Our Futures: Youth and Sexually Transmitted Diseases," School of Journalism and Mass Communication, University of North Carolina at Chapel Hill, February 2004.
This report includes a primer on the most common STDs.

Committee on Government Reform, U.S. House of Representatives, Minority Staff, "The Content of Federally Funded Abstinence-only Education Programs," December 2004, at www.democrats.reform.house.gov.
This report concludes that 80 percent of the most popular abstinence-education curricula contain "false, misleading or distorted" information.

Kirby, Douglas, "Emerging Answers," May 2001, The National Campaign to Prevent Teen Pregnancy, at www.teenpregnancy.org.
This widely cited report concludes that advising teens to delay sex but also providing information about contraceptives constitutes the most effective approach to sex education.

Rector, Robert, and Kirk A. Johnson, "Teens Who Make Virginity Pledges Have Substantially Improved Life Outcomes," Heritage Foundation, Sept. 21, 2004.
Researchers for the conservative think tank conclude that teens who take virginity pledges have better life outcomes.

Web Sites

Justice Talking: http://www.justicetalking.org/view-program.asp?progID=426#laws.
The Dec. 9, 2003, "Justice Talking," a radio program distributed by National Public Radio was a debate on the topic, "Abstinence-Only" between a Bush administration official and an advocate for sexuality education.

Kaiser Family Foundation: www.kff.org.
This Web site contains daily news reports on HIV/AIDS and STDs.

For More Information

Abstinence Clearinghouse, 801 East 41st St., Sioux Falls, SD 57105; (605) 335-3643; www.abstinence.net. A nonprofit educational organization that promotes sexual abstinence.

Advocates for Youth, 2000 M St., N.W., Suite 750, Washington, DC 20036; (202) 419-3420; www.advocatesforyouth.org. Established in 1980 to help young people make informed decisions about their sexual health through comprehensive sex education, including all birth-control options.

Alan Guttmacher Institute, 120 Wall St., 21st Floor, New York, NY 10005; (212) 248-1111; www.guttmacher.org. A private research organization (formerly the research arm of Planned Parenthood) that publishes special reports on topics pertaining to sexual and reproductive health and rights with the mission to protect all reproductive choices.

American Foundation for AIDS Research, 120 Wall St., 13th Floor, New York, NY 10005-3908; (212) 806-1600; www.amfar.org. One of the world's leading organizations dedicated to supporting AIDS research, prevention and funding.

American Social Health Association, P.O. Box 13827, Research Triangle Park, NC 27709; (919) 361-8400; www.ashastd.org. A non-governmental group that seeks to improve public health, focusing specifically on sexually transmitted diseases and prevention.

Centers for Disease Control and Prevention, 1600 Clifton Rd., Atlanta, GA 30333; (404) 639-3311; www.cdc.gov/std. The federal agency charged with improving Americans' health and quality of life by preventing and controlling disease and injury.

Heritage Foundation, 214 Massachusetts Ave., N.E., Washington, DC 20002-4999; (202) 546-4400; www.heritage.org. A research institute that formulates and promotes conservative public policies, including abstinence-only sex education.

Institute for Youth Development, P.O. Box 16560, Washington, DC 20041; (703) 433-1640; www.youthdevelopment.org. Advocates a comprehensive message to youth to completely avoid five risk behaviors — alcohol, drugs, sex, tobacco and violence.

International Center for Research on Women, 1717 Massachusetts Ave., N.W., Suite 302, Washington, DC 20036; (202) 797-0007; www.icrw.org. A nonprofit organization that seeks to improve the lives of women in poverty, focusing on issues affecting their economic, health and social status.

National Campaign to Prevent Teen Pregnancy, 1776 Massachusetts Ave., N.W., Suite 200, Washington, DC 20036; (202) 478-8500; www.teenpregnancy.org. Seeks to reduce teen pregnancy by one-third by 2005; works to try to find common ground between the advocates of abstinence-only and comprehensive sex education.

Sexuality Information and Education Council of the U.S. (SIECUS), 130 West 42nd St., Suite 350, New York, NY 10036-7802; (212) 819-9770; www.siecus.org. Since 1964, SIECUS has worked to promote sexuality education, protect sexual rights and expand access to sexual health.

5

Child Welfare Reform

Tom Price

Sally Ann Schofield was sentenced in Augusta, Maine, to 20 years in prison for killing her 5-year-old foster child in 2002. Logan Marr suffocated after being bound to a highchair with 42 feet of duct tape. More than 900,000 children were abused or neglected in the United States in 2003 and 1,390 died. Today about a half-million children live in foster homes under the jurisdiction of state child welfare agencies.

AP Photo/Joel Page

From *CQ Researcher,*
April 22, 2005.

D aisy Perales, a 5-year-old San Antonio girl, died on Dec. 1, 2004, a week after she was found unconscious and bleeding, with head trauma, bruises, a fractured rib and a lacerated spleen. She weighed just 20 pounds.

Texas Child Protective Services had investigated her family seven times. Daisy was one of more than 500 Texas children to die of abuse or neglect from 2002 to mid-2004. The agency had looked into at least 137 of the cases. [1]

At the beginning of 2003, in Newark, N.J., police entered a locked basement to find Raheem Williams, 7, and Tyrone Hill, 4. Both were starving and covered with burns and excrement. The next day, police found the body of Raheem's twin, who had been dead for more than 30 days. The state Department of Youth and Family Services had received repeated warnings that the children were being abused. [2]

"Our system is broken, and we need to make monumental changes," New Jersey Human Services Commissioner James Davy declared a year later, after more scandals surfaced. [3]

A decade earlier, police in Chicago had discovered 19 children, ages 1 to 14, living in a filthy two-bedroom apartment with a half-dozen adults. Police described a horrific scene of dirty diapers, spoiled food, roaches and dog and rat droppings. One child had cigarette burns, cuts and bruises. The Illinois Department of Children and Family Services had been in contact with six of the children. [4] Following the discovery, the department placed the children with various caregivers, later admitting it had lost track of them. The department eventually confessed it had a backlog of 4,320 uninvestigated complaints of abused or neglected children.

U.S. Probe Faults State Programs

No state child welfare programs fully comply with federal child safety standards, according to a three-year investigation by the Bush administration. Sixteen states did not meet any of the seven federal standards (below) used to assess children's programs, and no state met more than two of the standards.

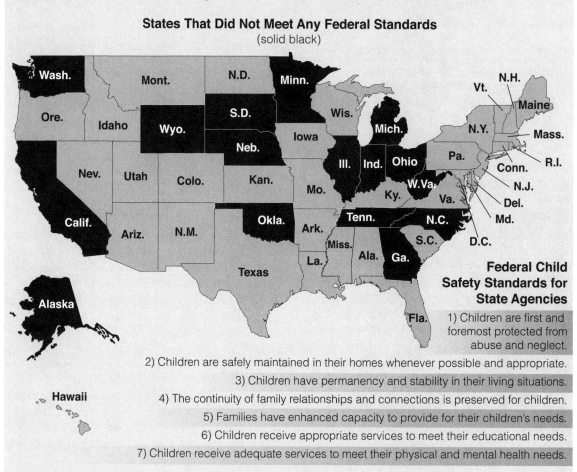

States That Did Not Meet Any Federal Standards
(solid black)

Federal Child Safety Standards for State Agencies

1) Children are first and foremost protected from abuse and neglect.

2) Children are safely maintained in their homes whenever possible and appropriate.

3) Children have permanency and stability in their living situations.

4) The continuity of family relationships and connections is preserved for children.

5) Families have enhanced capacity to provide for their children's needs.

6) Children receive appropriate services to meet their educational needs.

7) Children receive adequate services to meet their physical and mental health needs.

Source: U.S. Department of Health and Human Services

But then consider these hopeful signs of reform:

- Legislation being considered in Texas this year would increase spending on child welfare programs, improve training for caseworkers and encourage the administration to reduce caseloads. Republican Gov. Rick Perry calls reform an "emergency issue." [5]
- New Jersey is planning to hire hundreds of new child welfare workers, speed investigations and reduce caseloads to no more than 25 children or 15 families per worker — down from the current maximum of more than 40 children and 20 families. Children who have lived in institutions for 18 months or more will be moved into "familylike" settings. An independent committee of child welfare experts, appointed in a lawsuit settlement, has approved the plan. [6]
- And Illinois has been transformed into "sort of the

gold standard" for child welfare, in the words of Sue Badeau, deputy director of the Pew Commission on Children in Foster Care, a bipartisan group of political leaders and child welfare experts that promotes child welfare reform. After the state's child welfare scandal in the mid-1990s, new leadership and a new philosophy have turned the Illinois system around, says Mark Testa, co-director of the University of Illinois' Children and Family Research Center and former research director of the state children's services department.

The department reduced caseloads and focused on keeping families together or quickly placing children in alternative permanent-living situations. It obtained federal waivers from regulations preventing subsidies for placements with relatives, such as grandparents or aunts and uncles. As a result, Illinois has reduced the number of children in foster care from 52,000 in 1997 to fewer than 17,000 today, according to Testa.

So it goes in the American child welfare system: Scandal triggers public outrage which spurs reform, leaving children's advocates and child welfare workers constantly ricocheting between hope and despair. Meanwhile, more than 900,000 American children age 17 and younger were abused or neglected in 2003. [7]

"Reading the newspapers of late has been more like reading a horror novel, with case after case of abuse and neglect," said Texas state Sen. Jane Nelson, reflecting the nationwide despair generated by the unending reports of children who were mistreated while supposedly being protected by state agencies charged with doing so. [8] But, as the Republican author of reform legislation, Nelson also represents the potential for improvement that gives advocates hope.

Not a single state received a passing grade last year when the U.S. Health and Human Services Department

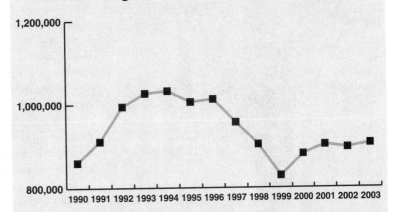

Nearly 1 Million Children Are Maltreated

More than 900,000 children in the United States were victims of abuse or neglect in 2003, about a 5 percent increase over the 1990 total. Most of the cases involved neglect, but 19 percent involved physical abuse and 10 percent sexual abuse.

Abused or Neglected American Children, 1990-2003 *

*2003 is the most recent year for which data are available

Source: Child Trends Data Bank, based on Department of Health and Human Services Reports, 1990-2003.

(HHS) completed its review of state and local child welfare systems, and 16 states did not meet *any* of the seven federal child-care standards used to evaluate the programs. But the first eight states given follow-up reviews met all their initial targets for improvement, says Wade F. Horn, the department's assistant secretary for children and families.* [9]

State and local officials throughout the country agree on the need for substantial improvements in their child welfare systems, and even critics acknowledge that significant improvements are under way. Private organizations are adding to the ferment, from public-interest law firms demanding reforms in court to foundations that are supporting innovation. The Bush administration has offered up its plan for restructuring federal funding of child welfare, and both Republicans and Democrats in Congress agree not only on the need for reform but also on how that reform should be carried out.

---

* The states are: Arizona, Delaware, Indiana, Kansas, Massachusetts, Minnesota, Oregon and Vermont.

Foster child Daphane Irvin, a senior at Chicago's South Shore High School, hopes to become an actress. Only 2 percent (1,900) of all foster care adoptions in 2002 were older teens, ages 16 to 18. Another 19,500 teens "aged out" of foster care without being adopted and must face the transition to adulthood alone.

"The consensus is: Where we can, we should protect the family," says Fred H. Wulczyn, an assistant professor at the Columbia University School of Social Work and a research fellow at the University of Chicago's Chapin Hall Center for Children. "Where we need to place kids in foster care, we should proceed to permanent placement — such as with adoptive parents — as soon as possible."

Child welfare workers, government officials and children's advocates agree that it's best for children to live with their parents in healthy families, and that agencies should help families stay together. When children must be removed from their parents because of abuse or neglect, it's best to quickly return the children home safely or to place them permanently with adoptive parents or relatives.

Failure to do so can have disastrous consequences, as Maryland residents learned in early April.

Maryland houses 2,700 children in 330 privately operated group homes that are not adequately supervised by state agencies, according to an investigation by *The Baltimore Sun.* [10] In some of those homes, children have been denied needed medical treatment, served inadequate food, assaulted by employees and even supplied by employees with illegal drugs. At least 15 group home residents have died since 1998.

Children often are placed in group homes — which cost the state far more than foster family homes — when there is no other place for them. "There were some providers who were good, but there were others who we would have chosen not to be bothered with, but we had no choice," said Gloria Slade, former child placement supervisor for the Baltimore Social Services Department.

Maryland Human Resources Secretary Christopher J. McCabe said the state will recruit more foster parents to reduce the need for group homes. But Charlie Cooper, who manages the Maryland Citizens' Review Board for Children, said the state must offer a wider range of children's services. [11]

"You have a lot of things going on at the same time" to improve services to children, says Susan Notkin, director of the Center for Community Partnerships in Child Welfare, a nonprofit organization that funds and consults with agencies implementing innovative programs. "A lot of innovation is being tested. There's a lot of interest in looking at the financing."

Madelyn Freundlich, policy director for Children's Rights, a New York-based advocacy organization, agrees. "There is a lot of energy in the field right now," she says. "There has been a joining together of public agencies and the private sector to really look at foster care, and there is a growing awareness among the general public about foster care and the support needed to provide the right services for kids and families."

But the challenge is complex. And the road from good intentions to effective accomplishments is neither short nor straight. There are stark disagreements about how much spending should be increased (or whether it should be increased at all), how much federal control should be exercised over federally funded state and local programs, and which reform proposals are most likely to be effective.

Widespread agreement on the need for reform represents just "superficial consensus," says Douglas J. Besharov, director of the American Enterprise Institute's (AEI) Social and Individual Responsibility Project and a former director of the U.S. Center on Child Abuse and Neglect.

"The Democrats who say they want to give states more flexibility want to make it open-ended [entitlement] spending," Besharov, a University of Maryland public affairs professor, says. "This is just an excuse to put in more money, while Republicans say they're looking for ways to cap expenditures. It's just like we're all in favor of long life and fighting cancer, but getting from here to there requires a lot more agreement than what I see."

As the nation struggles to help children from troubled families, here are some of the questions child welfare experts are trying to answer:

Do state and local governments do enough to keep families together?

Most headline-grabbing child welfare horror stories spring from parents mistreating children whom the system has failed to protect. But many child welfare experts believe the more common problem stems from agencies removing children from parents too frequently. It's not that the children didn't need protection but that agencies failed to provide early services that could have kept the kids safe and at home.

In fact, concern about taking children from their parents is so prevalent that a common measure of agency success is reducing the number of youngsters removed from their homes. Several private organizations are promoting reforms designed to improve services to troubled families before the children have to be removed. But there's still a long way to go.

Illinois' newfound reputation for quality stems in part from cutting its foster care population by two-thirds since the mid-1990s and removing fewer than half as many children from their parents each year, Testa says. Improvement in New York City's system is marked by a foster care caseload that dropped from just under 50,000 in the mid-1990s to just below 20,000 today, according to Columbia University's Wulczyn.

Nationwide, the foster care caseload also is declining, but it did not peak as early and is not falling as rapidly as in Illinois and New York. In 1999, nearly 570,000 American children lived in foster homes — an historic high. That number dropped to just above 520,000 in 2003, the most recent figure available. But the dip wasn't because fewer children were removed from their homes; it was because states did a better job of returning foster children to their parents or placing them in other permanent homes. [12]

Because child welfare systems differ from state to state, Wulczyn says, "it's hard to come up with one over-arching statement about where the system is, except to say that it's not as good as it should be, but it's better than it was."

Illinois succeeds, Testa says, because it is "doing a better job making family assessments, working with families who can take care of their kids in the home and not putting those children unnecessarily into foster care." Child welfare experts would like to see that approach expanded throughout the country.

"Most places do not have the services and support that families need, so they would never get put into the child welfare system in the first place," says Judy Meltzer, deputy director of the Center for the Study of Social Policy, who serves on panels monitoring court-ordered reforms in New Jersey and Washington, D.C. "The infrastructure does a really bad job of being able to reach out and work with families before they get to the point where crises occur and kids have to be removed from their homes."

Meltzer and others say that even the best child welfare agencies can't provide those services by themselves. "If we think child welfare agencies alone will do it, we will always be stuck," says Wanda Mial, senior associate for child welfare at the Annie E. Casey Foundation, a leading operator and funder of programs for disadvantaged children.

"Government can't do it alone," either, says Notkin, whose Center for Community Partnerships promotes cooperation among many public and private organizations.

Parental substance abuse causes or exacerbates 70 percent of child neglect or abuse incidents, says Kathryn Brohl, author of the 2004 book *The New Miracle Workers: Overcoming Contemporary Challenges in Child Welfare Work*. [13] Abuse also stems from poverty, poor housing, ill health, lack of child care, parental incompetence, domestic violence, arrest and imprisonment, Brohl adds. Some children enter the child welfare system because they run afoul of authorities by committing a

Judges' Hearings Help Kids Feel Loved

So, I [see] you want to be a cosmetologist," Judge Patricia Martin Bishop said to the teenager sitting before her. "What's that?" the girl asked.

"Someone who fixes your hair, does your nails — things like that," Bishop replied.

"I can't even do my own hair," the girl exclaimed. "I want to be a lawyer."

Bishop, the presiding judge in the Child Protection Division of Cook County Circuit Court in Chicago, looked at the girl's caseworker, who explained why she had changed the girl's answer on a questionnaire about her future. "I changed it to cosmetologist because she's reading at such a low level she'll never be a lawyer."

But Bishop quickly set the caseworker straight: "I'm not convinced she can't become a lawyer until we help her get through high school and give her the support she needs to get into college and get her through college and get her through law school. Until we've made some concerted effort to help her achieve her dreams, I'm not prepared to channel her to our dreams for her."

That moment, Bishop says, demonstrated exactly why she created "benchmark hearings" for teenagers.

Since 1997, Illinois has reduced its foster care rolls from 52,000 to fewer than 17,000, thus reducing demands on the court. Bishop was able to relieve Judge Patricia Brown Holmes of her regular caseload, and now they both conduct special hearings for unadopted teens about to leave foster care for independence.

The benchmark hearings are held when the child is 14, 16 and 17 $^1/_2$. The children, as well as their caseworkers, teachers, doctors, coaches and other adults with whom they have important relationships, attend the meetings, which can last up to two hours. "I require the psychiatrist to face me and tell my why this kid's on meds," the judge explains. "I make the basketball coach come in and tell me how basketball helps or hurts this kid."

Every Illinois foster child attends a juvenile court hearing every six months, but they can be brief, Bishop says. The benchmark meetings tend to be longer because the judges want to get a clear picture of the child's capabilities and needs.

"The idea is to look at kids more holistically," Bishop explains, "to coordinate with the agencies, to help [the teens] for the present and for their dreams for the future. If there are unresolved issues after a benchmark hearing, I keep it on my benchmark calendar and have follow-up hearings."

The needs for follow-up can vary widely. "A girl came to one of my benchmarks wearing sandals and a short skirt in dead of winter," the judge says. "She had moved from one group home to another, and her allowance hadn't kept up with her so she couldn't buy the things she needed. I kept

crime or frequently skipping school, says Mial, a former child welfare worker in Philadelphia.

To avoid removing children from their parents in these circumstances, Brohl and other experts say, child welfare workers must be able to call on other agencies to address such problems as soon as they are discovered — or even before.

According to social psychologist Kristin Anderson Moore, who heads the Child Trends research organization, the most effective ways to deter child abuse and neglect include "helping people establish healthy marriages before they have children, helping teenagers delay child-bearing and helping parents delay having second births."

Some "very rigorous studies" have shown that starting home-visitation programs shortly after birth can reduce abuse and neglect by 50 percent, says Shay Bilchik, pres- ident of the Child Welfare League of America. A visiting nurse trains new parents, monitors the well being of the child and arranges for additional services needed by the family. "If you track those babies 15 years down the road," Bilchik says, "home visitation has been shown to reduce those babies' entering into the criminal world."

Rep. Wally Herger, R-Calif., chairman of the House Ways and Means subcommittee that oversees child wel- fare, noted that the federal government spends 10 times as much on state and local foster care and adoption ser- vices as it does on programs designed to hold families together.

"As a result," he said, "rather than focusing on the prevention of abuse and neglect, today's funding struc- ture encourages the removal of children and breakup of families. That is unacceptable." [14]

the case on my benchmark hearing calendar until we were able to resolve the allowance problem."

At another hearing, Bishop discovered that a boy had maintained a relationship with his mother, whose parental rights had been terminated years before — a not uncommon occurrence. "His mother had continued drugging," Bishop says. "My position was, if he's maintained this relationship it's incumbent upon us to make it work as best we can. We put the mother back into [drug-treatment] services. She got clean. We sent this kid back home before he turned 18."

Presiding Judge Patricia Martin Bishop of Chicago created "benchmark" hearings to protect teens' rights — and their dreams.

Cook County Courthouse

parental rights. Sometimes it can continue to be the child welfare system.

Bishop is authorized to keep a foster child within the jurisdiction of the Department of Children and Family Services until age 21. And, using private donations, the department can even provide higher-education assistance until age 23.

Bishop doesn't have empirical data to establish the value of benchmark hearings, but she has heard encouraging anecdotes. "Lawyers who didn't want to do this now are requesting that I extend this down to age 12," she says. "Kids come and say, 'I want Judge Holmes to have my case, or Judge Bishop to have my case.'

"The state is such a poor parent. We [judges] can look a child in the eye and talk about what he or she hopes to do in the future. They feel as if they're heard. They feel as if they've gotten attention. They feel loved."

Adolescents need relationships that will help them make the transition to adulthood when they leave foster care, Bishop explains. Sometimes the relationship can be as unlikely as with a drug-addicted mother who had lost her

---

There are deep disagreements about how that problem should be fixed, however.

"I don't have any doubt Wally cares about kids," says Rep. Jim McDermott of Washington, the ranking Democrat on Herger's subcommittee. "It's a question of how you do it."

Does the federal government give state and local child welfare agencies enough financial support and flexibility?

As they lobbied on Capitol Hill last month, volunteers from the Child Welfare League of America boldly proclaimed their top legislative priority on oversized campaign buttons pinned to their lapels: "No caps on kids!"

The slogan is shorthand for their opposition to President Bush's proposal to convert the main source of

federal child welfare funding — the foster care entitlement — into a flexible, capped block grant, or a single grant that the states can spend in various innovative ways with less federal control.

Under current law, states are entitled to federal reimbursement for every foster child whose parents would have qualified for welfare under the old Aid to Families with Dependent Children program in 1996. Overall, the federal government pays about half the nation's $22 billion child welfare bill, according to an Urban Institute study, while the rest comes from state and local governments. [15]

The welfare league argues that not only should the existing entitlement regime be preserved but also that the federal government should increase spending on various child welfare programs.

Number of Foster Kids Has Declined

The number of foster children began declining after peaking in 1999, due largely to a rise in adoptions. Even so, more than a half-million American children were in foster care in 2003, a 31 percent increase over 1990.

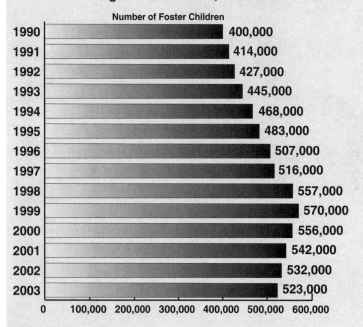

Number of Foster Children Ages 17 and Under, 1990-2003*

Number of Foster Children

Year	Number
1990	400,000
1991	414,000
1992	427,000
1993	445,000
1994	468,000
1995	483,000
1996	507,000
1997	516,000
1998	557,000
1999	570,000
2000	556,000
2001	542,000
2002	532,000
2003	523,000

0   100,000   200,000   300,000   400,000   500,000   600,000

* 2003 is the most recent year for which data are available

Source: Child Trends Data Bank, based on Department of Health and Human Services Reports, 1990-2003

warn that eliminating the entitlement could leave them with less in the long run.

The administration proposes giving states the option of accepting a block grant that could be spent on foster care and other services. Unlike the entitlement, the grant would not rise and fall with changes in the foster care caseload. For the first five years, each state would receive the same amount it would have received under the entitlement program based on the caseload change during the previous five years. That means states that had declining caseloads would receive less federal money. After five years, Congress would decide how to continue to fund the program.

Some states have implemented well-regarded innovations by obtaining waivers from federal regulations, leading administration officials to contend that allowing flexibility works. Pointing to the drop in welfare rolls that followed similar welfare reforms in the mid-1990s, the administration also argues that flexibility allows the states to be more effective while cutting costs. [16]

"We think if states are better able to focus money on prevention — which is cheaper than intervention — there would be less need for expensive out-of-home-care, in the same way that when states focused on work instead of simply cash, welfare caseloads declined," Horn says.

States would be hard pressed to shift money from foster care to other services, however, because child welfare systems already are underfunded, contends Liz Meitner, vice president for government affairs at the Child Welfare League. "We think a better strategy is to increase investments for prevention that will ultimately reduce the number of kids in foster care," Meitner says.

The Pew Commission on Children in Foster Care proposed maintaining the entitlement and beefing up federal aid while increasing flexibility. [17]

However, HHS Assistant Secretary Horn says groups like the Child Welfare League "live in a dream world where money grows on trees," adding that he himself prefers to live "in the world of the achievable."

Both sides agree that child welfare agencies should be able to spend more federal money on helping families stay together and on alternatives to traditional foster care, which receives the bulk of federal aid today. The administration contends this can be accomplished by letting states spend their existing federal foster care allotment for other activities, such as helping troubled families or supporting guardians. But many child welfare advocates argue that the agencies need more money and

The commission calculated it would cost $1.6 billion annually just to extend federal aid to all foster children. Acknowledging the pressure to contain federal spending, the commission proposed extending aid to all but cutting the amount given for each child, so total federal aid would not rise. The commission suggested hiking other, more flexible, federal grants by $200 million the first year and by 2 percent above inflation in later years.

"Every child who experiences abuse or neglect deserves the protection of both the federal and state governments," said commission Chairman Bill Frenzel, former Republican representative from Minnesota, making a key argument against ending the entitlement. [18]

"Child welfare has traditionally been the safety net for vulnerable children and families," Freundlich of Children's Rights says. "It does not have waiting lists. It's had to be there for the children."

Block grant opponents point to the crack cocaine epidemic that devastated many families and caused child welfare caseloads to soar in the 1980s and '90s. Without the entitlement, states would have had to spend much more of their own money or agencies could not have cared for all the children coming through their doors. Many warn methamphetamine abuse could become the next crack. They also note that, over time, block grant programs haven't kept pace with inflation, and funding for some has declined.

The Social Services Block Grant, for example, dropped from $3 billion in 1981 to $1.7 billion in 2003, according to the Child Welfare League. Had it tracked inflation, she says, it now would total more than $6 billion.

But Assistant HHS Secretary Horn replies that if states reduce foster rolls they would receive more money through a block grant program than through an entitlement program. That's because the entitlement, which is based on the number of children served, would drop if the rolls dropped, while the block grant would not. If caseloads rise significantly, he adds, the administration plan includes an emergency fund that states could tap.

The federal government can't afford to give states both flexibility and an entitlement, the American Enterprise Institute's Besharov argues. "The only way to give states flexibility in a federal grant program is to cap it. Otherwise, they will steal you blind."

Besharov suggests extending the waiver option, which gives the states supervised flexibility, and "tying it to rigorous evaluations" to document what works best.

Testa, of the Children and Family Research Center, also supports more waivers, although he doesn't share Besharov's fear of entitlements. "We have to invest a lot more in demonstrations that will prove what works," he says. "We should be giving states permission to innovate but requiring them to demonstrate that what they're doing is working."

Because states have to match the federal funds under current law, he adds, they will not be motivated to spend more than they need.

Does the child welfare system prepare foster adolescents for adulthood?

Mary Lee's foster care judicial reviews always seemed the same. She'd wait for hours in the courthouse, then have what felt like a one-minute session during which the judge would "pat me on the back and say everything's great."

Then, when she was 16, a judge actually asked: "Mary, what do you want for your life?" And she told him.

"I said I want a family," she recalls. "I want to be adopted. I want to know that when I go to college I'm going to have a family to come home to, that I'm going to have a dad to walk me down the aisle and grandparents for my children. And if I stay in foster care, when I leave I'm not going to have anything. I'm going to be totally on my own."

A week before her 18th birthday, after five years in foster care, Mary was adopted by Scott Lee, her caseworker, and his wife in Montgomery County, Tenn. Now 23, Mary has graduated from Vanderbilt University and plans to attend law school. She traces her good life and bright future to that moment the judge asked her about her dreams.

"Adoption is not about your childhood," she explains. "It's about the rest of your life. You always need a mom and a dad. You always need your grandparents. You always need the family support."

Mary's happy-ending story is, unfortunately, rare. According to the latest available statistics, 92,000 teens ages 16 to 18 lived in foster homes in 2002 — 17 percent of the total foster population. Just 1,300 of them were adopted that year — 2 percent of all foster care adoptions. That same year, 19,500 teens "aged out" of foster care, usually by turning 18, and many of them faced the transition to adulthood the way Mary Lee feared she would face it — alone. [19]

CHRONOLOGY

1800-1900 *Charitable organizations open "orphan asylums." Courts allow child protection societies to remove children from homes. Later, child-protection organizations pay families to take in homeless children.*

1853 Children's Aid Society of New York is founded and begins sending homeless children to Western families on "orphan" or "baby" trains in 1854.

1872 New York Foundling Asylum begins putting unwanted infants and toddlers on westbound "baby trains."

1900-1930s *First juvenile courts created. Child welfare agencies increase supervision of foster homes.*

1912 U.S. Children's Bureau established.

1935 Social Security Act provides federal funds for rural children's services, social-worker training.

1960-1970s *Federal role expands, focus intensifies on preserving families and alternatives to adoption.*

1961 Federal aid extended to poor foster children; more children's services are offered in urban and rural areas.

1962-69 Child-care professionals are required to report suspected abuse.

1974 Child Abuse Prevention and Treatment Act provides federal funds for protecting endangered children.

1976-79 Child welfare agencies try to reduce need for foster care. California, New York and Illinois subsidize adoptions.

1977 Foster care caseloads total about 550,000.

1980s-2000 *Single-parent households, unmarried births, child abuse and neglect reports all soar. Demands for reform increase. Lawsuits force improvements in state and local child welfare systems.*

1980 Congress creates federal adoption-assistance program. Social Security Act becomes main source of federal child welfare support.

1986 Foster caseload drops below 300,000; crack cocaine epidemic soon causes foster care rolls to soar.

1993 Federal government grants waivers for states to test innovative child welfare services.

1993-94 Discovery of 19 children living in squalor, death of another, spur shakeup of Illinois child welfare system.

1995 Foster caseloads hit nearly 500,000.

1997 Adoption and Safe Families Act increases federal support for adoption, family preservation.

1999 Foster caseloads peak at 570,000. Federal government increases aid for youths aging out of foster care.

2000s *Courts get federal money to reduce abuse and neglect backlogs, improve information technology.*

2001 Federal government offers new education assistance for aging-out youths.

2002 Authorities report 900,000 confirmed cases of child abuse or neglect nationwide, including 1,390 deaths.

2003 Foster rolls decline to 525,000. General Accounting Office says high caseloads and low salaries inhibit recruitment and retention of effective child welfare workers.

2004 Concern arises that a methamphetamine epidemic could raise foster care rolls. Pew Commission on Children in Foster Care argues that states need more child welfare money and flexibility. About 20 states receive waivers to offer support services not normally funded by federal programs.

2005 President Bush asks that federal foster care funding be converted to block grants. Illinois, now representing child welfare's "gold standard," cuts foster care population by two-thirds since mid-1990s and reduces average caseload from more than 50 to fewer than 20.

Four years after leaving foster care, nearly half of these older teens had not graduated from high school, a quarter had been homeless, 40 percent had become parents and fewer than a fifth were self-supporting, according to the Jim Casey Youth Opportunities Initiative, which works with those young people. [20]

"Effective middle-class families parent their kids into their 20s, and these kids are cut off at 18," Moore of Child Trends notes. "From age 18 to 24 is a time kids need contact and care and monitoring from adults."

After Chris Brooks left foster care in Nevada at age 19, he slept in a car and on friends' couches. At age 18, Terry Harrak figured out how to sleep and scrounge food amid the bustle of a busy hospital in Northern Virginia.

But both Chris' and Terry's stories have happy endings, thanks to serendipitous relationships with caring adults. A professor studying homeless youth "took me under his wing" and "became kind of like an uncle," Chris says. Now 23, he attends college in Las Vegas and mentors homeless youth. While living in a shelter, Terry met a Child Welfare League staff member who was looking for homeless young people to testify before Congress. Now 25, she attends college and works as the league's youth leadership coordinator, staffing an advisory council on which Chris and Mary serve.

Chris and Terry both say they were ill-prepared for independent living. And both cite the need for ongoing relationships and training in such basic skills as balancing a checkbook, filling out a tax form and applying for college aid.

"Historically, in child welfare we never thought about the permanent lifetime relationships that these kids need," says Gary Stangler, head of the Casey program for older teens and former director of the Missouri Social Services Department. "If we got them to age 18 alive, we did our job.

"Adoption, especially the older you get, is difficult and uncommon. So the solution was training for independent living, which is the opposite of permanent lifetime relationships."

Stangler has observed "an awakening to the fact that we were doing a very poor job for kids once they left the foster care system without the support we take for granted for our own kids." Slowly, he says, things are getting better.

Legislation passed in 1999 provides federal aid for housing and education for former foster youths, but many young people do not know how to apply for it. States are allowed to keep them on Medicaid beyond age 18, but most don't. Private organizations and some states are helping older teens build the adult relationships they need. And a few courts are institutionalizing the kind of court procedure that turned Mary Lee's life around.

In Chicago, the Cook County Circuit Court's Child Protection Division conducts "benchmark hearings" when foster children turn 14 and 16 and six months before they age out. (*See story, p. 102.*) The hearings can last up to two hours. Participants include the most important individuals in the children's lives, such as caseworkers, teachers, doctors and adults with whom the children have or might build long-lasting relationships.

"All of us were grappling with how could we, the court, get a handle on this road to being independent," says Patricia Martin Bishop, the division's presiding judge, who established the hearings. "The thought was, if we had more time to concentrate on each of these kids, we'd get a better handle on what needs they have that aren't met."

Among the questions Bishop requires the children to answer during the hearings: "What do you want to do when you get out of school? What do you intend to do with your life?"

BACKGROUND

Orphan Trains

In the beginning, America's child welfare system provided a kind of residential vocational education: Families took in needy children, then fed, clothed and trained them in a trade. Such apprenticeships were common, even for youngsters who were not parentless or poor. But it was considered an especially attractive way to place orphans and other children whose parents couldn't care for them. The child got a home and learned a trade; the host family benefited from the child's work. [21]

In the early 19th century, religious and charitable organizations began opening orphan asylums, which became the most common means of caring for children without parents between 1830 and 1860.

Also in mid-century, Charles Lorring Brace organized the Children's Aid Society of New York, which created the "orphan train" or "baby train" movement. Urban centers like New York attracted hordes of immigrants

How Illinois Reformed a Broken System

Three times, the Illinois Children and Family Services Department took Joseph Wallace away from his mentally ill mother, and three times the youngster was returned to her. There was no fourth time, because on April 19, 1993, she tied an extension cord around the 3-year-old's neck and hanged him from a transom in their Chicago apartment. [1]

Early the next year, Chicago police discovered 19 children living in a squalid, two-bedroom apartment with a half-dozen adults. Again, the department knew about six of the children but had left them with their mothers. [2]

Although the tragedies were only tiny tips of an enormous iceberg of bureaucratic failure, they shined a media spotlight on the Illinois child welfare system and outraged the public. In the end, they spurred dramatic reforms in the system, making it a font of successful innovation.

"They've addressed preventing kids from coming into foster care in the first place, as well as strengthening reunification for children who return home safely and strengthening alternative forms of permanency through subsidized guardianship and adoption," says Sue Badeau, deputy director of the Pew Commission on Foster Care, who says the system is now the "gold standard" of child care.

The Illinois system was "sort of average" in the 1980s, became "a mess" by the mid-'90s and now is one of the best, says Jill Duerr Berrick, associate dean of the School of Social Welfare at the University of California, Berkeley. "We've seen tremendous innovation coming out of Illinois."

Illinois probably ran America's worst child welfare system in the mid-1990s, says Mark Testa, co-director of the University of Illinois' Children and Family Research Center. It had the nation's highest prevalence of children in foster care — 17.1 per 1,000 — where they remained in care longer than children in other states. The total foster care rolls soared from 20,000 in the late-'80s to 52,000 in 1997. But when horror stories repeatedly hit the media, public outrage triggered changes.

Feeling intense pressure from the public, the state legislature and a lawsuit by the American Civil Liberties Union, Republican Gov. Jim Edgar appointed a new department director, Jess McDonald. He launched a comprehensive overhaul of the system and hired Testa as in-house research director.

"Lawsuits are critical to reform," says Marcia Robinson Lowry, executive director of Children's Rights, a New York organization that sues local and state governments to get them to improve child welfare systems. "There is sustained pressure for reform because of a court order."

McDonald and Testa discovered a system engaged in self-destruction. It was taking custody of thousands of children who didn't need to be removed from their homes, which limited caseworkers' ability to take care of children who really were in danger.

"The state was stepping in and taking these kids into protective custody because they were living with someone other than their parents — grandmother, aunt, uncle — even though they were living safely," Testa explains.

who took difficult, dangerous and sometimes deadly jobs. Diseases like typhoid, diphtheria and cholera also hit the poor especially hard. Deceased adults left orphans or single parents who couldn't support their children. And as immigrants or the offspring of immigrants, many of the children had no extended families they could turn to for support.

Besides worrying about the children's well being, Brace warned they might grow up to be violent criminals, referring to them as the "dangerous classes." He convinced businessmen to support shipping the children west, where they presumably would live healthy and wholesome lives on farms.

The first orphan train carried children to Dowagiac, Mich., in 1854. Over the next 80 years, some 150,000 to 200,000 children were shipped to states in the West. In 1872, the New York Foundling Asylum, which took in unwanted babies, began putting infants and toddlers on the trains, a practice that lasted into the 20th century. As in colonial days, the farmers benefited from the labor of the children they took in.

In the 1870s growing public concern about child abuse and neglect spurred the founding of societies for the prevention of cruelty to children, and courts began to empower them to remove children from neglectful homes.

"Children were building up in long-term foster care because there were no pathways for moving kids into more permanent homes, and folks weren't asking the relatives if they were willing to adopt. There was this myopia of only recognizing nuclear families, and if you're not in a nuclear family you're taken into the child welfare system."

The new managers forced the department to stop taking children who were living safely with relatives and start offering those families services available to nuclear families. "That reduced the number of kids coming into foster care right off the bat," Testa says. "But large numbers were still remaining in long-term foster care, so moving kids out needed attention."

The Illinois child welfare system delivers most foster care services through private contractors rather than local government agencies. "The financial incentives were all geared toward keeping kids in foster care," Testa explains, because they were paid only for foster children. "There was no reward for moving kids into permanent homes."

The state began paying incentives for adoption and reunification with parents, and the foster rolls dropped again.

The state also sought a waiver from federal rules in order to use some of its federal foster care funds to subsidize guardianships. Guardianship does not require termination of parental rights as adoption does, but it creates a permanent relationship between the child and the guardian and removes state supervision. Many relatives willing to care for children do not want to adopt, Testa says, because that would require termination of the biological parents' rights.

Since obtaining the waiver in 1997, Illinois has moved more than 8,000 children from foster care to guardianship, Testa says, reducing state costs and freeing caseworkers to concentrate on families that really are in trouble. During the decade of reform, the average worker's caseload has dropped from more than 50 cases to fewer than 20, Testa says.

"Illinois takes far fewer kids into foster care than many other states," he explains, "because we're doing a better job making family assessments and working with families who can take care of their kids with some help."

Now the department's biggest challenge is helping older adolescents who remain in foster care and are less likely to be adopted. "The solution is to attach every child as early as possible to a permanent family, a mentor, someone who's going to care about them," Testa says.

One hurdle to adoption is that older adolescents lose foster services that help in the transition to adulthood. The department has obtained a new federal waiver to extend those services after adoption or while the child is in guardianship. The department also is working with universities to support former foster children while they're in school. And it's developed a program to recruit families to host college students during vacations and to maintain connections with them during the school year.

"The Illinois system has not achieved perfection," Berrick says, "but it's certainly made a remarkable turnaround."

[1] Phillip J. O'Connor and Zay N. Smith, "Woman Charged In Son's Hanging," *Chicago Sun-Times*, April 20, 1993, p. 3.

[2] Phillip J. O'Connor and Ray Long, "Police Rescue 19 Kids In Filthy Apartment," *Chicago Sun-Times*, Feb. 2, 1994, p. 1; Colin McMahon and Susan Kuczka, "19 Kids Found In Filth," *Chicago Tribune*, Feb. 2, 1994, p. 1.

What we now know as foster care took root in the last two decades of the 19th century, when some child protection organizations began to pay families to take in homeless children so the children would not have to work. As the century neared its end, states began to organize charity boards that tended to favor home placements over institutional care.

The modern child welfare system began taking shape in the early 20th century. In 1912, the federal government created the U.S. Children's Bureau, now part of the Health and Human Services Department, to conduct research and distribute information to state children's agencies. States began to create separate juvenile court systems, which ordered more children into government care. In the 1920s, child welfare agencies began to exercise greater supervision of foster homes. And the New Deal brought federal money into the picture.

The Social Security Act of 1935 made the Children's Bureau responsible for administering the new Aid to Dependent Children program, later known as Aid to Families with Dependent Children, or AFDC. Congress intended the program to preserve poor families that otherwise might not be able to afford to keep their children at home. Aimed primarily at widowed mothers, it supported state aid programs for children living with a parent or other relative. States also received federal assistance

Linda and Mike Hurley and adopted daughter Courtney pose for their first family photo after signing adoption documents in Tampa on June 4, 2004. Child welfare agencies around the nation are seeking adoptive parents or guardians to help older foster children make the transition to adulthood.

to establish or strengthen children's services in rural areas and to train child welfare workers.

The federal government didn't extend aid to foster children and to urban services until 1961. To receive that aid, the foster child had to come from a family with income low enough to qualify for AFDC. Assistance also was offered for a broader range of child services, including family preservation.

Child Abuse and Crack

Also during the early 1960s, Denver physician Henry Kempe called public attention to the "battered child syndrome," revealing that many hospitalized youngsters whose injuries had been attributed to accidents actually had been abused by a parent or other caregiver. Before the decade ended, all 50 states passed laws requiring doctors, teachers and other child-care professionals to report suspected abuse. Congress followed suit in 1974 with the Child Abuse Prevention and Treatment Act (CAPTA),

which provided federal funds for child protection services, including procedures for reporting and investigating abuse and protecting endangered children.

During the late-'70s, child welfare agencies began focusing on moving children from foster care into permanent homes and on helping families avoid the need for out-of-home placements in the first place. Advocates of the shift in focus said it was better for children and would cost less than foster care.

Congress established a national adoption-information exchange program in 1978. California, New York and Illinois became the first states to subsidize adoptions in order to counteract the financial penalty suffered by foster parents who lose their foster payments when they finally adopt their foster children.

In 1980, Congress created a federal adoption-assistance program and merged it with the old AFDC foster care funds. Known as Title IV-E of the Social Security Act, it is now the main source of federal support for child welfare. The law required states to make "reasonable efforts" to keep children with their parents or return them as soon as possible. When families couldn't be reunited, the law declared placement with relatives or adoption to be superior to long-term foster care.

These efforts collided with the crack cocaine epidemic and other social pathologies from the mid-1980s through early-'90s.

From 1980 to 1994, single-parent households increased from 22 percent to 31 percent of all families. Births to unmarried teens soared from 27.6 per 1,000 females in 1980 to 44.6 in 1992. In 1993, 2.9 million child abuse and neglect reports were filed, up from 1.7 million in 1984. [22]

Foster caseloads — which dropped from a little more than 500,000 in 1977 to fewer than 300,000 in 1986 — soared back to nearly 500,000 by 1995. [23]

Federal and state governments, with support and prodding from private organizations, continued to press for family preservation and adoption as better alternatives to foster care.

In 1993, Congress authorized $1 billion over five years to help states strengthen troubled families. More federal money was distributed to help courts improve their handling of foster care and adoption cases. Congress gave the Health and Human Services secretary authority to grant waivers so states could use federal child welfare grants to finance innovative programs.

President Clinton declared adoption to be a national priority in 1996, saying "no child should be uncertain about what 'family' or 'parent' or 'home' means." The 1997 Adoption and Safe Families Act provided more incentives for adoption and family preservation. The Foster Care Independence Act of 1999 increased federal funding for counseling and other services for youths making the transition from foster care to adulthood. The money could be used for housing and other living expenses, and states could extend Medicaid coverage beyond the youths' 18th birthday.

In 2000 Congress authorized federal aid to help courts reduce backlogs of abuse and neglect cases and improve information technology systems. New federal educational assistance for so-called aging-out youths — those leaving the system — was authorized in 2001.

CURRENT SITUATION

Rigid Rules and Budgets

When Katie Sutton's grandchildren wanted to sleep over at a friend's house, Philadelphia child welfare caseworkers had to investigate the friend's family first. If she wanted to take a child to the doctor, she had to get a caseworker's instructions. When she wanted to take them across the nearby border into New Jersey, she had to get a caseworker's permission.

To Sutton, who had custody of five grandchildren as a foster parent, this was more than a nuisance.

Investigating a friend's family felt like "a way of invading their privacy and just automatically assuming that they have a bad background," she explained. For the grandchildren, the frequent involvement of caseworkers sent the message that "we're foster care kids, we don't belong anywhere, we have a label and we're different from everyone else." [24]

The children don't feel different anymore, because Sutton has become their permanent legal guardian, and they have left government supervision behind them. She hadn't wanted to adopt because she didn't want to terminate her son's parental rights. He's not a bad father, she said, just immature and emotionally and financially unable to care for his offspring. She couldn't afford to keep them outside the foster care system until Pennsylvania offered to subsidize her guardianship.

Caseloads Are Double Recommended Levels

The average American child welfare caseworker oversees two-dozen or more children — twice as many as child advocate and accreditation organizations recommend. Some caseworkers manage as many as 110 cases.

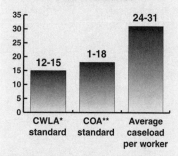

Number of cases per child welfare worker

* Child Welfare League of America

** Council on Accreditation for Children and Family Services

Source: "HHS Could Play a Greater Role in Helping Child Welfare Agencies Recruit and Retain Staff," U.S. General Accounting Office, March 2003

Her story encapsulates the state of the U.S. child welfare system today. Rigid rules and tight budgets make it difficult for agencies to tailor services to the specific needs of individual children and families.

But federal, state and local governments — often in cooperation with private organizations — are moving toward more flexible policies that emphasize holding families together and placing children in alternative permanent homes when that's not possible.

It's common for relatives not to want to adopt, even when they're willing to make permanent homes for grandchildren, nieces or nephews, Testa at the University of Illinois says. "They don't want to get embroiled in an

Stephen McCall of Brooklyn, N.Y., has been a foster parent for five years for, from left, Marshawn, Maleek, Brandon and Marcus. New York's child welfare agency is encouraging more potential foster parents to take adolescent and special-needs children.

adversarial battle with a daughter or sister," he explains. "Many of them feel it's odd that they'd have to adopt someone to whom they were already related."

In Sutton's case, Pennsylvania uses state funds to help her give the grandchildren a stable home. Sixteen other states do the same, while nine redirect surpluses from their share of the federal welfare program. Another nine have negotiated waivers with the HHS to spend some of their federal foster-care funds on subsidies for guardians. [25]

Waivers have become an important vehicle for reform of the child welfare system, just as they were for welfare reform in the mid-1990s. About 20 states have used them in varied ways, including for guardian assistance, drug-abuse treatment for parents, training of staff in private and public child services agencies, adoption promotion and other services to children and families not covered by federal foster care assistance. [26]

Whole Child Approach

Some state and local agencies have teamed up with private organizations and volunteers to improve the way they do business.

Some 70,000 volunteer court-appointed special advocates — or CASAs — represent the interests of children under court supervision throughout the country, for instance. Started in Seattle in 1976, the CASA movement has grown to 930 local programs that are united in

the National Court Appointed Special Advocate Association. [27] The volunteer builds a relationship with a child and tells the court whether the child is receiving the care and services the judge has ordered.

Child welfare workers often don't have enough time to keep close watch on the children in their charge, says Kenneth J. Sherk, who helps lead an organization that supports CASAs and children in the Phoenix-area child welfare system. "They're overworked and underpaid and all bogged down in red tape, and often as not things just don't get done for these kids," Sherk explains. "The CASAs tell the court and the Foster Care Review Board here when a child needs counseling, dental work, new clothes, school books — the basic needs."

In 2002 child welfare agencies in St. Louis, Louisville, Cedar Rapids, Iowa, and Jacksonville, Fla., agreed to work with the Center for Community Partnerships in Child Welfare. The center funds and advises efforts to bring a broad array of public and private organizations and individuals together to help troubled families. It's now working in 80 communities, Director Notkin says.

"The problems of families at risk of child abuse and neglect are complex," Notkin explains. "Therefore, it's necessary to develop a neighborhood network of services and support that involves public agencies, private agencies, nonprofits, the business community, the faith community, neighbors and relatives."

The center also stresses creation of a unique plan for each family, Notkin says. "If substance abuse is a problem, make sure someone from substance-abuse treatment is at the table," she explains. "If job training is needed, the job-training folks need to be there."

A key component is the participation of neighborhood volunteers who may tutor the parents in the skills of parenting, help to care for the children and help integrate the family into the community. "Our fundamental principle is that in order to have safe children we need strong families, and strong families need healthy communities that they're connected to," Notkin says.

Comprehensive approaches must be advocated, says Rosemary Chalk, director of the National Academy of Sciences Board on Children, Youth and Families, because "there's no sense of overall accountability for the whole child within the child welfare system."

"We know these kids are in bad shape and in many cases may have serious health problems or serious educational deficits," she explains. "But no one is stepping

Should states be allowed to convert federal foster care funds into capped block grants?

YES Wade F. Horn, Ph.D.
Assistant Secretary for Children and Families, U.S. Department of Health and Human Services

Written for The CQ Researcher, April 2005

States should be allowed to convert the Title IV-E foster care entitlement program into a flexible, alternative-financing structure. President Bush's proposed Child Welfare Program Option would allow them to do that. But the president's proposal is not a block grant. Its very name, Child Welfare Program Option, says it all: It is an option. If a state does not believe it is in its best interest to participate in this alternative, it may continue to participate in the current title IV-E entitlement program.

The states for many years have criticized the Title IV-E program as too restrictive. For instance, it only provides funds for the maintenance of foster children who have been removed from a home that would have been eligible for assistance under the old welfare program and for child welfare training. Under current law, Title IV-E funds cannot be used for services that might prevent a child from being placed in foster care in the first place, that might facilitate a child's returning home or that might help move the child to another permanent placement.

Under the proposed Program Option, states could choose to administer their program more flexibly, with a fixed allocation of funds over a five-year period. States would be able to use funds for foster care payments, prevention activities, permanency efforts, case management, administrative activities and training of child welfare staff. They would be able to develop innovative systems for preventing child abuse and neglect, keeping families and children safely together and quickly moving children toward adoption and permanency. They also would be freed from burdensome income-eligibility provisions that continue to be linked to the old welfare program.

Although states would have greater flexibility in how they use funds, they would still be held accountable for positive results. They would continue to be required to participate in Child and Family Services Reviews and to maintain the child safety protections, such as conducting criminal-background checks and licensing foster care providers, obtaining judicial oversight for removal and permanency decisions, developing case plans for all foster children and prohibiting race-based discrimination in placements. States also would be required to maintain their existing level of investment in the program.

Thus, the proposal allows — but does not force — states to enhance their child welfare services while relieving them of unnecessary administrative burdens. This option for flexible funding represents good public policy.

NO Shay Bilchik
President and CEO, Child Welfare League of America

Written for The CQ Researcher, April 2005

It is too common an occurrence to read a newspaper or listen to the news and learn about yet another seriously abused or neglected child or a child welfare system struggling to protect the children in its care. Recently, every state, the District of Columbia and Puerto Rico had the performance of their child welfare system measured as a part of a federal review. States fell short in a variety of areas, including having excessive caseloads, inadequate supervision, inadequate training and lack of treatment services.

Each of these shortcomings relates to a failure to provide resources that would support high-quality performance — resources that should be provided through investments made by the federal, state and local governments responsible for protecting abused and neglected children.

Yearly, states confirm nearly 900,000 reports of abuse and neglect. There are more than 550,000 children in the nation's foster care system. Too many of these children stay in foster care far longer than necessary because of the lack of appropriate support services. In fact, nearly 40 percent of abused and neglected children don't receive treatment to address the emotional trauma they have experienced. In addition, much of this abuse could have been avoided through prevention services.

There is indeed a need for greater flexibility in the use of federal funds to help address these service gaps. Proposals that condition flexibility on capping federal funding, however, are shortsighted and reflect a lack of responsiveness to the results of the federal review. While it may seem difficult to argue against an option being presented to the states that trades funding level for flexibility, it actually is quite easy when it is being presented as the federal government's solution to the problems facing our nation's child welfare system. Such a proposal is tantamount to a freeze on the federal commitment to protecting children and contradicts the vital role that the federal government plays in keeping children safe.

Flexibility is needed, but new federal investments are also needed so that fewer children are hurt and more parents can safely care for their children. The federal review clearly tells us that this is the case. It seems a fair demand, therefore, that our federal leaders bring forward a reform proposal that presents serious solutions to the trauma and horror that confront our abused and neglected children — and no less.

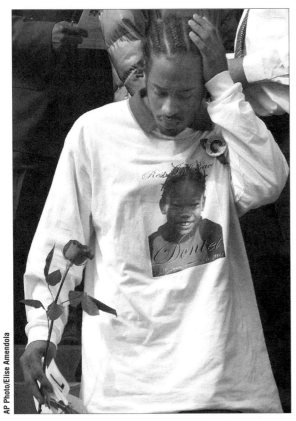

AP Photo/Elise Amendola

A mourner leaves the funeral service of Dontel Jeffers, 4, in Boston's Dorchester section on March 16, 2005, wearing a photo of the abused child on his shirt. Dontel died in a foster home where he had been placed by the Department of Social Services. The boy's relatives claim his foster mother beat him.

up and saying we're prepared to deal with the whole child."

Such services work, child welfare experts say, but the demand exceeds the supply. In a study of mothers who received drug abuse treatment, for example, slightly more than half had custody of their children before entering treatment while three-quarters had custody six months after completing treatment, the Child Welfare League reported. Three-quarters of parents with children in the child welfare system need treatment, the league said, but only a little more than 30 percent receive it. [28]

In 2003 authorities received about 2 million child abuse or neglect reports involving more than 3 million children. Agencies found that more than 900,000 of the children had been neglected or abused and that 1,390 had died. Most of the confirmed cases involved neglect, but 19 percent involved physical abuse and 10 percent sexual abuse. [29]

Although most agencies prefer to keep children with their parents, about 525,000 lived in foster homes in 2003, a number that has steadily declined since peaking at 570,000 in 1999. The Congressional Budget Office estimates that the number of federally supported foster care children will drop from 229,000 this year to 225,000 next year and 162,000 by 2015. Because federal aid goes only to children from families with very low income, only about half of the foster caseload receives a federal subsidy. [30]

Many child welfare workers complain that this caseload exceeds the capabilities of the work force, and the Government Accountability Office (GAO) has endorsed that view. "A stable and highly skilled child welfare work force is necessary to effectively provide child welfare services," Congress' nonpartisan investigating arm said in a 2003 report. [31] However, workers' salaries tend to be too low to attract and maintain a well-qualified staff, and caseloads tend to be higher than those recommended by widely recognized standards, the agency found. (*See graph, p. 111.*)

"Large caseloads and worker turnover delay the timeliness of investigations and limit the frequency of worker visits with children," the GAO said. [32] In reviewing the performance of state child welfare agencies, HHS attributed many deficiencies to high caseloads and inadequate training. [33]

The Child Welfare League suggests a caseload of 12 to 15 children per worker, and the Council on Accreditation for Children and Family Services recommends no more than 18, GAO said. [34] Actual caseloads last year ranged from nine to 80, with medians ranging from 18 to 38 depending on the type of cases a worker was handling, according to a survey by the American Public Human Services Association. [35]

Beginning caseworkers earned a median salary of about $28,500 in 2002, and the most experienced workers about $47,000, the Child Welfare League reported. [36] Child welfare administrators complain about losing workers to jobs in schools, where the workers can continue to work with children while earning more in a safer environment. [37] Child welfare staff turnover ranges from 30 to 40 percent annually.

To induce workers to stay in their jobs, Rep. Stephanie Tubbs, D-Ohio, has introduced legislation to forgive their college loans. Ohio Republican Rep. Mike DeWine introduced a similar bill in the previous Congress but had not done so again this year.

OUTLOOK

Hope and Fear

Children's advocates view the future of child welfare with optimism and concern. Their hope springs from the reform movements spurring changes in many state and local programs, the trends in child welfare policies that seem to be moving in effective directions and the agreement among liberals and conservatives that more attention must be focused on early services to troubled families and speedy placement of foster children into permanent homes.

They worry that the federal financial squeeze might strangle child welfare funding and that a threatened increase in methamphetamine addiction could imitate the devastating crack cocaine epidemic of the 1980s and '90s and cause caseloads to soar once more.

"You have a lot of things going on, a lot of innovation being tested, a lot of interest in looking at the financing," says Notkin, of the Center for Community Partnerships in Child Welfare. "You also have, in the last few years, some really horrific stories coming to the attention of the public that dramatize the crisis in child welfare.

"The question is whether there will be enough political will to honestly confront the problems of the child welfare system, which are reflective of and connected to other problems in our society."

The Child Welfare League's Bilchik foresees "a three- to five-year window where we're going to see tremendous change in practice and a continuing push for reduction of federal support. Either states are going to ratchet up their support in tough economic times or we're going to see a reduction in the level and quality of care.

"I think we're going to go through another cycle where they push for less investment, which will result in more harm for children and that will lead to recognition that more resources are needed," he says. "At the same time, good practices will be adopted as we get better at keeping kids closer to home, reducing the number of times they move and placing them more often with kin."

Columbia University's Wulczyn predicts foster care rolls will shrink because "we're doing a better job of providing appropriate services," but he adds a caveat: "as long as we don't experience an unexpected social upheaval that mimics the crack cocaine epidemic."

The Casey Foundation's Stangler expects agencies to do "a much better job of promoting permanency arrangements for older youth. And I expect states to get better at connecting the dots between emancipating youth, education and the work force."

He looks to expansion of current programs through which families volunteer to provide home-like relationships to former foster children, offering them a place to come home to during college vacations, for instance, and adults to whom they can turn for parent-like guidance year-round.

An important challenge, says Meltzer, of the Center for the Study of Social Policy, is getting other parts of society to solve problems that shouldn't have been left to child welfare agencies to fix. "Ultimately, the child welfare systems have become services of last resort for a lot of problems related to poverty, mental health and substance abuse," she explains. "Figuring out how you build up resources so fewer kids and families need child welfare intervention is where you want to go."

HHS Assistant Secretary Horn is confident that the government and child welfare community know more today than 15 years ago about how to prevent child abuse and neglect. "I'm very encouraged by the renewed focus on helping families form and sustain healthy marriages," he adds, "because two parents in a healthy marriage don't come home one day and decide to abuse and neglect their children. Parents in unhealthy, dysfunctional and violent households do."

Rep. McDermott concedes the possibility of "some improvements here or there. But, if you're digging the kind of debt hole we've created, the first ones who are sacrificed into the hole are the kids."

"Republicans and Democrats do care a lot about kids," says Mial of the Casey Foundation. "What it comes down to is how well connected are they to what's happening."

Research and education are needed, for child welfare workers as well as for politicians, she adds.

And despite Horn's optimism about knowledge gained in the last 15 years, she says, "We know how to send kids to adoption. We don't necessarily know how to keep kids in a family or how to reunite them with their family."

NOTES

1. Lomi Kriel, "Bill to Overhaul Kid Agency Is Filed," *San Antonio Express-News*, Feb. 4, 2005, p. A8. And Robert T. Garrett, "New bill on child abuse proposed; Police would become involved in most reports of juvenile injuries," *The Dallas Morning News*, Dec. 2, 2004, p. A4.

2. Suzanne Smalley and Brian Braiker, "Suffer the Children," *Newsweek*, Jan. 20, 2003, p. 32.

3. Leslie Kaufman, "State Agency For Children Fails Its Tests, U.S. Says," *The New York Times*, May 22, 2004, p B5.

4. Phillip J. O'Connor and Ray Long, "Police Rescue 19 Kids In Filthy Apartment," *Chicago Sun-Times*, Feb. 2, 1994, p. 1; Colin McMahon and Susan Kuczka, "19 Kids Found In Filth," *Chicago Tribune*, Feb. 2, 1994, p. 1.

5. Michelle M. Martinez, "Senators Giving CPS Reform Bill a Thumbs up," *Austin American-Statesman*, March 3, 2005, p. B1; "Senators Approve Protective Services Bill," *Austin American-Statesman*, March 4, 2005, p. B6.

6. Richard Lezin Jones, "Child Welfare Plan Approved," *The New York Times*, June 13, 2004, Section 14NJ, p. 6; Jones, "Monitor Approves Child Welfare Plan," *The New York Times*, June 10, 2004, p. B4; Jones, "New Jersey Plans to Lighten Load for Child Welfare Workers," *The New York Times*, June 9, 2004, p. B5; Jones, "Plan for New Jersey Foster Care Removes Many From Institutions," *The New York Times*, Feb. 16, 2004, p. B1.

7. "The Number and Rate of Foster Children Ages 17 and Under, 1990-2003," Child Trends Data Bank, available at www.childtrendsdatabank.org.

8. Robert T. Garrett, "Changes Urged for Care Agencies," *The Dallas Morning News*, Dec. 8, 2004, p. 4A.

9. "Trends in Foster Care and Adoption," U.S. Department of Health and Human Services, Administration for Children and Families, August 2004, available at www.acf.dhhs.gov/programs/cb/dis/afcars/publications/afcars.htm.

10. Jonathan D. Rockoff and John B. O'Donnell, "State's Lax Oversight Puts Fragile Children at Risk," *The Baltimore Sun*, April 10, 2005, p. 1A.

Additional stories in the series, "A Failure To Protect Maryland's Troubled Group Homes," published April 11-13.

11. Rockoff and O'Donnell, "Leaders Vow To Fix Group Homes," April 14, 2005, p. 1A.

12. Child Welfare League of America press release, 2004.

13. House Ways and Means Committee, Human Resources Subcommittee, "Hearing to Examine Child Welfare Reform Proposals," July 13, 2004, transcript and documents available at http://waysandmeans.house.gov/hearings.asp?formmode=detail&hearing=161&comm=2.

14. Roseana Bess and Cynthia Andrews Scarcella, "Child Welfare Spending During a Time of Fiscal Stress," Urban Institute, Dec. 31, 2004, available at www.urban.org/url.cfm?ID=411124.

15. "Budget in Brief, Fiscal Year 2006," U.S. Department of Health and Human Services, pp. 6 and 98, available at http://hhs.gov/budget/06budget/FY2006BudgetinBrief.pdf.

16. For background, see Sarah Glazer, "Welfare Reform," *The CQ Researcher*, Aug. 3, 2001, pp. 601-632.

17. "Fostering the future: Safety, Permanence and Well-Being for Children in Foster Care," Pew Commission on Children in Foster Care, May 18, 2004, available at http://pewfostercare.org/research/docs/FinalReport.pdf.

18. House Ways and Means subcommittee hearing, *op. cit.*

19. "The AFCARS Report" (Adoption and Foster Care Analysis and Reporting System), U.S. Department of Health and Human Services, August 2004, available at www.acf.dhhs.gov/programs/cb/publications/afcars/report9.pdf.

20. www.jimcaseyyouth.org/about.htm.

21. Except where noted, information for this section is drawn from these sources: Rachel S. Cox, "Foster Care Reform," *The CQ Researcher*, Jan. 9, 1998. Kasia O'Neill Murray and Sarah Gesiriech, "A Brief Legislative History of the Child Welfare System," Pew Commission on Children in Foster Care, available at http://pewfostercare.org/research/docs/Legislative.pdf; Mary-Liz Shaw, "Artist Recalls the Rough Rumbling of the Orphan Trains," *Milwaukee Journal Sentinel*, Feb. 2, p. E1; Mary

Ellen Johnson, "Orphan Train Movement: A history of the Orphan Trains Era in American History," Orphan Train Heritage Society of America, available at www.orphantrainriders.com/otm11.html.

22. "National Study of Protective, Preventive and Reunification Services Delivered to Children and Their Families," U.S. Department of Health and Human Services, 1994, available at www.acf.hhs.gov/programs/cb/publications/97natstudy/introduc.htm#CW.

23. Margaret LaRaviere, "A Brief History of Federal Child Welfare Legislation and Policy (1935-2000)," the Center for Community Partnerships in Child Welfare, Nov. 18, 2002, available at www.cssp.org/uploadFiles/paper1.doc.

24. Press conference, Washington, D.C., Oct. 13, 2004, transcript, pp. 7-9, available at www.fosteringresults.org/results/press/pewpress_10-13-04_fednews-bureau.pdf.

25. *Ibid.*, p.12, for updated waiver figure. Also: Mark Testa, Nancy Sidote Salyers and Mike Shaver, "Family Ties: Supporting Permanence for Children in Safe and Stable Foster Care With Relatives and Other Caregivers," Children and Family Research Center, School of Social Work, University of Illinois at Urbana-Champaign, Oct. 2004, p. 5, available at www.fosteringresults.org/results/reports/pewreports_10-13-04_alreadyhome.pdf.

26. "Summary of Title IV-E Child Welfare Waiver Demonstration Projects," U.S. Health and Human Services Department, May 2004, available at www.acf.hhs.gov/programs/cb/initiatives/cwwaiver/summary.htm.

27. "History of CASA." Available at www. casanet.org/download/ncasa_publications/history-casa.pdf.

28. "The Nation's Children 2005," the Child Welfare League of America, pp. 2-3.

29. *Ibid.*, p. 1. Also: "Child Maltreatment 2002," Health and Human Services Department, available at www.acf.hhs.gov/programs/cb/publications/cm02/summary.htm.

30. Child Trends Data Bank, *op. cit.* Also: "CBO Baseline for Foster Care and Adoption Assistance," Congressional Budget Office, March 2005, available at www.cbo.gov/factsheets/2005/FosterCare.PDF.

31. "HHS Could Play a Greater Role in Helping Child Welfare Agencies Recruit and Retain Staff," General Accounting Office, (now called the Government Accountability Office) March 2003, available at www.gao.gov/new.items/d03357.pdf.

32. *Ibid*, pp. 3-4.

33. *Ibid*, p. 21.

34. *Ibid*, p. 14.

35. "Report From the 2004 Child Welfare Workforce Survey: State Agency Findings," American Public Human Services Association, February 2005, p. 22, available at www.aphsa.org/ Home/Doc/Workforce%20Report%202005.pdf.

36. Child Welfare League of America National Data Analysis System, available at www.ndas.cwla.org/data_stats/access/predefined/Report.asp?ReportID=86.

37. General Accounting Office, *op. cit.*, pp. 3, 11.

BIBLIOGRAPHY

Books

Brohl, Kathryn, *The New Miracle Workers: Overcoming Contemporary Challenges in Child Welfare Work*, CLWA Press, 2004.
A veteran child welfare worker and family therapist explains new challenges facing workers and administrators, including meeting legislature-imposed timelines for case management, working collaboratively with clients, understanding diverse cultures and nontraditional families, keeping up with research, improving pay and training and overcoming worker burnout.

Geen, Rob, editor, *Kinship Care: Making the Most of a Valuable Resource*, Urban Institute Press, 2003.
A collection of essays edited by an Urban Institute researcher examines how child welfare agencies are using relatives as foster parents, how this differs from traditional foster care, and how the caregivers describe their experiences.

Shirk, Martha, and Gary Stangler, *On Their Own: What Happens to Kids When They Age Out of the Foster Care System*, Westview Press, 2004.
A journalist (Shirk) and the former director of the Missouri Social Services Department (Stangler) who

now runs a program for older foster children offer alternately inspiring and heartrending stories of 10 young people who must leave foster care and learn to live on their own without the family and community relationships that most young people lean on as they make the transition from teen to adult.

Articles

Campbell, Joel, "Encourage Access to Juvenile Courts: The Time Is Right for Lifting Juvenile Court and Child Welfare System Secrecy," *The Quill*, Aug. 1, 2004, p. 36.

A leader of the Society of Professional Journalists' Freedom of Information Committee argues that one way to improve the child welfare system is to let the news media into juvenile courts.

Colloff, Pamela, "Life and Meth," *Texas Monthly*, June 2004, p. 120.

Methamphetamine is destroying families in East Texas — an epidemic child welfare authorities worry could spike foster care rolls nationwide.

Humes, Edward, "The Unwanted," *Los Angeles Magazine*, Jan. 1, 2003, p. 64.

The reporter exposes a dysfunctional Los Angeles children's home.

Rockoff, Jonathan D., and John B. O'Donnell, "A Failure to Protect Maryland's Troubled Group Homes," *The Baltimore Sun*, April 10-13, 2005.

In a four-part exposé, the authors reveal child abuse, neglect and even death within Maryland's state-supervised group homes for children.

Reports and Studies

"Fostering the Future: Safety, Permanence and Well-Being for Children in Foster Care," the Pew Commission on Children in Foster Care, May 18, 2004, available at http://pewfostercare.org/research/docs/FinalReport.pdf.

This influential report by a blue-ribbon panel headed by two former U.S. representatives — Republican Bill Frenzel of Minnesota and Democrat William H. Gray III of Pennsylvania — explores the need to improve the child welfare system. The commission argues for more flexibility and more federal funds while acknowledging need to moderate federal spending.

"HHS Could Play a Greater Role in Helping Child Welfare Agencies Recruit and Retain Staff," General Accounting Office (now the Government Accountability Office), March 2003, available at www.gao.gov/new.items/d03357.pdf.

A report by Congress' nonpartisan investigating arm presents evidence that child welfare agencies' effectiveness suffers because caseworkers are underpaid and given too many cases to manage.

Testa, Mark F., "Encouraging Child Welfare Innovation through IV-E Waivers," Children and Family Research Center, School of Social Work, University of Illinois at Urbana-Champaign, January 2005; http://cfrcwww.social.uiuc.edu/briefpdfs/cfrc.

An academic study by the former research director of the Illinois Departm ent of Children and Family Services examines how states have used waivers of federal regulations to spend federal funds on innovative programs and suggests how to use waivers more effectively. Testa is co-director of the University of Illinois' Children and Family Research Center.

Vandivere, Sharon, Rosemary Chalk and Kristin Anderson Moore, "Children in Foster Homes: How Are They Faring?" Child Trends Research Brief, December 2003; www.childtrends.org/files/FosterHomesRB.pdf.

An analysis of surveys of children and families concludes that foster children are less healthy than other children, have more developmental and behavioral problems and often have problems in school.

For More Information

Annie E. Casey Foundation, 701 St. Paul St., Baltimore, MD 21202; (410) 547-6600; www.aecf.org. Advocates, conducts research and supports programs to benefit disadvantaged children and families; known for its Kids Count Data Book, an annual compilation of state-by-state statistics.

Child Trends, 4301 Connecticut Ave., N.W., Suite 100, Washington, DC 20008; (202) 572-6000; www.childtrends.org. Conducts research about children and publishes reports and statistics on its Child Trends Data Bank.

Child Welfare League of America, 440 First St., N.W., 3rd Floor, Washington, DC 20001-2085; (202) 638-2952; www.cwla.org. America's oldest and largest child welfare organization advocates, suggests standards and educates welfare workers.

Children and Family Research Center, School of Social Work, University of Illinois, 1203 W. Oregon, Urbana, IL 61801; (217) 333-5837; http://cfrcwww.social.uiuc.edu. Leading university-based institution for studying children, families and child welfare services.

Children's Bureau, 370 L'Enfant Promenade, S.W., Washington, DC 20447; (202) 205-8618; www.acf.hhs.gov/programs/cb. Agency of the U.S. Health and Human Services Department that supports states' delivery of child welfare services, publishes reports and data on its Web site, maintains hotlines for reporting child and domestic abuse and runaway, missing or exploited children (1-800-4ACHILD).

National Court Appointed Special Advocate (CASA) Association, 100 W. Harrison, North Tower, Suite 500, Seattle WA 98119; (800) 628-3233; www.nationalcasa.org. Provides leadership, consultation and resources for more than 900 CASA programs across the country whose nearly 70,000 volunteers serve as advocates for 280,000 abused or neglected children.

Pew Commission on Children in Foster Care, 2233 Wisconsin Ave., N.W., Suite 535, Washington, DC 20007; (202) 687-0948; www.pewfostercare.org. Blue-ribbon, bipartisan panel that proposed more federal funding and more flexibility for states to spend it.

6

Social Security Reform

Mary H. Cooper

President Bush tells the National Summit on Retirement Savings he favors allowing workers to invest part of their Social Security payroll taxes in stocks. Democratic presidential nominee John Kerry opposes so-called privatization plans.

AFP Photo/Stan Honda

From *CQ Researcher*, September 24, 2004.

D emographers often describe the huge generation of baby boomers as a pig in a python, a population bulge so big it dwarfs both their parents' generation and their children's.

By most measures, the 77 million Americans born during the prosperous postwar period from 1946 to 1964 have dominated culture and politics. New schools rose to accommodate them; their protests ended the Vietnam War; and their tastes drove entertainment and consumer trends.

Now, as they near retirement, baby boomers may have yet another profound influence on American society: They could bankrupt the 70-year-old Social Security system.

"As the baby boomers start to retire, if the economy is slowing and the deficit is still bad, there's going to be some serious concern about whether or not they're even going to get all of their benefits," says Jeff Lemieux, executive director of the nonpartisan Centrist Policy Network, which analyzes Social Security reform proposals.

Only about 60 percent of the 47 million people who now receive Social Security benefits are retired, but the boomers' retirement will swell those ranks to the breaking point. Barring changes to current law, the Social Security trust fund will run out of money by 2053, according to the nonpartisan Congressional Budget Office (CBO). [1]

Demographers have warned for several decades that Social Security could not long survive the boomers' retirement without significant changes in the way the system collects and disburses revenue. [2] Spawned by the hardships of the Great Depression, Social Security was designed as a "pay-as-you-go" system, collecting payroll taxes from current workers and employers and using those funds to pay benefits to current retirees. Historically, the system stayed in

Low-Income Retirees Depend on Social Security

Low-income seniors received 82 percent of their retirement income from Social Security in 2001, while wealthy seniors depended on Social Security for only 19 percent of their income.

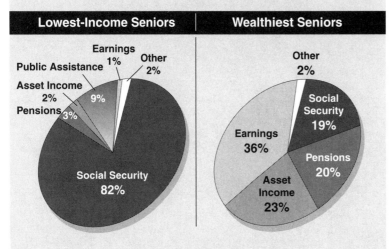

Sources of Income for Seniors, 2001

Note: Percentages for low-income seniors do not add to 100 due to rounding.

Source: "Income of the Aged Chartbook, 2001," Social Security Administration, 2003

advances have raised life expectancy, so future retirees will live longer and collect Social Security benefits longer than their predecessors. In fact, the combined impact of a larger retiree population and increased longevity suggests that Social Security's financial problems may outlive the boomers.

"This is not just a temporary problem that will go away when we get over the baby-boom bulge," says Michael Tanner, director of health and welfare studies at the libertarian Cato Institute. Rather than a "pig in a python," the boomers are "more like a python swallowing a telephone pole. The situation will never improve because life expectancies will continue to increase, while birth rates will likely continue to decline."

Policymakers have been reluctant to take on the politically thankless task of reforming Social Security. Indeed, the program is so popular it's known as the electrified "third rail" of U.S. politics — touching it can be political suicide. But with the approach of 2008, when the first boomers become eligible for Social Security benefits, politicians are acknowledging the system must be changed if it is to survive. *

The question is how. Early in his administration, President Bush set up a commission that recommended ways to "privatize" part of Social Security by allowing workers to invest a small portion of their payroll contributions in stocks held in personal investment accounts. The theory was that stocks would return higher dividends than the government's conservative bond investments.

Support for personal investment accounts runs high among conservatives eager to reduce the size and role of government in general — a sentiment famously characterized by Grover Norquist, president of Americans for Tax

the black because Social Security had a relatively large work force and small elderly population. In 1950, for example, 16 workers supported every retiree — more than enough to cover benefits. (*See graphs, p. 126.*)

Indeed, since 1983 payroll taxes have exceeded benefits paid, resulting in large surpluses in Social Security "trust funds" — the accounts used to pay benefits. [3] Money not needed to pay current benefits is invested in special-issue U.S. Treasury bonds. In early 2004, the Social Security system held $1.5 trillion in such bonds, which produced more than $80 billion a year in interest.

Over the years, the government has tapped into the trust funds to pay for unrelated programs, promising to pay the money back. But the boomers had fewer children than their parents, resulting in the "baby bust" of the 1970s and '80s. Thus, by 2040, when the last boomers will be well into retirement, only two workers will be supporting each Social Security recipient — too few to pay scheduled benefits at current tax rates.

Compounding the system's financial problems, medical

---

* Retiring workers may begin to receive reduced benefits at age 62. They receive full benefits by deferring retirement until their normal retirement age of 66.

Reform: "I don't want to abolish government; I simply want to reduce it to the size where I can drag it into the bathroom and drown it in the bathtub." [4]

Some proposals to privatize Social Security reflect the view that the private-enterprise system is a superior source of financial security for retirees than a government-funded entitlement program. Peter J. Ferrara, an associate law professor at the George Mason University School of Law, in Arlington, Va., and a former senior policy adviser on Social Security for Norquist's organization, has authored a plan that relies heavily on private investments. "Even though the stock market has a lot of ups and downs, over a lifetime of investment workers are certainly going to end up with a lot more through a system like this than they would under the pay-as-you-go Social Security system," Ferrara says.

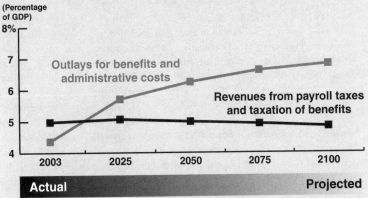

Outlays to Surpass Revenues in 15 Years

Social Security benefit payments will exceed revenues coming into the system beginning in 2019, according to Congressional Budget Office predictions. The revenue shortfall will force the program to pay benefits by drawing down its trust funds, which are expected to run dry by 2053.

Social Security Outlays and Revenues, 2003 to 2100
(As a percentage of gross domestic product)

Source: Congressional Budget Office, "The Outlook for Social Security," June 2004

Critics, including many Democrats, say personal accounts amount to a backdoor assault on one of the country's most successful entitlement programs. "What the folks who want to drown government in the bathtub are really trying to do with privatization is bankrupt the federal government," says Joan Entmacher, vice president for economic security at the National Women's Law Center, a Washington advocacy group. "It's terrifying."

The "dirty little secret" about personal investment accounts, she continues, is that rather than improving Social Security's long-term financial shortfall, "they would make it worse." A full 85 percent of payroll taxes paid by all of today's workers "go to pay benefits for our fathers, our grandmothers and the kid down the street whose parents were killed. If — instead of going into the Social Security trust fund — that money goes into private accounts [unavailable to Social Security], how are we going to pay those benefits?"

The stock market's recent plunge and recent corporate and stock market scandals that resulted in thousands of Americans losing their retirement nest-eggs

raise more red flags for critics of privatization plans. [5] Further, corporate America is abandoning traditional, defined-benefit pension plans in favor of defined-contribution schemes like 401(k)s that shift pension investment risks to workers, making Social Security the only secure source of retirement income that retirees can count on, they say. [6]

"In today's 401(k) world, 40 percent of workers work for employers who don't even offer a 401(k) plan, and fewer than 50 percent of private-sector workers take advantage of those plans," says Christian Weller, senior economist at the Center for American Progress, a liberal think tank in Washington. "Even those who favor privatization are aware of Social Security's value as an insurance system."

To date, the contenders in this fall's presidential election have taken a cautious approach to Social Security reform. Even Bush, who earlier spearheaded the call for privatization, has downplayed the issue. Sen. John Kerry, D-Mass., the Democratic nominee, rejects Bush's privatization scheme for Social Security but has yet to offer a detailed plan to resolve the system's impending funding

Major Proposals to Reform Social Security

Proposals to reform Social Security are designed to eliminate the funding gap that the program likely would face over the next several decades as baby boomers start retiring in droves.

Plans to "privatize" Social Security would supplement the current system, which pays defined, or guaranteed, benefits, with a voluntary system enabling workers to shift part of their payroll-tax contribution into government-managed personal investment accounts. [1] Returns on those investments would replace part of the defined benefits provided to retirees who choose to participate. Most of the plans offer several investment options in index funds, like the existing federal Thrift Savings Plan (TSP) that covers government employees. The plans differ in the amount of transition costs they entail, which result from the diversion of payroll-tax revenue from the Social Security trust funds to personal accounts.* Most plans include benefit cuts with or without payroll-tax increases. Among the plans being debated are proposals from:

Rep. Paul Ryan, R-Wis., and Sen. John Sununu, R-N.H. — Based on a proposal by Peter J. Ferrara of George Mason University, the plan allows workers to divert an average of 6.4 percent of earnings into personal investment account, more than any other major proposal. It would not cut Social Security benefits or raise payroll taxes. Workers who choose to stay with the current Social Security system would receive the benefits promised under current law; those who open investment accounts would be guaranteed to receive at least as much as they would receive in benefits under current law. The plan incurs much higher transition costs than other major proposals, according to Centrists.org, a nonpartisan group that analyzes public policy. [2]

Michael Tanner, Cato Institute — Workers could divert half of their payroll taxes — 6.2 percent — to private accounts. (The other half would pay disability and survivor benefits and part of the transition costs.) Workers who choose the private accounts would forgo the accrual of future traditional Social Security benefits. Workers who remain in the traditional Social Security system would receive benefits payable with the current level of revenue. The government would guarantee that workers' retirement incomes would be at least 120 percent of the poverty level. The plan requires Congress to figure out how to pay for remaining transition costs, suggesting cutting corporate subsidies and redirecting the savings to Social Security. [3]

President's Commission to Strengthen Social Security — The most closely watched of the commission's three proposals, Model 2, would allow workers to place up to 4 percent or $1,000 per year of payroll taxes into personal investment accounts, with the remainder going to the Social Security trust funds to pay current beneficiaries. Once retired, account holders would receive reduced benefits, based on the total amount diverted into their personal accounts. The plan would offer several investment options for Social Security retirement accounts, and those who fail to stipulate their investment allocations would have their holdings split among stocks and bonds. The plan would reduce retirees' initial benefits but continue to allow later benefits to rise with inflation.

Sen. Lindsey Graham, R-S.C. — Workers under age 55 either could "pay to stay" in the current system or join a hybrid system with personal accounts similar to the TSP. (Workers over 55 would remain in the current system.) Eligible workers could stay in the current system by paying an additional payroll tax of 2 percent. The hybrid system would pay lower benefits but increased minimum benefits

shortfall. And neither candidate is thought likely to offer a detailed solution to the shortfall before the election.

"The candidates have been quiet on Social Security all year, and that's largely because it's an election year," says Jeffrey R. Brown, a Social Security expert and professor of finance at the University of Illinois, Urbana-Champaign. "This, more than any other issue, is a topic that is difficult to express nuanced views about in a way that is easily digested by the electorate."

But even if both candidates continue to dodge the issue through the November elections, the next administration will face fundamental choices about the best way to ensure the system's long-term survival. Meanwhile, these are some of the questions policymakers are asking:

Does Social Security face an immediate funding crisis?

Government analysts predict that Social Security will begin taking in less revenue than it pays out in benefits

for low-income workers. The government would match voluntary contributions up to $500 for workers making less than $30,000 a year and guarantee a minimum benefit. Centrists.org calls the proposal moderately sized and somewhat more progressive — lower-income workers get relatively higher benefits, and higher-income workers get relatively lower benefits — than under current law, but with significant transition costs.

Reps. Jim Kolbe, R-Ariz., and Charles Stenholm, D-Texas — Beginning in 2006, workers under 55 could redirect 3 percent of their first $10,000 in earnings and 2 percent of their remaining taxable earnings to personal accounts. (For someone earning $30,000, the amount that could be invested would be about $733.) The government would match 50 percent of the contributions for workers earning less than $30,000 a year. Low-wage workers would receive a new minimum benefit. It would speed up the increase in Social Security's normal retirement age to 67 by 2011, with a small reduction in benefits for workers who retire early and a small increase in benefits for those who work beyond the normal retirement age. Centrists.org describes this personal-account plan as moderately sized, probably more progressive than current law and better than Graham's plan at limiting and paying for transition costs.

Laurence J. Kotlikoff, economist, Boston University, and Scott Burns, finance columnist — A new "personal security system" (PSS) would replace the retirement portion of Social Security (survivor and disability insurance would remain unchanged). The retirement portion of Social Security would cease to collect revenue, and a new federal retail sales tax would be used to pay off the transition costs. Current retirees would continue to receive their promised benefits, and current workers, once they retire, would

receive all the benefits owed them as of the plan's implementation date. Workers continue to pay payroll taxes to cover Social Security's survivor and disability benefits; the portion of payroll taxes no longer collected for Social Security's retirement system would go instead to PSS accounts. The government guarantees the principal amount that workers contribute to their PSS accounts. [4]

Robert M. Ball, former Social Security commissioner — Retains the system's current structure with minor benefit cuts and tax increases and offers private investment accounts. Part of the Social Security trust funds, now held only in Treasury bonds, would be invested in a broad index of stocks, overseen by a Federal Reserve-type board. Workers could choose to invest up to an additional 2 percent of their earnings in supplemental retirement savings accounts administered by Social Security.

Peter Orszag and Peter Diamond, economists, Brookings Institution — Plan offers no personal accounts and relies on tax increases to solve Social Security's funding shortfall, with a gradual increase in the $87,900 cap on taxable income and a new tax of 3 percent on earnings above the cap. It cuts benefits for higher-income workers and raises benefits for low-income workers, widows and widowers and workers qualifying for disability benefits. With no personal accounts, there are no transition costs. Centrists.org says the plan's downside is its permanent increase in the payroll tax, and that overall the plan is probably more progressive than current law.

---

[1] Social Security payroll taxes currently total 12.4 percent of earnings up to $87,900, half of which are paid by employers and half by employees.

[2] Centrists.org. The Web site provides assessments of most major Social Security reform proposals.

[3] See Michael Tanner, "Cato's Plan for Reforming Social Security," *Cato Policy Report*, May/June 2004, p. 3.

[4] See Laurence J. Kotlikoff and Scott Burns, *The Coming Generational Storm* (2004), pp. 155-162.

---

* Transition costs are the payroll tax revenues diverted to private accounts and thus unavailable to pay benefits under the existing system.

in about 15 years. After that, the system will be able to continue paying scheduled benefits for another three decades by drawing down the surplus in the Social Security trust funds. Around the middle of the century, however, that cushion will run out.

"We have a huge fiscal gap, a huge generational imbalance, which has been built up over years through this pay-as-you-go program," says Laurence J. Kotlikoff, an economics professor at Boston University. "It's now time for us to rec-

ognize that fact and collectively deal with it." In his recently published *The Coming Generational Storm*, Kotlikoff says it's not the boomers, but their children and grandchildren, who stand to suffer if Social Security reform is put off any longer. [7] "We do need social insurance; we just need to pay for it," he says. "And we can't let one generation's social insurance be paid for by bankrupting another generation."

Social Security's funding shortfall is even more worrisome, some analysts say, in the context of a rapidly wors-

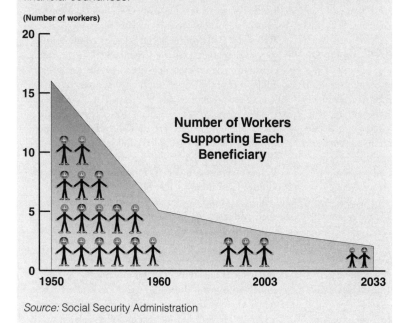

Fewer Workers Support Each Beneficiary

The number of workers paying into Social Security per beneficiary has dropped from 16 in 1950 to 3.3 today. In 2033, only two workers will be supporting each beneficiary, severely straining Social Security's financial soundness.

Number of Workers Supporting Each Beneficiary

Source: Social Security Administration

ening federal budget deficit and even graver financial shortfalls facing Medicare and Medicaid, the federal programs that provide health insurance program for seniors and the poor, respectively. [8]

"People often say that no action is taken until a crisis is upon us," says Maya MacGuineas, executive director of the Committee for a Responsible Federal Budget, a bipartisan, nonprofit group in Washington. "Today that crisis is really upon us. We have structural budget deficits, a huge deficit in Social Security and even larger deficits in our health-care programs. Then we have tax cuts that they're talking about making permanent with no plan for how to pay for them. Hopefully, this will push Congress to come up with a real kind of budget agreement, which is what we need to get back on the path towards fiscal soundness."

But other experts say predictions of Social Security's impending demise are overblown. "It's very important to consider the financial problems that Social Security is supposed to encounter from a long-term perspective,"

says Weller of the Center for American Progress. He points out that in their most recent annual report on the program's financial sustainability, the Social Security trustees predicted that the costs associated with the baby boomers' retirement would level off by about 2038. "Once the baby boomers have all died off, the program's cost stabilizes," he says. "Other than this demographic bulge, there's nothing really that makes the system unsustainable."

In fact, supporters of Social Security's current funding mechanism say calls for diverting payroll tax revenues to private investment accounts are little more than fearmongering on the part of those, like Norquist, who want to reduce the size of the government. "This is precisely a backdoor way of achieving that goal," says Entmacher of the National Women's Law Center. "While we might want to make some adjustments to the payroll tax, Social Security really is in a strong financial position."

Entmacher cites annual reports by the Social Security trustees and the recent CBO report as evidence that the system's projected shortfalls hardly amount to a crisis. The trustees' most recent annual report, published in March, predicted that the system's trust funds won't run out until 2042, 13 years later than the 2029 date the trustees forecasted in 1997, thanks in part to rising real wages since 1997. [9] And the CBO was even more optimistic, predicting the program wouldn't run out of trust fund money until 2052. "The privatizers aren't able to sell fear because the CBO confirms that Social Security can pay 100 percent of benefits until 2052," Entmacher says. "That's 50 more years."

But long before the trust funds actually run out of money, the surplus will begin to shrink. It's uncertain exactly when the system will begin paying more in benefits than it collects in payroll taxes — the trustees predict that will occur in 2018; the CBO says it won't happen until 2019. Such differences among the official forecasts are unimportant, some experts say. "The evidence is overwhelming that we are going to begin to run large deficits in the Social Security system sometime in the next two decades," says Brown of the University of Illinois. "Whether it's in 2018 or 2019, once we pass over into that period, absent some sort of a change in the way the system is structured, those deficits are going to grow larger every year."

Indeed, while experts differ widely over the gravity of Social Security's funding shortfall and the best way to solve it, everyone agrees that some adjustments are needed to ensure the system's long-term survival. They also agree that the sooner lawmakers make those changes, the easier it will be to pay for them. "There's no miracle here," says Alicia Munnell, director of the Center for Retirement Research at Boston College. "We just have to bite the bullet and acknowledge that it's going to require money. Then we can talk about what's the best way to do it."

Inaction — the path taken thus far — is no longer a viable option, most experts agree. "We could do nothing for a couple of decades, but then we would have very few options on the table apart from big tax increases or big benefit cuts," Brown says. "To do nothing is completely irresponsible and unrealistic."

Would privatization be good for future retirees?

Most proposals to privatize Social Security are voluntary and would allow workers to invest part of the money they now contribute as payroll taxes in stocks, bonds or a mix of the two, in privately held, government-administered accounts. In return, they would receive smaller monthly benefits when they retire than they would under the current system. Current beneficiaries and workers nearing retirement would retain promised benefits under most proposals.

Beyond those general terms, however, privatization schemes vary widely. The most sweeping proposal — by George Mason's Ferrara — would require the federal government to guarantee that beneficiaries' personal accounts return no less than the benefits they would have received through Social Security under current law.

"Even if Social Security could pay all its promised benefits, the real rate of return for most workers would be no more than 1.5 percent," says Ferrara. "The long-term return on stocks after inflation is 7 to 7.5 percent. So even if stocks during certain periods go up or down, the large gulf between private capital returns and the pay-as-you-

Former Enron employee Gwen Gray cries after telling union officials in Washington about her job layoff and her husband's death. The failure of many corporate pension funds has complicated the debate over Social Security reform.

go return means that we can take the risk off the worker so that he's guaranteed current-law benefits in any event."

Those higher investment returns, supporters of this approach maintain, will translate into greater consumer spending, boosting the overall U.S. economy. But critics say Ferrara's plan could bankrupt the system because it relies too heavily on the consistently robust growth of the stock market, an assumption they say is invalidated by the recent volatility of stock prices. "Peter Ferrara's proposal is a prime example of the notion that somehow privatization will accelerate economic growth and that over the long run it will ultimately pay for itself," says Weller of the Center for American Progress. "That's just silly economics."

Under some privatization proposals, administrative costs — mainly fees charged by brokers to manage workers' personal accounts — could reduce participants' account balances at retirement by as much as 30 percent, according to CBO estimates. [10] Boston University's Kotlikoff would reduce that burden by offering a single, internationally diversified portfolio. "This plan offers private investment in a collective, global mutual fund of stocks and bonds," he says. "Instead of having everybody investing on their own and paying whatever fees their brokers want to charge, everybody in our plan would be invested in exactly the same portfolio, and the whole thing would be administered by the Social Security Administration."

But critics say privatization would divert revenue from the Social Security trust funds to private accounts, reducing the amount of money available to pay benefits to current beneficiaries. Over time, when workers holding personal investment accounts retire and use the returns on those investments as part of their retirement income, privatization could save the system money. But until then, the payroll taxes diverted to those accounts would be a drain on Social Security, commonly described as the "transition costs" of privatization.

"Giving workers accounts costs money in the short run, because at the same time you're funding those accounts you're also paying Social Security benefits," says Lemieux of the Centrist Policy Network. "It's only in the long run, when people holding personal accounts get smaller regular Social Security benefits, that the savings to the system begin to take effect."

Many experts assess the viability of privatization plans according to the magnitude of the transition costs they would incur. Ferrara's plan has attracted the broadest criticism from supporters of Social Security because it would allow workers to divert a larger portion of their payroll to private accounts. "Some of the more conservative Republicans are entertaining a pie-in-the-sky or free-lunch proposal," says Lemieux. "This plan is just nuts. The transition costs would be so enormous they would greatly upset capital markets and possibly the economy. Over the next 75 years, Ferrara's plan would cost more than current law, and it would raise Social Security spending much higher than it would get even after all the baby boomers retire."

Other critics say privatization is the wrong approach to solving Social Security's funding problem because it undermines the federally guaranteed program at a time when other sources of retiree income are becoming less certain. U.S. employers are abandoning traditional, defined-benefit pension plans, which promise a monthly payment for life, in favor of defined-contribution plans, which shift the investment risk to the employee and future retiree. [11] Moreover, because employees generally are not required to participate in the defined-contribution plans — known as 401(k) plans — it's usually the lower-paid or less-educated workers who fare the worst, because they either feel they can't afford to set aside money for retirement or are unaware of the need to do so.

"We need a part of our retirement income that's secure and that we can count on," says Entmacher of the National Women's Law Center. "So much risk is already being shifted to workers, while employers are bearing less and less of that risk in private pensions. For that reason, we need Social Security to really be secure."

But many analysts who dismiss sweeping reforms such as Ferrara's still favor partial privatization as the only way to ensure Social Security's long-range survival. In addition, some proposals — such as one introduced by Reps. Jim Kolbe, R-Ariz., and Charles W. Stenholm, D-Texas — seek to enhance the system's progressivity by tailoring it in favor of low-income workers. * "The good reform proposals don't cut benefits so much for people who earned small amounts during their working careers, and they specifically boost personal accounts for those people," Lemieux says. "So I feel pretty confident that they would be even more progressive than current law."

Are benefit cuts or payroll-tax increases better alternatives to privatization?

Reducing benefits or increasing payroll taxes are the only alternatives to partial privatization to resolve Social Security's funding shortfall.

Lawmakers cut benefits in 1983 by gradually raising the age at which retirees become eligible to receive full benefits. Under current law, only workers born before 1938 may begin receiving benefits at the traditional eligibility age of 65. Anticipating Americans' increasing longevity, Congress phased in a gradual increase in the eligibility age, which eventually will reach 67 for those born after 1959. Workers of all ages may continue to take early retirement at 62 with reduced benefits, based on the expectation that they will receive them for a longer time than if they began receiving them at their normal retirement age.

Federal Reserve Board Chairman Alan Greenspan has suggested that the retirement age continue to increase to reflect longer life expectancies. But many analysts say further benefit cuts would deal an unacceptable blow to the entitlement program's promise to keep retirees and the disabled out of poverty.

"Social Security is already a bare-bones system," says Weller, of the Center for American Progress, who calcu-

---

* Progressivity means that poor workers get proportionally more benefits than wealthy ones.

lates that each one-year increase in the normal retirement age amounts to an 8 percent benefit cut. "About a third of households enter retirement woefully inadequately prepared, often with just Social Security to live on, which was never the intention. Cutting back Social Security benefits from their already low level is a dangerous proposition."

Some reform proposals would cut benefits less directly by changing the way they are calculated. Currently, Social Security adjusts benefits based on two formulas: Initial benefits are adjusted to reflect average wage increases in the economy, based on a wage-indexation formula, and subsequent benefits are adjusted for inflation using the cost-of-living index. But some reform plans would eliminate wage indexation and adjust benefits according to consumer price increases alone. "That would shrink the replacement ratio [the portion of pre-retirement earnings beneficiaries receive each month] of Social Security over time, from about 40 percent [of workers' earnings] right now to 20 percent or less within the next two or three decades," says Weller. "That's basically death by a thousand cuts, because every year relative benefits would be cut a little bit more. That's just a recipe for disaster."

Some analysts say changing the ways benefits are indexed is not only necessary but also fair. "You can call it a benefit cut, or you can call it a reduction in the growth of benefits," says Brown of the University of Illinois. "If you have future benefits grow with inflation rather than with real wage growth, future generations will continue to pay the current 12.4 percent payroll tax, but their benefits will grow with inflation and nothing more. Over 60 years, that would rebalance the system and do it in a very gradual way. People who are near retirement wouldn't be greatly affected, while people in their 20s and 30s today would have plenty of time to adjust. That would be a lot more feasible politically than cutting everybody's benefits today."

Others say increasing the payroll tax would make Social Security solvent over time. Today workers and

Average Low-Wage Worker Receives $701 Monthly

A typical low-wage worker who retired at age 65 in 2003 received $701 a month from Social Security, compared to $1,721 received by the average high-wage earner. Workers can maximize their monthly income by working until age 70 before claiming benefits.

Typical Social Security Benefits, 2003

Earnings	Age 62	Age 65	Age 70
Low	$572	$701	$833
Average	943	1,158	1,387
High	1,236	1,513	1,786
Maximum	1,404	1,721	2,045

Source: "Fast Facts & Figures About Social Security, 2003," Social Security Administration

employers split the cost of Social Security, with each paying 6.2 percent of workers' earnings, up to a maximum of $87,900 a year. Earnings above that cap are not subject to the payroll tax. Some analysts say raising the wage cap would be the fairest solution to the system's funding problems.

"Why should a secretary pay the Social Security tax on 100 percent of her income while her boss, who is more likely to be male, only pays tax on a portion of his?" asks Entmacher of the National Women's Law Center.

Some proposals, including the Kolbe-Stenholm bill, would increase tax payments by raising the earnings cap. "Most of the reform community is actually in favor of that to some extent," says Lemieux, including some privatizers who see an increase in the wage cap as a necessary means to cover the transition costs resulting from any shift to private accounts. "These transition costs amount to over a trillion dollars over the next 10 years, and we'd have to pay for that somehow."

Munnell, of the Center for Retirement Research, points out that benefits are already going to diminish, even without any additional changes to the system, thanks to the rising retirement age, an increase in Medicare premiums and the taxation of Social Security benefits. [12] Medicare Part B premiums, which are automatically deducted from Social Security benefits, are expected to rise from 6 percent of benefits for someone retiring today to 9 percent for those retiring in 2030. Because Social Security

CHRONOLOGY

1930s *Social Security is created to combat widespread poverty during the Great Depression.*

Aug. 14, 1935 President Franklin D. Roosevelt signs the Social Security Act, the nation's first major anti-poverty insurance program providing benefits to older Americans.

1939 Ida May Fuller of Ludlow, Vt., becomes the first retiree to receive a monthly Social Security check. Social Security is expanded to provide benefits to workers' survivors and the disabled.

1940s-1960s *A postwar population boom sets the stage for Social Security's future funding shortfall.*

1946 The first year of the baby boom starts a demographic bulge that will last for the next 18 years.

1950 Cost-of-living adjustments are applied to Social Security to protect benefits from inflation. . . . There are 16 workers for every retiree in the United States, more than enough to cover Social Security benefits.

1954 Congress expands Social Security to include benefits for disabled older workers and disabled adult dependents.

1960 Disability insurance is extended to cover disabled workers of all ages and their dependents.

1961 All workers are permitted to receive reduced, early-retirement benefits at age 62.

July 30, 1965 Medicare, the most far-reaching change to the Social Security system, becomes law, providing health insurance to Americans ages 65 and older.

1970s-1980s *Concern mounts over Social Security's solvency, as demographers warn of the coming baby-boom bulge.*

1972 Social Security's new Supplemental Security Income (SSI) program provides additional benefits to poor seniors

and begins covering the blind and the disabled — groups previously served by the states and localities.

1977 As Social Security benefit expenditures rapidly mount due to expanded coverage, Congress raises payroll taxes and increases the wage base — the maximum earnings subject to Social Security taxes — to restore the trust funds' financial soundness.

1983 Congress authorizes taxation of Social Security benefits, brings federal employees into the system and calls for an increase in the normal retirement age from 65 to 67, beginning in the 21st century.

2000s *Privatization proposals gather momentum.*

2001 President Bush's Commission to Strengthen Social Security recommends ways to reform the program that would introduce personal investment accounts.

2008 The first baby boomers reach age 62, making them eligible to receive reduced, early-retirement Social Security benefits.

2019 Social Security begins paying more in benefits than it receives in payroll tax revenues, forcing it to draw down its trust funds in order to pay benefits, according to Congressional Budget Office (CBO) predictions.

2009 The normal retirement age — the age at which retirees may receive full Social Security benefits — rises to 66.

2012 The first baby boomers turn 66, enabling them to receive full Social Security benefits.

2027 The normal retirement age rises to 67.

2040 With most boomers well into retirement, there are just two workers for each Social Security recipient, too few to pay scheduled benefits at current tax rates.

2052 The Social Security trust funds will run out of money, the CBO predicts.

Benefits Crucial to Older Women

Almost two-thirds of U.S. retirees now rely on Social Security for most of their income, largely due to the decline of traditional pensions in recent decades.

Social Security is especially vital for elderly women, but it does less to meet women's retirement needs than it does for men. Because of their longevity and work patterns, "women rely much more heavily on Social Security than men do for their economic security in old age," says Joan Entmacher, vice president for economic security at the National Women's Law Center.

The average American woman who reaches age 65 will live for another 20 years, four years longer than her male counterpart. But after her spouse dies, a widow receives only half her husbands' benefits, leaving her with reduced income to cover the higher medical costs that typically come with old age. Single women often fare even worse, having only their own benefits to live on in retirement.

Women also have fewer alternative sources of income during retirement than men, so they're more dependent on Social Security. They tend to accumulate less in savings and pension credits than men during their working years, mainly because they are more likely to work part time or take time off to raise children. [1]

Indeed, women typically work for 32 years, compared with 44 years for men. Part-time employment generally pays less than full-time work, and rarely provides pension coverage. Full-time female workers still make 75 cents for every dollar earned by men, a wage gap that makes it harder for women to save money for retirement. Because tradi-

tional pension benefits usually are calculated on the basis of years worked and earnings, even women with full pension coverage tend to receive lower benefits during retirement than their male counterparts.

Advocates of Social Security privatization say allowing women to save part of their payroll taxes in managed retirement investment accounts would help them prepare for a more comfortable old age.

But many women's-rights activists say privatization would further erode women's retirement security. For one thing, the current system favors lower-income recipients, a group that includes a disproportionate share of women. "Social Security has a progressive benefit formula, so that lower earners get a higher percentage of their pre-retirement earnings as benefits," says Alicia Munnell, director of the Center for Retirement Research at Boston College. "So to the extent that we move away from that benefit formula and into individual accounts, women would be hurt."

Another advantage of Social Security as it's currently designed is the automatic cost-of-living increase, which protects benefits from inflation. Virtually no private investment scheme or annuity offers such protection. "Because women live much longer than men, Social Security's inflation-indexed annuities are particularly valuable for women," Munnell says. "Again, to the extent that you move away from that, women will be hurt."

---

[1] See Alicia H. Munnell, "Why Are So Many Older Women Poor? Just the Facts on Retirement Issues," Center for Retirement Research at Boston College, April 2004.

---

benefits are taxed at a fixed rate, and future benefits will rise with inflation, the number of beneficiaries whose benefits will be taxed will grow over time.

"It's quite reasonable to fix the current system and keep its existing structure, but you need more money or benefit cuts to do that," Munnell says. "My preference is more money, because I'm not sure we want wage-replacement rates to go down further than they're already scheduled to go."

She supports an increase in the taxable-wage base, which former Social Security Commissioner Robert M. Ball and a few other reformers have proposed. "This can easily be done without going to personal accounts."

BACKGROUND

Roots in Industrialization

Social Security began during the Depression, but the concept of a publicly funded safety net to protect citizens from poverty is rooted in longstanding theory and practice. In his pamphlet, "Agrarian Justice," written shortly after the Revolutionary War, American patriot Thomas Paine described a social program to ensure the economic well being of the young and the elderly. Paine proposed creating a fund, financed through an inheritance tax, to provide a single payment of 15 pounds sterling to citizens

America's Changing Population

Most Americans were under age 50 at the end of the 19th century. But by 2080, because of the coming retirement of the baby boomers, longer life expectancies and the popularity of smaller families, there will be relatively fewer young people and more Americans over 50 — creating a demographic bulge resembling a "python swallowing a telephone pole," according to some demographers.

Makeup of U.S. Population, by Age and Gender

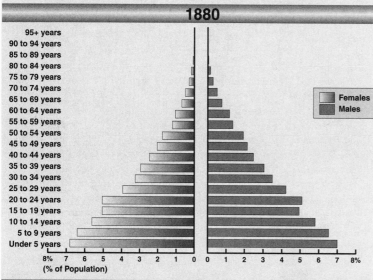

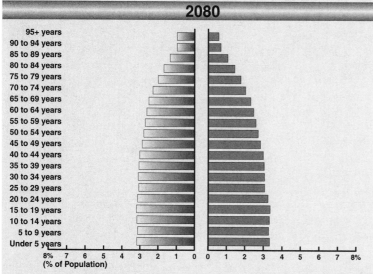

Source: "Population Aging: It's not just the Baby Boom," Center for Retirement Research

reaching age 21, to help them get started in life, and annual benefits of 10 pounds sterling to everyone 50 and older to prevent poverty in old age.

Paine's idea never made its way into public policy. Before the Industrial Revolution drew workers off the farms and into urban factories, in fact, people who could no longer work as a result of injury or old age relied on family for support and care. But the move to cities eroded that safety net, as extended families broke up into smaller, "nuclear" households composed of only parents and their children. Charities and a patchwork of state welfare programs were a poor substitute for family-based support. [13]

Only one segment of American society — war veterans — enjoyed government-provided income protection. The first solders' pension program started in 1776, before the signing of the Declaration of Independence. The Civil War Pension program, created in 1862, initially provided benefits to combat-disabled Union veterans and to widows and orphans of Union soldiers killed in action. Confederate veterans and their dependents received no benefits. The program was expanded in 1906 to include all surviving Union veterans and their widows. The last Civil War Pension recipient, a woman who married an elderly veteran while in her teens, died earlier this year. [14]

Working Americans became eligible for old-age benefits with the advent of company pensions, first introduced in 1882 by the Alfred Dolge Co., a piano and organ manufacturer. But private pensions were slow to gain acceptance. In 1900, only five companies in the United States offered pensions to workers.

Meanwhile, the steady move to cities, the breakdown of the extended family, increasing reliance on wage income for survival, together with an increase in life expectancy, were undermining the living standards of older Americans. By 1920, more people were living in cities than on farms. The vast majority of aging workers were simply fired when they were no longer able to perform up to standard. With no one to care for them and no income, millions of former workers faced the prospect of dying in poverty. Because of improvements in sanitation and health care, life expectancy increased by 10 years between 1900 and 1930, the fastest increase in recorded history. By 1935, the number of elderly Americans had reached nearly 8 million at a time when the traditional sources of care for this population were fast disappearing.

The plight of America's growing elderly population deteriorated even more rapidly after Oct. 24, 1929, when the stock market crashed, setting off the Great Depression. More than a quarter of working Americans lost their jobs, about 10,000 banks failed, and the gross national product — the value of economic output — plummeted from $150 billion before the crash to just $55 billion in 1932.

With few federal resources available to fight poverty, President Herbert Hoover (1929-33) called on Americans to volunteer their services and charitable contributions to alleviate the plight of the unemployed and the elderly. But with so much of the population facing financial hardship, Hoover's call went largely unanswered, leaving it up to the states to support the poor and elderly. By the 1930s, most states had established limited workers' compensation programs and state old-age "pensions" for older Americans who met financial-need standards. But these programs were of little value; none offered more than $1 a day to qualified beneficiaries.

As Congress began considering proposals for a new nationwide old-age safety net, conservative lawmakers favored adopting the state model, arguing that its need-based structure would limit the scope of the program and make it easy to end it once the economy recovered. But as the Depression persisted, calls for a different approach to social welfare — one that would reflect the permanent societal changes wrought by industrialization — began to take hold.

President Franklin D. Roosevelt signs the Social Security Act on Aug. 14, 1935. "We have tried to . . . give some measure of protection to the average citizen and to his family against the loss of a job and against poverty-ridden old age," he said.

Courtesy Social Security Administration

Social Security Act

President Franklin D. Roosevelt (1933-45) took office promising to shift the model for federal economic security policy from the state-based welfare assistance programs to new federal programs similar to "social insurance" plans then prevalent in Europe. First adopted in 1889 in Chancellor Otto von Bismarck's Germany, social insurance plans worked like commercial insurance plans, collecting premiums, or taxes, from a large pool of individuals (in this case working-age citizens) to pay benefits to those who meet eligibility conditions, such as disability and old age.

On June 8, 1934, Roosevelt announced his support for a similar approach in the United States. "Security was attained in the earlier days through the interdependence of members of families upon each other and of the families within a small community upon each other," he said in an address to Congress. "The complexities of great communities and of organized industry make less real these simple means of security. Therefore, we are compelled to employ the active interest of the nation as a whole through government in order to encourage a greater security for each individual who composes it."

Roosevelt sought to placate critics of such an expanded role for the federal government by adding: "This seeking for a greater measure of welfare and happiness does not indicate a change in values. It is rather a return to values lost in the course of our economic development and expansion."

Privatization supporters say stocks typically return higher dividends than the government's conservative bond investments. But critics say the stock market's recent plunge and numerous corporate and stock market scandals make personal investment accounts too risky for average workers.

On Aug. 14, 1935, Roosevelt signed into law the Social Security Act, which codified various recommendations of the presidential Committee on Economic Security. The new law created a social insurance program to pay retired workers age 65 or older a steady income for the rest of their lives.

"We can never insure 100 percent of the population against 100 percent of the hazards and vicissitudes of life," Roosevelt said. "But we have tried to frame a law which will give some measure of protection to the average citizen and to his family against the loss of a job and against poverty-ridden old age."

Though the law fell short of some supporters' goals, it provided the basic structure for today's Social Security program. Initially it paid benefits only to covered workers when they retired at 65. And, unlike the state old-age pension plans, it was funded through a contributory system, in which future beneficiaries contribute to their own retirement through payroll deductions made during their working lives. The law established a Social Security Board, made up of three presidential appointees, to administer the new program, but the Social Security Administration (SSA) replaced it in 1946, later incorporated into the Department of Health and Human Services.

Within two years all employers were registered, workers were assigned Social Security numbers and field offices were built. On Jan. 1, 1937, workers began acquiring credits toward their old-age benefits, and they and their employers began paying payroll taxes, known as FICA taxes (after the Federal Insurance Contributions Act, which authorized their collection). FICA taxes were placed in dedicated Social Security trust funds, to be used for paying benefits.

For the first three years Social Security paid each beneficiary a small, single, lump-sum payment because early recipients had not paid enough into the system to be vested for monthly benefits. By 1940, the trust funds had collected enough revenues to begin paying monthly payments.

In 1939 Congress expanded Social Security to cover workers' spouses, children under 18 and aged parents and provided survivors' benefits in the event of a worker's premature death. Lawmakers thus transformed the program from a retirement system for workers into a broader family income-security system.

The first retiree to receive a monthly Social Security check was Ida May Fuller of Ludlow, Vt., who retired in 1939 at age 65. Because of Social Security's pay-as-you-go financing arrangement, the retired legal secretary got a great return on her contribution. After contributing just $24.75 into the system over three years, she collected $22,888.92 in Social Security benefits before she died in 1975 at 100.

Later Amendments

By 1950, inflation had eaten away at the value of Social Security benefits, so Congress incorporated cost-of-living allowances (COLAs) that provided retroactive adjustments for beneficiaries in 1950 and 1952. A 1972 amendment made the COLA provision permanent.

Then, in 1954 Congress expanded the program to include disability insurance, initially limited to disabled older workers and disabled adult dependents. In September 1960, President Dwight D. Eisenhower (1953-61) signed into law an amendment extending coverage to all disabled workers and their dependents.

In 1956, Congress reduced from 65 to 62 the age at which women could choose to begin receiving their old-age benefits. Women who took the earlier benefits would receive smaller monthly checks, based on the actuarial notion that they would receive benefits for a longer period of time than if they waited until age 65. The same early-retirement option was extended to men in 1961.

In the 1960s, building on Roosevelt's vision of a strong governmental role in protecting Americans from poverty, President Lyndon B. Johnson launched a series of federal programs — known as the Great Society — including measures that strengthened the safety net provided by Social Security.

Johnson's primary proposal was Medicare — the federal program that provides health insurance to nearly all Americans age 65 and older. Signed into law on July 30, 1965, Medicare would become the most far-reaching change to the Social Security system. Within the next three years, nearly 20 million Americans enrolled in Medicare.

By the end of the 1960s there were calls to bring the old state and local welfare programs into the federal Social Security system to reduce waste and redundancy. In 1969, President Richard M. Nixon (1969-74) called on Congress to "bring reason, order and purpose into a tangle of overlapping programs."

The 1972 Social Security Amendments brought three "adult categories" — needy aged, blind and disabled — previously served by the states and localities with partial federal funding — under a single new Social Security program called Supplemental Security Income (SSI). More than 3 million people were shifted from the state welfare rolls to SSI.

The 1972 amendments also increased Social Security benefits for elderly widows and widowers, extended Medicare to individuals receiving disability benefits and those with chronic renal disease and increased Social Security benefits for workers who delay retirement past age 65.

Concerns about Social Security's soundness began to surface in the late 1970s. An economy beset by "stagflation" — inflation and minimal economic growth — and the demographic time bomb posed by the baby boom fueled predictions that the trust funds would soon be exhausted. To address the coming shortfall, Congress passed the 1977 Social Security Amendments, which increased the payroll tax, increased the maximum earnings subject to Social Security taxes and adjusted the way COLAs and the wage base are calculated. These changes restored the trust funds' long-term financial soundness for the next 50 years.

But within only a few years Social Security faced a serious short-term funding crisis due to the rapid growth in benefit expenditures. The crisis prompted President Ronald Reagan (1981-89) to appoint a panel headed by Greenspan (who began his tenure as Federal Reserve chairman in 1987) to recommend changes to the system. The 1983 amendments, based on those recommenda-

tions, authorized taxation of Social Security benefits, brought federal employees into the system and called for the gradual increase in the normal retirement age from 65 to 66 in 2009 and 67 in 2027.

Reagan oversaw the beginnings of a shift in philosophy toward the social safety net that had protected Americans from poverty since the Great Depression. He repeatedly called for tightening eligibility standards for welfare programs, decrying "welfare queens" he said were working the system to gain a free ride at the expense of honest, hardworking Americans. In 1995 Republicans took control of Congress, and began passing laws reflecting this philosophical shift.

The 1996 Contract with America Advancement Act, signed by Democratic President Bill Clinton on March 29, for the first time disqualified applicants for disability benefits under Social Security or SSI if drug or alcohol addiction contributed to their disabilities. The Personal Responsibility and Work Opportunity Act, signed five months later, ended the unlimited welfare entitlements provided under the Aid to Families with Dependent Children program that had been established by the 1935 Social Security Act.

The 1996 law limited the amount of time beneficiaries could receive welfare benefits and required recipients to work; it also ended SSI eligibility for most legal non-citizen aliens and tightened up eligibility standards for disabled children. After public outcry, Congress later relaxed some of the new restrictions on non-citizens and children.

Clinton signed two other bills aimed at encouraging Social Security beneficiaries to work. The 1999 Ticket to Work and Work Incentives Improvement Act established a new program providing vocational rehabilitation and employment services to help disability beneficiaries find productive work. The 2000 Senior Citizens' Freedom to Work Act allowed workers to receive benefits even if they continued to work past the normal retirement age.

CURRENT SITUATION

Privatization

When he made his acceptance speech at the Republican National Convention on Sept. 2, President Bush said, "We'll always keep the promise of Social Security for our older workers. With the huge baby-boom generation approaching retirement, many of our children and grandchildren understandably worry whether Social Security will be there when they need it. We must strengthen Social Security by allowing younger workers to save some of their taxes in a personal account, a nest egg you can call your own and government can never take away."

President Bush's support for shifting part of the Social Security tax revenues into personal accounts marks another philosophical departure from the social-insurance concept championed by Roosevelt. Like many of his supporters, Bush has often called for reducing the size of the federal government. As the main entitlement programs in the federal budget, Social Security and Medicare are prime targets for this effort.

Bush announced during his January 2001 inaugural address that he intended to reform Social Security and Medicare. That May he appointed the President's Commission to Strengthen Social Security and directed it to recommend ways to reform the program that would ensure three major goals: preserve the benefits of current retirees and those nearing retirement; return Social Security to sound financial footing; and enable younger workers to invest part of their payroll taxes in individual savings accounts outside of the Social Security system.

Supporters of the current system immediately denounced the commission as a rubber stamp for privatization. "The president, his staff and his allies are already committed to privatization," declared the liberal Campaign for America's Future after the commission was created. "Calling their process of arranging the details a 'commission' is an attempt to mislead the public about its process and purpose. In reality, it will amount to no more than a collection of individuals who support privatization." [15]

Treasury Secretary Paul H. O'Neill responded by defining Social Security as "a revolutionary idea for its time" that was fast running out of money. "This is all about happy times and doing the right thing while our generation is able to act," he said. [16]

The commission's final report, issued in December 2001, recommended several measures to meet Bush's goals. It offered three different models to ensure that Social Security would remain afloat over the long term. Model 2 of the report, widely viewed as the likely basis for the Bush administration's reform proposal, if it wins a second term, would eliminate wage indexation and rely entirely on consumer prices to adjust future benefits. Apart from changing the benefits formula, Model 2 would retain the current system for all who prefer it while allowing workers who wish to set up a private investment account with part of their payroll-tax contribution to do so.

Several reform plans have been introduced in recent months — including the Kolbe-Stenholm bill and one authored by Sen. Lindsey Graham, R-S.C. — both of which would provide for moderately sized, progressive personal accounts. In July, Rep. Paul Ryan, R-Wis., introduced a bill that incorporates Ferrara's more-radical privatization plan. "We're going to try to translate that into a very broad co-sponsorship on the Hill," George Mason University's Ferrara says, "ultimately with the goal of presenting it to the administration and making the case to them that this is, in fact, what they should adopt."

But with much of Congress facing re-election and concerns about the wars against Iraq and terrorism, proposals to overhaul Social Security have yet to receive extensive congressional consideration. Other than being introduced, says Lemieux of the Centrist Policy Network, "there hasn't been a lot of legislative activity on Social Security."

Eroding Pensions

Recent trends in private pension coverage add additional uncertainties to the debate over Social Security reform. Many traditional pension funds have been failing, threatening a major source of retirement income for American workers. Most recently, in a move that may be emulated by other troubled companies, United Airlines is considering scrapping its defined-benefit pension plan, which covers 120,000 workers, as part of a bankruptcy proceeding. The federal Pension Benefit Guaranty Corp. (PBGC), which protects pension benefits from corporate bankruptcies, would assume the airline's $8.3 billion pension obligations, but the move likely would mean reduced benefits for United workers. If other companies follow United's lead, the PBGC could be unable to cover benefits, requiring a taxpayer bailout reminiscent of the savings and loan crisis of the 1980s. [17]

That prospect — or the possibility that many retirees may stop receiving their pension checks altogether — gained further credence with a new study that concludes the agency will go broke by 2023 if pension funds continue to fail at the pace of recent years. [18]

Is privatization the best way to save Social Security?

YES — Peter J. Ferrara
Senior fellow, Institute for Policy Innovation

From testimony before the Senate Special Committee on Aging, June 15, 2004

I'm here to discuss . . . providing a progressive option for personal retirement accounts as a choice as compared to Social Security. The option . . . is designed to be progressive, which means lower-income workers can contribute a higher percentage of their taxes to the account than higher-income workers.

The option provides [for] . . . an average of 6.4 percent of the 12.4 percent [payroll-tax contribution] to go into personal accounts, a much larger account than has been proposed before. . . . The proposal makes no change in disability and survivors' benefits, and there is no change in Social Security benefits otherwise for anybody at any point — now or in the future. Because the advantages of a large personal account are so great, no other changes are necessary. . . . It preserves within the personal account the progressivity of Social Security so workers across the board would gain roughly the same percentage. . . .

There are five ways this proposal enhances progressivity for low- and moderate-income workers. First of all, it sharply increases future retirement benefits. . . . Large accounts do that much more than any other alternative because they're able to take more advantage of the better return in the private sector, so they provide very sharp increases. . . . [Workers who] invest over a lifetime, half-and-half in stocks and bonds at standard, market-investment returns, I calculate would gain a benefit increase of two-thirds compared to currently promised Social Security benefits. . . .

For most workers today, the real rate of return promised by Social Security — let alone what it could pay — is 1 to 1.5 percent. The long-term, real rate of return on corporate bonds is 3 to 3.5 percent. On stocks, I think the record will bear out 7 to 7.5 percent, so [there will be] much higher returns. And you see what we've done here is a vast improvement both on the basis of adequacy and of equity, because the returns are much higher, the future benefits are higher.

Also, under the reform plan low- and moderate-income workers would gain much greater accumulations of personal wealth than under Social Security. The chief actuary of Social Security has already officially scored this plan. He estimates that by 15 years after the reform plan is adopted working people would have gained $7 trillion in today's dollars in their own personal accounts. [T]his is the greatest advantage and breakthrough for working people that we could possibly adopt today.

NO — Christian Weller
Senior economist, Center for American Progress

From testimony before the Senate Special Committee on Aging, June 15, 2004

Privatization as an alternative to fixing Social Security within the parameters of the system is too risky and too costly, especially for low-income families.

Usually 80 percent of pre-retirement income is considered adequate for a decent standard of living. A substantial minority of households, typically one-third, falls short of this standard. The shortfalls are especially large for minorities, single women, workers with less education and low-wage workers. To make ends meet in retirement, these households will have to curtail their consumption, often severely, and rely on public assistance in retirement.

Retirement income adequacy also has worsened for the typical household over the past few years. Underlying this trend are three factors. First, pension coverage has remained low and declined in recent years. Second, retirement wealth has become increasingly unequally distributed. And, third, with the proliferation of defined-contribution plans, such as 401(k) plans, risks have shifted onto workers.

Against this backdrop, Social Security gains in relative importance. Its coverage is almost universal, [and] its benefits favor lifetime earners and [have] guaranteed, lifetime, inflation-adjusted benefits. Part of Social Security's importance results . . . from its other benefits, in particular disability and survivorship benefits. These benefits are often also at stake when Social Security benefits are reduced to pay for privatization. But we've got to keep in mind that Social Security benefits are bare bones. The average replacement ratio [the percentage of one's pre-retirement earnings provided by Social Security] in the United States is about half of that in Germany or Italy, and the average monthly benefit [for Social Security] was about $850 in 2002.

Social Security benefits were 80 percent of retirement income for households in the bottom 40 percent of the income distribution in 2000, meaning that the private sector is still not doing its job to help low-income workers. Yet Social Security trustees predict a financial shortfall in the long run. It is anticipated that by 2042 Social Security will have exhausted its trust funds and that tax revenue will cover only two-thirds of promised benefits. An immediate and permanent increase of the payroll tax by 1.9 percent would allow Social Security to cover all of that shortfall. . . .

With privatization, insurance is replaced with savings accounts. That is, the risks are privatized. These risks include the risk of misjudging the market and investing in losing assets. Another risk is the possibility of financial markets staying low for long periods of time. Moreover, workers face the risk that they will exhaust their savings during their retirement.

Meanwhile, a study by Munnell, of the Center for Retirement Research, documents the inability of 401(k)s and other defined-contribution plans to fill the gap created as private companies scale back or abandon their traditional pension programs. Despite the popularity of 401(k)s, she found that less than half of American workers are covered by an employer-provided pension plan, a figure that hasn't changed since 1979. And only one in four workers whose employers do offer 401(k)s chooses to participate in the plan, and fewer than one in 10 contribute the maximum allowable portion of their income. In addition, many employers offering 401(k)s have responded to hard economic times by cutting their matching contributions to the plans. [19]

These findings constitute a strong case against relying on private markets to solve Social Security's funding problems, Munnell says.

"We were stunned to find out what a poor mechanism 401(k) plans are, as currently structured, to provide retirement income," she says. Like 401(k)s, private investment accounts within Social Security require workers to be involved in the management of their retirement incomes, she notes. "These financial decisions are hard for people to make. They're not trained to do it, they don't have the time to do it, and to shift an even greater burden to the individual doesn't make any sense."

Ferrara says his plan addresses those concerns. "We designed the investment structure of the fund to make it easy for unsophisticated investors," he says. "There would be a list of private, managed investment funds approved and regulated by the government expressly for this purpose, and the investor only needs to pick one of those funds. Then the managers of those funds make all the sophisticated investment decisions for the investor."

Budget Concerns

When President Bush announced the formation of his Commission to Strengthen Social Security in May 2001, he said federal budget surpluses were enough to cover any costs incurred by the transition to a partially privatized system. "Our government will run large budget surpluses over the next 10 years," Bush said. "These surpluses provide an opportunity to move to a stronger Social Security system." [20]

That was before the terrorist attacks of Sept. 11, 2001. Since then, administration-supported tax cuts coupled with spending for counterterrorism initiatives and the war against Iraq have obliterated the budget surplus. This year, the deficit is expected to reach a record high of $445 billion, up from $375 billion in fiscal 2003.

Bush's initiative to add a drug benefit to Medicare, signed into law Dec. 8, 2003, will place an additional drain on the federal budget. The Medicare Prescription Drug, Improvement and Modernization Act, which would expand the federal health insurance program for some 41 million elderly and disabled Americans by offering partial coverage of prescription drug costs, is now expected to cost $534 billion over the next 10 years, $134 billion more than the administration had originally claimed. [21]

"Congress is still in shock and denial about the deteriorating budget," says Lemieux of the Centrist Policy Network. "They're still doing things the way they did a couple of years ago, when they thought they had a budget surplus and could pass tax cuts without paying for them and keep spending growing fast."

In light of the budget deficit, some analysts say moderate privatization plans offer a promising solution to Social Security's funding shortfall. "We have Medicare and Medicaid growing much faster than the gross domestic product, and we're looking at a very uncertain future in terms of how much money we're going to be spending on homeland security, defense and other programs," says University of Illinois Social Security expert Brown. He supports the commission's Model 2 plan for partial privatization of Social Security. "We have to put some serious constraints on how quickly Social Security can grow."

An essential and fair cost-saving element of the plan, Brown says, is its elimination of wage indexation in calculating initial benefits. "I don't see why the program has to grow faster than inflation," he says. "Why should my children get Social Security benefits that, after adjusting for inflation, are 30 percent higher than mine, even if we're [making the same amount of money today?]"

But other experts say the case for privatization evaporated with the federal budget surplus. "When some of the privatization proposals were developed we had a surplus, and they said we could take some of the surplus and use it to create private accounts," says Entmacher, of the National Women's Law Center. "Well, hello, not only is there no surplus anymore, but we're running gigantic deficits as far as the eye can see, and privatization actually makes it worse."

OUTLOOK

Campaign Debate

As the November presidential election nears, both major candidates are declaring their support for Social Security but skirting the details of plans to ensure the program survives the baby boomers' retirement.

Bush continues to push for partial privatization through private investment accounts, and he has not ruled out raising the retirement age. "It's very important in the Social Security system to say to boomers like me, nothing's going to change," Bush said at a campaign rally in Wheeling, W.Va. "We're in good shape. But if you're a younger worker, you better listen very carefully to the presidential debates on Social Security. The fiscal solvency of Social Security is in doubt for the young workers coming up. Therefore, I think young workers ought to be able to own a personal retirement account, a personal savings account, in order for Social Security to work."

Candidate Kerry opposes privatization, raising the retirement age or cutting payments. "As president, I will not privatize Social Security," Kerry said in accepting his party's nomination in July. "I will not cut benefits. And together, we will make sure that senior citizens never have to cut their pills in half because they can't afford lifesaving medicine."

The Democratic Party platform pledges to support "reform" but to fight privatization of either Social Security or Medicare. But it has provided no details about how to strengthen either program beyond fiscal discipline for Social Security and expanded prescription-drug coverage for Medicare. [22]

"I don't see anything that either the Republicans or the Democrats are advocating right now that would really responsibly deal with the long-term problems either with Social Security or Medicare," says Kotlikoff of Boston University. "The privatization proposal that the president is likely to propose if he's re-elected could well make things worse because it could cut taxes by more than it cuts benefits."

Meanwhile, Federal Reserve Chairman Greenspan is trying to heat up the debate by warning policymakers that reforms are urgently needed. "We owe it to our retirees to promise only the benefits that can be delivered," he said, suggesting that even the boomers — not just their children — may be in for an ugly surprise if changes are postponed much longer. "If we have promised more than our economy has the ability to deliver . . . as I fear we may have, we must recalibrate our public programs so that pending retirees have time to adjust through other channels. . . . If we delay, the adjustments could be abrupt and painful." [23]

Most analysts hope that the candidates will heed that warning and inform voters of their plans to resolve Social Security's fiscal problems as the campaign progresses. "Even if they don't provide highly detailed proposals, both candidates need to flesh out how they would reform the program," says MacGuineas of the Committee for a Responsible Budget. "If someone wants to lead this country, we need to know how they would fix the federal government's largest program. That's something the voters should have insight on."

NOTES

1. Congressional Budget Office, "The Outlook for Social Security," June 2004.

2. For background, see Adriel Bettelheim, "Saving Social Security," *The CQ Researcher*, Oct. 2, 1998, pp. 857-880.

3. See David Cay Johnston, "The Social Security Promise Not Yet Kept," *The New York Times*, Feb. 29, 2004.

4. From an interview with Mara Liasson, "Morning Edition," National Public Radio, May 25, 2001.

5. For background, see Kenneth Jost, "Corporate Crime," *The CQ Researcher*, Oct. 11, 2002, pp. 817-840, and David Masci, "Stock Market Troubles," *The CQ Researcher*, Jan. 16, 2004, pp. 25-48.

6. For background, see Mary H. Cooper, "Retirement Security," *The CQ Researcher*, May 31, 2002, pp. 481-504.

7. Laurence J. Kotlikoff and Scott Burns, *The Coming Generational Storm* (2004).

8. For background, see Adriel Bettelheim, "Medicare Reform," *The CQ Researcher*, Aug. 22, 2003, pp. 673-696; and Rebecca Adams, "Medicaid Reform," *The CQ Researcher*, July 16, 2004, pp. 589-612.

9. For more information on these estimates, see Thomas J. Healey, "Social Security's Surprising Turn," *The Washington Post*, June 25, 2004.

10. Congressional Budget Office, "Administrative Costs of Private Accounts in Social Security," March 2004.

11. See Cooper, *op. cit.*

12. See Alicia H. Munnell, "Just the Facts: The Declining Role of Social Security," Center for Retirement Research, February 2003.

13. Unless otherwise noted, information in this section is drawn from Social Security Online, "Brief History," March 2003.

14. Melissa Nelson, "Woman Recognized as Confederate Widow," The Associated Press, June 15, 2004.

15. Campaign for America's Future, press advisory, May 2, 2001.

16. Quoted in Glenn Kessler, "O'Neill Faults 'No Assets' Social Security," *The Washington Post*, June 19, 2001, p. E1.

17. See Mary Williams Walsh, "Bailout Feared if Airlines Shed Their Pensions," *The New York Times*, Aug. 1, 2004, p. A1.

18. Douglas J. Elliott, "PBGC: When Will the Cash Run Out?" Center on Federal Financial Institutions, Sept. 13, 2004.

19. Alicia H. Munnell and Anika Sundén, *Coming Up Short: The Challenge of 401(k) Plans* (2004).

20. From remarks in the Rose Garden, May 2, 2001.

21. See Walter Shapiro, "Politicians Fool Only Themselves with Medicare Bribe," *USA Today*, Aug. 13, 2004. For background, see Bettelheim, "Medicare Reform," *op. cit.*

22. See Dan Balz, "Democratic Platform Assails Administration," *The Washington Post*, July 4, 2004, p. A4.

23. Quoted in Martin Crutsinger, "Social Security Crisis Warned," The Associated Press, Aug. 28, 2004.

BIBLIOGRAPHY

Books

Katz, Michael B., *In the Shadow of the Poorhouse: A Social History of Welfare in America,* **Basic Books, 1996.**
A professor of history from the University of Pennsylvania traces the development of social policy in the United States, including Social Security.

Kotlikoff, Laurence J., and Scott Burns, *The Coming Generational Storm: What You Need to Know about America's Economic Future,* **MIT Press, 2004.**
A Boston University economist (Kotlikoff) and a finance columnist (Burns) suggest how Social Security and Medicare can survive the onslaught of 77 million retiring baby boomers and how individuals can protect their private savings.

Articles

Kirchoff, Sue, "Greenspan Urges Cuts to Benefits for Retirees," *USA Today,* **Aug. 30, 2004.**
Federal Reserve Chairman Alan Greenspan renews his controversial call to reduce Social Security benefits, even for baby boomers nearing retirement, to save the system from collapse.

Krugman, Paul, "Maestro of Chutzpah," *The New York Times,* **March 2, 2004.**
The liberal columnist argues that in the face of deepening federal budget deficits, Federal Reserve Chairman Greenspan should drop his call to cut Social Security benefits and instead push for a repeal or roll-back of the Bush-supported tax cuts that he says primarily benefit wealthy Americans.

McNeil, Donald G., Jr., "Demographic 'Bomb' May Only Go 'Pop!' " *The New York Times,* **Aug. 29, 2004, "Week in Review," p. 1.**
Falling birth rates are lessening the threat of global overpopulation and fueling concern over the negative impact of aging populations, especially in industrialized countries.

Porter, Eduardo, "Coming Soon: The Vanishing Work Force," *The New York Times,* **Aug. 29, 2004, Section 3, p. 1.**
The coming retirement of millions of baby boomers will create shortages of skilled workers in many fields and may force many boomers to postpone retirement.

Tanner, Michael, "Cato's Plan for Reforming Social Security," *Cato Policy Report,* **May/June 2004, p. 3.**
The libertarian think tank's solution for Social Security's shortfall is a combination of personal investment accounts and reduced benefits.

Reports and Studies

Congressional Budget Office, "The Outlook for Social Security," June 2004.
The CBO predicts Social Security's financial shortfall is not as imminent as earlier estimates indicated: Payments will start exceeding revenues in 2019, but the trust funds will not run out of money to pay benefits until 2052.

__, "Social Security: A Primer," September 2001.
This exhaustive analysis provides historical background, a description of Social Security's organization and programs and options for its future.

Favreault, Melissa M., and Frank J. Sammartino, "The Impact of Social Security Reform on Low-Income and Older Women," Urban Institute, July 2002.
Social Security benefits affect women of different ages, marital status and income levels in different ways. The authors point out the impact of several reform options on older women.

Ferrara, Peter, "A Progressive Proposal for Social Security Private Accounts," *IPI Reports*, Institute for Policy Innovation, June 13, 2003.
The most far-reaching and controversial of the major privatization plans would allow workers to divert a large portion of their payroll-tax contributions to private accounts.

Munnell, Alicia H., "Population and Aging: It's Not Just the Baby Boom," *Issue Brief*, Center for Retirement Research, April 2004.
The director of the Boston College-based center warns that the baby boomers' retirements will radically change U.S. society. Low birth rates since the mid-1960s and steady increases in longevity ensure that the United States will remain an aging society for the foreseeable future.

President's Commission to Strengthen Social Security, "Strengthening Social Security and Creating Personal Wealth for All Americans," December 2001.
The panel appointed by President Bush to devise ways to incorporate personal investment accounts into Social Security offers three main alternatives, one of which is expected to provide the model for a legislative proposal in 2005 if Bush wins re-election.

Social Security Administration, "The Future of Social Security," January 2004.
The report outlines current funding problems facing the program and proposals to allow workers to use part of their payroll-tax contributions to fund personal investment accounts.

For More Information

Cato Institute, 1000 Massachusetts Ave., N.W., Washington, DC 20001-5403; (202) 842-0200; www.cato.org. This libertarian think tank supports the introduction of private investment accounts to Social Security.

Center for American Progress, 1333 H St., N.W., 10th Floor, Washington, DC 20005; (202) 682-1611; www.americanprogress.org. A liberal think tank that supports the current structure of Social Security and opposes efforts to privatize them.

Center for Retirement Research, Boston College, Fulton Hall 550, 140 Commonwealth Ave., Chestnut Hill, MA 02467-3808; (617) 552-1762; www.bc.edu/centers.crr. Directed by Alicia Munnell, a former research director at the Federal Reserve Bank of Boston, the center studies issues related to Social Security and other sources of retirement income.

Centrist Policy Network Inc., 236 Massachusetts Ave., N.E., Suite 205, Washington, DC 20002; (202) 546-4090; www.centrists.org. A nonpartisan group that analyzes most of the major proposals to reform Social Security.

Committee for a Responsible Federal Budget, 1630 Connecticut Ave., N.W., 7th floor, Washington, DC 20009; (202) 986-6599; www.crfb.org. This nonprofit group analyzes all aspects of the federal budget and supports policies, including Social Security reform proposals, that strive to avoid deficit spending.

Institute for Policy Innovation, 1660 S. Stemmons Freeway, Suite 475, Lewisville, TX 75067; (972) 874-5139; www.ipi.org. A conservative group that supports Social Security privatization and other initiatives to reduce the size of the federal government.

National Women's Law Center, 11 Dupont Circle, N.W., Suite 800, Washington, DC 20036; (202) 588-5180; www.nwlc.org. A nonprofit group that analyzes the impact of public policy, including Social Security, on women and criticizes privatization efforts that would erode benefits to elderly women.

Social Security Administration, 6401 Security Blvd., Baltimore, MD 21235; (410) 965-3120; www.socialsecurity.gov. The federal agency that administers Social Security and Medicare.

7

Right to Die

Kenneth Jost

Three girls demonstrate at the Florida hospice caring for brain-damaged Terri Schiavo until her death on March 31. The case drew unprecedented national attention to end-of-life issues after state courts agreed with Schiavo's husband Michael that her feeding tube should be removed.

From *CQ Researcher,*
May 13, 2005.

Terri Schiavo and Barbara Howe lived far apart, but over the course of a decade-and-a half their lives converged toward tragically similar fates.

Terri Schiavo was a young wife in Florida with much to look forward to in 1990 when she suffered cardiac arrest that destroyed much of her brain and left her in a motionless, uncommunicative condition known as a "persistent vegetative state."

Barbara Howe had lived a full life as the wife of a Boston policeman and mother of three daughters when, in 1991, she was diagnosed with amyotrophic lateral sclerosis, or Lou Gehrig's disease.

Through the 1990s, Howe's condition slowly degenerated toward complete paralysis, while Schiavo's remained unchanging with no signs of possibly regaining full consciousness. And as their lives neared an end, their cases engaged the country in emotional debates about how to make decisions on medical care for patients no longer able to speak for themselves.

Howe understood what lay ahead after she was diagnosed. Even after advancing paralysis sent her to Massachusetts General Hospital in Boston in 1999, however, Howe remained adamant about one thing: She wanted doctors to keep her alive as long as she could enjoy her family. [1]

By 2003, Howe was paralyzed and breathing with a ventilator, pain-ridden and unable to communicate. But her oldest daughter, Carol Carvitt, said her mother's face would light up whenever Carvitt and her two sisters visited. So as her mother's legally designated health-care proxy, Carvitt insisted on life support for Howe, even after the hospital's end-of-life committee unanimously recommended in June 2003 that Howe be allowed to die.

Americans Support Schiavo's Tube Removal

Almost 60 percent of the public agreed with the decision to remove Terri Schiavo's feeding tube, while an overwhelming majority opposed Congress' and President Bush's interventions in the case.

Do you agree with the decision to remove Schiavo's feeding tube?

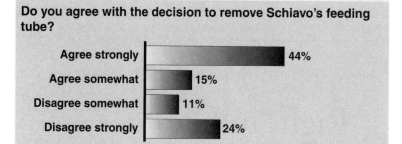

Agree strongly	44%
Agree somewhat	15%
Disagree somewhat	11%
Disagree strongly	24%

Do you think Schiavo's parents have the right to get a court to overrule the wishes of her husband?

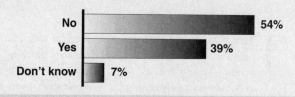

No	54%
Yes	39%
Don't know	7%

Was it right for Congress to intervene in the Schiavo case?

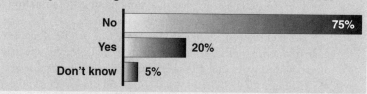

No	75%
Yes	20%
Don't know	5%

Was it right for President Bush to intervene in the case?

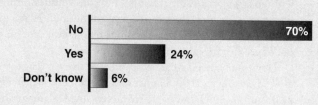

No	70%
Yes	24%
Don't know	6%

Source: Time poll, March 2005 (margin of error: +/- 3 percentage points)

"There is now 100 percent unanimous agreement that this inhumane travesty has gone far enough," Edwin Cassem, a psychiatrist and Jesuit priest who heads the committee, wrote in a summary later filed in court. "This is the Massachusetts General Hospital, not Auschwitz."

Carvitt's opposition forced the hospital's lawyers later that month to seek a court order permitting the withdrawal of life support. The wrenching legal battle spanned almost two years before reaching a conclusion on March 11, 2005: Carvitt and the lawyer representing her mother agreed to allow the hospital to turn off the ventilator on June 30.

"Part of Carol's decision was based on the realization the judge would have made the decision to turn off the ventilator even sooner. This way, her mom would live through June, rather than die in March," says Carvitt's lawyer, Gary Zalkin. [2]

Just as Howe's case was nearing its conclusion, Terri Schiavo's end-of-life legal battle was also entering its final stages — with unceasing media coverage — more than 1,300 miles away in Florida. [3]

Acting under a state judge's order, caretakers at a hospice in Pinellas Park on March 18 disconnected the feeding tube that had kept Schiavo alive for nearly 15 years. Her husband, Michael, had gone to court in 1998 asking to disconnect the tube that provided nutrition and fluids to her mostly motionless body.

Schiavo's parents, Robert and Mary Schindler, fought Michael's request bitterly and relentlessly in a battle that eventually engaged the entire nation — including President Bush and the U.S. Congress — in a debate over how to decide medical treatment for patients unable to speak for themselves.

The dispute raised centuries-old issues of religion and ethics against the backdrop of two late 20th-century developments: the widespread use of life-prolonging medical technology and the legal recognition of patients' rights of autonomy, including the "right to die."

Patients Lack Protection in Most States

Forty states and the District of Columbia generally allow physicians to refuse to comply with a patient's advance directives requesting life-sustaining measures. Laws in 12 states require hospitals to continue providing care while seeking to transfer the patient to a facility willing to provide care.

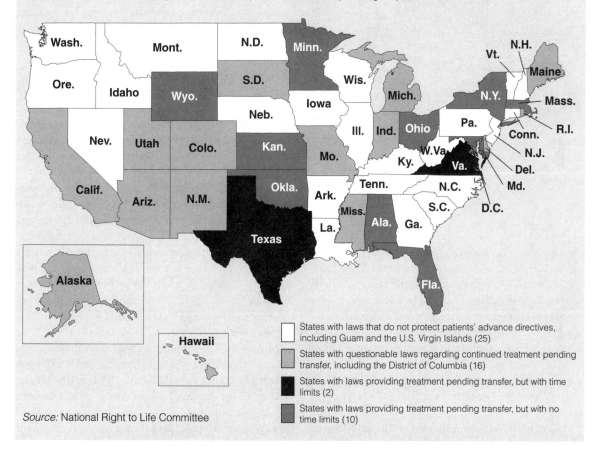

States with laws that do not protect patients' advance directives, including Guam and the U.S. Virgin Islands (25)

States with questionable laws regarding continued treatment pending transfer, including the District of Columbia (16)

States with laws providing treatment pending transfer, but with time limits (2)

States with laws providing treatment pending transfer, but with no time limits (10)

Source: National Right to Life Committee

In both the Howe and the Schiavo cases, however, the patients' rights were being exercised not by the patient but by a legal representative. In Schiavo's case, the question was how to determine her views on the basis of a few comments she made when she was in her 20s and had no reason to expect the fate that befell her. For Howe, the issue was how far to go in abiding by her clearly expressed wishes as her medical condition regressed beyond what doctors — but not her designated representative — thought she could bear.

Right-to-life groups see one common element, though: a too-casual acceptance of the idea that the government can lend its weight to allowing someone to die based on a diminished quality of life. "There is a mentality among some that can be described as a culture of death, a feeling that people with severe mental and physical disabilities have lives that aren't worth living," says Richard Doerflinger, director of the U.S. Conference of Catholic Bishops' secretariat of pro-life activities.

"We're not part of a culture of death," counters Charles Baron, who teaches law and medicine at Boston College and serves on the board of the right-to-die group Death with Dignity. "We're part of a movement that wants people to be free to decide how to get out, that wants to protect their right to get the medical care they want and the right to stop medical care that they don't want."

Supporters of Terri Schiavo's husband Michael demonstrate at Terri's Florida hospice on March 23, 2005. The day before, a federal judge had rejected a request from Terri's parents to reinsert her feeding tube.

Howe's case drew prominent news coverage in the Boston area but only limited attention elsewhere. Schiavo's case, by contrast, became the object of front-page coverage and constant cable news updates for weeks as lawmakers in Tallahassee and Washington — urged on by right-to-life and disability-rights groups — searched for legal steps to prevent the removal of her feeding tube. Broadcast and cable news stations and newspaper Web sites flashed word of her death instantly after the information broke on the morning of March 31.

Public opinion polls indicated solid majorities in favor of withdrawing Schiavo's feeding tube and strong criticism of the frantic legal and political efforts to block the eventual outcome.

Since Schiavo's death, opposing interest groups have drawn starkly different lessons from the outcome.

Right-to-life groups say state laws should be changed or a federal law enacted to make it harder to withdraw life support, especially nutrition and fluids administered by a feeding tube. "We are allowing imprecise, vague, general statements made [without] deep deliberation to control whether someone lives or dies," says Wesley Smith, a senior fellow at the Discovery Institute, a socially conservative think tank, and consultant to the International Task Force on Euthanasia and Assisted Suicide, which opposes both practices.

"This is a complex case with serious issues, but in extraordinary circumstances like this it is wisest to always err on the side of life," President Bush said on March 21, after signing legislation giving the federal government jurisdiction in the Schiavo case.

Right-to-die groups, however, say the calls for stricter regulation of end-of-life decision-making threaten the judicial and legislative gains made on behalf of patients' autonomy dating to the mid-1970s. "End-of-life decision-making is precious and in jeopardy," says Barbara Coombs Lee, president of the Oregon-based group Compassion and Choices. "It needs to be protected."

In Howe's case, right-to-life advocates see the need to rewrite state laws to prevent doctors from overriding a patient's expressed wishes to continue life support. (*See map, p. 145.*) "It is not and should not be the role of the doctor or health-care provider to decide whether a person's life should be preserved," says Burke Balch, an attorney with the National Right to Life Committee and director of its Robert Powell Center for Medical Ethics.

Right-to-die advocates acknowledge the case raises a difficult issue. "There is a real risk that physicians may refuse to prolong life under the pretext that treatment would be 'medically futile' when, in fact, the physician has decided that the particular kind of life of the patient does not merit prolongation," Baron says.

Meanwhile, the opposing groups continue to fight over the related issue of assisted suicide, legal in Oregon since 1997 but in no other state. [4] Advocates say the practice allows terminally ill patients to have a doctor's help in choosing how and when to die. "They have lived their lives according to their own terms, and they want to go out on their own terms," Baron says.

"It's not about autonomy," counters Doerflinger. "It's about the state classifying a group of people as having lives that are not as worth protecting as other people's lives."

The Bush administration is currently asking the Supreme Court to rule that federal law prohibits doctors from prescribing medications for use in ending a patient's life. Oregon contends the administration's stance intrudes on the state's traditional authority to regulate medical practice.

Right-to-life and disability-rights groups vowed to continue pushing in Washington and in state capitals for stricter laws, but popular and official attention to the issue dropped sharply after Schiavo's death. As those groups seek to regenerate interest — despite public approval of ending life support in cases viewed as hopeless — here are some of the major issues being debated:

Are "living wills" effective?

Amid the often fiercely partisan and personal debates over the Schiavo case, both camps seemed unanimous about one thing: the importance of using advance medical directives — or "living wills" — to set out instructions for providing or withholding medical care in the event of incapacity. With the Schiavo case over, the recommendation was repeated by, among others, the Bush administration's ranking health expert on the issue.

"It would be nice" if everyone had an advance medical directive, Donald Young, a physician and deputy assistant Health and Human Services secretary, told the House Subcommittee on Health on April 19. With wider use of living wills, Young said, "the kinds of decisions and discussions we're talking about today would be very rare."

Surprisingly, however, many experts describe living wills as only somewhat useful in the best of circumstances and potentially harmful in the event of intrafamily disputes like the Schiavo case. "A living will wouldn't have made any difference" in Schiavo's case, says Carl Schneider, a professor of law and internal medicine at the University of Michigan, Ann Arbor. The family would still have disagreed, he says, and the living will could not have settled the medical disputes over Schiavo's condition.

By most estimates, no more than one-fourth of Americans have living wills. Schneider, who has written extensively on patient autonomy and end-of-life decision-making, bluntly calls living wills "a joke" and does not have one himself. But he has designated a health-care proxy — his wife — and says that proxies, along with detailed conversations with physicians and family members, are the best means to have one's wishes about medical treatment carried out.

"A living will is almost always clinically useless," agrees Robert Burt, a Yale law professor who also has written extensively about end-of-life issues. "The important thing is to appoint a health-care proxy, somebody whom you deeply trust, whom you are willing to have thrust into what is inevitably a very emotionally taxing decision process if it comes to making decisions about discontinuing care."

Even with careful preparation, however, living wills have the inherent limitation of being prepared when the actual medical circumstances are unknown and to some

Circuit Judge Robert Greer ruled in February 2000 that Michael Schiavo's testimony showed that his wife Terri would not have wanted to be kept alive by extraordinary measures. The Florida Court of Appeals upheld that decision in June 2003. Four months later came the first of several political interventions in the case by Gov. Jeb Bush and the Florida legislature, President Bush and the U.S. Congress.

extent unknowable. "It's very strange well in advance of the situation to decide what you want and what you would not want," says Daniel Callahan, founder of the Hastings Center, a bioethics think tank in Garrison, N.Y. "People change their minds. They say things at age 40 or 50, and it's a different story at age 70 what they would be willing to put up with."

Some of the groups that advocate use of living wills acknowledge their limitations. "It's an imperfect tool, but it's the best tool we have," says Lee of Compassion and Choices. Her group urges people to be specific in their directives and stresses the importance of also designating a health-care proxy.

The American Bar Association (ABA) strongly recommends advance medical directives and provides information and forms on its Web site (*www.ABALawinfo.com*). But Charles Sabatino, assistant director of the ABA's Commission on Legal Problems of the Elderly, says standard forms "don't provide all that much guidance." Of those people who do have living wills, he says, most "don't take care of the other important task of talking about" their directives with physicians and relatives. Moreover, most people do not file their directives with their doctors. "They're not in the medical records at the time they need to be."

Public Support for Assisted Suicide Increases

Americans' support for assisted suicide more than doubled from 1950 to 2003, when nearly three-quarters of the public said doctors should be legally allowed to end the life of a patient with an incurable disease.

When a person has a disease that cannot be cured, do you think doctors should be allowed to end that patient's life by some painless means, if the patient requests it?

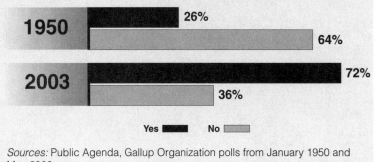

Sources: Public Agenda, Gallup Organization polls from January 1950 and May 2003.

Some of the limitations of living wills are institutional, Sabatino notes. Procedural requirements and such substantive provisions as the definition of "terminal condition" vary from state to state. A few states require use of a specific form. And the enforceability of living wills across state lines is, at best, not assured. [5] In addition, doctors are not required to follow advance directives, and many do not. In a recent survey, 65 percent of physicians responding said they would not necessarily follow a living will under some circumstances. [6]

For its part, the National Right to Life Committee (NRLC) complains that laws in all but 10 states allow doctors and hospitals to override advance directives if health-care providers conclude life-support measures are not medically warranted. "In most states, if you want life-saving treatment — or even food and fluids — there is no guarantee your wishes will be honored, even if you make them clear in a valid advance directive," says Dorothy Timbs, an NRLC legislative counsel.

Burt agrees, saying that doctors are too quick to conclude that life-support measures are futile. "The futility standard is a constant temptation for doctors to override the deeply troubled feelings of the family rather than working with the family, to bring them around and not strong-arm them," he says.

With all these limitations, Schneider argues simply that living wills should be abandoned. "Living wills do not and cannot achieve" the goal of patient autonomy, he says.

But ABA President Robert Grey says preparing an advance directive has the advantage of forcing people to begin thinking about end-of-life issues. "Whether you're old or young, healthy or ill, it's never too early to start thinking about who you want making decisions for you in an emergency, how you would want key health-care decisions handled, and what your basic desires are."

Should Congress regulate end-of-life decisions?

Lawmakers in Washington initially proposed to intervene in the Schiavo case with a broad measure that would have given the federal government jurisdiction over any withdrawal of food and fluids from incapacitated patients without written medical directives. When opposition threatened to delay the legislation, supporters drafted a new bill that applied only to Schiavo's case. [7] In the end, however, the measure failed to accomplish supporters' goal of reversing a Florida state court's rulings to permit withdrawal of Schiavo's feeding tube. Now, right-to-life supporters are renewing their push for sweeping federal legislation to regulate end-of-life decision-making.

"Current legal protections for vulnerable patients who need only food and water to survive are inadequate and confusing," says Doerflinger of the Catholic bishops' group. "We're in a society where it's a public scandal if an HMO refuses a liver transplant. But people in the richest nation in the world can starve to death in a nursing home where there's no clear indication that's what they would want to happen if they could express their wishes."

Opponents, however, continue to question the need for — or wisdom of — the federal government intervening in an area that for the most part has been left to the states. "End-of-life decision-making has traditionally been a matter of state regulation," Lee, of Compassion and Choices, says. "I believe it's best kept that way."

"Congress has nothing useful to contribute on this subject and shouldn't act in the swell of emotion about the Schiavo case," the University of Michigan's Schneider says. "We are talking about solutions to problems that are not very pressing at all."

Twice before the Schiavo case, Congress passed limited measures dealing with end-of-life issues. A nationwide controversy over an Indiana couple's 1982 decision to refuse possibly life-saving surgery for their infant son born with severe disabilities led two years later to a federal law prohibiting federally financed hospitals from withholding treatment from infants on the basis of disabilities. Later, in the wake of a 1990 Supreme Court decision explicitly upholding patients' rights to refuse life-support treatment, Congress in 1991 passed the Patient Self-Determination Act. [8] The law requires health-care institutions to develop written policies on advance directives and to inform patients of their rights to accept or refuse medical treatment.

Over time, the Schiavo case brought together antiabortion and disability-rights groups in a critique of state laws that specify when medical treatment can be withheld for incapacitated patients. Despite different political perspectives and affiliations, both movements now argue state laws have gone too far in empowering guardians or courts to reject life support without a clear expression of the patient's wishes.

"This is a civil-rights issue, a proper issue for federal standards," says Diane Coleman, president of the disability-rights organization Not Dead Yet. "While guardianship laws have traditionally been a state matter, if they're discriminatory, then there's a proper role for federal intervention of some kind."

"In these cases of vegetative state, we're generally dealing with medically stable patients who are generally tolerating the feeding well, but somebody decides that they shouldn't live any longer," Doerflinger says. "There, we feel society should have a role in protecting the helpless."

By contrast, right-to-die groups say calls for federal legislation or stricter state laws threaten the judicially recognized right to refuse medical treatment, including food and fluids. "There is a movement to make it harder and harder to articulate our wishes and to enforce our wishes," Lee says. "Social conservatives are asking for a higher and higher standard of proof to the degree that people who don't fill out advance directives may get no consideration of their wishes at all."

A 1983 auto accident left Nancy Cruzan, a healthy Missouri woman, in a persistent vegetative state at age 25. When Cruzan's parents' asked her hospital to disconnect her feeding tube, the hospital balked. Eventually the Cruzans' evidence of Nancy's views about life and death were ruled sufficient to disconnect the feeding tube. She died on Dec. 26, 1990.

"What's driving this is a certain amount of political pressure from people who do not want to allow complete autonomy of patients," says Boston College's Baron.

For now, the major legislative proposal being developed on Capitol Hill would require any hospitals that accept Medicare or Medicaid patients to establish a presumption against withdrawing food and fluids unless there is evidence of the patient's explicit wishes to the contrary. The proposal is to be introduced by Rep. Dave Weldon, R-Fla., a physician who sponsored the broad Schiavo case bill that was later shelved.

The Discovery Institute's Smith says it makes sense for the federal government to use its financial leverage over the Medicare and Medicaid programs to establish a stricter rule for withdrawing food and water than for terminating other life support. "If you don't want that, you should put it in writing," he says. If the patient had no written directive, and family members disagree, "we have to keep a presumption for life," he says.

But others say such legislation is best left up to the states. "Why is the federal government imposing this national regulation?" Baron asks rhetorically. "I don't find evidence that states are incapable of dealing with this on their own."

Existing state laws generally establish no presumption either way, according to the ABA's Sabatino. "If you build in a presumption of every treatment possible, you're going to skew the outcome in a lot of cases toward treatment," he says. "That may be good, but it may not be accurate. If you poll the public, most people say they wouldn't want to be kept alive in a situation like that."

Should states permit physician-assisted suicide for terminally ill patients?

David Prueitt thought he was ending his pain from terminal leukemia when he swallowed a legally prescribed, supposedly lethal dose of the barbiturate Seconal at his home in Estacada, Ore., on Jan 30, 2005. Instead, he fell into a coma for three days and woke up asking, "Why am I not dead yet?" He lived for nearly two weeks until finally succumbing to the cancer itself on Feb. 15. [9]

Prueitt's failed suicide was quickly seized on by opponents of Oregon's Death with Dignity Act, the state's voter-approved measure that authorizes physicians to assist terminally ill patients in ending their lives. "We've always been concerned that the dose would not always be lethal and that there would be complications," Kenneth Stevens, vice president of Physicians for Compassionate Choice, commented in early March. "In this situation, living is considered a complication."

Supporters of the law minimized the problem while promising to look for an explanation. "No medical procedure is 100 percent guaranteed," said Lee, one of the drafters of the original voter initiative.

Oregon's law has been under challenge almost constantly since voters first approved it, by a bare 51 percent majority, in 1994. The measure took effect only in 1997 after failed attempts to have it overturned by federal court or by a voter referendum. Since 2001, the Bush administration has been seeking essentially to nullify the law by contending that the federal Controlled Substances Act prohibits doctors from prescribing lethal substances. So far, federal courts have rejected the administration's arguments, but the U.S. Supreme Court has agreed to hear the government's appeal in October 2005.

In the seven years the measure has been in effect, 208 people have ended their lives under the law, according to the Oregon Department of Human Services. [10] The vast majority — 164 — had cancer. To use the law, a patient must first make three requests — two oral and one written — and be diagnosed by two doctors as terminal and expected to die within six months. The prescribing physician must inform the patient of feasible alternatives to suicide — such as hospice care and pain control — and must refer the patient for a psychological examination if needed.

Supporters of the law bristle at the term "assisted suicide" and insist the measure simply allows terminally ill patients the option of what Lee calls "a peaceful and humane death." "To call the hastening of an imminent death suicide is pejorative," Lee says. "To people who are terminally ill, the choice to continue living is not theirs to make."

Opponents say the law puts doctors and the government in the business of helping people kill themselves. "Suicide has happened through the centuries," says Gayle Atteberry, executive director of Oregon National Right to Life. "Our opposition is making it a state-sanctioned killing of yourself."

More particularly, opponents say patients have not used the law for the major justification that they claim proponents gave for allowing assisted suicide — relieving unbearable pain. According to physicians' reports to the state health department, patients who have availed themselves of the law most commonly cited end-of-life concerns such as a decreasing ability to participate in activities that make life enjoyable, loss of autonomy and loss of dignity. "Inadequate pain control or fear of inadequate pain control is the least of the reasons given for doing assisted suicide," Atteberry says. "The very premise on which this law was passed is not the reason people are using it."

But supporters contend that personal autonomy, not fear of pain itself, was always the major argument in favor of the law. "The overwhelming reason people [choose] assisted dying is because they fear the loss of control of their bodily functions and the degradation of the body and mind through a prolonged dying process," Lee says. She says that fear of being a burden on one's family ranks low in the list of concerns cited.

Opponents also contend the law has operated with little effective state oversight, allowing patients to shop for doctors willing to liberally construe the law's provisions. "When the prescription is written, the government doesn't independently verify any of the issues," says the Discovery Institute's Smith. "Oregon never contacts doctors who refuse to write prescriptions when requested. We don't know what's going on except through what the prescribing doctors write."

Lee counters that state reports and "a whole stack of research investigations" show there has been "no abuse" under the law. As to doctor-shopping, she says the law "respects the choice of patients and respects the choice of physicians. Physicians who do not wish to participate are free to do so, but their patients are also free to transfer their care to another physician who shares their values and their beliefs."

Despite the arguments, Lee claims — and Atteberry concedes — that the law is no longer controversial in Oregon itself. "It is simply not a hot political topic in Oregon," Lee says. She and other supporters cite Oregon's example in helping push similar legislation in other states — so far, without success.

Opponents are similarly looking beyond the state's border to press their arguments. "The best thing we can do is to pass on what we have learned about this experiment to other states that are contemplating it," Atteberry says.

BACKGROUND

Processes of Dying

The process of dying underwent far-reaching changes in the United States in the mid- and late-20th century, creating difficult ethical issues for doctors and patients — and eventually for judges and legislators. The professionalization of the practice of medicine combined with advances in public health and medical technology to change the *when*, the *where* and the *how* of the dying process. The new technology often was seen as merely prolonging the dying process, leading some patients and families to ask courts and legislatures to recognize a "right to die." [11]

The earliest Western source of medical ethics — the Hippocratic oath of ancient Greece — admonished doctors: "If any shall ask of me a drug to produce death, I shall not give it." Historian Peter Filene points out, how-

ever, that doctors in the 19th and 20th centuries routinely provided terminal patients with pain-relieving drugs — including opium and morphine — in sufficient doses to assure "a peaceful passing."

Efforts to legalize euthanasia — or "mercy killings" — failed in Ohio (1906) and New York (1939), but the Euthanasia Society of America — founded in 1938 — was encouraged by one poll showing 46 percent support for "mercy deaths under Government supervision for hopeless invalids." And in one celebrated case a New Hampshire jury in 1950 acquitted physician Hermann Sander of murder for administering lethal injections of air to a patient with terminal cancer. [12]

Americans' experience of death was meanwhile undergoing a gradual but radical transformation. In the 19th century, most people either died suddenly on the spot or slowly at home. By the late 20th century, the vast majority of people were dying of chronic conditions (87 percent, according to a study in 1982) and in institutions (80 percent, according to an official estimate in the 1980s). As bioethicist Robert Veatch points out, "the scene of a family gathered in the bedroom of the dying is now little more than a poignant memory." [13] People were also living longer: Life expectancy in the United States increased from 47.3 years to 75 years by the late 1980s, according to Veatch.

The practice of medicine was also changing. The family physician was being replaced by specialists who lacked the same close relationship with their patients and received in return a reduced measure of automatic confidence in their decisions. Meanwhile, new treatments and technologies were allowing doctors to prolong life. Most prominently, perhaps, the artificial respirator — successor to the less sophisticated "iron lung" of the 1950s — kept many patients alive after their natural breathing processes had deteriorated.

As early as the 1950s, however, some doctors and much of the public were viewing the new support technologies as a mixed blessing. A San Francisco doctor told *Time* in 1956 that too little attention was being given to the "God-given . . . right to die." [14] A year later, Lael Wertenbaker recounted in the widely discussed book *Death of a Man* how she helped her cancer-stricken husband Charles take his own life. Over the next decade, Filene writes, "a steady stream" of articles and books helped break the societal taboo about death-talk. And by the 1960s, he says, a right-to-die movement was forming

CHRONOLOGY

1950s-1960s *Advances in medical technology extend lives, prolong dying — prompting debates over end-of-life decisions.*

1957 Lael Wertenbaker's *Death of a Man* recounts how she helped her cancer-stricken husband to end his life.

Mid-1960s Right-to-die movement begins.

1970s-1980s *Courts recognize right to refuse life support, including food and fluids; states pass "living will" laws.*

1976 New Jersey Supreme Court upholds right to refuse life support, allowing parents of Karen Ann Quinlan to remove her from respirator; she survives, in persistent vegetative state, for another nine years. . . . California passes first state law to give legal effect to advance medical directives or "living wills"; seven states follow suit within a year.

1980 Pope John Paul II condemns mercy killing but reaffirms doctrine permitting withdrawal of extraordinary life-support measures in some cases.

1982 Indiana Supreme Court allows parents of infant son born with Down's Syndrome and obstructed esophagus to refuse surgery; case provokes national outcry, leads Congress to pass law in 1984 prohibiting hospitals from withholding treatment from infants because of disabilities.

1985 New Jersey Supreme Court rules that right to refuse treatment includes withdrawal of food and fluids.

1990s *Right-to-die, assisted-suicide argued in state courts and legislatures and before U.S. Supreme Court.*

1990 Terri Schiavo suffers cardiac arrest on Feb. 26 and lapses into "persistent vegetative state" lasting 15 years. . . . Supreme Court rules in Missouri case that states can require "clear and convincing evidence" of patients' wishes before permitting withdrawal of life-sustaining treatment; Nancy Ann Cruzan's case is returned to Missouri court, where after evidence of sufficient proof is presented, Cruzan is removed from life support and dies Dec. 26. . . . Congress passes Patient Self-Determination Act to require

health-care facilities to inform patients of procedures for advance medical directives.

1991 Initiative 119 is qualified for Washington state ballot to permit physician-assisted suicide; one week before election, Michigan physician Jack Kevorkian assists in suicides by two middle-aged women in Detroit; episode is seen as key to defeat of Washington initiative.

1992 California voters reject physician-assisted suicide initiative.

1994 Oregon voters narrowly approve Death with Dignity Act to allow doctors to prescribe lethal medications for terminally ill patients; opponents challenge measure in federal court, delaying implementation till 1997.

1997 U.S. Supreme Court, in related cases from New York and Washington state, finds no constitutional right to assisted suicide . . . Federal court lifts injunction against Oregon's assisted suicide law on Oct. 27; one week later, Oregon voters reject ballot measure to nullify the act.

1998 Michael Schiavo seeks court permission to remove wife's feeding tube; granted in February 2000, upheld by state appeal court in June 2003. . . . Michigan voters reject measure to legalize physician-assisted suicide.

2000-Present *Schiavo case becomes national battleground over end-of-life decision-making.*

2001 Attorney General John Ashcroft challenges Oregon assisted-suicide law by ruling that federal drug law prohibits doctors from prescribing lethal medications; Oregon officials win lower court rulings to nullify rule; Supreme Court agrees in February 2005 to hear case

2003 Florida legislature passes "Terri's law" to allow Gov. Jeb Bush to order Schiavo's feeding tube reinserted; Florida Supreme Court in 2004 rules law unconstitutional.

2005 Schiavo case dominates headlines as Terri's parents, backed by right-to-life and disability-rights groups, seek to prevent removal of feeding tube; Congress passes law for federal court jurisdiction over case, but state courts' decisions are upheld; feeding tube removed March 18; Schiavo dies March 31.

— fed by two of the decade's broader trends: the emphasis on individual self-realization and the equal-rights movements for blacks and women. [15]

Courts were dealing with the issue on a case-by-case basis until the tragic story of Karen Ann Quinlan culminated in a landmark right-to-die decision in 1976. [16] Quinlan, then 21, fell into a coma at a party on April 14, 1975. The cause was initially but never conclusively diagnosed as an overdose. She had been drinking and had taken Valium before or during the party. Whatever the cause, doctors were unable to restore her to consciousness. Her parents, observant Catholics, conferred closely with the treating physician and their priest before concluding that their daughter would not want to be kept alive in that manner and directing doctors to disconnect the respirator that was helping her breathe.

When the doctor refused, the parents sought out a legal aid lawyer, who agreed to file suit in New Jersey Superior Court claiming on Karen's behalf a right to remove life support — in effect, a right to die. After a nationally publicized trial, the judge rejected the plea. On appeal, however, the New Jersey Supreme Court unanimously ruled both that Karen had the right to terminate life support "as a matter of self-determination" and that her father could represent her wishes since she was unable to express them herself. Though the court never used the phrase, the decision established what came to be known imprecisely as the "right to die."

Politics of Dying

The Quinlan decision set the stage for legislators and courts throughout the country to recognize and define the right to refuse life-support treatments. State legislatures responded by passing laws authorizing the use of advance medical directives — so-called living wills — and the designation of health-care proxies. Courts extended the Quinlan doctrine to new situations, including the withdrawal of food and fluids. The Supreme Court, however, ruled that states could require a high standard of proof before allowing withdrawal of life support. Meanwhile, right-to-die organizations worked to establish a right to physician-assisted suicide but succeeded only in Oregon. [17]

Barely six months after the Quinlan decision, California became the first state to enact a living-will statute. The Natural Death Act, signed on Sept. 30, 1976, by Gov. Jerry Brown, applied only to terminally ill patients and required renewal of directives after five years. Within a year, seven states had followed California's lead. By 1992, all 50 states and the District of Columbia permitted either living wills or health-care proxies, or both. *

Quinlan herself defied medical expectations by breathing on her own after her respirator was disconnected, until she finally succumbed to pneumonia on June 11, 1985 — nine years later. By then, other state courts had extended the New Jersey court's ruling. In one of the first expansions, Massachusetts' highest court in 1977 ordered the withholding of chemotherapy treatments from a profoundly retarded man in his late 60s with terminal leukemia; the justices accepted a court-appointed guardian's view that the man would have chosen to forgo the "pain and fear" of treatment that could only extend his life by a matter of months. [18]

More significantly, New Jersey's high court in 1985 upheld a lower court's order allowing doctors to remove a feeding tube from an elderly woman with terminal cancer. The ruling had no direct effect: The woman had died before the court's order could be carried out. But because of the importance of the issue the justices took up the appeal and, in a 6-1 ruling, expanded the right to refuse treatment to include food and fluids. [19] The American Medical Association (AMA) reached a similar conclusion in the same year by adopting a policy to permit doctors to withdraw tubal nutrition and fluids from dying patients who request it or from irreversibly comatose patients.

In the early 1980s, a new controversy arose over the withholding of medical treatment from infants born with severe abnormalities. Right-to-life and disability groups reacted strongly to the death in 1982 of "Baby Doe," a boy born in Bloomington, Ind., with Down's Syndrome and an obstructed esophagus whose parents decided against potentially life-saving surgery.

The hospital's unsuccessful legal effort to perform the procedure against the parents' wishes went all the way to the U.S. Supreme Court. Two years later, Congress prohibited hospitals from withholding treatment from newborns because of disabilities; the impact of the law, however, has been unclear.

---

* All 50 states and the District of Columbia currently recognize health-care proxies; all states but three — Massachusetts, Michigan and New York — as well as the District of Columbia have laws recognizing living wills.

Making the Decision to End a Baby's Life

The birth of Wanda Hudson's son on Sept. 25, 2004, wasn't the wholly joyous event that most new parents dream about. Sun was born with a form of dwarfism that impairs lung and chest cavity development, and doctors at Texas Children's Hospital deemed his condition untreatable and fatal.

But Hudson held out hope, irrationally, doctors say, that her son would recover. In November 2004, after the hospital's bioethics committee endorsed the doctors' decision to discontinue treatment, Hudson filed suit to keep her son alive.

In early March 2005, a judge ruled that Texas law permitted the hospital to withdraw treatment, and a few days later — in what bioethicists say is a first in the United States — the hospital disconnected support despite a parent's objections and Sun died.

"This hospital was considered a miracle hospital. When it came to my son, they gave up in six months," Hudson said. "They made a terrible mistake." [1]

Bioethicists and physicians, however, appear to unanimously agree that ending Sun's care was the only ethical choice. The hospital issued a statement saying it had made "extraordinary efforts to provide the best possible care for Sun" and was "very grieved that no treatment could save this child." [2]

Infant end-of-life issues have been debated less publicly than those for adults throughout the last 50 years, and ethicists say the subject is just as unsettled.

The debate initially centered around the care of infants with serious, but not life-threatening disabilities, such as spina bifida and Down's Syndrome. Despite the suspicions of disability-rights groups, medical experts say nowadays there is no evidence that parents or doctors are trying to end care for infants with serious but not life-threatening disabilities.

"In the area of neonatology, nothing is really broken; the system is working," says Arthur Caplan, a bioethicist at the University of Pennsylvania. "Years ago, parents said, 'My kid has Down's; let them die,' and the doctors did. That doesn't happen now. We're more sophisticated about handicaps. There are more vocal protests from disability groups. And the impact of all of that has been felt in the health-care system."

But Stephen Drake, a research analyst at the disability-rights group Not Dead Yet, says disability discrimination still takes place. "We've lost a lot of ground in terms of minimum treatment," Drake says. "We need to have a set of guidelines — like the 'Baby Doe' regulations," which would specify, for instance, what "terminal" means and how low one's survival chances need to be for life support to be discontinued.

Drake was referring to a set of short-lived federal regulations — requiring physicians to provide life-sustaining medical procedures to all infants — enacted after a baby born with Down's Syndrome and an obstructed esophagus in Bloomington, Ind., in 1982 was allowed to die after his parents decided against potentially life-saving surgery. The hospital sued to perform the procedure against the parents' wishes, but three courts, including the Indiana Supreme

The Supreme Court's first pronouncement in the issue came in the case of a Missouri woman, Nancy Ann Cruzan, who had been left in a persistent vegetative state at age 25 following a 1983 car accident. Four years later, her parents went to court to get her feeding tube withdrawn. The Missouri Supreme Court ruled, however, that in the absence of a living will, life support could be withheld only on the basis of "clear and convincing evidence" of the patient's wishes. By a 5-4 vote, the U.S. Supreme Court agreed in 1990 that states could establish a strict standard of proof in such cases. [20] The case returned to the state trial court, which found the Cruzans' evidence of their daughter's views suffi-

cient to disconnect the feeding tube; she died on Dec. 26, 1990.

Over the next decade, attention shifted to efforts to legalize physician-assisted suicide. In Michigan, physician Jack Kevorkian defied the medical establishment and legal authorities by avidly publicizing his work in helping patients to end their lives. In one dramatic episode, Kevorkian set up his so-called "mercitron" to administer intravenous injections of a lethal mixture of thiopental and potassium chloride to two middle-aged women in a rented state park cabin in Michigan in 1991. In a more dramatic instance, the CBS newsmagazine "60 Minutes" in November 1998 broadcast

Court, upheld the parents' decision. The case was awaiting U.S. Supreme Court action when "Baby Doe" died. [3]

A public outcry by right-to-life and disability-rights groups led to further federal involvement. The Reagan administration issued the so-called Baby Doe regulations, which required hospitals receiving federal aid to provide aggressive medical treatment for severely handicapped infants over their parents' objections. They were struck down by the Supreme Court in 1986 for infringing upon states' rights. [4] In the interim, however, Congress passed the Child Abuse Amendments of 1984, requiring that states make sure that all newborns are protected against disability discrimination, except in cases where treatment would be "futile." [5]

Since then doctors and hospitals have had difficulty interpreting the law, because it did not clearly define "futile." So far, however, it has not been directly challenged — and therefore illuminated — in the courts, and no real data has been collected on how hospitals are defining "futile," Drake says.

"We want the government to get a handle on what is actually being done at hospitals, in the nurseries, in terms of infants with disabilities," Drake says. "We need hard data, but you can expect groups connected with hospitals to holler and scream about any move in that direction."

In the states, only California, Virginia and Texas have laws establishing additional requirements for infant care, says the Rev. John Paris, a Boston College bioethicist. "Texas has a wonderful statute that deals with situations when the family is insisting on life-sustaining treatment that a hospital feels is inappropriate," Paris says.

The Texas statute, which was applied in the Sun Hudson case, was signed into law by then-Gov. George W. Bush in 1999. In cases where doctors think life-sustaining treatment is futile, the law allows relatives to try to make provisions for care in another facility. Approximately 40 other hospitals refused to take Sun, according to Texas Children's Hospital. [6]

In practice, Drake says, the Texas law only encourages all hospitals to adopt futile-care policies, which means "no hospital will take the child."

"What hasn't been reported is that other kids with Sun's condition have lived as long as eight years," Drake says. "While that might not mean a lot to a doctor, I suspect it means a lot to a parent. Where there are gray areas, you have to go with the parent's wishes."

The Rev. Paris disagrees that Sun's condition was borderline, but he understands the emotion behind the argument. "These are difficult, trying, complex issues that require very sensitive responses," he says. "But it's antithetical to the argument to say that dying babies should be kept alive regardless of the circumstances or their potential quality of life."

— *Kate Templin*

---

[1] Leigh Hopper, " 'Inside of Me, My Son Is Still Alive,' " *The Houston Chronicle*, March 16, 2005, p. A1.

[2] www.khou.com/news/health/stories/khou050315_mh_statement. 13ffb5535.html

[3] "Ethical and Legal Issues," Ch. 5, in Goldsmith, J. P., ed., *Assisted Ventilation of the Newborn*, 4th ed., 2003.

[4] The case was *Bowen v. American Hospital Association*, 476 U.S. 610.

[5] Jon Tyson, "Evidence-Based Ethics and Care of Premature Infants," *The Future of Children: A Publication of Princeton University and the Brookings Institution*, Vol. 5, No. 1, spring 1995.

[6] Hopper, *op. cit.*

Kevorkian's videotape of the injection death of another patient, Thomas Youk. Michigan authorities, who had failed in six previous attempts to convict Kevorkian, quickly brought charges against him in Youk's death and won a second-degree murder conviction and 10-25 year prison sentence in 1999. Kevorkian was denied parole in November 2004. [21]

Meanwhile, voters in three Western states considered legalizing physician-assisted suicide. In a seeming backlash to the Kevorkian story, voters in Washington state rejected a measure in November 1991; California voters rejected a similar measure in 1992. Oregon voters narrowly approved the Death with Dignity Act two years later, but opponents' legal challenge in federal court delayed its implementation until 1997.

Supporters of physician-assisted suicide filed their own legal challenges, claiming terminally ill patients have a constitutional right to choose the manner of their dying. The issue reached the U.S. Supreme Court in separate cases challenging New York and Washington state laws. The justices in 1997 unanimously rejected the right-to-die groups' arguments in both cases.

In the main opinion, Chief Justice William H. Rehnquist said state laws banning suicide were "rationally related" to the government's "commitment to the protection and preservation of human life." But he also said the ruling would allow the debate over the issue to continue — "as it should in a democratic society." In separate opinions, other justices appeared more sympathetic, with several explicitly saying that doctors could legally prescribe pain-killing medications even if they knew the treatment would hasten a patient's death. [22]

'Culture of Death'?

As the 1990s drew to an end, the broad legal acceptance of living wills and health-care proxies and the standoff on assisted suicide seemed to be ushering in a quiet period on right-to-die issues. But Pope John Paul II used a triumphal visit to the United States in 1999 to raise the issue by asking Americans to rally against what he called a "culture of death." Meanwhile, Michael Schiavo in 1998 had asked a Florida court for permission to disconnect his wife's feeding tube — touching off a bitter legal battle and emotional national debate over end-of-life decision-making.

Early in his tenure, the pope in 1980 had issued a "Declaration on Euthanasia" that restated Catholic teachings opposing mercy killing while approving the right to refuse extraordinary means for sustaining life. [23] The document called for distinguishing between "proportionate" and "disproportionate" interventions by weighing the cost, complexity and risks against the possible results and "taking into account the state of the sick person and his or her physical and moral resources." [24] But the pontiff made no such close distinctions when he flagged the issue in January 1999.

Recalling the United States' 19th-century debates over slavery, John Paul said abortion and euthanasia similarly relegated whole classes of people to the status of "nonpersons." He exhorted Americans to "resist the culture of death and choose to stand steadfastly on the side of life."

In a Vatican speech five years later, John Paul laid out a strict position against withdrawing food and water from incapacitated patients. Providing food and water, the pontiff told a Catholic medical group in March 2004, should be considered ordinary care, not artificial intervention. "As such," the pontiff said, "it is morally obligatory." [25]

With a change of political administrations in 2001, the federal government aligned itself with the right-to-life stance on a range of issues, including end-of-life decision-making. In a telling shift, Attorney General John Ashcroft in 2001 challenged Oregon's assisted-suicide law by issuing a regulation threatening doctors with prosecution or sanctions under the federal Controlled Substances Act for approving prescriptions for lethal drugs. But a lower federal court and the federal appeals court for Oregon both held the federal rule improperly intruded on states' traditional authority to regulate medical practice.

Meanwhile, the Schiavo case made only a slight blip on the news media's radar in 1998, when Michael sought to disconnect his wife's feeding tube. News coverage grew, along with protests from right-to-life groups, as courts upheld Michael's request despite opposition from Terri's parents, the Schindlers. Circuit Judge Robert Greer made the critical ruling in February 2000, holding that Michael's testimony about Terri's past comments showed she would not have wanted to be kept alive by extraordinary measures. The Florida Court of Appeals upheld that decision in June 2003.

Four months later came the first of several political interventions in the case. Florida Gov. Jeb Bush filed a federal court brief urging that Terri be kept alive. In the same month, Florida lawmakers passed a bill allowing Bush to intervene in the case, and he promptly ordered the feeding tube reinserted. In September 2004, however, the Florida Supreme Court ruled that "Terri's law" — as it was dubbed — amounted to an unconstitutional legislative intervention in a pending judicial case. The U.S. Supreme Court declined to hear the state's appeal to reinstate the law.

In February 2005, Greer stayed the removal of the feeding tube for a month, until March 18. With a seemingly final deadline imminent, right-to-life groups turned to Congress in what they depicted as an effort by Terri's parents to save her from a cruel death by starvation and dehydration at the hands of a now-estranged husband. Michael kept a generally low profile, but his lawyer George Felos sought to rebut the arguments by pointing to Greer's finding that Michael was acting caringly and sincerely in what he viewed as Terri's best interests. Under Greer's order, the feeding tube was removed on March 18.

With Republican leaders convening an extraordinary weekend session March 19-20, Congress passed a law authorizing federal courts to assume jurisdiction over the Florida state court proceeding. President Bush flew to Washington from his ranch in Texas to sign the bill in the early morning hours of March 21.

The next day, U.S. District Judge James Whittemore in Tampa refused to order the feeding tube reinserted, essentially upholding the state courts' decisions. The ruling stood up despite a flurry of desperate pleas by the Schindlers and Florida authorities to the federal appeals court in Atlanta and the U.S. Supreme Court, which refused to intervene. With the whole country now watching, Terri died on March 31.

CURRENT SITUATION

Federal Standards Eyed

Political interest in the issues raised by the Schiavo case is way down on Capitol Hill judging from the sparse attendance at two legislative hearings held within three weeks of her death. Republican lawmakers who led the fight to intervene in the case are taking a lower profile, while Democrats — who raised no objections at the time — are openly questioning the need for federal legislation to set stricter standards for end-of-life decisions.

Republicans have also backed away from the sharp criticism of the federal judiciary made by, among others, House Majority Leader Tom DeLay, R-Texas, for refusing to override the state courts' decisions to permit the removal of Schiavo's feeding tube. On the day of Schiavo's death, DeLay warned that judges who reviewed the case would have to "answer for their behavior." In subsequent days, President Bush and Senate Majority Leader Bill Frist, R-Tenn., both declined to second DeLay's criticism; and the House leader himself apologized two weeks later for what he termed "inartful" remarks. [26]

Some observers see the diminished interest in the case as a reaction to polls showing strong disapproval of Congress' role. "When you get 82 percent saying they think Congress did the wrong thing, that's everyone," said Andrew Kohut, director of the Pew Research Center for the People and the Press. [27]

Right-to-life and disability-rights groups are urging Congress to enact legislation to establish a federal presumption against withdrawing food and water from incapacitated patients. The limited attendance by majority Republicans and explicit doubts about the need for legislation from several Democrats made clear that Congress will be slower to act on broad legislation than it did in passing the Schiavo bill — if it acts at all.

Only three of the 20 members of the Senate Health, Education, Labor and Pensions Committee attended a hearing on April 6, just six days after Schiavo's death. Two weeks later, hearings held by the House Subcommittee on Criminal Justice, Drug Policy and Human Resources drew five members, but only two stayed for most of the session. [28]

In contrast to the predominance of traditional anti-abortion groups in the lobbying and protests before Schiavo's death, disability-rights advocates dominated the witness lists at both congressional hearings. The Bush administration's representative at the House hearing said he had no legislative recommendations but offered to look at any proposals introduced in Congress.

The Senate hearing was technically rescheduled from a March 28 session that Republicans had tried to use to block removal of Schiavo's feeding tube by subpoenaing her as a witness — a maneuver blocked by state and federal courts. In opening the hearing, Chairman Michael Enzi, R-Wyo., said the session was about "more than Terri Schiavo." But the other senators present used the occasion to rehash the arguments for and against Congress's intervention in the case.

"Families facing these painful decisions deserve better than political theatrics from the United States Congress," Sen. Edward M. Kennedy, D-Mass., said. "Instead, our role in Congress should be to support families as they make end-of-life decisions."

Sen. Richard M. Burr, R-N.C., countered by calling criticism of Congress' action unfair. "We set a precedent with everything we do in Congress, but we also set a precedent with everything we choose not to do," Burr said. "We should set a precedent that you do stop, and you do ask questions — and possibly you act."

Rep. Michael Souder, R-Ind., opened the House subcommittee hearing by calling for "a federal presumption in favor of life" to ensure that incapacitated Medicare or Medicaid patients are "not denied ordinary care such as hydration or nutrition without due process and full exercise of their rights as human beings."

As the first witness, Rep. Weldon of Florida outlined a proposal along those lines but said he had not yet drafted specific legislation. A federal standard "would presume that vulnerable adults would want to be fed and given fluids unless they had explicitly expressed otherwise," Weldon said.

'I Want to Stop It From Happening Again'

For five years, Terri Schiavo's parents and other family members fought a fierce battle in the courts, in the media and in the streets to block her husband Michael from withdrawing the feeding tube that was keeping her alive. Then, on March 31, the fight came to what Terri's brother Bobby Schindler describes as "an abrupt halt."

Terri's death left the family "numb," Schindler says. "We didn't expect it to happen."

The bad blood between the Schindlers and Michael appears to have started in 1993 when they said they wanted some of the medical malpractice judgment that Michael had won against Terri's doctor the previous year: $750,000 for her and $300,000 for himself. (Her money was put in trust for her care.) Terri's 1990 heart attack that cut off oxygen to her brain had been caused by a potassium imbalance due to bulimia, an eating disorder that doctors had failed to diagnose. [1]

The bad blood continued even after Terri's death. The parents wanted their daughter buried in a Catholic service, but Michael had her body cremated — as he said she would have wanted.

Barely two weeks after Terri's death, however, Schindler was back helping to get media attention for the issues raised by his sister's case. He traveled from the family's home in Florida to Washington for an April 15 news conference held by the National Right to Life Committee criticizing state laws that allow doctors in some cases to override a patient's wishes in withdrawing life support, including food and water.

Afterward, Schindler said he plans to take a leave from his job teaching science at a Catholic high school in Tampa to continue working on the issues. "I want to focus on what happened to Terri and prevent anything like that from ever happening again," he says. "We're too comfortable with this whole quality-of-life mentality."

Schindler says his sister's death — 13 days after her feeding tube was removed under a state court order — was not peaceful and painless, as Michael's lawyer George Felos maintained. "Terri died a horrible death," Schindler says.

Michael Schiavo was designated Terri's guardian under Florida law, which — like the laws in 34 other states — gives priority first to a patient's spouse and then to the patient's parents or other relatives. The Schindlers unsuccessfully sought to remove Michael as guardian by pointing out that he was living with another woman and that they had two children together. "Michael's loyalties were for his family, not for Terri," Schindler says.

State courts made a mistake in the case, Schindler says, by giving too much weight to "casual comments" that Terri made about not wanting to be kept alive by extraordinary means. He blames media misinformation and slanted survey questions for poll results suggesting that most people believe the case was handled fairly and the legal outcome was correct.

Michael Schiavo retreated from the public spotlight in the final weeks before Terri's death and has remained out of sight since. For him, the case is over. In one postscript, the Florida Department of Children and Families released a report finding no evidence that Terri had been abused or mistreated during her final years at the Hospice House Woodside in Pinellas Park, as right-to-life groups had repeatedly charged. [2]

For Schindler, the fight continues. "We're heading down a dangerous path, and it's going to be tough," he says. "But I'm passionate about this, and I want to do whatever I can to stop it from ever happening again."

---

[1] William R. Levesque, "As Schiavo Settlement Disappeared, So Did a Relationship," *The St. Petersburg Times*, March 30, 2005, p. 1A.

[2] Graham Brink, "DCF found no signs Terri Schiavo abused," *The St. Petersburg Times*, April 16, 2005, p. 3B.

Democratic lawmakers questioned the approach. "The Schiavo case teaches us that the most important thing to help families is to encourage the use of living wills," Rep. Elijah E. Cummings, D-Md., said. He noted that he is cosponsoring a bill by Rep. Sander Levin, D-Mich., aimed at increasing awareness of advance directives and increasing help in their preparation.

A second Democrat, D.C. Delegate Eleanor Holmes Norton, complained that Republicans' criticisms of the court rulings that allowed the removal of Schiavo's feeding tube gave an inaccurate picture of the practice. "Every day of the week feeding tubes are given up because a court intervened or the family made that decision," Norton said. "No family would ever make that decision if a patient experienced starvation or dehydration."

Should Congress make it harder to withdraw food and fluids from incapacitated patients?

YES

Wesley J. Smith
Senior Fellow, Discovery Institute, and Attorney, International Task Force on Euthanasia and Assisted Suicide

Written for The CQ Researcher, May 2005

Terri Schiavo is dead. But the campaign she inspired to protect profoundly disabled people from medical discrimination is far from over. Indeed, Terri's court-ordered dehydration, justified by statements she allegedly made in casual conversations 20 years ago, cries out for increased federal protection of our most vulnerable citizens.

This is a delicate matter that requires a proper balance. Nobody wants federal agents lurking at patients' bedsides.

What to do?

- *Amend the Americans with Disabilities Act.* The ADA protects disabled people from discrimination. But it does not apply explicitly in the medical context where anti-disability bias can be deadly. This omission needs to be remedied so that lethal non-treatment decisions are never imposed on disabled patients by others based on discriminatory "quality-of-life" concepts.

- *Differentiate feeding tubes from other forms of care:* Feeding tubes should be distinguished legally from medical treatment in institutions that accept federal payments. Unlike removing a respirator or antibiotics, withdrawing artificial nutrition and hydration causes death in every case. Moreover, denying food and water is deeply symbolic, strongly implying that the patient does not have a life worth living. Patients should be able to refuse such care. But the decision should be the patient's — and it should be unequivocal. Those who do not want feeding tubes should put their desire in writing in case they become incapacitated. Absent that, there should be a strong federal legal presumption against death by dehydration of people with cognitive impairments in institutions that receive federal money.

- *Permit all patients to have feeding tubes:* Anecdotal evidence suggests that some hospices refuse dying patients who wanted feeding tubes, perhaps fearing that government bureaucrats will construe such care as impermissible. Surely we can all agree that food and water should never be refused when it is wanted. Congress should review the law and amend it as necessary to ensure that no federally funded medical facility is permitted to refuse wanted nutrition and hydration whether provided orally or through a feeding tube.

These suggestions are temperate, reasonable and strike a proper balance between assuring patient autonomy and preventing others from ending the lives of incapacitated people prematurely. A society founded on the inalienable right to life should do no less.

NO

Arthur L. Caplan
Chairman, Department of Medical Ethics, and Director, Center for Bioethics, University of Pennsylvania

From testimony before the House Subcommittee on Criminal Justice, Drug Policy and Human Resources, April 19, 2005

The question [about feeding tubes], coming as it does in the wake of the Terri Schiavo case, presumes that something is broken in the existing system of legal protections for those who once could — but as a result of illness or injury can no longer — speak for themselves about medical treatment. I think this argument is deeply flawed.

Despite all the attention that the Schiavo case generated suggesting otherwise, the system currently in place has worked well and continues to work well in ensuring that the rights of those to have or not have medical treatment consistent with their personal values and choices are respected.

Congress ought to both understand and respect the current system, which relies on the foundational values of the right to liberty and to privacy and includes one key procedural protection: that families or those close to us can best speak for us if we cannot communicate for ourselves about our medical care.

Those who know a person best can say what that person would have wanted either on the basis of conversations and discussions or by substituting their own judgment, using their knowledge of their loved one's beliefs about medicine and life. There is no role for Congress or any other institutional third party to try and insert itself into the substantive decision-making process.

Let me stress that the core value that protects each one of us is that no one has the right to make anyone of us do anything that we do not choose to do. This means that it would be wrong and indeed unconstitutional for Congress to create any presumption in favor of medical care or treatment for a once-competent person who can no longer communicate.

What must be created is a legal system that listens carefully and intently to try and discern the wishes of a person unable to make a decision. Only if no such information can be discerned would any presumption make sense, and even then Congress would have to act with great care in trying to decide what can be presumed about medical care for every American given the range of values and views that exist.

Again, the key protection of individual rights is not what Congress thinks is best for each person when it comes to health care, nor what any particular religious, or disability or disease-advocacy groups or any other organized interest group thinks. What matters — and what only matters — is what the individual thinks.

In his testimony, Weldon, who as a practicing physician previously specialized in internal medicine, cited a National Right to Life Committee report criticizing state laws allowing doctors to withdraw life support despite patients' wishes to continue it. He said the report pointed to "a chilling trend that substitutes utilitarian judgments of medical bioethicists for the minimum care and compassion required for incapacitated citizens."

Under questioning, however, Weldon acknowledged that as a physician he had withdrawn food and fluids in some cases. "There is a fine line between providing care and prolonging the dying process," Weldon said. He added later, "Most physicians get this right."

Assisted Suicide Argued

Right-to-die groups are hoping to make California the second state to legalize physician-assisted suicide after narrowly winning approval of the proposal in the first of several committees with jurisdiction over the bill. At the same time, the Bush administration is hoping the Supreme Court will agree with its arguments — rejected by lower federal courts — that Oregon doctors face sanctions under federal law for prescribing medications to help patients end their lives.

The California measure cleared the Assembly Judiciary Committee by a 5-4 vote on April 12 following emotional testimony from supporters and opponents. [29] Like the Oregon law, it would allow mentally competent, terminally ill patients to obtain a prescription for lethal medication. The bill would impose a 15-day waiting period, require agreement from two doctors on the prognosis and mandate counseling for patients suffering from depression or other psychological disorder.

Assemblyman Lloyd Levine, a Democrat cosponsoring the bill with Assemblywoman Patty Berg, recalled that his grandmother had suffered either extreme pain or extreme sedation as she was dying from a debilitating illness. "All I could think of was that there's got to be a better way," he told the panel. Former Oregon Gov. Barbara Roberts told the committee that the law had been used sparingly in her state.

But Marilyn Golden, representing the Disability Rights, Education and Defense Fund, said the law would give patients a "phony form of freedom" because they would be "steered toward assisted death." And Michael Sexton, president of the California Medical Association, said instead of assisted suicide, patients should be provided better pain therapy, end-of-life care and hospice services.

Proponents of the measure include Compassion and Choices and the California chapters of the American Civil Liberties Union and the National Organization for Women. Opponents include the California Hospital Association and the California Catholic Conference. Following the Judiciary Committee's vote, the bill went to the Assembly Appropriations Committee, where action was pending as of early May.

Similar bills were introduced this year in Vermont and Hawaii. The Vermont measure is bottled up in the House Health and Human Services Committee following an April 12 hearing; the Hawaii legislature shelved a similar bill in March. [30]

At the Supreme Court, the Bush administration is seeking to reinstate the "interpretive rule" that Attorney General Ashcroft issued on Nov. 9, 2001, construing that Oregon's assisted-suicide law ran afoul of the federal Controlled Substances Act. "Assisting suicide is not a 'legitimate medical purpose' within the meaning of [the law]," Ashcroft wrote. On that basis, he said that "prescribing, dispensing or administering federally controlled substances to assist suicide" violates the statute. In a 2-1 decision, however, the 9th U.S. Circuit Court of Appeals said Ashcroft's "unilateral attempt to regulate general medical practices" exceeded his authority under the statute. [31]

In its legal filings with the high court, the administration argues that the appeals court's "erroneous" view of the relationship between federal and state authority would mean that federal regulation of drugs would depend "on the vagaries of each state's notions of what constitutes a 'legitimate medical purpose' or 'treatment,' no matter how far outside the mainstream of accepted medical practice a particular State's views may be."

Attorneys for Oregon and for a doctor and a pharmacist who joined in the suit counter that Ashcroft's ruling infringed on "the States' historic police powers over the practice of medicine." The federal drug law "lacks any suggestion that it intended to appoint the attorney general as a national medical review board, with general authority to re-determine the validity of every prescription that conforms to state law," the state's lawyers write.

The high court granted review in the case on Feb. 23 and is due to hear arguments in early October. A decision would be due by July 2006.

OUTLOOK

Understanding Death?

Some 2.5 million people die in the United States each year, the vast majority with no public debate about how their lives ended. The Schiavo case was "a freak," says the University of Michigan's Schneider. "It was wildly untypical of end-of-life-cases."

Most patients also do not end up in persistent vegetative states (PVS). Although there is no precise census of PVS cases, estimates from the 1990s placed the number in the United States somewhere between 10,000 and 35,000. [32]

But few PVS disputes reach the courts. "In the vast majority of situations, we have family members and medical personnel getting together and gradually talking these things out," says Baron at Boston College.

In fact, says ABA expert Sabatino, since the Quinlan case in the 1970s, only about 250 appellate court decisions on end-of-life issues have been handed down — "not a huge volume for an area of law for 30-plus years."

And while many right-to-life groups sharply criticized the courts' intervention in the Schiavo case, Sabatino says courts must be available to settle disputes even though most agree that end-of-life questions are not best decided in court. "The courts are there when the differences of opinion are irreconcilable," he says.

In the Schiavo case, right-to-life groups failed in their strategy to get federal courts to override the state court's decision. "It's not clear that a purely procedural remedy will necessarily . . . bring greater protection to people who are denied food or fluids," says Balch of the National Right to Life Committee. "So what needs to be pursued is some substantive provision."

The federal proposal — a difficult-to-overcome presumption in favor of continuing food and fluids — faces major hurdles in a sharply divided Congress with more pressing domestic and foreign issues to address. Many political observers discount the measure's legislative prospects because of the perceived backlash.

But Balch and other right-to-life advocates question the phrasing of most of the polls, saying they tilt toward the right-to-die position. He also says a broadly applicable bill may seem a more appropriate congressional response than the law that applied only to Schiavo's case. In addition, he says the growing involvement of disability-rights groups — a traditional Democratic constituency — may help ease the partisan divide on the issue.

For their part, right-to-die advocates insist Congress has no business getting involved. "That would be Congress overstepping its authority," Lee of Compassion and Choices says of the federal presumption proposal, "and imposing unnecessary and onerous burdens on persons who want to make their wishes known."

"It would be a big mistake for the federal government to get involved here," Baron says. "There is nothing to indicate that the states are not dealing with the question of determining the wishes of someone once they're not competent to express their wishes themselves."

In some cases changing state laws might be easier than getting federal legislation passed. That's one reason the NRLC is focusing on amending state laws that allow health-care providers to use their medical judgment to disregard the wishes of patients or their representatives. But medical and hospital lobbies are likely to oppose laws that invade their professional expertise.

For his part, Yale law Professor Burt says state laws should be revised to eliminate presumptions that determine — as in the Schiavo case — who speaks for the patient in the absence of a designated health-care proxy. "That automatic appointment . . . shuts out other people who are also deeply and possibly equally important to the patient and who have perhaps an equal stake," he says. Rather than setting up an adversary legal proceeding, Burt says, laws should require all interested family members to agree before any decision is made to withdraw life support.

Meanwhile, assisted suicide is still a tough sell in state legislatures despite increasing public support for the idea, and handicapping the Supreme Court case on the Oregon law is tricky. In a previous 9th Circuit case, the justices reversed a decision that would have allowed California's medical marijuana law to take precedence over federal drug policy. On the other hand, Ashcroft's interpretation of the federal drug law to regulate medical practice may go beyond what the justices are willing to read into the statute.

Despite their divisions, advocates and experts on both sides generally agree that the Schiavo case has prompted useful debate about end-of-life issues. "These are very, very important questions," says Baron, of Death With Dignity. "It's extraordinarily important for the mind of the public to be focused on these issues."

Yet Burt cautions that death remains ultimately beyond human ability to comprehend, much less control. He writes: "We would do better to admit, as W. H. Auden acknowledged, that 'Death is not understood by Death; nor You, nor I.' " [33]

NOTES

1. Background drawn from Liz Kowalczyk, "Hospital, Family Spar Over End-of-Life Care," *The Boston Globe*, March 11, 2005, p. A1.

2. See "Lawyer Changes Mind Over Life Support," *The Boston Globe*, March 22, 2005, p. B2; Liz Kowalczyk, "Hospital, Family Agree to Withdraw Life Support," *The Boston Globe*, March 12, 2005, p. B1.

3. Voluminous coverage of Schiavo case can be found on various print and broadcast news organizations' Web sites, including the two major local newspapers: the *St. Petersburg Times* (www.stptimes.com) and the *Tampa Tribune* (www.tampatrib.com).

4. For background, see Richard L. Worsnop, "Assisted Suicide Controversy," *The CQ Researcher*, May 5, 1995, pp. 393-416.

5. See Charles P. Sabatino, "National Advance Directives: One Attempt to Scale the Barrier," *NAELA Journal*, spring 2005.

6. Steven B. Hardin and Yasmin A. Yusufaly, "Difficult End-of-Life Decisions: Do Other Factors Trump Advance Directives?" *Archives of Internal Medicine*, July 2004, pp. 1531-33; cited in Time, April 4, 2005, p. 29.

7. See Keith Perine and Seth Stern, "Bush Signs Bill Giving Schiavo's Parents Access to Federal Court," *CQ Today*, March 21, 2005.

8. For a summary of the act and its effects in operation, see Institute of Medicine, *Approaching Death: Improving Care at the End of Life* (1999), pp. 202-203.

9. Background and initial quotes drawn from Don Colburn, " 'Why Am I Not Dead Yet?' " *The [Portland] Oregonian*, March 4, 2005, p. A1.

10. "Seventh Annual Report on Oregon's Death with Dignity Act," Oregon Department of Human Services, March 10, 2005, http://egov.oregon.gov/DHS/ph/pas/docs/year7.pdf.

11. Background drawn from Peter G. Filene, *In the Arms of Others: A Cultural History of the Right-to-Die in America*, 1998. See also Ian Dowbiggin, *A Merciful End: The Euthanasia Movement in Modern America*, 2003; Derek Humphry and Mary Clement, *Freedom to Die: People, Politics and the Right-to-Die Movement*, 1998; Robert M. Veatch, *Death, Dying, and the Biological Revolution: Our Last Quest for Responsibility* (rev. ed.), 1989.

12. Filene, *ibid.*, pp. 5-9. The Gallup Poll is cited without specific date.

13. Veatch, *op. cit.*, p. 3.

14. "The Right to Die," *Time*, Jan. 9, 1956, p. 67, cited in Filene, *op. cit.*, p. 9.

15. *Ibid.*, p. 67.

16. The case is In re *Quinlan*, 355 A.2d 647 (N.J. 1976). For Filene's account of the successive stages of the case, see pp. 11-46, 76-95, 125-133.

17. Title and narrative of this subsection taken from Filene, *op. cit.*

18. The case is *Belchertown State School v. Saikewicz*, 370 N.E.2d 417 (Mass. 1977).

19. The decision is In re *Conroy*, 486 A.2d 1209 (N.J. 1985).

20. The decision is *Cruzan v. Director, Missouri Department of Health*, 497 U.S. 261 (1990).

21. A detailed chronology can be found on a Web site maintained by Kevorkian's attorney, Geoffrey Fieger, www.fansoffieger.com.

22. The decisions are *Washington v. Glucksberg*, 521 U.S. 702 (1997), and *Vacco v. Quill*, 521 U.S. 793 (1997).

23. Sacred Congregation for the Doctrine of the Faith, "Declaration on Euthanasia," May 5, 1980, www.vatican.va.

24. Quoted in Veatch, *op. cit.*, p. 82.

25. See Nicole Winfield, "Pope declares it immoral to remove feeding tubes from people in vegetative states," The Associated Press, March 20, 2004.

26. See Sheryl Gay Stolberg, "Majority Leader Asks House Panel to Review Judges," *The New York Times*, April 14, 2005, p. A1. DeLay's original remarks are reported in Carl Hulse and David D. Kirkpatrick, "Even Death Does Not Quiet Harsh Political Fight," *The New York Times*, April 1, 2005, p. A1.

27. Quoted in Gwyneth K. Shaw and Gail Gibson, "For Congress, a Quiet Retreat from Schiavo," *The Baltimore Sun*, March 27, 2005, p. 1A.

28. For coverage of the Senate hearing, see Kate Schuler, "End of Life Hearing Draws Little Notice After Fury," *CQ Today*, April 6, 2005. Some coverage of the House hearing can be found in Tamara Lytle, "Schiavo Battle Prompts Proposal on Feeding," *Orlando Sentinel*, April 20, 2005, p. A18.

29. Account taken from Jim Sanders, "Assisted suicide bill passes initial test," *The Sacramento Bee*, April 13, 2005, p. A3. The California measure is AB 654.

30. See Terri Hallenbeck, "Decision time on assisted suicide," *The Burlington Free-Press*, April 15, 2005; Mary Vorsino, "Doctor-assisted suicide bill fades at legislature," *Honolulu Star-Bulletin*, Feb. 6, 2005. The Vermont measure is H168; the Hawaii bill is SB1308.

31. The citation to the regulation as published in the *Federal Register* is 66 Fed. Reg. 56,607 (2001). The appeals court decision is *Oregon v. Ashcroft*, 368 F.3d 1118 (CA9 2004). At the Supreme Court, the case is *Gonzales v. Oregon*, 04-623.

32. Estimates from an American Medical Association body in 1990 and a *New York Times* article in 1994 are cited in Filene, *op. cit.*, p. 160 n. 104.

33. Quoted in Robert A. Burt, *Death Is That Man Taking Names: Intersections of American Medicine, Law, and Culture*, 2002. The English-born American poet W.H. Auden made the observation in his poem "We're Late."

BIBLIOGRAPHY

Books

Burt, Robert A., *Death Is That Man Taking Names: Intersections of American Medicine, Law, and Culture*, **University of California Press, 2002.**
A Yale law professor argues that efforts to rationalize end-of-life decision-making collide with an inevitable "ambivalence" about death and that procedures should be designed "with the conscious goal of amplifying this ambivalence in the minds of all participants in such decisions."

Dowbiggin, Ian, *A Merciful End: The Euthanasia Movement in America*, **Oxford University Press, 2003.**
A professor at the University of Prince Edward Island relates the history of the euthanasia movement in the United States from its origins in the elitist eugenics organizations of the early 20th century and its emergence as a broader-based movement in the 1930s through the passage of Oregon's Death with Dignity Act and other legal and political battles in the 1990s. Includes detailed notes, 11-page bibliography.

Filene, Peter G., *In the Arms of Others: A Cultural History of the Right-to-Die in America*, **Ivan R. Dee, 1998.**
A professor of history at the University of North Carolina-Chapel Hill traces the history of the right-to-die movement, focusing primarily on the major legal cases on the issue. Includes detailed notes.

Humphry, Derek, and Mary Clement, *Freedom to Die: People, Politics and the Right-to-Die Movement*, **St. Martin's Press, 1998.**
Two leaders of the right-to-die movement in the United States provide a thorough account of its origins, growth and status. Includes notes, detailed chronology and text of the Oregon law. Humphry founded the Hemlock Society (now called End-of-Life Choices) and headed the organization until 1992; he now heads the Final Exit Network. Clement is a lawyer and president of Gentle Closures, an organization that assists in addressing end-of-life concerns.

Rothman, David J., *Strangers at the Bedside: A History of How Law and Bioethics Transformed Medical Decision Making*, **Aldine de Gruyter, 2003.**
The director of Columbia University's Center for the Study of Society and Medicine traces the birth of bioethics as a distinct branch of science and medicine in the mid- to late 20th century and the new discipline's role in examining and raising awareness of end-of-life issues. Includes notes.

Schneider, Carl E. (ed.), *Law at the End of Life: The Supreme Court and Assisted Suicide*, **University of Michigan Press, 2000.**
Nine contributors examine the implications of the Supreme Court's 1997 decisions rejecting a constitu-

tional right to physician-assisted suicide. Includes text of decisions. Schneider is a professor of law and internal medicine at the University of Michigan-Ann Arbor.

Smith, Wesley J., *Forced Exit: The Slippery Slope from Assisted Suicide to Legalized Murder* **(rev. ed.), Spence Publishing, 2003.**

A senior fellow at the conservative Discovery Institute provides a strongly argued case against assisted suicide. Includes detailed notes.

Veatch, Robert M., *Death, Dying, and the Biological Revolution: Our Last Quest for Responsibility* **(rev. ed.), Yale University Press, 1989.**

A nationally prominent professor at Georgetown University's Kennedy Institute of Ethics examines the social and ethical problems of death and dying caused by a biological revolution that he says "has made living easier but dying harder." Includes detailed notes, bibliography and list of cases.

Articles

Eisenberg, Daniel, "Lessons of the Schiavo Battle," *Time,* **April 4, 2005, pp. 23-30.**

The cover story gives a comprehensive summary of the Schiavo case following her death on March 31. A separate story in the package examines Oregon's assisted-suicide law (Margot Roosevelt, "Choosing Their Time," pp. 31-33).

Fagerlin, Angela, and Carl E. Schneider, "Enough: The Failure of the Living Will," *Hastings Center Report,* **March/April 2004, pp. 30-42.**

The authors strongly argue that "living wills" have not produced results and should be abandoned. Schneider is a professor and Fagerlin a researcher at the University of Michigan in Ann Arbor.

Sabatino, Charles P., "National Advance Directives: One Attempt to Scale the Barriers," *1 NAELA Journal 131* **(Spring 2005).**

An American Bar Association expert gives up-to-date information on the status of advance directives with recommendations for improvements.

Reports and Studies

Institute of Medicine, *Approaching Death: Improving Care at the End of Life,* **National Academy Press, 1997.**

The medical branch of the National Academy of Sciences thoroughly examines end-of-life care in the United States and makes recommendations for improvements. Includes detailed lists of references, organizations.

For More Information

American Bar Association Commission on Law and Aging, 740 15th St., N.W., Washington, DC 20005-1022; (202) 662-8690; www.abanet.org/aging. Litigates and advocates on issues associated with aging.

Compassion and Choices, P.O. Box 101810, Denver, CO 80250; 800-247-7421; www.compassionindying.org. Works to assure freedom of choice at the end of life by advocating for assisted suicide rights.

Death with Dignity National Center, 520 S.W. Sixth Ave., Suite 1030, Portland, OR 97204; (503) 228-4415; www.deathwithdignity.org. Advocates for Oregon's Death With Dignity law, which makes legal physician-assisted suicide.

Final Exit Network, P.O. Box 965005, Marietta, GA 30066; (800) 524-3948; www.finalexitnetwork.org. A non-profit organization that holds that voluntary euthanasia and physician-assisted suicide are appropriate life endings.

Hastings Center, 21 Malcolm Gordon Road, Garrison NY 10524-5555; (845) 424-4040; www.thehastingscenter.org. An independent, nonprofit bioethics research institute that explores questions in health care, biotechnology, and the environment.

National Right to Life Committee, 512 10th St., NW, Washington, DC 20004; (202) 626-8800; www.nrlc.org. Nation's largest pro-life lobby working against abortion rights, euthanasia and infanticide.

Not Dead Yet, 7521 Madison St., Forest Park, IL 60130; (708) 209-1500; www.notdeadyet.org. Disability-rights group that opposes assisted suicide and euthanasia.

United States Conference of Catholic Bishops, Secretariat for Pro-Life Activities, 3211 Fourth Street, N.E., Washington, DC 20017-1194; (202) 541-3070; www.usccb.org. Advocates the protection of human life from conception to natural death.

8

Supreme Court's Future

Kenneth Jost

Chief Justice William H. Rehnquist administers the oath of office to President Bush on Jan. 20, 2005, as the first lady looks on. Conservatives praise Rehnquist in particular for decisions involving federalism and church-state issues. Liberals note his dissent on civil rights and civil liberties issues — notably, abortion rights and affirmative action.

From *CQ Researcher*,
January 28, 2005.

For three months, Chief Justice William H. Rehnquist had been out of public view while battling thyroid cancer. But when he emerged at the presidential inauguration on Jan. 20 to administer the oath of office to President Bush, Rehnquist showed the same kind of determination that he had demonstrated a decade earlier when — in the midst of Washington's worst blizzard in years — he kept the Supreme Court open while the rest of the federal government closed down.

Appearing pale and frail, the chief justice walked slowly with a cane as he came out of the Capitol at 11:45 a.m. to take his seat on the platform. Moments before noon, Rehnquist made his way unaided to the lectern, removed his cap and, from memory, gave the 35-word oath to Bush.

Rehnquist wore a scarf partly obscuring the tracheotomy tube inserted during his original hospitalization in October to help him breathe. His voice was somewhat hoarse, his delivery unhesitating. "He looked surprisingly good, impressively good," David Garrow, a legal historian and lecturer at Emory University School of Law in Atlanta, remarked. [1]

Rehnquist's brief appearance — he left before Bush's speech — dampened somewhat the three-month swirl of speculation about his possibly imminent retirement as the nation's 16th chief justice. "It may be that [the] outing could ease, somewhat, the anxious expectation that a change at the court is about to happen very soon," veteran Supreme Court reporter Lyle Denniston wrote on SCOTUSBlog, a popular Web site for coverage of the court. [2]

Still, Rehnquist's 33-year tenure on the court, including nearly 18 1/2 years as chief justice, is inevitably drawing to a close. At 80,

Rehnquist Court Has Overturned Many Precedents

Under Chief Justice William H. Rehnquist the Supreme Court has left standing many of the best-known liberal precedents of the Warren and Burger Court eras. But it has also overturned many significant, though lesser known, prior rulings — notably, those protecting the rights of defendants and prison inmates; restricting government aid to parochial schools; and limiting private suits against state governments. In the past three terms, however, the court also has expanded constitutional rights by overturning restrictive rulings — with Rehnquist among the dissenters.

Name of Case (Date)	Ruling
Thornburgh v. Abbott (1989) Prison officials may bar publications if action is reasonably related to maintaining discipline, security.	
Coleman v. Thompson (1991) State inmate may not file federal habeas corpus petition after failing to abide by state court procedural rules.	
Arizona v. Fulminante (1991) Use of a coerced confession at trial does not necessarily require reversal of a conviction if evidence amounted to "harmless error."	
Payne v. Tennessee (1991) "Victim impact statements," including evidence of victim's character and impact of crime on victim's family, may be used against capital defendant in sentencing hearing.	
Planned Parenthood of Southeastern Pennsylvania v. Casey (1992) Ruling generally reaffirmed *Roe v. Wade* abortion rights decision, but — overruled later decisions by unholding "informed consent" and 24-hour waiting-period provisions.	
Adarand Constructors v. Peña (1995) Racial preferences in federal contracting can be upheld only if they are narrowly tailored to serve a compelling government interest — the strict standard applied previously only to state governments.	
Seminole Tribe of Florida v. Florida (1996) Congress cannot use its power to regulate interstate commerce to authorize private suits against state governments for monetary damages.	
Hudson v. United States (1997) A defendant can be criminally prosecuted, even after having been fined in a civil enforcement action.	
College Savings Bank v. Florida Prepaid Postsecondary Education Expense Board (1999) State governments are not subject to private damage suits in federal court merely because they engage in commercial activity.	
Mitchell v. Helms (2000) Governments can lend instructional equipment to parochial schools without violating the constitutional prohibition against establishment of religion.	
* Ring v. Arizona (2002) Juries, not judges, must make any factual determinations needed to impose the death penalty.	
* Atkins v. Virginia (2002) Executing mentally retarded offender violates constitutional ban against cruel and unusual punishment.	
* Lawrence v. Texas (2003) State anti-sodomy laws are unconstitutional.	
* Crawford v. Washington (2004) Prosecutor cannot introduce testimonial statement from unavailable defendant unless the defendant has prior opportunity for cross-examination.	
* Rasul v. Bush (2004) Foreign nationals captured during the Afghanistan war and held at Guantanamo Bay Naval Base can bring habeas corpus petitions in federal court to challenge the legality of their detentions.	

* Rehnquist dissented.

he is the second-oldest person to serve as chief justice. * His total service is the eighth-longest among the 102 justices since the court was established in 1789. [3]

Rehnquist's legacy is more than longevity, however. He joined the court as its most conservative member in 1972 and leaves as the leader of a court with a generally conservative record in most areas, including criminal law and many civil rights and civil liberties issues. He is also universally credited with running the court efficiently and collegially.

If, as is widely expected, Rehnquist announces his retirement by the end of the court's current term in late June, President Bush would get his first opportunity to name a member of the high court — and the chance to fill the first vacancy in more than 10 years.

Bush has said that he would appoint justices in the mold of Rehnquist's fellow conservatives, Justices Antonin Scalia and Clarence Thomas, both of whom are being touted by many conservatives for elevation to chief justice. The selection of Scalia, Thomas or another staunch conservative could touch off a fierce fight in the Senate between a Republican majority fortified after the 2004 elections and a Democratic minority that blocked action on 10 of Bush's federal appeals court nominees during the president's first term. (*See p. 180.*)

"It's really up to the president to decide whether we'll have a Supreme Court fight and how big it will be," says Michael Comiskey, an associate

---

* The actual title is Chief Justice of the United States.

professor of political science at Pennsylvania State University and author of a new book on Supreme Court nominations. "If he nominates someone committed to the agenda associated with Justices Thomas and Scalia, there will be a fight. If not, I don't think there will be, at least for this first vacancy."

Conservatives praise Rehnquist in particular for decisions in two major areas: federalism and church-state issues. Douglas Kmiec, a constitutional-law expert at Pepperdine University School of Law in Malibu, Calif., credits Rehnquist with "recalibrating" state-federal relations in favor of the states and leading the court to be "more accommodating toward religious participation in government programs and religious expression in public places."

Liberals acknowledge — and criticize — Rehnquist's impact in those areas and also note that he remains a dissenter on some civil rights and civil liberties issues — notably, abortion rights and affirmative action. [4] "He was part of moving the court in a much more conservative direction, but ultimately in a way that disappointed conservatives," says Erwin Chemerinsky, a professor at Duke University Law School in Durham, N.C. "In some key areas, where conservatives would have wanted to see more, it didn't happen."

Rehnquist was nominated for the court in 1971 by President Richard M. Nixon, who campaigned for president in 1968 on a promise to shift the court to the right, in particular on criminal law issues. He was elevated to chief justice in 1986 by President Ronald Reagan, who campaigned in 1980

Rehnquist Court Struck Down 40 Laws

Under Chief Justice Rehnquist the Supreme Court has struck down on constitutional grounds parts of 40 federal statutes passed by Congress. Rehnquist himself wrote several of the decisions limiting powers of Congress vis-à-vis the states but dissented from some of the rulings expanding free-speech protections. Major rulings from the past 10 years include:

Name of Case (Date)	Statute
* **United States v. National Treasury Employees Union (1995)** Ban on honoraria for federal civil servants.	
Rubin v. Coors Brewing Co. (1995) Ban on listing alcohol content on beer containers.	
United States v. Lopez (1995) Gun Free School Zones Act.	
Seminole Tribe of Florida v. Florida (1996) Indian Gaming Regulatory Act.	
* **Denver Area Educational Telecommunications Consortium, Inc. v. Federal Communications Commission (1996)** Indecency provisions of 1992 cable act.	
City of Boerne v. Flores (1997) Religious Freedom Restoration Act.	
Reno v. American Civil Liberties Union (1997) Communications Decency Act.	
Printz v. United States (1997) Brady Handgun Violence Prevention Act.	
Eastern Enterprises v. Apfel (1998) Coal Industry Retiree Health Benefit Act.	
Clinton v. City of New York (1998) Line Item Veto Act.	
Alden v. Maine (1999) Fair Labor Standards Act (suits against states).	
Greater New Orleans Broadcasting Association, Inc. v. United States (1999) Limits on broadcast advertising of casinos.	
* **Saenz v. Roe (1999)** Welfare reform law (authorizing lower benefits for new state residents).	
Kimel v. Florida Board of Regents (2000) Age Discrimination in Employment Act (suits against states).	
United States v. Morrison (2000) Violence Against Women Act (private suits in federal courts).	
* **United States v. Playboy Entertainment Group, Inc. (2000)** Telecommunications Act (cable indecency provision).	
Dickerson v. United States (2000) Statute aimed at overriding Miranda.	
University of Alabama v. Garrett (2001) Americans with Disabilities Act (suits against states).	
* **Legal Services Corp. v. Velazquez (2001)** Restriction on welfare rights suits.	
United States v. Hatter (2001) Social Security taxes for U.S. judges.	
Bartnicki v. Vopper (2001) Anti-wiretapping law (civil liability).	
United States v. United Foods, Inc (2001) Mushroom promotion act.	
* **Ashcroft v. Free Speech Coalition (2002)** Child Pornography Prevention Act.	
* **Thompson v. Western States Medical Center (2002)** Food and Drug Administration Modernization Act (advertising restrictions).	
Federal Maritime Commission v. South Carolina State Ports Authority (2002) Shipping Act (private complaints against states).	
McConnell v. Federal Election Commission (2003) Bipartisan Campaign Reform Act (minor provisions).	
* **United States v. Booker (2005)** Sentencing Reform Act.	

* Rehnquist dissented.

President Bush says he would appoint justices in the mold of Justices Antonin Scalia, left, and Clarence Thomas, both of whom are being touted by many conservatives for elevation to chief justice.

on a pledge to name "strict constructionists" to the high court. The two Republican chief executives both advocated "judicial restraint" and said the Supreme Court should "interpret" rather than "make" the law.

By many measures, however, the Rehnquist Court has been very assertive: It has struck down parts of 40 laws — a quarter of the 160 such decisions handed down throughout U.S. history. In another measure of judicial activism, it overturned about 40 earlier precedents — typically, but not always, throwing out liberal in favor of conservative rulings.

Rehnquist's success in pushing a conservative agenda has been limited, however, mainly by the votes of two moderate conservatives — Reagan's first and last Supreme Court nominees: Sandra Day O'Connor and Anthony M. Kennedy, respectively. Separately or sometimes together, O'Connor and Kennedy have joined a bloc of four moderately liberal justices to preserve some liberal precedents and on occasion extend rights into new areas. They also sometimes vote or write separately from their conservative colleagues to limit the impact of new rulings in such areas as federalism, church-state issues and property rights.

With most court watchers expecting Bush to choose another conservative as Rehnquist's eventual successor, a significant change in the balance of power on the court could await departures by one or more of the other jus-

tices. Speculation focuses on O'Connor — age 74 — and John Paul Stevens, at 84 the court's oldest justice and also its most liberal.

Both O'Connor and Stevens appear to be in good health, however, and neither one has given any public indication of thinking about retirement. As the senior associate justice, Stevens has presided over the court's public sessions — and presumably its private conferences — in Rehnquist's absence.

A contentious Supreme Court nomination would rekindle memories of the two most recent high court confirmation battles: the Senate's rejection of Reagan's nomination of archconservative Robert Bork in 1987 and its narrow approval of Thomas' nomination in 1991. It would also come against the present-day backdrop of a sharp partisan fight in the Senate over Democrats' use of the filibuster to prevent votes on some of Bush's judicial nominees during the first term. (*See* "*At Issue,*" *p. 181.*)

Senate Majority Leader Bill Frist of Tennessee is vowing to prevent use of the filibuster in the new Congress — even at the risk of a Senate rules change that Democrats say would lead to all-out partisan warfare in the chamber. Democrats say the filibuster is a time-honored Senate tradition to safeguard political minorities and insist they used the device in Bush's first term only against a handful of nominees with extreme conservative views.

As court watchers keep an eye on Rehnquist's health, and interest groups gear up for an expected confirmation fight, here are some of the major questions being debated:

Has William Rehnquist been a successful chief justice?

The Supreme Court ended its term in June 2002 with Chief Justice Rehnquist on the winning side of most of the major decisions, including a long-awaited ruling upholding the use of vouchers at parochial schools. [5] Linda Greenhouse, *The New York Times'* longtime Supreme Court correspondent, credited Rehnquist with a "triumphant year."

Two years later, however, Rehnquist was on the losing end of many of the year's major rulings, including most of the 5-4 decisions. In her June 2004 wrapup, Greenhouse wrote that the previous term "may go down in history as the term when Chief Justice Rehnquist lost his court." [6]

Should Justices' Health Problems Be Revealed?

Chief Justice William H. Rehnquist has been slow and sparing in releasing details of his medical condition since disclosing he was being treated for thyroid cancer in late October 2004. Most Supreme Court watchers appear content with the limited disclosure, but a prominent legal historian and several newspaper columnists say the public deserves more information about his condition, treatment and prognosis.

David Garrow, a lecturer at Emory Law School in Atlanta and a Pulitzer Prize-winning author, says the public has "a right to know" whether Rehnquist is still capable of performing his duties as chief justice through the end of the Supreme Court's current term in late June.

Garrow notes that several justices have stayed on the bench after their mental competence had come into question. In the most recent instance, Justice William O. Douglas suffered a debilitating stroke on New Year's Eve 1974 but retired — more than 10 months later — only after the other justices formally resolved not to count Douglas' vote in any case where it might be decisive.

"The court's own history is so unfortunately replete with instances of incapacitated justices or partially incapacitated justices continuing to attempt to perform their jobs that it's incumbent on the press and Congress to ensure that only fully mentally competent justices are casting votes," Garrow says.

Other court watchers, however, appear largely unconcerned. "I would have disclosed the information that is available sooner, but I wouldn't say that there's any right to more detailed information," says Thomas Goldstein, a Washington lawyer who appears frequently before the court.

Garrow contrasts the limited information about Rehnquist's condition to the detailed disclosures about such elected officials as President Bush and Vice President Dick Cheney. But Richard J. Lazarus, director of the Supreme Court Institute at Georgetown University Law Center in Washington, says judges need not make such disclosures because they are not subject to the electorate.

"I don't expect that [Supreme Court justices] have an obligation to make public their physicals and the details of their problems, and treatments and medicines," Lazarus says. He says Rehnquist's obligation is to tell the public about his condition when it begins to affect his job — but not before.

Rehnquist's illness was disclosed by the court's public information office on Oct. 25, only after he had been admitted to Bethesda Naval Hospital outside Washington three days earlier. A press release said Rehnquist "under-went a tracheotomy" — cutting a hole in the windpipe to aid breathing — "in connection with a recent diagnosis of thyroid cancer." The release said Rehnquist would be on the bench Nov. 1.

News stories noted that thyroid cancer is typically treatable but that the type of the disease most common in elderly patients — anaplastic thyroid cancer — is usually fatal within a year or less. Some doctors said the decision to perform a tracheotomy indicated the cancer was too advanced for surgical removal of the thyroid. [1]

Rehnquist did not return to the bench on Nov. 1. Instead, he issued a statement saying his plan had been "too optimistic" and that he was recuperating at home while "continuing to take radiation and chemotherapy on an outpatient basis." After Rehnquist missed all of the November and December arguments, the court's public information office told reporters on Dec. 13 that the chief justice would vote in those cases only if the other eight justices were tied.

Garrow says Rehnquist's decision not to participate in the cases argued in November showed that he did not have "the strength or the mental concentration" needed to go through all the materials. In that light, he says it would be odd for Rehnquist to cast the decisive, tie-breaking vote on a case without having heard his colleagues' deliberations.

At least three newspaper columnists have argued for greater disclosure about Rehnquist's condition, but Garrow concedes his concerns are not widely shared. "I've been surprised that the intense secrecy has not generated more editorial criticism," he says. [2]

For his part, Lazarus says the information about Rehnquist's condition does not suggest any mental impairment. He also notes that three other current justices have been successfully treated for cancer and remained on the court afterwards: Sandra Day O'Connor, for breast cancer; John Paul Stevens, prostate cancer, and Ruth Bader Ginsburg, colon cancer.

"The suggestion that one can go on with one's life, including one's professional life, doesn't strike me as a bad message," Lazarus says.

---

[1] The text of the release and subsequent statements along with links to some of the major coverage can be found on SCOTUSBlog (www.goldsteinhowe.com/SCOTUSBlog) on or shortly after the dates in question.

[2] See Steve Chapman, "Has Rehnquist Outstayed His Time?" *Chicago Tribune*, Dec. 16, 2004, p. C27; Ellen Goodman, "Who Monitors the Health of Justices?", *The Boston Globe*, Jan. 6, 2005, p. A11; Jane Eisner, "Why the State of Rehnquist's Health Is Our Business," *Philadelphia Inquirer*, Jan. 9, 2005, p. D1.

The Rehnquist Court's Legacy . . . and Issues to Watch

Abortion — *Roe v. Wade* largely reaffirmed; ban on "partial birth" abortions overturned — over Rehnquist's dissents; reworked "partial birth" statute pending in lower courts.

Affirmative Action — Racial redistricting, minority preferences in government contracting restricted; limited use of racial preferences in college admissions upheld — with Rehnquist dissenting.

Church and State — Vouchers for students at private, parochial schools upheld, capping line of cases easing barriers to government funding for students at church-affiliated schools, religious groups at public universities; organized prayer barred at graduations, football games (Rehnquist dissenting); religious groups guaranteed equal right to after-hours use of public school facilities.

Death Penalty — Habeas corpus challenges by death row inmates limited, capital punishment reaffirmed but barred for mentally retarded offenders (Rehnquist dissenting); challenge to executing juveniles argued, awaiting decision.

Elections and Campaigns — McCain-Feingold limits on unregulated "soft money," corporate- or union-financed issue advertising upheld; states given leeway to set low limit on campaign contributions; Rehnquist dissents on both.

Federalism — Private damage suits against states for violating many federal laws barred in federal, state courts; use of commerce power to federalize criminal law, civil suits

The Rehnquist Court overturned the ban on "partial birth" abortions; a reworked statute is now pending in lower courts.

Getty Images/Alex Wong

limited; gun law requiring states to administer federal regulatory scheme struck down.

Freedom of Speech — Federal law to limit children's access to Internet porn struck down, revised statute cast in doubt — over Rehnquist's dissents; commercial-speech protections enlarged.

Gay Rights — Anti-gay ballot initiative, anti-sodomy statutes struck down (Rehnquist dissenting); military's "don't ask, don't tell" policy left standing, new challenge developing; gay-marriage case unlikely in near future.

Privacy — No right to assisted suicide; drug testing for high-school students upheld.

Property Rights — Landowners guaranteed compensation if regulations bar economically viable use of property; local governments limited in power to gain public use of private land as condition of development; major challenge to use of eminent domain for private development to be argued in February.

Terrorism — Bush administration's effort to block judicial review for U.S. citizens, Guantanamo detainees held as "enemy combatants" rejected (Rehnquist dissents in the Guantanamo case); new cases will fill in procedures; challenges to provisions of USA Patriot Act developing slowly in lower courts.

Torts — Punitive damages limited, ordinarily to no more than 10 times amount of compensatory damages; state court suits against health maintenance organizations for denying coverage held pre-empted by federal law.

Despite the year-to-year fluctuations in Rehnquist's scorecard, observers across the ideological spectrum agree that in many respects he has been a significant and effective chief justice. "He'll be remembered as one of the crucial chief justices in history," says Sean Rushton, executive director of the Committee for Justice, a conservative group founded in 2002 to back President Bush's judicial nominees.

Rehnquist came on to the court, Rushton says, "with a very distinct philosophy that was out of fashion when he was first named and that has gradually come, partly through his writings and the force of his leadership, to be much more the mainstream of American jurisprudence."

"He will leave a court that's more conservative than the one that he found, and he can take credit for being one of the most visible leaders at a time of the evolution of the court," says Michael Gerhardt, a professor with generally liberal views at William and Mary Law School in Williamsburg, Va. "He might not have won on everything, but it's much more to his liking than when he first got there."

The court's new doctrines on federalism and church-state issues are Rehnquist's major accomplishments and reflect views he held from his earliest days as an associate justice — then, typically in dissent.

As chief justice, Rehnquist helped craft separate lines of decisions somewhat limiting Congress' powers over areas traditionally reserved to the states. In a pair of rulings, Rehnquist wrote decisions holding that Congress could not use its power to regulate interstate commerce to support either a ban on firearms possession near schools or a statute allowing federal suits by victims of gender-motivated violence. [7] In a second area, Rehnquist led a series of decisions limiting Congress' ability to authorize private citizens to sue state governments for damages when states violate federal laws. [8]

The 2002 ruling on vouchers culminated a series of decisions — including a pivotal opinion in 1993 by Rehnquist — that loosened the rules on government aid for students at religiously affiliated schools. [9] In a separate but related doctrinal area, the Rehnquist Court in 1995 also held, on free-speech grounds, that state universities cannot prevent religious publications from receiving subsidies from student activity funds. [10]

Pepperdine University's Kmiec credits Rehnquist with working to establish the new doctrines "quite systematically." But Todd Gazianao, who follows the Supreme Court for the conservative Heritage Foundation, says he is "disappointed" that Rehnquist has not moved as fast or as far in some areas as he and other conservatives might have wanted.

For their part, liberal advocates disagree with those decisions and fault Rehnquist in other areas, such as narrowing procedural protections for suspects and criminal defendants and cutting back federal courts' roles in school desegregation and other racial justice cases. [11] "He's certainly taken the court in a direction that elevates form over substance, that removes the ability of the federal government as a protector of ordinary people," says Nan Aron, executive director of the liberal Alliance for Justice.

"There is erosion of fundamental rights and liberties," says Ralph Neas, president of the liberal advocacy group People for the American Way, adding that O'Connor's and Kennedy's roles as swing votes on some issues — for example, abortion and affirmative action — have limited Rehnquist's impact.

"A chief justice has a fair amount of influence," Gaziano notes, "but he's still just one person."

Apart from ideological issues, experts and advocates on all sides agree on Rehnquist's contributions in maintaining a collegial atmosphere at a court that has sometimes seen jealousies and resentments among the justices. "Throughout his tenure, he maintained the respect of his colleagues," Gerhardt says. "That's no mean feat."

Marci Hamilton, a professor at Yeshiva University's Benjamin Cardozo School of Law in New York City, also credits Rehnquist with prodding justices to get opinions out more quickly and with facilitating public access to the court's work via the Internet. "It is now extremely easy to get all of the Supreme Court's cases from a variety of sources," Hamilton says. "That is a huge, huge development."

"He's made significant changes in constitutional law," says Suzanna Sherry, a professor at Vanderbilt Law School in Nashville. "Different people will evaluate whether they're good changes or bad changes differently, but you can't say he didn't do anything."

Will President Bush change the balance of power on the Supreme Court?

From 1969 to 1991, Republican presidents made 11 consecutive appointments to the Supreme Court, decisively shifting its prevailing ideological orientation from liberal to conservative. Yet several of those appointees also have cast pivotal votes to safeguard abortion rights, affirmative action and gay rights and to limit the death penalty, school prayer and anti-pornography measures. [12]

Bush's selection of a new chief justice will give him an opportunity to put his stamp on the high court. And most court watchers expect Bush to choose someone who will at least match, if not surpass, Rehnquist's conservatism.

"The president is genuinely conservative, the most conservative president we've had since Herbert Hoover," says political scientist Comiskey. "I think he's going to be more ideological in nominating justices than Ronald Reagan was."

However, a Bush chief justice may have only minimal effect on the court in the short run, many court watchers note. "You replace Rehnquist, you don't change the balance of power," Hamilton says.

The long-run impact, however, could be greater, some experts say. "The chief justice is the face and the voice of the court," says William and Mary's Gerhardt. "The potential impact is huge because it will influence the tone of the court and the stature of the court."

More immediate changes in the balance of power depend on the unknown intentions of other justices: chiefly, Stevens and O'Connor, who along with Rehnquist are the court's oldest members. There is also occasional speculation about Justice Ruth Bader Ginsburg, who is 71 and — like Stevens and O'Connor — a cancer survivor in seeming good health.

Replacing Stevens with a conservative would leave the remaining three liberals in a significantly weakened position. Replacing O'Connor with a more consistent conservative would strengthen the conservative majority by limiting the liberal bloc's ability to gain a fifth vote and by eliminating the need to write conservative decisions narrowly to hold her vote.

For now, Stevens and O'Connor appear comfortable in their posts. Even before Rehnquist's health problems, Stevens had been wielding extra influence by his power, as the senior associate justice, to assign opinions when Rehnquist was in the minority. "Stevens seemed to be much more personally influential," Thomas Goldstein, the Washington lawyer who founded SCOTUSBlog, noted recently. As for O'Connor, Hamilton, one of her former law clerks, says bluntly: "She's going to be there forever. The woman's not leaving Washington."

Stevens' or O'Connor's eventual departure would seemingly set the stage for a potentially higher-stakes Supreme Court fight than the Rehnquist succession. "Democrats may decide that the nomination to replace Rehnquist is not the time to fight," says Comiskey. "The time to fight is if or when the president gets the chance to replace any of the justices who are less conservative than Rehnquist."

Any Supreme Court nomination raises the question of a president's ability to predict the votes of a future justice. Some presidents have been surprised by their appointees: President Dwight D. Eisenhower was disappointed by the liberal records of two of his appointees — Chief Justice Earl Warren and Associate Justice William J. Brennan Jr. On the other hand, most justices generally reflect the political and legal views of the presidents who appointed them.

Among the current justices, Comiskey says only Stevens and David H. Souter have voted differently — both more liberal — than could have been predicted at the time of their nominations. Souter was described as a "stealth nominee" at the time of his appointment by President George H. W. Bush in 1990 because of his unknown views on most issues.

Conservatives expect the current President Bush to avoid a "surprise" appointment, pointing to the conservative cast of his more than 200 first-term appointments to federal district and appeals courts. "The president's past performance has been the best indicator of what he's likely to do when there's a vacancy on any court at any level," says Gaziano at the Heritage Foundation.

Yet Hamilton says that even if the president finds a reliable conservative to appoint, the Supreme Court's traditions, including its respect for precedent, limit any chief executive's ability to reshape the law.

"Any president who thinks he has the unilateral power to dramatically change the court's precedents is fooling himself," Hamilton says. "It would be an extremely irresponsible jurist who comes on the court with the intent of overturning a vast body of law. Anybody who comes on the court gets moderated, whether it's Brennan or Rehnquist."

Should the Senate limit filibusters against judicial nominees?

When Chief Justice Warren decided in 1968 to retire, President Lyndon B. Johnson nominated as his successor

Abe Fortas, a longtime friend and political adviser whom Johnson had named as an associate justice only three years earlier. But Fortas ran into a buzzsaw of criticism over his liberal views, ties to Johnson and questionable ethics in accepting a $15,000 fee to give a law school seminar arranged by his former law firm.

Fortas' nomination never came to a vote, however. Sensing a victory in the presidential election, Republicans combined with some Southern Democrats to use the Senate's established tradition of unlimited debate to prevent a floor vote. An effort to cut off the "filibuster" in October 1968 gained a bare 45-43 plurality — well short of the two-thirds majority then needed to stop debate. Fortas then asked President Johnson to withdraw his nomination.

The Fortas nomination ushered in a new period of partisan conflict over high court seats that saw the Senate defeat two successive nominees by Nixon in 1969 and 1970 and Reagan's nomination of Bork in 1987. The partisanship spilled over into lower court nominations as well. Senate Democrats defeated two of Reagan's lower court nominees and one from the first President Bush. After Republicans gained control of the Senate in 1994, they bottled up dozens of President Clinton's federal court nominations.

Now Democrats have retaliated by using the filibuster to block floor votes on 10 of President Bush's nominees to federal appeals courts. Republican senators and conservative advocates are crying foul, insisting the president is entitled to an up-or-down vote on the Senate floor on nominees for any federal judgeship, including the Supreme Court.

"It's primarily the president's prerogative to select a candidate on the basis of ideology," says Rushton, of the Committee for Justice. The Senate "should give the president deference on an individual's judicial philosophy, and ultimately they should allow any nominee who has majority support when he reaches the Senate floor to come to a vote."

Liberals counter that Senate rules and traditions support use of the filibuster to block judicial nominees on ideological grounds. "History and precedent are clear," Aron, of the Alliance for Justice, says. "If the president picks nominees solely because of their partisanship, then the Senate has every right to oppose them."

Under current rules, a motion to invoke "cloture" and cut off a filibuster requires a three-fifths majority — 60 votes if all 100 senators are voting. With a 51-vote majority before the 2004 election, Republicans were unable to get the needed 60 votes to overcome Democrats' filibusters.

Bush responded in early January 2005 by resubmitting the names of most of the blocked nominees along with the names of some district court selections whose nominations also had not been acted on. Democrats called the move confrontational.

With a fortified 55-vote majority, Republicans are considering a plan to confront the filibuster issue with a seemingly technical but highly explosive tactic known on Capitol Hill as "the nuclear option." Under the plan, Senate Majority Leader Frist or another Republican would ask Vice President Cheney, as the Senate's presiding officer, to rule that a simple majority is sufficient to cut off debate on a judicial nomination. Cheney's ruling could then be sustained if backed by a simple majority of senators present and voting.

Conservatives say the parliamentary maneuver is proper. "There's nothing that would prevent the Senate from changing" the existing rules on cloture, Pepperdine's Kmiec says. Liberals disagree. "The filibuster is a procedure that is allowed by the rules of the Senate," Gerhardt says, "and those rules govern what should happen to it."

Some Republican senators are queasy about the proposed tactic, warning that it could hurt Republicans when they are next in the minority. "We were meant by the framers of the Constitution to have the minority have influence," Sen. John McCain, R-Ariz., said. [13]

Conservative partisans, however, are pressing Frist to take some action. "This a real test of Dr. Frist's leadership," says the Heritage Foundation's Gaziano. "There are many of us who care about the courts, who care about the delays in the judicial process that filibusters engender and the unfairness to the nominees, the unfairness to the presidency, the unfairness to the courts. And we will be extremely disappointed if Dr. Frist doesn't get it done."

But liberal advocates and experts defend the filibuster. "If the filibuster is eliminated for judicial nominations, then there truly is no check on President Bush's ability to put anyone he wants to on the courts," Duke University's Chemerinsky says. "In a system of checks and balances, that can't be right."

CHRONOLOGY

1970s *Supreme Court shifts to right under Chief Justice Warren Burger.*

1971 President Richard M. Nixon nominates William H. Rehnquist as his fourth appointee to the court; after 68-26 confirmation, he takes office Jan. 7, 1972, as court's most conservative justice.

1973 *Roe v. Wade* ruling establishes woman's right to abortion during most of pregnancy; Rehnquist is one of two dissenters.

1975 President Gerald R. Ford nominates John Paul Stevens to court; Stevens evolves from judicial moderate to liberal on most issues.

1978 *Regents of University of California v. Bakke* upholds limited use of racial preferences in higher-education admissions; Rehnquist dissents.

1980s *Rehnquist is elevated to chief justice by President Ronald Reagan, seeks to shift court to the right.*

1981 Sandra Day O'Connor is nominated and unanimously confirmed as first woman to serve on Supreme Court; assumes pivotal role between conservative and liberal blocs.

1986 Rehnquist is nominated and confirmed, 65-33, as chief justice; staunch conservative Antonin Scalia is unanimously confirmed for Rehnquist's seat.

1987-88 Senate rejects Reagan's nomination of Robert Bork after bitter fight; Reagan turns to moderate-conservative Anthony M. Kennedy, who easily wins confirmation in 1988.

1990s *Court remains closely divided but steers conservative course on many issues.*

1990, 1991 President George H.W. Bush names David H. Souter and Clarence Thomas to Supreme Court; Souter develops liberal stands; Thomas, after a bitter confirmation fight, stakes out bold conservative positions.

1992 O'Connor, Kennedy and Souter join in pivotal opinion largely reaffirming *Roe v. Wade*; Rehnquist dissents.

1993, 1994 President Bill Clinton's two appointees — Ruth Bader Ginsburg and Stephen G. Breyer — strengthen liberal bloc.

1995 Rehnquist opinion throws out federal law banning guns near school zones as beyond congressional power; blockbuster term includes other conservative decisions limiting minority preferences in government contracting, lowering courts' role in school desegregation.

1996 Rehnquist writes first in line of decisions limiting private damage suits against state governments in federal, and later state, courts.

2000-Present *Supreme Court watchers expect retirements after near-record period with no vacancies; Senate Democrats block some of President Bush's appointments to federal appeals courts.*

2000 Sharply divided Supreme Court votes 5-4 to bar Florida vote recount, paving way for George W. Bush's election as president.

2002 Rehnquist opinion in *Zelman v. Simmons-Harris* upholds use of vouchers at private and parochial schools.

2003 Supreme Court again upholds limited use of racial preferences in university admissions; *Lawrence v. Texas* throws out state anti-sodomy laws; Rehnquist dissents on both issues.

June 2004 Supreme Court rebuffs Bush administration tactics on enemy combatants; Rehnquist dissents from one of rulings and several other major decisions of term.

Fall 2004 Rehnquist on Oct. 25 discloses treatment for thyroid cancer; misses arguments in November and December but works from home; returns to work at court building, unannounced, during week of Dec. 20.

Jan. 20, 2005 Rehnquist swears in President Bush for second term; stronger than expected appearance cools speculation somewhat about retirement.

BACKGROUND

'Storm Centre'

The Supreme Court has been politically controversial since its founding, with fights in the 19th century over federal powers and slavery and in the 20th century over economic regulation, racial issues and criminal law. "We are very quiet there," Justice Oliver Wendell Holmes Jr. famously wrote in 1913, "but it is the quiet of a storm centre." Ideological battles have often played out in confirmation fights between presidents seeking to shape the court to their views and senators reluctant or unwilling to go along with the president's choices. [14]

The court under Chief Justice John Marshall (1803-1836) laid the foundation for the national government's powers over the states and the court's own power to rule federal or state laws unconstitutional. Thomas Jefferson denounced the court's rulings both while he was president and after leaving the White House. Marshall's successor as chief justice, Roger Taney (1836-1864), shifted the court's rulings toward states' rights and helped craft the infamous pro-slavery decision in the Dred Scott case in 1857. Abraham Lincoln owed his election as president to his strong criticism of the ruling as illegitimate both before and during the 1860 campaign.

In the late 19th and early 20th century, the court limited federal powers to protect civil rights and backed business interests with decisions barring a federal income tax and limiting federal or state regulation of economic affairs. The court's conservative stance prevailed through the first years of President Franklin D. Roosevelt's New Deal in the 1930s — prompting FDR's unsuccessful "court-packing" proposal to name up to six additional justices in 1937. Roosevelt's nine appointments to the court over the next six years, however, created a majority that recognized government's power over economic matters and set the stage for a shift to the left on racial, civil liberties and criminal justice issues.

In the 19th century, presidents had often encountered difficulties with Supreme Court appointments. Eighteen of the 63 nominations from 1811-1894 were either withdrawn, postponed, deferred or rejected by the Senate. "The biggest factor was ideology," Comiskey says. A Whig-controlled Senate defeated Democrat Andrew Jackson's initial nomination of Taney to be associate justice. Anti-slavery Northern Republicans blocked James Buchanan's lame-duck nomination of Jeremiah S. Black in 1861 because they found his views on slavery unacceptable. After the Civil War, the Republican-controlled Senate rejected Ulysses S. Grant's nomination of Ebenezer R. Hoar because he supported civil-service reform and had opposed the impeachment of President Andrew Johnson.

An era of good feeling prevailed, however, through most of the 20th century. From 1894 to 1968, only one Supreme Court nomination failed. Democrats and progressive Republicans combined in 1930 to defeat President Herbert Hoover's nomination of John J. Parker, opposing him as insensitive to racial and labor issues. But a few successful nominees drew opposition because of their views, including two of the court's greatest justices: Louis D. Brandeis, confirmed in 1916, 47-22, despite criticism that he was too liberal; and Charles Evans Hughes, confirmed in 1930 as chief justice, 52-26, despite criticism that he was too conservative.

Under Chief Justice Warren (1954-1969), the court drew perhaps the strongest and most sustained criticism in history for a series of liberal decisions — some of them unanimous, others closely divided. The court in the 1950s outlawed racial segregation and nullified some anti-subversive legislation. In the 1960s, it moved to enforce constitutional rights for suspects, barred government-sponsored prayer in public schools and forced reapportionment on rural-dominated state legislatures. Warren's successor, Warren E. Burger (1969-1986) — appointed by Republican Nixon — was a judicial conservative who presided over an often-fractious court with a tenuous conservative majority and a still-strong liberal bloc. Its major rulings included the 7-2 abortion-rights decision in *Roe v. Wade* (1973) and the fractured decision in the *Bakke* case (1978) upholding limited use of racial preferences in college admissions.

The ideological battles over the Warren Court's decisions triggered a new era of Supreme Court confirmation fights, with the Senate rejecting three presidential nominees in less than three years. After the filibuster of Johnson's nomination of Fortas as chief justice in 1968, the Democratic-controlled Senate rejected two Nixon nominees to succeed Fortas after his ethics-compelled resignation in 1969: Clement F. Haynsworth in November 1969 — mainly because he had failed to step out of cases in which he had a financial interest — and G. Harrold Carswell in April 1970, because of an undistin-

Professors Challenge Lifetime Tenure

An assortment of noted law professors with varying ideological views are challenging one of the most basic constitutional provisions about the U.S. Supreme Court: lifetime tenure for the justices.

Viewed by the Framers as necessary to safeguard the independence of the judiciary, lifetime tenure now allows justices to stay on the bench too long, the professors argue. The result, they say, is a danger of arrogance on the part of the justices and political stultification for the court. And they believe that Congress could change the system by passing a law — not a constitutional amendment — effectively establishing 18-year terms for the justices, with lifetime tenure as "senior justices" after active service on the court.

Whatever its merits, the proposal is viewed by leading Supreme Court watchers as having scant likelihood of adoption. But the lead authors of the proposal — veteran law professors Roger Cramton at Cornell and Paul Carrington at Duke — are urging the Senate Judiciary Committee at least to hold hearings on the idea. "A problem exists that can only grow worse and therefore needs legislative attention," Cramton and Carrington wrote in a letter to the committee on Jan. 19, 2005. [1]

Cramton and Carrington — who each has logged nearly 50 years in academia — note that the combination of increased life expectancy and presidential appointment of younger justices has markedly increased the average length of service on the Supreme Court. Since 1971, the average tenure for justices has increased from 16 to 25 years, the average age at retirement from 70 to 79 and the average length of time between appointments from two to three years. The Founders "could not foresee that lifetime tenure would result in persons holding so powerful an office for a generation or more," they say.

Justices are disinclined to retire, the professors argue, because of the power of the position and their ability — unlike lower court judges — to control their own workload. The court under Chief Justice William H. Rehnquist has reduced the yearly output of signed decisions from 120 or more to around 75. With the increased tenure and less frequent vacancies, Cramton and Carrington contend, each appointment becomes more politically charged, and presidents turn to younger nominees in hopes of affecting the court's decisions for a generation or longer.

To remedy the problem, the professors propose that one justice or chief justice be appointed every two years. The court would continue to function with nine members, but after 18 years a justice or chief justice would become a "senior justice" — available for assignments but not participating in the court's regular work. To avoid the issue of retroactivity, the proposal would not apply to any of the court's current members.

The proposal has been endorsed in principle by 30 law professors ranging across the ideological spectrum from staunch conservatives such as Northwestern's Steve Calabresi, co-founder of the Federalist Society, to unbending liberals such as the University of Michigan's Yale Kamisar. Walter Dellinger, acting U.S. solicitor general under President Bill Clinton and now a professor at Duke, is also among the endorsers.

Some court watchers, however, discount both the need for the proposal or its feasibility. "We've had this system for a long, long time, and it hasn't caused any problems yet," says Thomas Goldstein, a Washington lawyer and founder of SCOTUSBlog, which provides daily Web reports on the high court.

"I don't think that there's even the beginning of a consensus within popular opinion or in Congress that a justice who has been there 30 years has obviously overstayed his or her welcome," says David Garrow, a legal historian and lecturer at Emory Law School.

Garrow also says the proposal is "hopelessly complicated" and would have to be adopted by constitutional amendment, not by statute. Goldstein agrees. "If you have to be honest about it, you have to amend the Constitution," he says.

Dennis Hutchinson, a lecturer and associate dean at the University of Chicago and co-editor of the annual academic journal *The Supreme Court Review*, agrees with some of the concerns behind the proposal but also says a constitutional amendment would be required either to establish limited terms or mandatory retirement at a fixed age. "We have a written Constitution and an understood constitution," Hutchinson says. "And the understood constitution says they're justices for life."

In their letter to the Senate committee, Cramton and Carrington acknowledge the issues of complexity and constitutionality. The proposal, they say, is "not as simple as we might wish." As for the validity of the proposal, they say that it has "good prospects of being upheld as constitutional."

---

[1] For background, see Tony Mauro, "Profs Pitch Plan for Limits on Supreme Court Service," *Legal Times*, Jan. 3, 2005, p. 1; Linda Greenhouse, "How Long Is Too Long for the Court's Justices?", *The New York Times*, Jan. 16, 2005, "Week in Review," p. 5.

guished record and past opposition to integration. Amid the rejections, however, the Senate unanimously approved Nixon's first nomination — of Burger as chief justice in 1969.

Rehnquist's Court?

With Burger's retirement in 1986, President Reagan sought to solidify the court's conservative core by elevating Rehnquist to chief justice and appointing another strong conservative, Scalia, as associate justice. Rehnquist and Scalia proved to be as conservative as expected, but subsequent appointments left the court closely divided between conservatives and liberals. In some years, Rehnquist's impact was seen as substantial; in other years, less so.

Early in Rehnquist's tenure as chief justice, the court showed twin strains of conservatism — a de-emphasis of racial justice issues and a distaste for expansive civil remedies — with a series of rulings in 1989 disadvantaging plaintiffs in job discrimination suits under the Civil Rights Act of 1964. Congress, then under Democratic control, responded with a 1991 law overturning those rulings.

In other areas, though, the court's new stance on civil rights stood up. The court tightened the rules on racial preferences for government contracts — first for states in 1989, then for the federal government in 1995. Two rulings written by Rehnquist in the 1990s signaled federal courts that they could free school districts from desegregation decrees. And a line of cases beginning in 1993 established constitutional rules against using racial redistricting to help elect African-American or Hispanic lawmakers.

Conservative Majority, Liberals in Dissent

The Supreme Court consists of a sometimes-fragile conservative majority and a fairly cohesive bloc of four liberal-leaning justices. There have been no changes in membership for more than 10 years. The average age of the nine justices is now over 70.

Getty Images/Joyce Naltchayan

The Conservatives	The Swing Votes	The Liberals
1. William H. Rehnquist Born: Oct. 1, 1924 Joined court in 1972; nominated by Nixon. Appointed chief justice in 1986 by Reagan. *Crafted shift on states' rights, church-state issues*	**4. Sandra Day O'Connor** Born: March 26, 1930 Joined court in 1981; nominated by Reagan. *Pivotal vote to uphold racial preferences by colleges*	**6. John Paul Stevens** Born: April 20, 1920 Joined court in 1975; nominated by Ford. *Most protective of rights of suspects, defendants*
2. Antonin Scalia Born: March 11, 1936 Joined court in 1986; nominated by Reagan. *Strongest voice against pornography, gay rights*	**5. Anthony M. Kennedy** Born: July 23, 1936 Joined court in 1988; nominated by Reagan. *Shift on abortion saved Roe v. Wade*	**7. David H. Souter** Born: Sept. 17, 1939 Joined court in 1990; nominated by G.H.W. Bush. *Strongest voice for church-state separation*
3. Clarence Thomas Born: June 23, 1948 Joined court in 1991; nominated by G.H.W. Bush. *Most willing to re- examine old decisions*		**8. Ruth Bader Ginsburg** Born: March 15, 1933 Joined court in 1993; nominated by Clinton. *Staunch liberal on civil rights, women's issues*
		9. Stephen G. Breyer Born: Aug. 15, 1938 Joined court in 1994; nominated by Clinton. *Backs congressional, federal prerogatives*

In criminal law, three decisions in 1991 signaled a narrower view of constitutional protections by making it harder for inmates to use federal habeas corpus to chal-

The constitutionality of the Ten Commandments monument at the Texas State Capitol in Austin is the focus of upcoming Supreme Court arguments. Chief Justice Rehnquist has voted in past cases to ease the rules requiring separation of church and state.

overturn the *Roe v. Wade* abortion rights ruling, and anti-abortion groups thought a case challenging a restrictive Pennsylvania abortion statute gave the justices the vehicle for doing so. But a surprising coalition of three Republican-appointed justices — O'Connor, Kennedy and Souter — wrote a pivotal opinion reaffirming what they called *Roe's* "essential holding," while giving states slightly more discretion to regulate abortion procedures. Eight years later, anti-abortion groups were again disappointed when the court struck down a state ban on the "dilation and extraction" procedure, labeled by opponents as "partial-birth abortions."

Rehnquist proved more successful in the 1990s on his signature issues of federalism and church-state relations. On federalism, his 1995 decision striking down the Gun-Free School Zones Act warned against congressional intrusion into police powers reserved to the states. His 1996 ruling on an obscure federal law about Indian gaming was the first in a line of decisions reviving states' rights to limit private suits against state governments. On church-state issues, his 1993 opinion allowing taxpayer funds to pay for an interpreter for a deaf student attending a parochial school paved the way for the 2002 decision permitting religious schools to be included in voucher plans.

On civil liberties, Rehnquist's 1997 decisions rejecting a right to assisted suicide embodied his reluctance to use the Constitution's Due Process Clause to establish new individual rights. He also took a narrow view of the First Amendment's Free Speech Clause — often in dissent, as in the 2004 decision blocking Congress' second try to keep Internet porn away from children. On the other hand, Rehnquist joined with the court's conservatives in a series of rulings giving property owners somewhat greater protections against environmental or other land use regulations.

Through the 1990s, the court remained tenuously divided between conservative and liberal blocs on many of the issues. Thomas' appointment to the court in 1991 — narrowly approved following tumultuous hearings on charges of sexual harassment by his former aide, Anita Hill — strengthened the conservative wing. But conservatives were disappointed by Kennedy and outraged by Souter's seeming evolution into a staunch liberal. Clinton's appointments of Ginsburg and Breyer then somewhat solidified the liberal wing. The result often was to leave O'Connor with the decisive vote, leading observers at times to refer to the "O'Connor Court." [15]

lenge state convictions, allowing use of "victim impact statements" in death penalty cases and weakening the rule against use of coerced confessions. Through the years, the court showed impatience with most death penalty challenges and generally backed police in search-and-seizure and interrogation cases. But Rehnquist did write the 2000 decision that reaffirmed the *Miranda* rule on police interrogation, striking down a 1968 law Congress passed to limit the rule.

The court's seeming conservative shift stalled in 1992, however, on the emotional issue of abortion. Both the Reagan and Bush administrations had urged the court to

Despite the ideological fault lines, the justices generally appeared to maintain good relations with each other. And Rehnquist was credited with running the justices' private conferences efficiently and keeping his own and his colleagues' opinion writing on schedule. "He'll be remembered as a great chief justice," Pepperdine's Kmiec says. "Someone who was collegial to work with and very civil at all times, plus somebody who got his work done."

Bush's Judges

The Rehnquist Court was never more closely nor more sharply divided than in December 2000, when the conservative majority paved the way for George W. Bush to become president by effectively stopping the vote recount in the pivotal state of Florida. Court watchers anticipated one or more retirements during Bush's first term, but none came. However, Bush pleased conservative groups with the general pattern of some 200 judicial nominations during his first four years in office, even as some were sharply criticized by liberal interest groups and blocked from confirmation by Senate Democrats.

With 25 electoral votes, Florida emerged as critical in the 2000 presidential election after election-night tallies in the rest of the country left Vice President Al Gore with 267 electoral votes and Bush with 246. When Bush appeared to have won Florida with a narrow lead, Gore pressed for a recount. The Florida Supreme Court approved a statewide recount, but Bush asked the U.S. Supreme Court to block it. The court did, in a 5-4 ruling on Dec. 12, split along conservative-liberal lines. The majority found an equal-protection violation in the state high court's failure to set clear standards for the recount, while the liberal dissenters said the state courts should have been given time to develop uniform rules. [16]

Following custom, Rehnquist administered the oath of office to Bush on Jan. 20, 2001. With Republicans in control of the White House and both houses of Congress, many court watchers expected Rehnquist or O'Connor or both to retire. Neither did. Meanwhile, Republicans lost control of the Senate in June, when Vermont's James Jeffords left the GOP, became an independent and agreed to vote with Democrats in organizing the chamber. Whatever Rehnquist or O'Connor may have been contemplating — and neither said anything publicly — the partisan change in the Senate greatly affected judicial politics for the next 18 months.

Bush began putting his stamp on the federal bench by announcing 11 nominees for federal appeals courts on May 9, 2001. [17] Most on the list had solid conservative records as state court judges, academics or lawyers in private or government practice. A second batch announced in the summer had a similar conservative cast. Bush voiced hopes for smooth confirmations, but liberal interest groups accused him of appointing "right-wing ideologues."

By the end of 2002, Bush had won confirmation of 100 nominees, while two had been defeated in committee and another 29 were not acted upon. Republicans regained control of the Senate in the 2002 elections, and Democrats turned to the filibuster to block votes on Bush nominees they viewed as too conservative. By the end of 2004, Bush had filled 203 federal judgeships — nearly one quarter of the federal bench. But the Democrats' success in blocking 10 appeals court nominees from floor votes infuriated Bush and Senate Republicans and conservative interest groups.

Campaigning for re-election, Bush complained about Democrats' tactics while Republicans pulled out all stops to defeat Senate Minority Leader Tom Daschle in his bid for re-election from South Dakota. Neither Bush nor his Democratic opponent, Sen. John Kerry of Massachusetts, devoted much attention to the Supreme Court in their respective campaigns. But in a closed-door session with major Republican contributors in September, Bush said that he expected to have at least one high court appointment shortly after inauguration and as many as four by the end of a second term. [18]

An announcement in late October that Rehnquist was suffering from cancer caught official Washington and most court watchers largely by surprise, although some reporters recalled in hindsight that Rehnquist had been somewhat hoarse and appeared weak during oral arguments earlier in the month. The limited information from the court's public-information office and Rehnquist's chambers forced court watchers and medical experts to speculate on his condition, but it seemed to point to a serious, even grave, condition. In any event, Rehnquist's stated intention to return to the bench in November proved overly optimistic.

Nonetheless, Rehnquist was said to be continuing to work on cases from his home. In December, the court said Rehnquist had accepted Bush's invitation to administer the oath of office at the inauguration. And in early January, the public-information office acknowledged

Some Potential Supreme Court Nominees

Samuel Alito Jr.
(Judge, 3rd U.S. Circuit Court of Appeals)
Appointed: Bush, 1990
Age: 54
Education: A.B., Princeton U.; J.D., Yale U.
Residence: West Caldwell, N.J.

Emilio Garza
(Judge, 5th U.S. Circuit Court of Appeals)
Appointed: Bush, 1991 (Reagan, District Court, 1988)
Age: 57
Education: B.A., M.A., Notre Dame U.; J.D., U. of Texas
Residence: San Antonio

Edith Jones
(Judge, 5th U.S. Circuit Court of Appeals)
Appointed: Reagan, 1985
Age: 54
Education: B.A., Cornell U.; J.D., U. of Texas
Residence: Houston

J. Michael Luttig
(Judge, 4th U.S. Circuit Court of Appeals)
Appointed: Bush, 1991
Age: 50
Education: B.A., Washington and Lee U.; J.D., U. of Virginia
Residence: Vienna, Va.

Michael W. McConnell
(Judge, 10th U.S. Circuit Court of Appeals)
Appointed: Bush, 2002
Age: 49
Education: B.A., Michigan State U.; J.D., U. of Chicago
Residence: Salt Lake City

Theodore Olson
(Partner, Gibson, Dunn & Crutcher)
(U.S. Solicitor General, 2001-2004)
Age: 64
Education: B.A., U. of the Pacific; J.D., U. of California, Berkeley
Residence: Great Falls, Va.

John G. Roberts Jr.
(Judge, D.C. U.S. Circuit Court of Appeals)
Appointed: Bush, 2003
Age: 50
Education: A.B., Harvard U.; J.D., Harvard U.
Residence: Chevy Chase, Md.

J. Harvie Wilkinson III
(Judge, 4th U.S. Circuit Court of Appeals)
Appointed: Reagan, 1984
Age: 60
Education: B.A., Yale U.; J.D., U. of Virginia
Residence: Charlottesville, Va.

Source: CQ Judicial Staff Directory, 2004

that Rehnquist had returned to the Supreme Court building to do some work in the week before Christmas. He remained out of public view, however, until the inauguration.

CURRENT SITUATION

Rampant Speculation

The White House is officially maintaining a discreet silence on potential Supreme Court vacancies, but the no-comment stance is only adding to the rampant speculation in legal and political circles about possible high court candidates. More than a dozen possible candidates have been mentioned — all of them conservative, almost all of them sitting federal or state court judges. Bush's intentions or preferences remain unknown.

Much of the speculation focuses on the possibility that Bush would elevate a sitting justice — most likely, Scalia or Thomas — to the chief justiceship if Rehnquist retires and nominate a second person as associate justice. Historically, most presidents have not followed this pattern but have chosen a chief justice from outside the court. Rehnquist was only the third sitting associate justice to be elevated to chief.

In some instances, according to Comiskey, presidents have preferred to choose a chief justice from outside the court to avoid creating any resentment among justices passed over for the post. In addition, he says, an outside appointment is politically easier for presidents. "They only need to make one [nomination] and risk one confirmation fight," he says.

Should the Senate limit filibusters on Supreme Court and other judicial nominees?

YES

Sen. John Cornyn, R-Texas
Member, Senate Judiciary Committee

Written for The CQ Researcher, January 2005

Under our Constitution and Senate traditions, every judicial nominee who is supported by a majority of senators has been confirmed — until now. Unfortunately, some groups are now demanding — for the first time in our nation's history — that President Bush's nominees be supported by a supermajority of senators, or else be denied even the courtesy of an up-or-down vote, through the unprecedented use of an obstructionist tactic known as the filibuster.

The rules governing the judicial-confirmation process should be the same regardless of which party controls the White House or the Senate. No one would say that 51 percent of voters is needed to elect a Democrat to office, but a 60-percent vote is required to elect a Republican. Likewise, a majority of senators have always had the power to confirm a judicial nominee, whether the president is a Democrat or Republican.

In fact, the Senate has always confirmed judges who enjoyed majority but less than 60-vote support — including controversial Clinton nominees Richard Paez, William Fletcher and Susan Oki Mollway, and Carter appointees Abner Mikva and L. T. Senter.

This new supermajority requirement is wrong. As law Professor Michael Gerhardt once wrote, such a rule "is problematic because it creates a presumption against confirmation, shifts the balance of power to the Senate and enhances the power of the special interests."

The filibuster is hardly sacrosanct. At least 26 laws on the books today abolish the filibuster in a number of policy areas.

Nor is there anything extraordinary about a majority of senators acting to craft Senate rules and procedures. The constitutional authority of a majority of senators to enact rules and procedures was expressly stated in the Constitution, unanimously endorsed by the Supreme Court over a century ago and dutifully supported and exercised by the Senate on countless occasions since. Such authority has also been recognized — indeed, praised — by leading Senate Democrats, including Sens. Robert Byrd, D-W.Va., and Ted Kennedy, D-Mass. And Sen. Charles Schumer, D-N.Y., acknowledged the legitimacy of such authority at a Judiciary subcommittee hearing just two years ago.

The authority to restore Senate traditions by majority vote has been disparaged by some as a "nuclear" tactic. But what is truly nuclear is the radical alteration of the confirmation process — not the attempt to restore Senate tradition by traditional means.

NO

Sen. Patrick J. Leahy, D-Vt.
Member, Senate Judiciary Committee

Written for The CQ Researcher, January 2005

The high-pitched rhetoric and raw threats from partisans on the other side of the aisle regarding judicial nominations do not fit the facts. With Democratic support, 204 of President Bush's judicial nominees were confirmed during his first term — more than in the first terms of Presidents Reagan, George H.W. Bush and Clinton — and there now are fewer federal court vacancies than at any time in the last 16 years.

And while Republicans blocked more than 60 of President Clinton's judicial nominees — mostly anonymously and without hearings or votes — the 10 judicial filibusters in the 108th Congress were used sparingly and only as a last resort after the majority systematically bent, broke or changed longstanding Senate rules and practices that protect the rights of senators in defending the interests of their states.

In fact judicial filibusters, though rare, are neither unprecedented nor unconstitutional. The current Senate Republican leader participated in a judicial filibuster just five years ago.

No president has ever expected that every judicial nominee will be confirmed, because under our Constitution judicial appointment and confirmation authority is split between the president and the Senate. More than two-dozen Supreme Court nominees have been rejected, either through inaction or failing confirmation votes. The Constitution simply has never required an up-or-down vote on every nomination. By giving the Senate the power to advise and consent, the Framers clearly left open the possibility of withholding consent.

The "nuclear option" would destroy rules protecting the fundamental freedom of debate, one of the pillars that define the Senate as a unique deliberative body. Changing the Senate's rules would damage democracy and Senate procedures and traditions, shift power to the White House and irreparably weaken one of the only checks on the fitness of the unelected judiciary.

One of the Senate's great strengths is its role as a continuing body with continuing rules that have been respected under both parties. Its rules must not be changed to give whoever is in the majority the power to jerry-rig the results it desires, like a child's game of "King of the Hill."

The filibuster is one of the only incentives for a president to choose moderation over extremism in appointments that will affect the American people's constitutional rights for decades after he has left office. The solution is consultation that will result in judges with unblemished records of fairness and proven commitments to constitutional rights.

But Kmiec, who worked at the Justice Department during the Rehnquist-Scalia appointments, expects Bush to follow Reagan's example and elevate a sitting justice. "It's a great opportunity to make a double appointment," he says.

Many conservatives see the elevation of Scalia or Thomas as a way to strengthen the court's conservative wing. White House officials leaked word in November that the president was considering Thomas for the post. More recently, though, some conservatives are questioning whether Scalia or Thomas would moderate their views if named as chief justice.

"It may be best for conservatives if those two distinct conservative voices stay as associate justices where they can push the envelope," says Rushton of the Committee for Justice. "They may be the popular choice of the conservative movement, but it may be preferable to have a conservative from outside the court placed in the chief's position."

All the widely mentioned candidates from off the court are largely unknown to the public, with the possible exception of Theodore Olson, who served as U.S. solicitor general from 2001 until his resignation in June 2004. A Washington lawyer well known in legal, political and media circles, Olson also represented Bush in the two Supreme Court arguments in the 2000 presidential election dispute.

Among the most frequently mentioned candidates are three federal appellate judges: J. Harvie Wilkinson III and J. Michael Luttig of the Richmond, Va.-based 4th U.S. Circuit Court of Appeals; and Samuel Alito Jr. of the Philadelphia-based 3rd Circuit. All three are viewed as legal conservatives, although Wilkinson, a former law clerk to Justice Lewis F. Powell Jr., is regarded as more moderate and pragmatic than Luttig or Alito.

Also mentioned are two other federal appellate judges — staunch conservatives and Texans Emilio Garza and Edith Jones, who both serve on the New Orleans-based 5th Circuit. Two others sometimes mentioned are recent Bush appointees to appellate judgeships, both with extensive experience as Supreme Court advocates: Michael W. McConnell, a former law professor now on the 10th Circuit in Denver, and John G. Roberts Jr., a former Washington lawyer now on the D.C. Circuit.

Liberal interest groups are preparing for an all-out fight if Bush chooses a hard-line conservative. "We expect that he will — but hope that he will not — fulfill his pledge to his base, the right wing of the [Republican] party," says Neas, of People for the American Way.

"That will engender a tremendous confrontation battle. We've got to expect that and prepare for that."

Conservative groups are similarly mobilizing. "We expect the left will come out with daggers drawn," the Committee for Justice's Rushton says, "and we intend to defend the president's nominee from unfair attack."

Business as Usual?

Midway through its current term, the Supreme Court appears to be getting its work done at its customary pace despite Rehnquist's illness. By the end of January, the court had issued 15 decisions — exactly the same number it had completed at the comparable point of the 2003-2004 term. The court has scheduled a total of 73 cases to be decided before the justices begin their summer recess at the end of June.

As senior associate justice, Stevens presides over the court's public sessions and announces at the beginning of each day that Rehnquist reserves the right to participate in the case being argued on the basis of briefs and transcripts of the arguments. In December, however, the court said Rehnquist would not vote in any of the cases argued in November except to break a tie.

With Rehnquist participating in absentia, the court ruled Jan. 12 on one of its major cases: a constitutional challenge to the Federal Sentencing Guidelines. [19] In a bifurcated decision, the court ruled, 5-4, that the guidelines unconstitutionally allowed judges instead of juries to decide factual issues needed to raise a defendant's sentence. But with Justice Ginsburg switching sides, a different 5-4 majority cured the problem by declaring the guidelines to be advisory for federal judges instead of mandatory as Congress provided in creating the system in the 1980s.

The ruling followed a 5-4 decision in June that found a similar state sentencing system unconstitutional. Rehnquist had been among the dissenters in that case. The decision to apply the same ruling to the federal scheme had been expected, but the solution — making the guidelines advisory — caught most observers by surprise and confounded predictions about the ruling's effects.

Justice Department officials voiced concerns that the ruling would result in sentencing disparities of the sort that Congress had sought to eliminate. For their part, defense lawyers said they hoped and expected judges would impose shorter sentences than the guidelines had required in some cases, especially drug and white-collar offenses. Meanwhile, some members of Congress criticized the ruling and called for legislation to restore the original version of the guidelines as much as possible.

Among the cases already argued but not decided, the most prominent is a constitutional challenge to the execution of juvenile offenders. The justices appeared divided along conservative-liberal lines in the arguments, with O'Connor and Kennedy both giving mixed signals as to their likely votes. Rehnquist, who dissented when the court in 2003 barred execution of mentally retarded offenders, seemed likely in October to vote the same way in the new case. [20]

The court has three more two-week argument sessions scheduled. The most closely watched dispute perhaps will be two cases scheduled for March 2 challenging the display of the Ten Commandments on public grounds. Earlier, the justices will hear arguments on Feb. 22 in a case challenging a Connecticut city's use of the power of eminent domain to acquire homeowners' property and turn it over to a private company for development. [21]

Through January, the court had issued only two decisions under Rehnquist's name — both argued in October, one issued in November and the other in December. Both were unanimous and written in Rehnquist's normal style: compact and to-the-point. He has not written any separate concurring or dissenting opinions. Apparently, Rehnquist is participating in the court's case-screening work, since there has been no notation otherwise in the regularly issued lists of cases granted or denied review.

Some observers say Rehnquist's absence must be having some impact on the court's work. "There is no way he could be as engaged as he was in the day-to-day administration of the court and in the voting in the cases," says Richard Lazarus, director of the Supreme Court Institute at Georgetown University Law Center in Washington. "The fact is there is deliberation. They convince each other through their writing. There is no question that there is an impact."

But SCOTUSBlog founder Goldstein sees no effect from Rehnquist's absence — except that the atmosphere in the courtroom "has been a little more relaxed." Rehnquist is well known as a stickler for courtroom decorum.

"You can speculate that [Rehnquist's absence] has been disruptive," Goldstein says, "but it's just speculation."

OUTLOOK

Waiting and Watching

President Bush begins his second term with a full plate of foreign policy challenges — most notably, in Iraq — and an ambitious domestic agenda topped by an already contentious plan to partly privatize Social Security. After the narrowest re-election of any president in U.S. history, Bush is claiming a mandate for his foreign and domestic policies alike and promising to spend the "political capital" gained in his election to fight for his proposals.

Combined with the sweeping rhetoric of his inaugural speech, Bush's uncompromising stance leads many Supreme Court watchers to expect that the president will be similarly bold in picking strong-minded conservatives for any vacancies on the court during the next four years — including the chief justice's position if Rehnquist retires. Senators in both parties and interest groups on both sides are girding for a fight.

For his part, though, Rehnquist pleaded for some cooling of judicial politics in what seems likely to have been his final annual report on the federal judiciary, released at the end of 2004. [22] In a four-page passage, Rehnquist noted that criticism of judges "has dramatically increased in recent years" and noted with disapproval recent attempts in Congress to bring political pressure on federal judges.

As one example, Rehnquist noted the law passed in 2003 requiring collection of information on sentencing on an individual, judge-by-judge basis. (The so-called PROTECT Act was ruled unconstitutional in the decision on the Federal Sentencing Guidelines issued two weeks after the report.) Rehnquist also noted that there had been "suggestions" to impeach federal judges whose decisions were regarded as "out of the mainstream" and some bills to limit federal courts' jurisdiction over some constitutional issues.

Rehnquist warned against the use of impeachment to remove judges because of their decisions. But he also said the federal judiciary is "subject ultimately to the popular will because judges are appointed and confirmed by elected officials." And, after acknowledging the likelihood of further challenges to judicial independence, he concluded by saying, "Let us hope that the Supreme Court and all of our courts will continue to command sufficient public respect to enable them to survive basic attacks on the judicial independence that has made our judicial system a model for much of the world."

Rehnquist's remarks drew wide praise. "He has been a very credible, nonpartisan advocate for the independence of the judiciary," says William and Mary law Professor Gerhardt. And Bush himself drew enthusiastic applause when he told a post-inauguration luncheon with members of Congress that he was "touched" that Rehnquist came to administer the oath. "That was an incredibly moving part of the ceremony," Bush said.

The White House is still offering no reliable clues, however, about the president's inclinations on future Supreme Court vacancies. Some Democrats in Congress voice the hope — but not the expectation — for a non-confrontational choice. "If they send us someone who is completely objectionable, we are going to have a big fight," says Sen. Byron L. Dorgan of North Dakota, chairman of the Senate Democratic Policy Committee.

For the moment, though, Rehnquist's stronger-than-expected physical appearance is making Supreme Court watchers rethink their schedules and turn instead to the court's docket while the White House and Congress turn to immediate concerns. The next battle over the Supreme Court — if it is to be a battle — is yet to come.

NOTES

1. Quoted in Keith Perine, "Rehnquist Administers Oath, Perhaps for Last Time," *CQ Today*, Jan. 20, 2005.

2. Lyle Denniston, "The Chief Justice at the inaugural," SCOTUSBlog, Jan. 20, 2005 (www.goldsteinhowe.com/blog/).

3. Chief Justice Roger Taney (1836-1864) died in office at the age of 87. Justices with longer tenure include, in order of longevity, William O. Douglas, Stephen J. Field, John Marshall (chief justice), Hugo L. Black, the first John M. Harlan, Joseph Story, and William J. Brennan Jr.

4. For background, see Kenneth Jost, "Abortion Debates," *The CQ Researcher*, March 21, 2003, pp. 249-272, and Kenneth Jost, "Affirmative Action," *The CQ Researcher*, Sept. 21, 2001, pp. 737-760.

5. For background, see Kenneth Jost, "School Vouchers Showdown," *The CQ Researcher*, Feb. 15, 2002, pp. 121-144.

6. See Linda Greenhouse, "Court Had Rehnquist Initials Intricately Carved on Docket," *The New York Times*, July 2, 2002, p. A1; "The Year Rehnquist May Have Lost His Court," *ibid.*, July 5, 2004, p. A1. Rehnquist dissented in nine out of 17 5-4 decisions in the 2003-2004 term.

7. The decisions are *United States v. Lopez*, 514 U.S. 549 (1995) (Gun-Free School Zones Act); *United States v. Morrison*, 529 U.S. 598 (2000) (Violence Against Women Act).

8. The first ruling in the series is *Seminole Tribe of Florida v. Florida*, 517 U.S. 44 (1996).

9. The voucher ruling is *Zelman v. Simmons-Harris*, 536 U.S. 639 (2002); Rehnquist's earlier decision was *Zobrest v. Catalina Foothills School District*, 509 U.S. 1 (1993).

10. The case is *Rosenberger v. Rector and Visitors of University of Virginia*, 515 U.S. 819 (1995).

11. For background, see Kenneth Jost, "School Desegregation," *The CQ Researcher*, April 23, 2004, pp. 345-372.

12. For background, see Kenneth Jost, "Rethinking the Death Penalty," *The CQ Researcher*, Nov. 16, 2001, pp. 945-968.

13. Quoted in Keith Perine, "Parliamentary Toolbox Full of Options to Renovate Filibuster Rules," *CQ Weekly*, Jan. 10, 2005, p. 60.

14. For background, see Kenneth Jost, *The Supreme Court A to Z* (3d. ed.), 2003; David G. Savage, *Guide to the U.S. Supreme Court* (4th ed.), 2004.

15. For a portrait, see Jeffrey Rosen, "A Majority of One," *The New York Times Magazine*, June 3, 2001, p. 32.

16. For background, see Mary H. Cooper, "Voting Rights," *The CQ Researcher*, Oct. 29, 2004, pp. 901-924; Kathy Koch, "Election Reform," *The CQ Researcher*, Nov. 2, 2001, pp. 897-920, and Kenneth Jost and Gregory L. Giroux, "Electoral College," *The CQ Researcher*, Dec. 8, 2000, pp. 977-1008.

17. For background, see Kenneth Jost, "Judges and Politics," *The CQ Researcher*, July 27, 2001, pp. 557-600.

18. The comment was first reported by Ron Suskind in "Without a Doubt," *The New York Times Magazine*, Oct. 17, 2004, p. 44.

19. The case is United States v. Booker, 04-404. For background, see Kenneth Jost, "Sentencing Debates," *The CQ Researcher*, Nov. 12, 2004, pp. 925-948.

20. The case is *Roper v. Simmons*, 03-633.

21. The Ten Commandments cases are *Van Orden v. Perry*, 03-1500, and *McCreary County v. American Civil Liberties Union of Kentucky*, 03-1693; the eminent domain case is *Kelo v. City of New London*, 04-108.

22. The complete report is available on the Supreme Court's Web site: www.supremecourtus.gov.

BIBLIOGRAPHY

Books

Abraham, Henry J., *Justices, Presidents, and Senators: A History of the U.S. Supreme Court Appointments from Washington to Clinton* (rev. ed.), Rowman & Littlefield, 1999.
A professor emeritus at the University of Virginia provides a comprehensive history of the political and legal backgrounds of Supreme Court appointments.

Comiskey, Michael, *Seeking Justices: The Judging of Supreme Court Nominees*, University of Kansas Press, 2004.
An associate professor of political science at Pennsylvania State University, Fayette, analyzes the confirmation process, rejecting criticisms of the Senate's role in examining nominees.

Keck, Thomas M., *The Most Activist Supreme Court in History: The Road to Modern Judicial Conservatism*, University of Chicago Press, 2004.
A political scientist at Syracuse University's Maxwell School traces the evolution of judicial conservatism since the 1930s.

Maltz, Earl M. (ed.), *Rehnquist Justice: Understanding the Court Dynamic*, University of Kansas Press, 2004.
Individual contributors provide interpretive portraits of each Rehnquist Court justice. Maltz is a Rutgers University professor.

Tushnet, Mark, *A Court Divided: The Rehnquist Court and the Future of Constitutional Law*, W.W. Norton, 2005.
A Georgetown law professor analyzes the Rehnquist Court.

Yalof, David Alistair, *Pursuit of Justices: Presidential Politics and the Selection of Supreme Court Nominees*, University of Chicago Press, 1999.
A political scientist at the University of Connecticut examines presidential nominations from the Truman through Reagan administrations, with a brief discussion of nominations by former presidents George H.W. Bush and Bill Clinton.

Articles

Perine, Keith, "Fiercest Fight in Partisan War May Be Over Supreme Court," *CQ Weekly*, Jan. 10, 2005, p. 58.
The article sets the stage for an anticipated Senate fight over confirmation of President Bush's nomination of a successor to Chief Justice William H. Rehnquist, who is battling thyroid cancer.

On the Web

The Supreme Court Web site (www.supremecourtus.gov) provides the court's current and recent opinions, orders, argument calendars and docket information on cases. It also includes a link to an American Bar Association Web site (http://www.abanet.org/publiced/preview/briefs/home.html) that posts the parties' briefs, as they become available, in cases to be argued. Older Supreme Court decisions are available on several academic or commercial Web sites; one of the most popular is FindLaw.com. For current reportage, see SCOTUSBlog, a site founded by Washington lawyer and court watcher Thomas Goldstein (www.goldstein-howe.com/blog).

For More Information

Alliance for Justice, 11 Dupont Circle, N.W., 2nd Floor, Washington, DC 20036; (202) 822-6070; www.afj.org. Supports judicial independence and protection of the environment, civil rights and reproductive freedom.

Committee for Justice, 1275 Pennsylvania Ave., N.W., 10th floor, Washington, DC 20004; (202) 481-6850; www.committeeforjustice.org. Defends and promotes constitutionalist judicial nominees to the federal courts.

Federalist Society, 1015 18th St., N.W., Suite 425, Washington, DC 20036; (202) 822-8138; www.fedsoc.org. A group of conservatives and libertarians that believes "the separation of governmental powers is central to our Constitution."

People for the American Way, 2000 M St., N.W., Suite 400, Washington, DC 20036; (202) 467-4999; www.pfaw.org/pfaw/general. Promotes protection of First Amendment rights and opposes "the influence of the radical right."

Supreme Court Institute, Georgetown University Law Center, 600 New Jersey Ave., N.W., Washington, DC 20001; (202) 662-9350; www.law.georgetown.edu/sci/. Promotes understanding of Supreme Court decision-making.

9

Gang Crisis

William Triplett

A wall mural in East Los Angeles marks the 18th Street gang's turf. At least 21,500 gangs are active nationwide, in small communities as well as cities. Recent immigration has energized violent Latino and Asian gangs like Mara Salvatrucha and the Oriental Playboys.

Vertical text along image: National Youth Gang Center/Michelle Arciaga

From *CQ Researcher,*
May 14, 2004.

In June 2001, Fredy Reyes-Castillo met four fellow Latino immigrants at a gas station in Reston, an affluent Northern Virginia suburb. With its upscale malls and subdivisions, it's what drug dealers call a "green area" — full of kids with money.

The four were members of Mara Salvatrucha, or MS-13, a nationwide Latino street gang infamous for its drug dealing and violence. Reyes-Castillo, 22, was not a member, but that day he pretended to be. When the real gangsters realized he didn't understand MS-13 slang or sport gang tattoos, they beat him to death so brutally it took weeks to identify his body. [1]

Three months later, in nearby Alexandria, MS-13 members walked into a McDonald's and spotted an acquaintance, Joaquim Diaz, 19. Diaz was not an MS-13 member and didn't pretend to be.

However, one of the gang members, Denis Rivera, suspected Diaz had joined a rival gang. Rivera and another gang member convinced Diaz to accompany them to Washington to buy marijuana. But Diaz soon found himself in a remote area where he was slashed, stabbed, run over and then mutilated.

Rivera's girlfriend, Brenda Paz, later told police Rivera had bragged that he had tried to behead Diaz, comparing it to "preparing a chicken." But his knife had been too dull, so he had cut out Diaz's larynx instead. Paz entered the federal Witness Protection Program but left before Rivera went on trial. Weeks later her pregnant body was found on the banks of the Shenandoah River, stabbed to death. Police believe MS-13 was responsible. [2]

Newspapers across the country report scores of similar crimes in places like Reston that, until now, have not known gang violence. Even Utah, which historically has enjoyed a relatively low crime

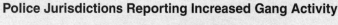

Gang Activity Jumped 50 Percent in 2002

Forty percent of police agencies reported an increase in local gang activity in 2002, a 50 percent rise over 2001, according to a research agency funded by the Department of Justice. Nationwide, there were some 21,500 gangs and 731,000 gang members in 2002.

Police Jurisdictions Reporting Increased Gang Activity

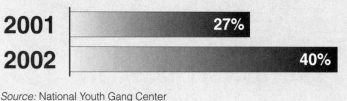

2001   27%

2002   40%

Source: National Youth Gang Center

rate, has at least 250 gangs with 3,000 members operating in the Salt Lake City region alone. [3]

Gang experts say the U.S. gang problem, which had diminished in the 1990s, has worsened dramatically in recent years. In 2001, for instance, 27 percent of police agencies polled by the National Youth Gang Center (NYGC), a research agency funded by the Department of Justice (DOJ), said gang activity was increasing in their jurisdictions. In 2002, however, the figure had jumped to more than 40 percent, with at least 21,500 gangs — and more than 731,000 members — active nationwide. [4] In addition to MS-13, the major groups include the Bloods, Crips, Black Gangster Disciples Nation, Almighty Latin Kings Nation and various so-called Jamaican posses, as well as outlaw motorcycle gangs and prison gangs.

Perhaps most alarmingly, the National Alliance of Gang Investigators Associations (NAGIA) says gangs have morphed from an urban scourge into a nationwide threat. "Gang membership has crossed all socioeconomic, ethnic and racial boundaries and now permeates American society," said an NAGIA report. "The gang problem today is much more pervasive and menacing than at any [other] time in history." [5]

Wesley McBride, president of the California Gang Investigators Association, told a Senate Judiciary Committee hearing on gang violence in September 2003 that while gang activity may wane periodically, it usually roars back at record levels. "While there have been occasional declines in gang activity over the years," McBride said, "the declines never seem to establish a record low [and]

the climactic rise at the end of the decline almost always sets a record." [7]

Moreover, authorities say, today's gangs are surprisingly well organized. The organizational chart of Chicago's 7,000-member Gangster Disciples — recovered during execution of a search warrant — was described by a federal prosecutor as "more sophisticated than many corporations." More than half the size of the Chicago Police Department, the gang had formed a political action committee, bought legitimate businesses and even sponsored community events, the prosecutor said. [9]

In the wake of the Sept. 11, 2001, terrorist attacks on the United States, gangs have even drawn the attention of the State Department and the Department of Homeland Security. Having already diversified from drug dealing into auto theft, extortion, property crimes and home invasion, some East Coast gangs have begun trafficking in fraudulent identification papers that could be used by terrorists trying to enter the country illegally.

While experts agree gangs are a serious problem, few agree on the causes or remedies. Even the definition of a gang is controversial. Some law enforcement officials say a youth gang is three or more 14-to-24-year-olds associating mainly, if not exclusively, to commit crimes. Others, like David Rathbun, a juvenile probation official in Fairfax County, Va., have simpler criteria for identifying gangs: "If it walks like a duck and quacks like a duck, it's probably a duck."

Because different authorities define gangs differently, national figures on gang activity and membership are often only "informed estimates," says NYGC Executive Director John Moore. But according to his organization's "fairly reliable" estimates, he says, 49 percent of U.S. gang members are Latino, 34 percent are black, 10 percent are white and 6 percent are Asian. While Latino and Asian gangs tend to be the most violent, white gangs have expanded into the most new territory over the last decade. [10]

Gangs also commit a disproportionate amount of urban violence. In Rochester, N.Y., for example, gang members who participated in a survey represented only 30 percent of the violent offenders in the region but committed 68 percent of the violent offenses. In Denver, gang members were only 14 percent of those surveyed but admitted to 79 percent of all violent, adolescent offenses committed in the city. [11] In fact, Moore says, 35 percent of Denver's homicides are gang-related.

Many gang victims are potential witnesses, police say. When not killing witnesses, gangs routinely intimidate them, usually through assault or rape. The U.S. attorney in New Orleans recently told Congress that witness intimidation had increased 50 percent in the previous year. [12] "Gangs have even been known to kill police officers who serve as witnesses against them," McBride said. [13]

Yet, the statistics can be tricky. For instance, the data show that overall gang membership and activity in smaller communities have decreased somewhat, but remain as high as ever — if not higher — in large cities and surrounding suburbs, Moore says. "They have decreased in smaller areas, but that's not where their strength ever was," he says.

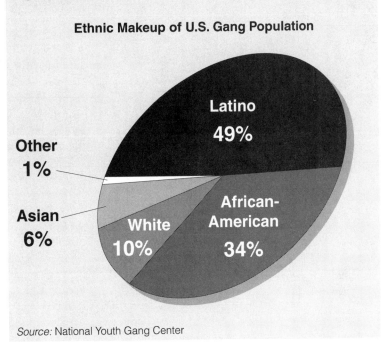

Most Gang Members Are Latino, Black

Nearly half of all U.S. gang members are Latino, and more than a third are black, according to a research agency funded by the Department of Justice. White gangs reportedly have expanded into the most new territory over the last decade, while Asian gangs have moved into the Northeast, and Latino, black and Asian gangs have migrated into the South.

Ethnic Makeup of U.S. Gang Population

Latino 49%
Other 1%
Asian 6%
White 10%
African-American 34%

Source: National Youth Gang Center

As law enforcement officials and policymakers try to assess America's gang problem, here are some of the questions under debate:

Is government doing enough to combat the problem?

Traditionally, state and local authorities have dealt with gangs, since they were not considered a federal problem. In addition to law enforcement, policymakers have tried a variety of prevention programs, such as midnight basketball, designed to give adolescents socially acceptable alternative activities. Other programs, such as vocational training, have offered at-risk youth the promise of legitimate jobs, since unemployment is a major reason kids join gangs.

As gangs migrated — or "franchised" themselves, as some officials describe it — from Los Angeles and other major cities, many police departments set up special gang units. Authorities felt they were keeping pace with the problem until gangs began increasing in the late 1980s and early '90s, when insufficient resources prevented police from keeping up. Since then, state and local authorities say they haven't been able to keep up with the increase. If the federal government would provide more resources, local law enforcement authorities say they could do more.

Several federal agencies assist in the fight against gangs. Since gang crime often involves guns, the Bureau of Alcohol, Tobacco, Firearms and Explosives (BATFE) investigates gangs. Similarly, gangs' frequent involvement with illegal drugs draws attention from the Drug Enforcement Administration (DEA).

Perhaps foremost among federal anti-gang agencies are the 75 FBI Safe Streets Gang Task Forces (SSGTFs) operating around the country. The SSGTFs emphasize "identification of the major violent street gangs [and] drug enterprises [that] pose significant threats," Grant D.

California Gang Investigators Association

Bloods gang members from Los Angeles display their gang signs and colors. Gang members generally don't wear their colors in public nowadays to avoid trouble from police or rival gangs.

Ashley, assistant director of the FBI's Criminal Investigative Division, told the Senate Judiciary Committee. [14]

"SSGTFs operate under the premise of cooperation between local, state and federal agencies," says Jeff Riley, chief of the FBI's Safe Streets and Gang Unit. "Once established, the SSGTFs are charged with bringing the resources of all the participating agencies to bear on the area's gang problem. This includes using sensitive investigative techniques, with an emphasis on long-term, proactive investigations into the violent criminal activities of the gang's leadership and hierarchy."

Moreover, when appropriate, U.S. attorneys "actively and creatively" prosecute gang crimes in federal courts, according to three U.S. attorneys who testified last September before the Judiciary Committee. In addition to using traditional narcotics and firearms statutes, federal prosecutors are using the Racketeer Influenced and Corrupt Organizations (RICO) law — successfully used to weaken the Mafia — against gangs. The U.S. attorney in Southern California recently convicted 75 members of the 18th Street and Mexican Mafia gangs under the RICO law. [15]

The DOJ also administers the Office of Juvenile Justice and Delinquency Prevention (OJJDP) and the Gang Resistance Education and Training (GREAT) program, which tries to develop positive relationships among local law enforcement, families and at-risk youths.

But McBride says federal law enforcement efforts have been ineffective because they have not been properly coordinated with state and local efforts. For instance, he says Los Angeles law enforcement agencies "hardly ever hear from" the FBI task force on gangs based in Los Angeles.

"You can almost compare [the situation] to the 9/11 hearings," says McBride, referring to the recent commission hearings that revealed a crucial lack of communication between various intelligence agencies before the terrorist attacks. "That's much like what's happening in the gang world."

Riley responds that the SSGTF in Los Angeles is located near the heart of the Watts section and focuses on inner-city gang activity, rather than on the more suburban activity McBride has been battling.

Fairfax County's Rathbun says the FBI task force in Northern Virginia, as well as U.S. immigration officials, works well with local officials, but he acknowledges that the level of cooperation varies from region to region.

But McBride, who recently retired from the Los Angeles County Sheriff's Department after 28 years of fighting gangs, contends that federal prosecution has not been effective. "You'd think they're prosecuting gang members right and left," says McBride, referring to the testimony at last September's Senate Judiciary Committee hearing. "I can tell you that U.S. attorneys don't want to see a gang case. They're very hard to prosecute, very labor-intensive and in their [U.S. attorneys'] defense, they simply can't handle all the cases — we probably arrest 40,000 gang members a year just in L.A. But don't say the feds are doing a great job of prosecuting gang members."

Many state and local authorities say they are best equipped to prosecute gangs, if the federal government would provide the necessary funding. Robert McCulloch, prosecuting attorney of St. Louis County, Mo., and president of the National District Attorneys Association, says 180 gangs with about 4,000 members are fighting a violent turf war in St. Louis. But he says most cases will never be prosecuted because he can't offer witness protection.

"Prosecutors across the county believe witness intimidation is the single, biggest hurdle facing successful gang prosecution," he said. In Denver, a defendant allegedly ordered a sexual assault on a female witness scheduled to testify in a gang homicide. In Savannah, a gang murder occurred in front of 300 people, but no one would identify the assailant. [16]

Most state and local jurisdictions cannot afford witness-protection programs or the training and overtime needed for gang investigations. The state budget crisis and tax cuts have sapped local funds, and the war on terrorism has forced the redeployment of anti-gang units. [17]

"There are already plenty of laws to prosecute gangs," says Beryl Howell, a former legislative director for Sen. Patrick J. Leahy, D-Vt., who worked on anti-juvenile-crime legislation in the mid-1990s. The obstacles to pursuing gangs effectively, she says, are "resource issues, not legal issues."

Sens. Orrin G. Hatch, R-Utah, and Dianne Feinstein, D-Calif., hope to remedy that with the Gang Prevention and Effective Deterrence Act of 2003. The bill would authorize approximately $100 million in federal funds annually for five years to underwrite area law enforcement efforts in jurisdictions with "high-intensity interstate gang activity." Another $40 million a year would fund prevention programs.

The Hatch-Feinstein bill would do more than provide desperately needed funds, says Bill Johnson, executive director of the National Association of Police Organizations and a former Florida prosecutor. It would also make participation in a "criminal street gang" and recruiting people to commit "gang crimes" federal offenses, punishable by 10 to 30 years in prison.

"It won't be the only solution, by any stretch of the imagination," he continues. "But if used properly, it'll help crush some of these gangs that really do overrun neighborhoods and communities."

But others are concerned that the bill would expand the federal role in fighting gangs, and in the process hamper local prosecutions. For instance, by redefining some state offenses as federal crimes, the bill could curtail state prosecutors' discretion in bringing charges and negotiating plea agreements, because defendants would be facing federal as well as state prosecution for gang crimes.

"We should be wary of making a federal crime out of everything," said Sen. Leahy. [18]

But Feinstein argues: "It used to be that gangs were local problems, demanding local, law-enforcement-based solutions. But over the last 12 years, I have seen the problem go from small to large and from neighborhood-based to national in scope. What were once loosely organized groups . . . are now complex criminal organizations whose activities include weapons trafficking, gambling, smuggling, robbery, and, of course, homicide. This is why we need a strong federal response."

Is There a Gang in Your 'Hood?

The following quiz can help neighborhoods measure potential gang activity. A score of 50 points or more indicates the need for a gang-prevention and intervention program:

In your community:

- Is there graffiti? (5 points)
- Is the graffiti crossed out? (10)
- Do the young people wear colors, jewelry, clothing, flash hand signs or display other behaviors that may be gang related? (10)
- Are drugs available? (10)
- Has there been a significant increase in the number of physical confrontations? (5)
- Is there an increasing presence of weapons? (5)
- Are beepers, pagers or cell phones used by the young people? (10)
- Has there been a "drive-by" shooting? (15)
- Have you had a "show-by" display of weapons? (10)
- Are truancies and/or daytime burglaries increasing? (5)
- Have racial incidents increased? (5)
- Is there a history of local gangs? (10)
- Is there an increasing presence of "informal social groups" with unusual names containing words like: kings, disciples, queens, posse, crew? (15)

Scoring Key

0-20 points = No Problem	50-65 points = You Have Problems
25-45 points = Emerging Problems	70+ points = You Have Serious Problems

Source: Tennessee Gang Investigators Association

The Violence of Mara Salvatrucha

David Rathbun has seen a lot of youngsters come through the juvenile justice system in Fairfax County, Va., near Washington, D.C. But he can't shake the memory of the 11-year-old charged with murder.

The boy and his 16-year-old brother belonged to Mara Salvatrucha, a Latino gang known for its violence. The two boys were out early one morning, "looking for trouble," says Rathbun, a juvenile-probation official. When they thought a youth across the street flashed a rival gang's sign at them — a gesture of disrespect — they crossed the street and stabbed him to death.

Violence is a gang's normal stock-in-trade, but gang experts say Mara Salvatrucha — or MS-13 — has made shootings, stabbings, hackings, beatings and rapes its brazen specialties. The gang originated in Los Angeles among refugees of El Salvador's civil war of the 1980s and rapidly spread around the country. The gang was formed in Los Angeles to protect Salvadoran immigrants from other, hostile Latino immigrants, according to veteran gang investigator Wesley McBride. The theory was: strike back twice as violently as you were attacked, and they'll leave you alone. Many MS-13s had been guerrilla fighters in El Salvador's bloody civil war.

MS-13 began as a merger between immigrants who'd been involved with La Mara — a street gang in El Salvador — and former members of the FMNL, a paramilitary group of Salvadoran guerrilla fighters called "Salvatruchas."

MS-13's victims have included innocent people caught in the middle as well as other gang members. In 2002, MS-13's Los Angeles cell reportedly dispatched several members to Fairfax County with instructions to kill a county police officer "at random." They didn't succeed. [1]

The Justice Department says MS-13 now has about 8,000 members in 27 states and the District of Columbia, and 20,000 more members in Central and South America, particularly El Salvador. The gang is involved in smuggling and selling illegal drugs, but different cells (or cliques, as they're sometimes called) may be involved in other activities, including providing "protection" to houses of prostitution, Rathbun says.

The independent National Gang Crime Research Center (NGCRC) ranks gangs by their violence level, with 1 being least dangerous and 3 the most dangerous. MS-13 is ranked a 3. Center Director George W. Knox describes MS-13's level of violence as "extraordinary." [2]

An investigator with the Orange County, Calif., district attorney's office says the gang participates in a broad range of criminal activities across the country. "MS members have been involved in burglaries, auto thefts, narcotic sales, home-invasion robberies, weapons smuggling, car jacking, extortion, murder, rape, witness intimidation, illegal firearm sales, car theft and aggravated assaults. . . . [C]ommon drugs sold by MS members include cocaine, marijuana, heroin, and methamphetamine. Mara Salvatrucha

Others are concerned about the historic conflicts between federal and state/local investigations and prosecutions. While SSGTFs are designed to work cooperatively with local authorities, differences remain in their investigative priorities. For instance, federal investigators' concentration on building cases over time will usually net more convictions, but local authorities often need to respond more quickly to community complaints, usually with street sweeps that can interfere with federal investigations.

Should gun laws be tightened to combat gang violence?

More than 350,000 incidents of gun violence, including 9,369 homicides, were committed in 2002, according to Michael Rand, chief of victimization statistics at the Justice

Department's Bureau of Justice Statistics. But no one knows what percentage of those murders were committed by gang members, partly because of disagreement over what constitutes gang-related crime. To some officials, if two gang members commit an armed robbery, the crime can only be considered gang-related if they share the proceeds with the rest of the gang. To others, any armed robbery committed by gang members qualifies as gang-related.

According to the BATFE, 41 percent of the 88,570 guns used in crimes in 46 large cities in 2000 were traced to people age 24 or younger. [19] Of course, no one knows how many of them were gang members.

But as a recent Justice Department survey concluded: "Although both gang members and at-risk youths admitted

gang members have even placed a 'tax' on prostitutes and non-gang member drug dealers who are working in MS 'turf.' Failure to pay up will most likely result in violence." [3]

One of the gang's signatures is a military-style booby trap used to protect a stash of illegal drugs. The trap usually consists of a tripwire rigged to an anti-personnel grenade.

Joining the gang requires potential members to be "jumped in." Several gangs observe this ritual, which involves a group-administered beating. Typically, gang members surround the candidate and then attack him; other gang members evaluate how well he defends himself and his ability to endure punches. MS-13's jumping-in lasts for 13 seconds.

Most MS-13 members are between ages 11 and 40, but leaving the gang is often difficult. The father of the two

AFP Photo

Police arrested this Mara Salvatrucha leader last year in San Salvador, El Salvador. Thousands of the gang's most violent U.S. members have been deported.

boys who stabbed the suspected rival gang member to death is also an MS-13 member; the mother wholeheartedly supports her husband's and sons' memberships, Rathbun says.

The 16-year-old was tried as an adult and sentenced to a maximum-security prison, but Rathbun has hope for the 11-year-old, who took school classes when he was in the county's juvenile system. "He had a probation officer that worked very closely with him, and his sense of self-worth increased as he did better academically. He stayed in touch with the gang, but he wasn't participating any more. I don't think his father will ever be out of MS-13, but, knock wood, I think we may have changed the son's course."

[1] "Focus on Gangs: Salvadoran MS-13 Rated Among Most Violent," *Emergency Net News*, Aug. 24, 2002; http://www.emergency.com/polcpage.htm.

[2] *Ibid.*

[3] Al Valdez, "A South American Import," National Alliance of Gang Investigators Associations, 2000; http://www.nagia.org/mara_salvatrucha.htm.

significant involvement with guns, gang members were far likelier to own guns, and the guns they owned were larger caliber." More than 80 percent of gang members surveyed said either they or their fellow members had carried concealed guns into school, while only one-third of at-risk youths said they or their friends had done the same. [20] The most popular weapons were 9mm semiautomatic pistols. [21]

"Gangs, like any criminals, can never be as effective without firearms," says Joe Vince, a retired BATFE analyst. "Absolutely, guns are a tool of the trade for gangs — you've never heard of a drive-by with a knife."

Vince regularly investigated gangs' gun-show purchases, where unlicensed firearms dealers are exempt from the Brady Handgun Violence Prevention Act, which requires licensed sellers to perform a criminal background check before selling a weapon. Since it is illegal for anyone to sell a firearm to a buyer with a criminal record, gangs often send buyers who don't have criminal records to gun shows. [22]

Such "straw purchases" are also illegal, but unscrupulous unlicensed dealers pretend not to recognize a suspicious purchase, even when an 18-year-old is trying to buy a dozen guns at once, Vince says. "We found a lot of gangs sending someone who didn't have a record to gun shows, and he'd be on a cell phone talking to the gang leaders and saying, 'Hey, this guy's offering this, and that guy's offering that,' " Vince says.

"Some dealers even advertise that they're not licensed, so you can buy from them no-questions-asked," says Garen Wintemute, director of the Violence Prevention Research Program at the University of California, Davis.

In Chicago — which now may have the nation's largest and most active gang population — gangs are blamed for 45 percent of last year's 598 homicides. [23] Authorities also believe Chicago has more illegal firearms than any other city: In 2003, Chicago police seized more than 10,000 illegal guns; Los Angeles police recovered just under 7,000 and New York City under 4,000. [24]

Gun control advocates maintain that tougher gun laws and more stringent enforcement of them could cut gang violence. "Wherever you can reduce the availability and accessibility of firearms to criminals, you reduce violent crime," Vince says. "People just cannot be as violent without a gun."

However, Erich Pratt, communications director for Gun Owners of America (GOA), says, "We've yet to discover any gun control legislation that successfully keeps guns out of the wrong hands. Washington, D.C., is certainly the epitome of that — you have a draconian gun ban there that doesn't let anybody own any guns, and yet the bad guys continue to get firearms."

Data compiled by the Bureau of Justice Statistics show that handgun homicides started decreasing in 1993 — a year before Congress enacted the Brady law — and continued to fall through 2000.

But a study in the *Journal of the American Medical Association* suggests no link between the decrease and the Brady law. "We find no differences in homicide or firearms homicide rates in the 32 . . . states directly subject to the Brady Act provisions compared with the remaining [18] states," the researchers wrote. [25]

Wintemute says the results could be interpreted in two equally valid ways: "One is that the Brady law never went far enough from the beginning," he says, "or that the Brady law is a failure and we should get rid of it."

Supporters of the law say that at the least it has prevented the crime rate from worsening. But Andrew Arulanandam, public affairs director for the National Rifle Association (NRA), says the law's stringent record-keeping provisions make that unlikely.

"You mean to tell me that some guy who's going to commit a heinous crime is going to leave a paper trail?" Arulanandam asks. Gang members are "not going to be deterred by a firearm law. More often than not, they'll obtain the firearm by illegal means."

But record-keeping is diminishing. Because of a provision in the Omnibus Appropriations bill, passed last January, federal authorities who run criminal background checks on gun buyers are no longer required to keep a record of the check for 90 days. In fact, they must now destroy the record within 24 hours.

Moreover, Eric Howard, spokesman for the Brady Campaign to Prevent Gun Violence, says the Department of Justice recently found that Brady background checks blocked more than a million potential purchasers from buying guns. "This flies in the face of what [the NRA] says all the time: That these guys aren't going to get background checks, they'll get guns elsewhere," Howard says. "Well, these guys aren't the sharpest knives in the drawer." The Brady law could very well have kept the nation's crime rate lower than it might otherwise have been in the past decade, Howard argues. [26]

Nonetheless, some states enforce the Brady law less stringently, so gangs go to those states. For instance, gangs in Chicago have established a gun-running pipeline into Mississippi, where Brady enforcement and local gun laws are generally more relaxed. [27]

Opponents of gun control say this proves their point: Regardless of how many prohibited purchases are blocked, criminals will always find a way to get firearms. The best deterrent, they say, is not to limit the number of guns on the street but to increase them — by allowing law-abiding citizens to carry concealed weapons. "States that have adopted concealed-carry legislation are seeing the greatest and most dramatic decreases in the murder rate," Pratt says.

The gun problem is like the drug problem, says the NRA's Arulanandam. "Drugs are outlawed, but people get their hands on them."

The BATFE's Vince agrees with the comparison, but he and other gun control advocates want to close the gun-show loophole, which the gun lobby says would penalize law-abiding, unlicensed dealers.

"If you focus law enforcement only on gun users but not on dealers," he says, "that's like saying we're going to go after everyone that shoots heroin but not the cartel."

Should more minors be tried as adults for gang crimes?

An undercover Chicago police officer working a drug deal in the depressed Humboldt Park neighborhood in April noticed two young men run into an alley. Seconds later, he heard gunshots and saw the men running out. A third man lay dying in the alley.

As the cop chased the suspects, they turned and fired at him. He continued chasing them and eventually caught them. One was 18, the other 15. Both were members of the Maniac Latin Disciples. "I wanted to shoot a Cobra" — a rival gang — "to prove how tough I was," the 15-year-old reportedly said. He was charged as an adult with first-degree murder. [28]

In colonial days, children sometimes faced adult charges and just as often were incarcerated with adults; sometimes they were executed. [29] In the late 19th century, however, social reformers argued that juveniles were developmentally different from adults and could be rehabilitated. The nation established a juvenile justice system — with separate statutes and penalties — at the beginning of the 20th century.

But in cases involving violent crimes, prosecutors sometimes try minors as adults, triggering debate over the tactic's effectiveness and justification. A surge in juvenile crime beginning in the late 1980s — largely triggered by a crack epidemic — led many minors to be charged as adults. A 1989 Supreme Court ruling allowing states to execute juvenile offenders 16 and older has kept the debate alive.

Currently, state prosecutors decide whether minors charged with violent felonies should be charged as adults. But the proposed Hatch-Feinstein bill would allow federal prosecutors to try any gang member 16 or older as an adult.

The legislation has triggered debates over whether more minors should be tried as adults, and whether the federal government should be trying minors at all. "We're always uncomfortable when furthering policies that take things that should be state matters and throw them into federal courts," the GOA's Pratt says. "We agree that if you do an adult crime, you do the adult time, but we think the states [should] handle it."

"The feds don't have any infrastructure set up to deal with juveniles, so they usually defer to the states, and wisely so," says Rathbun of Fairfax County. "We've had a couple of murder cases where the feds got involved, and it was useful because [the accused] got harsher sentences. But that's just a handful of our cases."

However, former legislative director Howell believes that federal authorities can more effectively prosecute gangs than state or local authorities. "The gang problem warrants federal attention because it quickly overtakes local and state boundaries," she says. "It can overtake national boundaries, too."

For example, as a federal prosecutor Howell once went after members of the Flying Dragons, which ran gambling and Mah Jong parlors in New York's Chinatown. But the gang also smuggled heroin from Hong Kong. The investigation had to contend with the respective requirements and laws affecting New York and Hong Kong authorities, not to mention language and cultural complications between both cities.

But prosecuting juveniles as adults won't solve the gang problem, she says. "Where does that get you?" she asks. "The younger you send kids to prison, the better-educated they become at being criminals. Adult prisons have lost much pretense, if they ever had any, of being rehabilitative. With the juvenile system, there's at least a pretense of rehabilitation."

Federal prosecution of minors as adults would be "a good law to have on the books and threaten with, but it's not going to help much," adds McBride, of the California Gang Investigators Association. States have tougher provisions on minors and gangs than federal agencies, he notes, and states aren't making any demonstrable headway against gangs by prosecuting minors as adults.

Trying minors as adults "is an effective tool the same way a sledge hammer is an effective tool," says the National Association of Police Organizations' Johnson. "It ought to be used sparingly, but in those cases where it's necessary, then it ought to be used."

More than 60 child-advocacy organizations oppose the Senate bill's provision to prosecute juveniles as adults for gang crimes. "I understand the desire to respond to gang violence," said Marc Schindler, a staff attorney for the Youth Law Center. "But this is the wrong way to do it. It's basically going to throw kids away to the adult system." [30]

Even law-and-order hard-liners acknowledge that the threat of severe punishment alone will not deter gangs. "A lot of gang members are in gangs because their parents didn't give a rat's behind about them," says McBride, echoing experts on all sides of the issue. "How do you make a momma care for her kid? You can't legislate that."

The best deterrent to gangs, many experts say, is to have parents involved with their children's lives, but in today's economy, that's often nearly impossible. Some observers attribute the rise in immigrant gangs to the fact that both parents often work multiple jobs and have little time to spend with their kids.

CHRONOLOGY

1950s *Southern blacks migrate to Northern inner cities; classic era of teen street gangs; wave of Puerto Rican immigrants arrives in New York City.*

Sept. 26, 1957 Leonard Bernstein's hit musical "West Side Story" opens on Broadway. It looks unflinchingly at the growing menace of gang warfare.

1960s *Gangs take on traits from civil rights, Black Muslim and radical youth movements; government channels some gangs into anti-poverty work.*

1961 President John F. Kennedy signs Juvenile Delinquency and Youth Offenses and Control Act, creating a federal committee to address youth crime.

1967 President's Task Force on Juvenile Delinquency calls for community efforts to curb youth crime. . . . Senate probes fraud in federal grant program for Chicago's Blackstone Rangers gang.

1970s *Police officials and academics shift their strategies on gangs from social work to suppression and control.*

Aug. 21, 1974 Congress creates Office of Juvenile Justice and Delinquency Prevention.

1975 Justice Department launches first national gang survey.

1980s *Latino and Asian immigrants make Los Angeles the nation's gang capital; crack cocaine arrives in inner cities; Reagan administration declares war on drugs.*

1982 FBI designates motorcycle gangs as national investigative priority within its organized-crime program.

1985 California creates State Task Force on Youth Gang Violence; L.A. Police Chief Daryl F. Gates vows to eliminate gangs in five years.

Late 1980s Highly profitable crack cocaine becomes the product of choice for drug-dealing gangs, sparking fights over the most profitable turf and a spike in violent crime.

1988 President Ronald Reagan signs Anti-Drug Abuse Act. . . . California convenes State Task Force on Gangs and Drugs; Los Angeles police crack down on gang neighborhoods.

May 15, 1989 Administration of first President George Bush bans imports of semiautomatic assault weapons used by street gangs.

1990s *Gangs expand out from inner cities; government, police and academics coordinate comprehensive approach to the gang problem.*

1995 Gang homicides in Los Angeles hit a record 809 deaths . . . more than half of all violent crime in Buffalo, N.Y., is gang related.

1997 FBI estimates that 50,000 gang members are active in Chicago. . . . Congress attempts to overhaul the U.S. juvenile justice system, but the bill deadlocks over juvenile sentencing and gun control.

1999 Congress again addresses juvenile justice, but House and Senate negotiators again stall over gun control.

2000s *Police say gang violence begins to rise; Asian and Latino gangs account for most juvenile violence; Congress again attempts to pass anti-gang legislation.*

Sept. 11, 2001 Terrorist strikes against the U.S. cause many police departments to reassign special gang units to counter-terrorist duties.

January 2004 Congress passes Omnibus Appropriations bill, which contains a provision voiding the Brady law's requirement that the National Instant Criminal Background Check system maintain records of criminal checks for 90 days; gun control advocates claim this will make it harder for authorities to trace crime guns to gang members and other criminals.

April 2004 Senate Judiciary Committee begins consideration of the Gang Prevention and Effective Deterrence Act, sponsored by Sens. Dianne Feinstein, D-Calif., and Orrin Hatch, R-Utah. Committee approval is expected in May.

Whatever the causes, the rise in gang crime has made some authorities open to anything that might help. Los Angeles County's sheriff recently estimated that the 96,000 gang members in his jurisdiction commit half the violent offenses each year. "We believe there are teenagers close to 18 who are committing heinous adult acts, and they should be treated as an adult," said Steve Whitmore, a spokesman for the L.A. sheriff's office. [31]

BACKGROUND

Early Gangs

The youth gang phenomenon dates back at least to the days of St. Augustine (A.D. 354-430), who wrote in his *Confessions* of the pleasures of stealing pears with adolescent accomplices: "My pleasure was not in those pears, it was in the offense itself, which the company of fellow sinners occasioned." [32]

In 17th-century London, youth gangs with such names as the Mims, the Bugles and the Dead Boys terrorized the citizenry by breaking windows, destroying taverns and fighting, each group wearing different-colored ribbons. And Charles Dickens often wrote about gangs in the 19th century, perhaps most famously the gang of boy orphans run by the money-grubbing Fagin in the classic *Oliver Twist*.

In the United States, the first recorded youth gang was the Forty Thieves, founded in about 1825 in Lower Manhattan. Others appeared in Philadelphia in the 1840s, such as the Bouncers, the Rats and the Skinners. Mostly they defaced walls with graffiti and carried pistols and knives.

Immigrants usually formed gangs for self-protection. Often not speaking the language of their new country and unfamiliar with its customs, they found assimilation extremely difficult. Discrimination added a sense of victimization to their existing feelings of alienation, and they saw gangs as a refuge from a hostile environment.

Waves of Irish immigrants in New York in the 19th century soon begat such gangs as the Bowery Boys and the Dead Rabbits, who waged three-day rumbles that

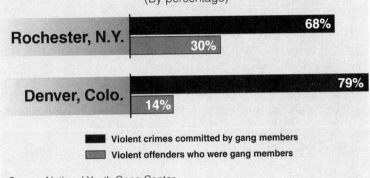

Gangs Commit Most Violent Teen Crimes

Gang members make up a small percentage of violent offenders but commit a disproportionate amount of teenage violent crime, as shown by statistics from Rochester, N.Y., and Denver, Colo.

Violent Crimes Committed by Gang Members
(By percentage)

Rochester, N.Y. — 68% / 30%

Denver, Colo. — 79% / 14%

■ Violent crimes committed by gang members
■ Violent offenders who were gang members

Source: National Youth Gang Center

forced helpless police to call in the Army. Their nonchalance toward violence was remarkable: A member of the Plug Uglies is said to have attacked a stranger and cracked his spine in three places just to win a $2 bet. [33] Female gang members also were known in the mid-19th century, among them the celebrated street fighters Hellcat Annie and Battle Annie. [34]

Early New York gangs, as brutally portrayed in the 2002 movie "Gangs of New York," often sold their services to labor unions and company operators maneuvering in the rough and tumble world of politics. "By 1855," a city historian wrote, "it was estimated that the Metropolis contained at least 30,000 men who owed allegiance to gang leaders and through them to the leaders of Tammany Hall and the Know Nothing, or Native American Party." [35] During the Civil War, Irish gang members were blamed for the anti-conscription riots in which many blacks were lynched.

The German and Italian immigrants who arrived in the late 19th century produced equally violent gangs. Some would commit crimes for hire: A slash on the cheek with a knife cost $10; throwing a bomb, $50; murder, $100. "It might be inferred that the New York tough is a very fierce individual [but] it is only when he hunts with the pack that he is dangerous," noted social reformer and photographer Jacob Riis. [36]

When Girls Join Gangs

In Augusta, Ga., six members of an all-girl gang corner a 22-year-old woman on the street and savagely beat her. [1] In San Antonio, Texas, two girls slash a rival gang girl's face with a broken bottle. [2] In Buffalo, N.Y., female members of a mixed gang transport narcotics and sometimes sell drugs on the streets. [3]

Gang members are usually seen as young men wearing distinctive clothes or colors, using a common slang and hand signals and fighting with gangs from other neighborhoods. If females are in the picture at all, they're usually viewed as supporting players — girlfriends, perhaps, or maybe sisters, but never gang members in their own right. Yet, female gangs have existed in America at least since the 19th century.

Relatively little is known about female gangs, however, and most of the knowledge has been acquired only in the last 20 years. Sexist stereotyping has largely been responsible for the lack of awareness, according to the Justice Department's Office of Juvenile Justice and Delinquency Prevention (OJJDP). Researchers historically perceived gangs in terms of vandalism, theft and assault — generally considered male provinces.

"It was often assumed that females did not take part in such behavior, so early researchers were not interested in the delinquency of female gang members," wrote sociologist Joan Moore and criminologist John Hagedorn in an issue of the Juvenile Justice Bulletin devoted to female gangs. [4]

When gang activity escalated in the 1980s and '90s, researchers began noticing that female gangs were either autonomous entities or affiliates of male gangs. With names like Latin Queens, the female counterpart to Latin Kings, and Sisters of the Struggle, they usually had their own identities and structures.

No one knows how many female gangs exist. Law enforcement surveys tend to show that between 4 and 11 percent of gang members are female, but social-service surveys show higher numbers.

Although little is known about female gang activity, some research and anecdotal reports show that most girl gangs are involved in delinquency or non-violent crimes, with drug offenses ranking near the top of the list. Female gang members commit fewer violent crimes than male gang members and in general are more prone to property crime. [5]

"The biggest difference between female gangs and male gangs is violence," says Hagedorn, a professor of criminal justice at the University of Illinois. "Girls are very seldom involved in homicide. The difference between males and females on this issue is massive."

Still, he acknowledges, female gang members can sometimes be just as violent as males. In the mid-1990s, an 11-city survey of eighth-graders revealed that more than 90 percent of male and female gang members admitted to having commit-

The most notorious of the early immigrant gangs in New York was, of course, the Mafia, or La Cosa Nostra ("Our Thing"), which originated as a criminal organization in Sicily. The Mafia rose to power by extorting neighborhood shopkeepers for "protection" money against arson. It consolidated its power during Prohibition, when it controlled the illegal distribution of liquor in many U.S. cities.

By the turn of the century, Jewish gangs and Chinese gangs had been added to the ethnic stew in New York's Bowery, Chinatown and in such rough neighborhoods as Hell's Kitchen on the West Side. During Prohibition, many youth gangs became involved with adult bootleggers. In Southern California, waves of Mexican immigrants arrived to form the first so-called barrio gangs.

But the worst gang problems plagued Chicago. In 1927 criminologist Frederick M. Thrasher published the

first major book on the problem, *The Gang: A Study of 1,313 Gangs in Chicago*, in which he analyzed gangs of every ethnic and racial stripe: Polish, Irish, Anglo-American, Jewish, Slavic, Bohemian, German, Swedish, Lithuanian, black, Chinese and Mexican. "The gang is a conflict group," Thrasher wrote. "It develops through strife and warfare."

The ethnic character of American gangs continued to manifest itself. In the 1930s, the rising numbers of blacks migrating from the South to New York, as well as new immigrants from the British West Indies, set up the first rivalries among black gangs. In the early 1940s, gangs of Latino youths in Southern California frequently clashed with U.S. servicemen stationed in the area, eventually provoking the so-called Zoot Suit Riots, named for a flashy clothing style then popular among Latinos.

ted one or more violent acts in the previous 12 months. Moreover, 78 percent of female gang members reported having been in a gang fight, 65 percent acknowledged carrying a weapon and 39 percent said they had attacked someone with a weapon. [6]

Within mixed gangs, males commonly boast that the females are their sex objects, a claim that has perpetuated the "sex slave" stereotype of female gang members. But OJJDP research done in conjunction with the National Youth Gang Center shows that females deny this, insisting that females of any position or authority in the gang are respected precisely because they do not allow the males to exploit them sexually. Sexual exploitation does occur, they say, but almost always involving girls or young women who are not members of the gang.

Currently, most female gangs are Latina and African-American, though the numbers of Asian and white female gangs have been increasing.

Regardless of ethnicity or race, many girls join gangs for the same reasons as males — seeking friendship and self-affirma-

Female gang members commit fewer violent crimes than male gang members, primarily property and drug offenses.

tion. Sometimes the lack of job opportunities pushes girls and young women to join gangs, as it does boys and young men. But many female gang members share a common pain of childhood, which they have tried to escape by seeking refuge in a gang. "Research consistently shows that high proportions of female gang members have experienced sexual abuse at home," Hagedorn and Moore write.

There's another important difference between female and male gang members: Females tend to leave a gang sooner because they get pregnant, usually by age 18.

[1] See "Woman Reports Gang Assault," *The Augusta Chronicle*, Feb. 22, 2004, p. B3.

[2] See Elda Silva, "'Homegirls' Gets Personal, Introspective," *The San Antonio Express-News*, Jan. 29, 2004, p. 1F.

[3] See Lou Michel, "The Bloods, Settling Debts with Death," *Buffalo News*, Dec. 16, 2003, p. A1.

[4] See Joan Moore and John Hagedorn, "Female Gangs: A Focus on Research," *Juvenile Justice Bulletin*, March 2001, p. 1.

[5] *Ibid*, p. 5.

[6] *Ibid*, p. 6.

Seeking Respectability

The classic youth-gang era began after World War II, when Americans migrated from the farms to the cities. The first "teenage" subculture emerged in the postwar period, and gangs severed their earlier ties to adult organized crime.

In Los Angeles, two black gangs appeared — the Businessmen and the Home Street Gang. In the 1950s, CBS News correspondent Edward R. Murrow drew nationwide attention to the conditions that produce gangs with the documentary "Who Killed Michael Farmer?" about the death of a handicapped young man at the hands of a Bronx street gang.

Society responded to gangs by trying to build long-term relationships with gang members and by sponsoring dances or athletic contests, such as a New York City Youth Board program that sought to reduce gang tensions. "Participation in a street gang or club," a 1950 Youth Board document read, "like participation in any natural group, is part of the growing-up process. . . . Within the structure of the group the individual can develop such characteristics as loyalty, leadership and community responsibility. . . . Some gangs . . . have developed patterns of anti-social behavior . . . [but] members can be reached and will respond to sympathy, acceptance, affection and understanding when approached by adults who possess those characteristics and reach out to them on their own level." [37]

In the 1960s, the Hell's Angels motorcycle gang gained national exposure and greatly influenced the younger, more ethnic urban gangs. "By 1965," wrote counterculture journalist Hunter S. Thompson, later of

AFP Photo/Mike Nelson

The Rev. Greg Boyle, a Jesuit priest, runs a jobs program in East Los Angeles for gang members who want to stop being criminals.

Rolling Stone fame, "[gangs] were firmly established as All-American bogeymen." Meanwhile, the decade's civil rights movement, urban riots and radical politics spilled over into the world of gangs, particularly among blacks, many of whom would become attracted to revolutionary groups like the Black Panthers.

With President Lyndon B. Johnson's War on Poverty pouring millions of federal grant dollars into inner cities, some criminal youth gangs decided to join the Establishment, heralding either an optimistic or opportunistic approach to addressing social problems, depending on one's viewpoint.

In New York City in 1967, for example, leaders of the Puerto Rican gang Spartican Army decided they wanted a role in bettering the social and economic conditions of their Lower East Side neighborhoods. Borrowing from Johnson's Great Society rhetoric, they took the name the Real Great Society and applied for a grant from the federal Office of Economic Opportunity (OEO). They were turned down, but their well-publicized efforts (profiled in *Life* magazine) attracted private foundation money. They opened a Real Great Society nightclub, a child-care service and a leather-goods store, all of which blossomed briefly but failed within a year. [38] They then organized summer classes for inner-city youths and finally won an OEO grant.

In Chicago, meanwhile, another experiment in gang respectability was under way. In 1967, the Blackstone Rangers, led by a fervent black nationalist, Jeff Fort, began toying with the notion of doing anti-poverty work

with a radical white clergyman, John Fry, who was affiliated with a community-organizing group named for Chicago's Woodlawn neighborhood. Because the group opposed Chicago's powerful mayor, Richard J. Daley, its anti-poverty programs had never received federal grant money, over which Daley had de facto control.

But the possible turnaround of the Blackstone Rangers was too tempting to Washington. In June, the OEO awarded the Woodlawn Organization and the Blackstone Rangers $927,000 to operate anti-poverty programs for a year.

Daley was furious at fellow Democrats in the Johnson administration, but he did not have to fume for long. The Woodlawn program quickly became known as a monumental boondoggle: Only 76 of 800 participants in its jobs program got jobs; bookkeeping was lax; gang members encouraged each other to quit school and be paid from the federal grant; by autumn, Fort had been arrested on murder charges. [39]

In Washington, Sen. John L. McClellan, D-Ark., chairman of the Government Operations Committee, held widely publicized hearings into the Woodlawn grant. Many blamed the OEO for poor judgment. While under indictment, Fort appeared as a witness but refused to speak. (The murder charges against him were later dismissed.)

In May 1968, OEO shut down the Woodlawn project, just weeks after the Blackstone Rangers were given credit for keeping Chicago relatively calm during the urban riots that followed the assassination of the Rev. Dr. Martin Luther King, Jr. The idealistic notion of giving government money to reformed gang members had suffered a crippling blow.

The impact of Chicago's gang experiment during the days of the War on Poverty would be felt for decades. Chicago gang members continued to receive foundation money for nearly 20 years. Fort was sentenced to prison in the early 1970s for fraud committed with the OEO grant. In prison, he converted to Islam and changed the Rangers' name to El Rukns (Arabic for "the foundation").

When he and some fellow gang members emerged from prison in the late 1970s, they threw themselves into the violent drug trade. Dozens of El Rukns members were sent to prison in the early 1980s. In 1987, Fort was sentenced to 75 years in prison for soliciting money from Libya to fund terrorist operations in the U.S. [40]

In the 1980s, crack cocaine became the product of choice for drug-dealing gangs: Highly addictive and inexpensive, crack provided a profit margin greater than powdered cocaine. Gangs soon were fighting over the most profitable turf — markets — giving rise to drive-by shootings and a spike in violent crime.

War Refugees

In El Salvador, civil war in the early 1980s prompted many refugees — and former guerrillas — to flee to the United States. The Mara Salvatrucha, or MS-13, gang emerged from a rapidly swelling population of Salvadoran immigrants in Los Angeles. Other gangs with roots in the Central American immigrant communities of Southern California also formed, and violence frequently erupted between them and the area's long-established Mexican gangs.

Asian gangs began appearing around the same time, mostly as a result of massive Asian immigration, including the "boat people," refugees from war-ravaged Southeast Asia. The gangs of Vietnamese, Cambodian and Laotian refugees had roots in the region's refugee camps following the Vietnam War and the post-war atrocities committed by the Khmer Rouge in Cambodia. [41] By the late 1980s and early '90s, Asian gangs had footholds from West Valley City, Utah, to Manhattan. "When I was a prosecutor in New York," Howell recalls, "the Vietnamese gangs were as violent as anybody."

Throughout the late 1980s and early '90s, many Latino gang members in L.A. headed north to Chicago, already teeming with black, white and mixed-race gangs. In 1991, the city's homicide rate hit a record 609 deaths. In response, Mayor Richard M. Daley recalled the gang-grant scandal from the era when his famous father had run city hall. The younger Daley lashed out at the liberal "social workers" of the 1960s and '70s who had "coddled" the teenage gang members who were now, as adults, Chicago's drug kingpins.

In an effort to reduce the nation's crime rate, Congress in 1996 enacted a law that allows deportation of non-citizens sentenced to a year or more in prison for anything ranging from petty theft to murder. Since then, in what constitutes the largest dragnet in the country's history, more than 500,000 "criminal aliens" have been deported to more than 130 countries, including many gang members who originally immigrated to the United States with their parents to escape poverty or civil war. [42] While the tactic has effectively reduced the number of criminals in the United States, it has overwhelmed the receiv-

ing countries, particularly in Latin America and the Caribbean, which have seen crime rates skyrocket since 1996.

Many of the deported have joined local gangs — often home-country versions of the gangs they belonged to in the United States. El Salvador and Honduras have suffered particularly sharp rises in violent gang crime, with beheadings, shootings, rapes and hackings now commonplace, police say. Moreover, vigilante groups often hunt down gang members and murder them on sight — a practice both U.S. and Latin American officials say only causes retaliation and escalation. [43]

By 1997, the chief of the FBI's violent-crime section estimated that Chicago had 50,000 active gang members — more than the combined area membership of the Moose, the Elks, the Knights of Columbus and the Shriners. [44] Meanwhile, in the previous 16 years approximately 7,300 people had died in gang violence in Los Angeles.

But Chicago and L.A. were not alone. In 1995, police blamed gangs for 41 percent of Omaha's homicides, and more than half of all violent crime in Buffalo. In Phoenix, gang-related homicides jumped 800 percent between 1990 and '94. [45] While the overall violent-crime rate across the country was dropping, violent juvenile crime remained high.

In response, lawmakers drafted the Violent and Repeat Juvenile Justice Act of 1997. The House passed its version of the bill, but the Senate's version — opposed by countless advocacy groups — never made it to a floor vote. Liberals felt it was too harsh, citing its intention to prosecute juveniles as adults and house them with adults in prison. Conservatives felt it penalized law-abiding gun merchants and owners.

Congress tried again in early 1999 with Democrats and Republicans apparently determined to compromise on the issue. But the bipartisan spirit was shattered in April, when two teenagers in Littleton, Colo., went on a shooting rampage at Columbine High School, killing 13 people before turning the guns on themselves. [46] Both the House and Senate passed juvenile crime bills, but liberals and conservatives deadlocked over gun control, effectively killing the bills in conference.

Starting in 1995, juvenile violent crime began falling, and continued falling through 2001, but in 2002 authorities began seeing an upsurge in gang violence. [47] Latino and Asian gangs were committing the most violent offenses, particularly along the Northeast Corridor. Of the two, the Latinos have drawn the most attention because their numbers are currently the largest. And among the Latinos, MS-13 is widely considered the most dangerous.

CURRENT SITUATION

Invisible Crisis

If many Americans are unaware of the country's gang crisis, it may be because some police departments don't want them to know about it. The National Alliance of Gang Investigators Associations says many law enforcement agencies have refused to cooperate with its nationwide survey of gang activities.

"We're getting so many of those forms back from [police] departments refusing to fill them out," McBride says. "The local authorities say, 'We don't want to ruin our economy, because companies won't move here if they know we have gangs!' " McBride says. "I even had one executive tell me that people don't have a right to know, and no sense scaring them. I was flabbergasted. People absolutely have a right to know and need to know how many gangs are out there."

But sometimes the agencies don't respond because of poor record keeping, he says. In Denver, for example, police records show that the city's 17,000 gang members committed only 89 of the 59,581 crimes in 2002. "I heard that figure, and I just wanted to laugh," said a member of the metropolitan police department's gang crimes unit. [48] Moore, of the National Youth Gang Center, says officers often do not know immediately that a crime is gang related; when they find out, they rarely revise the initial police report.

Another problem is the cyclical nature of gangs and gang prevention. Police departments often set up gang units and then dissolve them once they believe the situation is under control, only to see the problem worsen again. "There's just no continuity of incident reporting," Moore says, so police records on gangs are "notoriously slack."

Four years ago, when acknowledging a gang problem carried less stigma than it does today, the NAGIA assembled a national picture of gangs and gang activities that many say is still essentially accurate. Starting in the late 1990s, gangs began penetrating into suburban areas in the Northeast and Mid-Atlantic regions, particularly in upstate New York, eastern Pennsylvania and Northern Virginia. Increasing numbers of Asian gangs were migrating into the Northeast, while two Latino gangs — the

Latin Kings and the Netas — had become involved in political and social causes to establish some legitimacy. [49]

Along with the increase in gangs has come an increase in crime. Last September, for instance, Christopher Christie, U.S. attorney for Newark, N.J., reported that for the third straight year, the city's murder rate had risen, as well as the number of handguns recovered by police. "The rise in violence and unlawful gun possession corresponds directly to a substantial increase in documented gang activity beginning in 1999," he said. [50]

The South also has seen increased activity among established Asian and Latino gangs, and several Latino and black gangs from Chicago have expanded into the region, particularly in drug dealing. [51] In Charlotte, N.C., authorities have been fighting white motorcycle gangs along with the black Kings, but as in Northern Virginia, the most violent and visible gang is MS-13. [52]

In the Chicago area, gangs have been growing more sophisticated and organized. Asian and Latino gangs account for the greatest growth throughout the region, with the latter expanding in direct relation to a widening of the methamphetamine market. Chicago-based gangs have also extended their reach into various regions of the West, where the epicenter of gang activity continues to be Los Angeles.

National Gang Policy?

Investigating gangs that appear to be operating in several regions is complicated, because different gang factions often have different interests. "Gangs are, more often than not, locally based, geographically oriented criminal associations," Sen. Leahy recently said. "Even gangs that purportedly have the same name on the East and West coast are not necessarily affiliated with one another." [53]

What is needed, McBride says, is a national gang policy that spells out an accepted definition of a gang and gang-related activity and a national gang intelligence center, similar to the Department of Justice's National Drug Intelligence Center.

"We need massive federal aid to local government in a multifaceted approach — it can't be just cops," he continues, adding that the approach should coordinate probation, corrections and community-based programs, as well as prevention and intervention programs. Coordination and communication among all relevant authorities, which currently is lacking, also must be beefed up, he says. "And it all has to be long term. The

Would the Gang Prevention and Effective Deterrence Act proposed by Sens. Orrin Hatch and Dianne Feinstein help in the fight against gangs?

YES

Sen. Orrin G. Hatch, R-Utah

From a statement before the U.S. Senate, Oct. 15, 2003

Mr. President, I rise today to introduce a comprehensive, bipartisan bill to increase gang prosecution and prevention efforts.

The Gang Prevention and Effective Deterrence Act of 2003 also increases funding for the federal prosecutors and FBI agents needed to conduct coordinated enforcement efforts against violent gangs.

Additionally, this bill will create new, criminal, gang-prosecution offenses, enhance existing gang and violent-crime penalties to deter and punish illegal street gangs, propose violent-crime reforms needed to prosecute effectively gang members and propose a limited reform of the juvenile-justice system to facilitate federal prosecution of 16- and 17-year-old gang members who commit serious acts of violence.

Once thought to be only a problem in our nation's largest cities, gangs have invaded smaller communities. Gangs now resemble organized-crime syndicates who readily engage in gun violence, illegal gun trafficking, illegal drug trafficking and other serious crimes.

Recent studies confirm that gang violence is an increasing problem in all of our communities. The most current reports indicate that in 2002 alone, after five years of decline, gang membership has spiked nationwide.

While we all are committed to fighting the global war on terrorism, we must redouble our efforts to ensure that we devote sufficient resources to combating this important national problem — the rise in gangs and gang violence in America.

We must take a proactive approach and meet this problem head on if we wish to defeat it. If we really want to reduce gang violence, we must ensure that law enforcement has adequate resources and legal tools, and that our communities have the ability to implement proven intervention and prevention strategies, so that gang members who are removed from the community are not simply replaced by the next generation of new gang members.

Federal involvement is crucial to control gang violence and to prevent new gang members from replacing old gang members. I strongly urge my colleagues to join with me in promptly passing this important legislation.

NO

Jeralyn Merritt
Criminal Defense Attorney, Denver, Colo.

From talkleft.com: the politics of crime, Dec. 21, 2003

Sens. Diane Feinstein, D-Calif., and Orrin Hatch, R-Utah, have teamed up to sponsor a terrible bill — one that panders to irrational fear but resonates politically.

It is rife with new categories of crimes, added punishments for having a gun or being a gang member and myriad "think twice" measures hoping gang members will reconsider before committing a crime.

Anyone who knows gangs knows that lawmakers cannot conceive of a law that would lead a hard-core gang member to "think twice." We already have enough gang- and gun-related sentencing "enhancements" to send a 17-year-old who has never been in trouble with the law to prison for 35 years to life. And that's without his ever touching a gun or ever being an actual member of a gang. We need to overhaul these enhancements, not add to them.

Gangs are not all that mysterious. Reformers know what works with them and what doesn't. Gang experts, intervention practitioners, social scientists, researchers and enlightened law enforcement officials all agree. What works is prevention, intervention and enforcement.

You prevent kids from joining gangs by offering after-school programs, sports, mentoring and positive engagement with adults. You intervene with gang members by offering alternatives and employment to help redirect their lives. You deal with areas of high gang-crime activity with real community policing.

There are ways that money could make a difference in curbing gangs — but the Feinstein-Hatch bill doesn't acknowledge them.

Law enforcement doesn't need more tools; it needs more officers. Real community policing requires different deployment, which can happen only with increased personnel. Although the Feinstein-Hatch bill would also allocate $200 million for prevention and intervention, more than three-quarters of that money would be administered by law enforcement. That is as misguided as having Homeboy Industries — a gang rehab center — enforce a gang injunction.

What's really going on here is politics. Feinstein and Hatch's ill-advised bill will neither prevent nor deter gang-related crime. It's time to stop funding wasteful law enforcement initiatives and listen to those who know what works — and it's not the politicians. This turkey of a bill needs to die a fast death.

problem with going to federal funding agencies is you get little grants for 18 months at most. That's not enough."

Newark's Christie has called for a special, multi-level unit that would target an entire gang operation — much like the Mafia was targeted — not simply the most visible members on the streets. "It is not uncommon for a single gang to be involved in drug dealing, firearms trafficking, murder, robbery, money laundering and, more recently, mortgage fraud," he said. To deal with such broad-based activities, he suggests, the U.S. attorney's office should lead a team consisting of the FBI, DEA, BATFE and the Marshals Service, along with local authorities. [54]

Without such broad-based coordination and information sharing, many investigations and prosecutions languish, authorities say. Investigations are also hindered by the lack of funds to adequately protect witnesses. "For many prosecutors, a witness-protection program simply consists of a bus ticket or a motel room," said McCulloch, of the National District Attorneys Association, who has pleaded for federal funds for such programs. In Denver, he points out, the number of prosecutions has dropped sharply because of the lack of protection while the number of gang crimes "has increased tremendously." [55]

Lately, Congress appears to be listening: In addition to making some gang activities federal offenses, the proposed Gang Prevention and Effective Deterrence Act would provide approximately $100 million of federal assistance for state and local law enforcement and $40 million for prevention programs over five years. In the Senate the bill was scheduled for markup in mid-May and expected to pass largely intact. A House companion bill has yet to be submitted.

Johnson of the National Association of Police Organizations predicts the measure will eventually become law. "Maybe not in this Congress before the [November presidential] election," he says, "but I do think it will pass. It won't be a cure-all but another tool in the box that will marginally and incrementally help bring down gangs and make communities safer."

However, Denver criminal-defense attorney Jeralyn Merritt calls it "a terrible bill" that "panders to irrational fear but resonates politically." In a scathing criticism of the proposal on the Web site *talkleft.com*, she argues: "We already have enough gang- and gun-related sentencing 'enhancements' to send a 17-year-old who has never been in trouble with the law to prison for 35 years to life. And that's without his ever being an actual member of a gang. We need to overhaul these enhancements, not add to them.

"Gangs are not all that mysterious. Reformers know what works with them . . . What works is prevention, intervention and enforcement. You prevent kids from joining gangs by offering after-school programs, sports, mentoring and positive engagement with adults. You intervene with gang members by offering alternatives and employment to help redirect their lives. You deal with areas of high gang-crime activity with real community policing."

OUTLOOK

More Violence?

In Northern Virginia, probation official Rathbun thinks authorities at every level of government have begun to realize the size and scope of the gang threat. As he puts it, "It's kind of the problem *du jour* now."

But whether effective policies will soon emerge is an open question, he says. "There's still lots of crazy things," he says. "We've got a directive from our agency now that says we can't question anybody about their immigration status, which seems stupid."

Moore, of the National Youth Gang Center, expects gang violence to continue its cyclical patterns, with upswings followed by downturns. "Some cities experience a big flare-up in gang violence every year," he says. "They've either never recognized the problem and it bubbles up to the surface, or they think they've dealt with the problem, but it comes back up again."

To U.S. Attorney Christie in Newark, nothing short of a full-scale, coordinated assault by law enforcement agencies at all levels is going to make a difference. Gang crime is, he said, "the new organized crime in the United States, an organized crime that destroys families, corrupts our children and lays waste to neighborhoods in our most vulnerable communities. We must mount a fight comparable to the fight against La Cosa Nostra in past decades if we expect to have the same success." [56]

But the FBI's Riley believes the resources are coming "at a slow pace." Given the FBI's priority on combating terrorism, Riley envisions "probably a 10-year progression to get [anti-gang resources] to the point I'd like to see." Meantime, he expects increasing gang activity as a result of continued immigration and "the phenomenon of the media making the 'gangsta' lifestyle appealing."

But he's also somewhat optimistic. "I see more cooperation between federal agencies — the FBI, the [BATFE] and the DEA and even the Marshals Service."

Although federal legislation may help bring the problem under control, changing demographics and the inherent dangerousness of gang activity may help staunch the growth of gangs over the long-term, says Johnson of the National Association of Police Organizations. "The Baby Boomlet will get older, and as they do, they'll mature and calm down," he says. "As this generation ages, there will be a decrease in the general crime rate. Plus, the really bad ones either get caught or killed. Gang [activity] is a very high-risk business."

McBride of the California Gang Investigators Association doubts that either the proposed legislation or more federal funds will eliminate the problem. "After you get some federal grants, the statistics decrease, and then the politicians walk away saying the problem's solved," he says. "Then, surprise, surprise — the problem's right back."

But if done right, he says, the legislation could help. "If the funding goes for local prosecution and for local gang units, that's going to be a tremendous help. But if it stays federally based, it's not going to have the impact they want it to have."

Rathbun, who deals with juvenile gangs daily, is pessimistic. Some gangs that had seemed to disband in Northern Virginia, such as TRG, are revitalizing, and becoming shrewder.

"The kids are less apt to get the tattoos now, and less apt to dress like gang-bangers," he says, so authorities are less apt to immediately recognize them. Their actions, however, won't be any different than before. Rathbun says the rival 18th Street Gang and the Latin Kings, as well as the new South Side Locos, are beginning to move into MS-13 territory.

"We're expecting turf battles," he says. "Machetes, knives and guns. I think it's going to be a bad summer."

It has already begun with machetes. A 16-year-old boy thought to be a South Side Locals member was walking along a suburban street on May 10 when reputed MS-13 members jumped him and nearly hacked his hands off. His screams woke residents, who called police. Doctors saved both hands, but four fingers were permanently lost, and it is too soon to tell if he will recover use of his hands. [57]

"They were trying to send a message," said Robert Walker, a former Drug Enforcement Administration special agent who runs a gang-identification training program for law enforcement officers. "Gangs deal in what we call the three R's. The first is reputation, and they want to do all they can to build that. The second is respect . . . and the third is retaliation or revenge."

NOTES

1. See Maria Glod, "Man Gets 30 Years in Gang Slaying; Va. Judge Cites Brutal Beating in Sentencing 1 of 4 Charged," *The Washington Post*, Sept. 28, 2002, p. B6. See also Maria Glod, "Gangs Get Public's Attention: Dozen Actively Contributing to Area Crime," *The Washington Post*, Sept. 18, 2003, p. T1.

2. See Maria Glod, "Prosecutors Describe Gang-Style Execution as MS-13 Trial Opens," *The Washington Post*, Nov. 6, 2003, p. B6. See also Maria Glod, "Guardian of Slain Woman Replaces Her as Witness; Authorities Believe Teen was Silenced by Gang," *The Washington Post*, Nov. 7, 2003, p. B4.

3. Sen. Orrin G. Hatch, opening statement before Senate Judiciary Committee hearing on "Combating Gang Violence in America: Examining Effective Federal, State and Local Law Enforcement Strategies," Sept. 17, 2003.

4. Office of Juvenile Justice and Delinquency Prevention, U.S. Department of Justice, "Highlights of the 2001 National Youth Gang Survey," April 2003. See also Neely Tucker, "Gangs Growing in Numbers, Bravado Across Area," *The Washington Post*, Sept. 18, 2003, p. A1.

5. National Alliance of Gang Investigators Associations, "Threat Assessment, 2000."

6. Office of Juvenile Justice and Delinquency Prevention, *op. cit.*

7. Wesley McBride, testimony before Senate Judiciary Committee hearing, Sept. 17, 2003.

8. *Ibid.*

9. Patrick Fitzgerald, testimony before Senate Judiciary Committee hearing, Sept. 17, 2003.

10. National Youth Gang Center, www.iir.com/nygc/faq.htm#q6.

11. *Ibid.*

12. Eddie Jordan, testimony before Senate Judiciary Committee hearing, Sept. 17, 2003.

13. McBride, *op. cit.*

14. Grant D. Ashley, testimony before Senate Judiciary Committee hearing, Sept. 17, 2003.

15. Debra Yang, testimony before Senate Judiciary Committee hearing, Sept. 17, 2003.

16. Robert McCulloch, testimony before Senate Judiciary Committee hearing, Sept. 17, 2003.

17. For background, see William Triplett, "State Budget Crisis," *The CQ Researcher*, Oct. 3, 2003, pp. 821-844.

18. See Keith Perine, "Senators Pushing for Increased Federal Role in Fighting Crime Linked to Gangs," *CQ Today*, April 9, 2004.

19. Bureau of Alcohol, Tobacco and Firearms and Explosives (BATFE), "Crime Gun Trace Reports: National Report," June 2002, pp. ix, x.

20. C. Ronald Huff, "Criminal Behavior of Gang Members and At-Risk Youths," presentation to the National Institute of Justice.

21. BATFE, *op. cit.*

22. For background, see Richard L. Worsnop, "Gun Control," *The CQ Researcher*, June 10, 1994, pp. 505-528, and Kenneth Jost, "Gun Control Standoff," *The CQ Researcher*, Dec. 19, 1997, pp. 1105-1128.

23. Fitzgerald, *op. cit.*

24. See David Heinzmann, "Gangs Run Gun Pipeline from Delta to Chicago; Lenient Laws Make Buying Weapons Easier in South," *Chicago Tribune*, Feb. 5, 2004, p. C1.

25. Jens Ludwig and Phil Cook, "Homicide and Suicide Rates Associated with Implementation of the BHVPA," *Journal of the American Medical Association*, Aug. 2, 2000, Vol. 284, p. 585.

26. Jost, *op. cit.*

27. Heinzmann, *op. cit.*

28. See Carlos Sandovi, "Teen Charged in Humboldt Park Gang Rival's Killing; Police say Suspect also Took Shots at Undercover Cop," *Chicago Tribune*, April 21, 2004, p. C2.

29. For background see Brian Hansen, "Kids in Prison," *The CQ Researcher*, April 27, 2001, pp. 345-376.

30. See Lisa Friedman, "Anti-Gang Bill Draws Critics; Juvenile Advocacy Groups Oppose Adult Sentencing," *Los Angeles Daily News*, Nov. 24, 2003, p. N4.

31. *Ibid.*

32. Quoted in Armando Morales and Bradford W. Sheafor, *Social Work: A Profession of Many Faces* (1989), p. 415.

33. For background see Charles S. Clark, "Youth Gangs," *The CQ Researcher*, Oct. 11, 1991, pp. 753-776.

34. Anne Campbell, *The Girls in the Gang* (1984), p. 9.

35. Quoted in Irving A. Spergel, *Crime and Justice: A Review of Research*, "Youth Gangs: Continuity and Change," Michael Tonry and Norval Morris, eds., Vol. 12 (1990), p. 172.

36. Quoted in James Haskins, *Street Gangs: Yesterday and Today* (1974), p. 48.

37. *Ibid*, p. 99.

38. *Ibid*, p. 112.

39. See Nicholas Lemann, *The Promised Land* (1991), p. 245.

40. See Michael Abramowitz, "Street Gang Convictions Challenged in Chicago," *The Washington Post*, Dec. 22, 1992, p. A3.

41. See Matt Canham and Tim Sullivan, "Asian Gangs a Scourge: Violent Rivals in the Vietnamese, Lao and Cambodia Communities are Settling Scores at Malls, Amusement Parks; Asian Gangs Target Their Own People," *The Salt Lake Tribune*, April 14, 2003, p. D1.

42. The Associated Press, "U.S. Deportees Cart Crime to Native Lands," *Los Angeles Times*, Jan. 4, 2004, p. A5.

43. Kevin Sullivan, "Spreading Gang Violence Alarms Central Americans," *The Washington Post*, Dec. 1, 2003, p. A1.

44. Steven Wiley, testimony before Senate Judiciary Committee hearing on gang violence, April 23, 1997.

45. Sen. Dianne Feinstein, statement before Senate Judiciary Committee hearing on gang violence, April 23, 1997.

46. For background, see Sarah Glazer, "Boys' Emotional Needs," *The CQ Researcher*, June 18, 1999, pp. 521-544 and Kathy Koch, "School Violence," *The CQ Researcher*, Oct. 9, 1998, pp. 881-904.

47. National Center for Juvenile Justice, "Juvenile Arrest Rates by Offense, Sex, and Race," May 31, 2003.

48. See Chuck Plunkett, "Gangs' Hidden Fingerprint," *The Denver Post*, Nov. 9, 2003, p. A1.

49. National Alliance of Gang Investigators Associations, *op. cit.*

50. Christopher Christie, testimony before Senate Judiciary Committee hearing, Sept. 17, 2003.

51. National Alliance of Gang Investigators Associations, *op. cit.*

52. See Arian Campo-Flores, "Gangland's New Face," *Newsweek*, Dec. 8, 2003, p. 41.

53. Sen. Patrick Leahy, opening statement before Senate Judiciary Committee hearing, Sept. 17, 2003.

54. Christie, *op. cit.*

55. McCulloch, *op. cit.*

56. Christie, *op. cit.*

57. Maria Glod and Tom Jackman, "Teen's Hands Severed In Northern Va. Machete Attack," *The Washington Post*, May 11, 2004, p. B1.

BIBLIOGRAPHY

Books

The Truth about Street Gangs, Gang Prevention Inc., 2001.
This publication is designed to help communities identify and understand gangs, focusing on how they operate and how they conceal their activities.

Hernandez, Arturo, *Peace in the Streets: Breaking the Cycle of Gang Violence*, Child Welfare League of America, 1998.
Hernandez tells the riveting story of his experience as a young teacher in South Central Los Angeles and the positive effect he had on the gang members who were his students.

Kinnear, Karen L., *Gangs: A Reference Handbook*, ABC-CLIO, 1996.
This compendium on juvenile gangs by a journalist focuses on their activities, membership, motivations and their relation to society and the law.

Lloyd, J.D., ed., *Gangs*, Greenhaven Press, 2002.
A collection of informational essays by a journalist examines why gangs exist, their history, their day-to-day actions and what can be done to lessen the damage they do.

Articles

"U.S. Deportees Cart Crime to Native Lands; More than 500,000 have been banished under 1996 law," The Associated Press, *Los Angeles Times*, Jan. 4, 2004, p A5.
The federal government's tactic of deporting non-U.S. citizens convicted of crimes has sent many gang members back to their homeland, where they resume gang activity.

Campo-Flores, Arian, "Gangland's New Face," *Newsweek*, Dec. 8, 2003, p. 41.
The surge of Latino gangs is reflected in their relatively new and overwhelming presence in Charlotte, N.C.

Canham, Matt, and Tim Sullivan, "Asian Gangs a Scourge; Gunplay: Violent rivals in the Vietnamese, Lao and Cambodian communities are settling scores at malls, amusement parks; Asian Gangs Target Their Own People," *Salt Lake Tribune*, April 14, 2003, p. D1.
Asian gangs wreak havoc in the greater Salt Lake area, mostly within the immigrant community but sometimes outside of it.

Heinzmann, David, "Gangs run pipeline from Delta to Chicago; Lenient laws make buying weapons easier in the South," *Chicago Tribune*, Feb. 5, 2004, p. 1.
To skirt tough gun control laws, Chicago gangs use the proceeds of illegal drug sales to buy weapons in Mississippi.

Jackson, Chriscia, "Asian gangs have reputation for living 'giang ho,' or crazy life," Associated Press, May 25, 2000.
A look at the violence and destructiveness of Asian gangs as seen in the story of two juvenile members of Vietnamese gangs in Port Arthur, Texas.

Plunkett, Chuck, "Gangs' Hidden Fingerprint," *The Denver Post*, Nov. 9, 2003, p. A1.
Plunkett details the extensive gang activity throughout the Denver area and the police department's lack of accurate records on gangs.

Tucker, Neely, "Gangs Growing in Numbers, Bravado Across Area," *The Washington Post*, Sept. 18, 2003, p. A1.
Latino gangs are growing rapidly in Washington, D.C., and other areas of the country not previously known for intense gang activity.

Reports and Studies

"Highlights of the 2001 National Youth Gang Survey," Office of Juvenile Justice and Delinquency Prevention, Department of Justice, April 2003.
This annual survey documents national trends, activities and developments among youth gangs.

"National Youth Gang Center Bibliography of Gang Literature," Office of Juvenile Justice and Delinquency Prevention, U.S. Department of Justice, 1997.
An exhaustive bibliography of gang literature — dating as far back as the 1940s — reviewed and compiled by the National Youth Gang Center for the Office of Juvenile Justice and Delinquency Prevention.

Huff, C. Ronald, "Comparing the Criminal Behavior of Youth Gangs and At-Risk Youths," National Institute of Justice, Department of Justice, October 1998.
A survey shows that criminal activity of youth-gang members is significantly higher than that of at-risk youths.

Moore, Joan, and John Hagedorn, "Female Gangs: A Focus on Research," *Juvenile Justice Bulletin*, Office of Juvenile Justice and Delinquency Prevention, U.S. Department of Justice, March 2001.
This summary of research attempts to address the imbalance between research on male and female gangs.

Reed, Winifred L., and Scott H. Decker, "Responding to Gangs: Evaluation and Research," National Institute of Justice, U.S. Department of Justice, July 2002.
A comprehensive review of recent research about gang behavior as well as anti-gang strategies.

For More Information

Bajito Onda, P.O. Box 270246, Dallas, TX 75227; (214) 275-6632; www.bajitoonda.org/bajito.html. Foundation dedicated to giving Latino youths positive alternatives to gangs, drugs and violence through education.

Juvenile Justice Clearinghouse, P.O. Box 6000, Rockville, MD 20849-6000; (800) 851-3420; http://ojjdp.ncjrs.org/programs/ProgSummary.asp?pi=2. A component of the National Criminal Justice Reference Service that maintains information and resources on juvenile-justice topics.

National Alliance of Gang Investigators Associations; www.nagia.org. An online coalition of criminal-justice professionals dedicated to promoting a coordinated anti-gang strategy.

National Criminal Justice Reference Service, P.O. Box 6000, Rockville, MD, 20849-6000; (800) 851-3420; http://virlib.ncjrs.org/juv.asp?category=47&subcategory=66. A federally funded service that provides information on jus-

tice and substance abuse to support research, policy and program development worldwide.

National Major Gang Task Force, 338 S. Arlington Ave., Suite 112, Indianapolis, IN 46219; (317) 322-0537; www.nmgtf.org. An independent organization specializing in intervention, management strategies, networking, training and information-sharing regarding gangs.

National Youth Gang Center, P.O. Box 12729, Tallahassee, FL 32317; (850) 385-0600; www.iir.com/nygc. A Department of Justice-funded group that collects and analyzes information on gangs.

Office of Juvenile Justice and Delinquency Prevention, 810 7th St., N.W., Washington, D.C. 20531; (202) 307-5911; http://ojjdp.ncjrs.org. A Justice Department office providing leadership, coordination and resources on preventing juvenile delinquency and victimization.

10

Alternative Energy

Mary H. Cooper

California Gov. Arnold Swarzenegger fills a hydrogen-powered Hummer at the dedication of the state's first hydrogen fueling station in Los Angeles, on Oct. 22, 2004. To spur the development of hydrogen vehicles, Schwarzenegger has launched a program to build a "hydrogen highway" in California with 150 hydrogen-fueling stations. Advocates predict hydrogen fuel cells eventually will replace fossil fuels for most U.S. energy needs and launch a pollution-free industrial revolution.

From *CQ Researcher*, February 25, 2005.

With its menacing grille and high back end, the new sedan looked like what you'd expect from Detroit. But beneath the shiny, slightly bulbous exterior, the Sequel was unlike any other new vehicle unveiled in January at the North American International Auto Show in Detroit.

Under the hood was the device that many energy experts believe will power the United States into the future — a hydrogen fuel cell.

"The Sequel is not a gimmick or a ploy," says Assistant Energy Secretary David K. Garman, who heads the Office of Energy Efficiency and Renewable Energy. "U.S. automakers know their current business is not sustainable. They realize that personal transportation will need a completely different look and feel if they're going to stay in business in the 21st century. They want to take the car out of the environmental equation, and hydrogen is the only way to do that."

Engines powered by hydrogen require no imported fuel and emit virtually no pollutants, and the government has subsidized research on them for many years. In hopes of bringing vehicles like the Sequel to market, the Bush administration, in partnership with the auto industry, wants to increase spending on hydrogen research by $1.2 billion over the next five years. Fuel-cell advocates predict hydrogen fuel cells eventually will replace highly polluting fossil fuels — oil, coal and natural gas — for most U.S. energy needs and help launch a new, pollution-free industrial revolution. (*See story, p. 222.*)

Critics say the Bush administration is still too heavily focused on the use of fossil fuels, despite its support for fuel-cell research. Moreover, they say the administration is not putting enough effort into developing other alternative energy sources, such as solar.

U.S. Oil Imports Expected to Rise

The federal government estimates that U.S. oil imports will increase by 60 percent from 2002 to 2020 in response to falling domestic oil production and increasing U.S. oil needs.

(Millions of barrels per day)

Legend: Net Imports, Domestic Production

Source: Energy Information Administration, U.S. Department of Energy

Perhaps surprisingly, hydrogen fuel cells have been around since an English inventor crafted the first rudimentary model in the late 19th century. But except for limited use in manned space missions, fuel cells have served little practical purpose in the modern age, when abundant fossil fuels met the energy needs of a rapidly industrializing world.

The current push to accelerate technologies like hydrogen fuel cells arises from growing concerns about the threats to U.S. national security and the environment posed by continued reliance on fossil fuels. In 1970, for the first time, rising energy needs — mainly to power cars and trucks — forced the United States to begin importing more oil than it produced. Most of the Earth's remaining, proven petroleum deposits lie in the tumultuous Middle East. Iraq, for example, where more than 1,400 U.S. troops have died in the war to topple Saddam Hussein, holds the third-largest known oil reserves in the world. [1]

Even if peace comes to the Middle East, the problem of diminishing oil supplies will not go away. Despite improved methods for extracting crude from deep deposits under the ocean floor and other previously inaccessible deposits, oil is a finite resource that eventually will dry up. No one knows exactly when global oil production will start to decline; estimates range from five to 30 years from now. [2] But the impact of oil's eventual demise is already becoming apparent: As supplies dwindle, oil prices rise and threaten the U.S. economy.

Although average gasoline prices have dropped since climbing well above $2 a gallon last May, global oil prices hit $51 a barrel in February 2005, up from $28 two years ago, and most analysts predict further increases. The Energy Information Administration (EIA) predicts oil prices will decline to $25 a barrel in 2010 as new supplies reach the market but then climb to $52 a barrel by 2025, which some environmentalists say vastly understates the problem. [3]

As rapidly developing economies in India, China and other Asian nations boost the market for passenger cars, added pressure is being put on oil prices at the same time that global oil supplies are expected to decline. In China, for example, the EIA projects that energy use for transportation will grow by more than 5 percent a year through 2025. [4]

"As we reach peak global production of oil, the price inevitably will skyrocket," says Jeremy Rifkin, president of the Foundation on Economic Trends and a long-standing advocate of hydrogen-fuel development. "It may go down to $40 a barrel temporarily, but we're never going back to $30. It's probably going to reach $80 a barrel within the next five years."

As oil prices rise, alternative-energy sources like hydrogen fuel cells — now much more expensive than fossil fuels — will become more cost effective. Meanwhile, after a slow start in the U.S. market, hybrid cars like the Toyota Prius and

Honda Insight, which run on both gasoline and electricity, are in such high demand that automakers are coming out with new models, including SUVs. Federal tax credits for hybrids and state laws allowing hybrids to use limited-access rush-hour lanes are further fueling consumer demand.

Besides forcing the United States to rely on Middle East oil, continued reliance on burning fossil fuels for energy also releases carbon dioxide, the main "greenhouse gas" that most scientists agree causes global warming. [5] Emissions from gasoline- or diesel-fueled vehicles also contribute to urban smog, along with the burning of coal and, to a lesser extent, natural gas, to generate electricity and heat buildings. [6]

Recent scientific findings suggest that global warming is already devastating the environment. Polar ice sheets and high mountain glaciers around the world are melting faster than earlier predicted, while droughts and erratic weather patterns are blamed on rising surface temperatures. [7]

"There is a general consensus that if the planet warms by more than two degrees C, we'll be taking an enormous risk," Joseph Romm, Garman's predecessor at Energy during the Clinton administration, says. "Global warming is why we should be willing to consider spending a lot of money to develop a whole new energy system."

While most scientists and lawmakers agree that Americans must change their energy supplies and consumption patterns, they differ widely over the best way to achieve that goal. The Bush administration's energy blueprint, first proposed in 2001, has failed to become law because many lawmakers oppose its emphasis on expanding domestic production of oil and gas by drilling in untouched areas, such as the Arctic National Wildlife Refuge (ANWR).

Even Bush's Hydrogen Initiative, announced in 2003, has come under criticism for relying on fossil fuels to produce the hydrogen itself. Although it is abundant

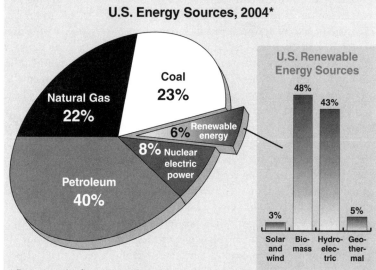

Renewables Make Up Sliver of Energy Pie

About 6 percent of the nation's total energy is provided by renewable sources, mainly hydroelectric power and biomass. Petroleum is the main fossil fuel, providing 40 percent of the nation's total energy, mostly for transportation.

U.S. Energy Sources, 2004*

Coal **23%**

Natural Gas **22%**

6% Renewable energy

8% Nuclear electric power

Petroleum **40%**

U.S. Renewable Energy Sources

Solar and wind **3%**
Biomass **48%**
Hydroelectric **43%**
Geothermal **5%**

* Based on the first 10 months

Note: Percentages do not add to 100 due to rounding.

Source: Energy Information Administration, "Monthly Energy Review," January 2005

in nature, hydrogen is bound to other atoms or molecules to form compounds such as water, so other energy sources are needed to make it available for use in fuel cells. (*See p. 220.*)

"Bush's plan is a Trojan horse that represents the interests of the same energy industry that they've been representing from the get-go," says Rifkin, who calls the product of Bush's vision "black hydrogen." Bush's energy plan is "a way for the administration to say to the public that we're going clean, but with the idea that the public will never ask where they plan to get the hydrogen from."

Rifkin and other advocates call for renewed efforts to promote non-fossil energy sources, such as wind turbines, solar panels, geothermal and biomass facilities that harvest energy in ways that do not release pollutants or carbon dioxide. Whether those sources are used to generate electricity for direct consumption or to produce what Rifkin calls "green hydrogen" for fuel cells, advocates say the United States should do more to promote non-fossil energy sources.

"Resources like wind are not only widely available in the market but are sufficiently abundant to meet all U.S. electricity, or even total energy, needs," says longtime sustainable-energy advocate Amory Lovins, chief executive of the Rocky Mountain Institute.

Bush continues to press for fuel-cell development. "Hydrogen fuel cells represent one of the most encouraging, innovative technologies of our era," he said in an address about energy independence at the National Building Museum on Feb. 6, 2003. "If you're interested in our environment, and if you're interested in doing what's right for the American people, if you're tired of the same, old endless struggles that seem to produce nothing but noise and high bills, let us promote hydrogen fuel cells as a way to advance into the 21st century. If we develop hydrogen power to its full potential, we can reduce our demand for oil by over 11 million barrels per day by the year 2040. That would be a fantastic legacy to leave for future generations of Americans."

Bush's energy bill, including his hydrogen program, is again pending before Congress, where the Republican majority — strengthened in last fall's elections — hopes to overcome opposition this year. Energy Secretary Samuel Bodman reiterated administration support for increasing domestic oil production, including drilling in ANWR, at his recent confirmation hearing. "ANWR has been part of the energy policy that this administration has proposed," he said. "And I would expect to be an energetic advocate for it." [8]

"As the energy bill has been a long time coming, I personally think that it is time that we finally get the job done in this Congress," said House Energy and Commerce Committee Chairman Joe L. Barton, R-Texas, at a Feb. 9, 2005, hearing on energy policy. "We have a world where there is a growing global energy demand, and also, unfortunately, we still have global energy instability. I think it's time that the United States of America take control of its own fundamentals for our energy future."

Even critics of the bill say there is enough public agreement today on the need for clean domestic-energy sources to enable lawmakers to come up with compromise energy legislation. "There is a large, hidden consensus on energy in the United States," Lovins says. "If we just did the things we all agree on, then the stuff we don't agree on would become largely superfluous."

As lawmakers debate Bush's energy proposals, here are some of the questions they will ask:

Will hydrogen replace fossil fuels as America's predominant energy source?

Until recently, the vision of a "hydrogen economy" — cars zipping silently around smog-free cities and households generating their own electricity — was little more than a pipe dream. But that was before technological breakthroughs, rising oil prices, ongoing turmoil in the oil-rich Middle East and growing recognition of the environmental dangers associated with fossil fuels.

Skeptics began to give hydrogen new attention after Jan. 28, 2003, when President Bush announced in his State of the Union address that he planned to launch a $1.2 billion federal Hydrogen Initiative. "With a new national commitment, our scientists and engineers will overcome obstacles to taking these cars from laboratory to showroom, so that the first car driven by a child born today could be powered by hydrogen and pollution-free," Bush said. "Join me in this important innovation to make our air significantly cleaner and our country much less dependent on foreign sources of energy."

Bush said his initiative, along with his earlier FreedomCAR program in partnership with Detroit, would help U.S. automakers bring reliable, affordable vehicles powered by hydrogen fuel cells to market by 2020. The initiative would also help develop hydrogen units to generate electricity for homes and businesses, which could wean consumers from the electricity grid as well.

A handful of visionaries long have foreseen a world free of fossil fuels. But today hydrogen fuel cells are squarely in the mainstream of the ongoing debate over energy policy, uniting many conservative Republicans and liberal environmental advocates.

"A fascinating aspect of the hydrogen program the president is promoting is that it addresses security, opportunity, ownership and innovation — four tenets crucial to this administration," says Rhone Resch, executive director of the Solar Energy Industries Association.

"We support the president's program because fuel cells are the wave of the future," says Eron Shosteck, spokesman for the Alliance of Automobile Manufacturers. "All of our companies are investing billions of dollars a year into finding new, advanced technologies to run on alternative sources of energy."

Many environmental advocates support a shift to hydrogen because they see it as the key to halting the pollution associated with fossil fuels. The nuclear, coal and natural-gas industries also support the switch, largely because they want to become the chief suppliers of the fuel needed to produce usable hydrogen — such as by using an electrical current to split water (H_2O) into its component parts of hydrogen (H) and oxygen (O). (*See diagram, p. 215.*)

"The peculiar politics of hydrogen is making for some strange bedfellows in this debate," says the Rocky Mountain Institute's Lovins. Nonetheless, he adds, "Some environmentalists think if the White House, major oil companies and the nuclear power industry favor hydrogen, it must be bad. Conversely, some other folks think that if the environmentalists are in favor of it, it must be bad."

Hydrogen skeptics tick off a long list of obstacles to hydrogen, starting with production problems. "Hydrogen is not like oil, coal and natural gas — primary sources of energy created over the course of millions of years that you can dig in the ground and find," says former Energy Assistant Secretary Romm. "Hydrogen is like electricity: It is made from something else." In light of mounting evidence that global warming poses a grave environmental threat, he adds, "that something else clearly has got to be a zero-carbon fuel."

That would rule out coal and natural gas, unless scientists could devise a way to "sequester" the carbon as it is released from burning those fuels by capturing and burying it underground. Carbon sequestration is a major research focus of the administration's Hydrogen Initiative. "We can capture carbon dioxide from coal combustion today," says Assistant Energy Secretary Garman. "We just can't yet do it affordably enough to make hydrogen fuel cells compete with gasoline. And that's the real issue."

But some experts say there's no way to guarantee that the sequestered carbon would not eventually escape into the atmosphere, causing a potentially catastrophic overload of carbon dioxide, the main greenhouse gas responsible for global warming.

"There is no way that we know of to economically sequester carbon dioxide," Rifkin says. "And even if you could sequester it, how could you guarantee that such a huge volume of carbon dioxide would remain in that state underground and never seep out for all of eternity?

President Bush gets a briefing on hydrogen fueling systems from an Air Products Inc. official at the National Building Museum on Feb. 6, 2003. The president's proposed $1.2 billion federal Hydrogen Initiative aims to help U.S. automakers bring hydrogen-powered vehicles to market by 2020 and develop hydrogen units to generate electricity for homes and businesses.

If we thought nuclear waste disposal was problematic, this is a far greater problem." [9]

The carbon sequestration problem prompts many experts to say the key to a hydrogen economy is harnessing non-polluting renewable energy sources — such as solar power — to produce the hydrogen. "Hydrogen is absolutely ideal from the environmental point of view, particularly if you generate it using a renewable source," says Bob Thresher, director of the Energy Department's National Wind Technology Center at the National Renewable Energy Laboratory (NREL) outside Boulder, Colo.

Safety is another barrier to widespread use of hydrogen fuel. Hydrogen is not only highly flammable but also invisible when it burns, making auto accidents involving fuel-cell cars potentially more dangerous. But advocates say hydrogen's extreme buoyancy makes it likely to quickly disperse from the site of a leak, and thus unlikely to remain in concentrations high enough to ignite. [10]

Delivering hydrogen fuel to consumers poses another major obstacle. Converting the nation's 167,000 gasoline stations into hydrogen stations would cost billions of dollars. (Twenty-seven hydrogen-fueling stations in California and other states have

Little U.S. Electricity Comes From Renewables

Renewable-energy sources, such as wind and solar power, account for nearly 20 percent of the world's electricity but only 10 percent of U.S. power. Most of America's electricity comes from burning fossil fuels and nuclear energy.

Sources of the World's Electricity

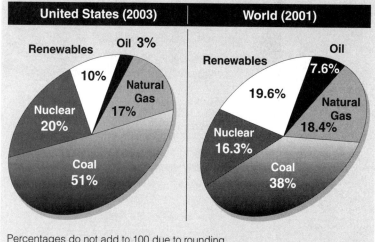

United States (2003) | World (2001)

United States (2003)
Renewables 10%
Oil 3%
Natural Gas 17%
Nuclear 20%
Coal 51%

World (2001)
Renewables 19.6%
Oil 7.6%
Natural Gas 18.4%
Nuclear 16.3%
Coal 38%

Percentages do not add to 100 due to rounding.

Source: "International Energy Outlook 2004," Energy Information Administration

Are efforts to develop hydrogen technology diverting funds from more promising energy sources?

President Bush's Hydrogen Initiative relies heavily on electricity from nuclear and coal-fired plants to produce hydrogen. His fiscal 2006 budget request called for increasing spending on research into hydrogen technologies, next-generation nuclear power plants and "clean coal" technology.

Of the Energy Department's $23.4 billion proposed 2006 budget, $260 million would be earmarked for hydrogen research, $56 million for a government partnership with the beleaguered nuclear industry and $286 million for coal research — $13 million more than Congress appropriated for clean-coal research in fiscal 2005.

Critics like the Rocky Mountain Institute's Lovins say reducing coal emissions would enable the United States to continue relying on its abundant coal reserves to generate electrical power and produce hydrogen. But he dismisses research on nuclear energy as a waste of money — even as a means to produce hydrogen.

"The nuclear and coal industries have latched on to hydrogen as a potential savior," Lovins says. "This may be true for the coal industry, because coal is extremely good at pulling hydrogen out of steam, and we may figure out ways to sequester the carbon. But it's hard to even imagine a cost-effective way to make hydrogen from any thermally generated electricity." And that doesn't even account for the environmental risks associated with using and disposing of nuclear fuel.

Administration officials defend the investments in coal and nuclear energy. "The ability to make hydrogen from a variety of different resources makes a lot of sense," Garman says, "because one whole sector of our economy, the transportation sector, is almost exclusively dependent on petroleum. Hydrogen can fuel much of the transportation sector, and yet be produced from a variety of domestic energy resources. Those include renewables, but candidly, they also include nuclear and coal."

been built to supply the first generation of zero-emission test vehicles.) [11]

Given these and other obstacles to creating a hydrogen-based energy system, a National Academy of Sciences panel concluded that fuel-cell cars would not begin to have a major impact on the auto market until at least 2025. [12]

But hydrogen advocates like Lovins say most of the obstacles have been overblown. "Much of what has been written on both sides about hydrogen is simply wrong," he says. [13] He says the claims that producing hydrogen from natural gas would add to carbon emissions, for example, ignore the fact that far more emissions are produced by gasoline-powered cars than would be released in producing hydrogen for fuel cells.

But the skeptics say the obstacles to developing a cost-effective hydrogen-based energy system are significant. "I wouldn't say it's impossible, but it certainly is not going to happen in the first half of this century," Romm says. "And it's important for people to understand it may never happen at all."

However, critics complain that while Bush's 2006 budget proposal would boost spending for coal and nuclear energy, it calls for no significant new funds for researching renewable-energy technology. Indeed, Garman's own Energy Efficiency and Renewable Energy division would receive $353 million — $30 million less than it received in 2005. The budget would maintain funding for solar energy ($84 million) and wind energy ($44 million) close to 2005 levels but cut spending for research on biomass and bio-refinery — extracting energy from plants — by $30 million. Energy-efficiency programs would also be cut; a program to help improve energy efficiency in buildings, for example, would receive $58 million in 2006 — 15 percent less than current spending. [14]

Some energy experts say the current drive to develop fuel cells depletes the federal budget for bringing to market other non-polluting, renewable-energy sources that are on the verge of becoming commercially viable. "Hydrogen is a very promising technology," says Bracken Hendricks, executive director of the Apollo Alliance, a coalition of labor, environmental and business groups that promotes energy independence. "It can provide an important, non-polluting energy source if it's linked to renewable-energy generation. But it's a long-range solution, and there are vast opportunities that can be captured immediately with existing technology."

The alliance prefers, among other things, using existing wind turbines to generate electricity; putting advanced internal-combustion engines and hybrid cars on the road to improve fuel economy and spur domestic auto industry employment; and developing biofuels that derive energy from agricultural-waste products and grasses. [15]

"These are substantial opportunities — that the Bush plan misses — to invest in measures that conserve energy and create large numbers of good jobs in sectors like high-skilled construction to retrofit buildings,"

How a Fuel Cell Works

A fuel cell operates much like a battery, but it does not run down or require recharging. It produces electricity and heat as long as fuel is supplied. A fuel cell consists of two electrodes (the anode and cathode) sandwiched around an electrolyte. Hydrogen fuel is fed into the anode, and oxygen from air enters the cathode. A catalyst causes hydrogen atoms to split into protons and electrons, which enter the cathode. The proton passes through the electrolyte. The electrons create a separate current that can be utilized before they return to the cathode, to be reunited with the hydrogen and oxygen in a molecule of water.

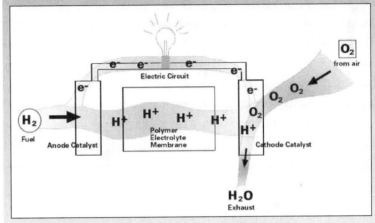

Source: Department of Energy

Hendricks says. "The Bush plan puts all of our eggs in one basket and looks at the hydrogen car as a silver bullet. But that's likely to be 30 to 50 years down the road, so it does very little in the near term for energy independence."

But Secretary Bodman says the Bush energy plan provides "numerous provisions to expand our domestic production of traditional energy resources, modernize our energy infrastructure, expand our use of renewable-energy sources such as wind and solar power, make wiser use of energy and pursue new forms of energy production that would help reduce pollution and lessen America's dependence on foreign oil." [16]

Is the United States losing its competitive edge in developing alternative-energy sources?

Several decades ago, the United States led the world in developing innovative energy technologies. Solar power, which uses photovoltaic cells to convert the sun's energy into electricity, and wind farms, which generate power using huge wind-driven turbines, resulted from intensive federal research programs spawned by the 1970s energy crises. [17]

As oil prices plummeted in the 1980s, so did U.S. government funding for renewable-energy research. However, other countries increased government spending on alternative energy and gained, according to some, a competitive advantage over the United States.

The Kyoto Protocol was a landmark in the push to develop alternative energy in Europe, Japan and other industrialized countries. Vice President Al Gore signed the international treaty to curb greenhouse-gas emissions in 1997, but Bush repudiated it four years later, saying it shackled the U.S. economy. The agreement, which on Feb. 16, 2005, went into effect in 141 countries, including all the major industrialized nations except the United States and Australia, requires member countries to reduce greenhouse-gas emissions by 5 percent below 1990 levels by 2012. [18] The European Union (EU), whose member nations also signed the treaty, has set an even more ambitious decrease — 8 percent — by 2012. [19]

To meet that goal, European governments are investing heavily in alternative-energy technologies, especially wind turbines. "Wind energy is the fastest-growing energy source in the world," says Thresher of NREL. "In the past five years, it's been growing by up to 30 percent a year, but most of that growth is in Europe." Germany's more than 16,000 windmills generate 39 percent of the world's wind energy, making it the leading global producer. Denmark generates 20 percent of its electrical power from wind turbines, and Spain is not far behind. [20]

But even with the loss of federal support, wind energy is fast becoming competitive with coal, natural gas and other electricity sources in the United States. Since 1980, when the first commercial wind farms were built in California, the cost of wind-generated electricity has fallen from almost 50 cents a kilowatt hour to around 4 to 6 cents — similar to the cost of power generated from coal or natural gas. As a sign of wind's promise, two years ago General Electric bought the largest U.S. wind-energy producer from a bankrupt Enron. [21]

The United States has lost its global edge, however, in solar energy, another highly promising alternative

source. "The United States accounted for about half of global solar production in 1997, but today we account for less than 10 percent," says Resch, of the Solar Energy Industries Association. "Policies adopted by other countries have created markets that are much more robust than what we have in the United States." Japan is now the world leader in solar energy, which, together with wind, provides 10 percent of the country's electricity. [22]

While no one expects the Bush administration or Congress to boost government subsidies for renewable energy to European levels, experts say lawmakers could help make American producers more competitive by establishing permanent tax incentives to develop and use alternative-energy sources. Current federal tax credits for producing renewable energy and buying hybrid vehicles, for example, are subject to change each year. "If we've dropped the ball on renewable energy, it's because you can't count on the tax credits," Thresher says. "With tax credits always in limbo, we have a chaotic market, where it's either feast or famine."

The European Union's Kyoto obligations mean that it will have to produce 22 percent of its electricity — 12 percent of its total energy — from renewable sources by 2010, says Rifkin, who advises the European Commission on energy policy. But because solar and wind power are only available when the sun is shining or the wind is blowing — and cannot be used to power automobiles — the EU launched an aggressive program to develop hydrogen technology. "You can't use solar or a windmill on your car," he says, "and that's what pushed the EU to begin moving toward a 'green' hydrogen future."

However, Europe may run into competition from the United States on hydrogen fuel cells — the one area where the Bush administration appears determined to dominate the alternative-energy market. Indeed, Rifkin says, Europe's plan to develop hydrogen technology spurred the administration to launch the Hydrogen Initiative two years ago.

"There's nothing like a little competition to get things moving," Rifkin says. "When American companies found out what was happening in Europe, they launched a big lobby push at the White House because they didn't want to fall behind Europe on this."

BACKGROUND

Mixed Messages

The Industrial Revolution depended on fossil fuels for its energy. Coal — far more efficient than wood — enabled James Watt's steam engine to drive factories, steel mills and trains, establishing a pattern of economic development centered on industrial cities connected by rail.

After the Texas oil boom at the turn of the 20th century, petroleum was refined into gasoline and diesel to fuel the internal-combustion engine — propelling the United States to the forefront of the global economy. And when Henry Ford's assembly lines began churning out inexpensive Model Ts, Americans rapidly turned to automobiles as their chief form of transportation, spurring suburban development and the construction of a vast network of roads and highways. Natural gas, initially burned off as a useless byproduct of oil extraction, became a key energy source for heating buildings, cooking and generating electricity.

For most of the 20th century the United States enjoyed seemingly endless supplies of coal, oil and natural gas. Even after oil imports began to account for a growing portion of the energy mix in the late 1950s, America's growing reliance on foreign oil went unnoticed amid the postwar economic boom.

That complacency ended on Oct. 20, 1973, when Arab members of the Organization of Petroleum Exporting Countries (OPEC) embargoed oil exports to the United States in retaliation for its support of Israel in the Yom Kippur War. [23] World oil prices skyrocketed, and gasoline prices followed suit, prompting panic buying and long lines at gas stations. In response, lawmakers created the Energy Research and Development Administration, to ensure adequate energy supplies, and the Strategic Petroleum Reserve, a 700-million-barrel federal stockpile to reduce future disruptions of oil imports.

The 1973 energy crisis also prompted policymakers to implement energy-conservation measures, notably the 1975 CAFE (corporate average fuel economy) standards requiring automakers to reduce fuel consumption in new cars. Under the standards, U.S. automobiles were required to achieve an average of at least 27.5 miles per gallon fuel efficiency (20.7 mpg for light trucks) by 1987. Because Detroit's Big Three automakers were slow

to improve the fuel economy of their automobiles, Japanese companies like Toyota and Honda quickly made inroads in the U.S. market with their inexpensive, fuel-efficient models.

In 1977, President Jimmy Carter's National Energy Plan called reducing America's reliance on foreign energy sources "the moral equivalent of war." At his request, Congress elevated energy policy to a top national priority, creating the Cabinet-level Department of Energy in August 1977. Regulations requiring more-efficient building insulation and appliances effectively reduced energy consumption, the cheapest and most effective way to reduce dependence on foreign energy sources. Congress passed tax incentives to spur research into alternative-energy sources, such as solar, wind and geothermal energy. Federal dollars also flowed into the construction of nuclear power plants until 1979, when an accident at the Three Mile Island nuclear facility in Middletown, Pa., raised concerns about the industry's safety and halted new reactor construction.

Federal support for alternative-energy development was strengthened by the Public Utility Regulatory Policies Act (PURPA), part of the National Energy Act signed by Carter on Nov. 9, 1978. Instead of directly funding research and development, PURPA helped create a market for renewable-energy sources by requiring utilities to include them in the mix of fuels they used to generate electricity.

But Carter's ambitious energy plan came to naught after the Iranian Revolution of 1978-79 ushered in a fundamentalist Muslim regime, and the flow of Middle East oil was again disrupted. This second energy crisis, together with Carter's inability to free 52 American hostages from the U.S. Embassy in Tehran, helped ensure his loss to Ronald Reagan (1981-1989) in the 1980 presidential election. Reagan and his Republican administration reversed Carter's focus on alternative-energy sources. Reagan opened federal lands to oil and coal mining and sent U.S. warships to protect Persian Gulf shipping lanes. He allowed government subsidies for alternative-energy sources to expire in 1985, and federal funding for alternative-energy research dropped from $1 billion in 1981 to $116 million in 1989. [24]

Reagan's push to deregulate U.S. businesses immediately affected the energy sector: Natural-gas price regulations were lifted in 1989 — a trend that continued under Reagan's successor, Republican George H. W.

CHRONOLOGY

1970s *Energy crises spur research into non-oil energy sources.*

October 1970 U.S. oil production peaks at 10 million barrels a day, beginning a period of gradual decline and increasing reliance on oil imports.

Oct. 20, 1973 Arab members of the Organization of Petroleum Exporting Countries (OPEC) embargo oil exports to the U.S. in retaliation for American support for Israel in the Yom Kippur War.

1975 Federal CAFE (corporate average fuel economy) standards are introduced, requiring automakers to reduce fuel consumption in new cars.

1977 President Jimmy Carter calls his National Energy Plan to reduce U.S. reliance on foreign energy sources "the moral equivalent of war." Congress creates the Cabinet-level Energy Department, elevating energy policy to a top national priority.

Nov. 9, 1978 To spur commercialization of renewable-energy sources, Carter signs the Public Utility Regulatory Policies Act, requiring utilities to use some renewables in generating electricity.

1979 An accident at the Three Mile Island nuclear power plant in Middletown, Pa., casts doubt on the potential for nuclear power to safely meet the country's electricity needs.

1980s *Amid falling oil prices and Republican opposition to government subsidies, spending on alternative-energy research and development plummets.*

1980 The first commercial power-generating wind farms are built in California.

1985 Federal subsidies for alternative-energy industries expire, while federal funding for renewables research begins to plummet to about one-tenth of previous levels.

1987 Automakers are required to achieve an average of at least 27.5 miles per gallon (mpg) for cars and 20.7 mpg for light trucks.

1990s *Despite support for non-polluting energy sources by*

the Democratic Clinton administration, a Republican-dominated Congress limits funding for renewable energy.

July 1992 President George H. W. Bush signs the precursor agreement to the Kyoto Protocol, an international treaty to reduce emissions of carbon dioxide and other greenhouse gases believed to cause global warming.

1997 Vice President Al Gore signs the Kyoto Protocol requiring the U.S. to cut its carbon emissions by 5 percent below 1990 levels by 2012.

December 1998 Global crude oil prices fall to $10 a barrel, fueling a surge in consumer demand for sport-utility vehicles (SUVs) and other gas guzzlers.

2000s *A Republican administration and a Republican majority in Congress press for increased domestic production of fossil fuels.*

May 2001 President George W. Bush's National Energy Policy downplays the environmental impacts of energy use, including global warming, and calls for intensified domestic production of oil, coal and natural gas in previously off-limits places like the Arctic National Wildlife Refuge (ANWR). It also recommends research to develop new, safer nuclear reactors to generate electricity.

Jan. 28, 2003 In his State of the Union address, Bush introduces his Hydrogen Initiative, a $1.2 billion effort to spur development of non-polluting cars that run on hydrogen fuel cells by 2020.

2004 American Physical Society concludes that major scientific breakthroughs will be necessary for the president's Hydrogen Initiative to successfully produce a commercially viable hydrogen-fueled car by 2020.

Feb. 10, 2005 As Congress prepares to take up Bush's energy bill, Sens. John McCain, R-Ariz., and Joseph I. Lieberman, D-Conn., reintroduce their Climate Stewardship Act calling for a domestic "cap-and-trade" system for curbing carbon emissions. On Feb. 16 the Kyoto Protocol goes into effect in 141 countries, but not the United States.

2025 Energy Department predicts that oil prices will climb to $52 a barrel after declining to $25 a barrel in 2010, as new supplies reach the market.

Bush. The 1992 Energy Policy Act opened the door for electric-utility deregulation, while reinstating some of Carter's earlier incentives for conservation and renewable-energy development. The small renewable-energy industry received a further boost in June 1992, when Bush signed the precursor agreement to the Kyoto Protocol, an international treaty that formally committed signatory nations to reduce greenhouse-gas emissions to 1990 levels by 2012. Such a drastic reduction in emissions by the world's largest emitter of fuel-related carbon dioxide would require a significant shift to non-fossil fuels.

However, the discovery of oil in the North Sea and Nigeria kept oil prices low during the 1980s and '90s, removing much of the economic incentive to develop alternatives to fossil fuels. In December 1998, crude oil prices hit an all-time low of $10 a barrel. Lured by affordable gasoline, American motorists abandoned small cars for larger sedans and SUVs, which were classified as light trucks and thus subject to less-stringent fuel-efficiency standards.

Despite the resulting decline in fuel efficiency, Congress in 1996 barred the National Highway Traffic Safety Administration (NHTSA) from even considering raising CAFE standards above original levels.

After Democrat Bill Clinton (1993-2001) took over the White House in 1993, his energy policy reflected mounting concern about the dangers of global warming. He declared the reduction of carbon emissions a top national priority, and in 1994 ordered all executive agencies to reduce energy consumption to 30 percent less than 1985 levels by 2005. However, a Republican-dominated Congress rejected Clinton's proposals to increase federal support for alternative-energy sources that could have reduced those emissions.

Bush's Energy Policy

Shortly after Bush was inaugurated in 2001, Vice President Cheney convened a blue-ribbon panel to develop an energy policy for the new Republican administration. As a former chief executive officer for Halliburton Co., a major supplier of oil and gas industry products and services, Cheney was criticized for refusing to reveal the proceedings of his advisory group, reputed to have drawn heavily from advocates of the oil, coal and nuclear industries. A court suit challenging the secrecy is pending.

The world's first hydrogen energy station began pumping in 2002 in Las Vegas. It's part of a $10.8 million, public-private demonstration project. A hydrogen generator produces hydrogen by reforming natural gas and sends the hydrogen to storage tanks in gaseous form. It then can be pumped into hydrogen-fueled vehicles. Hydrogen not used for vehicles is directed to a fuel cell that generates power for the Las Vegas electrical grid for general consumer use.

Getty Images/David McNew

Bush released his National Energy Policy in May 2001. [25] It emphasized the need to shore up energy supplies and downplayed the environmental impacts of energy use, including global warming. The report called for intensified domestic production of oil, coal and natural gas, with the pristine Arctic National Wildlife Refuge no longer off-limits. The policy also recommended research to develop new, safer nuclear reactors to generate electricity. Although 103 nuclear power plants generate 20 percent of electricity in the United States, no new plants have been ordered since 1973. [26]

The plan said renewable-energy sources probably would not account for more than 6 percent of total energy supplies through 2020. Meanwhile, the president's first budget proposal slashed spending for renewable-energy research and development by 50 percent and cut by 28 percent funding for a Clinton-era research partnership with U.S. automakers to develop cleaner and more efficient vehicles. The plan also emphasized research into "clean-coal" technologies that would allow the United States to continue exploiting its abundant coal resources by sequestering, or capturing, the carbon released from burning coal before it escapes into the atmosphere as carbon dioxide.

Major Alternative Energy Sources

Energy sources that regenerate and can be sustained indefinitely, sometimes called "green" renewables, contribute much less to global warming and climate change than exhaustible fossil fuels like petroleum and coal, which pollute when they are burned. Currently, renewable-energy sources provide about 6 percent of the nation's total energy output.

Hydrogen — Unlike fossil fuels or renewable-energy sources like solar or wind energy, hydrogen is not converted directly into electricity. Rather, it must be produced from hydrogen-containing materials — like water, natural gas or methane — using electricity generated from another fuel. The hydrogen is then stored in a tank located adjacent to a fuel cell — which uses the hydrogen to run vehicles, machinery or appliances. The tank has to be refilled periodically at a hydrogen fuel station.

Hydrogen fuel cells are non-polluting: Their only byproducts are water and heat. And because hydrogen is abundantly available, fuel-cell technology could potentially free countries from dependence on foreign energy sources.

Hydrogen molecules are typically separated from other materials by electrolysis or steam reforming. [1] Electrolysis uses electric current to split molecules of water (H_2O) into hydrogen and oxygen. As the gases bubble up through the water tank, the hydrogen can be captured and stored. Steam reforming combines steam and a hydrocarbon — such as methanol (CH_3OH) — at high pressure and temperature to produce hydrogen and carbon dioxide.

Wind — Windmills have been used to generate electricity in remote locations in the United States since the early 1900s. But after the 1973 OPEC oil embargo caused oil and gas prices to spike, the federal government began funding research into new wind-power technology. NASA developed the first modern wind turbines in the mid 1970s. By 1979, after a second round of oil-price shocks, federal funding for wind-power research and development exceeded $50 million a year. However, when oil prices fell during the Reagan administration, federal funding for wind-power research plummeted, dropping to $17 million by 1982. [2]

Wind power continued to develop, however, in several states. California began installing wind farms in 1983, and by 1990 the state was producing more than half the world's wind power. Since then, European countries, led by Germany, have taken the lead in wind generation by heavily subsidizing the construction of wind farms.

Solar — Solar thermal energy results when solar radiation is converted into heat. This can be done with a simple, passive solar heating system, such as south-facing windows opening onto a dark-colored stone floor, which stores and slowly releases the heat into the surrounding room. In more complex rooftop systems, solar panels containing a fluid — such as water or oil — are heated by sunlight, and the fluid is then pumped through a continuous circuit of pipes to heat interior rooms.

Environmentalists and Democratic lawmakers immediately attacked the plan for its continued reliance on fossil fuels. Then-Senate Minority Leader Tom Daschle, D-S.D., proposed barring drilling in ANWR and increasing funding for renewable-energy technology. Neither approach, however, garnered enough support to become law during the first Bush administration.

While the energy bill was stalled in Congress, the administration helped traditional energy industries by easing regulations aimed at curbing air pollution. [27] In particular, the president repudiated the Kyoto Protocol and proposed new rules that would weaken Carter-era Clean Air regulations. Known as New Source Review, the regulations required utilities and some other indus-

tries to install "scrubbers," or filters, to reduce emissions of major air pollutants from coal-fired plants. The rule changes, which pit industrial users of coal against environmentalists, are the subject of litigation now before the U.S. Court of Appeals for the D.C. Circuit. [28]

Hydrogen Initiative

The Bush energy policy's most innovative feature is its aggressive push to leapfrog existing alternative fuels, such as solar and wind energy, and develop an energy portfolio based largely on hydrogen.

Presented in 2003, Bush's Hydrogen Initiative would provide $1.2 billion to develop commercially viable hydrogen fuel cells to power vehicles and generate electricity. A

Solar photovoltaic technology converts solar radiation into electricity, which can be used for any purpose. Developed by Bell Labs in the early 1950s, photovoltaics got a boost from federal funding after the energy crises of the 1970s. By 1981, Boeing and Kodak had improved the technology's efficiency with the first thin-film photovoltaic cells. But, as with wind energy, leadership in solar technology has shifted to Europe and Japan, especially after Germany's Siemens AG bought California-based ARCO Solar in 1990, then the world's largest photovoltaic company.

Geothermal — Technology converting underground steam to electricity originated in Italy in the early 1900s, but the first commercial-scale geothermal facility in the United States did not appear until 1960, when Pacific Gas & Electric installed a 10-megawatt unit in California, called The Geysers. Federal support to develop geothermal facilities peaked in the late 1970s at about $100 million a year and now stands at around $30 million a year. Nevertheless, the United States maintains a leading position in the global geothermal industry; since 1985, U.S. developers have added nearly 1,000 megawatts of geothermal electric generating capacity outside The Geysers, and California Energy is the world's largest geothermal company.

Biomass — Half the world's population burns wood for heating and cooking, which contributes to deforestation, causes air pollution and exacerbates global warming by releasing carbon dioxide. But organic matter can be an important source of renewable energy. Moreover, unlike other renewable-energy sources, biomass can be converted directly into transportation fuels. Ethanol, a form of alcohol, is made by fermenting carbohydrate-rich plants such as corn to produce a gasoline additive that reduces harmful emissions. Biodiesel, which can be made from recycled cooking oils and animal fats, can be used alone or added to regular diesel fuel to reduce emissions. Biomass can also be converted into a fuel oil to generate electricity or be burned directly to produce steam for electrical generation or other industrial uses. Critics oppose ethanol because they say it takes more net energy to produce ethanol than is saved by burning it.

Wave Energy — Traditional hydropower, which converts the energy of moving river water into electricity, is a major source of power in the West. But a vast, largely untapped reserve of energy is held in the waves, tides and even the heat of the world's oceans. Tidal energy can be captured by erecting a dam across the opening of a tidal basin and using traditional hydropower technologies to turn turbines to generate electricity from the elevated water in the basin as the tide recedes. Britain, whose western coastline has some of the most powerful wave action in the world, is launching a program to capture wave energy to generate electricity. Wave energy is still in the research stage in the United States.

---

[1] See Richard Tarara, "Hydrogen: A Key Component of Energy in the Future," St. Mary's College, Department of Physics, April 30, 2001; stmarys.edu.

[2] Unless otherwise noted, information on renewables comes from the Energy Information Administration, www.eia.gov.

related program — the FreedomCAR (an acronym for cooperative automotive research) initiative introduced in 2002 — would spend $500 million to help the auto industry develop automobiles powered by hydrogen fuel cells by 2020. Together, the two programs brought total funding for hydrogen research to $1.7 billion over five years.

"Hydrogen power will dramatically reduce greenhouse-gas emissions, helping this nation take the lead when it comes to tackling the long-term challenges of global climate change," Bush said. "One of the greatest results of using hydrogen power, of course, will be energy independence for this nation. . . . If we develop hydrogen power to its full potential, we can reduce our demand for oil by over 11 million barrels per day by the year 2040." [29]

In 2003, the administration joined 15 countries and the European Union in the International Partnership for the Hydrogen Economy to coordinate international research and development of hydrogen technology. Besides Europe and the United States, the partnership includes Australia, Brazil, Canada, China, India, Japan, South Korea and Russia. Taken together, it accounts for $35 trillion in economic output and two-thirds of global energy consumption and carbon dioxide emissions.

In 2004, the Energy Department issued a detailed timetable for developing hydrogen fuel cells. [30] But the administration's hydrogen programs quickly came under scrutiny. The American Physical Society last year concluded that major scientific breakthroughs would be nec-

Jeremy Rifkin's World Without Oil

It's hard to imagine a world without oil, but Jeremy Rifkin can — and in the not-very-distant future. Rifkin and other boosters say a wholesale switch to hydrogen will open the door to an entirely new way of life free of air pollution and dependence on imported oil and less threatened by global warming.

"This is an extraordinary opportunity," says Rifkin, president of the Foundation on Economic Trends in Washington, D.C. "When you look at the great economic changes in history, which are very infrequent, they occur when two things happen: A basic change in the way we use the energy of the planet and a basic change in the way we communicate with each other to organize that energy."

The author of 16 books on the impact of scientific and technological changes on society, Rifkin is one of the most outspoken advocates of a "hydrogen economy" relying on fuel cells to meet virtually all the world's energy needs.

In Rifkin's vision, explained in his 2003 book, *The Hydrogen Economy*, a complete transformation to hydrogen fuel cells will bring more far-reaching changes to global society than simply curbing pollution and ending oil dependence.

"The whole 19th and 20th centuries revolved around the geopolitics of fossil fuels," he says. In his view, fuel cells could destroy that dynamic. Just as personal computers and the Internet have ushered in a "second industrial revolution" in com-munications, Rifkin says, fuel cells could trigger a "third industrial revolution" by enabling individual households to generate the power they need and even sell any excess to the power grid.

"The fuel cell is analogous to the personal computer," he says. "With the PC we generate our own information; with a fuel cell you can generate your own energy."

Once hydrogen fuel cells are widely available, Rifkin foresees a new role for the ubiquitous automobile. Because cars are parked for most of the time, they could be used as "power stations on wheels," plugged into homes and offices to provide electricity for myriad uses. They also could feed excess power to the grid through a so-called distributed energy system.

Such a system could free consumers from centralized utilities — and the utility bills and vulnerability to blackouts they entail, Rifkin says — and also have radical implications for society in general.

"Whoever controls the energy in a civilization controls the civilization itself," Rifkin says. "If you move from elite, top-down energy systems like nuclear, coal and oil to energy generated by renewable sources that you [use to produce hydrogen and] then store with fuel cells and can even share with other consumers, then you will have true power to the people."

Hydrogen also holds great promise for developing nations, Rifkin says. "Two-thirds of the people on Earth have never placed a phone call, and a third of them have no

essary for the Hydrogen Initiative to successfully produce a commercially viable hydrogen-fueled car by 2020. Among the biggest obstacles, the physicists concluded, are the high cost of fuel-cell production methods and the lack of a suitable material to use in building a safe hydrogen fuel tank. [31]

CURRENT SITUATION

Ambivalent Consumers

When it comes to their cars, Americans appear ambivalent about changing longstanding energy habits. Absent strong disincentives to waste energy, such as high gasoline prices or taxes, they ignore warnings about U.S. dependence on foreign oil or the environmental harm caused by driving gas-guzzlers, as shown by the huge popularity of SUVs over the past 10 years. [32]

This seeming disregard for energy use has its roots in U.S. history. "This country was built around an abundance of resources," says former Energy official Romm. "Even as late as the 1950s, the United States produced twice as much oil as the rest of the world combined."

But when rising energy prices hit consumers' pocketbooks, attitudes appear to change — at least among some consumers. When two "oil shocks" drove up gasoline prices in the 1970s, many consumers abandoned their U.S.-made gas-guzzlers in favor of efficient Japanese cars and spent millions insulating their houses. Last year, when the price of gasoline hit the $2-per-gallon mark, demand for hybrid cars such as the Prius spiked, after

electricity," he says. "So this is about more than energy security or the environment; it's also a critical means to establish a new economy for the 21st century for the entire planet and bring in the marginalized and peripheral parts of the human race that have never been involved in globalization. The reason they're powerless is literally because they don't have any power."

Critics of switching to a hydrogen economy say the focus on fuel cells ignores the technology's drawbacks and diverts attention from solar, wind, geothermal and other renewable, non-polluting resources that are on the verge of becoming competitive alternatives to fossil fuels. But Rifkin says the critics miss the point.

"It's very frustrating because this is not rocket science," he says. "Solar, wind and geothermal energy sources are intermittent, so once they start contributing 15 percent or so of total energy production, you have to have a

Jeremy Rifkin predicts that hydrogen fuel cells will change the world in ways far more profound than simply curbing pollution and ending oil dependence.

way to store that energy, which is what the hydrogen fuel cell will do."

For now, Rifkin's vision has found its most receptive audience in Europe, where he is advising the European Commission on developing fuel-cell technologies. The commission has committed more than $2 billion over the next several years for research into sustainable-energy projects, with hydrogen energy to be used as the critical storage carrier for renewable energy. Within eight years, he says, Europe hopes to generate 22 percent of its electricity by renewable sources such as wind and solar power, with hydrogen fuel cells storing the excess.

The European plan would continue to use natural gas to generate electricity, but will be subsidizing renewable-energy industries with an eye to replacing fossil fuels. "Europe is not saying no to fossil fuels," Rifkin says, "but Europe is committed to a renewable-energy future [based on] the hydrogen fuel cell."

having stalled when first introduced eight years earlier. Now buyers are on waiting lists to buy hybrids.

That ambivalence — or at least the splintered nature of the U.S. automobile market — is reflected in the wide range of choices available to American car buyers. Even as automakers begin offering several models of fuel-efficient hybrid cars — including a hybrid version of Ford's small Escape SUV — they also are churning out large sedans with V-8 engines and powerful sports cars reminiscent of the pre-oil embargo era of the 1960s. [33]

"We're responding to consumer demand," says Shosteck of the Alliance of Automobile Manufacturers. "We're doing our part by offering a vast array of vehicles that get very high mileage and working on all these advanced technologies, such as hybrids and vehicles that run on fuel cells, advanced diesel engines and alternative

fuels. But we can only go half way. We need consumers to do the other half — that is to buy these vehicles in large numbers."

But consumers are sending lawmakers mixed messages about alternative energy sources outside the auto showroom. Some states encourage consumers to buy hybrid vehicles by allowing hybrid drivers to use restricted lanes on heavily congested commuter routes even when they do not have any passengers. Restricted lanes are generally reserved for multiple-passenger vehicles during rush hours. But after Virginia endorsed such a rule on its restricted lanes leading into Washington, and single-driver hybrid cars suddenly began crowding onto the restricted lanes, other drivers complained; state legislators are now reconsidering the measure. [34]

London is one of nine European cities testing hydrogen-powered buses during a two-year trial to reduce greenhouse-gas emissions and noise pollution. Mayor Ken Livingstone called the buses the "greenest, cleanest and quietest ever."

Other alternative-energy sources have engendered popular resistance as well. Environmental advocates complain that birds and bats are endangered by the spinning turbines in windmills, which are finally on the verge of becoming cost-effective alternatives to coal-fired power plants. And Europeans complain about the noise and unsightliness of windmill farms, which are far more ubiquitous in Europe than here.

"The tendency in Europe now is to place wind farms offshore," says Thresher of NREL. "Not only is the wind more constant offshore, but you can also get the windmills away from people, so they don't have to look at them as much."

One federally supported effort to conserve energy has been an unqualified success among consumers. The voluntary Energy Star program, launched in 1992, certifies products such as building materials and appliances that meet minimum standards for energy efficiency. Last year alone the program saved $8 billion in energy costs. [35] Energy Star has become so widely accepted that its standards have become the minimum consumers will accept.

"The Energy Star label on a replacement window, for example, is almost the price of admission into the mar-

ket today," explains the Energy Department's Garman. Because most replacement windows meet the standards, he says, "The manufacturers tell me that if their products fail to qualify for the Energy Star label, they will soon be out of business."

State Alternatives

While the debate over energy policy has been stalled in Congress, many state governments have taken steps to increase the use of alternative-energy sources.

California, long the leader in innovative state energy policy, continues to apply the most sweeping measures to wean itself from polluting fossil fuels, including the country's most stringent mandates requiring automakers to offer low-emissions automobiles. [36] Gov. Arnold Schwarzenegger also has set up a program to build a "hydrogen highway" in California, with at least 150 hydrogen-fueling stations, to spur the development and sale of hydrogen vehicles. So far, 27 stations have been built nationwide. [37]

Because electrical power is regulated at the state level, some recent state energy initiatives are changing the source of consumers' electricity. California, Texas, New York, Massachusetts and 13 other states have adopted so-called renewable energy-portfolio standards, which require utilities to buy set percentages of their electricity from wind farms and other renewable sources. Ironically, Texas — with its longstanding emphasis on oil and gas production — now has one of the most aggressive renewable standards, signed into law in 1999 by then-Gov. George W. Bush. Under the law, utilities are required to add 2,000 megawatts of renewable energy to their total energy mix by 2009. [38]

Wind farms are contributing the bulk of this additional electricity, largely because rising natural-gas prices are making wind-energy prices competitive in many parts of the country. [39] But solar advocates see a growing role for photovoltaic solar panels as well.

"Photovoltaics has tremendous potential in all the states, not just the desert Southwest," says Resch of the Solar Energy Industries Association. One reason is strictly economics: Installing a solar photovoltaic system creates 35 jobs for every megawatt it generates, Resch estimates, compared with three or four jobs created per megawatt of electricity generated from natural gas or coal. "State governors and legislatures are recognizing that increasing photovoltaic use in their states is going to

Should U.S. energy policy focus on developing hydrogen fuel cells?

YES

David Garman
Assistant Energy Secretary for Energy Efficiency and Renewable Energy

From testimony before the House Science Committee, March 3, 2004

A little more than one year ago the president announced a pioneering plan to transform the nation's energy future from one dependent on foreign petroleum to one that utilizes the most abundant element in the universe — hydrogen. This solution holds the potential to provide virtually limitless, clean, safe, secure, affordable and reliable energy from domestic resources.

To achieve this vision, the president proposed that the federal government significantly increase its investment in . . . hydrogen production, storage and delivery technologies, as well as fuel cells — with the goal of enabling an industry decision by 2015 to commercialize hydrogen fuel-cell vehicles.

We won't realize the full potential of a hydrogen economy for several decades. Phase I technology development will lead to a commercialization decision by industry only if government-sponsored and private research is successful in meeting customer requirements and in establishing a business case that can convince industry to invest. . . .

Our focus today is the research and development to overcome the technical barriers associated with hydrogen and fuel-cell technologies — including lowering the cost of hydrogen production and fuel-cell technologies, improving hydrogen storage systems and developing codes and standards for hydrogen handling and use. . . . Over the past year our progress has increased confidence that the 2015 goal is realistic and attainable. . . .

Our focus on hydrogen fuel-cell vehicles does not come at the expense of support for conservation and gasoline hybrid vehicles as a short-term strategy for reducing oil use, [air] pollutants and greenhouse-gas emissions. . . .

However, it will take a revolutionary approach like hydrogen fuel cells to provide the fundamental change that will allow us to be completely independent of oil and free of carbon in the tailpipe. Incremental changes available in the near term will not overcome the increasing demands for a limited supply of oil. . . .

Achieving the vision of the hydrogen-energy future is a great challenge. It will require careful planning and coordination, public education, technology development and substantial public and private investments. It will require a broad political consensus and a bipartisan approach. Most of all, it will take leadership and resolve.

By being bold and innovative, we can change . . . our dependence upon foreign sources of energy; we can help with the quality of the air; and we can make a fundamental difference for the future of our children.

NO

Joseph Romm
Former Acting Assistant Secretary of Energy; author of The Hype about Hydrogen: Fact and Fiction in the Race to Save the Climate

From testimony before the House Science Committee, March 3, 2004

Hydrogen and fuel-cell cars are being hyped today as few technologies have ever been. In his January 2003 State of the Union address, President Bush announced a $1.2 billion research initiative, "so that the first car driven by a child born today could be powered by hydrogen and pollution-free." The April 2003 issue of *Wired* magazine proclaimed, "How Hydrogen Can Save America." In August 2003, General Motors said the promise of hydrogen cars justified delaying fuel-efficiency regulations.

Yet, . . . a number of recent studies raise serious doubts about the prospects for hydrogen cars. In February 2004, a prestigious National Academy of Sciences panel concluded, "In the best-case scenario, the transition to a hydrogen economy would take many decades, and any reductions in oil imports and carbon-dioxide emissions are likely to be minor during the next 25 years." And that's the best case.

Realistically, . . . a major effort to introduce hydrogen cars before 2030 would undermine efforts to reduce emissions of heat-trapping greenhouse gases like carbon dioxide — the main culprit in last century's planet-wide warming of 1 degree F.

As someone who helped oversee the Department of Energy's program for clean energy, including hydrogen, for much of the 1990s . . . I believe that continued research into hydrogen remains important because of its potential to provide a pollution-free substitute for oil in the second half of this century. But if we fail to limit greenhouse-gas emissions over the next decade — and especially if we fail to do so because we have bought into the hype about hydrogen's near-term prospects — we will be making an unforgivable national blunder that may lock in global warming for the U.S. of 1 degree Fahrenheit per decade by mid-century. . . .

The longer we wait to deploy existing clean-energy technologies, and the more inefficient, carbon-emitting infrastructure that we lock into place, the more expensive and the more onerous will be the burden on all segments of society when we finally do act.

If we fail to act now to reduce greenhouse-gas emissions — especially if we fail to act because we have bought into the hype about hydrogen's near-term prospects — future generations will condemn us because we did not act when we had the facts to guide us, and they will most likely be living in a world with a much hotter and harsher climate than ours, one that has undergone an irreversible change for the worse.

Wind turbines near Palm Springs, Calif., generate electricity from the consistently strong winds. Wind energy is considered the fastest-growing energy source in the world. In Germany, more than 16,000 windmills generate 39 percent of the world's wind energy.

mean jobs and that it's good economic policy as well as good energy policy," he says.

The economic benefits from state renewable-energy mandates are already beginning to materialize. Pennsylvania, for example, recently enacted renewable standards requiring 18 percent of the state's electricity to come from renewable sources by 2018. A controversial provision includes waste coal as an acceptable source, even though coal is the dirtiest source of electricity. But encouraging utilities to burn this coal would also remove a serious source of water pollution. The provision also gained the support of the United Mine Workers, who would gain jobs from utilizing the waste coal to generate electricity.

"There are jobs to be created in building and operating advanced coal plants that will operate using waste coal," says Hendricks of the Apollo Alliance. In addition, adoption of the new portfolio standards already has drawn business investment. The Spanish wind turbine manufacturer Gamesa, she says, recently announced that it would build a new plant in Pennsylvania's economically depressed coal country.

"They feel that there's a huge potential for wind energy in Pennsylvania and the mid-Atlantic region," Hendricks says. "Pennsylvania has the manufacturing

infrastructure, it has skilled labor and now it has a new portfolio standard that tells industry that the state is going to support new energy technology being produced there."

Some experts predict that regional and state climate differences will determine the energy mix triggered by the new portfolio standards. "If you live in Arizona, you're probably looking at more solar energy," Thresher says. "If you live in North or South Dakota, you'll probably want to use wind as your primary source, and if you live in the Farm Belt, some of the marginal land may be used to grow crops for biomass. These renewable sources would ultimately be used to produce hydrogen, which will likely be the fuel of choice 50 years down the road."

OUTLOOK

Energy Bill

When the 109th Congress convened in January, Republican leaders expected to quickly push through President Bush's energy bill, which has failed to win passage since it was submitted three years ago. Last fall's elections boosted the Republican majority to 55 seats in the Senate — just five short of the 60 needed to break a filibuster, which Senate Democrats and moderate Republicans have used to block the bill in the past. Republicans also now hold a comfortable, 31-seat majority in the House, which has passed the bill.

Senate Majority Leader Bill Frist, R-Tenn., appeared confident that the new Senate would pass the energy bill and included it among the first 10 pieces of legislation to be considered this year. "In the last Congress we probably spent as many days on the floor [on energy] as on any other bill," he said at a Jan. 24 press conference where he laid out his main legislative priorities. "I'm very excited about moving us toward energy independence in the future, and we're confident we can do that in this Congress."

But Republican confidence in early passage of the energy package has since waned. In early February, House Republican leaders abandoned a plan to take up the energy bill right away because it would cost more than allowed under the president's fiscal 2006 budget request. "It's not ready, and I don't know, frankly, when it will be ready," said House Majority Leader Tom DeLay, R-Texas, who predicted the bill would not come up for the vote for at least another month. [40]

The delay in congressional action on energy may give opponents of the plan time to build support for alternative proposals. "The administration's energy policy is a very mixed bag," says Lovins of the Rocky Mountain Institute. "There are a few good things in it, but most of it comes from the traditional hogs-at-the-trough mentality, which is not a good way to make policy."

By far the most controversial portion of the measure is the plan to expand domestic production by opening the ANWR to drilling. Not only is there insufficient evidence that the refuge holds significant oil deposits, critics say, but the trans-Alaska pipeline that would be used to transport it to the Lower 48 is aging and vulnerable to attack. Even the major oil companies that stand to profit from ANWR's development have recently backed away from the idea. [41]

"The oil companies aren't in the least interested in drilling in the Arctic refuge," Lovins says. "And even if they were, and they found oil there, it would be a grave threat to national security" because of the vulnerability of the pipeline.

But proponents aim to keep the ANWR provision in the bill. "ANWR sits neatly within those categories of what it is that we're looking for when we're seeking increased domestic production in this country, a decreased reliance on foreign sources of oil, an ability to provide for this country in a manner that can be balanced, that can be done in concert with the environment," said Sen. Lisa Murkowski, R-Alaska. "With the technology that we're utilizing up north, we can do it right. We just need the permission of Congress to go there." [42]

Critics also charge that the bill does little to reduce the U.S. contribution to global warming. The president's call for hydrogen research, they say, is not enough to offset the mounting emissions of greenhouse gases ensured by the plan's call for intensified use of fossil fuels. Sens. John McCain, R-Ariz., and Joseph I. Lieberman, D-Conn., are likely to use the delay in action on the energy bill to build bipartisan support for their Climate Stewardship Act, which would establish a domestic "cap-and-trade" system for curbing carbon emissions. Such a system would offer a powerful incentive for businesses to invest in clean, renewable energy sources.

McCain and Lieberman agree with many environmental advocates that fighting global warming has to be a major imperative of energy policy. "We must take a

more active role in finding a solution," McCain said on Feb. 10 as he and Lieberman reintroduced the bill and promised further proposals to spur development of technologies to harness non-fossil energy sources.

Challenging fellow Republicans who doubt the threat of global warming is big enough to warrant abandoning fossil fuels, McCain said, "Given the high stakes involved — the future of our children and our grandchildren, not to mention the future of the planet as we inherited it — which approach are you willing to bet on?"

NOTES

1. After Saudi Arabia and Canada. U.S. Energy Information Administration, www.eia.doe.gov.

2. See Tim Appenzeller, "The End of Cheap Oil," *National Geographic*, June 2004, pp. 80-109.

3. Energy Information Administration, "Annual Energy Outlook: 2005," February 2005.

4. Energy Information Administration, "International Energy Outlook 2004," April 2004.

5. For background, see Mary H. Cooper, "Energy and the Environment," *The CQ Researcher*, March 3, 2000, pp. 161-184.

6. For background, see Mary H. Cooper, "Global Warming Treaty," *The CQ Researcher*, Jan. 26, 2001, pp. 41-64; for information on the scientific debate over global warming, see William Triplett, "Science and Politics," *The CQ Researcher*, Aug. 20, 2004, pp. 661-684.

7. See Juliet Eilperin, "Arid Arizona Points to Global Warming as Culprit," *The Washington Post*, Feb. 6, 2005, p. A3.

8. Bodman, a chemical engineer who served as Treasury deputy secretary during Bush's first term, spoke Jan. 19, 2005, before the Senate Energy and Natural Resources Committee. On Feb. 1 he was confirmed to replace outgoing Energy Secretary Spencer Abraham.

9. For background, see Brian Hansen, "Nuclear Waste," *The CQ Researcher*, June 8, 2001, pp. 489-512.

10. For a comparison of hydrogen pros and cons, see Joseph Romm, *The Hype about Hydrogen* (2004), and Amory B. Lovins, "Twenty Hydrogen Myths, Rocky Mountain Institute, 2003; www.rmi.org.

11. See Energy Information Administration, "A Primer on Gasoline Prices," Aug. 3, 2004; and "Worldwide Hydrogen Fueling Stations," www.fuelcells.org.

12. Committee on Alternatives and Strategies for Future Hydrogen Production and Use, National Research Council, "The Hydrogen Economy" (2004).

13. For background, see Lovins, *op. cit.*

14. See Mary O'Driscoll, Ben Geman and Brian Stempeck, "DOE: Nuclear, Hydrogen Among Budget Winners," *Greenwire*, Feb. 7, 2005.

15. Apollo Alliance, "The Ten-Point Plan for Good Jobs and Energy Independence," www.apolloalliance.org.

16. From Bodman's Jan. 19, 2005, Senate Energy and Natural Resources Committee testimony.

17. For background see Mary H. Cooper, "Alternative Energy," *The CQ Researcher*, July 10, 1992, pp. 573-596.

18. For background see Mary H. Cooper, "Global Warming Treaty," *The CQ Researcher*, Jan. 26, 2001, pp. 41-64.

19. See "U.N. Conference on Climate Change: EU Set to Keep Momentum in the Global Fight Against Climate Change," European Union, Dec. 3, 2004, www.europa.eu.int.

20. See Robert Collier, "Germany Shines a Beam on the Future of Energy," Scripps Howard News Service, Dec. 21, 2004.

21. For background on Enron's bankruptcy, see Kenneth Jost, "Corporate Crime," *The CQ Researcher*, Oct. 11, 2002, pp. 817-840.

22. Collier, *op. cit.*

23. For background, see Nicole Gaouette, "Middle East Peace," *The CQ Researcher*, Jan. 21, 2005, pp. 53-76; and Mary H. Cooper, "Oil Diplomacy," *The CQ Researcher*, Jan. 24, 2003, pp. 49-72; and Mary H. Cooper, "Energy Security," *The CQ Researcher*, Feb. 1, 2002, pp. 73-96.

24. Cooper, "Energy Security," *ibid.*

25. National Energy Policy Development Group, "National Energy Policy," May 2001.

26. See Mark Holt, "Nuclear Energy Policy," Dec. 17, 2004, Congressional Research Service.

27. For background, see Mary H. Cooper, "Bush and the Environment," *The CQ Researcher*, Oct. 25, 2002, pp. 865-896.

28. See Lily Henning, "Circuit Reviews New EPA Rules on Pollution," *Legal Times*, Jan. 31, 2005, p. 1.

29. Bush spoke at the National Building Museum in Washington, D.C., Feb. 6, 2003.

30. U.S. Department of Energy, "Hydrogen Posture Plan," February 2004.

31. American Physical Society, "The Hydrogen Initiative," March 2004.

32. For background, see Mary H. Cooper, "SUV Debate," *The CQ Researcher*, May 16, 2003, pp. 449-472.

33. See Earl Swift, "The New Power Surge," *Parade*, Jan. 23, 2005, pp. 8-9.

34. See Steven Ginsberg and Carol Morello, "As Hybrid Cars Multiply, So Do Carpooling Gripes," *The Washington Post*, Jan. 7, 2005, p. A1.

35. www.energystar.gov.

36. For information on California's energy policy, see Cooper, "Energy Security," *op. cit.*

37. "California Rolls Toward Hydrogen," *Wired News*, wired.com, April 21, 2004.

38. See Marc Gunther, "Taking on the Energy Crunch," *Fortune*, Feb. 7, 2005, p. 97.

39. See Matthew L. Wald, "Wind Power Is Becoming a Better Bargain," *The New York Times*, Feb. 13, 2005, p. A17.

40. See Ben Evans, "Costs of Bill, Senate Schedule Slow Energy Legislation," *CQ Weekly*, Feb. 14, 2005, p. 407.

41. See Maureen Lorenzetti, "Oil Firms Lower Pressure on Push to Drill in Alaska," *CQ Weekly*, Jan. 24, 2005, pp. 157-158.

42. Testimony before Senate Energy and Natural Resources Committee, Jan. 19, 2005.

BIBLIOGRAPHY

Books

Deffeyes, Kenneth S., *Hubbert's Peak: The Impending World Oil Shortage*, Princeton University Press, 2001.
Geophysicist M. King Hubbert predicted correctly in 1956 that U.S. oil production would peak in 1970. The author, Hubbert's former colleague, predicts that a similar peak in global production will occur by 2006.

Hoffmann, Peter, *Tomorrow's Energy: Hydrogen, Fuel Cells, and the Prospects for a Cleaner Planet,* MIT Press, 2001.
A supporter of policies to encourage the development of hydrogen fuel cells describes steps to move toward a hydrogen-based economy.

Lovins, Amory B., *et al., Winning the Oil Endgame: Innovation for Profits, Jobs, and Security,* Rocky Mountain Institute, 2004.
By gradually substituting biofuels, natural gas and hydrogen for oil, the United States can wean itself from oil and profitably emerge from the transition, saving $130 billion per year by 2025.

Rifkin, Jeremy, *The Hydrogen Economy: The Creation of the Worldwide Energy Web and the Redistribution of Power on Earth,* Tarcher Putnum, 2003.
By enabling consumers to generate their own electricity, hydrogen fuel cells stand to reduce poverty and eliminate global struggles linked to dependence on fossil fuels.

Roberts, Paul, *The End of Oil: On the Edge of a Perilous New World,* Houghton Mifflin, 2004.
While other industrial nations are developing alternative-energy sources and cutting greenhouse-gas emissions, the Bush administration is calling for more fossil-fuel production and refuses to support mandated cuts in carbon emissions called for in the Kyoto Protocol.

Romm, Joseph J., *The Hype About Hydrogen: Fact and Fiction in the Race to Save the Climate,* Island Press, 2004.
Hydrogen fuel cells may be ready for use in factories and residences by 2010, but not for widespread transportation use until 2040. Meanwhile, the United States must speed the adoption of existing renewable energy sources and technologies to improve energy efficiency.

Articles

Appenzeller, Tim, "The End of Cheap Oil," *National Geographic,* June 2004, pp. 80-109.
Efforts are under way to squeeze usable oil out of tar sands and drill for previously inaccessible deposits. But Americans have yet to appreciate the myriad consumer products that are made from oil — and the difficulty of replacing this dwindling resource.

Glick, Daniel, "The Big Thaw," *National Geographic,* September 2004, pp. 12-33.
Scientific evidence is mounting that temperatures are rising faster than earlier predicted and that burning fossil fuels is the culprit.

Wald, Matthew L., "Questions About a Hydrogen Economy," *Scientific American,* May 2004, pp. 64-73.
Hydrogen fuel cells offer solutions to many of our current energy woes, but converting from fossil fuels to hydrogen presents formidable technical problems.

Reports and Studies

Energy Information Administration, "Annual Energy Outlook 2005," Feb. 11, 2005.
The Energy Department's latest long-range forecast predicts that oil prices will fall over the next five years as new reserves are found, but then rise slowly to about $52 a barrel by 2025 as demand outpaces production.

Lovins, Amory B., "Twenty Hydrogen Myths," June 20, 2003, Rocky Mountain Institute.
A supporter of efforts to bring non-polluting hydrogen fuel cells to market says claims that hydrogen is too expensive or dangerous are overblown or wrong.

Makower, Joel, Ron Pernick and Clint Wilder, "Clean Energy Trends 2004," Clean Edge Inc., 2004.
A research firm concludes that government policies such as requiring use of renewable energy and offering tax credits will be needed if renewable energy sources like solar and wind energy are to replace fossil fuels.

National Commission on Energy Policy, "Ending the Energy Stalemate: A Bipartisan Strategy to Meet America's Energy Challenges," December 2004.
Experts representing industry, consumers and government list energy-policy priorities they say everyone should endorse, such as expanding domestic oil production, strengthening vehicle-efficiency standards and doubling government funding for energy research and development.

U.S. Department of Energy, "Hydrogen Posture Plan: An Integrated Research, Development, and Demonstration Plan," February 2004.
A detailed strategy, based on President Bush's 2003 Hydrogen Initiative, for encouraging production of vehicles powered by hydrogen fuel cells and construction of the infrastructure needed for the transition to a hydrogen economy.

For More Information

Alliance of Automobile Manufacturers, 1401 I St., N.W., Suite 900, Washington, DC 20005; (202) 326-5500; www.autoalliance.org. A trade association representing nine U.S. and foreign automakers.

Apollo Alliance, Institute for America's Future, 1025 Connecticut Ave., N.W., Suite 205, Washington, DC 20036; (202) 955-5665; www.apolloalliance.org. A coalition of labor, environmental and business organizations that supports energy independence as a source of good jobs.

Energy Information Administration, EI 30, 1000 Independence Ave., S.W., Washington, DC 20585; (202) 586-8800; www.eia.doe.gov. The Energy Department's main source of information about every aspect of energy use, including fuels, consumption and forecasts.

Foundation on Economic Trends, 1660 L St., N.W., Suite 216, Washington, DC 20036; (202) 466-2823; www.foet.org. A research and advocacy organization that promotes cutting-edge technologies such as hydrogen fuel cells.

National Renewable Energy Laboratory (NREL), 1617 Cole Blvd., Golden, CO 80401-3393; (303) 275-3000; www.nrel.gov. The Energy Department's renewables research unit.

Rocky Mountain Institute, 1739 Snowmass Creek Rd., Snowmass, CO 81645-9199; (970) 927-3851; www.rmi.org. An environmental organization that supports energy efficiency and independence.

Solar Energy Industries Association, 805 15th St., N.W., Suite 510, Washington, DC 20005; (202) 682-0556; www.seia.org. The national trade association of manufacturers, dealers and installers.

11

Smart Growth

Mary H. Cooper

Shops, cinemas and outdoor dining share the neighborhood with new high-rise apartment and office buildings in Bethesda, Md. The popular mixed-use "infill" development — an example of the smart-growth trend — is two blocks from a subway stop and a 10-minute train ride from Washington, D.C.

CQ Press/Kathy Koch

From *CQ Researcher*,
May 28, 2004.

Nestled beside Virginia's Blue Ridge Mountains only 30 miles west of Washington, Loudoun County has long cherished its rolling pastures and dense woodlands.

Today, however, the rooftops of suburban housing developments pepper the bucolic countryside, and the county has emerged as a flashpoint in the acrimonious national debate over policies designed to deal with suburban sprawl.

Indeed, Loudoun was recently "crowned" as America's fastest-growing county. In just over three years, more than 50,000 people moved to Loudoun, boosting the population by more than 30 percent and spurring construction of thousands of new homes. [1]

"It is sad to see Loudoun following the lead of [neighboring] Fairfax County in its mass destruction of open space, wetlands and agricultural lands for the sake of development and greed," complained county resident Dennis Desmond. "Each day we see traffic grow, an increase in demand on limited freshwater supplies, and an increase in the pollution of groundwater, streams, ponds and the air." [2]

The county's explosive growth led to controversial, new anti-sprawl, or "smart growth," policies. Alarmed by the pace of development in eastern Loudoun, the county's Board of Supervisors last year set strict new limits on new-home construction in the rural western region, still dominated by dairy farms. The board reduced by 80,000 the number of new homes allowed to be built over the next several years and raised the minimum lot size from three acres per house to 10, 20, and in some areas, 50 acres per house. These restrictions, they hoped, would concentrate growth in the eastern, developed area and protect the remaining open space.

Many States Are Adopting Smart-Growth Measures

At least 20 states have passed statutes to discourage sprawl and promote smart growth, and many of them are now seeking additional reforms. Fifteen states currently have efforts under way to enact their first anti-sprawl laws.

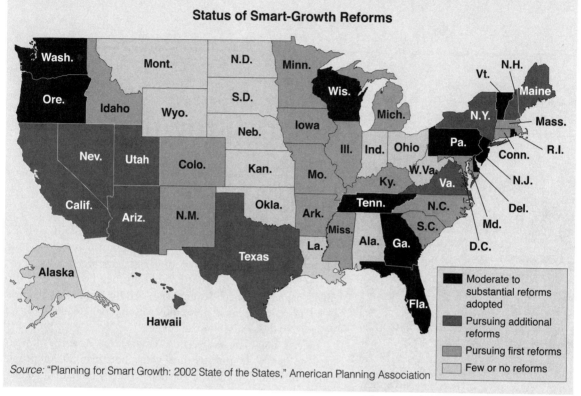

Status of Smart-Growth Reforms

Legend:
- Moderate to substantial reforms adopted
- Pursuing additional reforms
- Pursuing first reforms
- Few or no reforms

Source: "Planning for Smart Growth: 2002 State of the States," American Planning Association

But builders and some property owners complained the policies shut out developers and violated property rights. Farmers said the new rules denied them the right to sell off a few small parcels to pay rising property taxes — thus driving them off their farms.

Last fall, county voters elected a new, pro-development majority to the board, which has since overturned many of the building restrictions, renewing the controversy over Loudoun's future.

"Being No. 1 [in growth] doesn't worry me," says Stephen J. Snow, one of the new county supervisors who led the rollback of building restrictions. "I firmly believe in the American dream. So whatever we can do to help people raise themselves in life through home ownership is a good thing."

Building restrictions, he says, infringe on Americans' right to choose where to live. "People ought to have

access to the land," he says. "Take a look at our history, including the Oklahoma land rush, when they gave people land. Why? To create the American dream.

"How can a black or Hispanic family on the rise ever hope to buy 50 acres in Loudoun County?" he asks. "That's only for the wealthy. All we get from these policies is economic segregation. That is just so un-American it's beyond the pale."

With the nation losing 365 acres of open space every hour to developers' bulldozers, it's little wonder that the controversy dividing Loudoun County is echoing in communities across the country. [3] And much of the new growth is occurring in areas that have not had to deal with rapid growth before. While Los Angeles County — the perennial poster child for suburban sprawl — remains the nation's most populated county, rural counties like Loudoun are growing much faster. Indeed, half of the country's 10 fastest-growing counties are in predominantly rural Georgia, as suburban Atlanta development spills onto farmland far from downtown. (*See chart, p. 236.*)

Of course, suburban sprawl has been around for decades. But its environmental and cultural impact is becoming increasingly apparent as development expands farther from urban centers. Besides devouring open space and wildlife habitat, new suburbs degrade the quality of life in other ways, environmentalists say: By spending more time commuting, residents exacerbate both traffic congestion and air pollution. As runoff-absorbing trees and fields are paved over, stormwater that normally would have been absorbed into the ground ends up in streams, rivers and low-lying areas, often causing flooding or polluting waterways with salt, chemicals and microbes picked up on the way.

Sprawl also has homogenized the American cultural landscape, erasing much of the local character that distinguished a New England village, say, from a Kansas railroad town or a community that grew up around a California mission. Over the course of several decades, local ordinances separating residential from commercial and industrial areas have produced a seemingly endless patchwork of isolated bedroom communities where residents must drive in order to reach shops, schools and other destinations. Miles of strip malls filled with national chain stores flank major roadways, producing little to differentiate one community from another.

Some critics have even demonized sprawl as the source of contemporary ills ranging from homicidal alienation to obesity. (*See sidebar, p. 234.*) The movie "Bowling for Columbine," for instance, largely blamed the 1999 massacre by two teenagers at Columbine High School in suburban Littleton, Colo., on alienation caused in part by their community's sprawling development. In a similar vein, author James Howard Kunstler calls the suburbs "a

U.S. Cities With Worst Sprawl

Smart-growth advocates say Riverside, Calif., has the nation's worst sprawl. Two-thirds of Riverside's residents live more than 10 miles from a central business district, and fewer than 1 percent live in areas with enough population to support mass transit. Nearly all of the other most-sprawling cities are in the South or West.

The 10 Most-Sprawling Metropolitan Regions

Metropolitan Region	Rank
Riverside-San Bernardino, Calif.	1
Greensboro-Winston-Salem-High Point, N.C.	2
Raleigh-Durham, N.C.	3
Atlanta, Ga.	4
Greenville-Spartanburg, S.C.	5
West Palm Beach-Boca Raton-Delray Beach, Fla.	6
Bridgeport-Stamford-Norwalk-Danbury, Conn.	7
Knoxville, Tenn.	8
Oxnard-Ventura, Calif.	9
Fort Worth-Arlington, Texas	10

Source: "Measuring Sprawl and its Impact," *Smart Growth America*, Oct. 17, 2002

vast and evil setting," complaining of "the whole destructive, wasteful, toxic, agoraphobia-inducing spectacle that politicians proudly call 'growth.' " [4]

But while environmentalists, historic preservationists and other critics decry sprawl as dehumanizing, developers and property-rights advocates like Snow see sprawl as evidence that the American free-enterprise system works, creating wealth and well-being and allowing people to live where they choose. "For me, growth is neither good nor bad," says Samuel R. Staley, president of the Buckeye Institute for Public Policy Solutions in Columbus, Ohio. "As long as what we're doing is trying to accommodate the housing needs and preferences of people, I'm pretty happy with it." (*See "At Issue," p. 247.*)

Like sprawl itself, smart growth means different things to different people. "To paraphrase the old Supreme Court observation, smart growth is like pornography — there's no uniform definition; you just know it when you see it," says Clayton Traylor, senior vice president for state and local political affairs at the

Sprawl and Obesity Go Hand in Hand

Suburban development has long been criticized for consuming open space and exacerbating air pollution caused by traffic congestion. Now health experts are blaming sprawl for the twin American health ills — obesity and heart disease.

For years, public-health officials have warned of a rising epidemic of obesity in the United States. By 2000, 64 percent of adults in the United States were either overweight or obese, according to the Centers for Disease Control and Prevention (CDC). Both conditions are implicated in the rising incidence of heart disease, adult-onset diabetes and certain cancers. [1]

The trend is especially noticeable among children. Since the 1960s, the incidence of overweight and obesity among American children and adolescents has more than tripled, to about 15 percent. Obesity in children is especially alarming, experts say, because obese children are more likely to become obese adults, when the health consequences of overweight most often arise. [2]

Although overeating and poor diet, including the consumption of fatty junk food and high-calorie sodas, are the primary causes of overweight, the lack of physical exercise is another crucial factor, experts say. More than half of American adults fail to meet the surgeon general's recommendation for 30 minutes of moderate physical activity five days a week. More than a quarter don't get any exercise at all, the CDC reports. [3]

Experts say Americans' love affair with the automobile, encouraged by postwar suburban development, has contributed to the current obesity epidemic. A recent study found that counties with suburban sprawl have higher incidences of obesity and associated chronic illnesses, such as heart disease, than urban or rural counties. [4] By isolating residential areas from other parts of communities, sprawl forces people to drive to stores, schools and work. Even when destinations aren't too far away to reach by walking or bicycle, the lack of sidewalks along noisy, barren roadways usually discourages suburbanites from leaving their cars at home.

Americans' sedentary lifestyle is costing states and businesses billions of dollars in higher health-care premiums, lost productivity and increased workers' compensation payments, according to the National Governors Association. In Michigan, for example, 55 percent of adults are inactive, resulting in diseases that cost the state nearly $9 billion a year. [5]

To address the problem, in 2002 the association helped launch the Active Living Leadership initiative to help state and local governments advance more active lifestyles through zoning-law changes that encourage smart-growth — high-density, mixed-use communities with walkable streets, bike paths and public transit services. Thus far, the initiative has focused primarily on California, Colorado, Kentucky, Michigan and Washington.

Colorado boasts the lowest obesity rate in the country (17 percent of adults), but the state also has experienced the fastest increase in obesity over the past decade, prompting officials to look for ways to counter the trend by fighting sprawl. [6] For example, a 4,700-acre community being developed on the site of the old Stapleton Airport near Denver

National Association of Home Builders. "The home-building industry supports smart growth to the extent that we think better planning at the local level is needed. Good, comprehensive planning is smart, in and of itself, regardless of the pattern of development you're trying to achieve."

Some states, notably Oregon, have taken a stronger stand against sprawl, requiring all towns and cities to establish "urban growth boundaries" barring further development. And a growing number of local and even state governments are looking for ways to improve land-use planning by concentrating new construction in already-developed areas along transit corridors. A pioneer in this approach, known as "infilling," is former Democratic Gov. Parris Glendening of Maryland, who spearheaded Maryland's 1997 Smart Growth and Neighborhood Conservation Act. It required the state to deny or limit subsidies for new roads, sewers and schools outside state-identified "smart-growth" areas.

Infilling in older neighborhoods can help residents avoid driving to work and create people-friendly shopping, dining and entertainment meccas, replete with

entices residents out of their cars by incorporating walking and biking trails and public transit, built around a network of linked neighborhoods, each with retail and commercial sites within walking distance of schools and other amenities.

Simply changing land-use ordinances may go a long way toward improving Americans' health. For example, ordinances and school-board guidelines commonly discourage renovation of older, close-in schools and require that new schools be built on large sites, often 10 acres or more. As a result, schools are being shifted from established neighborhoods to the far edges of suburbia, too far for most pupils to walk or ride their bikes. [7]

But some experts say the link between suburban development and obesity is less clear than the studies suggest. "Many nutritionists would argue that diet is much more important than exercise in reaching and maintaining a healthy weight," says Samuel R. Staley, president of the Buckeye Institute, a Columbus, Ohio, organization that opposes strong government control over development. "If you're going to McDonald's every day, you probably aren't going to shave off

Americans' love affair with the automobile, encouraged by postwar suburban sprawl, has contributed to the obesity epidemic.

those extra pounds, no matter where you live."

In any case, Staley says, it's not the government's role to determine where people should live. "People should be allowed to make choices, even if they're poor choices," he says. "In this country you're allowed to be fat."

[1] Centers for Disease Control and Prevention (CDC), "National Health and Nutrition Examination Survey, 1999-2000." For background, see Alan Greenblatt, "Obesity Epidemic," *The CQ Researcher*, Jan. 31, 2003, pp. 73-104.

[2] American Heart Association, "Obesity and Overweight in Children," www.americanheart.org.

[3] CDC, "The Importance of Physical Activity," March 31, 2004, www.cdc.gov.

[4] Barbara A. McCann and Reid Ewing, "Measuring the Health Effects of Sprawl: A National Analysis of Physical Activity, Obesity and Chronic Disease," Smart Growth America and Surface Transportation Policy Project, September 2003.

[5] National Governors Association, "Story Idea: Smart Growth = Less Obesity?" March 15, 2004, www.nga.org.

[6] See Kirk Johnson, "Colorado Takes Strides to Polish Thin and Fit Image," *The New York Times*, Feb. 1, 2004, p. A12.

[7] See Constance E. Beaumont and Elizabeth G. Pianca, "Why Johnny Can't Walk to School: Historic Neighborhood Schools in the Age of Sprawl," National Trust for Historic Preservation, October 2002.

sidewalk-café ambiance. But infilling has its downsides. Some longtime residents complain that the high-rises dramatically alter a neighborhood's quality of life. And the new commercial areas can become victims of their own popularity if the resultant crowds, traffic congestion and parking problems end up producing more hassle than enjoyment.

Besides government-sponsored managed-growth initiatives, several architects and builders are combating sprawl on their own by creating so-called New Urbanist communities from scratch. They range from free-standing towns like Seaside, Fla., and suburban enclaves like Kentlands, Md., to infill neighborhoods carved out of abandoned urban parcels. They aim to reduce the need for cars and increase social interaction by mixing housing, retail and public construction in walkable communities, many with public transit. Design guidelines bring buildings close to streets and sidewalks, place some housing above stores and move parking lots behind buildings.

"New Urbanism is the design part of the overall smart-growth movement," says Glendening, who now heads the Smart Growth Leadership Institute, a

Sun Belt Is Burgeoning

Five of America's fastest-growing counties are in Georgia — primarily suburban Atlanta — with the others mostly in suburban communities in Sun Belt states.

Fastest-Growing U.S. Counties
(Percent change, 2000-2003)

County	Nearest Major City	Population Change
Loudoun, Va.	Washington, D.C.	30.7%
Chattahoochee, Ga.	Columbus	29.9
Douglas, Colo.	Denver	27.1
Rockwall, Texas	Dallas	26.8
Forsyth, Ga.	Atlanta	25.8
Henry, Ga.	Atlanta	25.7
Flagler, Fla.	Daytona Beach	24.8
Newton, Ga.	Atlanta	22.8
Paulding, Ga.	Atlanta	22.7
Kendall, Ill.	Chicago	22.0

Source: U.S. Census Bureau, "Population Estimates," April 1, 2000 to July 1, 2003

Washington, D.C.-based nonprofit. "The two efforts go hand in hand."

As the controversy in Loudoun County shows, population-driven development is fueling the debate about land-use policies — a debate that seems likely to intensify. As state and local governments examine ways to manage growth, these are some of the questions they are asking:

Do smart-growth policies contain sprawl?

Oregon's 30-year-old law requiring urban-growth boundaries around cities and towns is the nation's most far-reaching effort to contain sprawl — making it a bellwether for both advocates and opponents of smart-growth policies.

To supporters, the growth boundary around Portland has largely succeeded in fostering the kind of development its authors had intended — smaller houses with smaller yards, mixed-use neighborhoods, a well-utilized transit and bike-lane system, a thriving downtown — while preserving open space outside the city.

Critics acknowledge that the policy has curbed outward growth, but they contend the policy is an excessive

intrusion into the free market that denies residents the right to live in traditional suburbs. The American Dream Coalition, a property-rights group in Bandon, Ore., recently hosted a national conference in Portland to demonstrate what coalition leader Randal O'Toole sees as the downsides of smart growth: High-density living and congestion caused by government overreach. "I don't see it as a livable place to live," he said. "Our message is, 'Don't emulate Portland.' " [5]

But supporters of Portland's effort to counter sprawl say the policy is no more intrusive than zoning rules that established minimum lot sizes and separated residential neighborhoods from commercial and retail areas — rules that have spurred suburban sprawl since the late 1940s. "The 'Ozzie and Harriet' version of the American dream was not the result of invisible forces of the market," Rep. Earl Blumenauer, D-Ore., whose district includes Portland, told conferees. "[It] was the result of massive government engineering." [6]

Most other states with growth-management policies have used incentives and other less-stringent tools to focus new construction in and around already-developed areas. Maryland's smart-growth policies, for example, include a mix of tax incentives, siting of schools and other public buildings in developed areas and regulations that discourage construction in rural areas.

"We decided not to manage growth through regulation, but rather with a series of incentives and disincentives," Glendening says. "By doing that, we changed the bottom line. We wanted investors, builders and homebuyers to realize that they would get a better deal by purchasing in a smart-growth community."

Maryland's approach has had mixed results. A number of urban, infill projects in long-abandoned industrial areas of Baltimore have drawn new residents and retail centers, increasing the tax base and creating jobs in previously impoverished neighborhoods. Glendening cites the American Can factory, once on the Environmental

Protection Agency's (EPA) list of polluted industrial "brownfields." * "The site had been run-down, caught fire a number of times and was inhabited by vagrants and drug addicts," he says. With state assistance in cleaning up the site, a private developer built a mixed industrial and retail complex, creating more than 700 high-tech and retail jobs. "The whole neighborhood around the factory has taken off, and it now has the highest increase in assessed value for anyplace in Baltimore City."

But the smart-growth initiatives like Maryland's have been less successful in reducing traffic congestion — one of the main goals of the movement. This is particularly true when local efforts to preserve open space, such as Loudoun County's recently abandoned policies, are not coordinated with neighboring jurisdictions.

"If you prevent the development of land in part of a county in a fast-growing region like the Washington metropolitan area, you force the growth to move out even farther" — beyond the no-growth areas, says Anthony Downs, an expert on urban affairs at the Brookings Institution, a Washington think tank. People who move into new developments beyond the no-growth area must then drive even farther to reach their jobs, adding to air pollution. "So this kind of zoning really doesn't necessarily reduce traffic congestion; it just changes the character of the congestion. [Development just] arises farther out, and commuters are just driving through the areas being preserved from new development."

Likewise, urban-infill developments that come with smart growth can go too far or have unintended consequences. Many longtime residents of close-in suburban neighborhoods worry that development can reach a tipping point, overwhelming the qualities that drew them to those areas in the first place.

"The towering buildings that are going up now are a bit frightening," says Ellen Showell, a 30-year resident of Arlington County's bustling Rosslyn-Ballston corridor, along the subway line outside Washington, D.C. "Also,

The nation loses 365 acres of open space every hour to developers' bulldozers, much of that growth in areas that have never had to deal with rapid growth before.

I don't like seeing all the streets parked up. Where we used to have one or two cars parked outside our house, we now have a real city parking situation. Even though they've attempted to make this a pedestrian-friendly area, our society is still dependent on cars, and more people have brought more cars."

Showell and her husband supported Arlington's development plans through their local civic association and still embrace many of the changes the county government and developers have introduced. "They've really tried their best to keep a certain urban village feel to the neighborhood," she says. "We always loved the neighborhood's low-key lifestyle and getting to know the independent business owners over the years. We hope this won't be totally lost."

Many experts caution that it's too soon to judge the effectiveness of most smart-growth initiatives. "There is no one model or tool that is going to solve the problem of sprawl," says Glendening. "No one should expect that you can put in place anything that is reasonably acceptable politically that would instantly reverse current growth trends.

"We as a nation have worked hard for the last 60 years to get to the position where we are now," he continues, "and it's going to take at least a decade or two to start seeing any significant reversal of sprawl."

---

* A brownfield is a former industrial property whose reuse is limited to non-residential development because it contains a hazardous substance, pollutant or contaminant. The Environmental Protection Agency estimates that there are more than 400,000 brownfields in the United States. See www.epa.gov/brownfields; see also Mary H. Cooper "Environmental Justice," June 19, 1998, pp. 529-552.

Does managed growth reduce the supply of affordable housing?

By calling for a mix of apartments, condominiums, town houses and single-family homes in most new developments, smart-growth and New Urbanist designs attempt to end the longstanding economic segregation of neighborhoods between wealthy suburbs and poor downtowns. But that goal often proves elusive.

Arlington County launched an ambitious managed-growth policy three decades ago, when it decided to site its main segment of Metro, the region's new subway system, along a decaying thoroughfare and focus new development along that corridor. In order to preserve the single-family suburban neighborhoods that lay close to the proposed development area, county planners designated areas within a quarter-mile of each of the five Metro stations for high-rise office, apartment and condominium buildings. Outside those areas, density and building height were reduced, providing a transition to the single-family neighborhoods.

Arlington's gamble paid off; today the Rosslyn-Ballston Corridor, named for the Metro stations at either end of the county, is a bustling community whose eclectic mix of housing, shops, restaurants and county offices won it the EPA's National Award for Overall Excellence in Smart Growth in 2002. [7]

"Arlington's elected officials had the vision 30 years ago to use the Metro system to plan for the revitalization of an aging commercial corridor that was losing out to the new malls" being built in the outer suburbs, says Thomas H. Miller, coordinator of Arlington's planning commission. "The development occurred in a very linear fashion, so the single-family neighborhoods right on the periphery have really stayed intact."

Arlington's smart-growth success story has come at a cost, however. Small Sears bungalows built for a few thousand dollars in the 1920s and '30s now fetch close to $1 million. Even two-bedroom condos are going for $400,000, and affordable housing is scarce.

"Affordability is absolutely the biggest challenge we face," Miller concedes. "The people moving here now have the luxury of owning their automobile and living near Metro. The challenge is to get more affordable units and make sure that the people who need transit the most are actually able to live near transit." The county board is now considering a proposal to require developers to include more affordable units in residential projects along the corridor.

Moreover, so-called "greenfield" communities being built from the ground up in undeveloped areas also frequently fall short of expectations for affordable housing. New towns such as Mountain House, built on an open tract about 60 miles east of pricey, downtown San Francisco, are designed to offer housing for a broad range of income levels. But high demand for housing in the new community has driven prices beyond the reach of most moderate-income buyers. [8]

Some smart-growth critics say land-use regulations that focus development in certain areas and bar it in others inevitably drive up the cost of housing, to the disadvantage of less-affluent Americans. "Downzoning [reducing the number of houses allowed on a given tract of land] only creates more disparity in economic well-being," says Loudoun County's Snow. Most would-be buyers in western Loudoun were disadvantaged under the discontinued smart-growth rules because only the wealthy could afford single-family houses on the huge lots.

But sellers also lost out, in his view. "For many farmers their land is their 401(k) or pension," Snow says. When the county barred those farmers from selling small, single-family parcels — which would fetch more money per acre than the large, single-family parcels mandated under the smart-growth rules — they were deprived of their retirement income. "Under downzoning, a farmer's land that was worth $2 million suddenly fell in value to $700,000. That's a $1.3 million hit in the name of smart growth."

But simply overturning smart-growth rules and relying on market forces to direct development seems unlikely to reverse the lack of adequate affordable housing in wealthy suburban jurisdictions. According to a recent study of the Washington metropolitan area, the wealthiest suburban counties have the fewest affordable housing units. [9] And less-affluent residents are being driven out of housing markets across the country in other fast-growing areas.

"Many young workers cannot stay here," said former Secretary of Housing and Urban Development Henry Cisneros, calling for government intervention to increase the availability of affordable housing in the Los Angeles suburbs. "And those that can't leave are living in overcrowded, declining neighborhoods."

Without such intervention, he said, it will always be more profitable for developers to build higher-priced, single-family houses. "All the factors are against affordability." [10]

Are Americans wedded to suburban life?

The pull of the suburbs has been strong for upwardly mobile Americans since the streetcar and, later, the automobile enabled them to escape the grime, noise and crime of industrial downtowns. A suburban house with a yard is still what comes to mind as the American dream.

"Our polls show that the ideal housing solution is a four-bedroom, two-and-a-half-bath, single-family house with a garage," says Traylor of the National Association of Home Builders. "That's still what 75 percent or more of the people who are purchasing houses say they want."

The past few years of economic turmoil and job loss may have tempered those aspirations somewhat, at least temporarily. "With affordability issues, some buyers are having to make do with something less than that ideal solution, and town houses tend to be the default substitute," Traylor adds.

But the latest census data suggest that the traditional suburban house continues to be the preferred long-term housing goal for many Americans. "The fastest-growing counties are on the periphery of metropolitan areas, such as Atlanta, Washington, D.C., and Dallas," says William Frey, an urban-migration expert at the University of Michigan. "My guess is that there's a continuing desire to live within a major metropolitan area but without having to put up with all the hustle and hassle of living near the center of town, with its congestion and high housing costs."

Indeed, the rising cost of housing and worsening traffic congestion in cities and the close-in suburbs is contributing to the continued allure of the far suburbs, or exurbs. "The price of housing declines by at least 1.5 percent per mile as you move away from the center of a metropolitan area," says Downs at Brookings.

Meanwhile, many jobs are moving to small cities on the fringes of suburbs known as "edge cities," exempting some suburban residents from having to commute all the way into downtown. "The average distance people drive as their housing gets farther and farther from the center does rise," Downs says, "but it doesn't rise as much as their distance from the center."

Apart from such calculations, some property-rights advocates and critics of smart-growth policies say efforts to build more compact communities are doomed to failure because Americans will always prefer the bigger houses and yards that only the suburbs and rural developments can offer.

"Smart growth is the antithesis of the American dream," says Loudoun County's Snow, who sees conspiracy afoot in efforts to contain sprawl. "They're trying to get transit-oriented development and other things that actually deny people real homes," he says. "They want them to move into condos and apartments and ride bicycles. That's fine for [Beijing] and the rest of the communist bloc, but we should be about putting people into houses."

Most developers stop short of such sweeping condemnation of efforts to manage growth. Indeed, many in the building industry see promise in the kind of development that smart-growth planners and New Urbanist designers are promoting. Even the homebuilders' association now has a department that deals specifically with smart-growth issues. "We feel it's important to satisfy all housing desires," says Blake Smith, the department's spokesman. "Whether it's the higher-density urban lifestyle or the larger home on a larger lot, people should have a choice of where they live, and the homebuilders believe we need to be satisfying that demand."

In fact, areas where smart-growth policies have been on the books long enough to produce alternative patterns of development, such as Portland and Arlington, tend to be such hot real-estate markets that supporters see a more profound shift in consumer tastes away from the suburbs. What critics see as a failure to provide adequate low-cost housing, smart-growth advocates see as evidence that people are clamoring for more residential density, not less.

"What higher housing prices in smart-growth communities are really telling us is that this is where people want to live," says former Maryland Gov. Glendening. "We say, let people go ahead and choose to live where they want. If someone wants to live in what I consider to be a rather sterile subdivision of two-acre lots where you have to drive to get a quart of milk, let them go ahead and do it. But let's make sure that there are also choices for those people who would prefer to live in an area with a real sense of community, where they can walk down to the corner to get that quart of milk and hop on mass transit to get directly to work."

The retiring Baby Boomers are the wild card in the debate about whether Americans can be pried from their suburbs. City planners hope that retiring "empty nesters" from the huge Boomer generation will decide they no longer need the big yards and wide open spaces of the

CHRONOLOGY

1940s-1960s *Suburban development becomes firmly established, spurred by federal policies.*

1947 William Levitt sets the pattern for postwar suburban development with his legendary Long Island subdivision, Levittown. With its curved streets, small yards and garages, Levittown becomes a homogeneous residential enclave of middle-class families with children, whose residents depend almost entirely on their cars for transportation.

1956 The federally funded Interstate Highway System begins to take shape, eventually creating a 45,000-mile superhighway network that helps fuel suburban development.

1964 Developer Robert E. Simon builds Reston, on Virginia farmland outside Washington, D.C., as a free-standing new town with shops close to houses so residents won't need to drive to shop and socialize.

1970s-1990s *Some state and local governments try to limit suburban sprawl.*

1973 Oregon requires local governments to develop land-use and zoning plans to curb sprawl.

1979 Portland, Ore., adopts an "urban-growth boundary," beyond which most new development is barred.

1981 Miami architects Andres Duany and Elizabeth Plater-Zyberk design Seaside, Fla., as a free-standing, pedestrian-friendly new town that will become a model for New Urbanist designers.

1990 Washington requires fast-growing communities to develop growth-management plans.

1993 The nonprofit Congress for the New Urbanism is founded to promote high-density, mixed-use development along transit lines as an alternative to expanding suburban development.

1995 Minnesota passes the Livable Communities Act, which underwrites development of lightly contaminated "brownfield" sites to encourage retail and commercial use of already-developed areas.

1996 The Environmental Protection Agency (EPA) creates the Smart Growth Network — a partnership of more than 30 government, business and civic organizations — to share information on best practices for development.

1997 Congress approves $500,000 capital-gains tax exemption for a couple on profits from the sale of primary residences, which smart-growth advocates say will induce suburban dwellers to move to less-expensive, close-in housing. Maryland's Smart Growth and Neighborhood Conservation Act requires the state to deny or limit subsidies for new roads, sewers and schools outside state-identified "smart-growth" areas.

1998 President Bill Clinton signs the $217.9 billion Transportation Equity Act that boosts spending for both highways and mass transit systems. Oregon voters overturn an initiative to repeal Portland's urban-growth boundary.

January 1999 Vice President Al Gore identifies sprawl as a major environmental threat.

2000s *Population-growth pressures challenge anti-sprawl efforts.*

2000 The Centers for Disease Control and Prevention says 64 percent of Americans are obese and blames the epidemic, in part, on the lack of exercise due to an overreliance on automobiles. The Transportation Department reports that new-road construction has not kept up with the growing demand for roads accompanying suburban development.

2002 The National Governors Association helps launch the Active Living Leadership initiative to promote state and local zoning changes that favor walking, biking and transit over development that relies solely on cars for personal transportation.

2004 The U.S. Census Bureau projects that the number of people living in the United States will exceed 419 million — an additional 126 million people — by 2050.

suburbs, and will begin migrating back into the cities, perhaps into smart-growth enclaves close to commuter lines. (*See "Outlook," p. 249.*)

BACKGROUND

Early American Cities

Until the Industrial Revolution, the world's cities and towns typically arose on the banks of rivers, lakes and harbors or along major overland trade routes. [11] Often fortified against enemy attacks, they tended to be compact, densely populated and oriented toward the center, where a cathedral or government building provided an anchoring focal point for civic life.

American cities followed a slightly different model, based on British urban patterns. Protected by the English Channel from attack, London and other British cities began branching outward as early as the 16th century, as wealthy residents built rural estates to escape the crowding, filth and noise of urban life. Colonial cities, such as New York, Boston and Baltimore, also arose beside rivers and harbors that offered dockage for trading ships. Inland communities, such as St. Louis and Richmond, typically arose at the confluence of two rivers or at the "fall lines" of rivers — the point where riverboat traffic gave way to overland transportation. Like their English counterparts, wealthier Americans pushed urban boundaries outward, building fashionable neighborhoods, such as Boston's Beacon Hill, linked to the city center by a "mansion" street flanked by churches, clubs and libraries.

The Industrial Revolution and the growth of the railroad system in the late 19th century accelerated the outward development of American cities. Mills and factories arose along major transportation routes — roads, railroads and rivers, which also provided water power to fuel industrial production. Worker shantytowns that arose around exurban factories evolved into small communities separate from the nearby cities, such as Camden, N.J., across the Delaware River from Philadelphia.

Innovations in transportation continued to influence patterns of urban development. As railroads accelerated the westward migration of people and the creation of new towns and cities in the Midwest and West, local transit systems facilitated the outward migration of city residents. By the early 20th century, while blue-collar workers continued to live within walking distance of

their factory jobs, streetcars enabled the growing ranks of middle-class workers to live farther from their downtown offices. Wealthier families moved even farther out to "railroad suburbs," such as Philadelphia's Main Line communities.

This pattern, repeated in cities across the country, established a model for U.S. urban development that would persist for the next half-century — a vibrant downtown commercial district flanked by industrial areas, with residential neighborhoods both in town and extending along train and streetcar lines.

Cars Drive Development

With the advent of the automobile, transportation played an even greater role in shaping American communities. Henry Ford began mass-producing cars in the early 20th century, but it was not until the post-World War II economic boom that car ownership came within the grasp of millions of Americans. The car, more than any industrial innovation, was to break the traditional boundaries that had contained urban development, making way for the rise of the suburbs.

Federal policies in the 1950s and '60s facilitated the exodus from the cities. Home ownership became a key goal of federal incentives, particularly the home-mortgage income-tax deduction. Federally subsidized home-mortgage loans enabled returning GIs and other homebuyers of limited means to buy houses. But the loans often were restricted to houses in neighborhoods where housing values were considered safe from devaluation linked to poverty and crime. This restriction fostered the racial segregation of American communities and accentuated a widening divide between poor, minority, downtown neighborhoods and middle-class, white enclaves in the new suburban developments.

"It's a sad but true fact of our history that entire neighborhoods with any significant African-American population were redlined and excluded from eligibility for the home-loan guarantee," says Glendening of the Smart Growth Leadership Institute. "As a result, the federal loan programs were not only about helping people buy homes; they were almost forcing them to buy homes out there as opposed to the urban areas that had black populations."

The Interstate Highway System also fueled suburban development. Launched in 1956, it created a 45,000-mile network of federally financed superhighways. [12] Originally

Teardowns: The Dark Side of Smart Growth?

During the urban-renewal heyday of the 1960s-'70s, city governments routinely demolished abandoned inner-city houses, factories and stores and put up high-rise housing projects and office buildings, hoping to restore social and economic vitality to decaying downtowns.

But urban renewal produced mixed results: Many low-cost and public housing projects, often built in areas that no longer offered job opportunities, soon deteriorated into crime- and drug-ridden slums.

Today, a new wave of demolition and reconstruction is occurring in the nation's wealthier, close-in suburbs — and it is no less controversial. Dubbed by critics as the "teardown tsunami," the trend is rapidly transforming many longstanding neighborhoods, as older houses and mature trees are being replaced with large, multistoried houses that often bump up against property lines, dwarfing neighboring houses, blocking out sunlight, obstructing views and diminishing neighbors' privacy.

Moreover, what some call the "McMansionization" of old neighborhoods can "radically change the fabric of a community," said Richard Moe, president of the National Trust for Historic Preservation. "From 19th-century Victorians to 1920s bungalows, the architecture of America's historic neighborhoods reflects the character of our communities. Without proper safeguards, historic neighborhoods will lose the identities that drew residents to put down roots in the first place." [1]

Ironically, teardowns are largely a reaction to suburban sprawl and a consequence of the very smart-growth policies devised to curb it. Ever-increasing commuting distances, traffic jams and road rage are prompting many residents from the far suburbs, or "exurbs," to move closer to town, and the stock-market boom of the 1990s enabled many middle- and upper-income Americans to do just that.

But instead of trading their spacious suburban dwellings for smaller, older houses in the inner suburbs, these new urban immigrants demand the best of both worlds — large houses close to downtown amenities. Many are willing to pay top dollar for a large house, even if it is one of several squeezed onto a traditional quarter-acre lot. Indeed, the smaller yard, with its limited maintenance requirements, is especially appealing to exurban refugees tired of extensive lawn care.

Consumer demand and economics are driving the teardown trend. Historically, construction enhanced the value of land. Since the late 1990s, however, vacant land in the downtown and inner suburban neighborhoods has become increasingly scarce. As demand for real estate in these areas grew, land became more valuable than the structure on it.

Higher land values, in turn, make it harder for builders to turn a handsome profit by replacing a smaller teardown with just a same-size structure. According to the "Rule of Three," developers typically aim to sell new construction for three times what they paid for the property. [2] In order to maintain traditional profit margins, developers end up building two, three or more large houses — or a single McMansion — on a lot that once accommodated a single, small dwelling.

Similar financial incentives motivate local governments to tolerate and even encourage teardowns. Recent federal income-tax cuts have reduced the flow of revenues to states and localities, which are left to rely more heavily on alternative revenue streams — such as property taxes

envisioned to speed long-distance passenger and freight traffic, Interstate highways became major commuter arteries as well, enabling downtown workers to move beyond the older, "inner" suburbs to new developments miles from downtown. Because land values generally drop as one moves away from downtown, prospective home-buyers could afford more land and bigger houses in these new suburbs. And the four-lane Interstates made the tradeoff in commuting distances less onerous.

The design of postwar suburbs generally followed a pattern set by such developers as William Levitt. Levittown, the legendary Long Island subdivision he built beginning in the late 1940s, comprised more than 17,000 small, almost identical, inexpensive houses. With its curved streets and cul-de-sacs, small yards and garages, Levittown became a homogeneous middle-class enclave whose residents depended almost entirely on their cars for transportation.

— to fund libraries, police departments and other vital services. A housing lot that once produced revenues from a single dwelling can generate much more if it accommodates two or more units, all the more if they are large, opulent houses.

Teardowns are a mixed bag for nearby neighbors. The first teardown in a neighborhood may be welcomed as a signal that local real estate values — the main source of many homeowners' net worth — are rapidly rising. Homeowners already contemplating a move may quickly put their houses on the market to collect the windfall.

Huge, multistoried houses that replace smaller, older houses often dwarf neighboring structures, block sunlight, obstruct views and diminish neighbors' privacy.

furniture, old papers or even groceries. "The builder doesn't care," Barofsky said, "because he wrecks it anyway."

But not all neighbors welcome the change. Many long-term residents have set down permanent roots in their neighborhoods, leading them to feel entitled to a greater say in the community's appearance and character than a recent buyer — especially a developer interested purely in a money-making operation.

Some residents of older neighborhoods are beginning to take steps to slow or halt the pace of teardowns, aided by guidelines published by the National Trust to help communities and neighborhoods gain some control over local development. Although the Trust acknowledges the benefits of smart growth and channeling new development into already developed areas, it counsels communities to make sure new investment "respects the character and distinctiveness that made these neighborhoods so desirable in the first place." [4]

Developers who specialize in razing older houses tout the benefits to house sellers in marketing their properties as teardowns. "Until a few years ago, 'teardown' was practically a bad word," said Michael Barofsky, an Illinois Realtor who specializes in selling teardown houses. "Now it's come out of the closet and is almost desirable." [3]

Barofsky said convenience is luring more and more property owners to overcome their reluctance to abandon their homes to the bulldozer. Teardowns eliminate the need for lock boxes, open houses, home inspections, cleanup, costly repairs and the other hassles typical of house sales. Some sellers even leave behind their unwanted

[1] Quoted in National Trust for Historic Preservation, "Teardowns: Historic Neighborhoods, Nationwide," www.nationaltrust.org.

[2] See Patrick T. Reardon and Blair Kamin, "Paths of Destruction," *Chicago Tribune*, April 24, 2003, p. 1.

[3] Quoted in Rebecca R. Kahlenberg, "Is Your House a 'Teardown' Candidate?" *The Washington Post*, Oct. 25, 2003, p. F1.

[4] National Trust, *op. cit.*

Today, worsening urban traffic congestion is a major impetus to smart-growth programs across the country. As suburbs continue to spread farther from downtown jobs, commuters spend more and more time stuck in traffic jams. The migration of businesses from downtown to suburban locations has had mixed effects on traffic congestion: While it has eased pressure on roadways leading to and from city centers, it has also made it more difficult for workers to use public transportation.

As commuter traffic disperses in many different directions, mass transit lags behind in meeting commuters' changing needs, so more workers drive to work. As a result, even metropolitan areas with extensive bus and subway service, such as Washington, D.C., continue to suffer from jammed roadways. And because its acclaimed Metro system cannot keep up with the region's rapidly expanding suburban commercial development, the Washington region ranks

Struever Bros. Eccles and Rouse (Both)

Urban Transformation

Transformation of Baltimore's abandoned American Can Co. factory (top) into a vibrant retail and office center (bottom) exemplifies the urban "infill" development advocated by historic preservationists and other smart-growth proponents.

Anti-Sprawl Measures

Unlike older cities, which evolve over many years and include a mix of residential, industrial and commercial activities, the American suburbs have been shaped from the beginning by a desire to separate residential areas from commercial and industrial projects. Zoning ordinances created and enforced by local city and county governments have produced bedroom communities separated from industrial parks and commercial strip malls.

As the suburban boom continued in the 1960s-'80s, a few visionaries decided that zoning regulations alone were too blunt a tool to create attractive suburban communities. One of the first was Robert E. Simon, who in 1964 created Reston, a new Virginia town in what at the time was beyond the western suburban perimeter of Washington. Simon envisioned shops so close to houses that residents would not need to drive to shop and socialize. Although the suburbs have long since surrounded Reston, Simon's vision proved to be a success, and residents recently celebrated the town's 40th anniversary as an island of innovative development in one of the country's most congested metropolitan areas. [15]

Frustrated by failed efforts to contain sprawl, some state and local governments adopted stronger measures. In 1973, for instance, Oregon required all local governments to develop land-use and zoning plans to curb sprawl. Although opponents complained the measure violated property-owners' rights and reduced consumers' residential options, Oregon voters rejected efforts to repeal the law. In 1979, the Portland metropolitan area established an "urban-growth boundary" as well as a new regional government, Metro, to enforce the boundary.

just behind Los Angeles as the country's most congested metropolitan area. [13]

Moreover, new road construction has not kept up with suburban development. According to the Transportation Department, from 1980 to 2000 the number of vehicle miles traveled in the United States grew by 44 percent, while the total road space grew by less than 2 percent. [14]

In 1995, Minnesota passed the Livable Communities Act, which aimed to underwrite the development of brownfield sites, integrate affordable housing into new developments and develop mixed-use communities. The EPA granted its 2003 smart-growth achievement award to the Minneapolis-St. Paul metropolitan council, which used state funds provided by the Livable Communities Act to transform deteriorating inner suburbs into vibrant, mixed-use communities, such as St. Louis Park, built along Excelsior Boulevard. [16]

In 1997, Maryland's Gov. Glendening launched his smart-growth program. Rather than establishing urban-growth boundaries as Oregon had done, Glendening's program aimed to concentrate new development in partially developed areas with existing roads, utility lines and schools, thereby saving the state from having to build new infrastructure and preserving the state's rapidly dwindling rural green space.

Although most states have stopped short of adopting Oregon's statewide growth policy, many have followed Portland's example and established urban-growth boundaries, including California's fast-growing San Jose and Sonoma County, a largely rural, wine-producing region north of San Francisco.

Other local governments used traditional zoning ordinances to fight sprawl, as Arlington County did in response to construction of the Metro subway system. Arlington planners used zoning ordinances to focus high-density development along the Metro corridor, limiting intensive retail, commercial and high-rise apartment and condominium development to within a quarter-mile of each Metro station. Forty years later, the area is an award-winning, vibrant residential and retail community whose residents can walk to stores and take public transit downtown.

Consumers Prefer Bigger Houses, Lots

American homebuyers prefer larger houses and lots located away from cities, according to the homebuilders association. Meanwhile, they appear less interested in being able to get to work quickly and living closer to public transportation — features promoted by smart-growth advocates.

What Homebuyers Want
(In order of preference)

Feature	Percent saying it was "important" to "very important"
Houses spread out	62%
Less traffic in neighborhood	60
Lower property taxes	55
Bigger home	47
Bigger lot	45
Better schools	44
In a good neighborhood	43
Less developed area	40
Away from city	39
More luxury features	35
Closer to work	28
Shorter commute to work	23
Recreational facilities	22
Closer to public transit	13
Smaller house	10
Smaller lot	9

Source: "Smart Growth, Smart Choices," National Association of Home Builders

New Urbanism

The New Urbanism movement, another effort to create alternatives to the postwar suburban model, attracted support from many planners, architects and developers. Since 1993, the nonprofit Congress for the New Urbanism has called for more investment in central cities and decried sprawl as the leading cause of the separation of neighborhoods by race and income, environmental degradation, loss of open space and the lack of community identity in much of the country. The group's design guidelines for new communities espouse the following principles:

- Grid street layout, with wide sidewalks, bike lanes and, where feasible, public transit;
- Mixed-use development, including shops, offices and residential units of all types, including detached, single-family houses, town houses, condominiums and rental apartments;
- Buildings constructed close to the street, with windows and porches facing sidewalks to foster communication between occupants and pedestrians;
- Parking lots and garages behind buildings, ending the asphalt parking lots that surround strip-mall stores;
- Placement of schools, stores, libraries and other public facilities within safe walking or biking distance from residences;
- Community focal points, such as town squares or neighborhood centers, also within walking distance of residences;
- Clear boundaries around communities, with open space separating communities.

Some of the best-known New Urbanist communities, such as Seaside, in Walton County, Fla., Kentlands, in Gaithersburg, Md., and Laguna West, in Sacramento County, Calif., were built on previously undeveloped sites.

But the goal of saving open space and revitalizing deteriorating downtown areas makes such development especially suited for urban infill projects. City West, a 1,085-unit mix of affordable and market-rate rental units and owner-occupied houses in downtown Cincinnati was recently completed on the site of two failed public-housing projects. The new neighborhood has begun to draw both higher-income buyers eager to live near downtown amenities and lower-income renters, including some former residents who had fled the crime-ridden projects. [17]

CURRENT SITUATION

Policy Challenges

A major obstacle to the spread of New Urbanist designs is existing zoning laws, which often discourage mixing residential with commercial and retail uses and mandate large building setbacks from the street.

"Right now, it is easier to pave over a farm or tear down a forest and build a brand new subdivision or office park than to reuse or infill space in existing communities," says Glendening of the Smart Growth Leadership Institute. He cites historic Annapolis — Maryland's capital and one of the state's most popular tourist attractions — as a case in point.

"Everybody loves Annapolis," Glendening says. "It's got narrow streets, a wonderful mixture of single-family and multi-family residences, some over stores, and all the other attributes of the traditional neighborhood development pursued by New Urbanist designers. Yet if you wanted to go out and build a community like Annapolis today, it would be illegal in almost every state, including Maryland. Even after all the changes we've accomplished with our smart-growth program, it would take several years of variances to overcome existing zoning rules to create a town like Annapolis today."

Moreover, zoning rules governing school siting encourage suburban sprawl. [18] When older schools need renovation, most communities build a new, larger school outside of town or even beyond the suburban areas, where land is more plentiful and cheaper. "Common, existing guidelines dictate that schools have at least 30 acres of land, which means in most cases new schools will be built outside of town," Glendening says. "The first thing a family with young children looks for in a community is the condition of its schools. If they discover that the school has not been renovated in 30 years but that they've just built three new schools farther out, then that's where they're going to move."

Not only does this pattern fuel sprawl, but it also contributes to the growing incidence of obesity among American children. (*See sidebar, p. 234.*) [19] Rather than walking to a neighborhood school, Glendening says, "Everyone must either take the car to school, have a parent drive them or take a school bus. And it's all a result of these faulty guidelines that schools need to be on 30 acres."

Zoning regulations that encourage sprawl also drive up local governments' costs, which already are facing the worst budget crises in a half-century. [20] Suburban residential development costs governments more than commercial or retail development, because they require construction of schools, new roads and extensive utility hookups. "Residential development costs more in necessary services for every dollar in tax revenues that it generates," says Scott York, chairman of Loudoun County's Board of Supervisors. "It's important to expand the commercial tax base to help offset the cost of residential services."

Are smart-growth policies the best solution for suburban sprawl?

YES James E. McGreevey
Governor of New Jersey (Dem.)

From a speech before the N.J. Association of Counties, April 4, 2004

Whether we look at smart growth environmentally, economically or socially, it means the future of New Jersey.

We can't continue as we have in the past. It is not sustainable from any perspective. We must be mindful of where we build and how we build. We must design new policies that encourage the rebirth of our older suburbs, our great inner cities and the planned development of new, rural, town centers. We must preserve what is left of our open space and ensure the sanctity of our drinking-water supplies. . . . We cannot say we are serious about smart growth and continue to have development guidelines that lack enforcement mechanisms.

Our goal is to provide clarity and predictability so developers, municipalities and counties can understand their regulatory obligations prior to proposing any new development projects. . . . Together with the other municipal and county tools to direct and control growth, we will have the ability to reshape New Jersey's development patterns and make them more rational, responsible and predictable. . . .

The impacts of growth and sprawl do not adhere to the boundaries of a single community or town, [so] we cannot realistically address sprawl if we fail to engage in a greater level of regional planning. . . . So I am proposing . . . a mediation forum in which municipalities and counties can try to resolve their issues before heading to the courts. The purpose will be to find regional solutions to regional problems and to encourage municipalities to think about the impacts their development decisions have outside their borders.

Smart growth is about balance. I recognize the importance of economic development, the importance of jobs and the importance of keeping our state profitable. But I also recognize that in addition to our fiscal responsibilities, we have a responsibility to the land and environment that make up our state. Sprawl — and the unrestrained development that has jeopardized our water supplies, made our schools more crowded, our roads congested and our open space disappear — is the single greatest threat to our way of life in New Jersey.

We are trying to reverse decades' worth of thinking and policies in order to preserve our future. It will not be easy, but it is a fight from which we cannot back down or postpone. Every day we lose 50 acres to development — 50 acres of parks, farmland and open space that will never be reclaimed.

NO Samuel R. Staley
President, Buckeye Institute for Public Policy Solutions

Written for the CQ Researcher, April 2004

Smart growth is a political response to residential and commercial development outside core urban centers. Shifting land-use decisions to a politically driven planning process can significantly reduce the quality of life for the very people it is supposed to help by limiting housing choice, reducing housing affordability and lengthening commute times.

New Jersey is a case in point. Thirty-seven percent of its land is urbanized and a third is permanently locked up as open space (mainly through state parks), while its population density ranks ninth in the nation. State residents have access to a wide range of housing options, from the revitalized shorefront of Jersey City to the gritty urbanity of Newark to the housing subdivisions sprouting up in central Jersey, while remaining accessible to instate and out-of-state employment centers.

This diversity, however, could be at risk if smart-growth principles are implemented statewide. Leading the charge in New Jersey and perhaps the nation, Gov. McGreevey argues sprawl is the "single greatest threat to our way of life in New Jersey." The state must clearly outline the "regulatory obligations" of developers, cities and other governmental agencies to mitigate this threat — obligations that would presumably include conforming to a state plan to reduce sprawl. While the plan is voluntary for local governments, local officials are expected to ensure their plans conform with the state plan. In other words, housing with large yards and open floor plans should be discouraged as much as possible.

Thus, smart growth is not always about broadening choices. Smart growth can also be about imposing a one-size-fits-all concept of the neighborhood — as compact, high-density and transit-dependent — communitywide.

However, efforts that limit housing choices are likely to create new burdens. The most obvious may be limiting immediate access to open space in the form of yards. Moreover, statewide planning laws and higher densities have been found to increase housing prices, significantly reducing affordability. Research also has shown that transit riders spend a significantly larger share of their time commuting than automobile users.

Local policymakers should be cautious about adopting smart-growth principles too quickly. Housing options become scripted by state and regional planners, not the decisions of thousands of households haggling with developers and real-estate agents in the local housing market. The result could be less affordable, less competitive communities and neighborhoods.

In fact, cost containment had been a key justification for Loudoun's earlier smart-growth initiative. As the fastest-growing county in the nation, it accounts for an astounding 70 percent of Virginia's projected growth in public school enrollment over the next five years. [21] The county built 28 schools in the past eight years, and is scheduled to build an additional 23 over the next six years.

"We're piling on debt in order to build school after school after school in order to serve the growing population," York says. "Of course, the traffic situation also is becoming a nightmare around here, but there's very little money coming from the state government to deal with it."

Federal Impact

Although land-use decisions fall primarily within the jurisdiction of state and local governments, federal policies play an important role in shaping local development patterns. Environmental-protection statutes, such as the Clean Air and Clean Water acts, require state and local governments to meet federal mandates in controlling traffic-related smog and protecting waterways from the pollutants that stormwater washes from paved areas into streams and rivers.

The 1970 National Environmental Policy Act (NEPA) requires federal agencies to study and disclose the environmental impact of federally funded projects, like highways, and confer with the public before the projects are built. Supporters of deregulation have sought to undermine the NEPA process, saying it causes costly delays in highway projects, contributing to traffic congestion in fast-growing metropolitan areas. Reflecting that concern, President Bush in 2002 ordered the public-review process streamlined. [22]

Smart-growth supporters say federal policies — from income-tax deductions for interest on home mortgages to federally funded highway construction — have long underwritten suburban development. "The federal government has subsidized sprawl in a major way and continues to do so," says Glendening.

The federal government funds road-building and mass transit projects through a massive highway bill, reauthorized every six years. This year's renewal has bogged down over disagreements in funding levels: While President Bush requested $256 billion, the Senate approved a $318 billion highway bill in February, and

the House passed a $284 billion measure in March. Congressional leaders have yet to name members of a conference committee, which will work out a compromise. Meanwhile, Bush has threatened to veto any bill that exceeds the administration proposal. [23]

Developers generally disagree that the federal highway system has driven development away from cities and towns. "Some people think that if you build highways, then growth will follow," says Jim Tobin, legislative director for smart growth and environmental affairs at the National Association of Home Builders. "That's not the way it happens. Population is driving growth, home ownership and housing construction. The growth is already there; the transportation system — be it transit, highways or a mix — needs to accommodate that growth."

Some experts doubt that federal or state funding for new roads will relieve sprawl-related traffic congestion because commuters from the new communities they serve will eventually fill them to capacity. "The idea that traffic congestion can be eliminated through some kind of solution is a myth," says Downs of the Brookings Institution.

Flexible work hours and telecommuting could help alleviate congestion, he says, but only to a limited extent. "Congestion gets worse in part because it's a sign of prosperity and success, not necessarily a sign of defeat," he explains. "Traffic congestion is inevitably going to get worse in major metropolitan areas, and there's nothing we can do about it."

Anti-Sprawl Movement

But as congestion continues to clog metropolitan roadways, smog levels exceed allowable limits, and housing developments consume available open space, support is building in many parts of the country for curtailing sprawl. Reflecting that concern, the EPA has been supporting state and local smart-growth efforts for almost a decade.

EPA says its outreach into the state and local planning process could help protect the environment. "The built environment . . . has both direct and indirect effects on the natural environment," the agency states. "Where and how we develop directly impacts resource areas and animal habitat and replaces natural cover with impervious surfaces, such as concrete or asphalt. Smart growth [has] clear environmental benefits, including improved air and water quality, greater wetlands and open-space preservation and more cleanup and reuse of brownfield sites." [24]

To promote smart growth, EPA in 1996 created the Smart Growth Network, a partnership of more than 30 government, business and civic organizations that shares information on best practices for development. The effort gained momentum in January 1999, when Vice President Al Gore identified sprawl as a major threat to the environment.

But conservative activists criticize the EPA's new role, calling it an unwarranted intrusion into state and local affairs. "The federal government should not subsidize one side of a public-policy debate; doing so undermines the very essence of democracy," said a recent analysis by the CATO Institute, a libertarian think tank. "Congress should shut down the federal government's anti-sprawl lobbying activities and resist the temptation to engage in centralized social engineering." [25]

OUTLOOK

More Roads?

America's growing population seems likely to pose a serious challenge to efforts to limit further sprawl. By 2050, the Census Bureau projects, the number of people living in the United States will exceed 419 million — an additional 126 million people.

Although smart-growth proponents worry about the impact of this rapid increase in population, critics of smart growth question their motives. "A lot of concern about growth appears to stem from people's opposition to the idea of growth itself," says Staley of the Buckeye Institute. "But we live in a culture that is supposed to embrace tolerance for diversity and individuals. The whole idea underlying our government system is that just because we don't like more people is not a legitimate reason for preventing people from moving into a new community."

Staley concedes that more suburban development will likely add to the country's traffic congestion problems. "Traffic is a legitimate concern," he says. "But the issue is not so much that we have a lot of people commuting. It's more that we have not invested in the infrastructure upgrades necessary to keep people flowing.

"Our road investments lag development, and the result is all this congestion."

But traffic experts say accelerated road building will never solve the traffic problem. "If you build a lot more roads, you'd have to make the whole metro area a big cement slab," Downs, of the Brookings Institution, says. And expanding public transportation is not feasible, he says, because suburban residential areas are too low-density to support additional transit, and many Americans reject charging freeway tolls during peak hours to cut down on traffic, because it gives an advantage to those with money. "The last thing we could do is wait in line, and that's exactly what we're doing now — it's called congestion."

In Downs' view, traffic congestion is here to stay, regardless of population trends and smart-growth initiatives. "All metropolitan areas throughout the world have the same problem," he says, "and they all solve it the same way, which is with congestion."

Aging Baby Boomers

An important subset of America's growing population may determine the success or failure of future efforts to contain sprawl. The leading edge of the Baby Boom generation — the 78 million Americans born between 1946 and 1964 — is approaching retirement age. Many Boomers, who represent 28 percent of the U.S. population, were born and raised in the suburbs and raised their children there as well.

As the Boomers' children leave the nest, many planners wonder where this huge cohort will decide to spend its retirement years. If a large number decide to abandon the suburbs for alternative living arrangements, they will likely find that developers and local governments are eager to satisfy their housing needs. Retirees are in many ways ideal residents for localities trying to reduce expenses, because many are relatively well-off, with no children requiring schools, libraries and other services.

"Most governments — particularly in the fiscally constrained environment they're operating in right now — want to have their cake and eat it, too," Traylor, of the National Association of Home Builders, says. "They want Yuppie housing, built close to transit so they don't have to build new roads. They don't want children because they're very expensive to educate, and they don't want [less affluent] populations because they tend to require more social services."

Indeed, many local governments already provide attractive incentives for builders to construct specialized housing for aging Boomers and other active retirees.

"In many communities, if you want to build town houses or small single-family houses, the impact fees and other costs imposed by local governments are going to be exponentially higher than what you'd pay if you build a 55-and-older community," Traylor says.

Besides specialized retiree communities, many older Boomers may seek housing that has less space and no yard to maintain and is close to stores and other services — the kind of housing that New Urbanist communities provide. "In many cases, empty nesters prefer the higher density found with condominiums or apartments that have convenient access to amenities," says Glendening of the Smart Growth Leadership Institute. "If you build a high-density, mixed-use project right around mass transit, you will attract many retirees, who will want to spend the next 20-30 years of their lives there."

If Boomers lead a new reverse migration from the suburbs to the city, they will help relieve some of the pressure to build new suburban housing for America's growing population.

"When empty nesters and other seniors move back into urbanized areas, they leave houses behind in the suburbs that these additional millions of people can move into," Glendening says.

NOTES

1. U.S. Census Bureau figures released April 8, 2004, at *www.census.gov.*

2. From an April 20, 2004, letter to "Leesburg2Day.com," on online journal covering Loudoun County.

3. According to the Natural Resources Defense Council, www.nrdc.org.

4. See John King, "What's Sprawling Is Our Worship of Comfort," *San Francisco Chronicle*, Oct. 2, 2003, p. E1, and James Howard Kunstler, *The Geography of Nowhere* (1993), p. 10.

5. O'Toole spoke at the "Preserving the American Dream" conference, held April 15-18, 2004, in Portland, Ore. See Aimee Curl, "Conference Promotes Alternatives to Smart Growth," *Daily Journal of Commerce* (Portland, Ore.), April 19, 2004.

6. Quoted by Laura Oppenheimer, "Visitors Boo Portland Planning," *The Sunday Oregonian*, April 18, 2004, p. B1.

7. EPA's Smart Growth Program encourages states and localities to adopt managed-growth policies.

8. See John Ritter, "New Town's Challenge Is to Stick to Blueprint," *USA Today*, April 13, 2004, p. 15A.

9. Washington Regional Network for Livable Communities, "The Affordable Housing Progress Report," April 2004.

10. Quoted by Amanda Covarrubias, "'Recycling' Old Neighborhoods Urged," *Los Angeles Times*, April 9, 2004, p. B3.

11. Unless otherwise noted, information in this section is based on Jonathan Barnett, *The Fractured Metropolis* (1995). See also Mary H. Cooper, "Urban Sprawl in the West," *The CQ Researcher*, Oct. 3, 1997, pp. 865-889.

12. For background, see Mary H. Cooper, "Transportation Policy," *The CQ Researcher*, July 4, 1997, pp. 577-600.

13. See David Hosansky, "Traffic Congestion," *The CQ Researcher*, Aug. 27, 1999, pp. 729-752.

14. See Isaiah J. Poole, "Gas Tax Alternatives for a Nation on the Road," *CQ Weekly*, April 17, 2004, pp. 918-922.

15. See David Cho, "Reston Tosses a Party for 56,000 Neighbors," *The Washington Post*, April 18, 2004.

16. See "National Award for Smart Growth Achievement," www.epa.gov.

17. See Richelle Thompson, "City West Experiment Tests Idea of Mixing Incomes in Neighborhood," *The Cincinnati Enquirer*, Feb. 24, 2002.

18. For more information, see Rob Gurwitt, "Edge-ucation," *Governing*, March 2004, pp. 22-26.

19. For background, see Alan Greenblatt, "Obesity Epidemic," *The CQ Researcher*, Jan. 31, 2003, pp. 73-97.

20. For background, see William Triplett, "State Budget Crises," *The CQ Researcher*, Oct. 3, 2003, pp. 821-845.

21. See Rosalind S. Helderman, "School Growth Charts Put Loudoun on Top," *The Washington Post*, April 27, 2004, p. B1.

22. For information on public involvement in federal road-building projects, see Sierra Club and Natural Resources Defense Council, "The Road to Better Transportation Projects: Public Involvement and the NEPA Process" (undated), sierraclub.org.

23. See Isaiah J. Poole, "Chambers 'Not Close Yet' to Highway Bill Conference as Construction Season Wanes," *CQ Weekly*, April 24, 2004, p. 968.

24. "Environmental Protection and Smart Growth," www.epa.gov.

25. Peter Samuel and Randal O'Toole, "Smart Growth at the Federal Trough: EPA's Financing of the Anti-Sprawl Movement," Policy Analysis, Cato Institute, Nov. 24, 1999, p. 1.

BIBLIOGRAPHY

Books

Barnett, Jonathan, *The Fractured Metropolis: Improving the New City, Restoring the Old City, Reshaping the Region*, HarperCollins, 1995.
A city planner recounts the history of America's cities and the technologies that have shaped them, from the barge to the automobile. He calls for a national agenda to combat sprawl and improve the quality of city and suburban life.

Duany, Andres, Elizabeth Plater-Zyberk and Jeff Speck, *Suburban Nation: The Rise of Sprawl and the Decline of the American Dream*, North Point Press, 2001.
Leaders of the "New Urbanist" approach to development describe the pitfalls of suburban sprawl and outline design alternatives they say would greatly improve the quality of life in American communities by making it easier to walk or take public transit from home to school, work and other destinations.

Holcombe, Randall G., and Samuel R. Staley, *Smarter Growth: Market-Based Strategies for Land-Use Planning in the 21st Century*, Greenwood Publishing Group, 2001.
With the continuing spread of suburban development, state governments are playing a stronger role in planning decisions, traditionally the purview of local governments. The authors examine this trend and offer market-based alternatives to help shape development patterns.

Kunstler, James Howard, *Home from Nowhere: Remaking Our Everyday World for the 21st Century*, Free Press, 1998.
A noted critic of suburban sprawl calls for revised zoning and tax laws to promote alternative patterns of development that reduce dependence on the automobile and make more vibrant communities by combining residential housing with stores and offices.

Articles

Brooks, David, "Our Sprawling, Supersize Utopia," *The New York Times Magazine*, April 4, 2004, pp. 46-51.
For all the criticism of suburban sprawl, most Americans still choose to inhabit large houses in isolated, residential neighborhoods far from the city center, continuing the pattern that has dominated residential construction since World War II.

Frey, William H., "Gaining Seniors," *American Demographics*, November 201, pp. 18-21.
While Sun Belt communities continue to fill up with retirees, many elderly Americans are choosing to "age in place" in the same suburban communities where they raised their children.

Gurwitt, Rob, "Edge-ucation," *Governing*, March 2004, pp. 22-26.
A movement is taking hold to reverse the trend of building schools so far from most pupils' homes that they can no longer walk or bike to school.

O'Toole, Randal, "The Folly of 'Smart Growth'," *Regulation*, Fall 2001, pp. 20-25, fall 2001.
A critic of government regulation writes that Oregon's experiment with banning development outside urban boundaries has backfired, causing housing prices inside the boundaries to rise and failing to improve residents' quality of life.

Reports and Studies

Downs, Anthony, "Traffic: Why It's Getting Worse, What Government Can Do," *Policy Brief*, Brookings Institution, January 2004.
Because adults need to get to work every day, and children have to go to school, the author sees little hope of eliminating traffic congestion. But cities and states can take steps to reduce congestion, such as encouraging high-density development around transit stops, creating toll lanes on heavily used commuter roads and giving regional transportation authorities more power to coordinate planning in large metropolitan areas.

Heid, Jim, "Greenfield Development Without Sprawl: The Role of Planned Communities," Urban Land Institute, March 2004.

America's growing population cannot be accommodated by urban infill alone. But developing existing open space, or greenfields, need not be as destructive as it often is today. Careful planning can reduce the toxic emissions, stormwater runoff and visual pollution associated with suburban sprawl.

McCann, Barbara A., and Reid Ewing, "Measuring the Health Effects of Sprawl: A National Analysis of Physical Activity, Obesity and Chronic Disease," Smart Growth America and Surface Transportation Policy Project, September 2003.

By forcing residents to use their cars to commute from home to work, school and other destinations, the authors argue that sprawling suburban development is a key underlying cause of an alarming rise in the incidence of obesity, as well as heart disease, diabetes and other diseases related to overweight. McCann is a public-policy expert and Ewing an urban-studies professor at the University of Maryland.

For More Information

American Planning Association, 1776 Massachusetts Ave., N.W., Washington, DC 20036-1904; (202) 872-0611; www.planning.org. Tracks growth management legislation and provides model bills.

Congress for the New Urbanism, The Marquette Building, 140 S. Dearborn St., Suite 310, Chicago, IL 60603; (312) 551-7300; www.cnu.org. Promotes transit-oriented, mixed-use development as an alternative to traditional residential suburbs.

National Trust for Historic Preservation, 1785 Massachusetts Ave., N.W., Washington, DC 20036; (202) 588-6000;www.nationaltrust.org. Advocates curbing sprawl and revitalizing traditional downtowns and neighborhoods.

Reason Foundation, 3415 S. Sepulveda Blvd., Suite 400, Los Angeles, CA 90034; (310) 391-2245; www.reason.org. A libertarian organization that opposes smart-growth efforts as an unwarranted government intrusion into private life.

Smart Growth Leadership Institute, 1707 L St., N.W., Suite 1050, Washington, DC 20036; (202) 207-3355; www.sgli.org. Founded by former Maryland Gov. Parris N. Glendening to promote policies that curb sprawl.

U.S. Environmental Protection Agency, Development, Community and Environment Division (1808), 1200 Pennsylvania Ave., N.W., Washington, DC 20460; (202) 566-2878; smartgrowth@epa.gov. Manages EPA's Smart Growth program, which provides extensive information on state and local efforts to curb sprawl.

12

Big-Box Stores

Brian Hansen

Wal-Mart has grown into the world's largest company by offering "everyday low prices." But critics say big-box stores' ever-lower prices carry hidden costs for taxpayers, the community at large and the environment.

CQ Press/Kenneth Lukas

It's hard to miss the Wal-Mart store in the Denver suburb of Commerce City. At 155,000 square feet, it is nearly as large as three football fields. The low-slung, largely windowless building sits just off the main drag, Dahlia Street, on a 15-acre tract. Its parking lot is frequently full, even late at night. That's because, like thousands of other Wal-Marts across the country, the store never closes.

There are about 25 other Wal-Marts within 50 miles of Commerce City, as well as some 24 Home Depots, each store occupying at least 100,000 square feet. Other so-called big-box stores also abound, including Target, Kmart and Lowe's. In some Denver-area neighborhoods, mammoth, nationwide chain stores stand side by side like giant building blocks, with no local, independent businesses in sight.

Denver's experience is hardly unique. Big-box retailers in the United States are flourishing. More than 80 percent of American households purchased something last year from Wal-Mart, the nation's largest retailer — indeed, the world's biggest company of any kind. Home Depot is the nation's second-largest retailer and the fastest-growing retailer in U.S. history.

"People save time and money" by shopping at big-box retailers, says Jason Todd, government affairs manager at the International Mass Retail Association, which represents many big-box chains. "The stores also create quality jobs and generate tax revenues for the communities in which they're located."

But critics complain that the much-touted "everyday low prices" of big-box stores like Wal-Mart actually carry many hidden costs for taxpayers, the community at large and the environment, including: driving smaller stores out of business and turning downtown shopping areas into boarded-up ghost towns; exacerbating traffic con-

From *CQ Researcher*, September 10, 2004.

Study Cites Hidden Cost of Wal-Mart Jobs

The average Wal-Mart employee in California earns 31 percent less than the average employee at other large retail stores, according to the University of California at Berkeley Labor Institute. The study also found that fewer Wal-Mart workers are covered by company-based health insurance. As a result, Wal-Mart employees' families use more in taxpayer-subsidized public assistance — such as health care and food stamps — than the families of all large retail employees. Non-union Wal-Mart called the study biased because of the institute's strong ties to union labor.

Wal-Mart Wages vs. Other Large Retailers
(in California in 2001)

	Average Wages
Wal-Mart	$9.70
All big retailers in California	$14.01

Percentage Covered by Employer-Based Health Insurance
(in California in 2004)

Wal-Mart	48%
All large retailers	61%
Unionized grocers*	95%

Amount of Public Assistance Used Annually by Employees

Wal-Mart	$1,952
Large retailers	1,401

* In the San Francisco Bay area

Source: "Hidden Cost of Wal-Mart Jobs," University of California-Berkeley Labor Center, Aug. 2, 2004

gestion and suburban sprawl; undermining the nation's economy by creating a huge class of low-paid, non-union workers who can't afford basic needs such as health insurance or school lunches for their children; and forcing U.S. suppliers to manufacture products in low-wage countries overseas in order to meet demands for increasingly low prices. (*See sidebar, p. 264.*)

And because Wal-Mart is the world's largest wholesale buyer and employer, it has been able to crack the whip with both competitors and suppliers, forcing them to cope with its price-cutting policies in order to survive. And with some 1.5 million employees — more than the populations of 12 states — it is the world's largest private employer. As a result, the staunchly anti-union company — which is facing several class-action suits for allegedly violating fair-labor laws — is overhauling world employment practices, according to a report by the minority staff of the House Education and Workforce Committee.

"Wal-Mart's slogan should be 'Always low wages, always,' " Rep. George Miller, the committee's senior Democrat, said when he unveiled the report on Feb. 16, 2004. "Wal-Mart imposes a huge, often hidden, cost on its workers, our communities, and U.S. taxpayers. And Wal-Mart is in the driver's seat in the global race to the bottom, suppressing wage levels, workplace protections and labor laws."

But retail industry observers say Wal-Mart has wrung inefficiencies out of the supply chain and passed the savings along to consumers. "Wal-Mart is an outstanding operator, and suppliers learn how to supply goods faster, better, cheaper — in large part because of the challenges Wal-Mart puts toward them," says Dan Stanek, executive vice president of the retail consulting firm Retail Forward, Inc., of Columbus, Ohio. [1]

Nonetheless, many local policymakers have begun using zoning ordinances and other means to ban big-box retailers from their communities. The ordinances vary widely. Mequon, Wis., for example, prohibits retail stores larger than 20,000 square feet, while Santa Fe, N.M., sets the limit at 150,000 square feet.

Al Norman, an anti-big-box activist from Greenfield, Mass., estimates that the ordinances have derailed hundreds of proposed big-box stores in recent years. "More and more of these stores are being challenged, and it's slowing them down or stopping them in their tracks," Norman says.

The CBS television program "60 Minutes" dubbed Norman the "guru of the anti-Wal-Mart movement" after he kept Wal-Mart out of his hometown in the early

1990s. He now runs Sprawl-Busters, a group that opposes "megastores and other undesirable large-scale developments."

Big-box retailers denounce such efforts as illegal attempts to block competition. "There's nothing more going on here than an attempt by the unions and our competitors to try to stop our growth," says Robert S. McAdam, Wal-Mart's vice president of corporate affairs. "Instead of competing in the marketplace, they're trying to get government to preserve their profits."

But critics say big-box retailers themselves do not always operate on a level playing field with competitors, often demanding huge public subsidies from local and state governments before they will locate in an area. For instance, Wal-Mart — which last year made nearly $9 billion in profits — received at least $1 billion in state and local subsidies, according to a study released in May by the job-subsidy watchdog group Good Jobs First. [2] (*See sidebar, p. 258.*)

The anti-big-box movement has particularly targeted Arkansas-based Wal-Mart, which collected an astronomical $258 billion in revenues in 2003 — more than the combined revenues of General Motors, Microsoft and Coca-Cola. [3] And it is growing rapidly, having recently announced plans to move into perhaps its last marketing frontiers: big U.S. cities and overseas markets. On a single day last April, the giant chain opened 18 stores.

Big-box retailers come in two basic styles. Some, like Wal-Mart, Kmart and Target, sell everything from dog food to diamonds and operate "supercenters" that sell both groceries and general merchandise. Wal-Mart's supercenters are the biggest, sometimes covering 250,000 square feet, or nearly six acres, and carrying about 100,000 different products.

Other big-box retailers specialize in certain types of products, such as Barnes & Noble (books), Staples (office supplies) and Home Depot (home-improvement products). Atlanta-based Home Depot currently operates about 1,700 stores, each carrying about 40,000 different items. Stores average about 108,000 square feet, and have outdoor garden centers.

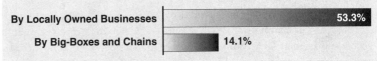

Big-Box Stores Hurt Maine Economies

Three times as much money stays in the local economy when goods and services are bought from locally owned businesses instead of at national chains and big-box stores, according to an analysis of the revenue and expenditures of eight local businesses in Maine by an anti-big-box store organization.

Percentage of Revenues Spent in Local and State Economy
(in Midcoast Maine region)

By Locally Owned Businesses	53.3%
By Big-Boxes and Chains	14.1%

Source: "The Economic Impact of Locally Owned Businesses vs. Chains: A Case Study in Midcoast Maine," Institute for Local Self-Reliance and Friends of Midcoast Maine, September 2003.

Americans love the convenience of big-box stores, especially the supercenters that feature one-hour photo centers, hair salons, banks, automotive centers and other services. Most also have acres of free parking — a huge attraction in today's car-cluttered culture. Brenda Hardy, of Montbello, Colo., patronizes Wal-Mart's Commerce City supercenter because, "Everything is under one roof, and you don't have to pay to park."

Wal-Mart's overarching business philosophy — to continuously cut prices — enables the Commerce City store to offer 50-foot garden hoses for just $4.96, large jars of Prego spaghetti sauce (with meat) for $1.72 and 20-inch flat-screen TVs for under $100.

McAdam says the low prices help bolster the nation's economy — and consumers' living standards — by allowing them to buy things they could not otherwise afford or to save for a rainy day. "If you're able to save 15 to 20 percent of your disposable income on what you have to buy for the necessities of life, you can spend that in other ways," McAdam says. "Maybe it's an extra night out on the town, or maybe you save up for a car or some other large purchase. Whatever it is, there's a benefit."

Wal-Mart's low prices also force competitors to lower their prices — a phenomenon known as the "Wal-Mart effect." Americans saved about $100 billion in 2002 thanks to Wal-Mart's low prices and the company's influence on its competitors, according to the New England Consulting Group, in Westport, Conn. [4]

Ira Kalish, global director of Deloitte Research in New York, says Wal-Mart has had a substantial positive impact on America's economy. "Wal-Mart has created a new economic model for retailing that focuses on low prices for consumers, and they've forced other retailers to do the same," he says. "This has effectively made consumers richer. It's like a tax cut, freeing up resources they can spend on other things."

Today, big-box retailers command large and growing market shares of many products. Nearly 40 percent of all book sales, for example, are captured by a handful of large chain stores, with just two companies — Barnes & Noble and Borders — accounting for more than a quarter of the total market. The office-supply market is similarly dominated by Office Max, Office Depot and Staples; and the hardware and building-supply markets by Home Depot and Lowe's.

No retailer, though, dominates more product markets than Wal-Mart. The company is the nation's top seller of many types of merchandise, including apparel, toys, cosmetics, diapers, CDs, DVDs and dog food. It currently commands the lion's share (about 30 percent) of sales of household staples such as toothpaste, shampoo and paper towels. Experts predict Wal-Mart will control half of this market by decade's end. [5]

But the intense competition from Wal-Mart and other discounters is taking a toll on other big retailers as well as mom-and-pop operations. For example, the once-dominant Toys "R" Us chain announced on Aug. 11 that it might abandon the toy business; it has about 17 percent of the $27 billion U.S. toy business, compared with Wal-Mart's 20 percent. [6]

"Bookstores, music retailers, electronics chains and supermarkets have all struggled to compete with Wal-Mart's low prices and its enormous power over its suppliers," *The New York Times* noted. [7]

Suppliers are equally squeezed by Wal-Mart's low-price policies. The company demands that suppliers constantly lower their wholesale prices, forcing some to close domestic manufacturing operations and ship jobs overseas. Levi Strauss & Co., America's iconic jeans maker, shuttered all its North American manufacturing plants in the past two years, eliminating some 5,600 jobs; foreign factories now handle the work. [8]

Stacy Mitchell, a researcher at the Washington, D.C.-based Institute for Local Self-Reliance, says the "savings" consumers derive by shopping at Wal-Mart and other big-box retailers carry hidden costs. In addition to millions of dollars in tax breaks and other government subsidies paid to big discounters, Mitchell notes, the companies often pay below-subsistence wages. According to the House report, the average Wal-Mart clerk made $8.23 an hour in 2001, or $13,861 a year — below the federal poverty line of $14,630 for a family of three.

Mitchell contends the company also offers inadequate health insurance plans, throwing more health-care responsibility onto taxpayers. "Wal-Mart encourages its employees to seek charitable and public assistance for meeting their health-care needs," the House study said.

Another study by researchers at the University of California, Berkeley, found that approximately 44,000 Wal-Mart employees in California cost taxpayers about $86 million annually due to their reliance on government services like public health care, subsidized housing, school lunches and food stamps. (*See table, p. 254.*) [9] Other studies have shown that local taxpayers often end up paying more for additional roads and public-safety services needed to support big-box stores than the extra tax revenues generated by the stores.

"There are lots of costs that don't show up on the price tags at stores like Wal-Mart," Mitchell says. "When you add it all up, these stores often don't even pay their own way, much less generate any net benefits for consumers and communities."

As Wal-Mart and other big-box retailers continue to expand, here are some of the issues being debated:

Do big-box retailers hurt locally owned businesses?

Independence, Iowa, population 6,000, once had a vibrant downtown. But after Wal-Mart opened a store nearby in 1984, local retailers began to disappear.

"Fourteen months later, the first local business went down: Anthony's, a department store that . . . had anchored Main Street for 30 years," *The New York Times Magazine* reported in 1989. Over the next four years, "about a dozen businesses closed . . . including a 100-year-old men's store, a furniture store and a sporting goods store. Most of the surviving shops are struggling to stay alive." [10]

A study by the National Trust for Historic Preservation found that 84 percent of all sales at new Wal-Mart stores came at the expense of existing businesses within the same county. Only 16 percent of sales came from outside the county — which critics say refutes the notion that Wal-Mart can act as a magnet drawing customers from a wide area and benefiting other businesses in town. [11]

While big-box stores usually get the blame for undercutting locally owned businesses, others say shoppers are at fault. "Wal-Mart offers consumers an additional shopping option," said Edward Fox, chairman of the J. C. Penney Center for Retail Excellence at Southern Methodist University. "If we choose to avail ourselves of that option, then we are the ones putting the downtown stores out of business." [12]

Wal-Mart's McAdam says the company is merely giving the customer what he wants. "It's not about whether you're small or large; it's about listening to your customers," he says. "Businesses that don't change and don't adapt to their customers' interests are the ones that may not succeed."

John Simley, a spokesman for Home Depot, says stores that struggle or close when his company comes to town are the ones that don't carry the right products, don't train their salespeople, or don't stay open in the evening. "The bottom line is, it's not us that's causing them problems — their customers are not choosing them anymore."

Small stores can co-exist with Home Depot if they adapt and find a niche, Simley says. He cites Curry Hardware in Quincy, Mass., which has a Home Depot practically next door and another a few miles away. Curry sells certain items, such as specialty paints, and provides services — like filling propane tanks and repairing windows and screens — that its big-box neighbors do not. "Business has been wonderful and we expect it to stay that way," said co-owner Sean Curry. "Home Depot hasn't been a problem for us." [13]

Bill Goldman, owner of Downtown Discount Fashions, a 6,000-square-foot independent clothing store and bridal shop in Rutland, Vt., tells a similar story: "They bring people into town [who then] filter around to the different specialty stores."

Locally owned businesses that can find a non-competitive niche do best, he says. "You don't try to compete with the big-box stores, because you can't. Wal-Mart is no competition to me. They don't carry what I carry [wedding gowns and bridal accessories]."

Brian Peltey, owner of Rutland Family Flooring, agrees. Although the Home Depot sells tile, carpeting and other flooring materials, it isn't hurting his much smaller, locally owned business. "I think they've driven some people to us," he says. "They fall down on the service end, so that's how we can compete."

When residents in Madison, Miss., complained about the design of a proposed Wal-Mart, the company built a store with a bricked exterior, a ceramic tile roof and white columns and arches to accommodate the community's quality-of-life concerns.

Courtesy Madison Mayor's Office

But critics say more typically big-box retailers steamroll local competitors. Steinbaugh Hardware in Louisville, Colo., just east of Boulder, had served the quaint downtown corridor for 104 years when a Home Depot store opened outside of town in August 1996. Five months later, Eagle Hardware opened a big-box store in the same area. Tom Steinbaugh, the fourth-generation Steinbaugh to head the family business, reluctantly closed in June 1997.

"The big boxes — we could fight one, but not two," an angry Steinbaugh said. "It's a punch in the face." [14]

Steinbaugh says his big-box competitors undercut him significantly on price. Experts say the large retailers' dominance in the marketplace gives them the clout to demand extremely low wholesale prices from manufacturers and suppliers — prices mom-and-pop stores cannot get. The big stores can then undercut the small stores.

Some experts say big-box retailers routinely violate laws regulating volume-related discounts and other pricing practices that might be used to weaken competitors. For instance, Wal-Mart is accused of regularly violating the Robinson-Patman Act, enacted in 1936 to prevent large chain stores from conspiring with manufacturers to drive small retailers out of business.

A suit filed by James McCrory, an independent tire dealer in Pompano Beach, Fla., alleges Wal-Mart and the Goodyear tire company are running such a scheme. McCrory says Goodyear sells certain tires to Wal-Mart at or

How Cities Subsidize Big-Box Stores

Lowe's is a $31 billion corporation. Yet the New Orleans City Council last year gave the giant home-improvement retailer $3.6 million in public funds to build a store near the French Quarter.

Target is a $48 billion corporation. But the Pennsylvania governor's office two years ago gave the company $5.8 million to build a distribution center in Chambersburg.

Even Wal-Mart — the world's largest company, with revenues of $258 billion in 2003 — caught a subsidy break. Birmingham, Ala., last year offered the giant retailer $10 million to build a store on the east side of town. And that's not all. According to a recent study, Wal-Mart — which last year made nearly $9 billion in profits — received at least $1 billion in various types of state and local government subsidies.

"The actual total is certainly far higher," said the study by the Washington, D.C.-based Good Jobs First, a subsidy watchdog group. "But the records are scattered in thousands of places, and many subsidies are undisclosed." [1]

To encourage new development, state and local governments often offer businesses various subsidies and tax exemptions on the premise that the jobs and future tax revenues they generate will outweigh the subsidy costs.

But critics say cities should not subsidize big-box stores, because studies show that the added financial burdens created by the huge stores — such as additional police services, employees' dependence on subsidized health care and other social benefits — far outweigh the jobs and tax revenues generated by the stores — even when they're not getting tax exemptions.

Moreover, says Jeff Milchen, executive director of the American Independent Business Alliance in Bozeman, Mont., when big-box stores receive subsidies, it unfairly disadvantages competitors who do not receive them. "Subsidies create a completely uneven, uncompetitive playing field," he says. "I have serious doubts as to whether Wal-Mart, Home Depot and other big-box retailers could succeed without the massive public subsidies they receive and use to support the operations of their stores."

The subsidies range from free or reduced-price land and infrastructure improvements to exemptions or rebates on sales, property and corporate income taxes; reduced utility rates, low-interest financing, subsidies to train and recruit workers, tax-exempt bond financing and outright grants.

For example, according to the Good Jobs First study, North Platte, Neb., gave Wal-Mart more than $15.2 million in subsidies to build a distribution center in 2003,

---

below cost and recoups its losses by charging him and other independent dealers more for the same tires. McCrory says the alleged scheme is significantly hurting his business.

"It doesn't take a rocket scientist to figure out what's going on," he says. "Wal-Mart is pulling this [expletive] all over the country."

Wal-Mart refutes the price-fixing allegation. "We are good bargainers; there's no question about that," McAdam says. "We just want a fair deal from our suppliers."

Wal-Mart and other big-box retailers also have been sued for violating state fair-pricing laws. Last year, for example, a judge in Oklahoma City ruled that three local Sam's Clubs, wholesale stores owned by Wal-Mart, had illegally sold gasoline at a loss to lure customers to buy other merchandise. He ordered the stores to raise their gas prices. The ruling helped "level the playing field" for independent gasoline marketers, said attorney Gary

Chilton, who filed the lawsuit on behalf of several convenience stores. [15]

Critics say big-box retailers also violate state laws against "predatory pricing" — selling goods at a loss simply to eliminate competitors. However, such charges are difficult to prove. For example, three independent pharmacists in Conway, Ark., initially won their 1991 suit charging the local Wal-Mart with trying to drive them out of business by selling items below cost. But the Arkansas Supreme Court overturned the ruling two years later, dealing a major setback to small businesses that had hoped predatory-pricing laws would help them compete with big-box retailers.

Do big-box retailers make communities less livable?

Critics say the thousands of cars and trucks attracted by big discounters cause additional traffic, air pollution, noise, sprawl and other detriments to the quality of life.

including up to $9.45 million in tax abatements, $3.2 million for a racking system, $1 million in special financing for the city to purchase land that was then granted to Wal-Mart, $1 million in federal Community Development Block Grant funds, $170,000 in waived city fees, $400,000 in job training funds and infrastructure improvements worth an unknown amount.

Some subsidies are structured as tax abatements, which allow retailers to keep — usually for a limited time — some or all of the taxes they would normally pay. Birmingham's deal with Wal-Mart, for example, requires the city to refund 90 percent of the sales taxes the store collects — expected to top $2.2 million a year — until the $10 million mark is reached.

Some subsidies generate little opposition. Others spawn firestorms of protest, such as Denver's efforts to revitalize Alameda Square, a run-down strip mall housing an Asian grocery store, a nail parlor and a martial-arts center. The city declared the area "blighted" in 1991 and offered special subsidized financing to any company that would buy and redevelop the site. Wal-Mart proposed building a 209,000-square-foot supercenter on the site that would generate up to $12.2 million in tax revenues annually.

City officials were ecstatic, but many Denverites were outraged at plans to subsidize the world's richest company. Publicly, the city said it was giving Wal-Mart about $10 million in special funding to take on the project, but documents obtained by the Front Range Economic Strategy Center, a group opposed to the deal, indicated the subsidy could balloon to $25 million over several years.

"It was pretty horrific," says Chris Nevitt, the group's executive director. "A lot of people got worked up about it. It was not a popular deal, to say the least."

City officials defended the deal, arguing that Wal-Mart could revitalize the site in a way that a smaller company could not. But even a company of Wal-Mart's size would balk at paying for all the infrastructure improvements needed at a site as dilapidated as Alameda Square, said Tracy Huggins, executive director of the Denver Urban Renewal Authority.

"There's a belief that because [Wal-Mart is] a large company, they could pay for those costs," Huggins said. "And they're right; they could. But will they? If it doesn't make sense for them from a financial standpoint, they can't do it." [2]

Wal-Mart backed out of the deal in April, unable to come to terms with the property owners. While some Denverites were upset by the development, others cheered.

"There's no reason taxpayers should be subsidizing the world's largest corporation," says Al Norman, a well-known anti-big-box activist from Greenfield, Mass. "It's corporate welfare."

---

[1] "Shopping for Subsidies: How Wal-Mart Uses Taxpayer Money to Finance Its Never-Ending Growth," Good Jobs First, May 2004.

[2] Quoted in Erin Johansen, "DURA Relied on TIF to Bring in Projects," *The Denver Business Journal*, Feb. 6, 2004, p. A3.

The stores become prime drivers of suburban sprawl, critics maintain, because they usually locate on the outskirts of communities where land is cheap enough to provide abundant parking. This chews up green space, forces people to drive further to shop and raises taxpayers' costs for road maintenance, police protection and other public services, critics note. At the same time, the low prices wreak economic havoc on small, locally owned stores on traditional main streets.

"Most people wouldn't choose to spend their vacations in towns full of big-box stores and strip malls," says anti-big-box activist Steve Bercu, owner of Book People, an independent bookstore in Austin, Texas. "They'd go to places like Nantucket, where they don't have those things. And why would you want to live somewhere where there's no character?"

But John La Plante, an adjunct scholar at the Mackinac Center for Public Policy in Midland, Mich., scoffs at the "quality-of-life" crowd that opposes discount stores. He says it is comprised mainly of quixotic dreamers, who yearn for a return to a "Norman Rockwell" era, and affluent elitists, who simply don't want their chic communities sullied with stores that cater to lower-income people.

"There's a nostalgia for a sort of existence that's not realistic in this day and age," La Plante says, "and there's definitely a class element [to blocking big-box stores], because it hurts people of lower incomes."

"It's called NIMBYism [not in my backyard]," says Raymond Keating, chief economist at the Small Business Survival Committee, which advocates for small business. Those who complain that Wal-Mart will destroy their quality of life are usually "a very vocal minority who want to freeze [their community] in time. On the flip side are the countless people who shop at the Wal-Mart or Home Depot, and they're basically voting with their dollars. What about the families that want to save a little bit of money by having a local Wal-Mart? Doesn't that enhance their quality of life?"

Many zoning ordinances place no size restrictions on stores in commercial districts. In Fargo, N.D., for example, the main shopping district in the city of 91,000 features Wal-Mart, Sam's Club, Kmart, Target, Kohl's, Home Depot, Lowe's and Best Buy, among others.

"Our [zoning] is pretty friendly to big-box development," says Mark Williams, an assistant city planner. "We look at a Wal-Mart development in the same way we would a 2,000-square-foot bike shop."

"People really like the big-box stores," says Fargo Mayor Bruce Furness, because of the low prices, the wide selection of goods under one roof and the ample free parking. And the sales and property taxes generated by the big-box stores are "very important to our economy," he adds.

Yet Fargo's willingness to accommodate big-box retailers apparently hasn't hurt its quality of life: It consistently ranks among the nation's best small cities for livability and as a place to work and raise children. [16]

But other communities take a decidedly different approach to planning. Easton, Md., for example, a quaint town with about 12,000 residents on Maryland's Eastern Shore, decided to limit retail stores to 65,000 square feet, a threshold based on the size of the town's existing buildings.

Easton adopted its size-cap ordinance in 2000, largely to block three proposed stores of about 170,000 square feet each. The town's planning and zoning commission predicted that increased traffic and demands for public services would compromise Easton's "unique and attractive small-town character." [17]

Dozens of other communities have capped retail store sizes, including Boxborough, Mass. (25,000 sq. ft.); Ashland, Ore. (45,000); Flagstaff, Ariz. (70,000); Taos, N.M. (80,000); and Stoughton, Wis. (110,000).

Big-box retailers say such caps are designed not to legitimately regulate land use but to specifically keep them out. Some have sued cities over the caps, saying they violate retailers' constitutional rights to conduct interstate commerce and to enjoy equal protection under the law. Some also say the caps violate certain state laws by using zoning to regulate competition.

Legal issues aside, some experts say size caps are counterproductive and can foster the very quality-of-life problems — such as increased traffic — that supporters of caps say they are designed to curtail. "There are many, many occasions where our [non-capped] stores actually reduce traffic," says Wal-Mart's McAdam. "You don't have to make as many trips [to different stores] to get everything you need."

Home Depot sometimes agrees to scale back stores in response to community concerns — but only up to a point, Simley says. The company would not, for example, agree to build a 40,000 square-foot-store where there's a clear need for a 180,000-square-foot store, he says, because doing so would result in parking gridlock, more frequent truck deliveries and other unpleasant consequences.

"If we open a smaller store than what's recommended to us, it would still attract the same number of customers," he says. "We determine square footage based on demand; we don't just say, 'The bigger the better.'"

Wal-Mart, too, says it will make reasonable modifications to accommodate community quality-of-life concerns. When residents in Madison, Miss., voiced concerns about the design of a proposed Wal-Mart, the company agreed to build a store with a bricked exterior, a ceramic tile roof and white columns and arches. "The store is absolutely gorgeous; it should be a national model for Wal-Mart," said Mayor Mary Hawkins-Butler. [18]

But other communities haven't been swayed, such as the Denver suburb of Thornton, where Wal-Mart wanted to build a 24-hour supercenter near a golf course surrounded by large homes. Wal-Mart promised a "neighborhood-friendly" store with a unique, pleasing design and parking lot lights that didn't bleed into the neighborhood, plus a gift of eight acres for community open space.

But many Thornton residents feared the store would remain a hulking, ugly box despite efforts to dress it up while drawing as many as 10,000 cars per day to the quiet community, scaring off the bald eagles that sometimes roost in the area. More than 6,000 residents signed a petition opposing the store, and some threatened to mount a campaign to recall the six City Council members who initially supported the proposal.

In June, the City Council reversed course and voted 7-2 against authorizing the rezoning proposal that Wal-Mart needed to build the store. "This was a real David vs. Goliath situation," said Thornton resident Joanne Flick, who spearheaded the grass-roots effort to block the store. "It wasn't appropriate to put a Wal-Mart or any other big box next to Thornton's only golf course." [19]

Do big-box retailers benefit local economies?

Supporters say the new jobs and additional sales- and property-tax revenues generated by big-box stores far outweigh any detrimental impacts. Plus, supporters say, by helping shoppers save money the stores foster job growth in other economic sectors through new consumer spending on everything from movies and health-club memberships to home improvements and new clothes.

Like hundreds of American communities, Hyannis, Mass., wrestled with the big-box question when BJ's Wholesale Club proposed a 69,000-square-foot grocery/general merchandise store in the picturesque town. The local policymaking body, the Cape Cod Commission, ultimately voted 7 to 6 (with two abstentions) to approve the store, which is slated for construction later this year.

"There were clear economic benefits for Hyannis and a substantial portion of the population," says Commissioner Lawrence Cole, who voted for the store. "If BJ's can provide people with what they want at lower prices, I can't see prohibiting them just because some people don't like big-box stores."

But Felicia Penn, executive director of the Cape Cod Smart Planning and Growth Coalition, which led the fight against BJ's, says it will hurt the town's few remaining local businesses. "It's not as if there's $35 million a year just sitting around unspent," says Penn, a local merchant herself, referring to BJ's projected first-year earnings. "All that money is going to have to come from other businesses, and that's going to suck the lifeblood out of our community."

Penn contends BJ's will produce a net loss of retail-sector jobs while drawing more traffic from neighboring communities. But the new tax revenues generated will not cover the additional road and infrastructure-maintenance costs required by the increased usage, she says.

A study commissioned by Barnstable, a community just north of Hyannis, supports Penn's hypothesis. The study by Tischler & Associates, a Bethesda, Md.-based consulting firm, found that locally owned "specialty retail" stores generate $326 in net tax revenues per 1,000 square feet per year. Conversely, the firm found, big-box stores cost Barnstable taxpayers more in services — such as road maintenance and police/fire protection — than the stores remit in taxes, creating net losses of $468 per 1,000 square feet annually. [20]

Other studies have reached similar conclusions. A 1993 study conducted for Greenfield, Mass., for example, concluded that a proposed Wal-Mart store would cost existing businesses $35 million in sales annually, leading to a net loss of 105,000 square feet of retail space (and the resulting lost property taxes). The study estimated that while the Wal-Mart would create 177 new jobs, it would cause local businesses to eliminate 148 jobs. [21] Greenfield residents rejected the proposed Wal-Mart in the wake of the study.

"What we find over and over again is that big-box retailers tend to destroy as many jobs as they create and end up costing taxpayers more than they contribute in revenues," says Mitchell of the Institute for Local Self-Reliance.

The National Trust study found that while local tax bases added about $2 million with each Wal-Mart, the decline in retail stores after the Wal-Mart opened depressed property values in downtowns and on shopping strips, offsetting the Wal-Mart tax gains. [22]

Some big-box advocates dismiss such studies outright, saying communities design them to produce the results they want to see. Others say they're inaccurate because they don't consider all of the relevant economic factors.

Home Depot's Simley says some studies ignore or gloss over the "multiplier" effect that Home Depot stores have on their host communities. The average Home Depot, Simley says, employs 150 to 175 people, creating a payroll of up to $5.5 million annually. About 80 percent of that stays in the local area, he says.

"That money goes to support other jobs in the community — jobs in grocery stores, clothing stores, restaurants and so forth," Simley says. "Depending on the locale, we've seen [job-creation] multipliers ranging from 1.8 to well over 3, so if we create 100 jobs, the net effect is between 180 to 300-plus new jobs."

Keating, of the Small Business Survival Committee, is skeptical about such studies, claiming, "If somebody is looking for a certain answer going in, they're going to get the answer coming out. When a Wal-Mart store opens, a lot of consumers go there and find wider selections and better prices, which are certainly good for those families and the economy in general."

Home Depot also benefits communities by providing residents with products to fix up their homes, which increases property values, Simley says. That creates more property tax revenues to spend on streets, parks, libraries and other amenities, he says.

CHRONOLOGY

1850s-1890s *Department stores, chain stores and mail-order houses replace small general stores.*

1858 R. H. Macy opens a small dry-goods store in New York City.

1859 The Great Atlantic and Pacific Tea Co. (A&P) is founded in New York City.

1872 Aaron Montgomery Ward distributes his first mail-order catalog.

1900-1930s *Small retailers say chain stores and mail-order houses are driving them out of business. State and federal efforts to level the playing field are unsuccessful.*

1902 James Cash Penney opens his first store in Kemmerer, Wyo. The J. C. Penney chain expands to more than 1,400 stores by 1930.

1912 Small merchants unsuccessfully lobby Congress to abolish the parcel-post system, saying mail-order firms are driving them out of business.

1931 California enacts the first "fair trade" law, designed to help small merchants compete against chain stores. Dozens of states follow suit.

1936 Congress enacts Robinson-Patman Act to prevent chain stores from driving independent retailers out of business.

1960s-1980s *Discount stores give rise to big-box retailers.*

1962 Kresge dime-store chain opens its first Kmart discount store in Garden City, Mich.; Dayton Corp. opens first Target store in Minneapolis; Sam Walton opens his first Wal-Mart in Rogers, Ark.

1970 Kmart is the nation's largest retailer with $2 billion in annual sales. Wal-Mart is far behind with $44.2 million.

1978 The first Home Depot opens in Decatur, Ga.

1979 Wal-Mart sales top $1 billion.

1988 The first Wal-Mart supercenter — a combination general merchandise/grocery store — opens in Washington, Mo.

1989 The first formal study of Wal-Mart's impact on rural America concludes that Wal-Mart raises overall retail sales in a community, but largely at the expense of small merchants.

1990s-Present *Local zoning laws try to limit the spread of big-box retailers.*

1990 Wal-Mart becomes the nation's top retailer, with $32.6 billion in sales.

1991 Wal-Mart opens its first foreign store, in Mexico City.

1993 An Arkansas court rules that Wal-Mart engaged in predatory pricing to drive three independent pharmacies out of business. The state supreme court overturns the ruling.

August 2001 Kmart slashes prices to compete with Wal-Mart. Five months later, Kmart declares bankruptcy.

Oct. 11, 2003 Some 70,000 union grocery workers in California strike over grocery chains' efforts to cut wages and benefits to better compete with non-union Wal-Mart. The strike eventually ends, with the grocery chains getting most of what they wanted.

March 2, 2004 In a victory for Wal-Mart, voters in Contra Costa County, Calif., overturn a zoning ordinance banning supercenter-type stores.

April 6, 2004 Voters in Inglewood, Calif., reject a ballot initiative that would have allowed Wal-Mart to build a supercenter without adhering to city zoning codes.

June 22, 2004 A federal judge grants class-action status to a gender-discrimination suit filed against Wal-Mart, covering about 1.6 million current and former employees, making it the largest workplace-discrimination lawsuit in U.S. history.

Aug. 11, 2004 Under pressure from discounters, Toys "R" Us announces it may exit the toy business; the firm's share of the U.S. market has dropped to 17 percent, compared to Wal-Mart's 20 percent and Target's 18 percent.

"Where we go, assessments increase," Simley says. "There's no other retailer, except maybe Lowe's, that can say that."

Moreover, Simley notes, economic-impact studies often improperly misanalyze the impact of "leakage," or residents leaving their communities to shop. In Old Saybrook, Conn., for example, town officials rejected a proposed Home Depot store as "incompatible" with the community's small-town character, Simley says. As a result, many residents began patronizing Home Depots in adjacent communities. He estimates the leakage at $20 million annually.

"People are leaving Old Saybrook because they can't get what they need," Simley says. "The economic reality is that there's an overwhelming demand for what we sell, but the people there have to go elsewhere."

BACKGROUND

Early Retailers

Modern-day big-box retailers evolved from the department stores, chain stores and mail-order houses that began supplanting small general stores after the Civil War. Department stores began appearing in big cities in the 1860s and '70s, such as Macy's in New York, Wanamaker's in Philadelphia and Marshall Field's in Chicago. By the turn of the century, department stores were in smaller cities and towns. [23]

With their wide range of merchandise, early department stores resembled big-box retailers. But many were known for high-end merchandise and meticulous customer service, not bargain-basement goods that customers had to rummage through themselves. Moreover, unlike today's single-story big boxes, many early department stores boasted several floors and exquisitely designed facades and interiors.

The late-19th century also saw the first chain stores, or "junior department stores," viewed by some as the closest ancestors to big-box retailers. Instead of replicating the glamorous shopping environments of their bigger retail cousins, they emphasized simplicity and low prices.

The nation's first major chain, the Great Atlantic and Pacific Tea Co. (A&P), was founded in New York City in 1859. Eventually, it expanded from just dealing in tea into a full-blown grocery outlet; by 1929, A&P operated 15,000 stores nationwide — triple the 5,000 stores Wal-Mart has worldwide today.

General-merchandise companies soon jumped on the chain-store bandwagon. Among the most successful was the J. C. Penney Co. James Cash Penney opened his first store in Kemmerer, Wyo., in 1902. By the mid-1930s, he had more than 1,400 stores across the country.

Some early general-merchandise chains were known as variety stores, or "5 and dimes," because nothing cost more than 10 cents (at least initially). Pioneers in this category included W. T. Grant and F. W. Woolworth.

Two of the most successful chains started out as mail-order houses. Aaron Montgomery Ward distributed his first catalog — a single sheet of paper listing 163 items — in 1872. By 1904, Ward's catalog — known to millions of Americans as the "Wish Book" — exceeded 500 pages. Sears, Roebuck and Co. published its first mail-order catalog in 1896, and by the turn of the century its more than 1,000 pages listed tens of thousands of items. Mail-order firms were especially popular in rural areas, which often had only small general stores. Sears began opening retail outlets in 1925; Ward's followed suit the next year.

Backlash

The early chain stores and mail-order houses — and, to a lesser degree, department stores — provoked a backlash similar to today's criticism of big-box retailers. Independent retailers complained bitterly that their larger competitors engaged in unethical and illegal practices to drive them out of business, mainly using their buying power to obtain lower prices from suppliers.

Some independents responded by publicly burning mail-order catalogs, or by playing on the era's racism, spreading rumors that Richard Sears and Montgomery Ward were black. In 1912, a coalition of independent merchants unsuccessfully lobbied Congress to cancel the fledgling parcel-post service, the mail-order firms' lifeline.

But anti-chain fervor continued. In 1922, author Frank Farrington implored merchants, wholesalers and the general public in his book *Meeting Chain Store Competition* to stop the proliferation of chains. And Shreveport, La., radio personality William K. Henderson urged listeners: "American people, wake up — we can whip these chain stores! We can drive them out in 30 days if you people will stay out of their stores."

But the chains' lower prices were just too seductive. Still, many state lawmakers were troubled by the chains' growing dominance and sought to level the retail playing field. Several states adopted "fair trade" laws that prohib-

Buy American? Not at Wal-Mart

Wal-Mart founder Sam Walton — the world's richest person when he died in 1992 — was a rags-to-riches billionaire. Raised in a backwater Arkansas town, he was famously frugal and down-to-earth: He shunned limousines, choosing instead to drive around in an old pickup truck.

"What am I supposed to haul my dogs around in, a Rolls-Royce?" Walton, an avid quail hunter, once quipped.

The first President George Bush extolled Walton as "an American original." Walton himself subtitled his autobiography, "Made in America."

Walton may have been made in America, but it's not easy to find American-made merchandise at Wal-Mart these days. The Levi Strauss jeans sold at Wal-Mart come from Mexico and Colombia. Fruit of the Loom boxer shorts are made in El Salvador, White Stag sweaters in the Philippines, Winnie-the-Pooh clocks in China — and the list goes on and on. Wal-Mart won't say what portion of its merchandise is imported, but the Columbus, Ohio, consulting firm Retail Forward estimates that it is about 60 percent.

However, in March 1985, Walton had announced that he was "firmly committed" to "buying everything possible from suppliers who manufacture their products in the United States." [1]

Walton touted the effort as a way to counteract the flood of cheap imports that was increasing the nation's trade deficit and prompting U.S. companies to eliminate manufacturing jobs. Wal-Mart pledged to buy U.S.-made items costing within 5 percent of equal-quality items from overseas. Some U.S. companies did lower their prices in order to sell to Wal-Mart. In 1988, Wal-Mart claimed it had converted some $1.2 billion in retail goods to U.S. manufacturers that otherwise would have been made overseas — creating or saving about 17,000 U.S. jobs.

Wal-Mart widely advertised its "Buy American" theme, and festooned its stores with red-white-and-blue banners that read, "Made in the USA," and "Keep America Working and Strong." It was a public relations windfall for Wal-Mart, especially among blue-collar Americans who had lost, or feared losing, their jobs due to foreign competition.

But eight months after Walton's death, NBC News correspondent Brian Ross interviewed then-Wal-Mart CEO David Glass on national television. Ross told Glass he'd recently visited numerous Wal-Mart stores and found clothing made in China and other countries on racks labeled "Made in the USA." Glass shrugged this off as a "mistake at the store level." [2]

Ross then played a videotape showing a Bangladesh factory where children as young as 9 were making shirts for Wal-Mart. Glass said Wal-Mart made a "concerted effort" not to buy merchandise made with child labor. But when Ross showed Glass photographs of the bodies of 25 children who had died in a fire at the same factory two years earlier, Glass replied, "Yeah. There are tragic things that happen all over the world." [3]

Other media investigations followed. After being forced to investigate its overseas suppliers, Wal-Mart announced it had adopted a set of standards to govern overseas suppliers. Other U.S. firms followed suit.

Wal-Mart's standards say the company "will not accept" products manufactured with any type of forced or prison labor. Workers must be at least 14 years old, even if local laws allow children to work at a lower age. Moreover, factory owners must "fairly compensate" workers and maintain "reasonable" work hours in accordance with prevailing labor laws.

---

ited chains from selling a product for less than the manufacturer's suggested retail price. While the new restrictions had some effect, court decisions in the 1950s and '60s diluted or voided most of them.

Many states also taxed the chains according to the number of outlets they operated. By 1939, 27 states had chain-store tax laws. Ironically, the tax laws may have done the anti-chain movement more harm than good: They encouraged the chains to build larger stores (instead of more stores), giving the independents even tougher competition.

The growing tide of angry independents finally prompted Congress to act in 1936. The Robinson-Patman antitrust act, known as the "anti-chain store act," made it illegal for chains to pressure suppliers into giving them volume-related discounts not offered to smaller retailers. It also prohibited suppliers from giving volume-related discounts to retailers — no matter how much they bought — that did not reflect their actual savings in manufacturing and/or delivering the goods.

Robinson-Patman was expressly intended to kill off

"Wal-Mart strives to do business only with factories run legally and ethically," the standards declare.

But critics say Wal-Mart and other U.S. retailers buy goods from countries like China precisely because they ignore their own labor laws. "U.S.-based corporations that invest in Chinese factories — a long list headed by Wal-Mart — owe some nice chunk of their profits to a work force toiling, to resurrect a line from Mao, under 'the barrel of a gun,' " Harold Meyerson, editor-at-large of the liberal *American Prospect* magazine, wrote recently. [4]

Wal-Mart remains popular with consumers even though most of its merchandise comes from overseas.

AFP Photo/Paul J. Richards

According to the House Education and Workforce Committee's recent minority staff report on Wal-Mart's labor abuses: "Workers in countries like China, Bangladesh and Honduras are suffering because of the stringent demands Wal-Mart makes of its suppliers. One factory worker reported working 19-hour days for 10- to 15-day stretches to meet Wal-Mart's price demands." [5]

Meanwhile, the Buy American program came under increasing attack. In 1998, the United Food and Commercial Workers International Union alleged that 80 percent of Wal-Mart's clothing was foreign-made and urged the Federal Trade Commission and all 50 state attorneys general to inves-

tigate Wal-Mart for "falsely" and "deceptively" concealing the practice.

"The time has come for American government officials to protect the integrity of our flag from crass, commercial abuse," said Doug Dority, then-president of the 1.4 million-member union. [6]

Wal-Mart abandoned its Buy American program in the late 1990s — not because of the union, it said, but rather because of the realities of economic globalization.

"There was a time when we really tried to buy product [domestically], but whether we like it or not, so much of everything is now sourced overseas," says Bob McAdam, Wal-Mart's vice president of corporate affairs. "And we are committed to providing people with the lowest possible price."

---

[1] Wal-Mart press release, March 13, 1985.

[2] Quoted in Bob Ortega, *In Sam We Trust* (1988), p. 223.

[3] *Ibid.*, p. 225.

[4] Quoted in Harold Meyerson, "China's Workers — And Ours," *The Washington Post*, March 17, 2004, p. A25.

[5] "Everyday Low Wages: The Hidden Price We All Pay for Wal-Mart," Democratic Staff of the House Committee on Education and the Workforce," Feb. 16, 2004.

[6] Quoted in F.N. D'Alessio, "Major Union and AFL-CIO Join Attack on Wal-Mart's 'Buy American' Program," The Associated Press, July 30, 1998.

---

the most despised chain store of all: A&P. While the giant chain was found guilty of violating the act, the conviction did not sink the firm. But a few decades later modern supermarkets forced it to close most of its stores. As for the Robinson-Patman Act, the federal government essentially stopped enforcing it in the 1970s.

"There really hasn't been any enforcement since the Nixon administration," says Carl Person, a New York lawyer. "It's really been devastating for people who rely on the government to create a level playing field."

Rise of the Discounters

Retailing changed markedly again after World War II, when the development of "discounting" allowed merchants to profit while undercutting the competition. Strategies included bypassing "the middle man" and buying goods directly from manufacturers; eliminating home delivery and other services; and, especially, operating out of low-rent facilities, often on the outskirts of town.

Many chain and variety stores embraced discounting, and the technique ultimately evolved into big-box retail-

Wal-Mart Accused of 'Union Busting'

When a pro-union flyer was found on the men's room floor at the Wal-Mart in Hillview, Ky., store manager Jon Lehman went into action. Following corporate policy, he immediately reported the incident to Wal-Mart headquarters in Bentonville, Ark., using the company's confidential "Union Hotline."

Within 24 hours, three company executives arrived in Hillview on a corporate jet. Lehman drove the officials to the store where he says they began "threatening, interrogating," making false promises to and "spying" on employees to determine who made the handbill. They scrutinized personnel files for clues and entered employees' biographical information and behavioral traits into a special matrix designed to identify likely union sympathizers. During the two-week investigation, they even monitored suspect employees' conversations.

The corporate sleuths didn't uncover the flyer's creator, but before departing they made employees watch two anti-union videos that portrayed union members as "crooks and thugs," Lehman says.

By spying on, intimidating and even firing employees thought to be union supporters, Wal-Mart routinely violates federal laws that protect workers' rights to unionize, according to officials at the United Food and Commercial Workers union (UFCW). "Union busting is a matter of policy at Wal-Mart," says Greg Denier, UFCW's director of communications. "Wal-Mart tells its managers that one of their primary duties is to identify and eliminate union activity. It's almost impossible to fulfill that mandate within the confines of the law."

Lehman resigned from Wal-Mart two years after the Hillview incident, feeling "outraged" over the incident and others like it and became a UFCW organizer. "I preached against the union for years," Lehman says now. "[Now] I'm trying to bring the truth back to Wal-Mart [employees] that the union can be a good thing."

So far, however, not one of Wal-Mart's 1.5 million employees — known as "associates" — is a union member. Wal-Mart says its stores are union-free because the employees are treated well — not because it is "anti-union," as critics charge. "We are not against unions; we just don't think they work for us and our associates," says Robert S. McAdam, Wal-Mart's vice president for state and local government relations.

Lehman says as a Wal-Mart manager he was given a 49-page policy manual, entitled "A Manager's Toolbox to Remaining Union-Free." It begins with the statement, "As a member of Wal-Mart's management team, you are our first line of defense against unionization," he says. The manual lists 25 early warning signs of union organizing, such as

---

ing. Among the movement's pioneers was the Kresge dime-store chain, which opened its first Kmart in Garden City, a Detroit suburb, in April 1962. By the end of 1963, there were 53 units.

Early Kmarts averaged about 100,000 square feet and typically were in shopping centers or strip malls, rather than crowded, downtown shopping districts. The outlying locations not only cut costs but also provided plenty of free parking — a convenience few downtown retailers could offer. By the late 1960s, Kmart was the largest discounter in America.

Woolworth launched a discount line, Woolco, in Columbus, Ohio, just three months after the first Kmart. Early Woolco stores were huge, up to 180,000 square feet. Like Kmarts, they usually were in shopping centers and strip malls with ample parking. Many also had

restaurants, pharmacies and automobile service centers, presaging today's "one-stop shopping" trend.

Other early discounters included the Dayton Corp., which also opened its first Target store in 1962, J. C. Penney (Treasure Island stores) and Gamble-Skogmo (Tempo stores) in 1964.

Wal-Mart Emerges

The 1960s also saw the emergence of Wal-Mart. Founder Sam Walton began his career in 1940 at J. C. Penney's, earning $75 a month as a management trainee. After a stint in the Army, Walton opened several Ben Franklin variety stores in Arkansas, Missouri and Texas.

Walton thought full-scale discount stores would succeed in small- and medium-sized towns — which he believed were underserved by the big chains. After two

"associates spending an abnormal amount of time in the parking lot before and after work" and "frequent meetings at associates' homes."

The manual tells managers they need to "understand what is considered legal and illegal conduct" in responding to union activities. It lists 25 examples of illegal activities, such as, "You cannot threaten associates with loss of their job if they sign a union authorization card."

Lehman says the store managers he knew usually adhered to the manual's guidelines. But he adds: "If you had a legitimate union scare or union activity in your store, the people from Bentonville would come in, and they would throw the book out the window."

Wal-Mart's McAdam denies the charge. "We don't do anything that's illegal; that's just not true," he says.

However, the National Labor Relations Board (NLRB), an independent government agency that enforces federal labor law, has filed at least 60 complaints against Wal-Mart in the last 10 years alleging it violated workers' right to organize. [1] Few other companies have as many complaints filed against them. Some have been thrown out, and many are still pending. But others have been upheld. In 2002, for example, a judge ruled that managers at three Las Vegas Wal-Marts had broken the law dozens of times by interrogating workers, confiscating pro-union literature and denying a promotion because a worker supported a union. [2]

In another well-known case, meat-cutters in Jacksonville, Texas, voted to unionize — the first union election in a Wal-Mart store. Eleven days later, Wal-Mart announced plans to phase out its meat-cutting departments throughout the company and instead sell prepackaged meat. Wal-Mart said it had been considering the move for more than two years, and that the timing was just a coincidence. The company refused to enter into contract negotiations with the Jacksonville butchers.

Last June, an NLRB judge ruled that Wal-Mart had illegally refused to bargain with the meat-cutters; Wal-Mart is appealing the decision.

Meanwhile, the UFCW is still trying to organize Wal-Mart workers in Las Vegas, where other service-sector jobs are highly unionized. Lehman says he's making some progress but adds that it's tough to take on the largest corporation in the world.

"The most prevalent reaction I get [from Wal-Mart employees] is fear," he says. "They want to talk to me, but they don't want to be seen talking to the union because they're afraid they could lose their jobs."

[1] For more information, see Abigail Goldman and Nancy Cleeland, "The Wal-Mart Effect: An Empire Built on Bargains Remakes the Working World," *Los Angeles Times*, Nov. 23, 2003, p. A1; Steven Greenhouse, "Judge Rules Against Wal-Mart on Refusal to Talk to Workers," *The New York Times*, June 19, 2003, p. A16; and Bob Ortega, *In Sam We Trust: The Untold Story of Sam Walton and How Wal-Mart is Devouring America* (1998).

[2] See Steven Greenhouse, "Trying to Overcome Embarrassment, Labor Opens a Drive to Organize Wal-Mart," *The New York Times*, Nov. 8, 2002, p. A28.

retail firms declined to back him, Walton mortgaged everything he had to open his first discount store in Rogers, Ark., in 1962. He called it "Wal-Mart Discount City." A sign announced: "We Sell for Less."

Walton was fanatical about keeping his overhead — and thus his prices — down. He paid his clerks about 60 cents an hour, well below the federal minimum wage of $1.15. [24] He shunned expensive racks and display cases, instead stacking his merchandise on tables or hanging it from metal pipes. Walton had claimed he would sell only first-class goods, but much of his merchandise was of poor quality, because many manufacturers refused to sell their top goods to an unproven discounter.

Nevertheless, the first Wal-Mart was wildly successful. Walton rushed to open more outlets, and by 1970 he had 38 stores in five states. By 1979, he had 276 stores in 11 states, with sales topping the $1 billion mark for the first time.

In 1983, Walton launched "Sam's Club," a line of warehouse-like stores where a nominal membership fee permits shopping for deeply discounted merchandise, usually purchased in large quantities. His first Wal-Mart supercenter — a combination grocery/general merchandise store — opened in Washington, Mo., in 1988. Another milestone came in 1991, when Wal-Mart opened its first international store, in Mexico City.

At his death in 1992, Walton was the world's richest man, with a fortune of more than $20 billion. The company's growth continued, and during the 1990s it leapfrogged over legendary firms such as General Motors to become the largest company in the world, both in sales and employees.

As Wal-Mart expanded, many communities welcomed the giant retailer, but critics began to emerge.

Iowa State University economist Kenneth Stone conducted the first formal study of Wal-Marts' impact on retail sales in 1989, focusing on 10 Iowa towns where the company had stores, and 45 communities where it did not.

Stone's findings were mixed, however, prompting both Wal-Mart supporters and critics alike to tout them as proof of their arguments. To the delight of supporters, towns with Wal-Marts experienced overall sales increases. But the increases came largely at the expense of small, independent retailers — as Wal-Mart critics had contended.

"It's kind of a zero-sum game when Wal-Mart comes to town," Stone says today. "What they take in doesn't come out of thin air — it comes out of other merchants' cash registers."

CURRENT SITUATION

Union Busting?

One of the most contentious aspects of the big-box debate revolves around Wal-Mart's impact on the grocery industry, which it entered only 16 years ago. By contrast, Kroger, which operates Ralph's, King Soopers and other chains, has been selling groceries for 122 years.

Nevertheless, Wal-Mart is already America's largest grocery chain. Its grocery sales come mainly from its more than 1,500 supercenters, which can be as large as four football fields (230,000 square feet).

Wal-Mart's grocery success is due in large part to its low labor costs. The staunchly anti-union company typically pays its employees between $7.50 and $8.50 per hour, compared to $13 to $18 per hour paid by traditional supermarket chains, which are heavily unionized. [25] In any event, Wal-Mart's lower labor costs help customers save up to 30 percent on their grocery bills, studies have found.

But critics say the cheap groceries carry a tremendous societal cost: When traditional supermarket chains cannot compete with Wal-Mart, they either must close stores or eliminate well-paying union jobs — some of the last well-paying jobs available to single mothers, retirees and people without college degrees.

Albertson's, for example, shuttered some 450 stores in 2002, including all 95 in the Wal-Mart strongholds of Houston, Memphis, Nashville and San Antonio, at a cost of more than 3,000 union jobs. Wal-Mart denies

frequent accusations that it engages in illegal "union busting," claiming a good labor-relations record. But at least 60 federal labor complaints have been filed against the company in the last 10 years. (*See sidebar, p. 266.*) [26]

Meanwhile, Wal-Mart faces other legal problems. It has denied knowingly using illegal immigrants to clean its stores and has reportedly been in talks to settle a Department of Justice probe into the matter. And a federal judge this year certified a class-action, workplace gender-bias suit against Wal-Mart, covering as many as 1.6 million current and former female employees.

Strike in California

California is the hottest spot in the grocery wars. For years Wal-Mart held off entering the state's heavily unionized grocery market, saying it needed time to build up its food-distribution system. But experts say the company really was mustering its resources to take on California's powerful unions.

In any event, in May 2002 Wal-Mart announced its intention to build 40 supercenters in California over the next four to six years. To prepare for the low-price competition, Kroger, Safeway and Albertson's scrambled to decrease the wages and benefits of thousands of workers at 852 California supermarkets.

Under the existing union contract, grocery clerks with just two years' experience could earn up to $17.90 per hour; $26.85 hourly on Sundays; and $53.70 per hour on holidays. Workers also received free, full health benefits. [27]

With the union contract set to expire last fall, the three companies jointly sought to charge workers for some of their health benefits, and lower the wages and benefits for new hires.

"We are seeking nothing more than a fair contract that will help us to remain competitive in the face of . . . increased competition from lower-cost operators," said John Burgon, president of the Ralph's chain. "The ability to manage costs is crucial to the long-term future of our businesses." [28]

But the United Food and Commercial Workers (UFCW) union rebuffed the companies' demands. Last Oct. 11, some 20,000 union workers in southern and central California went on strike at two Safeway subsidiaries, Vons and Pavilions. Kroger and Albertson's, in a show of support, locked out about 50,000 union workers the next day. In all, some 70,000 workers were walking picket lines.

Is Wal-Mart good for America?

YES
Robert S. McAdam
Vice President, State and Local Government Relations, Wal-Mart Stores, Inc.

Written for The CQ Researcher, September 2004

Wal-Mart offers everyday, affordable prices for American families across the country while providing good jobs and serving communities through volunteerism and charitable contributions.

W. Michael Cox, chief economist at the Federal Reserve Bank of Dallas, noted in *The New York Times:* "Wal-Mart is the greatest thing that ever happened to low-income Americans. They can stretch their dollars and afford things they otherwise couldn't."

Communities also benefit from increased economic activity and the revitalization of economically depressed areas spurred by Wal-Mart. Often, new businesses are established and existing businesses relocate near a new Wal-Mart. In Columbia, Md., after Wal-Mart took over a space abandoned by another retailer, *The Washington Post* commented that "Wal-Mart has quickly turned into a magnet" for new businesses.

Increased economic activity and lower prices yield jobs and economic growth. A recent Los Angeles County Economic Development Corp. study found Wal-Mart supercenters would save residents in a seven-county region $589 per household per year and create 36,400 jobs. Two-thirds of Wal-Mart jobs are full time. All pay above the federal minimum. In fact, the average wage is $9.98 an hour — higher in larger cities.

Clearly, people find value in working here: Our turnover rate — 46 percent — is one-third below the retail average. Our benefits are ranked the best in the retail industry. Both full- and part-time associates are eligible for benefits.

We provide career growth, too. Nine thousand hourly associates moved into management last year, joining two-thirds of our store management who started as hourly employees.

Part of our company's culture is giving back to the communities we serve through charitable contributions to local organizations. Corporate giving totaled $158 million last year.

In our communities, we've generated more than $52 billion in sales taxes and $4 billion in property taxes in the past decade. Wal-Mart is proud to purchase goods from 10,000 U.S. suppliers and export $2 billion of U.S.-made goods to our stores in 10 foreign countries.

Wal-Mart's value can be calculated in jobs, economic growth and charitable partnerships in communities throughout the country. Those numbers don't compare, however, to the rising standard of living U.S. families experience because of Wal-Mart's commitment to lowering costs and prices on everyday needs.

NO
Al Norman
Founder, Sprawl-Busters.com
Author, Slam-Dunking Wal-Mart: How You Can Stop Superstore Sprawl in Your Hometown

Written for The CQ Researcher, September 2004

The world's biggest retailer — some say the most admired retailer in America — is also the most reviled. Increasingly, Americans understand that Wal-Mart is more than just a chain store. It is a chain of exploitation that stretches from sweatshops in China to sales floors in California. Each link in the retail chain is forged in the heat of unfair advantage and abuse. Among other things, Wal-Mart:

- Watches 45 percent of its workers quit every year.
- Failed to make *Fortune* magazine's list of "100 Best Places to Work."
- Secretly collected life insurance benefits from its dead workers.
- Admits its wages are "not designed to fully support a family."
- Concealed violent crimes against shoppers at its stores.
- Asked taxpayers to subsidize the building of its empire.
- Spent 38 percent less on health care per worker than the average U.S. employer.
- Was sued in 32 states for forcing its employees to work "off the clock."
- Was sued by federal officials for discriminating on the basis of disability and sex.
- Has nearly 7,000 lawsuits pending against it at any point in time.
- Has more than 325 "dead" stores sitting empty in small-town America.
- Was busted for predatory pricing in the United States and Germany.
- Was caught using illegal workers to build and clean its stores.
- Imported more Chinese products ($12 billion) than any other retailer.
- Squeezes manufacturers on pricing so harshly that companies have been forced to transfer millions of factory jobs to Mexico or China.

Wal-Mart represents the end of competition, not the beginning. In 1989, its CEO, David Glass, predicted that half the nation's retailers would be out of business by the year 2000. The firm Retail Forward recently warned, "Wal-Mart will continue to steamroll the competitive landscape." Small-town America has been ravaged.

We are heading toward a "one-nation, one-store" marketplace. The battle will be won or lost in Wal-Mart's aisles. If Wal-Mart wins, America loses.

Wal-Mart has been slashing prices in Beijing since July 11, 2003, when the world's biggest retailer made its first foray into a major Chinese city. Opera performers celebrate the launch of a Sam's Club warehouse store in the capital city.

As the strike dragged on, many observers said the outcome could have serious implications for middle-class wage earners everywhere. "If the union loses this and has to give back a significant portion of their benefits, you're really moving down the road to everybody [becoming like] a Wal-Mart worker, with low wages and low benefits," said Paul Clark, a labor-relations expert at Pennsylvania State University. [29]

In early March, nearly five months after the strike began, the two sides agreed to a three-year contract. While the UFCW declared victory, the companies got most of the salary and benefit cuts they had sought for new hires.

"You're not going to be able to make a career out of it anymore," said Kerry Renaud, a veteran produce worker at a supermarket in Hollywood. "We [got] squeezed." [30]

Zoning Lawsuits

Wal-Mart is vigorously contesting anti-big-box zoning ordinances across the country. In February, for example, the company challenged a Turlock, Calif., ordinance banning retail stores larger than 100,000 square feet that sell groceries on more than 5 percent of their floor space. Wal-Mart says the ordinance is illegal because it outlaws some big-box stores — namely, its supercenters — while allowing others, such as Home Depots.

"[The city] cannot discriminate against Wal-Mart as opposed to other businesses in the area," said Wal-Mart attorney Timothy Jones. "Our belief is that Wal-Mart was the subject of the ordinance." [31]

The first of Wal-Mart's two lawsuits against the city contends the ordinance violates the company's constitutional rights to conduct interstate commerce and to enjoy equal protection under the law. The second alleges the city violated state law by using a zoning ordinance to regulate competition.

Mayor Curt Andre says the city will "vigorously defend" its ordinance. "The overwhelming majority of people that have talked to me have been fervent in their desire to keep any kind of superstore out of Turlock," he said. [32]

But other communities are having second thoughts about taking on the world's largest corporation. On March 30, county officials in Oakland, Calif., voted to rescind an anti-big-box ordinance rather than contest a Wal-Mart lawsuit alleging that the measure imposed "unusual and unnecessary restrictions on lawful business enterprises."

The measure, which the county had enacted only three months earlier, was nearly identical to Turlock's. [33] Other communities that have rescinded ordinances after Wal-Mart took or threatened legal action include Clark County, Nev. (Las Vegas)

In Los Angeles, meanwhile, the City Council voted, 14-1, on Aug. 11, 2004, to require developers seeking to build superstores — retail stores of 100,000 square feet or more that devote 10 percent or more of their floor space to food or other non-taxable items — to pay for an economic analysis before they can apply for, or get, a building permit.

The new law applies only to designated "economically vulnerable" areas of the city. City officials say the law is necessary because superstores like Wal-Mart supercenters and SuperTargets can have a devastating effect on local communities by lowering wages and driving out existing businesses.

Under the law, developers would have to analyze whether or not their proposed store would eliminate jobs, depress wages or harm surrounding businesses.

"This ordinance [ensures] that a superstore project would add to a neighborhood's economy and quality of life, not detract from them," said Mayor Jim Hahn.

Wal-Mart has spent millions of dollars lobbying city councils and residents in Los Angeles, Chicago and other large cities it hopes to move into, according to *The Washington Post.* [34]

Ballot Battles

Wal-Mart turned to voters instead of the courts to circumvent an anti-big box ordinance enacted in June 2003 in Contra Costa County, near Oakland. Using California's referendum process, Wal-Mart asked voters to reject the ordinance.

Wal-Mart spent some $1 million gathering signatures and distributing literature urging residents to overturn the measure — which they did on March 2, 2004, by a 54 percent to 46 percent vote.

"I hope this vote makes communities think twice about passing these ordinances," Wal-Mart spokeswoman Amy Hill said. [35]

Wal-Mart took an even more aggressive approach in Inglewood, a Los Angeles suburb that is 46 percent African-American and 46 percent Latino. The company first threatened a referendum and a lawsuit, which forced the City Council to repeal its 2002 anti-big-box ordinance. At that point, Wal-Mart could have built a store as long as it adhered to the rest of the city's zoning and environmental regulations.

Instead, Wal-Mart used the referendum process to ask voters to approve a supercenter on a 60-acre tract near The Forum, the former home of the Los Angeles Lakers. The 71-page ballot initiative described in minute detail Wal-Mart's plan for the site, from the design of the store's façade to the toilets in the restrooms.

It also declared the entire site would be exempt from Inglewood's planning, zoning and environmental regulations.

Wal-Mart spent more than $1 million promoting the initiative, inundating residents with phone calls, television commercials and mailers promising that the store would bring low-priced merchandise and good jobs to their community. "As far as I'm concerned, it's a no-brainer," Mayor Roosevelt Dorn said just before the vote, predicting the project would generate hundreds of jobs and millions of dollars in tax revenues. [36]

Supermarket workers and other UFCW union members mounted a campaign to defeat the plan, saying it would prompt other businesses to slash wages and benefits or eliminate good-paying jobs. Others were outraged over Wal-Mart's attempt to exempt itself from city regulations.

"They are driving a Mack truck through California land use, planning and environmental law and trying to create a Wal-Mart government on this 60-acre site," said Madeline Janis-Aparico, director of the Coalition for a Better Inglewood. "If they succeed in doing this, it will [become] their blueprint" for projects elsewhere. [37]

To the surprise of many pundits, Inglewood residents soundly rejected the proposal: 7,049 to 4,575.

"This shows . . . that Wal-Mart can't dupe people in this city to sign away their rights," said Inglewood resident Mike Shimpock. "If they spent $1 million here and lost by this margin, I doubt they'll try this elsewhere." [38]

But Wal-Mart officials said the defeat would not derail the company's expansion plans. "It's simply one store, one site in the list of hundreds we work on every year," McAdam said. "We're going to find ways to build stores and serve customers. We are not going to get pushed around by unions. We are here to state our case, and we are not going to go away quietly." [39]

OUTLOOK

More Expansion

Wal-Mart and Home Depot have especially aggressive growth agendas. Wal-Mart plans to open up to 495 new stores throughout the world this year, including 355 in the United States — an opening every 24 hours and 42 minutes. That would give Wal-Mart 3,368 stores in the United States and more than 5,000 stores worldwide. [40] Home Depot plans to open 175 new stores in 2004 — one every 50 hours. If the company stays on schedule, it will have more than 1,800 stores in North America by year's end. [41]

Many analysts speculate that Wal-Mart wants to get into other business sectors, such as automobile sales or banking. It has tried several times to buy a bank or a savings and loan but has been stymied by federal and state banking regulators. Nevertheless, the company recently partnered with a Memphis-based bank to establish Wal-Mart "Money Centers" in some stores. The banks carry Wal-Mart's imprimatur but are owned and operated by the Memphis firm.

Wal-Mart is tight-lipped about its banking aspirations, but many industry experts are worried. "Their goal is very clear: They want to have a Wal-Mart-owned bank branch in every store," said Kenneth Guenther, president of Independent Community Bankers of America. Wal-Mart banking would "inflict the black death" upon smaller competing banks, he warned. [42]

Meanwhile, most analysts say Wal-Mart will continue to consolidate its market share of product categories it now dominates, including groceries, sporting goods, household products, videogames, men's and women's apparel, toys and dog food. It is also rapidly expanding its overseas operations.

"The United States is 37 percent of the world's economy, which leaves 63 percent for international," said John Menzer, president of Wal-Mart's international division. "If we do our job, international operations should someday be twice as large as the United States." [43]

But critics like Sprawl-Busters' Norman say big-box retailers "will eventually take a hard fall." "If all you focus on is today, the siren-song of low prices will get you every time," he says. "It's important for people to understand that in the long run, their well-being and the well-being of their communities is bigger than the dimensions of their shopping carts."

NOTES

1. Quoted in Mary J. Thompson, "With low prices, Wal-Mart overwhelms competitors," *MSN Money*, Aug. 27, 2004.

2. "Shopping for Subsidies: How Wal-Mart Uses Taxpayer Money to Finance Its Never-Ending Growth," Good Jobs First, May 2004.

3. Revenues source: The companies' annual reports.

4. For background, see *ibid.*

5. See Anthony Bianco and Wendy Zellner, "Is Wal-Mart Too Powerful?" *Business Week*, Oct. 6, 2003, p. 100.

6. Constance L. Hays, "Toys 'R' Us Says It May Leave the Toy Business," *The New York Times*, Aug. 12, 2004, p. A1.

7. *Ibid.*

8. Quoted in "Levi Strauss Shuts All U.S. Plants," www.CBSNews.com, Sept. 25, 2003.

9. See Arindrajit Dube and Ken Jacobs, "Hidden Costs of Wal-Mart Jobs: Use of Safety Net Programs by Wal-Mart Workers in California," University of California at Berkeley Labor Center, Aug. 2, 2004. Available online at http://laborcenter.berkeley.edu/lowwage/wal-mart.pdf.

10. Quoted in Jon Bowermaster, "When Wal-Mart Comes To Town," *The New York Times Magazine*, April 2, 1989, p. 28.

11. "What Happened When Wal-Mart Came to Town? A Report on Three Iowa Communities with a Statistical Analysis of Seven Iowa Counties," by Thomas Muller and Elizabeth Humstone, National Trust For Historic Preservation, 1996.

12. Quoted in Rachel Sauer, " 'Wal-Mart Guilt' Doesn't Stop Shoppers," *The Milwaukee Journal Sentinel*, April 20, 2003, p. 5L.

13. Quoted in Alexander Reid, "Local Stores Compete with 'Big-Box' Chains," *The Boston Globe*, Feb. 3, 2002, p. B1.

14. Quoted in Gary Massaro, "Closing Store Leaves Big Gap," *The Rocky Mountain News* (Denver), April 6, 1997, p. A40.

15. National Association of Convenience Stores press release, April 1, 2003.

16. For example, *Expansion Management* magazine in May 2004 gave Fargo a "Five Star Community" rating, the highest level, in its annual Quality of Life Quotient. Components included affordable housing, available work force, standard of living, education levels, educational facilities, unemployment rates and peace of mind, described as the relative tranquility of a particular area. The same month, *Forbes* magazine named Fargo the second-best small city in the nation for businesses. For more information, see www.fmchamber.com/community/qualityoflife.html.

17. The zoning ordinance and the commission's report are posted on the town's Web site: www.town-east-onmd.com.

18. Quoted in Greg Harman, "Proposed Development Out of the Box," *The Biloxi* [Miss.] *Sun Herald*, Aug, 31, 2003, p. A1.

19. Quoted in John Rebchook, "Thornton Decision 'Dismays' Wal-Mart," *The Rocky Mountain News* (Denver), June 17, 2004, p. B13.

20. For more information, see the Smart Planning and Growth Coalition Web site at www.gotcommunity.org. The advocacy group is based in Barnstable, Mass.

21. Land Use, Inc., and RGK Associates, "Greenfield, Massachusetts: Fiscal and Economic Impact Assessment of the Proposed Wal-Mart Development," April 2, 1993.

22. Muller and Humstone, *op. cit.*

23. Unless otherwise noted, information in this and following paragraphs is based on Bob Ortega, *In Sam We Trust* (1998), pp. 18-71; and Sandra S. Vance and Roy V. Scott, *Wal-Mart: The Story of Sam Walton's Retail Phenomenon* (1994), pp. 16-38.

24. Ortega, *op. cit.*

25. Wal-Mart does not release salary data, but the figures cited reflect estimates by several sources, including Retail Forward, a consulting firm in Columbus, Ohio; researchers at the University of California, Berkeley, Labor Center and legal depositions given by former Wal-Mart employees in civil lawsuits filed against the company. See Charles Williams, "Supermarket Sweepstakes: Traditional Grocery Chains Mull Responses to Wal-Mart's Dominance," *The Post and Courier* (Charleston, S.C.), Nov. 10, 2003, p. 16E.

26. See Patricia Callahan and Ann Zimmerman, "Wal-Mart Tops Grocery List with its Supercenter Format," *The Wall Street Journal*, May 27, 2003.

27. From a joint statement issued by Albertson's, Ralph's and Vons, Oct. 6, 2003.

28. *Ibid.*

29. Quoted in Steven Greenhouse, "Labor Raises Pressure on California Supermarkets," *The New York Times*, Feb. 10, 2004, p. A14.

30. Quoted in Charlie LeDuff and Steven Greenhouse, "Grocery Workers Relieved, if Not Happy, at Strike's End," *The New York Times*, Feb. 28, 2004, p. A8.

31. Quoted in John Holland, "Wal-Mart Sues Turlock Over Ban," *The Modesto Bee*, Feb. 12, 2004, p. A1.

32. *Ibid.*

33. For background, see Karen Holzmeister, "County Repeals Ban on Big-Box Stores," *The Oakland* [Calif.] *Tribune*, April 1, 2004.

34. Michael Barbaro and Neil Irwin, "Wal-Mart in Talks to Build D.C. Store," *The Washington Post*, Aug. 11, 2004, p. E1.

35. Quoted in Erin Hallissy, "Wal-Mart Win Sends Strong Message; Giant Retailer Warns Local Communities on Future Ordinances," *The San Francisco Chronicle*, March 4, 2004, p. A21.

36. Quoted in John M. Broder, "Stymied by Politicians, Wal-Mart Turns to Voters," *The New York Times*, April 2, 2004, p. A1.

37. *Ibid.*

38. Quoted in Sara Lin and Monte Morin, "Voters in Inglewood Turn Away Wal-Mart," *Los Angeles Times*, April 7, 2004, p. A1.

39. Quoted in Jessica Garrison, Abigail Goldman and David Pierson, "Wal-Mart to Push Southland Plan," *Los Angeles Times*, April 7, 2004 (on Web site only).

40. Undated press release, "Wal-Mart Announces Expansion Plans for FY 2005."

41. Press release, Jan. 16, 2004.

42. Quoted in Alex Daniels, "Retailer Ties Name to Banking; Wal-Mart Venture Hints at Wider Ambitions, Observers Say," *The Arkansas Democrat-Gazette*, Jan. 21, 2004.

43. Quoted in Andy Rowell, "Welcome to Wal-World: Wal-Mart's Inexhaustible March to Conquer the Globe," *The Multinational Monitor*, Oct. 1, 2003, p. 13.

BIBLIOGRAPHY

Books

Mitchell, Stacy, *The Home Town Advantage: How to Defend your Main Street Against Chain Stores — And Why it Matters*, Institute for Local Self-Reliance, 2000.
Mitchell argues that "megastores" are economically disastrous and documents how some communities are keeping them out with zoning ordinances.

Ortega, Bob, *In Sam We Trust: The Untold Story of Sam Walton and How Wal-Mart is Devouring America*, Times Business, 1998.
A former investigative reporter portrays Wal-Mart's founder as a ruthless businessman.

Slater, Robert, *The Wal-Mart Decade: How a New Generation of Leaders Turned Sam Walton's Legacy into the World's Number One Company*, Portfolio, 2003.
A former *Time* reporter documents how Wal-Mart grew exponentially after founder Sam Walton's death in 1992.

Walton, Sam, with John Huey, *Sam Walton: Made In America: My Story*, Doubleday, 1992.
Walton describes his business philosophy and responds to his critics in his autobiography.

Articles

Bianco, Anthony, and Wendy Zellner, "Is Wal-Mart Too Powerful?" *Business Week*, Oct. 6, 2003, p. 100.
The authors conclude Wal-Mart's "everyday low prices" come at a cost to consumers and the nation's economy.

Fishman, Charles, "The Wal-Mart You Don't Know," *Fast Company*, December 2003, p. 68.
The author examines the impact — both good and bad — of Wal-Mart's cost cutting on suppliers and the U.S. economy.

Goodman, Peter S., and Philip P. Pan, "Chinese Workers Pay for Wal-Mart's Low Prices," *The Washington Post*, Feb. 8, 2004, p. A1.
Two reporters examine conditions at Chinese factories that supply Wal-Mart.

Greenhouse, Steven, "Wal-Mart, a Nation Unto Itself," *The New York Times*, April 17, 2004, p. B1.
The author examines how Wal-Mart is affecting America's economy and culture.

Kline, Mitchell, "How Big is Too Big? Zoning Plan Says Build Up, Not Out," *The Tennessean*, July 8, 2004, p. 1W.
The town of Ranklin, Tenn., is using zoning ordinances to limit the size and impact of big-box stores.

Murphy, Edward D., "Small Maine Retailers Scurry for Niches; To Beat Back the Big Boxes, They Stress Their Unmatched Level of Service, Attention and Expertise," *Portland Press Herald*, June 27, 2004, p. A4.
Murphy focuses on how small mom-and-pop retailers in and around Portland, Maine, are competing with megastores.

Saporito, Bill, "Can Wal-Mart Get Any Bigger? Yes, a Lot Bigger — Here's How," *Time*, Jan. 13, 2003, p. 38.
The world's largest company could double or even triple in the next few years.

Useem, Jerry, "One Nation Under Wal-Mart: How Retailing's Superpower — And Our Biggest, Most Admired Company — is Changing the Rules for Corporate America," *Fortune*, March 3, 2003, p. 64.
The author examines how Wal-Mart's low prices affect U.S. manufacturers.

Weiss, Eric M., "'Big-Box' Stores Leave More Than a Void," *The Washington Post*, Jan. 20, 2004, p. B1.
Communities suffer when their local big-box store goes out of business or shuts down to move to an even bigger location.

Wysocki, Bernard, and Ann Zimmerman, "Wal-Mart Cost-Cutting Finds a Big Target in Health Benefits," *The Wall Street Journal*, Sept. 30, 2003, p. A1.
Wal-Mart allegedly skimps on health benefits.

Reports and Studies

Dube, Arindrajit, and Ken Jacobs, "Hidden Costs of Wal-Mart Jobs: Use of Safety Net Programs by Wal-Mart Workers in California," University of California at Berkeley Labor Center, Aug. 2, 2004.
A critical study concludes that Wal-Mart employees in California cost taxpayers about $86 million annually due to their heavy reliance on subsidized housing and other public benefits.

Freeman, Gregory, *Wal-Mart Supercenters: What's in Store for Southern California?* Los Angeles Economic Development Corporation, January 2004.
A pro-Wal-Mart study concludes that consumers in a seven-county region in Southern California would save $3.7 billion annually once the company attains a 20 percent share of the grocery market, and that communities that ban Wal-Mart will lose significant tax revenues due to "leakage."

For More Information

American Independent Business Alliance, 222 South Black Ave., Bozeman, MT 59715; (406) 582-1255; www.amiba.net. Helps communities start independent-business alliances to fight big-box chains.

Institute for Local Self-Reliance, 927 15th St., N.W., 4th Floor, Washington, DC 20005; (202) 898-1610; www.ilsr.org. Promotes locally owned, independent retail businesses over the proliferation of chain stores.

National Trust for Historic Preservation, 1785 Massachusetts Ave., N.W., Washington, DC 20036; (202) 588-6219; www.nationaltrust.org. Generally anti-big-box, the Trust works to save historic commercial areas that "form our communities and enrich our lives."

Retail Industry Leaders Association, 1700 North Moore St., Suite 2250, Arlington, VA 22209; (703) 841-2300; www.imra.org. A trade group that promotes policies advantageous to big-box retailers. RILA members have more than $1 trillion in sales annually and operate more than 100,000 stores, manufacturing facilities and distribution centers nationwide.

Small Business and Entrepreneurship Council, 1920 L St., N.W., Suite 200, Washington DC 20036; (202) 785-0238; www.sbsc.org. Supports policies that help small businesses and entrepreneurship but is generally supportive of policies that favor big-box retailers.

Sprawl-Busters, 21 Grinnell St., Greenfield, Mass. 01301; (413) 772-6289; www.sprawl-busters.com. Helps citizens' groups fight unwanted big-box retail stores and provides news on big-box battles across the country.

13

Privatizing the Military

Mary H. Cooper

AFP Photo/U.S. Army

Civilian truck driver Thomas Hamill escaped from Iraqi kidnappers after 23 days in captivity. The Mississippi farmer came to Iraq to work for military contractor Kellogg, Brown and Root. Kidnapped contract workers have become pawns in the ongoing conflict in postwar Iraq. Private contractors serving as interrogators were also implicated in prisoner abuses at the U.S.-run Abu Ghraib prison in Baghdad.

From *CQ Researcher,*
June 25, 2004.

I raqi insurgents in Fallujah recently gave Americans a horrific glimpse into a little-known and increasingly controversial aspect of U.S. military operations. After ambushing a truck convoy and killing four U.S. security guards on April 28, they burned and mutilated the bodies and hung them from a bridge.

The four deaths, however, were not included in the Pentagon's list of American casualties in Iraq that day. In fact, although the men worked for the military, they weren't GIs. They were civilians employed by the military.

"We know that somewhere around 50 private military people have been killed in Iraq," says Peter W. Singer, author of *Corporate Warriors: The Rise of the Privatized Military Industry* and director of the Project on U.S. Policy Towards the Islamic World at the Brookings Institution. "Another 300 or so have been wounded. But these are only estimates because private military casualties don't show up on the public record."

Private military contractors in Iraq made news again in May when widespread prisoner abuses were reported at the U.S.-run Abu Ghraib prison in Baghdad. Three civilian interrogators were among the six soldiers implicated in the shocking physical and sexual abuse of Iraqi detainees. [1] But unlike their military peers, the contractors were not subject to military law and have not been charged under civil law either.

However, on June 18 the Justice Department charged a contractor working for the CIA in Afghanistan with assault in the beating of an Afghan detainee who later died in a U.S. prison there. David A. Passaro, a former Army Ranger hired to conduct interrogations, is the first civilian to be charged in connection with alleged prisoner abuses in Afghanistan and Iraq. [2]

Most Contractor Casualties Were in Iraq

More than 1,000 civilian contractors working for the U.S. government in Iraq and several other countries have died or been injured since September 2001, including more than 500 in Iraq.

	Deaths/Injuries
Iraq	529
Kuwait	317
Bosnia-Herzegovina	60
Colombia	52
Saudi Arabia	51
Germany	48
Afghanistan	44

Source: Department of Labor, based on insurance claims submitted to the U.S. government.

The slain guards in Fallujah and the civilian prison workers are part of a growing army of non-military personnel employed by scores of private contractors for the U.S. military in 50 countries around the world. Largely unnoticed by the American public, private contractors have assumed a growing role in the U.S. military for more than a decade.

Since the end of the Cold War in the early 1990s, policymakers have been reducing the size of the military and contracting out many non-combat jobs to private companies.

But after the U.S. victory in Iraq, violent resistance to the U.S.-led occupation forced the Pentagon to turn increasingly to private military contractors because the services were already stretched thin by downsizing and deployments in Afghanistan and other hot spots.

Private contractors now make up the second-largest contingent of forces in Iraq after the U.S. military itself — larger even than Britain's troop deployment. Most analysts say there are about 20,000 private military contractors (PMCs) in Iraq, including 6,000 who provide non-combat security, serving alongside 138,000 American GIs.

The armed personnel serve as guards, convoy escorts and bodyguards for U.S. officials in Iraq, including Ambassador L. Paul Bremer III, the American administrator of the Coalition Provisional Authority (CPA). [3]

"The role of private military contractors in Iraq is unprecedented, particularly given the numbers involved," says Marcus Corbin, senior analyst at the Center for Defense Information, an independent monitor of the military. "I can't think of any parallel in our military history."

Defense Secretary Donald H. Rumsfeld and other supporters of privatization say the military's use of contractors improves efficiency by freeing up soldiers for strictly combat operations. "There are a great many people [in Iraq] who are involved in various types of enterprises or activities that . . . need security," Rumsfeld said. "So a market [has been created] for security forces. And it's been a good thing that the security forces around this country and the world do a superb job." [4]

But some lawmakers and military experts worry that because contract workers are not bound by military law, privatization may erode accountability and blur the chain of command essential to military operations.

"How is it in our nation's interest to have civilian contractors, rather than military personnel, performing vital national-security functions such as prisoner interrogations in a war zone?" asked Michigan Sen. Carl Levin, senior Democrat on the Senate Armed Services Committee. "When soldiers break the law or fail to follow orders, commanders can hold them accountable for their misconduct. Military commanders don't have the same authority over civilian contractors." [5]

Privatization of military tasks has become a nearly $200-billion-a-year sector of the U.S. military-industrial complex. [6] In Iraq, previously obscure firms like North Carolina-based Blackwater Security Consulting, which employed the four guards killed in Fallujah, now operate beside well-known giants such as Halliburton Co., the oil and gas conglomerate formerly headed by Vice President Dick Cheney, and CACI, an information-technology firm based in Arlington, Va.

The value of civilian personnel services purchased by the Department of Defense increased from $100.5 billion in 1993 to $188 billion in 2004 — a rise of nearly 90 percent. [7] Many of those billions were earned through no-bid contracts. (*See sidebar, p. 280.*)

Rep. Janice D. Schakowsky, D-Ill., a longtime critic of the often-obscure process by which private companies receive government contracts, worries about the secrecy that surrounds Defense Department contracting. She has introduced legislation to expand congressional oversight and access to major contracts signed with private firms.

"I'm sure many important functions are done by these private contractors," she says. "But at the same time, the process masks just what the U.S. commitment is in places like Iraq and allows many of these activities to literally fly under the radar of the Congress and the consciousness of the American people."

When the United States relinquishes sovereignty to the Iraqi interim government on June 30, the role of private contractors in Iraq will not end, but may even increase due to an expected escalation of violence and a continued need for security for Iraqi officials and the U.S.-led $18.4 billion reconstruction effort.

But the legal status of the military contractors has yet to be clarified. Iraq's new interim prime minister, Iyad Allawi, insists that civilian contractors come under Iraqi law on June 30, ending the immunity from prosecution in Iraq they now enjoy for any incident involving their work. The Bush administration wants to extend that immunity after the handover. [8]

As the role of private military contractors grows in Iraq and elsewhere, these are some of the questions being raised:

Can the military do its job without military contractors?

Private contractors have had a longstanding role in providing support services to the military, both at home and overseas, in peacetime and at war.

During the Vietnam War, one company alone had more than 30,000 employees providing logistical support to U.S. troops, according to Doug Brooks, presi-

Defense Outsourcing Nearly Doubled

Spending on private contracts by the Department of Defense remained steady in the 1990s but nearly doubled in 2004.

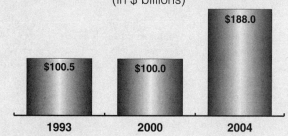

Purchases of Private Services by Defense Department
(in $ billions)

$100.5 — 1993
$100.0 — 2000
$188.0 — 2004

Increases in Outsourcing Outpace Spending

Purchases of private services by the Defense Department grew more than twice as fast as overall Defense spending in the last four years.

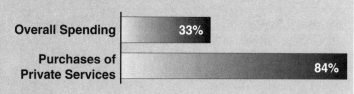

Increases in Defense Spending from 2000 to 2004*

Overall Spending — 33%
Purchases of Private Services — 84%

* First quarter only

Source: Charles L. Schultze, senior fellow emeritus, Brookings Institution, based on Commerce Department data.

dent of the International Peace Operations Association, an organization of military service providers. During the 1968 Tet Offensive, contractors suffered more casualties than the regular troops, he adds.

"There's never been a war or a time in history when private contractors haven't been used for one thing or another," he says. "The U.S. military needs contractors, and it always has."

The military traditionally has turned to private companies to build weapons and vehicles, construct bases and camps and provide food and other services for troops. For the past 15 years, however, private companies have supplied a widening array of products and services. Highly sophisticated weapons and equipment like satellite phones,

Controversy Surrounds Civilian Contractors

President Dwight D. Eisenhower's famous warning in 1961 about the rapidly growing "military-industrial complex" focused on the makers of tanks, ships and other military hardware.

His warning proved prescient. Hefty defense budgets and the emergence of the United States as the world's leading military power have turned the defense industry into a manufacturing behemoth. In fiscal 2003, procurement contracts to the top 100 Pentagon contractors totaled $209 billion. [1]

Since Eisenhower's prediction, a new category of defense contractors has emerged: Firms that provide workers to conduct security, interrogation and intelligence — work once performed exclusively by military personnel. After the Cold War ended more than a decade ago, the U.S. military turned increasingly to private military contractors to meet its security and intelligence needs around the world. About 60 such firms are operating in Iraq, and more than 20 in Afghanistan.

The multimillion-dollar global industry can be divided into three major sectors, according to Peter W. Singer, author of the 2003 book *Corporate Warriors: The Rise of the Privatized Military Industry*: [2]

- "Military provider firms" offer seasoned combatants — generally former members of U.S., British or South African special forces — to clients such as weak governments, insurgent forces or international oil or mining companies operating in hostile areas. Executive Outcomes provided forces in several African trouble spots in the 1990s, including Angola and Sierra Leone. London-based Sandline Co., which helped repel a 1998 coup attempt in Nigeria, embarrassed Britain by shipping arms to the region in violation of a U.N. arms embargo. Both firms have since disbanded.
- "Military consultant firms" train local police and military forces to fight in foreign conflicts. One of the leading such firms is Military Professional Resources Inc. (MPRI). Founded in 1987 and based in Alexandria, Va., it hires only American ex-soldiers and claims to work only on contracts approved by the U.S. government. MPRI's Defense Department contracts included training the Bosnian and Croatian armies in the 1990s.

Refraining from sending employees into battle has not protected military consultant firms from controversy, however. Employees of Falls Church, Va.-based DynCorp (purchased in 2003 by Computer Sciences Corp.), participated in a child-prostitution ring while working in Bosnia in the late 1990s, according to Human Rights Watch, Army investigators and two whistleblower lawsuits. [3] Although the employees were not immune from prosecution by local authorities for illegal acts committed outside their contractual mission, DynCorp fired them and returned them to the United States, where they did not face charges.

Lawmakers tried to close contractors' legal loopholes by passing the 2000 Military Extraterritorial Jurisdiction Act, which places Defense Department contractors overseas under U.S. legal jurisdiction. But because the alleged offenses in Bosnia preceded passage of the act, the DynCorp employees were not prosecuted. [4]

- "Military support firms" are farther removed from combat roles, at least in theory. The Halliburton Co. subsidiary Kellogg, Brown and Root (KBR) and other such firms provide logistics, intelligence, supply and global-positioning systems and laser designators used to precisely locate targets require skilled technicians to maintain and repair, and the armed services often hire contractors trained by the equipment producers themselves.

"The modern military cannot function without private contractors for some key roles," says Michael P. Peters, executive vice president of the Council on Foreign Relations, a New York City think tank. "Take avionics for aircraft. You need people who've actually built this stuff to be with you and maintain it, because you simply can't train enough 18-to-22-year-olds to have the level of knowledge, background and experience to keep this very, very sophisticated equipment running. If they were to ban all civilian contractors, the military would have a difficult time functioning at all."

Going to war in countries like Iraq and Afghanistan poses additional language and cultural barriers that the downsized U.S. military is ill-equipped to surmount on its own, Peters says, citing the civilian translators and interrogators at Abu Ghraib.

"When you get into a circumstance that is as big as Iraq, you have almost no other option than to hire private contractors," Peters says. "The military just doesn't have enough people to perform those functions."

other services to U.S. forces around the world. In Iraq, KBR truck convoys bring food and other supplies to a dozen or more Army camps. According to several KBR drivers, the company bilked American taxpayers by charging the Pentagon for repeatedly moving convoys of empty trucks between U.S. encampments, exposing the truckers to attacks by Iraqi insurgents.

CACI International Inc., another support firm, provides interrogators to U.S. forces administering prisons overseas under a so-called "blanket purchase agreement" that was originally signed with the Interior Department but subsequently utilized by the Pentagon. Steven Stefanowicz, a CACI employee, was one of three private contractors implicated in the recent prisoner-abuse scandal in Iraq. A contract translator employed by another firm, Titan Corp., also was named in an extensive Army report on the abuses by Maj. Gen. Antonio M. Taguba.

Allegations of fraud and waste by private contractors in Iraq continue to mount. At least 14 major contracts in Iraq, including a $7 billion deal for Halliburton to restore the country's oil industry, were awarded with limited or no competition, according to a report issued on June 14, 2004, by the General Accounting Office. [5]

"Increasingly, the administration is turning over essential government functions to the private sector, and it has jettisoned basic safeguards like competition and supervision that are needed to protect the public interest," said Rep. Henry A. Waxman, D-Calif., a vocal critic of Bush administration contracting practices. "We need more competition, not less. And we need to place the interests of the taxpayer ahead of the interests of the contractors." [6]

Administration spokesmen reject the allegations of contracting misdeeds, including recent charges that the office of Vice President Cheney, formerly Halliburton's chief executive officer, was instrumental in granting the oil-services giant its no-bid contract in Iraq. "The vice president was not informed" that Halliburton would get the contract, said Kevin Kellems, Cheney's spokesman. [7]

Meanwhile, a report by the Center for Public Integrity, a nonprofit investigative organization in Washington, D.C., found that 14 of the top private contractors in Afghanistan and Iraq made campaign contributions in excess of $1 million from 1990 through fiscal 2002. "Combined, those companies gave nearly $23 million in political contributions since 1990," the report said.

In addition, in classic Washington revolving-door style, top officers of many of these firms are former Pentagon officials, while many civilian officials at the Pentagon are former employees of major defense contractors. "The center's investigation found that . . . 13 [of the 14 top contractors] employ former government officials or have close ties to various agencies and departments." [8]

---

[1] U.S. Defense Department, Directorate for Information Operations and Reports, www.dior.whs.mil.

[2] Unless otherwise noted, information in this section is based on Singer's book, pp. 73-184.

[3] See Kelly Patricia O'Meara, "DynCorp Disgrace," *Insight*, Jan. 14, 2002.

[4] See Gail Gibson, "Prosecuting Abuse of Prisoners," *The Baltimore Sun*, May 29, 2004, p. 4A.

[5] See General Accounting Office, "Rebuilding Iraq: Fiscal Year 2003 Contract Award Procedures and Management Challenges," June 14, 2004.

[6] From a statement issued May 27, 2004.

[7] Quoted by Larry Margasak, "Official: Cheney Not Briefed on Iraq Work," The Associated Press, June 16, 2004.

[8] Maud Beelman, "Winning Contractors: U.S. Contractors Reap the Windfalls of Post-war Reconstruction," Center for Public Integrity, Oct. 30, 2003.

But critics say the widening prisoner-abuse scandal in Iraq and Afghanistan demonstrates a vital weakness in the military's growing reliance on civilian contractors to perform functions that traditionally have fallen to the military. "There is no room for U.S.-hired paramilitaries and mercenaries in an interrogation cell," said Rep. Schakowsky. "This is a dangerous and deadly mix that has contributed to the prisoner-abuse scandal in Iraq and could only lead to a more dangerous situation for U.S. military and civilian personnel at home and abroad, unless it is immediately stopped." [9]

Because many, if not most, security contractors are former soldiers, often with considerable combat experience, they are generally considered more effective at their jobs than new Army recruits. Young soldiers fresh out of training often suffer from the "22-year-old syndrome," panicking and firing their weapons in no particular direction when they come under fire, says an industry insider who requested he not be identified. "This tends to be damaging to local populations, buildings, that sort of thing."

On the other hand, Brooks says contractors, many of whom have as much as 20 years' experience in the field, tend to keep their cool under fire. "Combat is combat, of

Top 10 Military Service Providers

Some of America's largest corporations supply the U.S. military with basic services such as health insurance and computer and food services. Many smaller companies provide security services but do not appear among the Top 10, such as Titan* and CACI — whose employees have been implicated in the Abu Ghraib prisoner-abuse scandal in Baghdad. And some firms that provide interrogators and interpreters in Iraq do not appear on the Defense Department's list of contractors because they were hired through the Interior Department.

Major Providers of Military Services
(in $ billions, for FY2003)

	Value of Contracts
Lockheed Martin Corp.	$4.4
Northrop Grumman Corp.	3.5
General Dynamics Corp.	2.4
Halliburton Co.	2.4
Humana Inc.	2.4
Computer Sciences Corp.	2.0
Science Applications International	1.9
Health Net Inc.	1.8
Raytheon Co.	1.7
Boeing Co.	1.3

* Lockheed Martin is in the process of acquiring Titan Corp.

Source: "Procurement Statistics," Directorate for Information, Operations and Reports, Department of Defense

home, your career and your family for six or 12 months, live in a tent, get shot at and bombed. But it's beyond money. Your money is useless if you get blown up."

But critics warn that privatization has been taken to such an extreme that it may undermine the effectiveness of U.S. military operations.

"U.S. military doctrine says that we should not have private contractors in mission-critical roles, which are roles that affect the success or failure of operations," Singer says. "But there is a whole laundry list of roles that private contractors are playing in Iraq that violate that doctrine — everything from logistics, to training the Iraqi army, to protecting CPA installations and top government leaders, to escorting convoys, to conducting intelligence interrogations.

"If supplies break down," he continues, "if the local Iraqi army doesn't get trained properly, if CPA installations are overrun by rebels, if Paul Bremer gets killed, if our convoys are overrun by insurgent forces and if interrogators screw up at Abu Ghraib — all these things affect the success or failure of the operation."

course, but security contractors tend to be far more professional," he says. "When you hire somebody with that kind of experience, you're getting quite a product."

But critics point out that, unlike GIs, private contractors are free to walk away from their posts when the going gets rough, endangering U.S. forces in hostile areas.

That hasn't happened, Brooks says, even during the recent escalation of hostilities in Iraq. "It's true that you can't order a contractor to stay, and there were predictions at the beginning of the war that as soon as the shooting started all of these private companies would pull out," he says. However, since the Fallujah incident, security firms not only have maintained their presence but also have received more job applications, Brooks says. "People keep saying that they're only there for the money, but it's not just about money," he says. "Sure, money's important. You have to have enough money to leave your

Does privatization save taxpayers money?

In addition to freeing up military personnel for combat-related duties, privatization has been embraced by the Pentagon and other government agencies as a way to save money. The White House Office of Management and Budget recently projected that privatization would save more than $1 billion over the next three to five years, primarily because contractors bidding for government contacts are expected to find ways to reduce their costs. [10]

But that rationale has not always played out. During the 1980s, the Pentagon's payment of $640 for a toilet seat became the symbol of waste, fraud and abuse in military spending for goods and services and triggered efforts to increase oversight of the contracting process, including an effort to make contractors compete for government business. Later, Vice President Al Gore launched a campaign to "reinvent" a more efficient government, and reforms were introduced aimed at streamlining contracting procedures.

But charges of fraud and cronyism have continued to plague military contracting, as suggested by the current controversy over Halliburton's $7 billion no-bid contract to rebuild Iraq's oil industry. [11]

Indeed, reform efforts actually opened the way for new loopholes that helped avoid congressional oversight of Pentagon contracting practices. For example, the new "blanket-purchase agreement" allows a government department to avoid bidding out contracts by piggybacking onto another department's existing contract with a firm for unrelated services. In this way, the Defense Department contracted with CACI to provide interrogators for Iraq using an existing agreement the firm had for unrelated services with the Interior Department.

"The theory behind the blanket-purchase agreement was that the Defense Department can save overhead costs by contracting through other agencies," says Danielle Brian, executive director of the Project on Government Oversight, a nonprofit government watchdog group. "But in practice, we've lost any kind of control over who is getting the contracts and what price we're paying for them because there is no competition anymore. We also have no control over how prime contractors subcontract out the work to other firms."

Thanks to blanket-purchase agreements, Brian says, "CACI has become one of several full-service government contractors, which basically say, 'We may not have the experience or expertise in what you're looking for, but we'll get it. Just tell us what you need, and we'll figure it out.' "

The General Accounting Office (GAO) found that all of the 14 new contracts it examined were awarded without open competition, but it didn't find anything illegal. The GAO said the law allows for limited or no competition in awarding contracts "when only one source is available or to meet urgent requirements." [12]

Using civilians to carry out functions traditionally delegated to soldiers and military police represents another exercise in false economy, critics say. Many contractors are former Green Berets or Navy Seals — trained at government expense — who can make much more money doing the same work as private contractors rather than remaining in the military. Contract bodyguards in

American personnel at the Abu Ghraib prison threaten an Iraqi prisoner with dogs. At least two private military contractors have been implicated in the prisoner abuses, leading critics to question how private contractors working for the military are held accountable for possible crimes.

Iraq commonly earn twice as much or more than their military colleagues. [13]

"Military special forces are very expensive to train," Brian says. "By relying on contractors, the Defense Department is essentially spending a huge amount of money to train someone and then paying a company to make a profit off that taxpayers' investment."

Defenders of the "revolving door" between the military and the private sector say there's nothing wrong or novel about ex-soldiers using expertise gained at taxpayer expense to advance in the private sector. Airline pilots, for example, routinely get their training in the military. Indeed, Brooks, of the International Peace Operations Association, says the practice offers taxpayers a win-win opportunity.

"Basically, the taxpayer is getting double the service out of training a guy for one career," Brooks says. "When you train a military guy, you expect to use him while he's in the military. We're getting him when he's out of the military as well, so we're getting double the bang for the buck. I think it's brilliant."

Sometimes the savings to taxpayers is not obvious, say proponents of privatization, especially when contractors are often paid more than twice as much as a soldier for doing the same work. But proponents of military out-sourcing point out that recruitment, training, equip-ment, housing and health care inflate the cost for every soldier far above the base salary paid by the government.

"Say you pay a soldier $40,000 to do a job you'd have to pay a contractor $100,000 to do," says Peters of the Council on Foreign Relations. "By the time you add all those other costs, the actual cost of putting that $40,000 soldier in place may well exceed $100,000."

Moreover, Peters says, the savings realized from out-sourcing certain non-combat military services — such as translators and interrogators — are especially evident in places like Iraq. "Say we need 100 Arabic-speaking Army interrogators in Iraq," he says. "If you recruited 100 Arabic-speaking interrogators for Army service, you'd have to pay them to sit on the shelf to wait for a situation like Iraq. The overhead and investment [required] to keep that capacity in uniform is part of what you save when you're able to turn instead to the larger economy to find such people we can call upon when we need them for a discrete period of time — and without having to pay their retirement and other benefits."

Should there be more oversight of private military contractors?

The growing role of private contractors in the military has worried some lawmakers for years. Rep. Schakowsky has focused on the issue since visiting Colombia several years ago and learning that private contractors were play-ing a major role in U.S.-funded counternarcotics efforts. After the scandal erupted over the abuses of detainees in Iraq by both soldiers and contractors, Schakowsky wrote to President Bush asking him to suspend the use of pri-vate contractors in all Iraqi prisons pending further investigations into their conduct. (*See "At Issue," p. 293.*)

But she says the White House has yet to respond to her request. "The administration continues to say that they use these private military contractors because they're trained to do the job," she says. "But I think that's a mis-take, given the lack of clarity about whether they were involved in convincing or even ordering our military police to set the conditions for interrogations — in other words, to validate, if not direct, the abuses that occurred."

Corbin of the Center for Defense Information agrees, noting that their presence and participation in military operations, like the interrogations at Abu Ghraib, may make it unclear to soldiers who is actually in command.

"It's one thing if they're employed by and guarding private facilities," he says. "But having these semi-mili-tary, private contractors involved violates the fundamen-tal military principle of having a chain of command."

Industry advocates dismiss this concern, noting that as civilians, private contractors are not under anybody's orders technically, nor allowed to give orders. "They're given a contract, which says what they can and cannot do, and that's essentially their chain of command," Brooks says.

While he concedes that combat conditions like those in Iraq may blur the separation of authority, he says it occurs in a way that decreases, not increases, contractors' autonomy. "Because this is a martial-law situation, the local military commander can order contractors to do just about anything," he says. "And the contractors have to jump."

That doesn't satisfy Corbin, who says the military needs to establish a body of rules and procedures govern-ing private-contractor activities in war zones. "Just in terms of military operations, is the military supposed to go and rescue contractors when they come under fire?" he asks. "Or are contractors even supposed to go in to rescue the military? This is a new area, and both contractors and soldiers are woefully underserved in terms of operational procedures. They're just working it out on the fly."

Apart from confusion in the field, critics worry that contractors may answer more readily to their employers' and stockholders' interests than to those of the govern-ment's. "Who do they respond to?" Schakowsky asks. "Is it a CEO or a general?"

Singer of the Brookings Institution says a more wor-risome ambiguity surrounding private contractors is their legal status. "We have folks within a military operation, carrying on military roles, who are not part of the mili-tary," he says. "While the soldier who commits crimes is held accountable under the code of military justice, for contractors the situation is a little bit more confused." Because private contractors can't be court-martialed, they fall under one of two other systems, local law or U.S. extraterritorial law.

Singer rules out local law because, "There is no local law in Iraq." In any case, he says, "CPA regulations stipu-late that private military contractors are not subject to it."

Brooks says that concern is overstated because con-tractors are held to a higher legal standard when on over-seas missions than civilians in the United States.

If a contractor commits an offense that is below the level of a felony, the individual generally gets fired, he says. "If you run a red light in the States, you're not going to get fired from your job, but that's what happens in Iraq because the companies don't want to cross the military at all. It's harsh, because there's no real avenue for a person to appeal getting fired. But we're in a war, right?"

Contractors who commit a felony, Brooks says, are subject to the 2000 Military Extraterritorial Jurisdiction Act (MEJA), which places contractors working overseas under U.S. legal jurisdiction. But Singer says MEJA contains two important loopholes. First, he says, "it applies only to Pentagon contractors, not to those working for other government agencies." The CACI employees implicated in the Abu Ghraib abuses were working under a contract let by the Interior Department. "Also, it's unclear whether the law applies to subcontractors or to third-party nationals." Many of the contractors are citizens of Iraq or other countries.

Equally important, Singer says, the Pentagon has never written the regulations needed to implement MEJA. As a result, he says, "Not one of the 20,000 private military contractors on the ground in Iraq has been tried under MEJA. And we're led to take the fantastic leap of the imagination to conclude that over the course of one year not one person of those 20,000 has committed a crime of any kind, let alone any on the scale of Abu Ghraib."

Passaro, the CIA contractor charged with assault in Afghanistan, is the first civilian to be charged in the widening prison-abuse scandal. Six soldiers implicated in the Abu Ghraib abuses are currently under prosecution in Iraq; a seventh has already pleaded guilty. [14] But the two private military contractors who also were implicated in the scandal have not faced formal charges. [15]

"Donald Rumsfeld continues to say that those who have committed crimes will be prosecuted under other U.S. laws," Schakowsky says. "But it's unclear what those sanctions will be or that anyone will be sanctioned at all. This is a very, very murky area with many problems that are now coming to light in Iraq."

That legal ambiguity can also enable the government to avoid taking responsibility for mistakes or even criminal behavior by private contractors. In 2001, for example, an American company on contract for the CIA in the U.S. war on drugs mistakenly identified a small aircraft flying over Peru as a possible drug transport. Acting on the tip, Peruvian pilots shot down the plane, killing a U.S. mis-

sionary and her infant daughter. U.S. lawmakers reportedly were unsuccessful in obtaining information about the incident from the State Department or the CIA.

The alleged implication of civilian contractors in torture could open the door to other avenues for prosecution. A 1994 law makes it a crime for Americans to commit torture outside the United States. But as long as administration officials refrain from calling the abuses at Abu Ghraib "torture," it's unlikely that the contractors will be prosecuted under that law. [16]

BACKGROUND

Mercenary Armies

Throughout history, private armies have been the norm. Whether they were individual mercenaries signing on to bolster the ranks of organized armies or fully equipped professional armies, the ranks of the world's military forces more often than not have been driven by the profit motive. [17]

References to mercenaries date back more than 4,000 years to soldiers hired by King Shulgi of Ur (2094-2047 B.C.). The first record of a major conflict, the battle of Kadesh (1294 B.C.), speaks of hired Numidian soldiers in the army Egyptian Pharaoh Ramses II sent against the Hittites.

The first citizen armies mentioned in historical accounts were raised by Sparta and a few other ancient Greek city-states, but many other Greek forces relied on paid foreign soldiers who specialized in certain skills of war, such as cavalrymen from Thessaly and slingers from Crete.

Alexander the Great conquered the Persian Empire in 336 B.C. thanks in large part to mercenaries, including a 224-ship Phoenician armada. By the end of the First Punic War between the Romans and the Carthaginians in 241 B.C., the Carthaginians' reliance on mercenaries was so complete that failure to pay the victorious soldiers sparked a wholesale revolt known as the Mercenary War, which required yet more paid foreigners to quell. In 218 B.C., a largely mercenary force accompanied the Carthaginian general Hannibal in his march across the Alps in his campaign against Rome.

Like Greece, Rome relied initially on a citizen army but also on mercenaries with special skills, such as archery and cavalry. As the empire expanded and fewer Romans joined the far-flung forces, foreign mercenaries

CHRONOLOGY

1970s-1980s *U.S. military manpower peaks at more than 3 million personnel.*

1973 The draft is dropped in favor of an all-volunteer military.

Dec. 4, 1989 The United Nations adopts the International Convention against the Recruitment, Use, Financing and Training of Mercenaries. To date, however, only 25 countries have signed and ratified or acceded to the treaty; the United States is not among them.

1990s *Military outsourcing picks up as the Pentagon downsizes U.S. forces at the end of the Cold War.*

1993 A failed U.S. intervention to help the government of Somalia put down a rebellion galvanizes American public opinion against use of U.S. military forces in conflicts that pose no immediate threat to national security.

1994 The Federal Acquisition Streamlining Act expands agencies' authority to buy goods and services from private companies.

August 1995 After U.S. contractor Military Professional Resources Inc. (MPRI) helps Croatian forces defeat a Serbian attack, Croatia and Bosnia hire the Virginia-based firm to train their armed forces.

1996 The Clinger-Cohen Act allows the use of multi-agency contracts, enabling a single federal agency to handle contracts for other agencies.

2000s *Private military contractors serve in the "war on terrorism," prompting calls for greater oversight of these firms.*

2000 The Military Extraterritorial Jurisdiction Act (MEJA) places Defense Department contractors working overseas under U.S. legal jurisdiction.

Sept. 11, 2001 Terrorists attack the World Trade Center in New York City and the Pentagon, prompting President Bush to declare war on terrorism.

Oct. 7, 2001 U.S.-led coalition forces invade Afghanistan and rout its Taliban rulers but fail to capture Osama bin Laden, leader of the al Qaeda terrorist organization responsible for the Sept. 11 attacks.

2002 U.S. active-duty troop levels stand at 1.4 million after falling by more than one-half in three decades.

January 2003 Rep. Charles B. Rangel, D-N.Y., and Sen. Ernest Hollings, D-S.C., introduce the Universal National Service Act, which would require all American men and women ages 18-26 to perform a period of military or civilian service.

April 15, 2003 The United States, with Britain and several smaller countries, invades Iraq, topples Saddam Hussein and occupies the country.

April 28, 2004 Insurgents kill four U.S. private military contractors in Fallujah, Iraq, and hang their burned and mutilated bodies from a bridge.

May 2004 Three civilian contractors are implicated in a prisoner-abuse scandal at U.S. prisons in Iraq and Afghanistan.

June 14, 2004 An amendment is proposed to the fiscal 2005 Pentagon reauthorization bill that would bar the government from outsourcing the oversight of Iraq reconstruction to private companies unless the government "is entirely unable" to do the job with federal employees. It also bars the letting of private contracts "if there is even an appearance of conflict of interest for the private company."

June 16, 2004 Senators reject Democrats' proposals to prohibit the use of private contractors in combat missions or to interrogate prisoners and to increase the penalties for war profiteering by making it a crime to overcharge the government for goods and services in military contracts.

June 30, 2004 The U.S.-led Coalition Provisional Authority in Iraq is due to hand over the reins of government to an interim Iraqi administration. Thousands of private security contractors are scheduled to remain in Iraq, along with U.S. military personnel.

became key to Rome's military might; by the end of the third century A.D., the imperial army had more Germans than Romans in its ranks.

After the fall of the Roman Empire, European feudal rulers exacted military service from their serfs. But the feudal armies of Europe's Dark Ages continued to rely on mercenaries, especially for expertise in the latest war-making technologies of the time — the crossbow, early firearms and cannon. Nobles and kings often preferred mercenaries to conscripts, however, because arming serfs posed the risk of rebellion. The emergence of powerful cities, such as Venice and Florence, in 13th-century Italy gave rise to a new military organization. Units of contract soldiers and sailors participated in Europe's expanding local conflicts and in Crusades to the Middle East. By the end of the 14th century, mercenary troops had largely replaced feudal conscripts across Europe.

The growing power of mercenary armies posed a new threat to the European order. Rather than face unemployment at the end of hostilities, individual "free lances" began to form "companies" (from *con pane*, for the bread soldiers received for their services). These roving militias traveled the continent in search of war, offering their services to the highest bidder. During the Hundred Years War, companies were as feared as any official enemy, gaining a bloody reputation for extortion, killing unarmed civilians and destroying villages that refused to meet their demands for money and food.

As the free companies gained strength, kings mounted military campaigns away from home to keep them occupied. But the companies continued to grow more powerful, notably the 10,000-man Great Company in Italy and England's White Company. In Italy, nobles in Milan and other cities emulated their organization to mobilize local paid armies of *condottieri*, or contract soldiers, who eventually replaced their employers as the local ruling class. In 15th-century France, King Charles VII exploited the company model more successfully by taxing the country's growing middle class and permanently hiring several companies. In so doing, he kept them out of trouble and created Europe's first standing army since the Dark Ages.

Highly effective mercenary armies from Switzerland, southern Germany and Austria often determined the outcome of conflicts across Europe, and by the 17th-century European armies were essentially collections of highly paid, specialized mercenary units. War became such a lucrative enterprise that brokers who recruited and armed units and then leased them to warring governments were among the wealthiest men on the continent.

Citizen Armies

The Thirty Years War (1618-1648) marked a major shift in notions of statehood and military organization. Like their predecessors during the Dark Ages, mercenary forces inspired public loathing by looting the countryside during the conflict. But the gradual dissolution of the Hapsburg Empire marked the rise of national sovereignty and citizenship, and mercenary armies were slowly replaced with domestic citizen armies.

Advances in easy-to-use weaponry, notably the musket, contributed to the shift, since mercenaries had traditionally traded on their ability to offer specialized skills. In addition to requiring little training, muskets also gave a tactical advantage to the army with the largest number of soldiers to fire them, and rulers could more readily raise large numbers of troops through conscription than by hiring mercenaries. Meanwhile, Enlightenment notions of patriotism and citizenship made military service more appealing than during the era of serfdom.

"[P]eople were more willing to fight as citizens than as subjects," wrote Singer, of Brookings. "Those who fought for profit, rather than patriotism, were completely de-legitimated under these new conceptions." [18]

Paid military units continued to play an important role in conflicts, however. During the American Revolution, the British government hired some 30,000 mercenaries from the German state of Hesse-Kassel to help quell the colonists' uprising. Indeed, George Washington's 1776 defeat of the Hessian units was a key victory in the march to Independence.

Private military armies enjoyed a resurgence during the 200 years of European colonial expansion, when governments gave companies monopoly commercial rights to develop overseas holdings. The Dutch East India Co., English East India Co. and Hudson's Bay Co. fielded their own military units to defend their vast economic interests. Some of these private forces endured until the 20th century, when the companies' trade monopolies ended. But the legacy of the armed charter companies endured until the 1920s and '30s in parts of sub-Saharan Africa that lacked national governments and where private companies held sway — such as Rhodesia and Mozambique.

Return of Draft Considered Unlikely

The unpopularity of the Vietnam War — and the widespread perception that it was fought mostly by men from poor families who couldn't get draft deferments — helped push lawmakers to replace the draft in 1973 with today's all-volunteer army.

Since then, the services have met their manpower needs by offering college scholarships, technical training and other perks intended to help recruits "be all you can be," as the Army promises.

In the post-Cold War 1990s, the military shed jobs. The number of active-duty military personnel now stands at about 1.5 million, half the total during the Vietnam War.

But conflicts in the Balkans, the Middle East, Somalia and other far-flung places posed new challenges to the U.S. military. The challenges have intensified since the Bush administration launched its war on terrorism following the attacks of Sept. 11, 2001. The invasions and occupations of Afghanistan and Iraq have further strained the downsized military's capabilities.

To meet its growing manpower needs, the Pentagon has repeatedly extended duty tours in Afghanistan and Iraq. In Iraq alone, tours have been extended for 20,000 soldiers. [1] In early June, the Army barred soldiers scheduled for deployment to either country from leaving the service, even if their enlistments were up. [2]

Critics say the administration is placing too great a burden on overstretched troops as well as on the National Guard and reserves. Sen. John F. Kerry, the presumptive Democratic presidential candidate, called the administration's policy "a backdoor draft" and promised that if elected, he would add 40,000 military personnel to the active-duty armed forces by shifting funds currently earmarked for a controversial missile-defense system. [3]

"Let's be honest," says Peter W. Singer, a national security expert at the Brookings Institution, "the military designed the system so that you would use the National Guard and reserves if you got into a major war. This was meant to be a checking mechanism so that you wouldn't get into wars lightly. If there are situations where you don't think it's worth sending in the National Guard or the reserves, then maybe it's not worth doing it at all."

Some administration critics say restoring the military draft would be a better — and fairer — way to bolster troop levels. In January 2003, Rep. Charles B. Rangel, D-N.Y., and Sen. Ernest Hollings, D-S.C., separately introduced the Universal National Service Act, which would require a period of military or civilian service for American men and women ages 18-26 "in furtherance of the national defense and homeland security."

Introduction of the bills and renewed talk of the draft have spawned a flurry of Internet rumors that the administration is secretly planning to reinstitute obligatory military service shortly after the fall presidential election. But most analysts dismiss such rumors. [4]

Although Rangel's House bill has gained 14 co-sponsors, neither chamber has acted on the measure. Indeed, support for the draft proposals seems to be more a vehicle for criticizing the Bush administration's invasion and occupation of Iraq and the social inequities in the U.S. military than determined calls for restoration of the draft.

"I do not think that members of this administration and Congress would have been so willing to launch a war if they had known that their own children might have to fight it,"

With the exception of elite units, such as the French Foreign Legion or the Nepalese Gurkhas who still serve in the British and Indian armies, citizen armies raised under the aegis of sovereign nation-states became the dominant form of military organization. Most private military actors were individual mercenaries who hired out to businesses or rebel organizations in parts of the world where governments were weak, especially Latin America and Africa.

"Once at the center of warfare, by the start of the 20th century the international trade in military services was marginalized and mostly pushed underground," Singer writes. [19]

With the ascendance of the nation-state, for-profit military forces fell increasingly out of favor, and many governments even prohibited them. Meanwhile, the Geneva Conventions denied mercenaries the legal protections they provide for soldiers in combat.

Mercenaries' notoriety increased in the 1950s and '60s, when they helped fill the security vacuum left as European colonial powers withdrew from most of their

said Rangel. "Fact is, we are currently a nation in which the poor fight our wars while the affluent stay at home."[5]

As American casualties in Iraq mounted this spring, some Republicans echoed Democrats' concerns about relying on an all-volunteer military to fight terrorism. "Should we continue to burden the middle class, who represents most all of our soldiers, and the lower middle class?" asked Sen. Chuck Hagel, R-Neb.[6]

The Bush administration continues to support the all-volunteer army and reject suggestions that it is considering a return to the draft. "I don't know anyone in the executive branch of the government who believes it would be appropriate or necessary to reinstitute the draft," said Defense Secretary Donald H. Rumsfeld.

Although he acknowledged that the military is being stretched in Afghanistan and Iraq, Rumsfeld said the solution is better management of the professional military. "It simply requires changing the rules, changing the requirements, changing the regulations in ways that we can manage that force considerably better," he said.[7]

Military experts say the draft is unlikely to return anytime soon. "The political cost of cranking up something like the draft to meet a contingency that may not be there a couple of

U.S. Marines carry a wounded comrade to a helicopter while under heavy fire from North Vietnamese troops during Operation Hickory III in Vietnam in July 1967.

years from now would be tremendous," says Michael P. Peters, executive vice president of the Council on Foreign Relations, a New York City think tank.

"Frankly, most military people would not be in favor of reconstituting the draft because they've become very comfortable with the all-volunteer force. Despite what's been going on in Iraq, the military has been able to attract and bring into the active force a pretty steady flow of high-quality people to maintain the manpower levels they need."

[1] See Thomas E. Ricks, "Army Personnel Chief Aims to Keep Ranks Full," *The Washington Post*, May 28 2004, p. A21.

[2] See Bob Herbert, "Level With Americans," *The New York Times*, June 7, 2004, p. A27.

[3] See Dan Balz, "Kerry Says He Would Add 40,000 to Army," *The Washington Post*, June 4, 2004, p. A1. For background on missile defense, see Mary H. Cooper, "Missile Defense," *The CQ Researcher*, Sept. 8, 2000, pp. 689-712.

[4] See, for example, Jack Kelly, "Rumor Aside, Draft's Return Is Most Unlikely," *Pittsburgh Post-Gazette*, May 24, 2004.

[5] From a floor statement in the House of Representatives, May 5, 2004.

[6] Quoted in Robert Burns, "Defense Chief Sees No Need to Reintroduce the Military Draft," The Associated Press, April 22, 2004.

[7] Quoted in Guy Taylor, "Rumsfeld Rejects Idea of Returning to the Draft," *The Washington Times*, April 23, 2004, p. A1.

holdings in Africa. Led by such notorious figures as "Mad" Mike Hoare of Ireland and Frenchman Bob Denard, mercenaries known as *les Affreux* ("the Terrible Ones") fought in wars of succession in the former Belgian Congo and other areas throughout the decolonization period. Denard continued to participate in coups and attempted coups in Africa until 1995. Many mercenaries active in Africa received their training under the apartheid regime of South Africa, adding to their reputation for ruthless violence born of racism.

Downsizing the Military

The great wars of the 20th century were fought with conscripted or volunteer armies. After World War II, for almost the entire second half of the century, the United States and the Soviet Union, together with their respective allies in the North Atlantic Treaty Organization (NATO) and the Warsaw Pact, maintained huge standing armies, still composed almost entirely of citizen-soldiers.

But after the Soviet Union collapsed in 1991, ending the Cold War, the need for such large armies rapidly

Private security guards escort Afghan President Hamid Karzai (center) as he arrives in Afghanistan's Ghor province in July 2003. Many military contractors are retired Special Forces personnel.

diminished. Buoyed by the promise of a "peace dividend" that could be invested in other public sectors or returned to taxpayers as tax cuts, the United States and other countries downsized their militaries.

Since 1988, the Pentagon has shuttered 97 major military installations and reduced personnel at 55 facilities, saving $17 billion immediately and $7 billion annually, according to Citizens Against Government Waste. [20]

As U.S. policymakers were downsizing the military, they were also encouraging privatization of non-combat jobs. Military outsourcing began in 1973, when the draft was discontinued, near the end of the Vietnam War. To lure recruits, the Pentagon began contracting mundane jobs like cleaning and cooking to private firms. Throughout the 1980s and '90s, the Pentagon privatized more service jobs, including heavy construction, fuel supply and, especially, technical support — paying defense contractors to maintain and service the military's increasingly complex weaponry. The parallel trends of downsizing and outsourcing more than halved the number of active-duty troops — from more than 3 million in 1970 to 1.4 million by 2002. [21] A third of the reduction occurred during the 1990s.

Another rationale for privatizing the military, which intensified during the Clinton-Gore efforts to "reinvent government," was that inviting private companies to bid for contracts to provide military goods and services would result in even more cost savings. [22]

"Competition enhances quality, economy and productivity," states the Office of Management Budget's "Circular A-76," the executive branch's document on outsourcing. To make it easier for the Pentagon and other agencies to purchase goods and services from the private sector, Congress passed the 1994 Federal Acquisition Streamlining Act. And in 1996 lawmakers approved the Clinger-Cohen Act, enabling a single federal agency to handle contracts for other agencies. [23]

But the Cold War's end brought more than cost savings to the U.S. military. It also created a dangerous power vacuum that quickly sparked new and different threats to international security. As the superpowers withdrew from their previous areas of influence, long-simmering disputes erupted in countries — ranging from the former Yugoslavia to Rwanda and Sierra Leone — whose weak governments were unable to quell unrest on their own. These low-intensity conflicts were unlike those envisioned by Cold War planners, whose large armies and heavy equipment were ill suited to deal with the urban street-fighting and guerrilla tactics that characterized the new hostilities.

The United States learned this lesson the hard way in 1993 when it tried to help Somalia put down a rebellion. The effort ended with TV images of a dead GI being dragged through the streets of Mogadishu and galvanized U.S. public opinion against future interventions in conflicts that posed no immediate threat to national security.

Reflecting that reluctance, Congress restricted the role of U.S. troops in overseas conflicts. In trying to quell the supply of cocaine from Colombia, for example, the United States may deploy no more than 400 American soldiers. To get around the restriction, the U.S. is allowed to use up to 400 private military contractors to augment the official forces.

American private military contractors also played a major role in the Balkans. The August 1995 rout of Serbian forces in Croatia, for instance, was attributed to Virginia-based Military Professional Resources Inc. (MPRI), not Croatian forces. MPRI had first entered the region through a State Department contract to monitor sanctions against Serbia. After the battlefield victory, the governments of Croatia and Bosnia hired MPRI to help retrain and modernize their forces. [24]

Meanwhile, Western governments' fear of placing troops in harm's way and becoming mired in far-away conflicts has weakened the ability of multilateral forces to intervene in local and regional conflicts and subsequently keep the peace. Even as the number and intensity of global hostilities grew, the number of personnel in the United Nations' peacekeeping operations dropped from a peak of 76,000 in 1994 to about 15,000 just four years later. [25]

Yet the U.N. opposes the use of mercenary forces, having adopted on Dec. 4, 1989, the International Convention against the Recruitment, Use, Financing and Training of Mercenaries. So far, only 25 countries have signed and ratified or acceded to the treaty. The United States is not among them.

Despite continued societal ambivalence about private armies, mercenaries have flourished in the post-Cold War power vacuum, characterized by small wars and weak states. Military transformation and outsourcing have swollen the ranks of these modern freelancers, many of whom are former Warsaw Pact and NATO military personnel who found themselves out of work when their governments downsized them.

As demand for mercenaries' services has grown, new companies have emerged to provide a wide range of services, including logistical support; training local police forces; protecting officials and commercial sites; and armed combat.

CURRENT SITUATION

Modern Mercenaries

The role of private contractors in U.S. military operations has expanded greatly since the Sept. 11 terrorist attacks and the Bush administration's subsequent declaration of a war on terrorism. [26] At least 85 U.S. companies have contracts in Afghanistan or Iraq; about 15 of the firms are playing key roles in both countries, often filling jobs that contractors have long performed for the military, such as maintenance and repair of vehicles and aircraft, supervising supply lines and running logistics, driving supply trucks carrying food and fuel, setting up warehouses, preparing meals, cleaning bases, washing clothes and building military housing. [27]

But as the Abu Ghraib scandal and numerous civilian casualties in Iraq's escalating violence have shown, private military contractors are now performing duties more closely related to combat functions. As interrogators, translators and transcribers, they are closely involved in intelligence operations. And armed private contractors also help train local Iraqi police and soldiers and guard officials, military installations and convoys and non-military installations, such as oil pipelines and electrical stations.

> "The U.S. military is 35 percent smaller than it was at the end of the Cold War, but it has far more global commitments, and Iraq is the biggest military commitment in at least a generation. So there's a gap between the supply and demand of military personnel."
>
> — **Peter W. Singer**
> Author, *Corporate Warriors: The Rise of the Privatized Military Industry*

According to the Pentagon, private security companies in Iraq provide "only defensive services." [28] Brooks, of the contractors' association, says clear rules of engagement, established by the CPA, define what the approximately 6,000 security contractors may and may not do in Iraq. "They can defend themselves, they can defend what's in their contract — be it a person, a place or a convoy — and they can defend Iraqi citizens," he says.

The rules also define what types of weapons contractors may use on the job. "Essentially, they are limited to light weapons," Brooks says, "meaning weapons that one person can use alone, ranging from pistols to assault rifles," but not belted machine guns, grenade launchers or explosives. Companies may obtain special permits to

Armed guards aboard a helicopter operated by North Carolina-based Blackwater Security Co. patrol over Baghdad in May 2004. Four Blackwater guards were ambushed and killed in April.

carry larger weapons for convoy duty, he added.

Despite their conspicuous role, no one seems to know just how many private contractors are operating in Iraq. "The Defense Department doesn't care about the numbers; they hire a company to do something," Brooks says. "It's up to the companies that win contracts to determine how many people they're going to need to do the job. Some companies may use technology, and some may hire locals."

Likewise, the exact number of contractors who have been killed or wounded in Iraq is unknown because civilian casualties go largely unnoticed unless they are reported in the media. The Labor Department puts the death toll among civilian contractors in Iraq since April 2003 at 85, compared with 48 who have died in Afghanistan and other countries since 2001. But the totals do not reflect the mounting casualties resulting from the growing violence in Iraq over the past two months. [29] Meanwhile, as of June 15, 2004, 830 soldiers had died in Iraq, according to the Pentagon.

Cheney and Halliburton

Despite efforts to reduce the incidence of fraud and waste in Pentagon contracting practices, critics continue to complain about the department's dealings with the private sector. Much of the criticism has centered on Halliburton, one of the Pentagon's main suppliers in

Iraq; Vice President Cheney served as Halliburton CEO from 1995 until he became Bush's running mate in 2000. Cheney asserts that although he still receives deferred compensation from Halliburton he has no formal ties to the firm, which oversees the reconstruction of Iraq's oil industry, and provides other services through subsidiaries, such as Kellogg, Brown and Root. [30]

"I don't have anything to do with the contracting process," he said earlier this year, "and I wouldn't know how to manipulate the process if I wanted to." [31]

But new evidence appears to contradict Cheney's assertion. Rep. Henry A. Waxman, D-Calif., recently demanded information from Cheney's office about reports that he may have had a hand in Halliburton's winning its $7 billion, no-bid contract for the Iraqi oil-reconstruction project. [32] In addition, one of Halliburton's subsidiaries, Kellogg Brown and Root, is the military's single biggest contractor in Iraq, hired to transport food and other supplies to military installations around the country.

"Halliburton received $3.5 billion through its contract in Iraq last year alone," Rep. Schakowsky says. "So we're talking about a lot of money, but not a lot of oversight, accountability, clarity or sunlight on their activities." Schakowsky's proposed bill would require the Pentagon to show Congress any new contract worth more than $1 million for a private firm to do business in Iraq or Afghanistan. "Over the last four years, there have been more than $7 billion in contracts let for Iraq and Afghanistan," she says. "Let's remember, these are taxpayer dollars."

Allegations have also surfaced that Halliburton fraudulently charged the government — and exposed drivers to unnecessary danger — by repeatedly running convoys of empty trucks in some of the most violent areas of Iraq. According to 12 current and former employees, KBR drivers and escorts made more than 100 trips on trucks carrying nothing but "sailboat fuel." [33]

Under KBR's cost-plus contract, the firm can bill the government for every trip it makes, so frequent trips are in its interest. "No one knows exactly what they were charging," says Singer of the Brookings Institution. "The cost is estimated to be about $2,000 for each truck; there were 15 trucks in each convoy; and convoys run once or twice a day. So you can see how these services accrue over time."

KBR has said it never ran empty trucks unnecessarily. "KBR is not paid by the load or by the mission," said Patrice Mingo, the company's manager for public relations.

Does the Pentagon rely too heavily on private contractors?

YES

Rep. Janice D. Schakowsky, D-Ill.
Member, House Energy and Commerce Committee, Subcommittee on Oversight and Investigations

From a letter to President Bush, May 4, 2004

I am writing out of concern over recent news of abuse of prisoners being held by the United States at the Abu Ghraib prison in Iraq. In particular, I have questions about the role of civilian contractors in these abuses, the investigation into the abuses and rules of accountability for U.S. civilian contractors operating in Iraq. . . . This is yet another example of questionable adherence to international human rights laws by United States forces in Iraq.

It has been reported that, more than two months after a classified Army report found that contract workers were implicated in the illegal abuse of Iraqis, the companies that employ them (CACI International Inc. and Titan Corp.) say that they have heard nothing from the Pentagon and that they have not removed any employees from Iraq.

The sadistic abuses of Iraqis at a U.S. military prison raise serious questions about the accountability of U.S.-hired private military contractors who are involved in illegal activity. It has been widely reported that civilian contractors are not subject to the Uniform Code of Military Conduct and that the Department of Justice is reluctant to get involved in this issue. . . . I have long held that the use of civilian contractors to carry out military functions on behalf of the United States is a dangerous policy, in large part because of the lack of accountability and oversight that exists. In particular, I do not believe that private companies should be trusted with interrogation of Iraqi prisoners.

I believe that pending a thorough investigation and appropriate action, including but not limited to the dismissal and prosecution of those involved, all contracts with civilian firms for functions involving security, supervision and interrogation of prisoners, should be suspended. . . .

Furthermore, I would like to know the policy of your administration regarding the directives, rules and laws governing contractors that operate on behalf of the United States in Iraq. It is my hope that the individuals named in recent press reports were not ordered to conduct such atrocious activities by U.S. personnel. However, that is something your administration should unequivocally address. . . .

I maintain that the use of private military contractors by the United States military is a misguided policy [that costs] the American people untold amounts, in terms of dollars [and] U.S. lives and is damaging our reputation with the international community. It also impedes the ability of the Congress to conduct appropriate oversight and keeps the American public in the dark.

NO

Doug Brooks
President, International Peace Operations Association

Written for The CQ Researcher, June, 2004

In times of war, the Department of Defense has always relied on the private sector for essential services. From Valley Forge to Vietnam, private companies have been flexible and able to endure remarkable risks while supporting our troops. Private companies are able to tap into a pool of highly specialized professionals and a large network of local and U.S. reconstruction capabilities. They regularly utilize experienced military veterans while supporting and enhancing U.S. policies, lessening the burden on our young soldiers serving on the front. Consequently, our military is more focused, professional and cost effective.

Attempts by partisan analysts to turn the practice of private sector support into a political football are worrying. We must ensure adequate standards, transparency and accountability. However, we should remember that redundant bureaucracy, regulations and restrictions dangerously limit the flexibility that makes the private sector so enormously cost effective. The U.S. military is immensely capable, but to demand that it radically curtail its utilization of contractors would place unnecessary stress on our soldiers struggling to bring stability to volatile regions of the world.

Contrary to public opinion, the overwhelming majority of private military contracts are restricted to logistical and support services. The fact that the Pentagon also chooses to contract with private companies to provide security services to protect our reconstruction efforts is neither surprising nor worrisome. In the United States we have three times as many private guards as we do police, and while the threat levels are substantially higher in Iraq and Afghanistan, contractors are limited to defensive roles.

The companies use former military personnel for this hazardous duty, and all employees are under strict rules of engagement and are limited to light weapons. They are clearly not the rogue private army that critics allege. Nor are critics honest about the numbers. Three-quarters of the 20,000-strong private security employees are, in fact, Iraqis — the very people who should be providing security for their own country.

Policymakers should decide where we draw the line between military and civilian operations, not contractors. Whether or not we support the policies that got us involved, it is in everyone's interest that Afghanistan and Iraq be stabilized, reconstructed and democratized. The more successful the Pentagon's stability operations are, the quicker American troops can be brought home. Partisan quarrels should not obscure the inherent usefulness of the private sector.

Private contractors help Iraqi and U.S. military experts assess damage to an Iraqi pipeline near Basra. The Pentagon contractors are employees of Kellogg, Brown and Root, a subsidiary of Halliburton, the oil and gas conglomerate formerly headed by Vice President Cheney.

"So we would not be running trucks if they did not need to be run." [34]

Despite Halliburton's large investment in Iraq, the mounting scrutiny into its operations could jeopardize its prospects there. "Everybody knows convoys are getting blown up by bombs as they travel down the highways," says Corbin of the Center for Defense Information. "This scandal may actually get Halliburton kicked out of Iraq because if it's true, it's just beyond belief."

Lawmakers and Pentagon officials are stepping up investigations into allegations of waste and cost overruns among private contractors in Iraq. On June 15, government auditors described poor oversight and overcharges by firms providing troop support and reconstruction projects.

"We have no evidence to say there was willful fraud, based on the work we've done so far," said David M. Walker, head of the General Accounting Office (GAO). "But there have been very serious problems." [35] The House Government Reform Committee is expected to hear testimony in July from former Halliburton employees about allegations of overcharging by the contractor.

Tightening Oversight

Even the most hardened critics were surprised by one of the Pentagon's latest contracts, which called for a foreign company headed by a controversial foreign mercenary to be in charge of overseeing contracts in Iraq and coordinating contractor activities in a U.S.-led military operation. In May, the Army awarded the three-year, $293 million contract to a British security firm to guard employees of the Program Management Office, responsible for U.S.-funded contracts in Iraq, and to run a new operations center for contractors to help coordinate convoy and staff movements. The firm, Aegis Defense Services, was founded just two years ago by Tom Spicer, a controversial former British special forces officer who worked for warring parties in Sierra Leone and Papua New Guinea in the 1990s. [36]

Contracts with Aegis and many other firms could run into trouble if a measure adopted by the Senate on June 14 becomes law. Included as an amendment to the fiscal 2005 Pentagon reauthorization bill, the measure introduced by Sens. Ron Wyden, D-Ore., and Byron Dorgan, D-N.D., prohibits the government from outsourcing the oversight of Iraq reconstruction to private companies unless the government "is entirely unable" to do the job with federal employees. It also bars the letting of private contracts "if there is even an appearance of conflict of interest for the private company."

"The outsourcing of oversight on Iraq reconstruction is a costly, unsound practice that never should have been permitted in the first place, and it's time to close the door on it now," Wyden said. "This amendment can save American taxpayers untold additional dollars by placing accountability for Iraq reconstruction squarely with the Department of Defense." [37]

Senators have rejected two other Democratic amendments to the Pentagon bill aimed at enhancing congressional oversight of private military contractors. An amendment sponsored by Sen. Christopher Dodd, D-Conn., would have prohibited the use of private contractors in combat missions and to interrogate prisoners. Another, sponsored by Sen. Patrick Leahy, D-Vt., would have made it a crime to overcharge the government for goods and services in military contracts.

"It's unfortunate that Republican leaders have chosen to do the White House's bidding by killing stiff penalties for those who gouge the taxpayers," Leahy said after the June 16 vote defeating his measure. "We should be defending the public, not the war profiteers." [38]

Opponents said the proposals would jeopardize the effectiveness of U.S. forces at a time of growing violence in Iraq. "Congress should deliberate very carefully a criminal penalty of up to 20 years for these thousands upon thousands of companies that are currently engaged," said Senate Armed Services Committee Chairman John W. Warner, R-Va. [39]

OUTLOOK

After the Handover

The United States formally relinquishes its authority in Iraq on June 30, when it will turn over the reins of government to an interim administration, pending formal elections in January 2005. But the United States will maintain a robust military presence in the country long after the formal handover. It also will retain command over U.S. and Iraqi forces and control the $18.4 billion reconstruction effort. [40]

The Bush administration says it will maintain the current troop level of 138,000 in Iraq through 2005. But that may be hard to do. The Army has already extended soldiers' tours in Iraq, and while the service is currently meeting its recruiting goals, it may have trouble sustaining the planned troop levels over the long-term. [41]

"The U.S. military is 35 percent smaller than it was at the end of the Cold War, but it has far more global commitments, and Iraq is the biggest military commitment in at least a generation," says Singer. "So there's a gap between the supply and demand of military personnel."

All the options for increasing the number of troops on the ground in Iraq — expanding the military, calling up more National Guard reservists, reinstituting the draft and bringing in more allied forces — would be politically costly, he says. "Enlarging the military would force the administration to admit that they were wrong about how many troops would be needed to win the war in Iraq, restoring the draft would spark a huge outcry, and bringing in the allies would force the administration to make political compromises that it has shown it's not willing to make." Indeed, the leaders of NATO members France and Turkey rejected Bush's recent call to add NATO forces to the 138,000 U.S. contingent and 15,000 soldiers from Britain and 32 other coalition members after the handover. [42]

The manpower solution that imposes the least political cost to the administration, Singer says, is to rely even more heavily on private military contractors. "There are none of the costs associated with the other options, the public remains only limitedly aware of it, and when casualties happen there's not the same kind of outcry," he says. "In fact, they aren't even reported in the public record."

Indeed, most experts predict that private military contractors will continue to play an essential role in Iraq for the foreseeable future. "There aren't too many short-term solutions to the manpower problem in Iraq," says Peters of the Council on Foreign Relations. "Just about everybody in the active Army and Marine Corps is either in Iraq, on their way to Iraq or has just come back from Iraq. So there's not a lot of flexibility, and that's part of the challenge that the military faces."

NOTES

1. For background on Bush administration interpretations of prisoner protections, see David Masci, "Ethics of War," *The CQ Researcher*, Dec. 13, 2002, pp. 1013-1032.

2. See Curt Anderson, "CIA Contractor Charged in Detainee Death," The Associated Press, June 18, 2004.

3. The CPA, created by the United States in early 2003 to oversee reconstruction in post-conflict Iraq, will hand over authority to the interim Iraqi government on June 30. For background, see L. Elaine Halchin, "The Coalition Provisional Authority (CPA): Origins, Characteristics, and Institutional Authorities," CRS Report for Congress, Congressional Research Service, April 29, 2004.

4. From a television interview with WAVY-TV in Hampton Roads, Va., April 6, 2004.

5. Levin spoke May 7, 2004, at a Senate Armed Services Committee hearing on Iraqi prison abuses.

6. See P.W. Singer, *Corporate Warriors* (2003), p. 78.

7. Charles L. Schultze, senior fellow emeritus, Brookings Institution, based on Commerce Department data.

8. See Elisabeth Bumiller and Edward Wong, "Iraq Seeks Custody of Hussein; Bush Has Security Concerns," *The New York Times*, June 16, 2004, p. A1.

9. Schakowsky press release following the indictment of a CIA contractor for prisoner abuse in Afghanistan, June 17, 2004.

10. Office of Management and Budget, "Competitive Sourcing: Report on Competitive Sourcing Results, Fiscal Year 2003," May 2004.

11. Larry Margasak, "Committee to seek testimony from Halliburton executives," The Associated Press, June 15, 2004.

12. General Accounting Office, "Fiscal Year 2003 Contract Award Procedures and Management Challenges," June 2004.

13. See, for example, Andrew Buncombe, "You Don't Have to Be Poor to Work There, But It Helps," *The Independent* (London), June 15, 2004, p. 26.

14. See John Hendren and Mark Mezzetti, "U.S. Charges Contractor Over Beating of Afghan Detainee," *Los Angeles Times*, June 18, 2004 p. A6.

15. See Seymour M. Hersh, "Torture at Abu Ghraib," *The New Yorker*, June 15, 2004, p. 42.

16. See Adam Liptak, "Who Would Try Civilians of U.S.? No One in Iraq," *The New York Times*, May 26, 2004.

17. Unless otherwise noted, information in this section is based on Singer, *op. cit.*, pp. 19-39.

18. *Ibid.*, p. 31.

19. *Ibid.*, p. 37.

20. www.cagw.org.

21. See Council on Foreign Relations, "Iraq: Military Outsourcing," May 20, 2004, www.cfr.org.

22. For background on Clinton-era government downsizing efforts, see Susan Kellam, "Reinventing Government," *The CQ Researcher*, Feb. 17, 1995, pp. 145-168.

23. See Robert O'Harrow and Ellen McCarthy, "Private Sector Has Firm Role at the Pentagon," *The Washington Post*, June 9, 2004, p. E1.

24. See Eugene B. Smith, "The New Condottieri and U.S. Policy: The Privatization of Conflict and its Implications," *Parameters*, winter 2002-03, pp. 104-119. *Parameters* is a quarterly magazine published by the U.S. Army War College.

25. See David Shearer, "Outsourcing War," *Foreign Policy*, fall 1998, p. 70.

26. For background, see Kenneth Jost, "Re-examining 9/11," *The CQ Researcher*, June 4, 2004, pp. 493-516, and David Masci and Kenneth Jost, "War on Terrorism," *The CQ Researcher*, Oct. 12, 2001, pp. 817-848.

27. For more information, see Council on Foreign Relations, "Iraq: Military Outsourcing," www.cfr.org.

28. "Private Security Companies Operating in Iraq," an attachment to a letter from Defense Secretary Donald Rumsfeld to Rep. Ike Skelton, D-Mo., May 4, 2004.

29. James Cox, "Contractors Pay Rising Toll in Iraq," *USA Today*, June 16, 2004, p. 1A.

30. "Vice President Dick Cheney and Mrs. Cheney Release 2003 Income Tax Return," The White House, April 13, 2004, www.whitehouse.gov.

31. Quoted in "Cheney Faults 'Desperate' Attacks on Halliburton," CNN.com, Jan. 23, 2004. See also Robert O'Harrow Jr., "E-Mail Links Cheney's Office, Contract," *The Washington Post*, June 2, 2004, p. A6.

32. See Erik Eckholm, "Evidence Suggests Cheney Knew of Oil Contracts," *The International Herald Tribune*, June 15, 2004, p. 4.

33. See Seth Borenstein, "Trucks Made to Drive Without Cargo in Dangerous Areas of Iraq," Knight Ridder/Tribune News Service, May 23, 2004.

34. Quoted in Kathleen Schalch, "Halliburton Trucks Reportedly Traveling in Iraq Empty Instead of Hauling Supplies to Troops," National Public Radio, "Morning Edition," June 8, 2004.

35. Walker testified June 15, 2004, before the House Government Reform Committee. See Erik Eckholm, "Auditors Testify About Waste in Iraq Contracts," *The New York Times*, June 16, 2004, p. A13.

36. See Mary Pat Flaherty, "Iraq Work Awarded to Veteran of Civil Wars," *The Washington Post*, June 16, 2004, p. E1.

37. From a press release by Sen. Wyden's office, wyden.senate.gov.

38. From a press statement issued by Leahy's office on June 16, 2004.

39. Quoted in Carl Hulse, "Senate Rejects Harder Penalties on Companies, and Ban on Private Interrogators," *The New York Times*, June 17, 2004, p. A8.

40. See Jeffrey Gettelman, "Iraqis Start to Exercise Power Even Before Date for Turnover," *The New York Times*, June 13, 2004, p. A1.

41. See Monica Davey, "Recruiters Try New Tactics to Sell Wartime Army," *The New York Times*, June 14, 2004, p. A1.

42. See Glenn Kessler and Dana Milbank, "Leaders Dispute NATO Role in Iraq," *The Washington Post*, June 10, 2004, p. A6.

BIBLIOGRAPHY

Books

Pelton, Robert Young, *The Hunter, the Hammer, and Heaven: Journeys to Three Worlds Gone Mad*, The Lyons Press, 2002.
This journalistic account of wars in Sierra Leone, Chechnya and Bougainville (an island that recently seceded from New Guinea) includes a description of the role of private contractors in determining the outcome of modern conflicts.

Singer, P.W., *Corporate Warriors: The Rise of the Privatized Military Industry*, Cornell University Press, 2003.
Outsourcing military services enables the Defense Department to more efficiently manage U.S. military forces, but it also poses questions about congressional oversight of the military and the legal status of contractors overseas, the director of the Project on U.S. Policy Towards the Islamic World at the Brookings Institution writes.

Articles

Ante, Spencer E., "The Other U.S. Military," *Business Week*, May 31, 2004, p. 76.
Military contracting is a growing business, with billions of dollars in contracts in Iraq's reconstruction alone, but contractors appear to operate there with little oversight by Congress or executive agencies.

Avant, Deborah, "Mercenaries," *Foreign Policy*, July/August 2004, pp. 20-28.
A George Washington University political science professor answers several frequently asked questions about the use of private military contractors by the U.S. military.

Burger, Timothy J., and Adam Zagorin, "The Paper Trail," *Time*, May 30, 2004.
Vice President Dick Cheney's office rejects charges that Cheney, a former CEO of Halliburton, had a hand in the company's landing a lucrative, no-bid contract to restore Iraq's oil industry.

Cox, James, "Contractors Pay Rising Toll in Iraq, Insurgents Target Civilian Workers," *USA Today*, June 16, 2004, p. 1B.
Insurgents are attacking civilian contractors whose services are vital to Iraq's reconstruction.

Hersh, Seymour M., "Chain of Command," *The New Yorker*, May 17, 2004, pp. 38-43.
One in a series of articles by the author into the prisoner-abuse scandal at Abu Ghraib prison describes interrogation techniques used by U.S. soldiers and private contractors.

Schwartz, Nelson D., "The Pentagon's Private Army," *Fortune*, March 17, 2003, p. 100.
Even before the United States invaded Iraq last year, the U.S. military relied heavily on private contractors to provide essential services for troops.

Shearer, David, "Outsourcing War," *Foreign Policy*, fall 1998, pp. 68-81.
This review of the history of private military contractors raises the problem of their accountability to governments in an era of rapidly spreading regional conflicts.

Smith, Eugene B., "The New Condottieri and U.S. Policy: The Privatization of Conflict and Its Implications," *Parameters*, winter 2002-2003, pp. 104-119.
This article in the journal of the U.S. Army War College describes the rise of private military contractors in the wake of the Cold War's end and subsequent downsizing of the American military.

Reports and Studies

Beelman, Maud, "Winning Contractors: U.S. Contractors Reap the Windfalls of Post-War Reconstruction," Center for Public Integrity, Oct. 30, 2003.
The watchdog group examines allegations of fraud and cronyism between high-ranking government officials and companies that receive lucrative contracts with little congressional oversight.

General Accountability Office, "Military Operations: Contractors Provide Vital Services to Deployed Forces but Are Not Adequately Addressed in DOD Plans," June 2003.

The investigative arm of Congress finds that while the Pentagon considers private contractors to be part of U.S. forces in Iraq, it was unable to provide the cost of their contribution to the military mission.

House Committee on Government Reform, Minority Staff, Special Investigations Division, and Senate Democratic Policy Committee, "Contractors Overseeing Contractors: Conflicts of Interest Undermine Accountability in Iraq," May 18, 2004.

Democratic lawmakers criticize the Coalition Provisional Authority's hiring of private firms to oversee the work of private contractors in Iraq with which they have business ties.

For More Information

Citizens Against Government Waste, 1301 Connecticut Ave., N.W., Suite 400, Washington, DC 20036; (202) 467-5300; www.cagw.org/site/PageServer. Advocates the elimination of waste and inefficiency in government and publishes periodic exposés of pork-barrel spending.

Defense Procurement and Acquisition Policy, Defense Department, 3060 Defense, Pentagon, #3E1044, Washington, DC 20301-3060; (703) 695-7145; www.acq.osd.mil/dpap. The Pentagon's office for assessing procurement policies serves as a liaison between the Defense Department and its civilian contractors.

General Accounting Office, 441 G St., N.W., Suite 1139, Washington, DC 20548; (202) 512-3000; www.gao.gov. The investigative arm of Congress has conducted many studies of contracting practices of federal agencies.

International Peace Operations Association, 1900 L St., N.W., Suite 320, Washington, DC 20036; (202) 464-0721; www.ipoaonline.org. Represents private military contractors.

Project on Government Oversight, 666 11th St., N.W., Suite 500, Washington, DC 20001-4542; (202) 347-1122; www.pogo.org. A watchdog group dedicated to exposing government waste, fraud and corruption, especially in military contracting.

14

International Law

Kenneth Jost

Suspected al Qaeda terrorist Hamed Abderrahman Ahmed, a Spanish Muslim, was released after two years in custody at the U.S. Naval Base in Guantanamo Bay, Cuba. He will be tried in Spain and faces life in prison. Critics contend the Bush administration's harsh treatment of the Guantanamo detainees defies international law.

AFP/Getty Images/Christophe Simon

From *CQ Researcher*,
December 17, 2004.

A t first glance, the U.S. government's terrorism case against Salim Ahmed Hamdan seems rock solid. For nearly five years, the Yemeni native served as driver and sometimes bodyguard for Osama bin Laden, the infamous head of the al Qaeda terrorist network.

Hamdan also delivered weapons, munitions and other supplies to al Qaeda training camps inside Afghanistan, the government says, and learned of al Qaeda's role in the 1998 bombings of U.S. embassies in Kenya and Tanzania, the 2000 bombing of the *USS Cole* and the Sept. 11, 2001, attacks on the World Trade Center and the Pentagon.

But Hamdan — now in his third year of detention at the U.S. Naval Base at Guantanamo Bay, Cuba — insists he is not a terrorist. He says he took the job as bin Laden's driver in 1996 simply to earn a living.

Hamdan says Afghan bounty hunters turned him over to U.S. forces in Afghanistan in October 2001 and that he cooperated with the Americans in every way. For his troubles, he says he was physically abused in Afghanistan and then held in solitary confinement at Guantanamo Bay since June 2002.

Such factual disputes are regularly resolved in trials based on direct testimony and circumstantial evidence offered by prosecution and defense. For more than two years, however, the government has insisted that Hamdan be tried before a special military commission with limited procedural rights and no review in the regular judicial system.

The government suffered a major setback in the case on Nov. 28, 2004, when a federal judge in Washington, D.C., ruled the pro-

U.S. Businesses Sued for Rights Abuses Overseas

Foreign plaintiffs are using the federal Alien Tort Statute to try to win damages from U.S. and other multinational corporations for their roles in alleged human rights abuses in countries around the world. None of the plaintiffs has won a judgment since the first case was filed against Unocal Corp. in 1995. But business groups say the suits represent a major financial threat to companies operating overseas. Here are summaries of a few of the major cases:

Name of Case Issues. *Status*	(Citation/Case Number)
Aguinda v. Texaco, Inc. Ecuadorians sued Texaco for environmental damage attributed to an oil pipeline leak. *Dismissed on ground suit should be tried in Ecuador.*	**303 F.3d 470 (2d Cir. 2002)**
In re South African Apartheid Litigation Consolidated cases by South African citizens against more than 100, mostly U.S.-based, corporations seeking more than $200 billion in damages for alleged collaboration in murder, torture, forced relocation and other abuses under former apartheid policies. *Dismissed on ground complaints did not sufficiently allege violations of international law.*	**MDL 1499 (S.D.N.Y. 2004)**
Bano v. Union Carbide Corp. Victims of 1984 toxic gas disaster at Bhopal, India, chemical plant sued in U.S. court in 1999, for damages beyond a settlement approved in Indian court in 1991. *Alien Tort Statute claims dismissed; environmental claims reinstated.*	**273 F.3d 120 (2d Cir. 2001)**
Doe v. Exxon Mobil Corp. Eleven Indonesian villagers in northern region of Aceh, Sumatra, claim Exxon Mobil responsible for human rights abuses by military unit assigned to guard facilities. *Pending on defendants' motion to dismiss, supported by U.S. government.*	**01-CV-1357 (D.D.C.)**
Doe v. Unocal Corp. Plaintiffs filed parallel federal, state court suits claiming Unocal is liable for human rights abuses by Myanmar military in conjunction with construction of gas pipeline. *Unocal agreed to settle the case in December 2004 for a still-to-be negotiated amount.*	**BC 237-980 (Los Angeles County Superior Court)**
Sarei v. Rio Tinto PLC Plaintiffs charged a British-based company with destruction of a Papua New Guinea (PNG) rain forest as a result of copper-mining operations and with PNG government collaboration to suppress a civilian uprising against reopening of the mine. *Dismissed under "political question doctrine."*	**221 F. Supp. 2d 1116 (C.D. Cal. 2002)**
Sinaltrainal v. Coca-Cola Co. A Colombian trade union claims Coca-Cola hired paramilitary units to terrorize and murder trade union organizers at bottling plants in Colombia. *Pending trial.*	**01-CV-03208 (S.D. Fla.)**
Wiwa v. Royal Dutch Petroleum Co. Current or former Nigerians claim Royal Dutch Shell conspired with military government to unlawfully suppress Nigerian opposition movement. *Pending after appeal court reversed lower court's decision that case should be tried in Nigeria.*	**226 F.3d 88 (2d Circ. 2000)**

Sources: Center for Constitutional Rights; Institute for International Economics; International Labor Rights Fund

ceedings unlawful. U.S. District Judge James Robertson said the military commissions not only violated the Uniform Code of Military Justice (UCMJ) but also international law — specifically, the Geneva Conventions — by denying Hamdan prisoner-of-war status without a prior hearing to decide the question.

"The government must convene a competent tribunal . . . and seek a specific determination as to Hamdan's status under the Geneva Conventions," Robertson wrote in the 45-page ruling. "Until or unless such a tribunal decides otherwise, Hamdan has, and must be accorded, the full protections of a prisoner of war." [1]

Robertson's ruling represents the latest and perhaps the highest-profile example of the growing role of international law in legal disputes within the United States — and the growing controversy over that role. An increasing number of civil plaintiffs or criminal defendants are basing claims or defenses on international law, including — but not limited to — provisions of treaties ratified by the United States.

In recent cases, for example, the Supreme Court has been asked to look to decisions by international and foreign courts to determine the constitutionality of capital punishment of juvenile offenders or state anti-sodomy laws. The justices are also being asked to order a new hearing for a Mexican national facing execution in Texas on the ground that he was not allowed to see a Mexican consul before trial as required by an international treaty signed — and actively pushed — by the United States.

Meanwhile, lower federal courts have been asked to award damages to foreign plaintiffs for human rights violations committed overseas by foreign government officials or, in some cases, big multinational corporations. A Supreme Court ruling in June 2004 limited but did not completely bar such suits brought under a 1789 law, the Alien Tort Statute.

International law is a hard-to-grasp concept that inspires idealistic hopes for world peace among supporters and fears of loss of national sovereignty among skeptics. Its origins lie in what is called "customary international law" — practices such as diplomatic immunity or freedom of the seas that came to be accepted as binding by nation-states despite the lack of any international court or enforcement bodies.

Historically, the United States has favored and promoted an expanded scope of international law — through bilateral and multilateral treaties and creation of international forums, including the United Nations.

"International law has been an important vehicle for the United States to advance its interests and values and to mobilize international support for actions it wants to pursue," says Jane Stromseth, who teaches international law at Georgetown University Law Center in Washington.

Conservatives in the United States have often resisted these efforts — for example, by blocking U.S. participation in the League of Nations after World War I and periodically complaining about loss of U.S. sovereignty because of various international treaties or actions of the United Nations. More recently, consumer, environmental and labor groups have charged that the World Trade

U.N. Secretary-General Kofi Annan challenged President Bush's doctrine of "pre-emptive, unilateral, military force" in attacking Iraq. "From our point of view and from the [U.N.] Charter point of view, it was illegal," he said.

Organization (WTO) infringes U.S. sovereignty by establishing free-trade rules that limit the ability to support domestic producers or set strict environmental or consumer protection standards. (*See sidebar, p. 304.*)

The Bush administration has drawn waves of criticism for policies that critics say amount to defiance of or contempt for international law, including the decision to deny POW status to detainees at Guantanamo Bay. In explaining the decision to go to war against Iraq, Bush at times has advocated a policy of "preventive" or "pre-emptive" war that critics say violates the U.N. Charter's provisions on the use of military force. (*See "At Issue," p. 315.*)

The administration also has strongly opposed U.S. participation in the International Criminal Court (ICC), the permanent U.N. war crimes tribunal established in 2002 under terms of a 1998 treaty signed by 120 countries. Bush in 2002 revoked the U.S. signature to the treaty, fearing that American service members would be subject to prosecution before the tribunal. The administration insists that countries receiving American military aid agree to shield U.S. service members from prosecution before the tribunal.

"This administration has pursued more of a line that says if the rules don't suit us, we'll ignore them," says Anne-Marie Slaughter, dean of the Woodrow Wilson School of Public and International Affairs at Princeton University in New Jersey. "The view has been that we can afford to do that."

For now, Hamdan's lawyers are asking the Supreme Court to review his case quickly in hopes of an early resolution of the rules for military commissions at Guantanamo. The government says the case should follow normal procedure and go first to the U.S. Court of Appeals for the District of Columbia. The justices are expected to decide how to handle the case in January 2005.

As the administration continues to fend off criticisms of its policies, and U.S. courts continue to deal with a variety of international-law issues, here are some of the major questions being debated:

Should the United States give more weight to international law in foreign policy?

Barely two weeks after the 9/11 terrorist attacks, the Bush administration asked the United Nations Security Council to stiffen the international community's stand against terrorism. Unanimously and with unusual speed, the council approved a resolution requiring nations to seek to suppress terrorists and terrorist organizations by, among other things, freezing their assets, denying them safe haven and preventing movement across borders. "We are very encouraged by the Security Council's strong support and rapid, unanimous action," U.S. Delegate John Negroponte declared. [2]

Two years later, however, the administration bypassed the Security Council when it launched the U.S.-led invasion of Iraq. In his message to Congress on March 19, 2003, President Bush sought to justify the war as a means "to bring Iraq into compliance with its obligations" under Security Council resolutions. But the administration started the war without council approval because it could not muster the necessary nine votes in the 15-member council nor would it have been able to avert a possible veto from France and Russia — two of the five permanent members with veto power over resolutions. [3]

Administration officials and their supporters defend the invasion in terms of international law in part by claiming a right of self-defense under the United Nations Charter for either an actual attack or an "imminent threat" of attack. "The right to use force pre-emptively is not a novel concept in international law or in the history of the United States," says William Howard Taft IV, the State Department's legal adviser.

Critics disagree with the administration's so-called pre-emptive war doctrine, both as theory and in practice. And U.N. Secretary-General Kofi Annan told the BBC unequivocally that he considers the war in Iraq was not in conformity with the U.N. Charter. Asked pointedly about its legality, he said, "From our point of view and from the charter point of view it was illegal." [4]

"It is controversial that a country can act to prevent states from acquiring certain weapons in the future," says Stromseth, referring to the administration's claimed rationale to find and destroy Iraq's alleged weapons of mass destruction. The disputes over the legality of the invasion, she adds, left many countries reluctant to commit troops to the war or help support the post-conflict reconstruction.

Critics also say the administration weakened international support for its policies by skirting international law with its treatment of detainees after the Afghanistan war and prisoners captured in the Iraq war. "We have always been the strongest proponent of the Geneva Conventions," says Slaughter. "Effectively, we just said none of those rules applies here," leaving the impression "that this administration is inventing its own rules."

The administration, however, insists that the Geneva Conventions are out of date — written to govern the treatment of uniformed soldiers of nation-states, not clandestine members of terrorist networks. "This is a new circumstance that we've never seen before," says John Yoo, a law professor at the University of California, Berkeley, who helped devise the legal rationale for the administration's policies while serving as deputy director of the Justice Department's Office of Legal Counsel. "The last thing you would do is to say we ought to stay with the same categories and rules that we had on Sept. 10 — because those failed."

Even sympathetic international-law experts acknowledge misgivings with the administration's stances. "The U.S. legal case didn't quite make it, but I am strongly in favor of the invasion," says John Murphy, a law professor at Villanova University in Pennsylvania. "It pains me to say that, as an international lawyer."

The United States was forced to take action to oust Iraqi President Saddam Hussein because of obstructionism by France and Russia at the Security Council, Murphy says. "When you have . . . an ally actively undermining the efforts of the Security Council to require Saddam Hussein to comply with all the obligations, . . . and you have a person who's as evil as he was, it was necessary to remove him," Murphy says.

But Slaughter says the United States risks longer-term costs to foreign policy interests by acting unilaterally instead of following international law. "It's a way of reassuring other nations that we are not going to be a rogue elephant, that we're not simply going to crash around the international system and do what we want," she says. "It's important that other nations be reassured because otherwise they have every reason to start balancing against us."

Yoo counters that critics misunderstand international law, which he says depends as much on what nations do as what treaties they sign. "Some people . . . think nations cannot use force unless they're under threat of imminent attack or the U.N. Security Council authorizes it," he says. "Anyone who looks at the practice of states since 1945 can see that that's not the practice states have followed."

Slaughter and Stromseth see some need to change international law in the post-9/11 era. "There is scope for a new understanding of the right of self-defense against non-state actors," Stromseth says. Slaughter says some of the provisions of the Geneva Conventions do not apply in conflicts with a non-state enemy.

But they and others say the United States would be better served by seeking international agreement on any changes instead of acting on its own. "When we end up doing something unilaterally, we pay the price somewhere else," says Harold Hongju Koh, dean of Yale Law School and the State Department's human rights chief under President Bill Clinton. "We strain our alliance and we end up having trouble in other areas of our foreign policy."

Should the Supreme Court consider international and foreign law in making decisions?

Lawyers seeking to bar the execution of juvenile offenders in the United States often cite the prohibition against the practice by international treaty and by national law or practice in all but four other countries. * But when a

Defense Secretary Donald Rumsfeld and Chairman of the Joint Chiefs Gen. Richard Myers have maintained that holding the Guantanamo Bay detainees without trial does not violate the Geneva Conventions.

lawyer for the state of Missouri was asked during recent Supreme Court arguments whether the justices should take international or foreign law into account in deciding the issue, he bluntly said no.

"That's not for this court to decide," Missouri state solicitor James Layton said during the Oct. 13 argument in a case brought by death row inmate Christopher Simmons. "Congress should consider that. The legislatures should consider that. It's an important consideration, but it is not a consideration under the Eighth Amendment." [5]

The arguments provided the latest airing of an issue that has become a flash point between conservatives and liberals and some moderates both on and off the court. Liberal advocacy groups want the court to look to international and foreign law for possible guidance on some constitutional issues. "We can and, I believe, should look to international law as a way of informing our own judgments about our laws and our policies," says Virginia Sloan, executive director of the Constitution Project, a bipartisan group in Washington that filed a brief in support of Simmons' plea to the Supreme Court.

---

* The countries are: Iran, Saudi Arabia, Nigeria and Congo, according to Amnesty International.

Do Trade Treaties Challenge U.S. Authority?

The tiny Caribbean nation of Antigua and Barbuda recently taught the United States a potentially costly lesson in the power of international law. It won a ruling from the World Trade Organization (WTO) in November 2004 that two U.S. laws prohibiting Internet gambling — along with four similar state laws — violate a global agreement liberalizing trade in services. Antigua and Barbuda had complained before the WTO that its offshore gambling industry declined more than 50 percent after the United States cracked down on Internet gambling.

The Bush administration is appealing the ruling, arguing that states and the federal government can regulate gambling under their longstanding authority to protect public morals and public order. But legal scholars say the Antigua decision could encourage other countries to challenge any law restricting gambling, including gambling monopolies run by state lotteries and Indian tribes and limits on the number of slot machines or casinos allowed in a state.

"If Antigua can challenge federal and state laws related to Internet gambling, then other countries can challenge state laws related to bricks-and-mortar gambling," says Georgetown University law Professor Robert K. Stumberg. Moreover, he adds, "lots and lots of state laws" could conceivably be seen as restraints of trade and are now vulnerable to challenges from overseas corporations.

Antigua's WTO triumph underscores growing concern that international trade laws grant dispute-settlement tribunals broad, new powers that enable them to challenge the legality of a variety of federal, state and local laws both here and abroad, and, in at least two cases, have even challenged U.S. court decisions.

"There are grave implications here," California Supreme Court Chief Justice Ronald M. George said. "It's rather shocking that the highest courts of the state and federal governments could have their judgments circumvented by these tribunals." [1]

The controversial tribunals have been established by the WTO, created in 1995 to regulate global trade, and the North American Free Trade Agreement (NAFTA), adopted in 1994 to open up trade between Canada, Mexico and the United States. But because the trade arbitration panels give top priority to the free flow of goods and services above all other considerations, critics say they can force local, state and federal governments to either eliminate or weaken domestic laws that protect health, safety, the environment and worker rights.

WTO rulings that have raised concerns include cases in which countries have challenged U.S. laws designed to protect dolphins and sea turtles; Clean Air Act rules requiring clean-burning gasoline; and regulations to prevent the importation of invasive species into the United States. For its part, the United States has challenged or threatened to challenge, among other things, Japan's automobile efficiency and emission policies designed to meet an international anti-global warming treaty and a European Union ban on the sale of furs from animals caught with steel jaw leg traps.

Global trade advocates point out that a WTO tribunal cannot actually overturn or nullify a domestic law. The government whose law is declared a barrier to trade can either change the offending law or keep it on the books. But by retaining the law, the government must pay damages, which can range in the hundreds of millions of dollars. Most governments choose to change their laws rather than pay the damages. Often, say critics of the current global trade regime, the mere threat of a WTO challenge discourages lawmakers from even proposing certain environmental, safety or workers'-rights laws.

Moreover, under a little-known provision of NAFTA, called Chapter 11, broad, new powers are granted to corporations that some legal scholars and critics say redefine property rights in a way that goes far beyond the rights recognized by U.S. courts or enjoyed by U.S. companies. In fact, the U.S. Congress has repeatedly rejected the broader definition of property rights allowed under the new NAFTA provision. [2]

Under Chapter 11, any foreign corporation that might potentially lose money due to a government action, such as a local zoning law or a state court decision, may sue the national government for damages. The provision ostensibly was included to protect international investors from having their property expropriated by foreign governments, as Mexico did in 1938 when it nationalized its oil industry.

However, under the NAFTA provision corporations are claiming damages even though no actual property has been seized, but when the company perceives that a government action could *potentially* cut into a portion of its future profits. Already, more than 20 Chapter 11 cases have been filed, demanding almost $14 billion from U.S., Canadian and Mexican taxpayers as compensation for corporate "losses" that allegedly occurred due to local land-use decisions, environmental and public health policies, and even adverse court rulings. (American companies are not allowed to file such cases in U.S. courts.) [3]

For instance, in 1999 the Canadian methanol manufacturer Methanex Corp. sued the United States, demanding

$970 million in damages from U.S. taxpayers to compensate the company's anticipated loss of profits due to California's ban on the use of the gasoline additive methyl tertiary butyl ether (MTBE), a potentially carcinogenic chemical that was leaking into groundwater. Despite the environmental damage, Methanex claimed California's ban was an unfair restraint of trade under NAFTA. The case is still pending. [4]

In two unprecedented Chapter 11 cases foreign corporations that lost cases in U.S. domestic courts have taken those cases to be "reheard" under NAFTA's Chapter 11 provision. One case challenged the concept of sovereign immunity involving a contract dispute with the City of Boston, and the other challenged the rules of civil procedure, the jury system and a damage award in a Mississippi state court contract dispute. [5]

Having an international tribunal reviewing U.S. court judgments amounts to "the biggest threat to United States judicial independence that no one has heard of, and even fewer people understand," said Georgetown University law Professor John D. Echeverria. [6]

Recently, the Conference of Chief Justices, the National Association of State Attorneys General, the National League of Cities and the National Conference of State Legislatures have criticized the Chapter 11 provisions for impinging on state and court authorities.

University of Chicago law Professor Alan O. Sykes says concerns about NAFTA's two Chapter 11 challenges of U.S. court decisions are largely a tempest in a teapot — at least so far. "It could turn out to be a bigger deal down the road, but so far no great damage has been done by these cases." Technically, he points out, trade tribunals cannot overturn a U.S. court decision; they can only hold a state liable for damages if the tribunal finds the court's decision discriminated against a foreign corporation.

With regard to Chapter 11 decisions redefining corporate property rights, Sykes says, the NAFTA governments have issued a clarification that the provision was not meant to do that. "My feeling is that the arbiters have gotten the message that their decisions have gone too far. They've figured out which end is up, and are trying not to create all sorts of mess."

Critics of the global trading system particularly chafe at the secretiveness and lack of accountability of the often-anonymous three-judge panels that make WTO and NAFTA decisions. "Hidden beneath the 'free trade' cover was an entire, anti-democratic governance system under which policies affecting our daily lives in innumerable ways are decided out of our sight or control," says a Public Citizen assessment of NAFTA. [7]

Indeed, the Methanex case was heard by a three-judge panel in closed-door proceedings, and no one from the California state government or the environmental and consumer-protection groups that had fought for the MTBE ban were notified of the hearings, nor were they allowed to file briefs supporting the measure.

But Sykes dismisses charges that the international trade regime threatens democracy. "Democratically elected leaders signed these treaties because they felt it was in their national interest," he says. "Any time you agree to something under international law, you restrict a country's freedom of action." In exchange, the United States "gets a lot out of these treaties. We get less-expensive imported goods, lower inflation, access to foreign markets and protection for intellectual property abroad."

However, Georgetown's Stumberg says the secrecy is part of a pattern in which a growing number of "hot-button issues" that conservatives have long sought unsuccessfully in Congress and the U.S. courts — such as tort reform, "regulatory takings" reform, sovereign immunity, curtailment of states' regulatory powers and local permitting authority — are now being debated in inaccessible international venues.

"All the kinds of things that investors and governments fight about in U.S. courts are migrating over to these international forums," says Stumberg, adding that he did not think the migration was "by accident."

Indeed, NAFTA's architects knew exactly what they were doing when they wrote Chapter 11, contends Daniel Price, a Washington lawyer who helped to write the provisions. "The parties did not stumble into this. This was a carefully crafted definition. NAFTA checks the excesses of unilateral sovereignty." [8]

---

[1] Quoted in Adam Liptak, "Review of U.S. Rulings by Nafta Tribunals Stirs Worries," *The New York Times*, April 18, 2004, Sec. 1, p. 20.

[2] Under U.S. law, a company can claim damages from a "regulatory taking" only if its actual property has been rendered almost 100 percent useless because of a government action. But the international trade panels are interpreting Chapter 11 to mean that a company's property has been "taken" if a small percentage of its estimated future profits has been impacted. The U.S. government is including Chapter 11 powers in other bilateral and regional trade agreements currently being negotiated, and would eventually like to expand the powers to cover the entire Western Hemisphere under the proposed Free Trade Agreement of the Americas.

[3] "The Ten Year Track Record of the North American Free Trade Agreement: Undermining Sovereignty and Democracy," Public Citizen, 2004.

[4] See William Greider, "The Right and US Trade Law: Invalidating the 20th Century," *The Nation*, Oct. 15, 2001.

[5] The cases are *Loewen v. United States* (Mississippi) and *Mondev International Ltd. v. United States* (Massachusetts).

[6] Greider, *op. cit.*

[7] Public Citizen, *op. cit.*

[8] Greider, *op. cit.*

Conservatives strongly object, saying that international law has no place in interpretation of the U.S. laws and constitutional provisions. "The [Supreme Court's] limited role is to interpret the Constitution," Yoo says. "It's not to ask other countries what our Constitution means or what their constitution means."

The court itself has cited international law in two recent, high-profile decisions. When the court in 2002 prohibited execution of mentally retarded offenders, Justice John Paul Stevens noted in a footnote that "within the world community" the practice was "overwhelmingly disapproved." A year later, Justice Anthony M. Kennedy pointed to the invalidation of anti-sodomy laws by the European Court of Human Rights as a factor in the decision to declare laws banning gay sex unconstitutional in the United States as well. [6]

At least three other justices have commented favorably in public speeches about the use of international law: Sandra Day O'Connor, like Kennedy a moderate conservative, and liberals Ruth Bader Ginsburg and Stephen G. Breyer. On the other hand, Antonin Scalia, the high court's most outspoken conservative, has strongly criticized the practice.

Scalia complained about the citation of international law in his dissents in the earlier capital punishment and gay sex cases. He also sharply questioned Simmons' lawyer on the practice in the pending death penalty case. "It is my view that modern, foreign legal material can never be relevant to any interpretation of, that is to say, to the meaning of the U.S. Constitution," Scalia declared in a speech to the American Society of International Law in April 2004. [7]

Despite the sharp debate, some observers on both sides say the practical effect of the practice is minimal. "You get the sense that it's almost ornamental," Yoo says.

Likewise, Louis Michael Seidman, a liberal constitutional law expert at Georgetown University Law Center, doesn't think the citations "amount to much."

Still, conservative academics and advocacy groups are mounting a full-bore attack on the practice. "The idea that it makes one whit of a difference that many other countries do not execute people who are 16 or 17 makes no sense to me," says Richard Samp, chief counsel of the conservative Washington Legal Foundation. "World opinion is not what gives the authority to federal judges. It is the Constitution."

Speaking to a meeting of the conservative Federalist Society in Washington in November 2004, Pepperdine Law School Professor Roger Alford called the practice "inherently undemocratic" and "prone to judicial hegemony."

Michael Ramsey, a professor at the University of San Diego School of Law, agreed. "No one has adopted a principled theory for deciding when to look at foreign practices other than picking the ones they like," he said. "The use of international practices expressly adopts the view of courts as policy makers."

Liberal academics insist that the practice is far from new, but dates actually from the earliest days of the United States. "The earliest justices were all former diplomats," Koh says. "There was no federal law, only state law and international law."

International-law advocates also liken the practice to judicial decision-making within the United States. "Knowing how a very distinguished judge [in another country] has thought about the issue is no more troubling than a New Jersey judge considering how a California judge has ruled on the issue," Slaughter says.

"The fear among conservatives is that we'll somehow fall prey to some strange, exotic cultural practice from somewhere else," adds Richard Wilson, who directs an international human rights clinic at American University's law school in Washington. "There's very little likelihood that that will happen, and there's a possibility that we may learn something."

Should U.S. courts hear suits for human rights violations abroad?

The accounts in two federal court suits depict widespread abuses of Burmese workers by the Myanmar military during the construction of a natural gas pipeline in the Southeast Asian country — abuses ranging from forced labor and torture to rape and even killings. The suits' principal target is not Myanmar's military junta, however, but the Unocal Corp., the giant California-based, multinational oil and gas company.

The suits, filed under an obscure 18th-century U.S. law alternately called the Alien Tort Claims Act or Alien Tort Statute, seek millions of dollars in damages from Unocal on the theory that the company knowingly aided the enslavement and mistreatment of Burmese workers by the Myanmar military. Unocal denied wrongdoing, but after seeking to have the suits dismissed on legal grounds agreed with the plaintiffs' lawyers in December 2004 to settle the case by paying a still-to-be-negotiated amount for compensation and programs to improve living conditions in the region. [8]

The Unocal cases are the furthest advanced pending suits among dozens filed against current or former foreign government officials or multinational corporations since 1980, when a federal appeals court first opened the door to such suits. The so-called *Filártiga* decision by the New York-based 2nd U.S. Circuit Court of Appeals allowed a Paraguayan physician to sue a former Paraguayan police official for the torture death of his son. [9]

Human rights groups say the suits serve a valuable purpose by enlisting U.S. courts in the cause of promoting compliance with international law. "If we believe in a system of international law, it has to apply here," says Jennifer Green, a senior staff attorney with the New York-based Center of Constitutional Rights, which represents plaintiffs in the Unocal case. "It's necessary if we are committed to human rights law and the rule of universal standards."

But conservative groups and business lobbies say such suits threaten U.S. business and foreign policy interests and typically are out of place in U.S. courts. "The idea that somehow we owe it to the international human rights community to open up our courts to any and all violations of human rights that have occurred around the world is absurd," says the Washington Legal Foundation's Samp.

The dispute turns in part on the meaning of the elliptically phrased statute, contained in the original Judiciary Act of 1789. The law states that federal courts "shall have original jurisdiction of any civil action by an alien for a tort only, committed in violation of the law of nations or a treaty of the United States." Human rights groups say the statute broadly recognizes suits for violations of international law, while conservative and business groups say Congress must specifically authorize any such legal actions.

The Supreme Court split the difference between those views in June 2004 in its first ruling on the law since *Filártiga*. Six justices joined a majority opinion in *Sosa v. Alvarez-Machain* that limited use of the act to international-law violations recognized in the 18th century, such as piracy, or to other violations of norms "accepted by the civilized world and defined with . . . specificity." In a separate opinion for three members of the court, Justice Scalia said he would have limited the acts to suits specifically authorized by Congress. [10]

Human rights groups claimed the decision as a victory. The ruling "endorsed the standard used in the *Filártiga* case," Green says. Business groups took some comfort from restrictive language in the decision, but voiced disappointment that the majority left lower courts with some discretion to recognize new suits. "It leaves wiggle room," Samp says.

Business groups and business-oriented experts complain that suits open multinational corporations to the danger of huge damage awards or costly settlements. "Whenever there exists a deep-pocket defendant, there necessarily exist incentives to bring claims 'on spec' that involve both bold conjectures about facts and ambitious claims about unwritten law," says Paul Stephan, an international business expert at the University of Virginia School of Law in Charlottesville. One recent study found that more than 50 multinational corporations are defendants in alien tort suits with claims exceeding $200 billion. [11]

"I would hope that businesses in general don't subscribe to the theory that these gross human rights violations are a normal part of doing business," counters Green. "We're talking about things that are well defined in international law: torture, genocide. If they engage in those practices, they can expect to be hauled into court."

Critics also say the law can put U.S. courts at odds with the government's diplomatic stance toward other countries. "This kind of litigation has got to be limited because otherwise federal courts are going to be interfering with foreign policy of the executive branches," says former Justice Department official Yoo.

Koh, the State Department's human rights chief for three years, calls that argument "a red herring," arguing that the government "is always free to file a brief, and the court should take that into account." In the Unocal suit, Koh notes that the United States has had "a policy of wholesale condemnation" of the Myanmar government for three administrations.

BACKGROUND

'The Law of Nations'

The United States has professed allegiance to international law since its founding, championed international law throughout its history and played the major role in building the superstructure of international law institutions established since the end of World War II. Even when the United States flexed its diplomatic, economic or military muscle, it has only rarely challenged the idea

CHRONOLOGY

1945-1970s *United Nations founded under U.S. leadership, but peacekeeping machinery paralyzed by Cold War rivalry with Soviet Union.*

1945 U.N. Charter formally approved by 51 countries; creates Security Council as peacekeeping body, with U.S., Soviet Union among five nations with veto power; also establishes International Court of Justice (World Court).

1947 General Agreement on Tariffs and Trade (GATT) binds U.S., other signatories to free-trade rules; superseded by World Trade Organization in 1995.

1949 Geneva Conventions codify rules on treatment of prisoners of war, civilians.

1977 Geneva Conventions expanded to cover civil war, liberation conflicts.

1980s-1990s *Terrorist attacks on U.S. citizens, facilities here and abroad.*

1980 Federal appeals court in *Filártiga* case allows suit under Alien Tort Statute by Paraguayan dissident against Paraguayan police inspector for torture-murder of son; ruling revives use of previously obscure 1789 provision.

1983 U.S. invades Grenada, saying action necessary to protect U.S. citizens; invasion condemned by U.N. General Assembly.

1984-1986 World Court in 1984 backs jurisdiction over suit by Nicaragua claiming U.S. support for contras violates international law; Reagan administration next year terminates U.S. agreement to compulsory jurisdiction; court rules against U.S. in 1986.

1989 U.S. invades Panama, claiming right of self-defense; invasion later condemned by U.N. General Assembly, Organization of American States.

1993 Bombing of World Trade Center, later linked to al Qaeda; Clinton administration initiates criminal prosecutions of perpetrators.

1995 U.S. backs special international war crime tribunals for former Yugoslavia, Rwanda.

1996 Burmese citizens are first to use Alien Tort Statute to sue corporate defendant for rights abuses abroad.

1997 Kyoto Protocol calls on developed nations to reduce "greenhouse gas" emissions to reduce global warming.

1998 U.S. signs treaty to create permanent International Criminal Court to try war crimes cases, but President Bill Clinton does not submit it for ratification. . . . Bombing of U.S. embassies in Kenya, Tanzania, later linked to al Qaeda.

2000-Present *Bush administration often differs with other countries, world opinion on international-law issues.*

2001 President Bush rejects Kyoto Protocol . . . Terrorist attacks on World Trade Center and Pentagon by al Qaeda operatives on Sept. 11 leave nearly 3,000 people dead; U.N. Security Council passes U.S.-backed anti-terrorism resolution on Sept. 28. . . . U.S. leads international coalition to oust Taliban regime in Afghanistan for harboring al Qaeda; hundreds of detainees later transported to Guantanamo Bay Naval Base in Cuba.

2002 Bush revokes U.S. signature on International Criminal Court treaty . . . Supreme Court cites international practice in barring execution of mentally retarded offenders. . . .

2003 President Bush, bypassing U.N. Security Council, launches U.S-led invasion of Iraq in March. . . . Supreme Court in June cites ruling by European Court of Human Rights in striking down state anti-sodomy laws. . . .

2004 Supreme Court on June 28 rejects Bush administration's effort to bar court challenges by Guantanamo detainees; in separate decision next day, justices narrow scope of cases under Alien Tort Statute. . . . Justices in October consider plea to bar execution of juvenile offenders; decision due by June 2005. . . . Federal judge in November says military violating Geneva Conventions by failure to give Guantanamo detainees hearing on POW status. . . . High-level U.N. panel in November rejects doctrine of "preventive" use of force except when authorized by Security Council; U.S. disagrees.

that it was bound, like all countries, to follow the "law of nations." [12]

The authors of the Declaration of Independence in 1776 felt obliged by "a decent respect to the opinions of mankind" to set forth the causes for breaking away from Britain. They proceeded to lay out a detailed indictment of British rule to be judged by "a candid world." Two decades later, with a new nation and a new Constitution, the Supreme Court in 1793 explicitly recognized the applicability of international law. "The United States, by taking a place among the nations of the earth, [became] amenable to the law of nations," Chief Justice John Jay wrote. [13]

Later, as secretary of State, Jay made the first important U.S. contribution to international law by negotiating a treaty with Britain that called for the use of arbitration to resolve remaining Revolutionary War disputes. The Jay Treaty settled most issues between the two countries but provided that three disputes would be resolved by "commissions" composed of one or two members appointed by each party and a third or fifth member chosen by agreement or lot. The two countries also resorted to arbitration after the end of the War of 1812 and again after the Civil War, when the United States in the so-called *Alabama Claims* arbitration successfully sought damages from Britain for building warships for the Confederacy while professing neutrality. [14]

The United States claimed international law on its side in each of its three major international wars of the 19th century. The United States launched the War of 1812 by claiming that Britain — then at war with Napoleonic France — was violating its rights of neutral shipping by seizing U.S. ships and impressing American sailors along with any captured British subjects. President James K. Polk launched the U.S.-Mexican War in 1845 by depicting Mexico's land claims as a violation of the treaty ending the war of Texan independence. And the United States claimed to be backing Cuba's independence from its colonial ruler when it declared war against Spain in 1898. Territorial expansion may have been the main motive in 1845 and economic imperialism in 1898, but the cloak of international law was thrown over both conflicts.

In the aftermath of the Spanish-American War, the Supreme Court once again declared the country's commitment to international law, this time in a dispute arising from the seizure of two Spanish fishing boats off the Cuban coast. The owners of the boats sued to recover damages after the ships and their cargo had been sold as prizes of war. They claimed that international law exempted fishing vessels from capture during war. "International law is part of our law," the Supreme Court declared in its ruling in the boat owners' favor. The court noted that in imposing the blockade of Cuba, President William McKinley had instructed the Navy to follow "the law of nations applicable in such cases." [15]

The United States was primed to enter World War I by Germany's alleged violations of neutral shipping rights with its submarine warfare against U.S. passenger and freight-carrying vessels. In his message asking Congress to declare war against Germany in 1917, President Woodrow Wilson enlarged U.S. goals into "a crusade to make the world safe for democracy." With the war won, Wilson sought to create a new international body that would protect nations against foreign aggression and ensure worldwide peace. The League of Nations failed in both goals, in part because the United States declined to join and in part because its charter included no enforcement powers.

As the world's sole superpower after World War II, the United States set out to establish a new and more effective international body — the United Nations. In one crucial change from the League of Nations, the U.N. Charter created an enforcement tribunal: the Security Council.

The council — which now has 15 members — was given authority to determine the existence of a threat to the peace or an act of aggression and to authorize economic sanctions or military action in response. Security Council resolutions are theoretically binding on all member states. But in a bow to geopolitical realities, the five major World War II victors — the United States, Britain, France, the Soviet Union and China — were each given veto power over any council action. "We set about establishing a set of rules that would take power realities into account but would nevertheless establish rules that everyone would comply with," says Princeton University's Slaughter. [16]

The Rule of Law

The Cold War rivalry between the United States and the Soviet Union largely paralyzed the United Nations' peacekeeping machinery whenever the two nations clashed because both had veto power in the Security

The International Court of Justice, or World Court, cannot require participation or enforce its decisions. Judges arrive at the beginning of hearings to discuss Israel's controversial wall in the Occupied Territories.

Council. Meanwhile, the body of international law was growing through the operations of U.N. agencies and U.N.-supported treaty-making conferences. The United States sometimes supported and sometimes resisted the growing web of international laws.

Only once during the Cold War did the U.N. Security Council authorize military action against the wishes of one of the two rival superpowers. That came in 1950 when communist North Korea invaded the pro-Western South Korea, and the Soviet Union boycotted the Security Council meeting called to consider the crisis. Without a Soviet veto, the council authorized the United States to lead a multinational force to repel the invasion.

Over the next 40 years, the Security Council frequently voted to dispatch "peacekeeping" forces to trouble spots: the Suez Canal in 1956, Congo in 1960, the Kashmir region along the India-Pakistan border in 1965. But the council authorized military intervention only in 1990 — after the end of the Cold War — when it approved a resolution for a U.S.-led force to repel Iraq's invasion of Kuwait.

In the meantime, the laws of war had been consolidated and expanded in two major diplomatic conferences, both times with strong backing from the United States. The four Geneva Conventions — signed on Aug.

12, 1949 — codified rules for treatment of combatants and prisoners of war and extended protections to civilians. To distinguish combatants from civilians, troops are required to wear uniforms and carry arms openly. Combatants who follow the guidelines enjoy various protections, including requirements for humane treatment and limits on interrogation if held as POWs. The fourth convention bars attacks on civilians or the use of civilians as hostages. Two additional protocols signed in 1977 extended the rules to wars of self-determination and other internal conflicts.

The U.N. Charter also established the International Court of Justice (the ICJ or, colloquially, the World Court) as a successor to a comparable tribunal under the League of Nations. The 15-member court, which sits in The Hague, Netherlands, "has not lived up to hopes of many of its early supporters," according to the authors of a leading textbook. [17]

The court has jurisdiction only over countries, not individuals, and cannot require participation or enforce its decisions. In 1980, for example, Iran refused to comply with the court's judgment to release U.S. hostages.

The United States similarly refused to abide by the court's 1986 decision that its support for the Nicaraguan contras violated international law. [18] While the case was pending, the Reagan administration in 1985 decided to terminate U.S. agreement to compulsory ICJ jurisdiction over treaty or other international-law disputes — reversing a policy dating from the Truman administration.

The United States also drew criticism from the U.N. General Assembly for two military actions during the 1980s — the invasions of Grenada in 1983 and Panama in 1989 — though it was designated to lead the Security Council-approved intervention to expel Iraq from Kuwait in 1990.

In the 1990s, however, the Clinton administration strongly supported creation of limited-jurisdiction international tribunals to hear war crimes cases involving genocide and mass murder in the former Yugoslavia and Rwanda. [19] President Clinton also approved use of U.S. troops as part of a U.N. peacekeeping force in Somalia (1993) and backed NATO's intervention — without U.N. approval — twice in the former Yugoslavia: Bosnia (1996) and Kosovo (1999). Clinton also signed the international treaty establishing the International Criminal Court. Upon taking office, President Bush withdrew U.S. approval of the treaty.

International treaties covered an ever-growing list of activities during the second half of the 20th century. One of the first post-war treaties, the General Agreement on Tariffs and Trade (GATT), sought to liberalize trade rules by generally requiring member states to grant other nations equal access to markets and limiting preferential treatment of domestic producers. Signed in 1947, the GATT established a voluntary dispute-settlement system, which was superseded in 1995 by the WTO's mandatory dispute-settlement system.

Among other major treaties, the United States strongly supported pacts in 1970 and 1971 aimed at preventing airline hijackings and the 1987 Montreal Protocol restricting the use of ozone-depleting chlorofluorocarbons. On the other hand, the United States refused to sign the 1982 Law of the Sea Convention because of restrictions on deep-seabed mining. And currently the Bush administration opposes participation in the 1997 Kyoto Protocol, which calls on developed nations to reduce emission of so-called greenhouse gases implicated in causing global warming. [20]

Within the United States, meanwhile, the 2nd U.S. Circuit Court of Appeals in New York created a major new venue for international law disputes with its 1980 decision allowing two Paraguayan citizens to use the Alien Tort Statute to sue a former Paraguayan police official for the torture death of a family member. After the appeals court refused to throw the case out, a lower federal court awarded Joel Filártiga and his daughter $10 million in punitive damages, but they are believed never to have been able to collect any significant amount of the judgment. The 2nd Circuit later allowed Croats and Muslims from Bosnia-Herzegovina to bring a suit for torture and genocide against Radovan Karadzic, the former Serb paramilitary leader now believed to be hiding in Bosnia. A jury in 2000 awarded $4.5 billion in damages, but prospects of any recovery are nil.

Legal conservatives criticized the *Filártiga* case on the grounds that the federal courts' role in international disputes was unwarranted and unhelpful. Criticism grew as foreign plaintiffs sued multinational corporations for a variety of alleged international law violations overseas. Besides the suit by Burmese plaintiffs against Unocal, other noteworthy cases included suits against Royal Dutch Shell for allegedly conspiring with the Nigerian government to crush opposition to oil drilling in the country's Ogoni region; against Texaco for alleged environmental degrada-

tion in the Ecuadorian rain forest; and against an array of companies for alleged complicity with South Africa's former apartheid policies. As of summer 2004, plaintiffs had won judgments in none of the two-dozen such cases. [21]

The Post-9/11 World

The Sept. 11, 2001, terrorist attacks became a watershed in official U.S. attitudes toward international law. The United States won worldwide support for its initial response to the attacks. But a month later President Bush drew domestic and international criticism for his decision to circumvent Geneva Conventions provisions in the treatment of prisoners captured in Afghanistan.

Eighteen months later, in March 2003, Bush bypassed the U.N. Security Council in launching the invasion of Iraq. The administration then drew a new round of criticism with disclosures of alleged abuses of detainees at Guantanamo Bay and in Iraq. With criticism mounting, the Supreme Court in June 2004 issued two rulings rejecting the administration's legal basis for its policies toward the detainees.

Through the 1990s, the Clinton administration had sought criminal prosecutions for terrorist attacks on the World Trade Center (1993) and U.S. embassies in Kenya and Tanzania (1998). However, Clinton rejected an all-out military response other than a failed cruise missile attack on an al Qaeda base in Afghanistan and an alleged chemical weapons factory in Sudan after the embassy bombings. [22]

In September 2001, however, President Bush immediately promised military retaliation for the attacks on the World Trade Center and the Pentagon against al Qaeda and Afghanistan's Taliban government for harboring the terrorist network. Missile strikes on Oct. 7 marked the beginning of a military campaign that toppled the Taliban within two months and left thousands of Afghans and other, mostly Muslim foreigners in U.S. captivity.

In a speech to the U.N. General Assembly on Nov. 10, Bush vowed that the United States would defend itself "against terror and lawless violence." Three days later, Bush signed an order authorizing special military tribunals to try foreigners charged with terrorism, including acts unrelated to the Sept. 11 attacks. The order promised detainees would be treated "humanely," but administration officials said the Geneva Conventions did not apply.

The order prescribed loosened rules of evidence before the tribunals barred detainees from seeking legal review in any U.S., foreign or international court. "The conventional way of bringing people to justice doesn't apply to these times," White House Communications Director Dan Bartlett told reporters. An American Civil Liberties Union official called the order "deeply disturbing." [23]

By early 2002, some 600 foreigners had been transported from Afghanistan to the U.S. naval base at Guantanamo Bay, Cuba. Despite the order, lawyers representing some of the detainees filed *habeas corpus* petitions in federal courts challenging the conditions and procedures as violations of both U.S. and international law. The administration vigorously defended its position in and out of court. Through February 2004, Defense Secretary Donald H. Rumsfeld and other Pentagon officials were suggesting that the detainees could be held without trial for the duration of the war on terrorism.

Behind the scenes, however, Secretary of State Colin L. Powell and others reportedly were calling as early as October 2002 for releasing or transferring some of the less important detainees. [24] The State Department was responding in part to diplomatic pressure from such staunch U.S. allies as Australia and Britain about the detentions; a small number of Australians and Britons were among the captives, and four of them brought one of the *habeas corpus* petitions. Eventually, the administration began releasing some of the detainees, including one of the Britons. But the administration won a significant victory in March 2003 when the federal appeals court in Washington ruled that the Guantanamo detainees had no right to contest their confinement.

Meanwhile, Bush provoked new waves of criticism for advocating what came to be called a right of "preemptive self-defense" against potential attacks from enemy countries or terrorist organizations. In a May 2002 speech at the U.S. Military Academy at West Point, Bush said the United States would "impose pre-emptive, unilateral, military force when and where it chooses." Bush and other administration officials elaborated on the doctrine through the run-up to the war against Iraq even while seeking Security Council support for the planned invasion on other grounds — chiefly, enforcement of previous U.N. resolutions requiring Iraq to disarm.

Within the United States, the doctrine was widely criticized, though criticism receded as leading Democrats became reluctant to oppose Bush's evident intention to go to war. But U.N. Secretary-General Annan publicly challenged the Bush doctrine, as did France and Germany among other countries in opposing Security Council sanction for the invasion. Once major combat had ended in Iraq, criticism increased as doubts grew about Bush's allegations that Iraq had developed weapons of mass destruction — the administration's main justification for the war.

By late 2003 and early 2004, the Supreme Court had also stepped into the debate by agreeing to hear legal challenges to the Guantanamo policies along with separate cases brought by U.S. citizens held as enemy combatants in the United States. In June 2004, the court delivered an unmistakable rebuke to the administration by ruling, 6-3, that federal courts had jurisdiction under U.S. law to hear the detainees' challenges. Neither the majority opinion nor the dissent dealt with the detainees' international-law claims. [25]

In one of the U.S. citizen cases, however, six of the justices said the administration violated either international law or U.S. military regulations by refusing to give the detainee a chance to challenge his confinement before some impartial tribunal. [26]

CURRENT SITUATION

Policies Challenged

The Bush administration continues to face criticism at home and abroad for its policies in the war on terror and in Iraq. In perhaps the most stinging criticism, the International Committee of the Red Cross (ICRC) has charged that the military has subjected detainees at Guantanamo Bay to coercive interrogation and treatment "tantamount to torture."

Reports of the ICRC's claim surfaced in late November as federal courts in Washington were dealing with legal challenges to plans for military commissions to try some of the detainees on terrorism-related charges.

Barely a week later, the American Civil Liberties Union (ACLU) released a trove of government records documenting concerns lodged by Defense Department and FBI personnel about treatment of U.S. captives in Iraq, Afghanistan and Guantanamo.

Meanwhile, the New York-based Center for Constitutional Rights (CCR) is asking a German court to initiate a war-crimes investigation of U.S. officials and military personnel for alleged U.S. mistreatment of Iraqi captives at the Abu Ghraib prison in Baghdad.

"We vehemently deny any allegations of torture at Guantanamo, and reject categorically allegations that the treatment of detainees at Guantanamo is improper," the Pentagon said on Nov. 30, the day *The New York Times* detailed the ICRC's findings. [27]

The Geneva-based ICRC, which is not affiliated with the American Red Cross, declined to release the report. But the organization said it "remains concerned that significant problems regarding conditions and treatment at Guantanamo Bay have not yet been adequately addressed."

The Geneva Conventions specifically mention the ICRC as an organization to monitor treatment of POWs. It regularly sends inspection teams to POW detention centers while promising that any findings will be submitted in confidence to the host government. ICRC teams began visiting the Guantanamo facility in January 2002. In a report publicized in October 2003, the ICRC charged that holding detainees indefinitely without initiating legal proceedings was adversely affecting their mental health.

The Times story disclosed that an unreleased report in January 2003 raised the question of whether "psychological torture" was taking place. The July 2004 report went further, the *Times* said, by depicting the treatment as amounting to physical and psychological coercion aimed at breaking the prisoners' will.

Techniques used, according to the *Times*, included subjecting detainees to "humiliating acts, solitary confinement, temperature extremes and use of forced positions." The report continued: "The construction of such a system, whose stated purpose is the production of intelligence, cannot be considered other than an intentional system of cruel, unusual and degrading treatment and a form of torture."

The ICRC also charged that some medical personnel at the base were participating in planning for interrogation in what it described as "a flagrant violation of medical ethics." The Pentagon replied that detainees were receiving first-rate medical care and denied that medical files were "used to harm detainees." [28]

The documents released by the ACLU included reports by Defense Intelligence Agency (DIA) "debriefers" on allegedly abusive interrogation at Abu Ghraib in violation of the Geneva Conventions as late as May 2004. The DIA personnel said the military interrogation teams obstructed their work by ordering them out

Members of Amnesty International in Barcelona, Spain, call for the liberation of hundreds of detainees being harshly treated and held without trial at the U.S. Naval Base in Guantanamo Bay, Cuba.

of rooms during questioning and confiscating evidence of the alleged abuses. The records were obtained in Freedom of Information Act lawsuits brought by the ACLU in conjunction with CCR, Physicians for Human Rights, Veterans for Common Sense and Veterans for Peace. [29]

In Washington, meanwhile, a ranking government attorney acknowledged in court that evidence obtained by torture could be used in the military commissions planned for some of the Guantanamo detainees. Brian Boyle, principal deputy associate attorney general, made the statement in a hearing Dec. 2 in one of the challenges brought by detainees.

U.S. District Judge Richard Leon asked whether evidence obtained by torture would be admissible before the military's so-called combatant status review tribunals. Boyle answered that if the tribunals "determine that evidence of questionable provenance were reliable, nothing in the Due Process Clause [of the Constitution] prohibits them from relying on it." Boyle later specified that he did not believe torture had taken place at Guantanamo. [30]

Leon, hearing challenges filed by five detainees, expressed some doubts about interfering with the government's plans for the tribunals. The previous day, Senior Judge Joyce Hens Green, who was presiding over consolidated cases brought by 54 detainees, seemed more sympathetic to their objections. Both judges said they would try to issue rulings promptly. [31]

In the other development, CCR invoked a German law claiming universal jurisdiction over alleged war

> ### 'We vehemently deny any allegations of torture at Guantanamo, and reject categorically allegations that the treatment of detainees at Guantanamo is improper.'
>
> — Department of Defense, Nov. 30, 2004

crimes in filing a 102-page complaint stemming from the reported abuses at Abu Ghraib. Those named include Defense Secretary Rumsfeld, former CIA Director George Tenet and various U.S. military personnel.

Death Case Reviewed

The International Court of Justice (ICJ) wants U.S. courts to reconsider death sentences imposed on any foreign nationals denied treaty-granted rights to assistance from consular officials from their home countries before their trials. But the effect of the ICJ's ruling is uncertain as the U.S. Supreme Court considers a Mexican national's effort to use the decision to block his execution for participating in a 1993 gang-related murder in Texas. [32]

The international tribunal's 14-1 ruling on March 31, 2004, came in a case brought by Mexico on behalf of 51 Mexican nationals facing the death penalty for capital murder convictions in the United States. [33] Mexico charged the United States with violating the 1963 Vienna Convention on Consular Relations, which allows people arrested in a foreign nation to meet with diplomatic representatives from their own country and requires officials to advise detainees of that right.

An 18-member U.S. legal team, headed by State Department legal adviser Taft, argued before the tribunal in December 2003 that the Mexicans' rights had not been violated or, alternatively, that any failure to advise them of their rights had not affected their trials. But the court ruled that it was "clear" that the United States had committed "internationally wrongful acts" by "the failure of its competent authorities to inform the Mexican nationals concerned, to notify Mexican consular posts and to enable Mexico to provide consular assistance."

The court rejected Mexico's argument, however, that the violations required nullification of all the convictions. Instead, it said the United States should "permit review and reconsideration" of each case in order to determine whether the violation "caused actual prejudice" to the defendant. The court also said the United States had been making "considerable efforts" to ensure that law enforcement authorities comply with the treaty.

The enforceability of the tribunal's judgment in U.S. courts is uncertain. Six weeks after the ruling, the Oklahoma Court of Criminal Appeals on May 13 halted the execution of one of the Mexicans in the case, Osbaldo Torres; and Gov. Brad Henry commuted Torres' sentence later the same day. But the 5th U.S. Circuit Court of Appeals refused to bow to the ruling six days later in a case involving a Texas death row inmate, Jose Ernesto Medellin. The appeals court said Medellin's claim was "procedurally defaulted" because he had failed to raise the issue until after his trial and appeals in Texas courts.

In its ruling — and in an earlier decision in a case brought by Germany — the ICJ said use of procedural default rules to block review of a foreign national's plea violated the Vienna convention. But the 5th Circuit court said the U.S. Supreme Court had ruled the opposite way in a brief, unsigned decision in 1998 involving a Paraguayan facing execution in Virginia. [34]

Now, Medellin is asking the Supreme Court to determine whether U.S. courts must follow the ICJ's decision "as a matter of international comity and in the interest of uniform treaty interpretation." Medellin's petition is being

Should there be a right of pre-emptive self-defense?

YES
John Yoo
Professor of Law, University of California at Berkeley School of Law

Written for The CQ Researcher, December 2004

In the last five years, the United States has launched three wars against other sovereign nations — in Kosovo, Afghanistan and Iraq. It has also engaged in a global conflict against the al Qaeda terrorist organization. While other countries and legal scholars claim that these interventions violate international law, in reality they recognize an emerging standard for the use of force to prevent threats to international peace and security.

A narrow reading of the U.N. Charter requires that nations use force only in two circumstances: in self-defense against a cross-border attack or when authorized by the U.N. Security Council. By historical practice, nations have also recognized that force may be used to pre-empt attacks that have not yet occurred but are "imminent." Obviously, neither the United States nor other nations have obeyed this standard. During the Cold War, for example, the United States resorted to armed force many times in places like Vietnam, Grenada and Panama, yet the U.N. authorized the use of force only twice (in Korea and the first Iraq war).

A more flexible approach to the use of force is demanded by the significant changes in the international and technological environment. A strict U.N. standard might have made sense at the end of World War II, when the problem was vast wars between nation-states, and the U.S. wanted to reduce the level of international violence to zero.

Today, however, we are faced with the threat of terrorism, rogue nations and the proliferation of weapons of mass destruction (WMD). As we learned on Sept. 11, 2001, we may have little or no warning that a terrorist attack is "imminent." Nations may only have narrow windows of opportunity to strike at threats before they become difficult or impossible to stop. Rather than ask whether an attack is about to occur, we should ask whether the use of force is reasonable in light of the magnitude of potential harm that a terrorist or rogue nation could inflict.

The wars in Kosovo, Afghanistan and Iraq also make clear that the use of force cannot be limited to self-defense alone. A failed state, which can allow terrorists to flourish, or the reckless ambitions of a despotic tyrant present threats to international peace and security.

Requiring approval from the Security Council — filled with nations only too happy to use their vetoes to protect their parochial interests — to stop threats of terrorism, rogue nations and WMD only discourages efforts to supply the world with the most valuable international public good of all: stability and security.

NO
Mary Ellen O'Connell
William B. Saxbe Designated Professor of Law and Fellow, Mershon Center for International Security, The Ohio State University

Written for The CQ Researcher, December 2004

Today's law on self-defense is found in the United Nations Charter. It was written largely by the United States, and it allows unilateral force in self-defense only when an armed attack occurs. Any other situation in which a state wants to use significant armed force requires authorization through the collective decision-making process of the U.N. Security Council.

Thus, the law prohibits the use of armed force to pre-empt a future attack unless prior authorization is received from the Security Council. (The charter's rules on self-defense parallel very closely the self-defense rules in U.S. criminal law: You can't fight back until attacked and, anticipating an attack, you go to the authorities to prevent the attack.)

The United States wrote these rules with the Nazi example very much in mind — the Germans had claimed to be exercising lawful pre-emptive self-defense when they invaded their neighbors prior to and during World War II. Hard experience taught that states must be held to a standard where the necessity for using force is objectively demonstrated. The system of international law, perhaps more than other legal systems, needs such objective, bright-line rules. In the absence of an international police force and regular courts, it needs rules that are self-implementing.

The Iraq case reveals the genius of this system. Iraq never attacked the United States, therefore the United States had no right to "counterattack" in self-defense. The United States could not persuade the Security Council of the need to use force against Iraq. Nevertheless, the United States invaded, only to find that indeed there was no actual threat. Our country would have been far better off had it heeded the council's collective wisdom.

It is not surprising, and is perhaps hopeful, that the United States has turned back to the council for help regarding Iran and North Korea.

Until Iraq, the United States stood steadfastly by the charter rules as written, knowing that a breach of the rules sets a dangerous precedent. States are equal under international law; the rules work largely on the basis of reciprocity.

There is no special set of rules for superpowers. If the United States wants a rule prohibiting force — and it always has for the most basic moral considerations — it needs to respect that rule itself.

supported by Mexico and 13 other Latin American countries, the European Union and Amnesty International.

In addition, former U.S. diplomat L. Bruce Laingen, who was charge d'affaires in the U.S. Embassy in Tehran during the 1979 hostage crisis, is also backing Medellin's plea. Laingen argues that unless U.S. courts respect the consular treaty, other countries will retaliate, and U.S. citizens' rights abroad will be endangered.

Texas officials are urging the high court to stick with its 1998 decision, which it described as holding that Vienna Convention claims, "like constitutional claims, can be procedurally defaulted, even in a death penalty case." The Bush administration has not filed a brief with the Supreme Court, nor has any other state or private organization joined on Texas' side at this stage.

The justices had Medellin's case on their schedule for three consecutive weekly conferences in late November and early December 2004 before finally granting review on Dec. 10. Argument will be held in the spring with a decision due by the end of June.

Meanwhile, lower federal courts are beginning to apply the Supreme Court's decision narrowing the scope of suits brought under the federal Alien Tort Statute. In the first decision to apply the high court's ruling, a federal court judge in New York City has dismissed a sprawling suit by South Africans against U.S. and other multinational corporations for collaboration with the country's former apartheid policy of racial discrimination.

U.S. District Judge John Sprizzo sharply criticized the apartheid policy's other abuses to the more than 100 companies named as defendants. But he said that holding multinational companies liable for "doing business in countries with less than stellar human rights records" could have "significant, if not disastrous, effects on international commerce." [35]

OUTLOOK

Preventive Action

Nearly two years after the launch of the Iraq war, the United States remains at odds with the United Nations over the use of force in the post-9/11 world. The dispute is one of several international-law issues where the Bush administration is taking stands in conflict with U.S. allies and much of world opinion.

In a report released on Nov. 30, 2004, a high-level panel created a year earlier by U.N. Secretary-General Annan acknowledged the need for "a broader-based approach" to fighting terrorism and singled out al Qaeda as a "universal threat." But the report rejected arguments that an individual country could exercise a right of "anticipatory self-defense" and instead said only the Security Council could authorize preventive action in cases where no attack had occurred or was imminent.

"The risk to the global order and the norm of non-intervention on which it continues to be based is simply too great for the legality of unilateral preventive action, as distinct from collectively endorsed action, to be accepted," the report states. "Allowing one to so act is to allow all." [36]

A week later, Kim Hughes, assistant U.S. secretary of State for international organizations, commended the report for urging the Security Council to be "more proactive" in dealing with terrorism and nuclear proliferation. But Hughes said the United States has "serious concerns" about the panel's limited view of self-defense and would not feel obliged to seek Security Council approval to use force preventively.

"Even in a case where terrorists have a nuclear weapon, the report says a state should go to the Security Council first for authorization to take preventative military action," Hughes said in a Dec. 6 speech to the Baltimore Council on Foreign Relations. "Whether the council could decide soon enough for effective military action is another matter. Such constraints will never be acceptable to the United States."

The administration also continues to oppose two major international treaties negotiated in recent years: the Kyoto Protocol to limit emission of gases thought to cause climate change and the pact to establish the permanent International Criminal Court (ICC). The Kyoto treaty is set to take effect in February 2005. Bush rejected the treaty in 2001, calling for voluntary measures instead.

The administration has used diplomatic pressure, including the threat to cut off military aid, to persuade 97 of the 139 countries that have now signed the ICC treaty to protect U.S. service members from prosecution before the tribunal. [37]

Some observers say the administration's skeptical stance toward international law reduces international support for U.S. policies. "Increasingly, the United States has found itself at odds with several key players," says Villanova law Professor Murphy.

Berkeley's Professor Yoo minimizes the problem. "The cost to our reputation is probably not that much," he says.

The disputes over these and other treaties underscore the widening scope and complexity of multilateral agreements and what one professor calls the "receding importance" of so-called customary international law. J. Patrick Kelly, a professor at Widener University School of Law in Wilmington, Del., welcomes the trend, saying treaties provide more specific formulations of international law and also give a greater voice to developing nations — but at the expense of reducing the influence of the United States and other developed countries. [38]

Under the Constitution, treaties ratified by the Senate are part of "the supreme law of the land" (Article VI). Still, members of Congress and others periodically complain about the loss of U.S. sovereignty under international law even when treaties have been approved by the Senate. Specialists in the field generally discount the problem.

"It does interfere with our national sovereignty to some extent, but that's not a bad thing," says Michael Ramsey, a professor at the University of San Diego School of Law and self-described "mild skeptic" of international law.

"We decided it would be better for our national security and our national interests if we agreed to these things," Ramsey says, referring to the U.N. Charter and other treaties. "Sometimes you can promote your long-term interests best by giving up things. That's the nature of a contract."

"The world is too big for us to deal with by ourselves," says Yale's Koh. "We need to have mechanisms for dealing with problems globally, and international law is the means to do that. We need to have a strategy for using international law to achieve our own ends."

NOTES

1. The case is *Hamdan v. Rumsfeld*, Civ. No. 04-1519 (Nov. 8, 2004). Factual background drawn from documents filed with Hamdan's petition for *certiorari* before U.S. Supreme Court (docket number 04-702, filed Nov. 22), available at SCOTUSblog (http://www.goldsteinhowe.com/blog/).

2. For the text of Resolution 1373, see http://ods-dds-ny.un.org/doc/UNDOC/GEN/N01/557/43/PDF/N0155743.pdf?OpenElement. For coverage, see Serge Schmemann, "U.N. Requires Members to Act Against Terror," *The New York Times*, Sept. 29, 2001, p. A1.

3. See David E. Sanger with John F. Burns, "Bush Orders Start of War on Iraq; Missiles Apparently Miss Hussein," *The New York Times*, March 20, 2003, p. A1.

4. Quoted in Patrick E. Tyler, "U.N. Chief Ignites Firestorm By Calling Iraq War 'Illegal,' " *The New York Times*, Sept. 17, 2004, p. A1.

5. The case is *Roper v. Simmons*, 03-633. For background, see Kenneth Jost, "Sentencing Debates," *The CQ Researcher*, Nov. 12, 2004, pp. 932-934.

6. The cases are *Atkins v. Virginia*, 536 U.S. 304 (2002), and *Lawrence v. Texas*, 539 U.S. 558 (2003).

7. See Anne Gearan, "Supreme Court Justice Skeptical of Value of International Law to U.S. Courts," The Associated Press, April 2, 2004.

8. See Lisa Girion, "Unocal to Settle Rights Claim," *Los Angeles Times*, Dec. 14, 2004, p. A1.

9. The case is *Filártiga v. Pena-Irala*, 630 F.2d 876 (2d Cir. 1980).

10. The citation is 540 U.S. — (June 29, 2004). The decision barred a suit by a Mexican physician, Humberto Alvarez-Machain, against a former Mexican police inspector for abducting him and bringing him to the United States for trial.

11. Gary Clyde Hufbauer and Nicholas K. Mitrokostas, "Awakening Monster: The Alien Tort Statute of 1789," Institute for International Economics, July 2003, p. 7. The study was financed in part by a business lobby, the National Foreign Trade Council.

12. Background drawn in part from John F. Murphy, *The United States and the Rule of Law in International Affairs* (2004). See also Barry E. Carter, Phillip R. Trimble and Curtis A. Bradley, *International Law* (4th ed.), 2003.

13. *Chisholm v. Georgia*, 2 Dall. 419 (1793), cited in Louis Henkin, *Foreign Affairs and the Constitution* (1972), p. 127.

14. See Carter, *et al.*, *op. cit.*, p. 342.

15. The case is *Paquete Habana*, 175 U.S. 677 (1900).

16. For background on the Security Council, see David Masci, "The United Nations and Global Security," *The CQ Researcher*, Feb. 27, 2004, pp. 173-196.

17. Carter, *et al.*, *op. cit.*, p. 287.

18. The case is titled *Case Concerning Military and Paramilitary Activities In and Against Nicaragua*

(*Nicaragua v. United States of America*), [1986] I.C.J. Rep. 14 (Judgment).

19. For background, see Kenneth Jost, "War Crimes," *The CQ Researcher*, July 7, 1995, pp. 585-608.

20. For background, see Mary H. Cooper, "Global Warming Treaty," *The CQ Researcher*, Jan. 26, 2001, pp. 41-64, and Mary H. Cooper, "Bush and the Environment," *The CQ Researcher*, Oct. 25, 2002, pp. 865-896.

21. See Hufbauer and Mitrokostas, *op. cit.*, pp. 63-72.

22. See Kenneth Jost, "Re-examining 9/11," *The CQ Researcher*, June 4, 2004, pp. 493-516.

23. "Military Order of November 13, 2001: Detention, Treatment and Trial of Certain Non-Citizens in the War Against Terrorism," 66 Fed. Reg. 57,833 (Nov. 16, 2001), excerpted in Sean D. Murphy, *United States Practice in International Law, Volume 1: 1999-2001* (2003), pp. 438-441. For coverage, see Elisabeth Bumiller and David Johnston, "Bush Sets Option of Military Trials in Terrorism Cases," *The New York Times*, Nov. 14, 2001, p. A1.

24. See Tim Golden, "Administration Officials Split Over Military Tribunals," *The New York Times*, Oct. 25, 2004, p. A1.

25. The case is *Rasul v. Bush*, 540 U.S. — (June 28, 2004).

26. The case is *Hamdi v. Rumsfeld*, 540 U.S. — (June 28, 2004). Four of the justices, in a plurality opinion by Justice Sandra Day O'Connor, said the procedure violated military regulations; two justices, in a partial concurrence by Justice David H. Souter, said the procedure violated the Third Geneva Convention. The court dismissed on procedural grounds the second U.S. citizen case, *Rumsfeld v. Padilla*, 540 U.S. — (June 28, 2004).

27. Neil A. Lewis, "Red Cross Finds Detainee Abuse in Guantanamo," *The New York Times*, Nov. 30, 2004, p. A1. *The Times* said it had obtained a memorandum describing and quoting from the ICRC report but not the report itself.

28. *The Washington Post* had previously reported on the ICRC criticism of allowing military interrogators access to detainees' medical files. See Peter Slevin and Joe Stephens, "Detainees' Medical Files Shared; Guantanamo Interrogators' Access Criticized," *The Washington Post*, June 10, 2004, p. A1.

29. See Barton Gellman and R. Jeffrey Smith, "Report to Defense Alleged Abuse by Prison Interrogation Teams," *The Washington Post*, Dec. 8, 2004, p. A1.

30. The ACLU posted the documents at www.aclu.org/torturefoia. For coverage, see Michael J. Sniffen, "Evidence gained by torture can be used to detain enemy combatants at Guantanamo," The Associated Press, Dec. 3, 2004.

31. See Neil A. Lewis, "Fate of Guantanamo Detainees Is Debated in Federal Court," *The New York Times*, Dec. 2, 2004, p. A29, and Carol D. Leonnig, "Judge Questions Sweep of Bush's War on Terrorism," *The New York Times*, Dec. 2, 2004, p. A4.

32. Background drawn in part from Tony Mauro, "High Court on Collision Course With Int'l Law," *Legal Times*, Nov. 22, 2004, p. 1.

33. The case is *Avena and Other Mexican Nationals* (*Mexico v. United States of America*), 2004 ICJ 128 (Judgment of March 31), www.icj-cji.org. For coverage, see Marlisle Simmons and Tim Weiner, "World Court Rules U.S. Should Review 51 Death Sentences," *The New York Times*, April 1, 2004, p. A1.

34. The earlier ICJ decision is the *LaGrand* case (*Germany v. United States of America*), 2001 ICJ 104 (judgment of June 27). The Supreme Court decision is *Breard v. Greene*, 523 U.S. 371 (1998).

35. The case is *In re South African Apartheid Litigation*, MDL No. 1499 (S.D.N.Y. Nov. 29, 2004) For coverage, see Larry Neumeister, "Judge tosses out lawsuits seeking billions from U.S. companies," The Associated Press, Nov. 29, 2004.

36. United Nations, "A More Secure World: Our Shared Responsibility: Report of the Secretary-General's High-Level Panel on Threats, Challenges, and Change," Nov. 30, 2004 (http://www.un.org/secureworld/report2.pdf). For coverage, see Warren Hoge, "Report Urges Big Changes for U.N.," *The New York Times*, Dec. 1, 2004, p. A1.

37. See Joe Lauria and Farah Stockman, "Aid Cuts Threatened by U.S. Over Tribunal," *The Boston Globe*, Dec. 5, 2004, p. A1.

38. See J. Patrick Kelly, "The Twilight of Customary International Law," *Virginia Journal of International Law*, Vol. 49 (winter 2000), pp. 449-538.

BIBLIOGRAPHY

Books

Carter, Barry E., Phillip R. Trimble and Curtis A. Bradley, *International Law* **(4th ed.), Aspen Law & Business, 2003.**
The law school casebook provides comprehensive coverage of court decisions, executive branch action and other materials on international law issues. Carter is a law professor at Georgetown University; Trimble at the University of California, Los Angeles; and Bradley at the University of Virginia.

Damrosch, Lori F., Louis Henkin, Richard Crawford Pugh, Oscar Schachter, and Hans Smith, *International Law: Cases and Materials* **(4th ed.), West, 2001.**
The law school casebook thoroughly covers international law topics, including a succinct introduction to the history of international law. Includes a four-page guide to official and private Internet sources on international law. Damrosch and Smith are professors and Henkin and Schachter professors emeriti at Columbia University School of Law; Pugh is a professor at the University of San Diego School of Law.

Murphy, John F., *The United States and the Rule of Law in International Affairs,* **Cambridge University Press, 2004.**
The book analyzes and assesses the role of international law in U.S. foreign policy. Includes chapter notes. Murphy is a professor at Villanova Law School.

Murphy, Sean D., *United States Practice in International Law: Volume 1, 1999-2001,* **Cambridge University Press, 2002.**
The reference book combines original source material with explanatory narratives to cover U.S. practice in international law, topic by topic, from 1999-2001. The next volume covers 2002-2004 [forthcoming, 2005]. Murphy, a professor at George Washington University School of Law, is also coauthor with Thomas Buergenthal of *Public International Law in a Nutshell* (3d ed.), West, 2002.

Rose, David, *Guantanamo: The War on Human Rights,* **New Press, 2004.**
The British journalist presents a highly critical account of detention and interrogation policies at the Guantanamo Bay Naval Base as inconsistent with international law standards.

White, Richard Alan, *Breaking Silence: The Case That Changed the Face of Human Rights,* **Georgetown University Press, 2004.**
The book vividly recounts the torture-murder of Joelito Filártiga, teenaged son of a prominent Paraguayan opposition leader; the Filártiga family's use of the Alien Tort Claims Act to sue the responsible police inspector in U.S. courts and the impact of the court decisions in favor of the suit. White is a senior fellow at the Council of Hemispheric Affairs in Washington.

Articles

Alford, Roger P., "Misusing International Sources to Interpret the Constitution," *American Journal of International Law,* **January 2004.**
An associate professor at Pepperdine University School of Law argues against the Supreme Court's use of foreign and international law in constitutional interpretation.

Greene, Jenna, "Gathering Storm: Suits That Claim Overseas Abuse Are Putting U.S. Executives on Alert and Their Lawyers on Call," *Legal Times,* **July 21, 2003.**
The story gives an overview of issues surrounding suits against corporate defendants under the Alien Tort Statute.

Kelly, J. Patrick, "The Twilight of Customary International Law," *Virginia Journal of International Law,* **Vol. 40, winter 2000, pp. 445-539.**
A professor at Widener University School of Law argues that treaties are replacing customs and practices as the major sources of international law.

Neuman, Gerald L., "The Uses of International Law in Constitutional Interpretation," *American Journal of International Law,* **January 2004.**
A professor at Columbia University School of Law argues in favor of the Supreme Court's use of foreign and international law in constitutional interpretation.

Reports and Studies

Hufbauer, Gary Clyde, and Nicholas K. Mitrokostas, "Awakening Monster: The Alien Tort Statute of 1789," Institute for International Economics, July 2003.
The tract traces the history of the Alien Tort Statute and

strongly criticizes its recent use in broad-based human rights suits in U.S. courts against foreign officials and, in particular, multinational corporations. Includes summaries of 23 suits brought under the act since the seminal case, *Filártiga v. Pena-Irala* (1980). The study was partially funded by the National Council on Foreign Trade, a business group that opposes expansive use of the act.

United Nations, "A More Secure World: Our Shared Responsibility: Report of the Secretary-General's High-level Panel on Threats, Challenges and Change," Nov. 30, 2004 (www.un.org/secureworld/report2.pdf). The report is aimed at forging a "new security consensus" to deal with threats to peace and order posed by terrorism, failed states and nuclear proliferation. The United States, however, rejected one of the major premises — that only the Security Council can authorize the use of force as preventive action against a threat to stability.

For More Information

American Constitution Society for Law and Policy, 50 F St., N.W., Suite 5200, Washington, DC 20001; (202) 393-6181; www.acslaw.org. A progressive legal organization "working to ensure that the fundamental principles of human dignity, individual rights and liberties, genuine equality, and access to justice are in their rightful, central place in American law."

The American Society for International Law, 2223 Massachusetts Ave., N.W., Washington, DC 20008; (202) 939-6000; www.asil.org. Fosters the study of international law and promotes the establishment and maintenance of international relations "on the basis of law and justice."

Center for Constitutional Rights, 666 Broadway, 7th Floor, New York, NY 10012; (212) 614-6464; www.ccr-ny.org. "Dedicated to protecting and advancing the rights guaranteed by the U.S. Constitution and the Universal Declaration of Human Rights."

Federalist Society, 1015 18th St., N.W., Suite 425, Washington DC 20036; (202) 822-8138; www.fedsoc.org. A "group of conservatives and libertarians . . . founded on the principles that the state exists to preserve freedom, that the separation of governmental powers is central to our Constitution, and that it is emphatically the province and duty of the judiciary to say what the law is, not what it should be."

Institute for International Economics, 1750 Massachusetts Ave., N.W., Washington, DC 20036; (202) 328-9000 Fax: (202) 695-3225; www.iie.com. A nonpartisan research institution devoted to the study of international economic policy.

International Law Association, Charles Clore House, 17 Russell Square, London, WC1B 5 DR, England; (44) 20-7323-2978; www.ila-hq.org. American branch: c/o Carlos Pelayo, Davis Polk and Wardwell; 450 Lexington Ave., Room 1938; New York, NY 10017. Devoted to the study, clarification and development of both public and private international law, with about 50 branches worldwide.

Washington Legal Foundation, 2009 Massachusetts Ave., N.W., Washington, DC 20036; (202) 588-0302; www.wlf.org. Works "to maintain balance" in the courts and help the U.S. government "strengthen America's free-enterprise system" through litigation, publishing and educational efforts.

15

Middle East Peace

Nicole Gaouette

Moderate Palestinian leader Mahmoud Abbas greets supporters at the Jenin refugee camp in the West Bank on Dec. 30, 2004. Israel and the United States hailed his election as Palestinian Authority president on Jan. 9, 2005, as a positive step on the road to peace.

From *CQ Researcher*, January 21, 2005.

After 52 months of unrelenting violence, many Middle East observers hailed the Jan. 9, 2005, Palestinian election as the beginning of a more hopeful chapter in the intertwined histories of Israelis and Palestinians.

"We may be laying the foundation for the second working democracy in the Middle East," said Ziad Abu Amr, a former Palestinian cabinet member. [1]

Israeli Prime Minister Ariel Sharon made a congratulatory call to Palestinian President-elect Mahmoud Abbas, in which the leaders "agreed to continue their dialogue in the future." [2]

Yet it didn't take long for old patterns to re-establish themselves. On Jan. 13, two days before Abbas was sworn in, Gaza militants killed six Israelis, prompting Sharon to cut contact with the Palestinians until they make "a real effort to stop terror."

Even so, some observers see the landslide election of moderate Abbas as the new Palestinian president as one of several changes that make a peace settlement more possible than it has been in years. The death of longtime Palestinian leader Yasser Arafat in November 2004 paved the way for the election. A patchwork Israeli coalition should provide political stability during a year in which Sharon is determined to force Israelis out of settlements in the Gaza Strip. And President Bush says his own re-election will enable him "to use the next four years to spend the capital of the United States on" the creation of a Palestinian state. [3]

Such an optimistic scenario hardly seemed likely in September 2004, when the bloody Israeli-Palestinian conflict entered its fifth year, having claimed some 1,000 Israelis and more than 3,000 Palestinians. [4]

321

Divvying Up the Occupied Territories

The Palestinian-Israeli conflict revolves around the West Bank and Gaza Strip (inset), the occupied territories captured by Israel in 1967. In October 2004, Israel's parliament backed Prime Minister Ariel Sharon's plan to evacuate some 7,500 Israeli settlers in Gaza in summer 2005 and also to close four small West Bank settlements. President Bush supports allowing 200,000 settlers in some 200 larger Israeli settlements to remain in the West Bank. Meanwhile, despite Palestinian outrage and Israeli promises to the United States, Israel is expanding its settlements and erecting a 455-mile barrier between Palestinian and Israeli lands that annexes about 200,000 acres of Palestinian farmland.

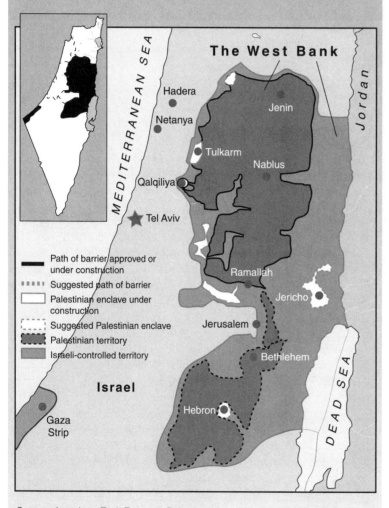

Source: American Task Force on Palestine

"The scarcest commodity lately in the Middle East has been hope," David Makovsky, director of the Project on the Middle East Peace Process at the Washington Institute, says. "We have a real window of opportunity here."

But Mouin Rabbani, a senior analyst at the International Crisis Group, a Brussels-based think tank, warns there is little time to waste. "The real question is: Is a two-state solution still viable?" Rabbani says. "The only real answer is that with every passing day it is less viable, and, if we haven't already passed the point of no return, we are fast approaching it."

Indeed, there are many factors to temper optimism: Four years of Palestinian suicide bombings and harsh Israeli reprisals have eroded the physical and psychological foundations needed for peace. The Palestinian Authority (PA) barely functions as the Palestinians' governing body, while the militant group Hamas has gained in popularity and wants Abbas to share power. And Palestinians generally see the United States not as an honest broker but rather as unabashedly pro-Israel.

Moreover, attempts to promote a settlement have been ignored or condemned. Palestinian violence has undermined Israel's political left, which has traditionally backed peace talks. In the absence of negotiations, Israel in 2002 began building an immense, 455-mile-long wall separating Palestinian and Israeli lands — and in the process annexed thousands of acres of Palestinian farmland. Meanwhile, Israel has steadily increased the size and number of its settlements in the occupied territories, deepening mistrust of Israeli intentions.

The United States and Israel say progress will depend on Abbas' performance, but he faces considerable challenges. The Palestinian Authority is "no longer national and barely exercises authority," said a sympathetic commentator. [5] In fact, the Israelis have demolished the PA's buildings, and its security forces have been disarmed, subsumed into militia groups or killed. Fatah, the Palestinians' core political party, is divided both ideologically and physically, with members in Israeli jails or unable to meet easily due to Israeli curbs on their movement. [6]

Meanwhile, Abbas' three constituencies — Americans and Israelis on one side, Palestinians on the other — wait impatiently for results. Besides rebuilding the PA, Palestinians want Abbas to eliminate corruption and improve their lives, which largely means restoring their ability to move freely inside the occupied territories. The United States and Israel want him to act against militant groups, but Hamas is legitimizing its popularity by winning seats in local elections. And while Hamas boycotted the presidential race, its members will run in July's legislative elections, which will demonstrate Hamas' strength compared to Abbas' Fatah. And Abbas — sober, silver-haired and seen as a quitter when the going gets tough — must accomplish all these tasks without Arafat's charisma or political power.

Sharon confronts his own internal battles, particularly from those within his own party who oppose his plan to evict some 7,500 Israeli Jews from 21 settlements in Gaza — a major part of his strategy to disengage from the Palestinians. (Sharon also would close four small West Bank settlements.) The coalition he assembled to pass the eviction measure gives him only a tenuous four-seat majority in the 120-seat Knesset, or parliament. [7] The withdrawal itself presents a more serious challenge — to both Sharon and Israel.

Settlers are furious about the prime minister's disengagement plan. Stone-wielding settlers referred to Israeli troops as Nazis when they tried to remove their illegal West Bank buildings in January. [8] Pro-settler army officers have encouraged soldiers to defy orders to evacuate settlements, earning Sharon's harsh criticism. [9] Senior Israeli army officials say they expect bloodshed. [10]

Yet, overall, the future of most Israeli settlements appears bright. Bush has promised Sharon that a peace agreement will allow most West Bank settlements to remain in Israeli hands, and a close Sharon aide has said the Gaza evacuation is meant to ensure Israeli control of the West Bank.

Despite promises to the United States to stop expanding settlements — and an obligation to do so under a Bush-brokered peace plan called the "Roadmap" [11] — Israel continues to build in the occupied territories and, some observers say, has even accelerated construction. [12] In late 2004, the government invited developers to submit bids for the construction of thousands of houses in large settlements. Palestinian villages cut off from their fields by the security barrier have watched Israeli contractors lay the foundation for new settlements on their farmlands. [13] Continued Israeli construction in the occupied territories will make a viable Palestinian state impossible, Rabbani and others contend.

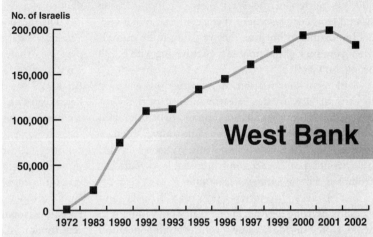

Israeli Settler Population Has Skyrocketed

Israel has expanded its settlements in the occupied territories. The number of Israelis in West Bank settlements has increased tenfold in the past 20 years and fifteenfold in the Gaza Strip.

Jewish Settlement Population, 1972-2002

No. of Israelis

West Bank

1972 1983 1990 1992 1993 1995 1996 1997 1999 2000 2001 2002

Source: Foundation for Middle East Peace, December 2004

"Regardless of the prime minister in Israel, regardless of peace talks, settlements have grown by 10,000 to 12,000 people every year since the Oslo Accords," says William Quandt, a foreign affairs professor at the University of Virginia, referring to Israel's 1993 agreement to withdraw from the Gaza Strip and the West Bank city of Jericho. There are now approximately 200,000 settlers in the West Bank, excluding those around Jerusalem, he notes. "If you continue at that rate, it's impossible to imagine they're going to be moved, when you think of the trouble they're having with 8,000 people [in Gaza]."

Settlement construction, along with the ever-rising security barrier, divides Palestinian parts of the West Bank into sections that Sharon proposes to connect with roads to provide "transportation continuity." [14] Many analysts, Israelis as well as Palestinians, say such a divided state would not be economically viable, which has prompted calls for a one-state solution. [15]

But Israel's supporters say that Israelis and Palestinians living together in one state would amount to demographic suicide because the area's Arab population is expected to eclipse Israel's 5 million Jews sometime between 2010 and 2015. [16] At that point, Israel would be unable to remain both Jewish and democratic if it wanted to retain control of the land between the Mediterranean Sea and the Jordan River.

The hard demographic realities Israel faces underlie the rhetoric about the conflict over the occupied territories and drive both left- and right-wing attempts to find a solution. Whether the answer turns out to be Bush's "Roadmap," Sharon's disengagement plan or some other option remains to be seen.

Meanwhile, here are some fundamental questions that Israelis and Palestinians are debating:

Does Arafat's death make Palestinian statehood more likely?

As Arafat's former bodyguards hauled his flag-draped coffin through throngs of weeping, shouting Palestinians in the West Bank city of Ramallah on Nov. 12, 2004, international diplomacy was rolling into high gear.

Within hours, President Bush announced that the Palestinian leader's death offered a new opportunity to achieve peace. "I believe we've got a great, new chance to establish a Palestinian state," he said. [17] Israeli politicians echoed Bush's optimism, calling Arafat's death an "his-

toric opportunity." [18] Jordan's King Abdullah II dubbed it "a moment shaped by both loss and hope." [19]

But some analysts say Palestinian statehood is still uncertain. They argue that Israeli actions and U.S. policies also have hindered progress and that those factors won't change. Moreover, Abbas, who lacks Arafat's political clout, must cope with an impoverished, badly divided society. [20]

"The general perception is that the chances for Palestinian statehood have increased, but different issues play into that," says Matthew Hodes, director of the Conflict Resolution Program at The Carter Center in Atlanta. "You have to look at the fragmentation of Palestinian society, the genuine intentions of the Israeli government and the real intentions of the U.S. in this conflict."

Israeli and Palestinian citizens themselves seem pessimistic. A November poll revealed that despite the drop in violence after Arafat's death, 49 percent of Israelis think it is impossible to make peace with Palestinians. [21] In December, pollsters found that 80 percent of Palestinians want reconciliation with Israelis, but 48 percent think it is impossible with Sharon in power. [22]

Moreover, before negotiations can even begin, Abbas must reform a political system bloated by patronage and corruption, stop violence against Israel, formulate a response to the Gaza pullout and West Bank settlement expansion and create a working relationship with Israel and the United States. He also will have to improve the security and economic welfare of ordinary Palestinians while contending with an infrastructure that has largely been destroyed by the conflict.

To avoid the minefields of internal conflict seemingly lurking everywhere, analysts say Abbas will have to integrate Islamist groups such as Hamas into the political system and incorporate the views of younger rebels within his Fatah party. [23] He has already survived one apparent assassination attempt. [24] But little progress "can be realistically achieved unless Israel and the U.S. actively cooperate," according to the International Crisis Group. [25]

Yet Sharon's intentions are unclear, particularly after Dov Weisglass, one of his closest aides, said in October 2004 that the upcoming Gaza pullout was meant to "prevent the establishment of a Palestinian state" by ensuring Israel retains control over the West Bank. [26] Weisglass said Israel has U.S. approval for this scenario. [27]

Sharon has told Palestinians that Israel wants "to live side by side in understanding and peace," adding, "We have no desire to rule over you; we have no desire to run your affairs." [28] But his terms sound untenable to many Palestinians.

"Sharon has spoken unequivocally about the kind of settlement he wants: No return of [Palestinian] refugees [to Israel], no 1967 borders for a so-called Palestinian state, no removal of settlements from the West Bank, no Jerusalem as a capital for the Palestinians," says Hisham Ahmed, a Palestinian political scientist at Bir Zeit University in the West Bank. "What's left?"

Outside the Middle East, however, the view is more upbeat. "Arafat represented the embodiment of the problem," says Danielle Pletka, vice president of foreign and defense policy studies at the conservative American Enterprise Institute (AEI). "I think he did an enormous disservice to his people by creating a culture of violence, corruption and rejection."

Makovsky of the Washington Institute says Arafat's death offers a chance to reform the Palestinian system, echoing the administration's view. Bush said after Arafat's death: "The responsibility for peace is going to rest with the Palestinian people's desire to build a democracy, and Israel's willingness to help them build a democracy." [29]

Yet Bush might not appreciate the fruits of Palestinian democracy. With regard to Arafat, he clearly wanted regime change. The president called for new Palestinian leadership in June 2002, but the United States did little to encourage elections while Arafat was alive. Had they occurred, Arafat would have won easily. Now, as the U.S. calls for democracy once again, voting may transform Hamas into a democratically elected political force, especially after the July legislative elections.

But some critics say democracy is not the real problem. "Defects in Palestinian democracy (by almost every measure less significant than in every other Arab country) did not cause the Israeli-Palestinian conflict any more than addressing them will solve it," a recent International Crisis Group report stated. [30]

"Arafat wasn't the main problem in the first place," adds James Zogby, president of the Arab American Institute. "The problems are very systemic," he adds, citing the Israeli settlements. "Palestinians have some very minimal demands that have to be met, Israel objects to those demands and the United States refuses to play the objective role of a mediator. That being the case, nothing has changed other than Arafat dying."

Palestinians walk along the Mediterranean Sea in January 2004 after Israeli troops closed local roads into Gaza City following attacks that killed an Israeli soldier and wounded five others.

Has the U.S. allied itself too closely with Israel?

In December 2004, Sharon outlined his achievements of the past year to the Herzliya Conference, an annual gathering of Israel's political elite. "The most important accomplishment is the understandings between U.S. President George Bush and me, which provide a new, more stable basis than ever before for the strategic understandings between Israel and the United States," the prime minister said.

During Bush's first term, U.S.-Israeli ties have grown stronger. America's "war on terror" has bolstered sympathy for Israel in its conflict with the Palestinians. Conservative Christian Zionists, who believe Israel has a Biblical right to the occupied territories, are among the president's most important domestic constituencies. (*See sidebar, p. 334.*) In addition, the war in Iraq and the U.S. campaign to encourage democracy in the Arab world have underscored the close ties Americans share with the sole democracy in the Middle East.

"American support not only makes it possible for Israel to go to great lengths for peace; it ensures the very existence of the Jewish state," said Amy Friedkin, then president of the influential American Israel Public Affairs Committee (AIPAC), on Sept. 11, 2003. "Alone in a region of dictatorships and states sponsoring terrorism, Israel adheres to the same core values of freedom and democracy that define America."

Yet some analysts have begun calling for a reassessment of U.S. policy toward Israel. In several recent books — such

Arabs Outnumber Israelis in the Territories

There are less than a half-million Israelis and almost 4 million Arabs in the Occupied Territories. On April 14, 2004, President Bush suggested that Israel should retain its major settlements.

Population Estimates, 2002

Occupied Territory	No. Israeli Settlements	Jewish Population	Arab Population
Gaza Strip	21	7,500	1,275,000
Golan Heights	30	20,000	20,000
West Bank	140	201,000	2,237,000
East Jerusalem	9	170,000	200,000
Total	200	398,500	3,732,000

Source: CIA Factbook and Foundation for Middle East Peace, "Report on Israeli Settlements in the Occupied Territory," December 2004

as *Imperial Hubris* by Michael Sheuer, a former senior U.S. intelligence official, and *America: Right or Wrong* by British scholar Anatol Lieven, the authors and other critics argue that the administration's seemingly unconditional support for Israel harms U.S. interests in the Middle East and makes it impossible for the United States to act as an honest broker between Israelis and Palestinians.

"There has been a historical shift in the first four years of this administration away from a position that has existed in one way or another in U.S. government since Truman: to tread a fine line [that allows the United States] to simultaneously have a very special relationship with the Israeli state, combined with an acceptance of a need to play that honest broker role," says The Carter Center's Hodes.

For Israel, U.S. friendship has produced unparalleled U.S. financial aid — some $80 billion since 1974 — and rock-solid U.S. support in the U.N. [31] In fact, say some analysts, Israel could not take the risks needed for peace, such as leaving West Bank areas it considers militarily important, without strong U.S. backing.

However, America's loyalty to Israel has produced bitter anti-American resentment in the Arab world.

Since the latest Israeli-Palestinian conflict reignited in September 2000 and the 2003 U.S. invasion of Iraq, Arab views of the United States have soured. When Western and Arab leaders met in Morocco in December 2004 to discuss regional political change, the conference ran aground when the Arab attendees began protesting "the Western bias toward Israel." [32]

"Our favorable ratings as a country — which were in the mid-teen or 20s range in 2002 — have sunk to single digits," says Zogby of the Arab American Institute. "Israel is certainly a factor in this. We ask, 'What should the U.S. do?' Invariably, it comes up: 'Be fair to the Palestinians.'"

Convicted terrorist Ramzi Yousef, claiming responsibility for the 1993 World Trade Center bombing, demanded that the United States halt all aid and ties to Israel. "The terrorism that Israel practices (which is supported by America) must be faced with a similar one," he wrote. [33]

Since 1998 terrorist leader Osama bin Laden repeatedly has decried the U.S.-Israeli alliance, and, indeed, justifies the Sept. 11, 2001, al Qaeda attack on the United States in part as punishment for America's support for Israel. [34]

Lieven, a senior associate at the Carnegie Endowment for International Peace, says the Israeli-Palestinian conflict "is certainly not the only motive, but is a very, very important contemporary motive for Arab anger at the United States and sympathy for al Qaeda."

Zbigniew Brzezinski, national security adviser during the Carter administration, believes the Arab-Israeli conflict could severely disrupt America's ties with Europe, and that a solution is "essential" to solving other U.S. security challenges. "To the extent that the Arabs perceive America as sponsoring Israeli repression of the Palestinians, America's ability to pacify anti-American passions in the region is constrained," he wrote. [35]

Palestinians themselves see bias in Bush's April 14, 2004, letter to Sharon backing Israel's claim to parts of the West Bank. A month later, 53 former U.S. diplomats charged that Bush had sacrificed U.S. credibility in the Arab world by tilting toward Israel. [36]

"By closing the door to negotiations with Palestinians and the possibility of a Palestinian state, you have proved that the U.S. is not an even-handed peace partner," said the letter writers, who included former ambassadors to India, Saudi Arabia, Syria, Qatar and Egypt.

But AEI's Pletka contends that Bush's actions reflect realism, not bias. "No recent president has believed that it is automatic that Palestinians will be given the option of the right of return" to their ancestral lands in Israel, she says, "not because those presidents are blindly [pro-Israel], but because they have a firm grip on reality and because the numbers just don't make sense if Israel is going to be a Jewish state."

However, several analysts say tensions plaguing the United States' relationship with the Arab world are not only the result of U.S. ties to Israel. "If the Jewish state had not come into existence, the United States would still have stood as an embodiment of everything that most of these Arabs considered evil," said Norman Podhoretz, godfather of the neoconservative movement and retired longtime editor of *Commentary* magazine. He argues Islamic terrorists are driven by a commitment "to the destruction of everything good for which America stands." [37]

"Arab-Islamic hatreds of the United States preceded the conquest of the West Bank and Gaza," writes Josef Joffe, a research fellow at Stanford University's Hoover Institution. "What really riles America-haters in the Middle East is Washington's intrusions into their affairs, be it for reasons of oil, terrorism, or weapons of mass destruction." [38]

Should Israel pull its settlers out of the Gaza Strip?

In October 2004, after a long summer of political skirmishing, Sharon won an unexpected victory — Israel's parliament backed his plan to evacuate settlements from the Gaza Strip. Outside the Knesset, protesters screamed predictions of Sharon's assassination and warned of a struggle that would pit Jew against Jew.

The evacuation, set to occur between July and September this year, promises to be a major turning point both for Israel and the Israeli-Palestinian conflict. Supporters say it will remove Israel from an untenable situation that costs lives and vast amounts of money. Advocates and opponents alike say the pullout will set a precedent for the evacuation of West Bank settlements. Sharon's detractors say it makes Israel look weak and hands Palestinian militants a victory.

But the plan has ramifications beyond the relocation of some 1,500 families. [39] For Israel's powerful settler minority, the battle against evacuation is also a struggle to maintain their political influence. Many observers fear a clash between Israel's army and its settlers. And analysts on both sides fear

an Israeli departure will produce a Gaza unequipped for economic survival or a dangerously unstable "Hamas-stan."

And some observers contend Sharon is using the Gaza pullout to avoid following the U.S.-backed "Roadmap" and indefinitely delay the creation of a Palestinian state. They cite statements by Sharon and Bush's pledge, made in support of Sharon's Gaza disengagement plan, that Israel could keep major West Bank settlements in the event of a peace agreement.

"The goal of the disengagement plan is to perpetuate Israeli control in most of the West Bank, and to repel any internal or external pressure for a different political solution," said Ephraim Sneh, a Labor Party legislator and former deputy defense minister. [40]

The Gaza Strip is a 139-square-mile wedge of land that runs along the Mediterranean Sea, bordered by Egypt to the south and Israel to the north and east. Israel seized Gaza from Egypt in the 1967 Arab-Israeli war and encouraged Jewish settlers to move there with tax breaks and cheap mortgages. Today, Gaza is one of the world's most densely populated areas — home to 1.3 million Palestinians whose cities and refugee camps surround the spacious communities of 7,500 Jewish settlers, a situation maintained only through the constant presence of Israeli soldiers. [41] Palestinians are forbidden from using the roads that connect the settlements, and Palestinian movement from town to town is blocked by Israeli army checkpoints.

Because Sharon is considered the father of the settler movement, his December 2003 proposal to evacuate the Gaza settlements met with outrage and shock. The anger ebbed somewhat after the October 2004 comments by his aide, Weisglass, who quipped that disengagement "supplies the amount of formaldehyde that is necessary so that there will not be a political process with the Palestinians." [42]

Sharon had previously said that "after the evacuation, there will be a very long period in which nothing else will happen." Referring to Bush's 2002 plan to establish a Palestinian state by 2005, he added, "We are not following the 'Roadmap.' I am not ready for this." [43]

Critics say this proves Sharon's oft-stated preference for a long-term interim agreement that would prevent further progress while inoculating Israel against criticism. "Sharon has convinced Western opinion that he has a peace agenda, that he wants to disengage," says Ahmed of Bir Zeit University. "But by submitting his own plan, Sharon has been successful in toppling an international plan, the road map."

Up to two-thirds of Israelis back Sharon's disengagement plan, because the Gaza Strip has no significant Jewish holy sites and because defending its settlers costs Israeli soldiers' lives. [44] The Knesset is budgeting about $550 million for disengagement in 2005, but costs are expected to soar as high as $1.2 billion. [45]

"The idea that almost 9,000 Israelis would be able to live in a small area with a Palestinian population of at least a million and a half was never viable," says Gerald Steinberg, a political scientist at Bar Ilan University outside Tel Aviv. "There is increasing discussion of the cost, in manpower and lives, and increasingly the answer is 'no.' People don't want their kids fighting and dying for Gaza."

But the settlers' leaders have called for civil disobedience, considered asking soldiers to resist evacuation orders [46] and sent young right-wing activists from the West Bank to Gaza to help protest disengagement. [47] In a written call to arms, Pinchas Wallerstein, the head of a settler council, described the pullout as "the immoral crime of uprooting Jews from their homes by force," and the settlers as people who had "made the wilderness bloom and protected the borders of the state." [48]

"This is a showdown," says Yossi Alpher, co-founder of Bitterlemons.org, an Israeli-Palestinian dialogue Web site, noting that a successful Gaza pullout would herald a waning of settler political power. "The minute you pull the plug on settlements, you get tremendous pressure for them to evacuate more."

Some analysts fear the pullout itself could trigger a civil war between settlers and the army. [49] Others warn about what follows a pullout, especially since Israel intends to control Gaza's entrances, water resources, sea and air space and reserves the right to enter at will. [50]

"There is 80 percent youth unemployment in Gaza. It is one of the most densely populated, poorest nations on Earth," Zogby says. "Israel will be turning this over to the Palestinians, saying, 'You govern this million-plus people in this cramped place with no jobs, no sewage, no hope.' It's a cruel joke more than it is a step toward peace."

Pletka also warns: "Gaza could become a beachhead for extremism, a terrorist enclave that can destabilize Egypt, Israel and the West Bank. It's a real risk."

BACKGROUND

Old Conflict

The conflict between Israelis and Palestinians — what one writer calls "their Hundred Years War" — is rooted in 19th-century Europe. [51] Russian pogroms in the 1880s sparked the first rush of Jewish immigration to Palestine, then part of the Ottoman Empire. Moreover, European anti-Semitism led to the birth of Zionism — a movement to create a Jewish homeland that gained momentum in the 1890s. The British government gave the idea an electrifying boost in 1917 with its Balfour Declaration calling for the creation of a Jewish "national home" in Palestine. [52] Jews based their claim on God's biblical promise of the land to Abraham and their historical presence there until the Romans dispersed them in 70 A.D. Britain backed them to serve its own political designs on the Ottoman lands. European Jews began arriving in the region, but the rush of immigration soon led to clashes with the Arabs there.

The violence intensified with the Arab revolt of 1936-1939, which prompted the British to propose partitioning Palestine into Jewish and Arab states. The Jews accepted, but the Arabs refused because they had made a pact with the British: In exchange for an Arab uprising against the Turks, all Arab provinces of the Ottoman Empire would get independence. [53] But after the Arab rebellion, the British, Russians and French divided up the Middle East among themselves and then gave part of Palestine to the Jews. It was seen as a great betrayal.

In November 1947, the United Nations proposed a similar partition plan that would have put Jerusalem under U.N. administration. Again, the Jews accepted, and the Arabs rejected the idea. Ongoing guerrilla fighting erupted into a war punctuated by Israel's declaration of independence on May 14, 1948.

The United States recognized Israel immediately, but Israel's declaration was rejected by Arab nations, which saw it as yet another colonial enterprise. [54] The next day at dawn, Egypt, Syria, Jordan, Lebanon and Iraq invaded in an attempt to crush the new nation.

Israel's decisive victory in 1949 made it a powerful new force in the region and gave it control over far more territory than the U.N. had allotted it. The war was a disaster, however, for the approximately 1.3 million Palestinians living in the area. [55] About half became refugees, fleeing to Egyptian-controlled Gaza, the Jordanian-controlled West Bank or to refugee camps in other Arab countries. Israel rebuffed attempts to repatriate these refugees, many of whom fled with house keys they have passed down from generation to generation in camps that have ossified into permanent cities.

While the region remained tense in the ensuring years, Israel built its economy and military with the help of foreign aid and constant immigration. Aside from the 1956 Suez Canal crisis, the region was quiet until 1967, when Egypt began massing troops on Israel's southern border. The U.N. had withdrawn troops meant to buffer the two countries, and the United States, mired in Vietnam, could offer little help. Israel launched a surprise attack on Egypt, Syria and Jordan, routing all in a six-day war that changed the region.

Israel's triumph demoralized its Arab neighbors and left it feeling invincible. The tiny nation had wrested the Sinai Peninsula and Gaza Strip from Egypt, the Golan Heights from Syria and the West Bank and East Jerusalem — home to the Temple Mount, Judaism's holiest site — from Jordan. Israel quickly began building settlements in the West Bank.

Israel's 1967 victory brought an international rebuke, however, when the United States and Soviet Union pushed Resolution 242 through the U.N. Security Council. The resolution demanded the "withdrawal of the Israeli armed forces from territories occupied in the recent conflict." [56] Israel's conquest was double-edged in other ways. The newly conquered territory came — like a Trojan horse — with more than 1 million Palestinian residents. [57] And the victory galvanized overseas Palestinian groups to organize resistance.

Palestinian identity had begun coalescing after Israel's victory in 1949. Convinced that Arab countries and others would do little to help the Palestinians, Arafat, then a university student in Cairo, founded Palestinian student unions and revolutionary groups. Palestinian nationalism flourished, leading to the creation of the Palestine Liberation Organization (PLO) in 1964.

Before long, PLO attacks on Israel and high-profile airplane highjackings brought international condemnation. But Arab nations gave the group recognition, admiration and funds. By 1970, the PLO — based in Jordan and led by Arafat — was confident enough to attempt a coup against moderate King Hussein. The group failed and re-established its base in Lebanon. Eighteen months later, PLO terrorists killed 17 people, including 11 Israeli athletes, at the 1972 Munich Olympics. [58]

David vs. Goliath?

On Oct. 6, 1973, Egypt and Syria launched an initially successful coordinated attack on Israel on the Jewish holy day of Yom Kippur. After three weeks of fierce fighting and a massive infusion of American aid, U.S. Secretary of State Henry Kissinger brokered a ceasefire in which Israel withdrew from Egyptian and Syrian land in exchange for security guarantees. [59] The U.N. Security Council called for talks on Israel's withdrawal from occupied lands and an end to hostilities — demands that had been outlined in Resolution 242 and soon known by the shorthand of "land for peace." [60]

The Yom Kippur War plunged Israel into depression and contributed to the hawkish Likud bloc's first victory over the Labor Party in 1977. Likud rejected the idea of "land for peace," arguing that the problem wasn't land, but Arab refusal to accept Israel. So the party was sympathetic to the growing number of Israelis who, for religious or political reasons, were determined to settle the land in a way that would prevent it from being returned to the Arabs. Under Likud leadership, Israeli settlements in the occupied territories expanded rapidly.

The 1970s also marked the beginning of significant attempts to reach a regional peace. During a historic trip to Israel in 1977, Egypt's President Anwar Sadat urged Israel to return the Sinai to Egypt in exchange for normal relations. The next year, Sadat, Israeli Prime Minister Menachem Begin and U.S. President Jimmy Carter met at Camp David and agreed that Israel would withdraw from the Sinai in exchange for full diplomatic relations with Egypt. The Camp David Accords also mandated an autonomy plan for the occupied territories that recognized the "legitimate rights of the Palestinian people." [61] The 1978 accords also promised Israel and Egypt ongoing U.S. aid — totaling about $125 billion since then — making the two countries the largest recipients by far of U.S foreign aid. [62]

Sadat's visit shattered Israel's isolation, but the hopefulness it created was quickly overshadowed: Egyptian militants assassinated Sadat in 1981. The next year, Israel invaded Lebanon in an attempt to destroy the PLO, which survived in part because the United States pressured Israel to let Arafat and his fighters leave for Tunis, Tunisia.

CHRONOLOGY

1881-1948 *Jewish immigration, spurred by genocidal European anti-Semitism, leads to the founding of Israel.*

1917 Balfour Declaration pledges Britain will help Jews establish a "national home" in Palestine.

1947 United Nations votes to partition Palestine into Jewish and Arab states. Jews accept the plan; Arabs reject it.

May 14, 1948 David Ben-Gurion declares the birth of Israel. . . . On May 15 Arab armies attack Israel, are defeated within months. War uproots up to 750,000 Palestinians.

1950s *Yasser Arafat begins organizing Palestinian students in Egypt.*

1960s-1980s *Victories in 1967 and 1973 strengthen Israel. Palestine Liberation Organization (PLO) begins hijacking jetliners but gains official recognition.*

1964 PLO is founded at first Arab League Summit.

1967 In Six-Day War, Israel captures Golan Heights, West Bank, Gaza Strip and Sinai Peninsula; U.N. Resolution 242 demands Israel's withdrawal.

1969 Arafat is elected chairman of PLO.

1970 Jordan's King Hussein crushes a PLO coup attempt; PLO flees to Lebanon.

1973 Israel repels surprise attack by Egypt, Syria in Yom Kippur War.

1978 At Camp David, Israel agrees to return Sinai to Egypt in exchange for normalized relations.

1980s-1990s *Israel's invasion of Lebanon and a Palestinian uprising make both sides more open to talks.*

1982 Israel invades Lebanon to crush the PLO; Arafat flees to Tunisia.

1987 Palestinians launch six-year Intifada in the occupied territories.

1990 Peace talks between Israel and the Palestinians continue.

1993 In February, Israeli and Palestinians begin secret peace talks in Oslo, Norway. In September, Arafat and Yitzhak Rabin sign the Oslo Accords, giving Palestinians control over Gaza and Jericho.

1996 Arafat is elected head of the new Palestinian Authority (PA).

1998 Arafat and Likud Party leader Benjamin Netanyahu agree to land-for-peace deal; conservative and religious Israeli groups later scuttle the plan.

2000-Present *Following the second Intifada, Palestinian elections provide new peace opportunities.*

2000 In July Arafat and Labor Party leader Ehud Barak fail to reach a peace agreement at Camp David. . . . Second Intifada begins. . . . In December Arafat and Barak again fail to agree on peace.

2001 Ariel Sharon comes to power.

2002 Israel reoccupies parts of the West Bank. . . . On June 24 President Bush announces his "Roadmap" plan to create a Palestinian state by 2005 but vows not to deal with Arafat. . . . In August Israel begins building a "security fence" encroaching into parts of the West Bank.

2003 Sharon is re-elected on Jan. 28. . . . On June 4 he pledges to support an independent Palestinian state.

2004 On April 14, Bush endorses Sharon's Gaza pullout, arguing that Palestinian refugees' "right of return" must be limited and that many of Israel's West Bank settlements should remain intact in a peace deal. . . . On July 9, International Court of Justice declares much of separation barrier illegal. . . . Sharon wins approval for Gaza pullout on Oct. 26. . . . Arafat dies in Paris on Nov. 11.

Jan. 9, 2005 Mahmoud Abbas is elected Palestinian president with 62 percent of votes but a turnout of only 42 percent of the voters.

Events of the 1980s tarred Israel's reputation as a David fighting for survival against an Arab Goliath. The trend began with the Lebanon invasion and was strengthened when Israeli troops sealed off two Palestinian refugee camps in Beirut, allowing only Israel's Christian Lebanese allies, who were seeking revenge against Palestinian Muslims, to enter. [63] When the Sabra and Shatila camps were opened, the International Red Cross estimated that some 2,400 men, women and children had been killed. [64] An Israeli inquiry found that Sharon, Defense minister at the time, bore "personal responsibility." [65]

Israel left Lebanon in 1985 but retained a 10-mile-wide "security zone" along its own border. Two years later, a popular uprising, or Intifada, erupted among Palestinians in the West Bank and Gaza, taking even the PLO leadership in Tunis by surprise. [66] Palestinians were rebelling against Israeli policies, particularly the confiscation of their land and water for Israeli settlements and their harsh treatment at the hands of Israeli troops. In 1988, the United States began talks with the PLO, negotiations that were boosted by the United States' 1991 success in pushing Iraq out of Kuwait. Then, in 1992, Yitzak Rabin led the Labor Party to power, introducing a new era of negotiation with the Palestinians. [67]

Peace Efforts

The two sides had begun talks in Madrid in 1991, but without success. Now, under Rabin, secret meetings in Oslo yielded an agreement for Israel's withdrawal from much of Gaza and the West Bank city of Jericho. Talks over the next five years were to decide arrangements for the rest of the occupied territories. In September 1993, Arafat and Rabin signed the Oslo Agreement in the White House Rose Garden, and — in a historic first — shook hands while a beaming President Bill Clinton looked on.

In July 1994, Arafat ended his 27-year exile from the occupied territories, returning in triumph to establish the Palestinian Authority (PA), which took over administrative control in some Palestinian areas. By the end of the year, Rabin had agreed to pull the Israeli army out of more West Bank cities, but extremists on both sides soon disrupted the momentum: In November 1995, an Orthodox Jew assassinated Rabin and not long after, Palestinian militants detonated three bombs in Israel, killing 54 people and damaging Israeli confidence in the peace process.

AFP Photo/Menahem Kahana

Israel's controversial security barrier will stretch 455 miles when complete and annex thousands of acres of Palestinian farmland.

The bombings undermined Rabin's successor, Shimon Peres, a key architect of the Oslo Accords. In May 1996, Peres lost a close election for prime minister to Likud leader Benjamin Netanyahu, who had pledged to slow the peace process down. [68] In 1998, Clinton brought Netanyahu and Arafat to rural Maryland to restart negotiations. The ensuing Wye River Memorandum quickly fizzled as Netanyahu's religious and settler supporters forced him to delay fulfilling Israel's obligations and then abandoned his coalition, triggering an election.

Ehud Barak and the Labor Party won that 1999 vote and re-engaged the Palestinians. By July 2000, Barak and Arafat met at Camp David with Clinton to discuss the most difficult "final status" issues, including Israeli settlements, the status of Jerusalem and Palestinian

Israel's Great Wall: Security Measure or Land Grab?

Nowhere is the division and distrust between Israelis and Palestinians more concretely expressed than in the 455-mile security barrier Israel is building. [1] Construction of the network of razor wire, concrete walls, ditches, patrol paths, fences and observation posts began in June 2002 and is slated for completion this year. [2] The barrier's route often juts and curves deeply into the occupied territories.

Barrier proponents argue that a peace settlement is impossible without a physical barricade to give Israelis a sense of security. Others, including the International Court of Justice in The Hague and Israel's Supreme Court, say the barrier violates basic Palestinian rights. [3]

Moreover, Palestinians and some Israelis who oppose the wall contend that rather than being constructed purely for security reasons, Israelis are using it to seize Palestinian land. As currently planned, the barrier will put 157,800 acres or 11.2 percent of the West Bank on the barrier's Israeli side. [4] And in Jerusalem, rather than separating Israelis and Palestinians, the barrier puts 220,000 Palestinians on the western, or Israeli, side.

"From a security point of view, it's problematic," says Yehezkel Lein, of the Israeli human rights group B'tselem.

In addition, in the northern West Bank the barrier cuts Palestinian villages off from their farmlands, accessible now only through military gates. Thousands of the estimated 875,000 Palestinians who live near the barrier have been cut off from their schools, hospitals, fields and workplaces. Other cities are completely encircled by the barrier, apart from an entrance checkpoint maintained by the Israeli army.

Critics also charge that, ultimately, the barrier will be used to determine the parameters of any future Palestinian state. The barrier's planned route around Jerusalem "will dismember the West Bank into northern and southern cantons and seal Jerusalem off from the West Bank," says Danny Seidemann, legal counsel for Ir Amim, an Israeli group devoted to political, economic and social issues in Jerusalem. "It is an attempt to dictate the ideal borders for a Palestinian state."

But proponents of the wall say it is necessary for peace. Uzi Dayan, a former Israeli national security adviser who now heads the Security Fence for Israel movement, says there can be no Palestinian state at all without the barrier, which languished on the drawing boards until dozens of Palestinian suicide bombings in Israel galvanized Israeli public opinion in favor of a barricade. [5]

"Without the fence, we'll never be effective in fighting terrorism," Dayan says. "Without effectively fighting terrorism, there will never be a two-state solution because you

refugees' "right of return." Both that meeting and a later summit in Egypt failed.

Barak's government and the peace talks were faltering in late September, when Likud leader Sharon strode onto the Haram al-Sharif, or Temple Mount, in Jerusalem. Control of the site, holy to both Muslims and Jews, is a difficult final-status issue, and Sharon had bitterly opposed Barak's suggestions that the area could be shared or placed under international supervision. Sharon's visit set off rioting that quickly metastasized into the second Intifada. In February 2001, Israelis responded to Sharon's steely vow to curb Palestinian violence and made him prime minister.

Sharon's election, along with George W. Bush's 2000 presidential victory and the Sept. 11, 2001, terrorist attacks, altered Middle East dynamics. Bush announced he would not be as involved in diplomacy as Clinton and Carter. For his part, Sharon refused to meet with Arafat while the Intifada raged. Arafat, increasingly isolated diplomatically, said he was powerless to stop it.

The conflict escalated in January 2002, when Hamas increasingly used suicide bombers to attack Israeli civilians and soldiers, and Israel began deeper and longer incursions into Palestinian areas. [69] In February, Saudi Crown Prince Abdullah called on Israel to withdraw from the occupied territories in exchange for normalized relations with the Arab world. The proposal received a brief sputter of interest. In March, the Israeli army confined Arafat to his damaged West Bank compound. In April, Israel reoccupied several Palestinian cities in an unsuccessful attempt to stop suicide bombers.

give a bunch of terrorists the key to disrupt it any time. If you want two states, you have to have a fence."

Settlers and right-wing Israelis initially opposed the barrier, fearing it would become a *de facto* border. However, they eventually embraced the idea but lobbied for changes in its route. As construction has progressed, the number of suicide bombings has dropped.

On July 1, 2004, Israel's Supreme Court ordered the Ministry of Defense to stop barrier construction around some parts of Jerusalem and reroute other sections, declaring that the barrier acted as "a veritable chokehold, which will severely stifle daily life." [6] It ordered the army to find a balance between humanitarian and security considerations.

A week later, the International Court of Justice in The Hague ruled that the barrier was illegal because it was built on West Bank land. [7] The U.N. General Assembly, which often opposes Israeli actions, soon followed with a resolution calling for the barrier's removal.

The Israeli government says the barrier is a reversible security measure. But Seidemann argues that simultaneous construction of Israeli settlements alongside the barrier in several areas will make the structure irreversible. Indeed, senior U.S. officials have said that Washington expects Israel to remove settlements on the eastern, Palestinian side of the barrier but would allow settlements on the Israeli side to remain. [8]

"Dovetailed with settlement activity, [the barrier] threatens to create the critical mass of political fact that fur-

ther undermines the feasibility of the two-state solution," Seidemann said. [9] He says U.S. silence on the issue — particularly on accelerated settlement construction around Jerusalem — can only lead to more violence.

Dayan dismisses Seidemann's objections. "People who oppose the fence, oppose it because it's a fence of definition," he says. "I agree that it does hurt. But more than 200 people have been killed in Jerusalem in the last four years. It does disturb [Palestinian] daily routines, but a security fence does not kill people."

---

[1] "Frequently Asked Questions about the Fence," Security Fence for Israel.

[2] http://www.securityfence.mod.gov. il/Pages/ENG/default.htm.

[3] Joseph Berger, "High Court Tells Israelis to Shift Part of Barrier," *The New York Times*, July 1, 2004, p. A1, and Rhoula Khalaf and Nikki Tait, "Israeli West Bank wall breaks law, judges rule," *The Financial Times*, July 10, 2004, p. 11.

[4] *Four Years — Intifada, Closures and Palestinian Economic Crisis,* The World Bank, Oct. 2004, p. 5.

[5] Nicole Gaouette, "Behind the Barrier," *The Christian Science Monitor*, Aug. 8, 2003, p. 1.

[6] Molly Moore, "Israeli Court Orders Changes in Barrier," *The Washington Post*, July 1, 2004, p. A1.

[7] Gregory Crouch and Greg Myre, "Major Portion of Israeli Fence is Ruled Illegal," *The New York Times*, July 10, 2004, p. A1.

[8] Chris McGreal, "Israelis hasten land grab in shadow of wall," *The Guardian*, Dec. 14, 2004, p. 12.

[9] Danny Seidemann, "Letting Israel Self-Destruct," *The Washington Post*, Aug. 26, 2004, p. A23.

The violence prompted Bush to call for Israel's withdrawal from the territories and for Palestinians to crack down on terrorist networks. Neither group complied. Bush's envoy, retired Gen. Anthony Zinni, failed to secure a ceasefire. In the atmosphere of unrelenting violence, Israel began its 450-mile security barrier. [70]

The 'Roadmap'

In June 2002, pressured by Arab states to act, Bush outlined his plan for a Palestinian state. The three-step "roadmap" was structured so final borders would be settled by the end of 2005. Bush also stressed that Palestinians had to reform their political system and elect "new leaders, not compromised by terror," a reference to Arafat. [71] The United States delayed publishing the roadmap until Sharon won a landslide re-election in

February 2003 and delayed again until political reforms brought Mahmoud Abbas, the first Palestinian prime minister, to power on April 29.

Abbas called peace a "strategic, irrevocable choice" for Palestinians the day his nomination was approved, but his appointment failed to generate any momentum. Sharon refused to ease conditions for Palestinians — most of whom lived under lengthy curfews with Israeli troops patrolling their city streets — until the PA pursued militant groups. Fearing a civil war and lacking popular support, Abbas insisted he would start with dialogue, not confrontation, in dealing with Hamas and others.

Though Hamas offered a ceasefire if Israel stopped attacks on its members, Sharon refused, concerned the group would use the time to rearm. [72] In the ensuing stalemate, Israel imposed the toughest restrictions on

Evangelical Christians Support Israel

Billboards began appearing across the United States in spring 2003, shortly after President Bush unveiled his "Roadmap" for an Israeli-Palestinian settlement. "Unto thy offspring will I give this land," they read, quoting from Genesis and exhorting readers to "pray that President Bush honors God's covenant with Israel. Call the White House with this message." [1]

The billboards were sponsored, in part, by a Christian Zionist group whose leader boasted, "We're in constant contact with the White House." While it is not clear how much the president's evangelical faith shapes his foreign policy, it is evident that Christian conservatives have become influential on matters concerning Israel and the Palestinians.

Evangelical Christians are intensely interested in the future of Israel because they believe the return of Jews to Israel signals the return of the Messiah and the beginning of the End Times — an apocalyptic battle between good and evil. They see attempts to divide the Holy Land as blasphemy or worse.

A separate Palestinian state is part of "Satan's plan," warns televangelist Pat Robertson. [2] "If the United States takes a role in ripping Jerusalem away from Israel and giving it to . . . a bunch of terrorists, we are going to see the wrath of God fall on this nation that will make tornadoes look like a Sunday school picnic." [3]

"Arguably, evangelicals are the strongest Zionists in the country, not the Jews," says Luis E. Lugo, director of the Pew Forum on Religion & Public Life. "They imbue [Israel] with theological significance, not just strategic or political significance, but a sense that God gave this land to the Jews."

Roughly a quarter of the U.S. electorate identify themselves as evangelicals. [4] In the 2004 election, 78 percent of them voted for Bush. In fact, support for Israel was a primary consideration for 31 percent of evangelical Christians when deciding whether to vote for the president or Sen. John Kerry. [5]

Evangelical concern for Israel increased in the last few years, says journalist Esther Kaplan, author of *With God on Their Side*, a critical look at Christian fundamentalist influence on the Bush administration. "I think the 'war on terror' framework dovetailed with commitment to Israel to create a confluence of ideas about Islam and the Palestinians as the enemy, along with this idea that God granted this land to the Jews," she says. "These two sets of religiously driven political beliefs merged after [the terrorist attacks of] 9/11 and took off."

Evangelical voters envision a peace settlement, but not in the West Bank. "Encourage peace by all means, but that doesn't mean the Jews have to be kicked off the land or give it away," explains evangelical broadcaster Janet Parshall,

Gaza since the second Intifada's start. In late May, Israel adopted 14 reservations to the roadmap, widely seen by Palestinians as gutting the plan of any substance. [73]

Suicide bombings and Israeli army strikes on refugee camps and cities continued. By September, Abbas resigned, saying he had been undermined by a lack of support from Arafat, the United States and Israel. [74] Despite the lack of official progress, in December 2003 a group of former Israeli and Palestinian government officials presented their own peace plan, the Geneva Accords. Sharon derided the proposal and presented his own plan to unilaterally declare new borders and withdraw from some settlements. [75]

In February 2004 Sharon offered details of his "disengagement" plan. It involved removing Israelis from 21 Gaza settlements and four in the West Bank and angered both settlers and Palestinians, who argued that Sharon's

plan violated the roadmap. The United States, however, praised it as a way to jump-start roadmap talks. In March, Israel assassinated the spiritual leader of Hamas, Sheik Ahmed Yassin, infuriating the Arab world.

Palestinian alienation deepened in April, when Bush released a groundbreaking letter to Sharon in which he placed the burden for peace squarely on the Palestinians and dismissed two longstanding bases for peace negotiations: Bush dismissed the "right of return" and deemed some West Bank settlements new "realities."

Arab leaders — angry about Bush's letter, the Iraq war and revelations about the U.S. military's mistreatment of Iraqi prisoners at Abu Ghraib prison outside Baghdad — pushed the United States to re-engage with the Palestinians. In May, Bush pledged to broker a "just peace." [76]

Nonetheless, the violence continued, with both sides roiled by internal political discord. Israel launched a mas-

who sees a solution in neighboring Jordan. "I think you could absolutely have two states, but you don't have to do it in [the West Bank]. You have a next-door neighbor, who, for all intents and purposes, is already a Palestinian state." She echoes Sharon, who has long advocated the idea that Jordan is Palestine.

Parshall believes the president's faith informs his approach to the Middle East. "I believe that, as an evangelical, [Bush] understands the importance of that land," she says. "He hasn't drawn borders. I remember clearly [National Security Adviser] Dr. [Condoleeza] Rice saying, 'All we want to do is get parties together.' "

This administration has been described as "the most resolutely 'faith-based' in modern times," [6] and Bush has told friends he felt called to run for president. [7] His policy on the Middle East has been more evidently pro-Israel than that of his recent predecessors. Yet some observers say that on Israel, Bush separates personal faith from public policy.

"My impression is that the president feels an obligation to protect Israel because they are an ally and a democracy that is surrounded by enemies from all sides," says Michael Cromartie, vice president of the Ethics and Public Policy Center. "It is a mistake to say that because the president is an evangelical Christian himself that some kind of Christian view of the End Times motivates his concerns. Rather, I think geopolitical realities on the ground are the chief motivating factor."

The president's personal faith is irrelevant given the political power evangelicals wield, says pollster James Zogby, president of the Arab American Institute. In 2003, the Zogby International polling firm asked Americans whether the U.S. should press Israel to leave the occupied territories. Overall, 55 percent said yes, and 45 percent said no. But 80 percent of evangelicals said no, he points out.

"This conservative grouping is the base vote of the Republican Party and is driving the debate," Zogby says. "They are the group the president cannot lose, and I believe he has tailored his position on this issue to meet that constituency."

---

[1] Rick Perlstein, "The Jesus Landing Pad," *The Village Voice*, May 18, 2004.

[2] "Pat Robertson: Only God Should Decide Gaza," NewsMax Wires, Oct. 4, 2004.

[3] www.patrobertson.com/Teaching/TeachingonRoadMap.asp.

[4] "Evangelicals and U.S. Foreign Policy," Luis E. Lugo, Pew Forum talk at Carnegie Endowment for International Peace, Nov. 18, 2004. For background, see David Masci, "Evangelical Christians," *The CQ Researcher*, Sept. 14, 2001, pp. 713-736.

[5] "Support for Israel Drives Evangelical Vote, Poll Finds," International Fellowship of Christians and Jews, Oct. 6, 2004. Also see Esther Kaplan, *With God on Their Side* (2004), p. 25.

[6] Howard Fineman, "Bush and God," *Newsweek*, March 10, 2003.

[7] Kevin Phillips, *American Dynasty* (2004), p. 233, and "The Faith of George W. Bush," Goodtimes Entertainment video.

---

sive incursion into Gaza to search for tunnels being used to smuggle weapons from Egypt, earning U.N. condemnation for the Palestinian death toll and destruction of homes. Kidnappings within the Palestinian community in Gaza underscored the tensions between Hamas and Arafat's Fatah party.

In Israel, right-wing groups increasingly vilified Sharon for the Gaza pullout plan. The rancor extended to the prime minister's Likud Party, which refused to approve the pullout or Sharon's attempts to bring Labor into his faltering coalition. In July, the International Court in The Hague ruled that much of Israel's security barrier was illegal, since most of the completed 120-mile portion had been built inside the West Bank. The U.N. General Assembly called for the barrier's removal.

In October, Sharon's former chief of staff and personal lawyer told an Israeli newspaper that the Gaza pull-

out was intended to freeze the peace process, "prevent the establishment of a Palestinian state" and strengthen Israel's hold on its West Bank settlements. [77] Sixteen days later, Israel's parliament approved the evacuation of Gaza settlements by September 2005.

On Oct. 29, an ill Arafat left his Ramallah compound — for the first time in more than two years — and flew to Paris for medical tests. His death there on Nov. 11, at age 75, spurred the first surge of optimism about peace in years. Abbas was quickly voted into Arafat's old job as head of the PLO and later approved as the main party's candidate for president of the PA. The United States pledged to give the Palestinians $20 million in direct aid. [78]

By the time Abbas was elected on Jan. 9, 2005, with 62 percent of the vote, the second Intifada had claimed at least 1,013 Israelis and 3,361 Palestinians. [79]

CURRENT SITUATION

U.S. Policy

Although President Bush has pledged to "spend the capital" of the United States to reach a Middle East peace settlement during his second term, his forays into peacemaking have had limited success. Few analysts expect him to plunge into assertive mediation in the years ahead. Thus, the onus will be on the Palestinians to create momentum that the U.S. can put its shoulder behind.

Bush's cautious approach results from watching his predecessor's failures and experiencing his own. Bush made it clear when first elected that he would not invest the kind of effort former President Clinton made to pull Israelis and Palestinians together. Events soon forced his hand.

The Sept. 11, 2001, terrorist attacks on New York and the Pentagon concentrated U.S. attention on the Middle East and set the stage for the U.S. attack on Iraq. In spring 2002, the need to win regional support for the Iraq invasion made Bush responsive to Arab leaders' concerns about spiraling Israeli-Palestinian violence. That summer he unveiled the roadmap to establish "a provisional state of Palestine" by 2005. [80]

But violence quickly eviscerated that initiative and, distracted by the war in Iraq, the United States retreated to a less active role. When Sharon unveiled his plan for a unilateral withdrawal of settlements from the Gaza Strip in December 2003, the administration described it as a courageous step that could break the impasse between the parties and restart progress on the roadmap.

The United States has not done much since Sharon's pullout announcement and its approval by the Israeli parliament. "The administration's thinking is that the time isn't ripe for a massive peace push, so it is better to concentrate on the smaller efforts that may end up being the foundation for a peace deal," wrote *Wall Street Journal* reporter Neil King Jr. [81] This emphasis on small steps dovetails with Sharon's vision of a long interim period preceding any final settlement. [82]

The changing of the guard at the State Department means that former national security adviser and Secretary of State nominee Condoleeza Rice will oversee these modest efforts. Colin L. Powell's term as secretary of State was often marked by tension between the White House and State Department over many aspects of Middle East policy. Powell often spoke about the need for Israel to stop settlement construction, while the White House remained silent.

Some observers say the good working relationship between Rice and Bush will be a boon for the peace process. "The chances of success are greater because of these personnel changes in the administration," says Makovsky of the Washington Institute. "You need a secretary of State who can say, 'I speak with the full authority of the president of the United States.' I think this secretary of State can do that in a way that the previous secretary of State, with all his accomplishments, couldn't."

In fact, on June 29, 2003, Rice called on Israel to redraw the boundary for the wall so that it annexes less Palestinian land.

Abbas and Hamas

With his gray hair, steel-rimmed glasses and banker's suits, Mahmoud Abbas has always looked more the technocrat than the revolutionary. That has been part of his appeal to U.S. and Israeli interlocutors looking for an acceptable face of Palestinian power. And while Abbas' moderation — and willingness to argue for it publicly — ensured foreign support for his candidacy, it will not guarantee Palestinian backing for his presidency.

The former lawyer and businessman won the Jan. 9 presidential election backed by the main Fatah party, but his power base is weak. Young Fatah reformers see the 69-year-old Abbas as part of Arafat's corrupt generation, and the old guard no longer trusts Abbas entirely after he courted the reformers during his brief 2003 tenure as prime minister. But his most difficult relationship will be with Islamic militants outside Fatah, particularly the politically popular Hamas.

In the late 1980s, Israel encouraged an Islamic movement in the Gaza Strip to compete with Arafat's PLO. The Islamic Resistance Movement — known by the Arabic acronym 'Hamas,' meaning "zeal" — was the result. Dedicated to Israel's destruction, Hamas accepts neither the 1993 Oslo Accords nor the legitimacy of the PA. Its suicide bombers have killed and maimed hundreds of Israeli civilians since the second Intifada began in 2000.

In the post-Arafat era, Hamas is using municipal and legislative elections to transform itself into a legitimate political party. It won 35 percent of the races in the December 2004 municipal elections but urged members to boycott the January presidential election. [83] The low 43 percent turnout for that race is seen as an indication

Will President Bush's April 14 proposal to Ariel Sharon advance the peace process?

YES   Bernice Manocherian
President, American Israel Public Affairs Committee

Written for The CQ Researcher, January 2005

In a letter to Prime Minister Ariel Sharon last April 14, President Bush laid out his vision for peace between Israel and the Palestinians, as well as his plan for getting there.

By reaffirming critical American security guarantees to Israel, this letter enabled the Jewish state to commit to a breathtaking risk for peace — withdrawing from all of Gaza and more than 300 square miles in the West Bank.

Together with the emergence of a new and potentially reformed leadership in the Palestinian Authority (PA), the president's commitment to the security of Israel has helped to lay the foundation for a possible resumption of political negotiations between the Israelis and Palestinians.

In his letter to Sharon, President Bush reiterated his vision of "two states living side by side in peace and security," Israel as "a Jewish state" within "secure, defensible borders," and a "viable, contiguous, sovereign and independent" Palestinian state.

The letter included two crucial assurances. First, Palestinian refugees would resettle in the Palestinian state "rather than in Israel." Second, Israel would not be expected to return to its 1949 borders as part of a final settlement with the Palestinians.

Both of these guarantees were based on simple logic and were also included in President Clinton's December 2000 peace plan: Palestinian refugees will go to the Palestinian state and Jewish refugees to the Jewish state, and the 1949 armistice line has never been recognized as a final border.

Based on these principles, Sharon was able to announce courageous and unprecedented Israeli steps toward peace.

Under Sharon's disengagement plan, Israel will commit to the largest Israeli territorial concession since it withdrew from the Sinai Peninsula in 1982. Israel will withdraw from Gaza and an area twice as large in the West Bank, giving more than 1.7 million Palestinians an unconditional opportunity to govern themselves.

Israel has also adopted severe restrictions on settlement growth and begun to dismantle unauthorized outposts in the West Bank and Gaza. It is undertaking humanitarian measures to improve the daily lives of Palestinians in those areas.

These steps have helped to provide the basis for future political negotiations between Israel and the Palestinians, provided the PA rids itself of corruption and cracks down on the terrorist groups that have killed more than 1,000 Israelis over the past four years.

By supporting a secure future, both for Israel and the Palestinians, the president's letter of April 14, 2004, strengthened prospects for peace in the Middle East.

NO   Ziad Asali M.D.
President, American Task Force on Palestine

Written for The CQ Researcher, Jan. 4, 2005

The predictable parts of the president's significant letter included his commitment to the vision he expressed on June 24, 2002, for two states living side-by-side in peace and security, and to his "Roadmap" as the route to get there.

The president's vision was for a Palestinian state that is viable, contiguous, sovereign and independent; supported by the international community as it develops democratic institutions; and energized by a free and prosperous economy and security institutions dedicated to maintaining law and order.

His support for the Disengagement Plan came as no surprise. Nor did his restated commitment to the "Roadmap." But the reassurances the president felt that he needed to provide to Israel for the risks included several significant and controversial points. The most salient was that any final agreement will be achieved only on the basis of mutually agreed changes that reflect new realities on the ground.

The president also referred to the responsibilities Israel assumes consistent with its statement that the barrier is a temporary, security barrier rather than a permanent, political barrier. Significantly, the president reiterated his commitment to a negotiated peace settlement between the parties in accordance with U.N. Security Council Resolutions 242 and 338. He also proposed resettling the refugees in Palestine rather than in Israel.

The president's unwavering commitment to Israel's security coincided with his repeated references to terrorism. In fact, he used the word terror, terrorism or terrorist 13 times in a two-page letter. One hopes that association with these words does not collectively burden the Palestinians.

Critics have pointed out that the reassurances President Bush gave to Mr. Sharon were unmatched by explicit reassurances needed by the Palestinians, such as withdrawal of Israeli Defense Forces, cessation of settlement building, relieving the oppressive measures against civilians, ending the occupation and acknowledging political rights in the old city and East Jerusalem. It remains to be seen what reassurances the president will give the new Palestinian president on his first visit to Washington.

For those of us who are more interested in a peaceful resolution than in scoring debating points, we must factor in the new Palestinian political realities, notably the passing of Chairman Arafat and the changes that have led to the democratic election of President Abbas.

The potential exists for cooperative relations between parties whose strategic interests in a two-state solution do not fundamentally contradict each other. The president has the unmatched opportunity to implement his vision by coordinating the efforts of an old ally with that of a new one.

Israeli police evict an Israeli settler at the illegal West Bank outpost settlement of Mitzpe Itzhar on Jan. 3, 2005. Israeli Prime Minister Ariel Sharon has proposed abandoning Israel's Gaza Strip settlements but retaining all but four in the West Bank.

of its influence. [84] Hamas' participation in the July 2005 legislative elections will provide a clearer picture of the distribution of power between the militant group and Fatah, but it is already evident that Hamas' attempt to reinvent itself will require compromises.

"The fundamental change will be what Hamas does in deed, not in word," says Rabbani of the International Crisis Group. "They won't recognize Israel, but they [also] won't obstruct a PLO leadership that can negotiate an end to the occupation."

Since Arafat's death, Hamas has asked Fatah for a power-sharing arrangement, offered Israel a 10-year truce and said it would accept creation of a Palestinian state in the West Bank and Gaza Strip. "That means Hamas accepts that the other party will live in security and peace," said Hamas leader Sheik Hassan Yousef. [85]

The shift is born of maturity, Hamas leaders said. [86] Desperation also may be a factor: Israel has assassinated Hamas' three most important founding members and scores of its field commanders in retaliation for suicide bombings. Hamas leadership in Gaza and the West Bank is now in hiding. Both the United States and Britain have designated Hamas as a terrorist group, damaging its fundraising capabilities. And any sign of peace tends to drain Palestinian support away from Hamas in favor of Fatah.

The Intifada has boosted Hamas' appeal among Palestinians because of its violence against Israel and the medicine and food it provided during the Intifada, when the PA all but ceased to function. Unlike Fatah, it distributed aid regardless of recipients' political leanings. For Abbas, Hamas' success presents a political Catch-22.

The United States and Israel have demanded Palestinian democratic reform. Those reforms are legitimizing Hamas, which the United States and Israel insist Abbas dismantle. Yet Abbas will need Hamas' help to run Gaza if Israel withdraws. [87] For now, he also lacks the power to confront the Islamists and has made it clear that he won't. "We will not forget those wanted by Israel," Abbas said on one campaign stop. "These are the heroes who are fighting for freedom." [88]

Professor Quandt, of the University of Virginia, says it will be some time before Abbas can address the challenge posed by Hamas. "His first order of business is to get his authority established," Quandt says. "He has to create a new base within Fatah, clean out the dead wood and the security forces, which are run by mini-warlords right now. He doesn't have anything to work with yet."

In the days before and after the presidential election, Hamas sent Abbas multiple reminders of its power. The group launched two attacks on Israeli soldiers, blasted homemade Qassam rockets into Israel and distributed flyers denouncing Abbas' remarks that the Intifada and the use of violence had failed. [89] The attacks served notice that Hamas can undermine Abbas' presidency with its attacks or bolster his position by remaining quiet.

Even so, many observers expect more Hamas strikes in the months leading up to the pullout from Gaza settlements, so the group can claim a victory for its tactics if and when Israel leaves. "Hamas wants it to happen under fire," says Quandt.

The Occupied Territories

Twenty-four hours before Palestinian elections began, Israeli troops pulled out of Palestinian cities. The day after, Jan. 10, the troops were back. Life, as Palestinians now know it, was back to normal: a stop-and-go series of Israeli checkpoints, highways open to Israeli settlers but closed to Palestinians and local roads blocked with piles of rubble, courtesy of the Israeli army.

Movement within the occupied territories has been an enormous challenge since Sharon reoccupied the West Bank in April 2002 in an effort to curb suicide bombings. Israel used many tools to strike back at militants, including mass arrests, assassinations and assaults on West Bank towns, but its controls on Palestinian movement have had the broadest effect on people and their livelihoods.

Dubbed "closure," these restrictions cover the movement of Palestinian people and goods within the occupied territories and between the territories and Israel proper. The separation barrier is part of the closure system, as are curfews enforced by army jeeps in Palestinian cities. Curfews, which can be implemented for 24 hours at a time for several consecutive days, affected more than 500,000 people daily for almost seven months in 2002. [90]

Israel has said it will withdraw troops when Palestinians can take responsibility for security, but the controls are likely to stay in place for now. From a security perspective, they are effective. In July 2004, Israeli Defense Minister Shaul Mofaz credited them with helping to cut the number of suicide bombers by 75 percent from 2003. [91]

"I don't want Israeli troops in the Palestinian towns," Mofaz said in January 2005. "We are there now because we have no other choice; we have to stop the suicide bombers. We don't want all these roadblocks and checkpoints to exist. . . . But if [Palestinians] will not be a partner and stop the violence, then we will stop the violence for them." [92]

While curfews have eased, the economic impact of closures continues to be devastating. They disrupt business, supply routes, raise transportation costs and cut the links between rural areas and urban centers. People are unable to reach work, children are cut off from school, and the ill are often unable to reach medical care. [93]

Within two years after the second Intifada began in September 2000, Palestinian per capita income had dropped 40 percent. By 2003, nearly half of all Palestinians had fallen below the poverty line and were living on less than $2.30 a day.

"The precipitator of this economic crisis has been 'closure,' " said a World Bank report. "Without major changes in the closure regime . . . there is no prospect of a sustained recovery of the Palestinian economy."

OUTLOOK

Many Uncertainties

The late Israeli politician Abba Eban once quipped that Palestinians never miss an opportunity to miss an opportunity. In the wake of Arafat's death and the elections that brought Abbas to power, Palestinians have arrived at another moment of opportunity — albeit one not entirely within their control. Most agree that while the spotlight rests on the Palestinians, future actions by Israel and the United States will also greatly affect the outcome of the Middle East's "Hundred Years War." [94]

Israel likely will focus on the upheaval surrounding the Gaza pullout and the wrenching prospect of army clashes with settlers, who are "fighting for their ideological lives right now," says Steinberg, the political scientist at Bar Ilan University.

The Bush administration will set itself small goals and avoid deep involvement in the conflict, analysts say. U.S. diplomacy will emphasize the need for Palestinian democracy, grounds for the optimism of some observers and the deep pessimism of others.

The pessimists say the focus on democracy is a screen for inaction, which will only stoke Palestinian anger that will undermine Abbas, boost militant groups such as Hamas and lead to further violence. Significant violence will prolong Sharon's unilateral approach to the conflict. Israelis will expand settlements, making it physically impossible for Palestinians to establish the state envisioned in peace negotiations of the 1990s.

"[Bush is] conditioning meaningful progress toward a settlement on secondary issues, such as Palestinian institutional reform," says International Crisis Group's Rabbani. "What it's effectively doing is procrastinating. The result is to make it increasingly less likely that a settlement will be reached while a two-state solution is still viable."

Makovsky of the Washington Institute counters that demands for democracy are not just a way to "push the can down the road" and delay peace talks, but are a genuine grassroots desire. "I see Abbas as signaling a real historical turning point," he says.

Supporters of democratic reform see a strong link between security and democracy. This view is championed most prominently by Soviet dissident turned Israeli Knesset member Natan Sharansky, who argues that democracies create stable, inherently peaceful societies. Though it may take "years, even decades," Sharansky writes, democracy would allow Palestinians to defuse belligerent leaders. [95]

Abbas may not last for decades, let alone years, though many say that his stewardship of this transition will have an enduring impact. "Abbas could undercut support for the Islamists by making progress in the peace process and improving economic conditions," said Khalil Shikaki of the Palestinian Center for Policy and Survey Research. "He could also buttress the institutions of

Palestinian democracy. . . . These institutions must outlast Abbas if democracy is to survive." [96]

Even so, "it's unclear whether there's a Palestinian leadership Israel can deal with," Steinberg says. "It will likely take any Palestinian leader a long time to get out of Arafat's shadow. The prospects of permanent-status negotiations still seem far down the road and that brings us back to unilateral policies, to a framework of Israel deciding what it can do in terms of drawing back from territory."

If the United States pushes ahead with talks, Lieven of the Carnegie Foundation sees little progress as long as Sharon leads Israel. "His terms will give Israel control over water, air space and access to the outside world. Not only will large settlement blocs within the occupied territories be annexed to Israel, but the Palestinian territories will be divided by Israeli-controlled roads and security zones to provide access and defense for those settlements. These are terms that no self-respecting nationalist movement can accept," he says.

If those terms do become the basis of an agreement, the University of Virginia's Quandt does not expect a Palestinian state to thrive economically or attract investment.

"This is not a picture of two viable states living side by side," he says. "I would be absolutely stunned if a 10-to-15-year period produced that."

NOTES

1. Greg Myre, "Mandate in Hand, Abbas Declares He's Ready for Talks," *The New York Times*, Jan. 10, 2005, p. A3.

2. Joel Greenberg, "Sharon calls Abbas to congratulate him," *The Chicago Tribune*, Jan. 12, 2005, p. 4.

3. Mike Allen and Glenn Kessler, "Bush Goal: Palestinian State by 2009," *The Washington Post*, Nov. 13, 2004, p. A1.

4. Chris McGreal, "Five Children Killed in Gaza Strip Battles," *The Guardian*, Sept. 30, 2004, p. 15.

5. Robert Malley, "Palestinians are in a deadly vacuum," *The Financial Times*, Sept. 29, 2004, p. 19.

6. *Ibid.*

7. Gil Hoffman, "Rabbi's blessing seals Sharon's unity coalition," *The Jerusalem Post*, Jan. 6, 2005, p. 1.

8. Bradley Burston, "The 3rd Intifada: Settlers take on their own army," *Haaretz*, Jan. 5, 2005.

9. Mohammed Daraghmeh, "Abbas Presses for Peace Talks," The Associated Press, Jan. 7, 2005.

10. Burston, *op. cit.*

11. "Report on Israeli Settlement in the Occupied Territories," Foundation for Middle East Peace, Nov.-Dec. 2004, p. 8.

12. Chris McGreal, "Israelis hasten land grab in shadow of wall," *The Guardian*, Dec. 14, 2004, p. 12.

13. *Ibid.*

14. Foundation for Middle East Peace, *op. cit.*

15. Tony Judt, "Israel: The Alternative," *New York Review of Books*, Oct. 23, 2003; www.nybooks.com/articles/16671.

16. Leon Wieseltier, "Must Peace Wait for Democracy?" *The New York Times Magazine*, Jan. 9, 2005, p. 15.

17. Allen and Kessler, *op. cit.*

18. Ephraim Sneh, "A once-in-a-lifetime opportunity," Haaretz, Nov. 12, 2004; www.commongroundnews.org/article.php?mode=8&id=419].

19. Abdullah II, "The Road From Here," *The New York Times*, Nov. 12, 2004, p. 22.

20. For background, see David Masci, "Prospects for Mideast Peace," *The CQ Researcher*, Aug. 30, 2002, pp. 673-696.

21. Etgar Lefkovits, "Post-Arafat polls: Still no peace partner," *The Jerusalem Post*, Nov. 29, 2004, p. 2.

22. Palestinian Center for Policy and Survey Research, Dec. 1-5, 2004 poll; www.pcpsr.org/survey/polls/2004/p14epressreleaseF.html.

23. "After Arafat? Challenges and Prospects," International Crisis Group, Dec. 23, 2004; www.icg.org/home/index.cfm?id=3197&l=1.

24. Molly Moore and John Ward Anderson, "Shots Fired Near New PLO Chief," *The Washington Post*, Nov. 15, 2004, p. A22.

25. *Ibid.*

26. Ari Shavit, "The Big Freeze," *Haaretz*, Oct. 1, 2004; www.fmep.org/analysis/interview_weisglass_10-01-04.htm.

27. John Ward Anderson, "Sharon Aide Says Goal Of Gaza Plan Is to Halt Roadmap," *The Washington Post*, Oct. 7, 2004, p. A14.

28. Joel Greenberg, "'Historic breakthough' possible, Sharon says," *The Chicago Tribune*, Dec. 17, 2004, p. 3.

29. Allen and Kessler, *op. cit.*

30. International Crisis Group, *op. cit.*

31. Zbigniew Brzezinski, "Hegemonic Quicksand," *The National Interest*, Winter 2003-2004, pp. 8 and 11.

32. Joel Brinkley, "Arab and Western Ministers Voice Different Priorities," *The New York Times*, Dec. 12, 2004, p. 28.

33. Steve Coll, *Ghost Wars* (2004), p. 250.

34. Osama Bin Laden, "Jihad Against Jews and Crusaders," ed. Walter Laqueur, *Voices of Terror* (2004), p. 410.

35. Brzezinski, *op. cit.*, p. 8.

36. Suzanne Goldenberg, "Former diplomats attack Bush," *The Guardian*, May 4, 2004, p. 2.

37. Norman Podhoretz, "World War IV: How It Started, What It Means, and Why We Have to Win," *Commentary*, September 2004, pp. 18 and 40.

38. Josef Joffe, "A World Without Israel," *Foreign Policy*, Jan-Feb 2005. p 42.

39. Foundation for Middle East Peace, *op. cit.*, p. 5.

40. Ephraim Sneh, "Sharon's plan will perpetuate war," Haaretz, Oct. 11, 2004; www.fmep.org/analysis/ sneh_sharons_plan_will_perpetuate_war.htm.

41. John Ward Anderson and Molly Moore, "After Gaza Win, Sharon Fights Political Doubt," *The Washington Post*, Oct. 30, 2004, p. A28.

42. Shavit, *op. cit.*

43. Greg Myre, "Sharon Doubts Gaza Exit Aids the Road Map," *The New York Times*, Sept. 15, 2004, p. 5.

44. Ben Lynfield, "Sharon stakes job on pullout," *The Christian Science Monitor*, Oct. 28, 2004, p. 1.

45. Nina Gilbert, "Knesset approves compensation bill," *The Jerusalem Post*, Nov. 4, 2004, p. 1.

46. Yaakov Katz, "Settler chiefs endorse civil disobedience," *The Jerusalem Post*, Dec. 21, 2004, p. 1.

47. Amos Harel and Nir Hasson, "West Bank youth move into Gaza to obstruct pullout," *Haaretz*, Jan. 2, 2005.

48. "Wallerstein's letter calls for civil disobedience," *The Jerusalem Post*, Dec. 21, 2004.

49. Burston, *op. cit.*

50. Martin Indyk, "The Day that Bush Took Gaza," *The Washington Post*, April 25, 2004, p. B1.

51. Glenn Frankel, *Beyond the Promised Land* (1996), p. 13.

52. Walter Laqueur and Barry Rubin, eds., *The Israel-Arab Reader* (2001), p. 16.

53. Dennis Ross, *The Missing Peace* (2004), pp. 19, 31 and 32.

54. Ross, *op. cit.*, p. 20.

55. David Masci, "Middle East Conflict," *The CQ Researcher*, April 6, 2001, p. 284

56. http://ods-dds-ny.UN.org/doc/RESOLUTION/GEN/ NR0/240/94/IMG/NR024094.pdf?OpenElement.

57. Ross, *op. cit.*, p. 22

58. For background, see Richard L. Worsnop, "Centennial Olympic Games," *The CQ Researcher*, April 5, 1996, pp. 289-312.

59. Ross, *op. cit.*, p. 26.

60. *Ibid.*

61. Martin Gilbert, *Israel: A History* (1998), p. 492.

62. For background, see Mary H. Cooper, "Foreign Aid After Sept. 11," *The CQ Researcher*, April 26, 2002, p. 365. For aid figures, see Clyde R. Mark, Congressional Research Service, "Israel: U.S. Foreign Assistance," Oct. 3, 2003, and "Egypt-United States Relations," Oct. 10, 2003, p. 3.

63. Gilbert, *op. cit.*, p. 509.

64. Tomas Kapitan, "Sabra and Shatilla massacre, 1982," *Encyclopedia of War and Ethics 1996*; www.globalpolicy.org/intljustice/general/2001/sab &shat.htm.

65. Laqueur and Rubin, *op. cit.*, p. 269.

66. Gilbert, *op. cit.*, p. 525.

67. *Ibid*, p. 551.

68. *Ibid*, pp. 594-595.

69. "It Can Only Get Worse," *The Economist*, Jan. 26, 2002.

70. Nicole Gaouette, "Behind the Barrier," *The Christian Science Monitor*, Aug. 8, 2003, p. 1.

71. Glenn Kessler, "Cutting Arafat Loose, But Not by Name," *The Washington Post*, June 30, 2002, p. A19.

72. James Bennet, "Sharon Gives Plan for Mideast Peace Qualified Support," *The New York Times*, May 24, 2003, p. 1.

73. Harvey Morris, "Palestinians fear 'road map' may lead to a dead end," *The Financial Times*, May 15, 2003, p. 9, and Harvey Morris, "Palestinian leader in fight to restore his credibility," *The Financial Times*, June 10, 2003, p. 8.

74. Chris McGreal, "Middle East crisis: Ridiculed and betrayed: Why Abbas blames Arafat," *The Guardian*, Sept. 8, 2003, p. 4.

75. John Ward Anderson and Molly Moore, "Sharon Threatens to Redraw Borders," *The Washington Post*, Dec. 19, 2003, p. A1.

76. Glenn Kessler, "Talks with Palestinian Officials to Resume," *The Washington Post*, May 7, 2004, p. A1, and Janine Zacharia, "Arab furor over Iraq grows," *The Jerusalem Post*, May 7, 2004, p. 1.

77. Anderson and Moore, Dec. 19, 2003, *op. cit.*

78. BBC News, "US Pledges $20 mln to Palestinians," Dec. 8, 2004, http://news.bbc.co.uk/1/hi/world/middle_east/4080061.stm.

79. Ben Lynfield, "Moves Toward Moderation," *The Christian Science Monitor*, Dec. 14, 2004, p. 1.

80. "Text of President Bush's address on the Middle East," *The Washington Post*, June 25, 2002, p. A12.

81. Neil King Jr., "Bush Plans New Strategy for Middle East," *The Wall Street Journal*, Dec. 29, 2004, p. A4.

82. Myre, *op. cit.*, Sept. 15, 2004.

83. John Ward Anderson and Molly Moore, "Hamas Won Power in West Bank Vote," *The Washington Post*, Jan. 6, 2005, p. A15.

84. John Ward Anderson and Molly Moore, "Palestinians Appear to Give Abbas A Clear Win," *The Washington Post*, Jan. 10, 2005, p. A1.

85. "Hamas to call truce," The Associated Press, Dec. 3, 2004.

86. "Hamas leader says would consider 10-year truce," *Haaretz*, Nov. 29, 2004.

87. Laura King, "Abbas Will Have to Win More Than Vote," *Los Angeles Times*, Jan. 7, 2005.

88. Bradley Burston, "The Abbas Problem: Partner or Yasser Redux," *Haaretz*, Jan. 3, 2005.

89. Sharmila Devi and Harvey Morris, "Gaza militants raise pressure on Abbas by striking at Israeli army," *The Financial Times*, Jan. 6, 2005, p. 7.

90. "Four Years — Intifada, Closures and Palestinian Economic Crisis," *The World Bank*, October 2004.

91. Chris McGreal, "Thwarted Hamas turns from bombs to politics," *The Guardian*, July 2, 2004, p. 18.

92. Steven Erlanger, "Israeli Defense Chief Hopeful About New Palestinian Attitude," *The New York Times*, Jan. 6, 2004, p. 3.

93. Unless otherwise noted, statistics in this section are from *The World Bank*, *op. cit.*

94. Frankel, *op. cit.*

95. Natan Sharansky with Ron Dermer, *The Case for Democracy* (2004).

96. Khalil Shikaki, "Among Palestinians, Evidence of Change," *The Washington Post*, Dec. 12, 2004, p. B1.

BIBLIOGRAPHY

Books

Gilbert, Martin, *Israel*, William Morrow, 1998.
One of Britain's most respected historians provides an invaluable and engaging chronicle of Israel's first 50 years; the detailed maps and index make the book highly accessible.

Grose, Peter, *Israel in the Mind of America*, Alfred A. Knopf, 1983.
A research associate at Harvard's Belfer Center for Science and International Affairs examines the U.S. role in Israel's founding as well as the history of American sympathy for Jews.

Laqueur, Walter, ed., *Voices of Terror*, Reed Press, 2004.
This compilation of writings about the use of violence as a political tool includes many primary source materials, including statements by Osama bin Laden.

Laqueur, Walter, and Barry Rubin, eds., *The Israel-Arab Reader*, Penguin Books, 2001.
This comprehensive research guide includes speeches, letters, treaties and other documents relating to the Arab-Israeli conflict.

Lieven, Anatol, "America: Right or Wrong," Oxford University Press, 2004.

A senior associate at the Carnegie Endowment for International Peace writes that U.S. policy in Israel isolates the United States from the international community and alienates Arab countries.

Oren, Michael, *Six Days of War*, Penguin Books, 2002.

The definitive history of the 1967 war that brought the West Bank, Gaza Strip, Sinai and Golan Heights under Israeli control.

Ross, Dennis, *The Missing Peace*, Farrar Strauss Giroux, 2004.

A former U.S. chief Middle East peace negotiator recounts the Madrid, Oslo and Camp David negotiations. He blames Yasser Arafat for the failed 2000 peace talks, but other writers fault both sides.

Sharon, Ariel, with David Chanoff, *Warrior*, Simon & Schuster, 1989.

The Israeli prime minister's gripping autobiography provides insight into the character of the man, the politician and the core events that have shaped Israel.

Articles

Bennet, James, "Sharon Coup: U.S. Go-Ahead," *The New York Times*, April 14, 2004, p. A1.

President Bush made significant commitments to Israeli Prime Minister Ariel Sharon when backing Sharon's plan to abandon Israeli settlements in the Gaza Strip.

Brzezinksi, Zbigniew, "Hegemonic Quicksand," *The National Interest*, winter 2003-2004, pp. 5-16.

The former national security adviser in the Clinton administration says major U.S. security concerns, such as containing weapons of mass destruction, will be easier to deal with once Arab-Israeli peace is achieved.

Kessler, Glenn, "Cutting Arafat Loose, But Not by Name," *The Washington Post*, June 30, 2002, p. A19.

The author describes the Bush administration's decisive June 2002 policy shift.

King, Neil, Jr., "Bush Plans New Strategy for Middle East," *The Wall Street Journal*, Dec. 29, 2004, p. A4.

The *Journal* reporter contends the United States will not push for peace but will concentrate on the small steps of Palestinian institution building; several critics contend the president will miss a crucial opportunity.

Podhoretz, Norman, "World War IV: How It Started, What It Means, And Why We Have to Win," *Commentary*, September 2004, pp. 17-54.

The magazine's editor-at-large, godfather of the neocon movement, discussed the challenge posed by Islamic terrorism and dismisses the U.S. alliance with Israel as a cause for Arab anger.

Reports and Studies

"After Arafat? Challenges and Prospects," International Crisis Group, Dec. 23, 2004.

The independent, conflict-resolution group examines the challenges posed by the Palestinian transition to a post-Arafat era and argues that despite the U.S. emphasis on Palestinian democracy, it is not and has never been the core problem.

"Evangelicals and Israel," Ethics and Public Policy Center, November 2003.

The Washington think tank provides a conservative overview of evangelical positions on the Israeli-Palestinian conflict.

"Four Years — Intifada, Closure and Palestinian Economic Crisis," *World Bank*, October 2004.

This report examines the economic impact of the Middle East conflict on the Palestinian territories.

For More Information

American-Arab Anti Discrimination Committee, 4201 Connecticut Ave., N.W., Suite 300, Washington, DC 20008; (202) 244-2990; www.adc.org. Dedicated to defending the rights of people of Arab descent.

American Israel Public Affairs Committee, 440 1st St., N.W., Suite 600, Washington, DC 20001; (202) 639-5200; www.aipac.org. Seeks to maintain and improve U.S.-Israel relations.

American Task Force on Palestine, 815 Connecticut Ave., N.W., Suite 200, Washington, DC 20006; (202) 887-0177; www.americantaskforce.org. Promotes creation of a Palestinian state alongside Israel.

Arab American Institute, 1600 K St., N.W., Suite 601, Washington, DC 20006; (202) 429-9210; www.aaiusa.org. Represents Arab-American interests in the United States.

Center for Contemporary Arab Studies, 241 Intercultural Center, Georgetown University, 37th & O St., N.W., Washington, DC 20057-1020; (202) 687-5793; http://ccas.georgetown.edu. Organizes lectures, conferences and artistic events exploring current issues.

Foundation for Middle East Peace, 1761 N St., N.W., Washington, DC 20036; (202) 835-3650; www.fmep.org. Publishes maps, news and analysis of settlement policy.

Institute for Palestine Studies, 3501 M St., N.W., Washington, DC 20007; (202) 342-3990; http://palestine-studies.org/final/en/index.html. Studies issues affecting Palestinian Arabs.

U.S. Institute of Peace, 1200 17th St., N.W., Washington, DC 20036; (202) 457-1700; www.usip.org. Founded by Congress to resolve international conflict.

Washington Institute for Near East Policy, 1828 L St., N.W., Suite 1050, Washington, DC 20036; (202) 452-0650; www.washingtoninstitute.org. Research institute that works to improve the effectiveness of U.S. Middle East policy.

16

Exporting Democracy

Peter Katel

A Ukrainian woman in Dityaki votes on Oct. 31, 2004. After a peaceful, U.S.-supported revolt, voters elected reform candidate Viktor Yushchenko. Supporters of President Bush's global campaign to spread democracy point to hopeful signs in Ukraine, Iraq, Kyrgyzstan and other nations, but skeptics caution that it takes more than an election to establish a true government of the people.

AFP Photo/Viktor Drachev

From *CQ Researcher*,
April 1, 2005.

Election day approached in Iraq amid fear that anti-U.S. insurgents would carry out their threat to "wash the streets with the blood of voters." [1]

The terrorists kept their promise, though the death toll was lower than many had feared. Mortar fire and suicide bombers killed at least 44 people. [2] Still, Iraqis braved the threats and waited in long lines to vote — and in big numbers. Indeed, a surprising 58 percent of Iraqis voted, nearly matching the 60 percent turnout in last fall's U.S. presidential election. [3]

"America's willful defeatists look particularly puny in light of the millions who turned out to vote because they believe in the new Iraq," *National Review Online* crowed. [4]

Even European skepticism weakened. "Thanks to [Iraqi voters], the 'de-freezing' of transatlantic relations could happen earlier than even optimists expected," a Polish newspaper editorialized. [5]

But President Bush has his sights set on more than just a democratic Iraq.

At his second inauguration, on Jan. 20, 2005, Bush declared: "[I]t is the policy of the United States to seek and support the growth of democratic movements and institutions in every nation and culture, with the ultimate goal of ending tyranny in our world." [6]

Critics said the president was taking on too great a challenge, but events quickly suggested that a democratic upsurge was building:

- Some three weeks after the Iraqi elections, Lebanese protesters accused Syria of killing a popular Lebanese politician and demanded the pullout of Syrian troops.

- Egyptian President Hosni Mubarak made a tentative move toward expanding voting after ruling for nearly a quarter-century without contested elections.

Majority of Nations Are Free or Nearly Free

Nearly two-thirds of the world's 6.4 billion population, or 4 billion people, lived in free or partly free societies in 2004, and the rest lived in "not free" societies. From 1994 to 2004, the number of free countries increased by 13 and not free countries declined by five (inset).

Free — Citizens enjoy high degree of political and civil freedom.

Partly free — Some restrictions exist on political and civil liberties, often accompanied by corruption, weak rule of law, ethnic strife or civil war.

Not free — Political process is tightly controlled and basic freedoms are absent.

Global Trends in Freedom

	No. of countries	
	1994	2004
Free	76	89
Partly free	61	54
Not free	54	49
Total	191	192

Source: "Freedom in the World," 2005 survey, Freedom House, www.freedomhouse.org.

- Democracy-averse Saudi Arabia began experimenting with municipal elections.
- Ukrainians watched the government of Viktor Yushchenko commence work following a peaceful,

U.S.-supported uprising that ultimately toppled an entire political class they considered corrupt.

- Finally, in late March protesters alleging corruption, repression and electoral fraud in Kyrgyzstan forced the longtime president to flee the country; he was replaced by an opposition leader as interim president pending new elections in June.

In almost each case, Bush supported moves toward democracy. For example, he pressured Mubarak to release a prominent democracy activist who had been imprisoned for months. And at a joint appearance with Russian President Vladimir Putin in Slovakia, Bush needled Putin about Russia's crackdown on independent journalists and political opponents, prompting Putin to retort that debating "whether we have more or less democracy is not the right thing to do." [7]

Putin was not the only one to question Bush's pro-democracy sentiments.

"It's very easy to talk about advancing the cause of freedom," Anthony H. Cordesman, a senior fellow at the Center for Strategic and International Studies, said after Bush's inaugural address, "but very often you have the practical reality that you have to deal with the world and governments as they are." [8]

"If the United States cannot eliminate poverty or raise test scores in Washington, how does it expect to bring democracy to a part of the world that has stubbornly resisted it and is virulently anti-American to boot?" asked political scientist Francis Fukuyama of Johns Hopkins University's School of Advanced International Studies. [9]

Such responses prompted a "senior" administration official to assure the skeptics that spreading democracy wasn't Bush's sole foreign-policy goal. [10]

But Bush's backers argue he should stay the course. If people in the Third World are against everything the United States is for, they ask, then why are all those Arabs and Afghans voting and demonstrating? Indeed, shortly before the Iraq elections, Afghans and Palestinians had voted in their own free elections.

"The good thing about this president is that he puts his money where his mouth is," says Adeed Dawisha, a longtime Iraqi exile and political scientist at Miami University, in Oxford, Ohio. "If we believe in democracy, it is our duty to see that other people benefit from it. Exporting democracy is part and parcel of one's belief in democracy."

Is Bush too aggressive? No, argued *Weekly Standard* Editor William Kristol, a leading conservative Republican. "[I]f Bush can succeed in Iraq, force Syria out of Lebanon and undermine the mullahs in Iran, then historians will say: Bush was willing to fight — and Bush was right." [11]

But challenges abound to Bush's global democracy campaign. In Iraq, for example, nearly two months after the elections Iraqis still had not formed an interim government.

Moreover, skeptics say it takes more than an election to establish a true government of the people — not to mention civil liberties for women as well as men, a free press, an independent judiciary and the other institutions that make up a democracy.

Fukuyama, who supports democracy promotion, especially in the Middle East, concludes that "the United States needs to be more realistic about its nation-building abilities and cautious in taking on large social-engineering projects in parts of the world it does not understand very well." [12]

One of the toughest cultural challenges for democratic change in the Middle East, for instance, will be conservative Islam's restrictions on women's rights. Muslim countries ruled by the strict Islamic legal code known as Sharia — espoused by some newly elected Iraqi politicians — severely limit women's rights to vote, work, own property, divorce, obtain an education and even drive a car.

Meanwhile, human-rights advocates note that some of the United States' best friends, such as Pakistan and Saudi Arabia, repress dissent but get little pressure from the Bush administration. Bush's own State Department calls Pakistani President Pervez Musharaff's human-rights picture "poor." [13]

But administration officials view Musharaff as a vital ally in the hunt for Osama bin Laden and in trying to halt the spread of nuclear weapons technology. "God bless him. . . . He is a moderate voice in the world, in the Muslim world," Secretary of Defense Donald H. Rumsfeld said last fall. [14] And Secretary of State Condoleezza Rice recently refused to criticize Musharaff for not giving up his post as army chief of staff, saying only that the United States expects "a commitment to a democratic path for Pakistan." [15]

Similarly gentle pressure is applied to oil-rich Saudi Arabia, where only practitioners of the state-endorsed form of Islam have freedom to worship. [16] Yet Bush has refrained from any public pressure on the monarchy, one of the United States' three biggest sources of petroleum. In his State of the Union address in February 2005, he said only: "The government of Saudi Arabia can demonstrate its leadership in the region by expanding the role of its people in determining their future." [17]

President Bush and Russian President Vladimir Putin meet the press after conferring in Bratislava, Slovakia, on Feb. 24, 2005. Bush told Putin he had concerns about Russia's crackdown on independent journalists and political opponents.

So-called "realists" have long advocated a light approach with powerful, undemocratic allies. Some repressive governments are worth supporting, the reasoning goes, because the dissidents they imprison are dangerous to the United States. Indeed, foreign policy realists worry that in the case of the Middle East, democracy might be bad for the United States because keeping allied governments in power is more important than defending the rights of imprisoned dissidents. [18]

"[M]any of the groups arguing against repression in those societies are fundamentalists and anti-American," said Harvard political scientist Samuel Huntington. "Promoting democracy and human rights are very important goals for the United States, but we also have other interests." [19]

A veteran democracy activist from Egypt dismisses that argument. Analysts like Huntington have fallen for a scare tactic about fundamentalists used by dictators "to frighten Westerners — 'the barbarians will come with democracy,' " says Saad al-Din Ibrahim, a visiting fellow at the Woodrow Wilson International Center for Scholars. He spent 14 months in prison in Egypt before being cleared in 2003 of illegally receiving foreign funds and of tarnishing Egypt's image abroad.

One of the best indicators of the Bush campaign's success, Ibrahim says, is Iraqis' responses to pollsters. "Everyone has said they would like to see the Americans out. 'But would you like to have them out immediately?' 'No.' "

Still, even some democracy advocates worry that President Bush may awaken more hope than can be delivered. Thomas Carothers, a former State Department lawyer who directs the Democracy and Rule of Law Project at the Carnegie Endowment for International Peace, says, "I see this as grabbing the theme by the throat. I say, just don't squeeze it to death."

As Bush continues his support for worldwide democracy, here are some of the questions being debated:

Should the United States be trying to export democracy?

Carothers and other experts say the success of exporting democracy depends largely on the conditions existing in the "importing" country, such as the quality of its judicial system and other institutions.

"[When] a society has underlying conditions favorable to the emergence of democratic government, if you remove the authoritarian government by force you can allow those underlying conditions to flourish," Carothers says. "If you don't have the underlying conditions, it's hard to create them."

For instance, Yale Law School Professor Amy Chua wrote, the sudden importation of democracy if combined with laissez-faire capitalism in developing countries without protective institutions can trigger violence against ethnic minorities that have held power in those countries for decades.

Some of those skeptical of Bush's policies in Iraq say deep-seated conflicts and rivalries between the majority Shiites and the two largest minority groups — the Sunnis and Kurds — could easily derail democracy efforts. Kurds and Shiites have been unable to agree on a new government, but continued terrorism against Shiites from Sunni insurgents may be more dangerous.

"Armed Shiites are pressuring their leaders for revenge," says Rawand A. Darwesh, an Iraqi Kurdish journalist on a Fulbright Scholarship to study at American University, in Washington. "A vigilante culture is emerging."

But Iraqi exile and democracy advocate Laith Kubba, a senior program officer at the federally funded but independently operated National Endowment for Democracy, says those ethnic tensions make democracy all the more necessary in Iraq. "Only checks and balances can ensure

Most Nation-Building Efforts Failed

The United States has led 16 nation-building efforts since 1900, but only four countries remained democracies 10 years after the U.S.-led projects ended, two scholars at the Carnegie Endowment for International Peace concluded. Germany and Japan were the two big successes, following their defeats in World War II. The two other positive outcomes came in tiny Grenada and Panama. Nation-building efforts by the United States acting alone have usually meant U.S.-run governments or surrogate regimes. None of the latter evolved into democracies, and only one U.S.-run occupation government (Japan) made the transition to democracy. Those results are a warning sign for the Bush administration's largely unilateral Iraq efforts, the Carnegie Endowment study said.

United States-Led Nation-Building Efforts Since 1900

Country	Population	Period	Duration (years)	Multilateral or Unilateral	Type of Interim Administration	Democracy After 10 Years
Afghanistan	26.8 million	2001-present	2+	Multilateral	U.N.	N/A
Haiti	7.0 million	1994-1996	2	Multilateral	Local	No
Panama	2.3 million	1989	1	Unilateral	Local	Yes
Grenada	92,000	1983	<1	Unilateral	Local	Yes
Cambodia	7 million	1970-1973	3	Unilateral	U.S. surrogate	No
South Vietnam	19 million	1964-1973	9	Unilateral	U.S. surrogate	No
Dominican Republic	3.8 million	1965-1966	1	Unilateral	U.S. surrogate	No
Japan	72 million	1945-1952	7	Unilateral	U.S. direct	Yes
West Germany	46 million	1945-1949	4	Multilateral	Multilateral	Yes
Dominican Republic	895,000	1916-1924	8	Unilateral	U.S. direct	No
Cuba	2.8 million	1917-1922	5	Unilateral	U.S. surrogate	No
Haiti	2 million	1915-1934	19	Unilateral	U.S. surrogate	No
Nicaragua	620,000	1909-1933	18	Unilateral	U.S. surrogate	No
Cuba	2 million	1906-1909	3	Unilateral	U.S. direct	No
Panama	450,000	1903-1936	33	Unilateral	U.S. surrogate	No
Cuba	1.6 million	1898-1902	3	Unilateral	U.S. direct	No

Source: Minxin Pei and Sara Kasper, "Lessons from the Past: The American Record on Nation Building," Carnegie Endowment for International Peace, May 2003

that no single community would run away with all the power," he says.

Other critics point out that the United States has not been successful at establishing stable or long-lasting democracies in the past. For instance, of the 16 democratic nation-building projects undertaken by the United States in the 20th century, democracy still existed in only four of them a decade after U.S. forces departed, according to the Carnegie Endowment for International Peace. (*See chart, p. 349.*) [20]

Moreover, the United States often has not been willing to stick around for the long haul in promoting democracy. Jennifer Windsor, executive director of Freedom House, an advocacy organization, says fledgling democracies in Latin America and elsewhere are paying the price for another U.S. shortcoming: "We throw a lot of money in the crisis situations and then lose interest." Haiti is an oft-cited example. (*See sidebar, p. 356.*) [21]

Policy shifts are another classic danger. After the 1991 Persian Gulf War, for instance, the United States initially

Rights Advocates Question Bush's Approach

In theory, human-rights activists ought to support President Bush's global democracy campaign. But a close examination of Bush's program shows big differences between Bush's approach and the policies pushed by human-rights groups.

For one thing, they question Bush's language. The National Security Strategy of 2002, in which Bush unveiled his democracy plan, makes no mention of "human rights," referring instead to "freedom" and "human dignity."

Human-rights experts say the omission is critical because "human rights" carries a precise definition in international law. The Universal Declaration of Human Rights commits signatories to respect individuals' rights to life, liberty and personal security, as well as the presumption of innocence and other liberties. [1]

Not using the term "human rights," according to advocates, suggests the administration seeks to avoid working through the international institutions responsible for enforcing the declaration. The effect, says Carroll Bogert, associate director of Human Rights Watch in New York, is "human-rights promotion without commitment."

Secondly, the administration is not applying equal standards to hostile governments and allied ones, critics say. "When are they going to push their friends?" Bogert asks. "Every state is reluctant to apply stringent human-rights criteria to its friends. That's why the multilateral character of human rights is important, why you need more than just one country brandishing its big stick."

Saudi Arabia and Pakistan are often cited as undemocratic allies that the United States treats with kid gloves. While administration supporters acknowledge that neither country meets democracy standards, they argue that Bush nonetheless has put effective pressure on both. Pakistan has gone from an ally of the Taliban dictatorship in Afghanistan to a fairly reliable anti-terrorism partner, says Clifford May, executive director of the Foundation for the Defense of Democracies. And Saudi Arabia's recent elections, though limited, were a step forward, he says. "If the incentives and disincentives being applied are producing progress," May says, "you don't want to go so fast that the enterprise crashes."

Planned elections in Egypt and the release of imprisoned Egyptian democracy activist Ayman Nour are other examples of how calibrated pressure can produce change, May argues.

As for the United States acting unilaterally, May says, "This administration attempts to work in multilateral fashion when possible," but overthrowing Saddam Hussein was worth taking on, even without U.N. backing.

Despite their concerns about the administration's human-rights record, groups like Human Rights Watch and Amnesty International spent years collecting evidence against Saddam's government that could provide the bulk of U.S. evidence against Iraqi defendants charged with human-rights violations. [2]

Human Rights Watch alone has issued some 80 investigative reports, inquiries and recommendations to U.S. and Iraqi officials since U.S.-led forces took Baghdad. [3] Among the topics: defects in the legal procedures to be used in the trials of Saddam and his top aides; evidence of torture by the new Iraqi government; the looting of records of the human-rights crimes of Saddam's regime and possible links between the Abu Ghraib detainee-abuse scandal and the Bush administration's decision not to apply international legal standards to treatment of prisoners captured in Afghanistan and elsewhere.

Human Rights Watch has criticized the law setting up the Iraqi Special Tribunal, which will be allowed to admit confessions obtained by torture or through interrogations without a lawyer present, the organization said. The group also faults the fact that judges and prosecutors will not be required to have experience in genocide and war crimes cases. [4]

Some tribunal judges say they would like experienced foreign judges sitting with them, but they say Iraq would reject such moves as outside manipulation. [5]

The choice between Iraqi-approved justice and an internationally approved trial perfectly mirrors the human-rights community's conflicted response to Bush's democracy agenda.

"Do we applaud the recent developments in the Middle East — people challenging autocratic governments, people voting? You bet," Bogert says. "But sometimes those moves forward need bolstering by something a little broader than just one country."

---

[1] "Universal Declaration of Human Rights," United Nations High Commissioner for Human Rights, www.unhchr.ch/udhr/lang/eng_print.htm.

[2] William Langewiesche, "The Accuser," *The Atlantic Online*, March 2005, http://theatlantic.com.

[3] All available at http://hrw.org.

[4] "Iraq: Tribunal's Flaws Raise Fair-Trial Concerns," Human Rights Watch, Dec. 17, 2004, http://hrw.org/english/docs/2004/12/16/iraq9907_txt.htm.

[5] Marlise Simons, "Iraqis Not Ready for Trials; U.N. to Withhold Training," *The New York Times*, Oct. 18, 2004, p. A11.

supported a Shiite and Kurdish uprising against Saddam Hussein but then changed course; thousands of Shiites and Kurds were later slaughtered by Saddam. Darwash notes that anti-U.S. Shiite leader Moqtada al-Sadr has made a big issue of the 1991 Shiite deaths.

"I personally am against Sadr — but he has arguments," Darwash says.

In Iraq, however, the Bush administration had no choice but to try to create a democratic state from the remnants of Saddam's regime, Kubba says. "America broke it, so they have to fix it," he says.

But American Enterprise Institute scholar Joshua Muravchik — whose 1992 book, *Exporting Democracy*, is credited with coining the expression — says the U.S. tendency traditionally has been to favor the status quo, especially if the regime in power was anti-Communist, had large deposits of oil or was particularily powerful.

During the Carter administration, known for promotion of human rights, "We were coddling whoever was powerful, Left or Right," says Muravchik, an early member of the so-called neoconservative movement launched by hard line anti-Soviet Democrats. "The Peoples Republic of China and the House of Saud were two regimes we didn't dare mess with. Instead, the United States got "very tough on human-rights violators from small countries like Guatemala and Mozambique."

Yet Bush may be trying to shift the pattern of Washington acting only in its own interest, says Morton Halperin, a senior vice president at the liberal Center for American Progress and hardly a Bush supporter. "The Bush administration actually supported a democratic transition in Ukraine, even though the government sent troops to Iraq," he says. Halperin also directs the Open Society Policy Center, which is part of billionaire investor George Soros' global democracy-building efforts. Soros contributed $15.8 million to anti-Bush efforts during the 2004 presidential campaign. [22]

Bush officials have also publicly criticized Saudi Arabia's human-rights record, according to Michael Kozak, acting assistant secretary of State. The department's 2004 global human-rights report noted the Saudis' lack of religious freedom and persecution of "everybody who isn't tied to the particular sect of Islam that is dominant in the country." [23] The report also cites accounts of corruption, torture and mistreatment of detainees and other violations of international standards by Iraqi forces in U.S.-occupied Iraq.

A member of the Royal Welch Fusiliers protects Iraqis going to vote in Amara on Jan. 30, 2005. At least 44 people died in attacks by insurgents, but a surprising 58 percent of Iraqis voted.

Is democracy taking root in Iraq and Afghanistan?

Egyptian democracy activist Ibrahim challenges the view that Iraq has no democratic tradition, pointing out that between 1920 and 1958 the British mandate (and quasi-protectorate) that created Iraq allowed for a free press and a multiparty electoral system for parliament. "Democracy could take root," he says. "There is no reason why it couldn't."

But Ibrahim acknowledges that with the terrorist insurgency democracy's chances may depend on how much longer non-insurgents will tolerate car bombs and similar mayhem.

"The great enemy of democracy is disorder," says Michael Mandelbaum, a professor of American foreign policy at the School of Advanced International Studies at Johns Hopkins University. "People may just say, 'We're sick of this; we want a government that is strong enough to suppress this violence, and we'll take whatever consequences,' " says Mandelbaum, author of *The Ideas that Conquered the World: Peace, Democracy, and Free Markets in the Twenty-First Century.*

That time may be fast approaching, given Iraqis' favorable response to the tough security rules instituted for the recent elections. Private cars were banned from streets and highways for two days before the vote, and the borders were closed.

"We Americans were taken aback by what could be called heavy-handed security procedures," says Matt Sherman, a State Department adviser in Iraq to the Iraqi interior ministry. "I'm saying, 'Guys, this is thin ice,' but Iraqis know the special security measures they have to take. And when I sat down with an Iraqi three days before the election and asked, 'Are you afraid to vote?' he said, 'I'm not afraid because I saw on TV that the government has taken very serious measures.'"

However, the minority Sunni community did not vote in large numbers. "We've got to focus right now on making sure that Sunnis participate in the process," Sherman says, because the country's new constitution — to be written by the new national assembly — can be vetoed by two-thirds of the voters of any three provinces.

The current interim constitution requires a two-thirds majority of legislators to approve selection of a president and two vice presidents, who in turn will pick a prime minister and cabinet. [24] In other words, Miami University's Dawisha says, "You've pushed them to form coalitions, to bargain and therefore to compromise on their more extreme views." Thus, he says, some of the nascent institutions usually deemed essential to democracy already have been established.

Meanwhile, Iraqi Kurds have their own demands. Most Kurds want their region to be somewhat independent from the central government and already have demanded that their army operate independently of the Iraqi military. [25] Kurds also may demand the right to expel Arabs brought into Kirkuk and other oil-rich areas in Kurdish territory under Saddam's "Arabization" policy.

For their part, many Iraqi women fear that democratization — ironically — could end up curtailing rights and freedoms they enjoyed under Saddam's secular regime, particularly if some of the newly elected and increasingly powerful conservative female politicians get their way. They have vowed to base the new Iraqi constitution on strict Sharia law, thus doing away with women's rights to inheritance, alimony and child custody as well as laws preventing girls under 18 from getting married and men from having more than one wife.

Despite all the doubts, Iraq seems further along toward democracy than Afghanistan. Yet there — despite a remaining Taliban presence in the south, widespread illiteracy and a heavily damaged road system — some 70 percent of eligible voters turned out on Oct. 9, 2004, to choose among 18 presidential candidates.

Foreign observers called the election legitimate. In a country with a long history of subjugation of women, 40 percent of voters were women.

"Democracy is a form of government, and you can't have it without a government," says Barnett Rubin, an expert on Afghanistan at New York University's Center on International Cooperation. "But there isn't a state in Afghanistan. The judiciary doesn't function; the local administrations are controlled by commanders who engage in the drug trade. Just having an election does not mean people govern themselves or have rights."

Bush administration officials acknowledge the problems, particularly the drug trade. In the past year, the amount of land planted in poppies skyrocketed 239 percent to 509,035 acres, according to the State Department. Production of opium gum, a heroin precursor, was 17 times greater than in the next-largest producing country, Burma. "Afghanistan's illicit opium/heroin production can be viewed, for all practical purposes, as the rough equivalent of world illicit heroin production," the State Department reported in March. [26]

U.S. officials fear that the estimated $7 billion in annual profits from the heroin trade will be used to finance the work of anti-U.S. and anti-democracy factions, says Robert Charles, assistant secretary of State for international narcotics and law enforcement. They include armed opponents of elected President Hamid Karzai of Afghanistan; the Islamic Movement of Uzbekistan, which aims to install Islamic governments throughout Central Asia — and remnants of al Qaeda and the Taliban.

"It took only $400,000 to $500,000 to pull off 9/11," Charles says. "These groups are dedicated to spurring violence. We know they represent a threat not only to Afghanistan but also the threat of power projection outside Afghanistan." Already, some of the drug money is going to warlords who control much of the country and who are, technically, the government's partners, Charles acknowledges.

Nevertheless, he points out, a criminal-justice system is being built. "Eighty-five percent of the mullahs, by one recent survey, said they did not want their communities involved in the drug trade," Charles says. "That is a very important social-cultural backbone on which to build. The threat is grave, but the opportunity for success is enormous."

Is the Bush administration making America safer by exporting democracy?

Many foreign-policy experts agree with the Bush administration that in the long run the world — and the United States — will be safer if more countries embrace democracy.

"There is a security payoff," says Adrian Karatnycky, a senior scholar at Freedom House. "You see it as Central and Eastern Europe have democratized, and to a lesser extent in democracies in Africa. As the world becomes more democratic, there are fewer cross-border wars and conflicts" and, thus, fewer breeding grounds for terrorism.

Bush has adopted this reasoning. In his State of the Union address, he said, "The only force powerful enough to stop the rise of tyranny and terror, and replace hatred with hope, is the force of human freedom. Our enemies know this, and that is why the terrorist [Abu Musab al-] Zarqawi recently declared war on what he called the 'evil principle' of democracy." [27]

But others, including members of the Bush administration, argue that — at least in the short run — U.S.-occupied Iraq has become a magnet and a new training ground for anti-U.S. terrorists. Central Intelligence Agency Director Porter Goss acknowledged that trend early this year. "Islamic extremists are exploiting the Iraqi conflict to recruit new anti-U.S. jihadists," he said. [28]

The ongoing bloodshed in Iraq is being nourished by the country's neighbors, who have a long track record of keeping conflicts going, says Ali Al-Ahmed, a Saudi-born democracy activist and founder of the Washington-based Saudi Institute, which advocates political reform and human rights in the kingdom. "Look at what Arab governments have done in the Palestinian-Israeli conflict; what have they done but fuel death and war?"

Israel has been able to build "a powerful, healthy, successful state . . . disrupting the Arab plan to undermine the state of Israel by using the Palestinians," says Al-Ahmed. And while he is optimistic that Iraq and other Middle Eastern countries can do the same, it won't be easy, he says, because the more Iran, Syria and Saudi Arabia feel pressured to democratize, the greater their incentive to fund and promote terrorism in Iraq.

Karatnycky and other democracy-promotion advocates agree that forcing rapid political change in the Middle East will be difficult because it challenges entrenched power. "There are a lot of groups in these areas whose interests are not served by democracy," says political scientist Dawisha. "Saddam's interests were not, and while other Arab leaders are not as brutal and malevolent, there are no democracies. You have a lot of very influential groups that benefit from that type of leadership who will fight — and fight ferociously — to protect their interests."

Meanwhile, members of the "realist" school of foreign policy — which views protecting U.S. interests as more important than promoting democracy — are not so sure that promoting free elections can make the world safer.

"The last thing any American would want are domestic circumstances in any Arab state to spin out of control and have the very people who have profound differences with the United States on top of the heap," Frank Wisner, a former U.S. ambassador to Egypt, said. "We certainly don't want fundamentalist, Islamic-controlled, radical-controlled regimes." [29]

But the American Enterprise Institute's Muravchik says that danger is exaggerated. "Such people who get elected will either not get re-elected — or they will be forced to moderate," because "Islam may be the answer to peoples' spiritual needs but not their economic needs," he says.

Muravchik concedes that the Iraq war has helped the terrorists gather new recruits but says that is inevitable. "We were attacked at Pearl Harbor and then went to war and were then subject to more attacks. Once you go to war, your enemy is going to try to hit you as hard as he can."

Others argue that the way in which the United States went to war in Iraq may have boosted anti-U.S. terrorism recruitment. "What was the need to rush — with no planning about putting in democratic structures or having enough personnel on the ground to maintain the infrastructure?" asks Matthew Spence, a Yale Law School student and former National Security Council staffer who is now an organizer of the Truman Project, a Democratic foreign-policy network. "There's a real danger that people can look at what was done in Iraq — democracy promotion done poorly — and conclude that it was wrongheaded."

Moreover, says a 2004 study by the CIA's National Intelligence Council, battlegrounds like Iraq could one day produce more competent terrorists. "Iraq and other possible conflicts in the future could provide recruitment, training grounds, technical skills and language proficiency for a new class of terrorists who are 'professionalized' and for whom political violence becomes an end in itself," the report said. [30]

CHRONOLOGY

1940s-1960s *As a postwar superpower, the United States focuses on countering the Soviet Union rather than supporting democracy.*

1946 George F. Kennan, a senior U.S. diplomat in Moscow, sends his famous "Long Telegram" advocating containment of the Soviet threat.

1953-1954 Covert U.S. actions overthrow pro-Soviet governments in Iran and Guatemala.

1956 Hungarians rise up against Soviet domination but United States does not intervene militarily.

1961-63 President John F. Kennedy steadily increases the number of U.S. military advisers in South Vietnam, fearing communist domination of Southeast Asia.

1970s-1980s *Americans become more wary of military interventions after Vietnam War ends; U.S. diplomacy focuses on human rights.*

1977 President Jimmy Carter pressures repressive governments in Africa and Latin America to improve human rights.

1979 Carter comes under attack as overly idealistic after anti-U.S. revolutionaries overthrow two U.S. allies, the Shah of Iran and dictator Anastasio Somoza of Nicaragua.

Feb. 26, 1986 Dictator Ferdinand Marcos of the Philippines, a longtime U.S. ally, is toppled.

June 12, 1987 Speaking in West Berlin at the Soviet-built Berlin wall, President Ronald Reagan challenges Soviet leader Mikhail Gorbachev to "tear down this wall!"

1986 "Iran-Contra" scandal erupts, revealing that the Reagan administration secretly sold antitank missiles to non-democratic Iran and used the profits to illegally finance the "contra" guerrillas in Nicaragua.

1990s *President George H.W. Bush's realism is followed by President Bill Clinton's policy of humanitarian intervention and nation-building.*

Feb. 27, 1991 U.S.-led military coalition forces Iraq to retreat from Kuwait in the Persian Gulf War, but Bush does not overthrow Hussein.

Aug. 1, 1991 Bush warns Ukrainians eager to break with the collapsing Soviet Union not to "replace a far-off tyranny with a local despotism." Interventionist conservatives are outraged.

1992-1999 Presidential candidate Clinton urges U.S. military intervention in the Balkans to halt Serbian "ethnic cleansing" of Muslims in Bosnia-Herzegovina, but as president he limits the U.S. role to organizing peace talks and air raids on Serbian positions by NATO.

2000s *Pro-democracy trend begins gathering strength.*

October 2001 U.S.-led coalition invades Afghanistan as part of its "war on terrorism" against Osama bin Laden and the Taliban government.

2002 Mikheil Saakashvili becomes president of Georgia after Rose revolution topples Eduard Shevardnadze. . . . President Bush unveils a National Security Strategy that includes a commitment to global democracy.

2003 Bush initially orders caucuses to choose Iraq's constituent assembly but Shiite leader Grand Ayatollah Ali al-Sistani demands elections.

April 14, 2004 Bush acknowledges that no weapons of mass destruction had been found in Iraq but that enabling Iraq to become peaceful and democratic is reason enough.

October-December 2004 Defying predictions, 70 percent of Afghans vote in the country's first presidential election and select U.S. ally Hamid Karzai. . . . Ukrainians cement their U.S.-supported revolt by electing reformer Viktor Yushchenko as president.

2005 Iraqis brave violence on Jan. 30 to vote for members of an assembly responsible for writing Iraq's constitution. . . . In the following weeks, citizens of Lebanon protest Syria's presence, Egypt's president authorizes multiparty presidential elections, Saudi Arabia holds limited municipal elections and protesters in Kyrgyzstan on March 24 force the longtime president to flee.

BACKGROUND

Wilsonian Idealism

The notion that the United States is an example to all nations of the benefits of self-government goes back to the Founding Fathers. [31] So does the conflict between those, like President Bush, who want to export that example and those content to let it speak for itself.

America "goes not abroad, in search of monsters to destroy. She is the well-wisher to the freedom and independence of all. She is the champion and vindicator only of her own," John Quincy Adams, then secretary of State, said during a July 4th address in 1821. [32]

Various 19th-century presidents, however, cited idealistic motives for going to war — and for exterminating the nation's Indian population. Now seen merely as justifications for seizing territory, their high-sounding declarations gave later declarations of moral purpose in foreign policy a bad name.

In the early 20th century, Democratic President Woodrow Wilson founded an interventionist school of U.S. foreign policy based on moral imperatives. Wilson cast his argument for entering World War I in idealistic terms, although he had practical reasons as well, such as preventing a loss of U.S. influence in the world.

In seeking a declaration of war, Wilson said America should fight "for democracy, for the right of those who submit to authority to have a voice in their own governments . . . and make the world itself at last free." [33]

But Congress rejected Wilson's dream of establishing world peace through his proposed League of Nations, blocking U.S. membership and setting the nation on a course of isolationism in the years before World War II.

Yet at the end of the Cold War, 80 years later, historian Mandelbaum writes, "the goal for which the United States had fought World War I had evidently been achieved: Much of the world was democratic." [34]

Idealists vs. Realists

World War II saw a flowering of the notion that the United States would help defeat the Axis powers not only to restore freedom to occupied democratic countries but also to spread democracy — even to colonies held by U.S. allies.

"[President Franklin D.] Roosevelt appears to have believed that the ruthless imperialism of the older colonial powers might be replaced by a liberal and benevolent American penetration that would be of advantage both to the natives and to American commerce," the late historian Richard Hofstadter wrote. [35]

But during the ensuing Cold War between the United States and the Soviet Union, spreading American benevolence wasn't always possible or even desirable. The main objective became avoiding war between two nuclear powers.

To maintain a balance of nuclear forces, the United States essentially accepted the existence of the Soviet Union's "sphere of influence" in the Soviet bloc. Thus, the United States did nothing to aid anti-Soviet uprisings in East Germany in 1953, in Hungary in 1956 and in Czechoslovakia in 1968. But when the Soviet Union tried to extend its influence into the Third World, the United States responded quickly. It overthrew — or supported the overthrow — of democratically elected governments in Iran, Guatemala, the Dominican Republic and Chile that were seen as pro-Soviet or Soviet-controlled. The resulting regimes were almost always repressive and brutal dictatorships.

In the late 1970s, President Jimmy Carter — elected after the dual traumas of Watergate and Vietnam — made human rights the new guiding principle for foreign policy. But conservatives derided Carter as someone who reserved human-rights criticism for right-wing governments, while cutting left-wing regimes considerable slack. They attacked him as soft on Soviet human-rights violations and incapable of protecting Third World allies.

Events seemed to bear out the critics. The Sandinista revolutionaries — Cuban allies — overthrew the U.S.-friendly Somoza dictatorship. And another friend of Washington, the Shah of Iran, was toppled and replaced by a dictatorship led by Shiite clergymen.

After conservative Republican Ronald Reagan won the White House in 1980, he named Jeane Kirkpatrick, then a political science professor at Georgetown University, as U.S. ambassador to the U.N. Kirkpatrick had once written: "No idea holds greater sway in the mind [sic] of educated Americans than the belief that it is possible to democratize governments any time, anywhere, under any circumstances."

But the one-time neoconservative Democrat's doctrine of supporting autocratic allies bumped up against the reality that some of these allies were more trouble than they were worth. One was Philippine President Ferdinand Marcos, whom United States officials persuaded to flee his

Is Democracy Faltering in Latin America?

Well before democratic activism began stirring in the Middle East, Latin America experienced a tidal wave of democratic change. But that tide is turning, in large measure because of the region's public-safety and economic crises. [1]

Popular disaffection for a system that hasn't lived up to expectations is prompting a return to authoritarianism in some countries, and some experts say the region offers a cautionary example to the Bush administration about unrealistic estimates of the speed with which democracy can take root in troubled countries and deliver results.

"Twenty years is not enough," says Eduardo Gamarra, director of Florida International University's Latin America and Caribbean Center, in Miami. "It's taken us 200 years, and we've still not consolidated democracy in this country. To expect democracy to be an overnight thing is very, very narrow-minded, at best."

According to the U.N. Development Program (UNDP), only 57 percent of the citizens in 18 nations polled in 2002 preferred democracy over other forms of government, compared with 61 percent six years earlier. Moreover, 45 percent of the respondents said they would support an authoritarian government if it could deliver economic results.

The disillusionment follows a democratization trend in every country in continental Latin America (Cuba and Haiti are not included). Twenty-five years ago, repressive military regimes were the norm in the region running from Mexico to Argentina; only three nations were democratic. Today, the UNDP says all 18 nations met the minimum standards for political democracy — legitimate, multiparty elections and peaceful transfers of power. [2]

However, full-fledged democracy, or citizen control over state actions, remains limited, which may explain why Latin Americans feel democracy is not meeting their expectations, the report said.

Indeed, the region has been plagued over the past decade by an economic crisis and a crime explosion in which drug cartels have replaced freelance gangs. [3]

"The Latin American hasn't stopped believing in democracy, but he tolerates dictatorships," says Ibsen Martínez, a political columnist for Venezuela's *El Nacional* newspaper.

Reflecting this ambivalence, even the word "democracy" has been expanded to cover governments that are anything but democratic, Martínez and others contend. In Venezuela, for example, critics of President Hugo Chávez say he promised voters "direct democracy" but has given them authoritarian rule. [4] Chávez also has embraced Cuba's Fidel Castro, prompting fears that communism may return to Venezuela.

Direct democracy is actually a form of rightist, strongman doctrine, Gamarra says. "It's sort of a throwback to the old corporatist movement" developed by fascist dictator Benito Mussolini in Italy, and Juan Perón, Argentina's strongman

country in 1986 after the "People Power" movement demanded his ouster and free elections.

So-called realists, including former Secretary of State Henry A. Kissinger, lamented the new emphasis on promoting democracy that led to the abandonment of Marcos. Opposing that view from within the administration was one of the architects of the Philippines operation, Paul Wolfowitz, later a key political strategist of the Iraq war and recently nominated to head the World Bank. [36]

Republican Transition

In addition to dealing with Iraq, both Presidents Bush — George H.W. and George W. — have wrestled with calls for democratic change in Ukraine. The elder Bush did not urge the Ukrainians to break with Moscow. In a speech in Kiev on Aug. 1, 1991, Bush said, "Americans will not support those who seek independence in order to replace a far-off tyranny with local despotism. They will not aid those who promote a suicidal nationalism based upon ethnic hatred." [37]

Angry interventionist conservatives mockingly dubbed Bush's talk the "chicken Kiev" speech. "Could Bush's words have left any doubt . . . that America was more concerned about keeping the Soviet Union intact under a single leadership than about fostering democracy?" two Heritage Foundation officials noted. [38] By comparison, the current President Bush supports a democratic transition in Ukraine.

from 1946-55. [5] "Rather than radical progressive, it's a conservative movement, an anti-modernization movement."

The Bush administration, Gamarra adds, does not understand this. Gamarra says he hosted a meeting at which Roger Pardo-Maurer, the Defense Department's deputy assistant secretary for Western Hemisphere affairs, said Chávez was using a "hyena strategy" of preying on weak countries in the region. [6] "You can't go around labeling presidents hyenas; it is absolutely counterproductive," Gamarra says.

Latin America's public-safety crisis has spurred calls throughout the region for crackdowns; in some countries there have been lynchings of suspected criminals, including a Peruvian mayor considered corrupt.

The U.N. documented 482 lynchings in Guatemala from 1996 to 2002, mostly in the countryside. [7] "These are indicators that the people believe in an immediate death penalty, with no judicial process," says political consultant Joaquín Villalobos, a former commander of the Farabundo Martí National Liberation Front, El Salvador's major guerrilla army in the civil war of the 1980s.

The power of the past is also reflected by Central America's variant of the crime explosion. In Guatemala alone, more than 500 women were murdered in 2004. In Honduras, El Salvador and Guatemala, urban crime is centered on Mara Salvatrucha and other youth gangs, some of which have established strong footholds in the United States. [8] "They have appeared in the three countries that have authoritarian, repressive pasts," Villalobos says.

"Today, the preference for repressive measures over preventive ones has made the trend grow."

Nevertheless, Villalobos and other experts do not predict a return to the military dictatorships that once dominated Latin America. Though they view the disillusion as real, they consider it largely cyclical. "We're not going to have revolution, nor counterrevolution, nor dictators," Villalobos says, "but disorder, yes."

---

[1] For background, see Kenneth Jost, "Democracy in Latin America," *The CQ Researcher*, Nov. 3, 2000, pp. 882-903.

[2] "Democracy in Latin America: Towards a Citizens' Democracy," United Nations Development Program, p. 27, http://democracia.undp.org/Default.asp? Idioma=2, February, 2005.

[3] Patrice M. Jones, "S. America tiptoes forward," *The Chicago Tribune*, Jan. 11, 2004, p. 3; Patrice M. Jones, "Latin America's quest for saviors," *The Chicago Tribune*, Jan. 26, 2003, p. 6; Richard Lapper, "Back to revolution," *Financial Times*, Feb. 21, 2002, p. 18, and Richard Lapper, "Democracy: a fragile plant in Latin America's political jungle," *Financial Times*, April 15, 1999, p. 8.

[4] Arthur S. Banks *et al.*, *Political Handbook of the World, 2000-2002* (2003), p. 1217.

[5] Robert D. Crassweller, *Peron and the Enigmas of Argentina* (1988), pp. 26, 88.

[6] For published comments by Pardo-Maurer, see Andy Webb-Vidal, "Washington Crafts Policy to Contain Chávez 'Subversion,' " *Financial Times*, March 14, 2005, p. 6.

[7] For background, see William Triplett, "Gang Crisis," *The CQ Researcher*, May 14, 2004, pp. 421-443.

[8] Juan Forero, "Electing force in Latin America," *The New York Times*, June 25, 2004, and Scott Johnson *et al.*, "Vigilante Justice," *Newsweek* (Atlantic edition), Dec. 20, 2004, p. 30.

War with Iraq further demonstrated differences in the Bushes' policies. The elder Bush assembled an international coalition to push Iraq out of Kuwait after Saddam invaded in August 1990. But Bush did not topple him.

"[O]ur practical intention was to leave Baghdad enough power to survive as a threat to an Iran that remained bitterly hostile to the United States," Secretary of State James A. Baker wrote. [39]

When George W. Bush was campaigning for office in 2000, he gave neoconservatives plenty of reason to believe that he was cast in his father's mold. In one of his debates with Vice President Al Gore, Bush criticized "nation-building," noting, "'I'm not so sure . . . it's the role of the United States to walk into a country and say, 'We do it this way; so should you.' " [40]

Of even more concern to Republican democracy advocates, President Bush followed the old realist line on the dangers of democracy in some parts of the world. For example, after Pakistan's Musharaff took power in a coup d'etat, Bush said, "It appears this guy is going to bring stability to the country, and I think that's good news for the subcontinent." [41]

But after the Sept. 11, 2001, terrorist attacks, Bush began talking about democracy building and acknowledging that, in the Middle East, at least, realism propped up autocracies within which extremist ideologies grew. Specifically, 15 of the 19 hijackers on 9/11 were from

Protesters in Beirut, Lebanon, on March 7, 2005, call for Syria to pull its troops out of the country and blame Syria for the death of former Prime Minister Rafiq Hariri, who was killed by a bomb after calling for Syria's withdrawal.

Saudi Arabia, a key U.S. ally whose conservative state religion, Wahhabism, deeply influenced bin Laden and his followers. [42]

In the words of commentator Christopher Hitchens, an advocate of war with Iraq, administration policy-makers concluded after 9/11 that it was time to raze "the political slum that the United States has been running in the region . . . the rotten nexus of client-states from Riyadh [Saudi Arabia] to Islamabad [Pakistan]." [43]

That view seemed to echo the long-held ideas of Wolfowitz, who by then had become deputy secretary of Defense. The United States, he said six months before the Iraq war, was already fighting "a war of ideas, a struggle over modernity and secularism, pluralism and democracy and real economic development." [44]

As Bush laid the groundwork for the war, he emphasized Iraq's alleged weapons of mass destruction (WMD) more than concern about democracy building. Wolfowitz even acknowledged in *Vanity Fair* that the Bush administration used WMD (and Saddam's alleged link to al Qaeda) to make a case for war because it was the one issue on which he and his colleagues all agreed. [45]

Nevertheless, the administration's 2002 National Security Strategy foreshadowed the administration's subsequent democracy-promotion efforts. [46] "History has not been kind to those nations which ignored or flouted the rights and aspirations of their people," the strategy's first page said.

At the time, news reports about the policy emphasized Bush's embrace of "preemption," or the right to strike first when an attack appears imminent. [47] But as veteran journalist James Mann observes in his best seller about Bush's foreign-policy team, the strategy was "breathtaking" in even more respects: "The ideals of Woodrow Wilson were to be revived, this time linked hand in hand with America's unprecedented military power." [48]

Yet events in Iraq were not kind to initial Bush administration predictions of either a quick campaign or an enthusiastic reception by Iraqis that would allow comprehensive political reform and infrastructure rebuilding. Even in neoconservative circles, some began to argue that the administration's forecasts grew from overblown ideas. Fukuyama of Johns Hopkins was the most prominent of the critics, questioning how the United States could fix Iraq if it couldn't improve Washington, D.C., schools.

CURRENT SITUATION

Politics Amid War

Nearly two months after Iraq's elections, efforts to hammer out a governing coalition continued. By early March 2005, the talks had led to the nomination of Ibrahim Jafari, the Shiite head of the religious Dawa party, as prime minister. He would represent the United Iraqi Alliance, a Shiite-dominated coalition that won a two-vote majority of 140 seats (later reduced to 138 by the defections of two politicians). [49]

However, under the interim constitution approval of major legislation will require two-thirds majorities, so a governing coalition will need more than a simple majority. The coalition-building was between the Shiite and Kurdish parties, since most Sunnis either boycotted the election or were terrorized into not voting.

The protracted negotiations were occurring amid resumed attacks by the insurgents. From Jan. 31 to March 9, at least 379 Iraqi civilians and 76 U.S. or coalition soldiers were killed. [50]

Among the dead were the only sons of Mithal Al-Alusi, an anti-Saddam Sunni who returned from exile to enter politics. On Feb. 8, Al-Alusi heard shooting outside his house in Baghdad. "I was running out with my gun to the area, but it was too late," Al-Alusi said during a recent visit to Washington. Ayman, 29, and Jamal, 19,

AFP Photo/Patrick Baz

were dead in their Jeep Cherokee, along with their body-guard. "The war is not finished," he says. "The change of regime does not mean we have finished the job. We have just started."

The relentless violence would seem to confirm the skepticism of those who have been arguing that democracy cannot be built in such conditions. But Michael Moreno, a 23-year-old Californian who volunteered to work in Iraq and is advising the Iraqi interior ministry, says by telephone, "I work with police, with senior officials in the ministry and with the lowest constable, and I see improvement. There will be many more deaths to come, but that's not to say that Iraqi security forces aren't building themselves up."

With the handover of sovereignty to a provisional government, the political environment has changed as well.

Earlier, under the U.S.-appointed Governing Council, the first U.S. administrator for Iraq, L. Paul Bremer III, vetoed an attempt to subject family matters to the Islamic legal code, Sharia. [51] Now, with U.S. vetoes out of the picture, some fundamentalist Shiite politicians — who include devout women — are renewing the effort, which would include allowing men to have multiple wives, letting husbands decide whether a wife can work and doing away with divorce and property ownership by women.

Theoretically, the two-thirds majority requirement would prevent Shiite fundamentalists from such unilateral actions. But Kurds, who normally would not support the family-law change, might not oppose it in return for their own autonomy. So goes one line of speculation, which a Kurdish official flatly rejected. [52]

More threatening to non-fundamentalists than a religiously based family code is a Sunni campaign of violence against women. The terrorists target women considered westernized and independent. In Mosul alone, 20 women have been assassinated. Meanwhile, some radical Shiites have threatened women, demanding that they fulfill their "traditional" roles. [53]

Jafari, the nominee to be prime minister, avoided a direct answer to an interviewer's question about women's concern over family law. "We won't make the new constitution based only on the Koran," he said. "Women will have their rights, and if there are women with competency and specializations to take high places in the government, it will be a pleasure for us." [54]

People Power

As the most culturally liberal and demographically complicated country in the Arab world, Lebanon might have been the most predictable site for a "people power" movement to surface. Still, the speed with which thousands of Lebanese hit the streets following the assassination of a former prime minister took the world by surprise.

Rafik Hariri was killed by a bomb on Feb. 14, 2005, not long after joining other politicians in calling for the withdrawal of Syria. A week later, street demonstrators in Beirut demanded a Syrian pullout and blamed Syria for Hariri's death. Hariri had quit as prime minister after Syria tried to change Lebanon's constitution so a Lebanese president it favored could remain in office.

The tens of thousands of demonstrators included Lebanon's Christian, Sunni and Druze (a split-off from Shiite Islam) communities but not the mainstream Shiites, the country's biggest population sector. [55] They are represented, above all, by Hezbollah (Party of God), which has a long cooperative relationship with Syria and which the United States considers a terrorist organization. It has 13 seats in the 128-member parliament and a 20,000-man militia that claims credit for forcing Israeli withdrawal from southern Lebanon in 2000.

Hezbollah made its views known with a rally in Beirut on March 8 that drew hundreds of thousands in support of Syria. Rather than demanding that Syria remain in Lebanon, the demonstrators protested against what their placards called "American-Zionist intervention."

Sheik Hassan Nasrallah, the main Hezbollah leader, challenged the Bush administration's claim that Lebanon was part of the U.S.-supported democracy wave. "You are wrong in your calculations in Lebanon," he said the next day. "Lebanon will not be divided. Lebanon is not Somalia; Lebanon is not Ukraine; Lebanon is not Georgia." [56]

Indeed, Lebanon did not seem to be moving toward a simple outcome, as in Ukraine. Nine days after pro-Syrian Prime Minister Omar Karami resigned under pressure from the anti-Syrian demonstrators, the Lebanese parliament voted him back to office. A possible explanation: Karami is one of the few Sunni politicians available, and the constitution requires the prime minister to be Sunni. [57]

Elsewhere in the region, responses to the democratic currents of the moment were coming from the summits of power rather than the streets.

In Egypt, President Mubarak's call for competitive presidential elections followed years of agitation by small groups of intellectuals rather than popular protests. One of those dissidents, Ayman Nour, was freed from prison only after public U.S. pressure. He had been charged with forging the legal documents required to form the Tomorrow Party. In a letter from prison published in Newsweek, Nour called the charge both false and absurd and said he was confined in a space 5 ft. 6 in. long by 2 ft. 3 in. wide by 39 inches high. "I hope to be released soon, but fear this detention may drag on," he wrote. [58]

Nevertheless, Nour was freed shortly after Secretary of State Rice suddenly canceled a trip to Egypt to signal U.S. displeasure over Nour's imprisonment. [59]

In Saudi Arabia, a drawn-out election process for half the seats on municipal councils, which have little power, was seen as the Saudi monarchy's response to calls for democratization lately echoed by the Bush administration. The elections (women are not allowed to vote) began in Riyadh, the capital, in February, and were to continue in other regions in March and April.

In Riyadh, the Wahhabi religious establishment backed at least five of the seven winners. In effect, a Saudi election observer charged, the clerics violated the prohibition on political parties. "We have enough religious power in our country, and they will increase it even more," one of the candidates not endorsed by the religious leaders said. [60]

But in Washington, Saudi exile Al-Ahmed takes another view. Noting that Wahhabis traditionally don't favor elections, he says, "People who are anti-democratic — suddenly they become involved [in elections]. If we have a democratic process, those people will come around and deal and bargain — that's a good thing. We have to deal with them; the best way is through a democratic process."

Al-Ahmed's optimistic take on the elections paralleled comments from within the kingdom by Shiite cleric Sheik Hassan al-Saffar, who said the Saudi elections, like those in Iraq, "ignited in people's minds the spark of thinking about their interests and aspirations." [61]

Tough Realities

In March, Afghan President Karzai appointed one of the country's most notorious warlords as military chief of staff. Gen. Abdul Rashid Dostum has been accused, among other things, of ordering Taliban prisoners in 2001 stuffed into shipping containers, where hundreds of them suffocated. Dostum has denied the charge. "Most Afghans want the factional commanders like Dostum to be held accountable for their crimes," John Sifton of Human Rights Watch said. [62]

For New York University's Rubin, Dostum's selection reflected the realities of building a government from the ground up in a country where a judicial system concerning war crimes does not exist, and where Dostum won 90 percent of the votes of his Uzbek compatriots.

"He was a very powerful man with no job and lots of followers with guns," Rubin says, adding that Dostum's "meaningless" new job will bring him to Kabul, where he can be watched.

Conditions for Afghan women, whose oppression under the Taliban was denounced by the Bush administration, also reflect the warlords' power. Women who wanted to run or had run for parliament felt threatened by regional strongmen, Human Rights Watch reported. "Although male candidates are also likely to confront problems due to political repression and insecurity, conservative political factions may target women simply because they are women." [63]

Nevertheless, a reported 40 percent of Afghanistan's 8 million voters in the October 2004 presidential election were women. The constitution requires 25 percent female representation in parliament's lower house and 17 percent in the upper house. "The problem is not the constitution," said Suraya Sobhrang, acting minister of women's affairs, "but its implementation." [64]

It remains to be seen whether Afghan women — who suffered brutal repression under the Taliban and continue to face harsh tribal marital traditions — will enjoy equal rights in the new Afghanistan. While educated urban women are free to work and study now, the daily lot of women in villages and remote tribal areas has not improved much, despite the end of Taliban rule and the arrival of electoral democracy.

In fact, doctors and human rights workers are discovering hundreds of cases of young women attempting suicide rather than continue to suffer the cruelties of forced marriage and beatings at the hands of their husbands or inlaws. "It takes different forms in different provinces," Karima Karimi, an officer of the Afghan Independent Human Rights Commission, told a reporter last year. "Some take tablets. Some cut their wrists. Some hang themselves. Some burn themselves." [65]

Has the war in Iraq helped to spread democracy?

YES

Clifford D. May
President, Foundation for the Defense of Democracies

Written for The CQ Researcher, March 2005

There were those who predicted that if American forces overthrew Saddam Hussein the Arab Street would rise in response. They were right. It's happening — for example, in Lebanon, where we are seeing demonstrations in favor of freedom and democracy unlike anything ever seen before in the Middle East.

"We love the American people," Louis Nahanna, a Lebanese demonstrator, told reporter Claudia Rosett during the massive, recent Beirut rally. "Please don't let Bush forget us. Your support is very important."

The toppling of the brutally oppressive Taliban regime and the historic elections that followed in Afghanistan, the Orange Revolution in Ukraine, the "Revolution of Purple Ink" in Iraq, new (and improved) elections in the Palestinian Authority and Saudi Arabia, the promise of more open politics in Egypt and, as noted, the Cedar Revolution now under way in Lebanon — these and other developments suggest we are living in a period of revolutionary promise.

President Bush's words and policies — including the use of military force in Afghanistan and Iraq — did not cause all this to happen. But none of this would have happened were it not for those words, policies and actions. Former *New York Times* correspondent Youssef Ibrahim, a vehement opponent of the Iraq war, recently wrote that, to his astonishment, there has been a lifting of "the fear that has for decades constricted the Arab mind . . . . [T]he U.S. president and his neoconservative crowd are helping to spawn a spirit of reform and a new vigor to confront dynastic dictatorships and other assorted ills."

The president's critics are not wrong when they say that we don't know how all this will end. Indeed, in 1989 the Berlin Wall fell, and a new era of freedom began for Eastern Europe. But in 1989 a pro-democracy movement also began in Tiananmen Square, and there it was crushed.

I would submit, however, that it is time to find out whether there is a democratic antidote to the poisons that have long been flowing through the Arab world. Yes, action entails risk. But so does inaction. The catastrophe of 9/11 was only the most dramatic consequence of a quarter-century of inaction, of denying that the rise of radical Islamism and terrorism were matters to be taken seriously.

We can do more than observe this experiment. Our enemies will do everything they can to stifle freedom, democracy and human rights. We must do everything we can to promote those ideas, everything we can to assist the brave men and women who are fighting for values we share.

NO

Melvin A. Goodman
Senior Fellow, Center for International Policy

Written for The CQ Researcher, March 2005

When the justifications for the invasion of Iraq — weapons of mass destruction and links to terrorism — were determined to be specious, the Bush administration contended that use of force would lead to democratic reform in Iraq and the Middle East. Recent elections in Afghanistan, Iraq and the Palestinian Authority even fostered the premature assumption that use of military power had precipitated the beginning of democratic transformation of the region.

Public protests among Iraqis, Palestinians and Lebanese also have been cited as calls for democracy, although these demonstrations have more to do with U.S., Israeli and Syrian occupation, respectively, than with liberal reform.

Democratic reform requires political and social stability, and the U.S. occupation of Iraq has created instability throughout the region, raising the possibility that Iraq will create a pro-Iranian Islamic government hostile to liberal values. It is much easier to overthrow dictators than it is to create liberal democracies in nations historically dominated by authoritarian governments and lacking traditions of law and liberty. A long-term U.S. military presence in Iraq presumably will lead to greater desecularization in the region, with faith-based regimes adopting anti-American, anti-Western policies.

Over the past year, moreover, we have seen setbacks to democracy throughout the former Soviet Union and sub-Saharan Africa. The increasingly chaotic situations in Bosnia, Haiti and Kosovo, where U.S. military power was applied, also argue against the forcible introduction of democratic reform.

It is more likely that the war against terrorism, particularly the use of preemptive military power, will compromise our own democracy rather than serve to expand democratic reform elsewhere. In addition to the use of torture at U.S. facilities in Iraq and Afghanistan, there has been an increase in the compromise of such basic rights as fair trial, adequate defense and freedom of communication for aliens and even American citizens. The United States held Jose Padilla and Yaser Hamdi, both U.S. citizens, as "enemy combatants," unable to contact their lawyers or gain access to the charges against them, until the courts eventually intervened on their behalf.

The USA Patriot Act contains serious infringements on civil rights, permitting secret searches and access to medical and financial records with minimal judicial oversight. The Patriot Act contains such a broad definition of "terrorism" that the legislation can be used against any political protester, including environmentalists and anti-abortion activists.

Commission officials estimate that hundreds of such cases occur each year, and President Karzai has ordered an investigation into the situation.

Meanwhile, in Ukraine, newly elected President Yushchenko is holding to a promise to investigate a September 2000 murder that came to symbolize the crimes of the old regime. The victim was journalist Heorhiy Gongadze, who had investigated official corruption. Yushchenko announced recently that Gongadze's killers had been arrested and were talking. Four days later, the former interior minister apparently committed suicide before meeting with prosecutors. [66]

But in several other former Soviet republics, including Moldova and Kyrgyzstan, opposition candidates were faring poorly in elections. "Many leaders in the former Soviet Union have begun seeking closer ties with Moscow because they have found that they need Moscow's help to stay in power," said Alexander Pikayev, a Moscow-based political analyst. [67]

But events seemed to be moving faster than many had anticipated. In Kyrgyzstan, President Askar Akayev fled the predominantly Muslim country on China's northwest border in late March after protesters reacting to allegedly rigged parliamentary elections began looting government and commercial buildings. In the hours before and after Akayev's departure, an imprisoned opposition leader was freed; state television was seized by the opposition; the newly elected parliament was installed, and an opposition leader was selected as interim president.

"The president left the country and the people made a coup d'etat," said Valeriy Dile, an independent deputy of the old parliament, adding that he doubted there would be any negotiations with the ousted Akayev because his regime "has been liquidated by the people." [68]

Some argue the Kyrgyz revolt could lead other Central Asian leaders — many considered more authoritarian than Akayev — to crack down on free speech and opposition activity. However, a successful transition to democratic rule in Kyrgyzstan, home to both Russian and American military bases, could spur democracy and greater U.S. influence in the region, which borders the oil-rich Caspian Sea area.

Paying the Bills

The Bush administration is not matching its rhetoric on democracy with money for programs, some democracy advocates say. "People are taking risks because they heard of the president's commitment, so the administration has to be there for them, so they don't get slaughtered," says Windsor of Freedom House. "Let's make this a priority."

According to *The Washington Post*, the National Endowment for Democracy has only received new funding for Middle East programs in the past two years, while funding has been cut for the endowment's democracy-building programs in Eastern Europe and the former Soviet Union by 38 percent and 46 percent, respectively. [69]

Democracy-building in Afghanistan and Iraq, by contrast, is well funded. For Iraq alone, Congress last year gave the endowment $60 million — an amount that equals the organization's total budget the previous year, spokeswoman Jane Riley Jacobsen says.

That magnitude of funding for high-intensity programs in one country runs counter to the endowment's usual approach — spending small amounts in countries long before mass movements organize themselves. Typical grant recipients are media and civil-society organizations advocating independent judges and other hallmarks of democratic societies.

"It is usually a very long-term commitment to democrats abroad that results in elections," Jacobsen says. "Obviously, in this case [Iraq] there was a real need for injection of substantial sums."

Windsor argues that the administration's funding policy is shortchanging the slow and patient work that is necessary to build support for democratic change among ordinary citizens.

Whatever the flaws they see in Bush's democracy campaign, some Democrats fault their own party for letting the president grab democracy as a global issue.

"The Democrats got disoriented," says former Sen. Bob Kerrey, D-Neb., president of New School University in New York. "They were angry about the misrepresentations about an imminent threat from Iraq, and they missed something terribly important: The president was proposing essentially a liberal intervention in another country in the cause of democracy."

Now, with democracy emerging in Ukraine and Lebanon, Kerrey says Democrats should be saying, "This is what we've been fighting about for 50 years, and we are not going to let our original anger about the Iraq war blind us to that." [70]

Kerrey was among 17 signers of a "Dear Democrats" letter that declared, "Our party will not cede to President Bush the high ground of liberal values in foreign policy."

The letter echoed human-rights community criticism of Bush for not leaning as hard on friendly, non-democratic governments. [71]

The mixture of criticism, self-criticism and praise can be heard from other administration critics. Bush's democracy initiative could serve as the basis for an international approach to fighting terrorism, billionaire political philanthropist Soros told an anti-terrorism conference in Madrid in March. But Soros also lambasted the administration for violating human rights in fighting terrorists, both by going to war, which inevitably claims innocent lives, and by practicing torture at the Abu Ghraib prison near Baghdad. [72]

Not all Democrats want to emulate Bush's foreign policy. Sens. Barbara Boxer of California, Edward M. Kennedy of Massachusetts, Robert C. Byrd of West Virginia, and Mark Dayton of Minnesota all used the confirmation hearings for Secretary of State Rice to attack the Iraq war, with Byrd calling it a "path of increasing isolation [and] a war that has no end." [73]

Nevertheless, the current of Democratic self-criticism is running strong.

If they don't support Bush's democracy efforts, warned the liberal *New Republic* magazine, "Democrats could well be branded as the party that opposes bringing human rights and responsible governance to people who don't yet benefit from them. And that could change U.S. politics for a generation." [74]

OUTLOOK

If at First . . .

The enormous scope of the administration's global democracy campaign, coupled with its early positive results, has left both skeptics and supporters cautious about predicting the future.

Skeptics argue that initial successes shouldn't be overblown. "The disintegration of Yugoslavia started with successful elections in Croatia and Slovenia," points out Marina Ottaway, a senior associate at the Carnegie Endowment. "What comes out of the [Iraqi] elections now is an extremely polarized situation. The demands of the main actors are very conflicting."

Business representatives worry that political changes carried out militarily, as in Iraq, can stall the rise of market-based economic changes. "In the absence of stability, you have constraints on outside investment coming in, especially Western and even domestic investment," says retired Army Lt. Gen. Daniel W. Christman, senior vice president for international affairs at the U.S. Chamber of Commerce.

Christman says slow-motion changes, such as China's swing to capitalism in the 1990s, are more favorable for long-term business development. "Participating in international economic engagement can lead to the kind of openness and transparency and institution-building that is so consistent with democratic reform," Christman says.

Democracy-promotion advocate Muravchik of the American Enterprise Institute observes that democracies that emerged after World War II took time to grow into the new political culture.

"There is a fairly familiar process in which democracy is implanted and then sinks roots," he says. "So that's a reason to be hopeful about Afghanistan and Iraq. The other side is that it's also a pretty familiar story that democracy doesn't make it on the first try. The French are on their fifth republic now."

Karatnycky of Freedom House notes that militarily induced change "has not been the model of most successful transitions." The "bottom-up movement" for change works best, while a violent climate is not conducive to democracy, he says. "The evidence of the past doesn't show that it's impossible, but that it's tougher."

Even supporters of the Iraq invasion and of Bush's democracy campaign say wars aren't foolproof methods of installing democracies. "There is an inevitable course in human history — capitalism and democracy and the arrival of a single world market," says Stephen Schwartz, a contributor to the *Weekly Standard* and author of *The Two Faces of Islam*, an analysis of Wahhabism.

But, Schwartz adds, "There is a difference between countries where a transition is possible and likely because the old system is exhausted, and a situation where you have a bloody dictator who will fight to the end. I've never called for American intervention in Saudi Arabia; surgery is not needed in every case. Surgery was needed in the Iraq case."

If there's one country familiar with theories of history's inevitable outcome, it's Russia, and the past tends to make Russians dubious of such theories. Nina Khruscheva, an international-relations specialist at New School University in New York, knows better than most how long tyrannical cultures can prevail. She is the great-granddaughter of Nikita S. Khruschev, the Soviet leader of the 1950s and early '60s who began the long transition from the state terror regime of Josef Stalin.

Khruscheva will be happy if Bush's campaign keeps racking up successes. But Russia's current slide back into authoritarian rule, despite predictions of its democratic future after the fall of the Soviet Union, leaves her with two questions: "If it doesn't work in Russia, how do we think it's going to work in Iraq? Why do we think that in the eight years of this administration, Bush is going to leave behind a greatly democratized world?"

NOTES

1. Dexter Filkins, "Iraqis Vote Amid Tight Security and Scattered Attacks," *The New York Times*, Jan. 20, 2005, p. A1.

2. Evan Osnos, "Emboldened Iraqis flock to cast ballots," *Chicago Tribune*, Jan. 31, 2005, p. 1.

3. John F. Burns and James Glanz, "Iraqi Shiites Win, But Margin is Less Than Projection," *The New York Times*, Feb. 13, p. A5; for U.S. percentage, see Brian Faler, "Election Turnout in 2004 Was Highest Since 1968," *The Washington Post*, Jan. 15, 2005, p. A5.

4. Cited in Steve Chapman, "After Iraq election, self-congratulation abounds," *Chicago Tribune*, Feb. 10, 2005, p. 27.

5. Robin Wright, "European Bitterness Over Iraq Dissipates," *The Washington Post*, Feb. 6, 2005, p. A21.

6. George W. Bush, "Inauguration 2005," www.whitehouse.gov/news/releases/2005/01/print/20050120-1.

7. Elisabeth Bumiller and David E. Sanger, "Bush and Putin Exhibit Tension Over Democracy," *The New York Times*, Feb. 25, 2005, p. A1.

8. Mark Silva and Stephen J. Hedges, "When vision meets reality," *Chicago Tribune*, Jan. 22, 2005, p. 1.

9. Francis Fukuyama, "The Neoconservative Movement," *The National Interest*, summer 2004, p. 7.

10. Steven R. Weisman and David E. Sanger, "Bush Speech Not a Signal Of New Policy, Aides Say," *The New York Times*, Jan. 22, 2005, p. A10.

11. William Kristol, "After 1/30/05," *The Weekly Standard*, March 7, 2005, http://weeklystandard.com/Content/Public/Articles/000/000/005/292bhhzj.asp.

12. Fukuyama, *op. cit.*, pp. 7 and 22-23.

13. "Country Reports on Human Rights Practices — 2004," State Department, Feb. 28, 2005, www.state.gov/g/drl/rls/hrrpt/2004/41743.htm.

14. "An Update on the Global War on Terror with Donald Rumsfeld," Council on Foreign Relations, Oct. 4, 2004.

15. Glenn Kessler, "In Asia, Rice Says North Korea More Isolated From Neighbors," *The Washington Post*, March 16, 2005, p. A17.

16. "A Country Study: Saudi Arabia," Library of Congress, December 1992, http://lcweb2.loc.gov/cgi-bin/query/r?frd/cstdy:@field(DOCID+sa0006).

17. www.whitehouse.gov/news/releases/2005/02/20050202-11.html.

18. For background, see Kenneth Jost and Benton Ives-Halperin, "Democracy in the Arab World," *The CQ Researcher*, Jan. 20, 2004, pp. 75-99.

19. "Q&A: A Head-On Collision of Alien Cultures," *The New York Times*, Oct. 20, 2001, p. A13.

20. Minxin Pei and Sara Kasper, "Lessons from the Past: The American Record on Nation Building," Carnegie Endowment for International Peace, Policy Brief, May, 2003, www.ceip.org/files/pdf/Policybrief24.pdf.

21. For background, see Peter Katel, "Haiti's Dilemma," *The CQ Researcher*, Feb. 18, 2005, pp. 149-172.

22. Leslie Wayne, "And For His Next Feat, a Billionaire Sets Sights on Bush," *The New York Times*, May 31, 2004, p. A3.

23. "Iraq, Country Reports on Human Rights Practices — 2004," Bureau of Democracy, Human Rights, and Labor, Feb. 28, 2005; "On-the-Record Brief on the Release of the 2004 Annual Report on Human Rights," Feb. 28, 2005, both at http://state.gov.

24. Anne Barnard, "Shi'ite Muslims, Kurds Big Winners in Iraq Vote," *The Boston Globe*, Feb. 14, 2005, p. A1.

25. *Ibid.*

26. "International Narcotics Control Strategy Report — 2005," State Department, www.state.gov/g/inl/rls/nrcrpt/2005/vol1/html/42366.htm.

27. George W. Bush, "State of the Union Address," Feb. 2, 2005, http://www.whitehouse.gov/news/releases/2005/02/20050202-11.html.

28. Dana Priest and Josh White, "War Helps Recruit Terrorists, Hill Told," *The Washington Post*, Feb. 17, 2005, p. A1.

29. "Wisner lauds Pro-Democracy Moves in Middle East, but Urges Caution," Council on Foreign Relations, March 1, 2005.

30. "Mapping the Global Future: Report of the National Intelligence Council's 2020 Project," National Intelligence Council, December 2004, p. 94, www.cia.gov/nic/NIC_globaltrend2020.html.

31. Background drawn from: Joshua Muravchik, *Exporting Democracy: Fulfilling America's Destiny* (1992); Michael Mandelbaum, *The Ideas That Conquered the World: Peace, Democracy, and Free Markets in the Twenty-First Century* (2003); James Mann, *Rise of the Vulcans: The History of Bush's War Cabinet* (2004); Richard Hofstadter, *The American Political Tradition And the Men Who Made It* (1948).

32. Quoted in Muravchik, *ibid.*, p. 19.

33. Quoted in Hofstadter, *ibid.*, p. 271.

34. Mandelbaum, *ibid.*, p. 34.

35. Hofstadter, *op. cit.*, p. 349.

36. Mann, *op. cit.*, pp. 131-137.

37. Francis X. Clines, "Bush, in Ukraine, Walks fine Line on Sovereignty," *The New York Times*, Aug. 2, 1991, p. A1.

38. Kim R. Holmes and Burton Yale Pines, "Read Bush's lips on foreign policy," *Chicago Tribune*, Sept. 12, 1991, p. 27.

39. Quoted in Lawrence F. Kaplan and William Kristol, *The War Over Iraq* (2003), p. 44.

40. David E. Sanger, "The 2000 Campaign: Foreign Policy; A Delicate Dance of the Interventionist and the Reluctant Internationalist," *The New York Times*, Oct. 12, 2000, p. A25.

41. Frank Bruni, "Pressed by a Reporter, Bush Falls Short in World Affairs Quiz," *The New York Times*, Nov. 5, 1999, p. A28.

42. Final Report of the National Commission on Terrorist Attacks Upon the United States, Official Government Edition" pp. 169 and 362, www.gpoaccess.gov/911/.

43. Christopher Hitchens, "Machiavelli in Mesopotamia: The case against 'regime change' in Iraq," *Slate*, Nov. 7, 2002.

44. Paul Wolfowitz, "Building a Better World: One Path from Crisis to Opportunity," Sept. 5, 2002 www.defenselink.mil/speeches/2002/s20020905-depsecdef.html.

45. Sam Tanenhaus, "Bush's Brain Trust," *Vanity Fair*, July 2003, p. 114.

46. The complete document is at www.whitehouse.gov/nsc/nss.pdf.

47. See, for example, Peter Slevin, "Analysts: New Strategy Courts Unseen Dangers; First Strike Could be Precedent for Other Nations," *The Washington Post*, Sept. 22, 2002, p. A1.

48. Mann, *op. cit.*, p. 328.

49. Salih Saif Aldin and John Ward Anderson, "Drawn-Out talks on Assembly Upset Iraqis; Political Wrangling Stalls Formation Of New Government," *The Washington Post*, March 6, 2005, p. A18.

50. www.iraqbodycount.net/background.htm. http://icasualties.org/oif/default.aspx.

51. Babak Dehghanpisheh *et al.*, "Iraq's Hidden War," *Newsweek*, March 7, 2005, p. 20.

52. *Ibid.*, and Farnaz Fassihi, "Iraqi Shiite Women Push Islamic Law On Gender Roles," *The Wall Street Journal*, March 9, 2005, p. A1.

53. *Ibid* (Dehghanpisheh).

54. "Interview with vice president of Iraq, Ibrahim al-Jaffari," Integrated Regional Information Networks [U.N. news service], March 2, 2005.

55. CQ Press, *The Middle East* (2000), p. 201.

56. Hassan M. Fattah, "Pro-Syria Party in Beirut Holds a Huge Protest," *The New York Times*, March 9, 2005, p. A1.

57. Jad Mouwad, "Lebanese Assembly Re-elects Pro-Syria Premier Who Quit," *The New York Times*, March 10, 2005, p. A12.

58. Ayman Nour, "Did I Take Democracy Too Seriously?" *Newsweek*, March 14, 2005, p. 28.

59. Glenn Kessler, "Rice Drops Plans for Visit to Egypt," *The Washington Post*, Feb. 26, 2005, p. A14.

60. Evan Osnos, "Saudi vote hands reformers a setback; Conservatives lead in capital," *Chicago Tribune*, Feb. 12, 2005, p. 1.

61. Neil MacFarquahar, "Saudi Shiites Look to Iraq and Assert Rights," *The New York Times*, March 2, 2005, p. A1.

62. "Rights Groups Dismayed by Afghan Strongman's Past," Reuters, March 2, 2005 [on *New York Times* web site].

63. "Between Hope and Fear: Intimidation and Attacks against Women in Public Life in Afghanistan," *Human Rights Watch Briefing Paper*, October 2004, at http://hrw.org.

64. "Afghanistan: Marking International Women's Day," Integrated Regional Information Networks [U.N. news agency], March 8, 2005 (available at www.alternet.org/thenews/newsdesk/IRIN.

65. Quoted in Carlotta Gall, "For More Afghan Women, Immolation Is Escape," *The New York Times*, March 8, 2004, p. A1.

66. Kim Murphy and Mary Mycio, "Former Ukraine official's death linked to probe of 2000 slaying," *Chicago Tribune*, March 5, 2005, p. 3.

67. Anna Dolgov, "Ex-Soviet States Look to Moscow," *The Boston Globe*, Feb. 18, 2005, p. A8.

68. David Holley, "Kyrgyzstan's Leader Endorses the Newly Elected Parliament," *Los Angeles Times*, March 29, 2005, p. A3; Steve Gutterman, "Kyrgyzstan Leader Reportedly Flees Country," The Associated Press, March 24, 2005; Dmitry Solovyov, "Kyrgyz Opposition Seizes Control, Akayev Vanishes," Reuters, March 24, 2005.

69. Peter Baker, "Funding Scarce for Export of Democracy," *The Washington Post*, March 18, 2005, p. A1.

70. For background, see David Nather, "Democatic 'Doves' vs. Internationalists," *CQ Weekly*, March 21, 2005, pp. 698-700.

71. "Our National Security Challenge: An Open Letter to Democrats," Progressive Policy Institute, March 11, 2005, www.ppionline. org/ppi_ci.cfm?knlgArea ID=450004&subsecID= 900020&contentID=253152.

72. "Soros slams US war on terror for violating human rights," Agence France-Press (English), March 10, 2005.

73. Carl Hulse, "Boxer is Loudest Voice of Opposition to Rice Nomination," *The New York Times*, Jan. 20,

2005, p. A6; Sheryl Gay Stolberg and Joel Brinkley, "In Senate, Democrats Assail Rice and U.S. Policy in Iraq," *The New York Times*, Jan. 26, 2005, p. A1.

74. "Grudging Respect," *The New Republic*, March 21, 2005, p. 7.

BIBLIOGRAPHY

Books

Carothers, Thomas, and Marina Ottoway, eds., *Uncharted Journey: Promoting Democracy in the Middle East*, Carnegie Endowment for International Peace, 2005.
Several authors explore the complications involved in trying to spread democracy in a region where it has never flourished.

Chua, Amy, *World on Fire: How Exporting Free Market Democracy Breeds Ethnic Hatred and Global Instability*, Anchor, 2004.
A Yale Law School professor argues that a combination of sudden democracy and laissez-faire capitalism in developing countries creates an outlet for violence against ethnic minorities with entrepreneurial cultures.

Halperin, Morton H., Joseph T. Siegle and Michael M. Weinstein, *The Democracy Advantage: How Democracies Promote Prosperity and Peace*, Routledge, 2005.
The authors offer the left-liberal perspective on how democracy promotes economic growth, instead of the other way around, as "realists" argue.

Mandelbaum, Michael, *The Ideas that Conquered the World: Peace, Democracy, and Free Markets in the Twenty-First Century*, Public Affairs, 2003.
A study of the global reach of doctrines that many Americans associate only with the United States.

Muravchik, Joshua, *Exporting Democracy: Fulfilling America's Destiny*, AEI Press, 1992.
A pioneering work by a neoconservative who first detailed the rationale for what eventually became the Bush democracy campaign.

Sharansky, Natan, and Ron Dermer, *The Case For Democracy*, Public Affairs, 2004.
In a book that George W. Bush has cited as a big influence on his thinking, a former Soviet dissident turned Israeli cabinet minister argues that people of all cultures and countries want democratic government.

Articles

Conquest, Robert, "Downloading Democracy," *The National Interest*, Winter 2004-2005.
A historian who is a towering figure among conservatives takes a critical look at the possibilities for spreading democracy.

Galbraith, Peter W., "As Iraqis Celebrate, The Kurds Hesitate," *The New York Times*, Feb. 1, 2005, p. A19.
Kurds are holding fast to their vision of independence, a former U.S diplomat warns, and they may break Iraq apart in the process.

Ibrahim, Youssef M., "Will the Mideast Bloom?" *The Washington Post*, March 13, 2005, p. B1.
A veteran journalist turned consultant reports that a democratic current is flowing and that some Arabs credit Bush for strengthening it.

Karatnycky, Adrian, "Ukraine's Orange Revolution," *Foreign Affairs*, March-April, 2005, pp. 35-56.
A veteran democracy advocate and Ukraine expert chronicles and analyzes the events that toppled a government.

MacFarquhar, Neil, "Saudi Shiites Look to Iraq and Assert Rights," *The New York Times*, March 2, 2005, p. 1.
Saudi Arabia's repressed Shiite minority takes heart from the Iraqi vote and from their own country's first elections.

Richburg, Keith B., "Leaders Who Opposed War Offer Cautious Praise," *The Washington Post*, Jan. 31, 2005, p. A11.
The successful Iraqi elections calm the stormy weather between the Bush administration and "old Europe."

Zakaria, Fareed, "What Bush Got Right," *Newsweek*, March 14, 2005, pp. 22-26.
The editor of *Newsweek International*, a skeptic on Bush's democracy policy, acknowledges its advances while warning that they may not continue.

Reports and Studies

Asmus, Ronald, *et. al.*, "A Transatlantic Strategy to Promote Democratic Development in the Broader Middle East," *Washington Quarterly*, Spring 2005.
A quartet of foreign-policy specialists lays out a long-term plan by which Western countries can translate vision into practical steps.

Goodson, Larry, "Bullets, Ballots, and Poppies in Afghanistan," *Journal of Democracy*, January 2005.
The chair in national security studies at the U.S. Army War College finds reason for optimism, though tempered by an opium boom, which promises profits for terrorists.

Spence, Matthew, "Policy Coherence and Incoherence: The Domestic Politics of American Democracy Promotion," Center on Democracy, Development, and The Rule of Law, Stanford Institute on International Studies, Jan. 20, 2005.
U.S. government agencies differ widely in their ideas and practices about how to spread democracy, a former National Security Council staffer writes.

For More Information

American Enterprise Institute, 1150 17th St., N.W., Washington, DC 20036; (202) 862-5800; www.aei.org. The conservative think tank's Foreign and Defense Policies program produces studies and commentaries on democratic transition.

Center for International Policy, 1717 Massachusetts Ave., N.W., Suite 801, Washington, DC 20036; (202) 232-3317; http://ciponline.org/nationalsecurity/index.htm. The center's scholars publish a steady stream of commentary and analysis from a left-liberal perspective.

Center on Democracy, Development, and the Rule of Law, Encina Hall, Stanford University, Stanford, CA 94305-6055; (650) 724-7197; http://cddrl.stanford.edu. Produces papers and proposals that explore the links between democracy and socioeconomic development.

Democracy and Rule of Law Program, Carnegie Endowment for International Peace, 1779 Massachusetts Ave., N.W., Washington, DC 20036-2103; (202) 483-7600; www.carnegieendowment.org. The think tank offers research papers, policy proposals and debates by a number of scholars.

Foundation for the Defense of Democracies, P.O. Box 33249, Washington, DC 20033; (202) 207-0190; http://defenddemocracy.org. The pro-administration advocacy group publishes research and commentary on democratization as it relates to anti-terrorism efforts and Middle East policy.

Freedom House, 1319 18th St., N.W., Washington DC 20036; (202) 296-5101; freedomhouse.org/. The democracy-advocacy organization publishes an annual survey of global democracy.

National Endowment for Democracy, 1101 15th St., N.W., Suite 700, Washington, DC 20005; (202) 293-9072; www.ned.org. The independent, congressionally funded organization offers news, research papers, public events and a magazine.

Saudi Institute, 1900 L St., N.W., Suite 309, Washington, DC 20036; (202) 466-9500; http://saudiinstitute.org. An advocacy and research organization that promotes democracy in Saudi Arabia.